The Classic 1000 Italian Recipes

The Classic 1000 Italian Recipes

Christina Gabrielli

foulsham

LONDON • NEW YORK • TORONTO • SYDNEY

foulsham

The Publishing House
Bennets Close, Cippenham, Berks SL1 5AP

ISBN 0–572–02848–2

Cover photographs © The Stock Market Photo Agency

Photographs by Carol and Terry Pastor

With thanks to the following companies for providing items for the photographs:
Terracotta and other tiles, including lemon-tree decorated tiles opposite page 192, from
Smith and Wareham Ltd Tile Merchants, Unit 2 Autopark, Eastgate Street,
Bury St Edmunds, Suffolk, IP33 1YQ. Tel: 01284 704188/7.
Web site: www.smithandwareham.co.uk.
Tiles, including Roman mosaic tiles opposite page 257 and white tiles opposite page 288,
from Fired Earth Ltd, 7 Giles Street, Norwich, Norfolk, NR2 1JL. Tel: 01603 618461.
Web site: www.firedearth.com.
Oil bottles, olive oils and glazed Italian pottery, including green-splashed dishes and bowls
opposite page 320, from O&Co., 15–19 Cavendish Place, London, W16 0QE.
Tel: 020 7907 0306. 26a The Market, Covent Garden, London, WC2E 8RF. Tel:
020 7240 0697. 13 Rose Crescent, Cambridge, CB2 3LL. Tel: 0122 3306 723. Web
site: www.olivers-co.com.

Printed in Great Britain by St Edmundsbury Press Ltd, Bury St Edmunds, Suffolk

C O N T E N T S

Introduction   7
Notes on the recipes   8
Antipasti   9
Soups   41
Snacks and Light Meals   59
Meat: Beef   79
       Poultry and Game   92
       Lamb 112
       Pork, Ham and Sausage 119
       Offal 127
       Veal 133
Fish 146
Vegetable Dishes 171
Pasta 196
Rice 250
Pizza 268
Breads and Biscuits 283
Salads 296
Desserts 311
Ice Cream and Sorbets 345
Condiments 356
Index 380

Introduction

Italy is a country positively vibrating with enthusiasm for life – and for food! It is rich in culture and natural resources. From glistening olives to fragrant, robust wines, sun-ripened tomatoes to creamy white cheeses, the Italian cook has a wide variety of ingredients to choose from and uses every one with skill and dexterity.

This book is crammed with recipes from every part of Italy. There are thick, hearty soups, delicate antipasti, magnificent meats, fish, and, of course, an abundance of pizza, pasta and rice dishes. And, to round off the book, a selection of popular Italian desserts and some of the coolest, creamiest and most refreshing ices you'll ever want to make.

Notes on the Recipes

When following a recipe use either metric, imperial or American measures, never a combination.

All spoon measurements are level   15 ml = 1 tbsp
                                     5 ml = 1 tsp

All eggs are medium unless otherwise stated.

● Most recipes call for fresh herbs unless dried are specifically stated. If you wish to substitute dried, use only half the quantity or less as they are very pungent. Frozen herbs are a better substitute for fresh than dried.

Always wash and dry fresh produce before use and peel, core or remove seeds when necessary.

All cooking times are approximate and should be used as a guide only.

Always bake food on the shelf just above the centre of the oven unless otherwise specified.

● You can increase or decrease the quantity of rice or pasta you use, according to appetites, in any recipe where they are cooked in an unspecified amount of water. For most risottos, however, if you change the quantity of rice, you must also change the quantity of liquid or it will not cook correctly.

Use dried pasta unless fresh is specified. If you substitute fresh, cook for 3–5 minutes only.

● There are some recipes for Italian breads in the book but there are many varieties readily available in supermarkets, so do try them.

Antipasti

Antipasti are appetisers. There are many regional specialities. Some are elegant and formal, others rustic and very simple. A classic antipasto is often served at lunchtime in Italy and will usually consist of a plate of thinly sliced cured meats: different types of prosciutto, pink mortadella, thinly sliced sausage wrapped in equally thinly sliced cured pancetta, small garlicky sausages and two or three kinds of salami. But whether you choose meat, fish, cheese, vegetables and in whatever style, I guarantee all these receipes are tempting and delicious!

Asparagi alla Parmigiana

Asparagus Parmesan-style

Serves 4

450 g/1 lb asparagus, trimmed
15 g/½ oz/1 tbsp butter
2 egg yolks
15 ml/1 tbsp vinegar
Salt and freshly ground black pepper
50 g/2 oz/½ cup Parmesan cheese, grated

Cook the asparagus in boiling salted water for about 8–10 minutes until tender. Drain and cut into even-sized lengths and place on a warmed serving plate in the shape of a pyramid. Place the butter in a saucepan and beat in the egg yolks. Add the vinegar and season with salt and pepper. Cook until thickened, stirring all the time. Do not allow to boil. Pour over the asparagus, sprinkle with the Parmesan cheese and serve at once.

Piatto di Antipasti

Antipasto Platter

Serves 6

1 red (bell) pepper
1 green (bell) pepper
6 spring onions (scallions)
2 carrots
2 celery sticks
100 g/4 oz mushrooms
½ cauliflower
½ cucumber
4 slices bread, toasted
15 g/½ oz/1 tbsp unsalted (sweet) butter
50 g/2 oz/1 small can anchovy fillets, drained
Piquant Garlic Sauce (see page 367)

Clean all the vegetables. Thinly slice the peppers. Finely chop the spring onions. Thinly slice the carrots and celery. Cut the mushrooms in half lengthways and the cauliflower into small florets. Peel the cucumber and slice into thin strips. Remove the crusts from the toast and butter the slices. Cut into fingers and lay the anchovy fillets on the bread. Arrange the anchovy toast fingers and all the vegetables in a ring on a platter and serve with the garlic sauce as a dip.

Topinamburi di Erbe

Artichokes with Herbs
Serves 4

450 g/1 lb Jerusalem artichokes,
scrubbed or scraped and cut in
even-sized pieces
15 ml/1 tbsp lemon juice
1 onion, sliced
1 garlic clove, crushed
5 ml/1 tsp fresh chopped basil
5 ml/1 tsp fresh chopped thyme
1 bay leaf
15 ml/1 tbsp oil
225 g/8 oz tomatoes, skinned and
chopped
30 ml/2 tbsp tomato purée (paste)
10 ml/2 tsp cornflour (cornstarch)
dissolved in 15 ml/1 tbsp water
Salt and freshly ground black pepper

Place the artichokes in a pan of cold water
and add the lemon juice. Bring to the boil
and cook for 8 minutes. Drain and refresh
under cold running water. Place the onion,
garlic, basil, thyme, bay leaf and oil in a
frying pan (skillet) and cook for 3 minutes.
Stir in the tomatoes. Bring to the boil and
add the tomato purée. Reduce the heat and
cook for 30 minutes, stirring occasionally.
Stir in the cornflour and cook, stirring, for
3 minutes to thicken the sauce. Discard the
bay leaf and add the cooked artichokes.
Heat for 3 minutes and season to taste.
Serve immediately.

Carciofi alla Romana

Artichokes in Wine
Serves 4

4 globe artichokes, leaves, stalks and
chokes removed
15 ml/1 tbsp lemon juice
300 ml/½ pint/1¼ cups chicken or
vegetable stock
15 ml/1 tbsp olive oil
30 ml/2 tbsp white wine
Salt and freshly ground black pepper

Place the artichokes in a pan with 10 ml/2
tsp of the lemon juice and the stock. Bring
to the boil, cover and simmer for 30 minutes until just tender. Remove the artichokes from the pan and drain on kitchen
paper. Heat the oil in a separate pan and
fry (sauté) the artichokes for 3 minutes.
Add the wine and remaining lemon juice
and cook for 3 minutes. Strain the stock
into the pan and cook over a high heat for
about 5 minutes until the liquid has
reduced slightly. Season to taste. Allow to
cool. Arrange the artichokes on small
plates, either whole or cut into small
pieces. Pour over the sauce.

Melanzane alla Panariello

Cold Aubergine Antipasto
Makes 20 rolls

2 small aubergines (eggplants)
Salt
75 ml/5 tbsp olive oil
60 ml/4 tbsp red wine vinegar
2 canned anchovies, drained and
*   chopped*
2 garlic cloves, finely chopped
30 ml/2 tbsp finely chopped fresh
*   parsley*
2 shallots, finely chopped
30 ml/2 tbsp capers
Freshly ground black pepper

Cut the ends off each aubergine, leaving it unpeeled. Stand each aubergine on end, and cut it lengthwise into the thinnest possible slices. Lay the slices on a plate and salt each one lightly. Place the slices flat in a colander, and allow them to drain for 30 minutes. Dry each slice with kitchen paper. In a large frying pan (skillet) heat 30 ml/ 2 tbsp olive oil and fry (sauté) the first batch of aubergine slices slowly on both sides, until they are cooked through. Remove the slices and roll them up. Place in a serving dish. Set aside to cool. Add more oil and fry the second batch. Combine the remaining oil, vinegar and the anchovies. Mash well until the anchovies dissolve in the sauce. Add the chopped garlic, parsley, shallots, capers and pepper to taste. Pour the sauce over the aubergine rolls and serve.

Asparagi con Formaggio

Asparagus with Cheese
Serves 4

450 g/1 lb asparagus
Salt
25 g/1 oz/2 tbsp butter, melted
50 g/2 oz/½ cup Parmesan cheese ,
*   grated*

Pour sufficient water into a frying pan (skillet) to give a 2 cm/¾ in depth. Add a pinch of salt and bring to the boil. Add the asparagus spears and cook for 5 minutes until almost tender. Drain, reserving the cooking liquid for further use as vegetable stock. Cut the asparagus into short lengths if preferred. Lay in a shallow flameproof dish. Cover with melted butter and grated cheese. Place under a hot grill (broiler) until the cheese starts to brown.

Formaggio Bolognese

Bologna Cheese
Serves 3–4

6 canned anchovy fillets, mashed
150 g/5 oz/⅔ cup Ricotta cheese
75 g/3 oz/½ cup olives, stoned (pitted)
*   and chopped*
15 ml/1 tbsp chopped fresh thyme
Juice of ½ lime
Salt and freshly ground black pepper

Blend the anchovies into the Ricotta cheese and mix until smooth. Stir in the olives and thyme. Mix in the lime juice and season with the salt and pepper.

Bresaola Antipasto

Cured Beef Starter
Serves 4

225 g/8 oz Bresaola (naturally cured
   beef), thinly sliced
1 garlic clove, crushed
5 ml/1 tsp freshly ground black pepper
Juice of ½ lemon
15 ml/1 tbsp virgin olive oil

Lay the Bresaola, slightly overlapping, on
a shallow plate. Blend the remaining
ingredients together. Sprinkle the Bresaola
with the dressing before serving.

Patate e Scalogne Caramellizare All' Aglio

Caramelised Potatoes, Shallots and Garlic
Serves 4–6

900 g/2 lb potatoes
12 garlic cloves, peeled but left whole
8–12 shallots, peeled but left whole
100 g/4 oz/½ cup butter, melted
2 sprigs of thyme
2 sprigs of rosemary
Salt and freshly ground black pepper
Ciabatta, to serve

Cut the potatoes in 2.5 cm/1 in chunks and
place in a very large saucepan with the
garlic, shallots, melted butter and 60 ml/4
tbsp water. Cover with a lid. Cook for 5
minutes. Season with the salt and pepper
and add the herbs. Pour into an ovenproof
dish and roast in a preheated oven at
220°C/ 425°F/gas mark 7 for 35 minutes or
until tender and golden. Serve hot with
Ciabatta bread.

Misto di Carote

Carrot Mix
Serves 4

450 g/1 lb carrots
2 celery sticks
2 potatoes
1 onion
15 g/½ oz/1 tbsp unsalted (sweet) butter
1 bay leaf
30 ml/2 tbsp Marsala wine
30 ml/2 tbsp chopped fresh sage

Dice the carrots, celery and potatoes and
finely chop the onion. Place the butter in a
saucepan and when hot fry (sauté) the vegetables for 3 minutes. Add the remaining
ingredients and continue cooking, stirring
occasionally, for 15 minutes or until tender. Remove the bay leaf before serving.

Pasticcine al Formaggio

Cheese Cakes
Serves 4

450 g/1 lb potatoes, grated
1 red onion, chopped
275 g/10 oz/2½ cups hard cheese,
   grated
30 ml/2 tbsp chopped fresh coriander
   (cilantro)
Freshly ground black pepper
25 g/1 oz/2 tbsp unsalted (sweet) butter

Mix the potatoes, onion, cheese, coriander
and pepper together in a bowl and shape
into 8 round cakes. Squeeze out any excess
liquid and leave to drain on kitchen paper
for 1 minute. Melt the butter in a frying
pan (skillet) and cook the cakes on each
side until brown and crispy. Serve hot or
cold.

Uova alla Sarda

Egg and Olive Antipasto
Serves 4–6

2 eggs
2 celery sticks
1 small red (bell) pepper
1 small green (bell) pepper
225 g/8 oz/1⅓ cups black olives, stoned
 (pitted)
225 g/8 oz/1⅓ cups green olives, stoned
 (pitted)
30 ml/2 tbsp olive oil
15 ml/1 tbsp chopped fresh oregano
Salt and freshly ground black pepper
Ciabatta bread, to serve

Boil the eggs until they are hard. Quickly drop into a pan of cold water. Shell and cut the eggs into slices and lay them in a flat dish. Clean the celery and chop into small pieces and place in a bowl. Chop the peppers finely and add to the celery. Cut the olives into quarters and stir into the celery with the olive oil. Add the oregano and season with the salt and pepper. Spoon the olives over the eggs and serve chilled with hunks of fresh Ciabatta.

Fritelle di Zucchini

Courgette Fritters
Serves 3–4

225 g/8 oz courgettes (zucchini),
 grated
45 ml/3 tbsp plain (all-purpose) flour
2 eggs
10 ml/2 tsp chopped fresh sage
1 garlic clove, crushed
Salt and freshly ground black pepper
75 ml/5 tbsp oil

Mix the courgettes, flour, eggs, sage and garlic in a bowl and season with salt and pepper. Heat the oil in a pan and drop 15 ml/1 tbsp of the mixture for each fritter into the hot oil. Cook until golden on both sides, drain on kitchen paper and serve hot.

Zucchini in Salsa di Pomodoro

Courgettes in Tomato Sauce
Serves 4

30 ml/2 tbsp olive oil
1 onion, sliced
2 garlic cloves, crushed
750 g/1½ lb courgettes (zucchini),
 sliced
1 large green (bell) pepper, chopped
225 g/8 oz tomatoes, skinned and
 chopped
10 ml/2 tsp chopped fresh basil
1 bay leaf
Salt and freshly ground black pepper
6 canned anchovy fillets, drained and
 chopped
50 g/2 oz/¼ cup Parmesan cheese,
 grated

Heat the oil and fry (sauté) the onion, garlic, courgettes and pepper for 7–8 minutes until the onion is brown. Stir in the tomatoes, seasoning, basil and bay leaf and reduce the heat. Simmer for 30 minutes until the sauce has thickened and the vegetables are soft. Discard the bay leaf and remove from the heat. Spoon the mixture into an ovenproof dish and scatter over the chopped anchovies and cheese. Grill (broil) for 5 minutes until the top is brown.

Finocchio in Besciamella al Formaggio

Fennel in Cheese Sauce
Serves 4

1 fennel bulb
25 g/1 oz/2 tbsp butter
30 ml/2 tbsp plain (all-purpose) flour
250 ml/8 fl oz/1 cup milk
120 ml/4 fl oz/½ cup single (light)
* cream*
Salt and freshly ground black pepper
50 g/2 oz/½ cup hard cheese, grated
15 ml/1 tbsp breadcrumbs
30 ml/2 tbsp grated Parmesan cheese

Trim the fennel fronds and reserve. Cut the head into chunks. Place in a steamer and steam over boiling water for 15 minutes until tender. Transfer to an ovenproof dish. Melt the butter and stir in the flour. Gradually stir in the milk and blend to a smooth paste. Cook gently for 2 minutes and stir in the cream, salt and pepper. Cook, stirring, for 1 minute and add the grated hard cheese. Pour over the fennel and sprinkle over the breadcrumbs and Parmesan cheese. Bake for 25 minutes in a preheated oven at 180°C/350°F/gas mark 4. Garnish with the fennel fronds.

Finnocchio alla Fiorentina

Florentine Fennel
Serves 4

900 g/2 lb fennel bulbs
250 ml/8 fl oz/1 cup water
Salt
50 g/2 oz/¼ cup unsalted (sweet) butter
25 g/1 oz/¼ cup plain (all-purpose)
* flour*
150 ml/¼ pt/⅔ cup milk
Freshly ground black pepper
30 ml/2 tbsp grated Caciocavallo
* or Parmesan cheese*

Trim the fennel and reserve the feathery fronds for garnishing. Cut the fennel into wedges and put in a saucepan. Pour over the water and bring to the boil, adding 2.5 ml/½ tsp salt. Lower the heat, cover the pan and simmer for 10 minutes. Drain, reserving the cooking liquid. Transfer the fennel to a warm ovenproof dish and keep warm. Melt the butter in a saucepan and sprinkle over the flour. Cook for a few seconds and gradually stir in the milk. Bring to the boil, stirring, until thick and smooth. Season with salt and pepper and pour over the fennel. Sprinkle the top with cheese and place under a hot grill (broiler) until lightly browned. Garnish with the reserved fennel fronds.

Cetrioli alla Fiorentina

Florentine Cucumbers
Serves 4

Salt
1 large cucumber, cut into chunks
30 ml/2 tbsp olive oil
2 garlic cloves, crushed
Freshly ground black pepper
60 ml/4 tbsp tomato purée (paste)
15 ml/1 tbsp chopped fresh thyme
15 ml/1 tbsp chopped fresh tarragon

Sprinkle salt over the cucumber pieces and allow to drain on kitchen paper for 10 minutes. Heat the olive oil in a frying pan (skillet) and add the crushed garlic. Cook until golden. Add the cucumber to the pan and fry (sauté) for 3 minutes. Blend in the remaining ingredients and simmer for 5 minutes. Transfer to a warmed serving dish.

Olive Ripiene

Stuffed Fried Olives
Serves 4

50 g/2 oz ham
50 g/2 oz/½ cup Parmesan cheese, grated
1.5 ml/¼ tsp grated nutmeg
20 large olives, stoned (pitted)
15 ml/1 tbsp plain (all-purpose) flour
1 egg, beaten
50 g/2 oz/1 cup breadcrumbs
Oil for frying

Mince the ham and add the grated cheese and nutmeg. Fill the olives with the mixture. Dip each of the olives, first in the flour, then in the beaten egg and lastly in the breadcrumbs. Fry (sauté) in hot oil and drain thoroughly. Serve hot or cold.

Fricassea di Carciofi

Fricassee of Artichokes
Serves 4

4 globe artichokes, leaves, stalks and chokes removed
25 g/1 oz/2 tbsp unsalted (sweet) butter
1 garlic clove, crushed
2 egg yolks
30 ml/2 tbsp water
Salt and freshly ground black pepper
15 ml/1 tbsp lemon juice
15 ml/1 tbsp chopped fresh parsley
25 g/1 oz/2 tbsp Parmesan cheese, grated

Simmer the artichoke hearts in plenty of boiling water for 30 minutes. Drain well and cut in quarters. Heat the butter in a saucepan and cook the garlic for 1 minute. Add the artichoke hearts and the measured water and cover with a lid. Simmer for a further 5 minutes, stirring occasionally. Beat the egg yolks with the lemon juice and grated cheese. Stir into the artichoke mixture and cook very slowly, stirring, for 5 minutes without boiling.

Antipasto di Formaggio di Capra

Goats' Cheese Antipasto
Serves 4

2 small goats' cheeses
15 ml/1 tbsp vinegar
30 ml/2 tbsp olive oil
Salt and freshly ground black pepper
Mixed salad leaves, to serve

Remove any crust from the cheeses and cut them both in half horizontally. Place the four halves in an ovenproof dish. Blend the vinegar, oil and salt and pepper together. Brush over the top of the cheeses and pour the rest around. Place under a hot grill (broiler) until browned on top and serve each cheese on a bed of salad leaves.

Zucchini alla Griglia

Grilled Courgettes
Serves 4

5 ml/1 tsp butter
8 courgettes (zucchini)
2 garlic cloves, crushed
5 ml/1 tsp salt
15 ml/1 tbsp chopped fresh oregano
75 g/3 oz/¾ cup hard cheese, grated

Grease a baking dish with the butter. Slice the courgettes in halves, lengthways and place in a large pan of boiling water. Cook for 1 minute and refresh in cold water. Drain well and arrange in the baking dish. Sprinkle with the garlic, salt and oregano. Spoon the cheese on top of the mixture and bake in a preheated oven at 200°C/ 400°F/gas mark 6 for 20 minutes.

Radicchio in Padella

Pan-roasted Radicchio
Serves 4

3 radicchio heads, trimmed
50 g/2 oz/¼ cup unsalted (sweet) butter
15 ml/1 tbsp olive oil
5 ml/1 tsp grated nutmeg
Salt and freshly ground black pepper

Wash the radicchio and dry on kitchen paper. Cut in halves and then quarters. Melt the butter in a frying pan (skillet) and stir in the oil. Lay the radicchio in the pan and cook for 4 minutes. Toss well and turn into a serving dish. Sprinkle with the nutmeg, a little salt and plenty of pepper.

Tortine di Patata all'Italiana

Italian-style Potato Cakes
Serves 4

1 large onion
225 g/8 oz/1 cup boiled and mashed
   potatoes
50 g/2 oz/¼ cup unsalted (sweet) butter
Salt and freshly ground black pepper
50 g/2 oz/½ cup plain (all-purpose)
   flour
2 egg yolks
1.5 ml/¼ tsp cayenne
15 ml/1 tbsp chopped fresh sage
Oil for frying

Grate or finely chop the onion. Mix the potato with the onion, butter and seasoning. Blend in the flour, egg yolks, cayenne and sage. Form into small even-sized cakes and fry (sauté) in hot oil until brown and crispy on the edges. Drain on kitchen-paper before serving.

Mozzarella in Carrozza

Crispy Fried Mozzarella
Serves 4

8 canned anchovies, drained
8 thick slices bread, crusts removed
8 slices Mozzarella cheese,
  cut 1cm/½ in thick
3 ripe tomatoes, skinned, seeded and
  sliced
Salt and freshly ground black pepper
3 eggs, beaten
Oil for frying
Chopped fresh oregano

Cut each anchovy in half. Cut the slices of bread in half. Cover eight slices of bread with cheese, anchovy and tomato and season with salt and pepper. Cover each with a slice of bread to make a sandwich and dip in the beaten egg. Turn to coat the other sides of the bread and leave to stand for 40 minutes. Heat the oil in a shallow frying pan (skillet) and cook the sandwiches until crisp and lightly browned on both sides. Drain and serve hot sprinkled with the oregano.

Polenta con Peperoni alla Grattella

Grilled Polenta with Peppers
Serves 4

2.5 ml/½ tsp salt
100 g/4 oz/1 cup polenta
15 ml/1 tbsp chopped fresh basil
25 g/1 oz/2 tbsp unsalted (sweet) butter
50 g/2 oz/½ cup hard cheese, grated
30 ml/2 tbsp olive oil
1 garlic clove, crushed
1 red, 1 green and 1 yellow (bell)
  pepper, seeded and cut in strips
75 g/3 oz spinach leaves, chopped
60 ml/4 tbsp white wine
10 ml/2 tsp rosemary vinegar

Bring 600 ml/1 pt/2½ cups water to the boil and add the salt. Whisk in the polenta and cook for 20 minutes over a low heat. Stir in the basil, butter and hard cheese and pour into an oiled tin (pan). Leave until cold. Heat the remaining oil in a pan and fry (sauté) the garlic and peppers for 2–3 minutes. Stir in the spinach. Pour in the wine and the vinegar and stir well. Remove from the heat and spoon into a serving dish. Turn the polenta out on to a board and cut into squares. Brush over with oil and grill (broil) for 5 minutes on each side to brown. Top the vegetables with the polenta. Serve hot.

Strati di Foglie di Vite

Layered Vine Leaves
Serves 4

12 vine leaves
30 ml/2 tbsp olive oil
8 large mushrooms, chopped
10 ml/2 tsp chopped fresh sage
5 ml/1 tsp chopped fresh parsley
Salt and freshly ground black pepper

Rinse the vine leaves under cold water and dry with kitchen paper. Arrange six vine leaves on the base of an ovenproof dish and sprinkle over 15 ml/1 tbsp oil. Lay the chopped mushrooms on top of the vine leaves and sprinkle over the remaining oil, herbs and seasoning. Cover with the remaining vine leaves. Cover with foil and bake in a preheated oven at 180°C/350°F/gas mark 4 for 25 minutes. Remove the foil and continue to cook for a further 5 minutes. Divide between four individual serving dishes.

Fritelle di Liguria

Liguria Fritters
Serves 6

1 large courgette (zucchini)
10 ml/2 tsp salt
75 g/3 oz/¾ cup plain (all-purpose)
  flour
2 eggs
30 ml/2 tbsp single (light) cream
2 large carrots, grated
1 small leek, finely shredded
Freshly ground black pepper
Oil for frying
Salad, to garnish
Hot Italian bread, to serve

Grate the courgette and place in a colander. Sprinkle with salt and leave to stand for 30 minutes. Squeeze out the moisture from the courgettes and drain on kitchen paper. Beat the flour, eggs and cream together and stir in the courgette, carrots and leek. Season with the pepper. Heat the oil and drop in tablespoons of the batter. Cook for 4 minutes, turning once, until the fritters are golden brown. Serve hot with a salad garnish and chunks of hot Italian bread.

Marinata di Aglio e Peperoni

Marinated Garlic and Peppers
Makes 2 jars

1 green (bell) pepper
1 red (bell) pepper
1 yellow (bell) pepper
2 shallots, sliced
2 sprigs of rosemary
4 garlic cloves, chopped
15 ml/1 tbsp whole peppercorns
90 ml/6 tbsp lemon juice
250 ml/8 fl oz/1 cup olive oil
90 ml/6 tbsp white wine

Cut the peppers into thin strips and pack into two preserving jars with the shallots, rosemary, garlic and peppercorns. Blend the lemon juice with the oil and wine and pour over the vegetables. Cover with tight-fitting lids and store for at least 24 hours. Use within 3 weeks.

Olive Mediterranea

Mediterranean Olives
Makes 450 g/1 lb

225 g/8 oz/1⅓ cups black olives
225 g/8 oz/1⅓ cup green olives
30 ml/2 tbsp chopped fresh marjoram
15 ml/1 tbsp chopped fresh oregano
2 bay leaves
2 garlic cloves, sliced
8 whole peppercorns
1 lemon, quartered
1 sprig of rosemary
Virgin olive oil

Place everything except the olive oil in a clean, wide-necked jar. Pour in the olive oil, then cover and seal with greaseproof (waxed) paper or foil and a lid. Store in a cool, dark place, shaking every 2 or 3 weeks. After 1 month the olives are ready for use. Drain well before serving as an antipasto. The oil can be used for salad dressings.

Lattuga e Piselli

Lettuce with Peas
Serves 4

1 bunch of spring onions (scallions)
50 g/2 oz/¼ cup unsalted (sweet) butter
1 round lettuce, shredded
450 g/1 lb peas, shelled (or 225 g/
  8 oz/2 cups frozen)
5 ml/1 tsp brown sugar
Salt and freshly ground black pepper
2.5 ml/½ tsp grated nutmeg

Chop the spring onions. Melt the butter in a pan and add the lettuce, spring onions peas and sugar. Cover and simmer gently for 5–8 minutes until the peas are tender. Season to taste with the salt and pepper. Transfer to a serving dish and sprinkle over the nutmeg.

Zucca Fritta

Fried Marrow

Serves 4

3 small marrows (squash), peeled
Oil for frying
1 garlic clove
2 eggs, beaten
50 g/2 oz/1 cup fresh breadcrumbs
Salt and freshly ground black pepper

Cook the marrow in boiling, salted water for 10 minutes. Drain. Cut each marrow into 1 cm/½ in slices and remove the seeds. Heat a little oil in a shallow pan. Crush the garlic and beat into the eggs. Dip each marrow slice into the beaten egg and then the breadcrumbs. Fry (sauté) the marrow for two minutes until brown on both sides, season and serve while still hot.

Pasta d'Olive, Acciughe e Pomodoro

Olive, Anchovy and Tomato Paste

Serves 8

2 × 50 g/2 × 2 oz/2 small cans anchovy fillets, drained
225 g/8 oz/1⅓ cups black olives, stoned (pitted) and finely chopped
30 ml/2 tbsp capers, drained and chopped
1 garlic clove, crushed
Freshly ground black pepper
15 ml/1 tbsp tomato purée (paste)
Italian Flat Bread (see page 289), to serve

Place all the ingredients except the tomato purée in a mortar or blender and pound to a rough paste. Add the tomato purée to form a spreadable consistency. Serve with Italian Flat Bread.

Cipolle Metrano

Metrano Onions

Serves 4

4 large onions
2.5 ml/½ tsp salt
1 garlic clove, crushed
225 g/8 oz/2 cups cooked chicken, chopped
1 small apple, grated
10 ml/2 tsp chopped fresh basil
5 ml/1 tsp chopped fresh oregano
Salt and freshly ground black pepper
45 ml/3 tbsp breadcrumbs
1 egg, lightly beaten
10 g/¼ oz/2 tsp butter
15 ml/1 tbsp olive oil

Peel the onions and place in a large saucepan. Pour over enough water to just cover and add the salt. Bring to the boil, cover the pan and simmer for 10 minutes. Remove the onions and cut across 2 cm/ ¾ in from the top of each. Discard the tops. Scoop out the middle of each onion leaving a shell. Chop the centres and place in a mixing bowl. Add the garlic, chicken, apple, basil, oregano, salt, pepper and breadcrumbs and beat in the egg.

Spoon the stuffing into the onion shells and dot with the butter. Place the stuffed onions in an oiled ovenproof dish and pour over the olive oil. Bake in a preheated oven at 160°C/325°F/gas mark 3 for 50 minutes, basting occasionally with the oil.

Verdura Mista con Olive

Mixed Vegetables and Olives
Serves 4–6

30 ml/2 tbsp white wine vinegar
150 ml/¼ pt/⅔ cup olive oil
15 ml/1 tbsp lemon juice
1 garlic clove, chopped
5 ml/1 tsp chopped fresh basil
Salt and freshly ground black pepper
2.5 ml/½ tsp cayenne
100 g/4 oz/⅔ cup green olives
1 small cauliflower, trimmed and
  broken into small florets
1 cucumber, peeled and finely diced
1 green (bell) pepper, sliced
1 red (bell) pepper, sliced
2 courgettes (zucchini), peeled and
  sliced
1 large carrot, diced
2 shallots, chopped
100 g/4 oz/1 small can pimientos,
  drained and chopped
10 ml/2 tsp capers

Place the vinegar, oil, lemon juice, garlic, basil, salt, pepper and cayenne in a large bowl and beat vigorously. Place all the remaining ingredients in the bowl and stir thoroughly. Cover and chill for 24 hours before using, stirring occasionally.

Funghi Ripieni con Spinaci

Mushrooms Stuffed with Spinach
Serves 4

8 large mushrooms, wiped clean
25 g/1 oz/2 tbsp butter, melted
1 small onion, chopped
½ garlic clove, crushed
450 g/1 lb spinach, cooked and
  chopped
Salt and freshly ground black pepper
10 ml/2 tsp lemon juice
75 g/3 oz Mozzarella, diced as small as
  possible

Remove the stalks from the mushrooms and place the caps in an ovenproof dish. Drizzle over half the melted butter. Set aside. Pour the remaining butter into a frying pan (skillet) and cook the onion for 2 minutes. Add the garlic and chopped mushroom stalks. Fry (sauté) for 5 minutes until the vegetables are soft. Add the spinach, salt, pepper and lemon juice to the pan and fry for 2 more minutes. Remove from the heat and spoon the mixture into the mushroom caps. Sprinkle over the Mozzarella cheese and place the dish in a preheated oven at 180°C/350°F/gas mark 4 for 15 minutes.

Fagiolini alle Nocciole

Nutty Beans

Serves 3–4

450 g/1 lb French (green) beans, cut
* in short lengths*
Salt
15 ml/1 tbsp olive oil
60 ml/4 tbsp walnuts, chopped
25 g/1 oz/¼ cup Parmesan cheese,
* grated*

Cook the beans in boiling, salted water for 8 minutes. Drain well. Heat the oil in a frying pan (skillet) and fry (sauté) the nuts for 2 minutes. Add the beans and cheese and mix together. Serve immediately.

Olive Fritte in Tegame

Pan-fried Olives

Makes 24

25 g/1 oz Mortadella
25 g/1 oz Mozzarella cheese
5 ml/1 tsp chopped fresh sage
1.5 ml/¼ tsp cayenne
24 large black olives, stoned (pitted)
5 ml/1 tsp plain (all-purpose) flour
1 egg, beaten
50 g/2 oz/1 cup breadcrumbs
Oil for frying

Place the Mortadella, Mozzarella, sage and cayenne in a food processor and blend for a few seconds. Split the olives and fill with the stuffing. Roll in the flour and then the egg. Dip into the breadcrumbs and fry (sauté) in the hot oil until crisp and golden. Drain on kitchen paper and serve.

Prosciutto di Parma, Formaggio e Fette di Melone

Parma Ham, Cheese and Melon Fingers

Serves 4

1 ripe melon, rind and seeds removed
225 g/8 oz Gorgonzola cheese
175 g/6 oz Parma ham, thinly sliced
15 g/½ oz/1 tbsp butter, softened
1 Rosemary Focaccia loaf (see
* page 287)*
Butter
15 ml/1 tbsp snipped fresh chives

Cut the melon and cheese into narrow fingers. Place a piece of each on a slice of Parma ham and roll up tightly. Secure with a cocktail stick (toothpick) and place on thinly sliced buttered Focaccia. Sprinkle with the chives.

Pâté di Olive e Basilico

Olive and Basil Pâté

Serves 4

75 g/3 oz/½ cup green olives, stoned
* (pitted)*
150 g/5 oz/⅔ cup Ricotta cheese
30 ml/2 tbsp chopped fresh basil
15 ml/1 tbsp capers, chopped
Salt and freshly ground black pepper
San Severo Pastries (see page 291), to
* serve*

Roughly chop the olives and stir into the Ricotta cheese. Add the basil and capers and season to taste. Serve with San Severo Pastries.

Peperoni in Salsa di Pomodoro

Peppers in Tomato Sauce

Serves 4

15 ml/1 tbsp oil
25 g/1 oz/2 tbsp unsalted (sweet) butter
1 small onion, finely chopped
225 g/8 oz green (bell) peppers, seeded and sliced
225 g/8 oz red (bell) peppers, seeded and sliced
1 garlic clove, crushed
5 ml/1 tsp chopped fresh sage
300 ml/½ pint/1¼ cups tomato juice
Salt and freshly ground black pepper

Heat the oil and butter in a frying pan (skillet) and cook the onion for 5 minutes until lightly coloured. Add the peppers and garlic and continue to fry (sauté) for 3 minutes. Stir in the sage and tomato juice. Season with the salt and pepper. Simmer, uncovered, for 10 minutes, stirring occasionally until the peppers are soft. Serve hot.

Zucchini Ripiene

Stuffed Courgettes

Serves 2–4

15 ml/1 tbsp virgin olive oil
4 large tomatoes, skinned, seeded and chopped
150 g/5 oz/⅔ cup Ricotta cheese
30 ml/2 tbsp chopped fresh parsley
2.5 ml/½ tsp grated nutmeg
45 ml/3 tbsp grated Parmesan cheese
1 egg yolk, beaten
4 large courgettes (zucchini), cut in half and scooped out

Heat the oil in a pan and cook the tomatoes for 5 minutes until pulpy. Set aside. Blend the Ricotta cheese, parsley, nutmeg and Parmesan cheese with the beaten egg yolk to form a stiff paste. Carefully fill each courgette half and place in an ovenproof dish. Pour the tomato sauce around the courgettes and cook for 15 minutes in a preheated oven at 190°C/375°F/gas mark 5.

Peperonata

Garlic and Tomato Peppers
Serves 6–8

30 ml/2 tbsp olive oil
1 red onion, sliced
1 onion, sliced
2 red (bell) peppers, thinly sliced
2 yellow (bell) peppers, thinly sliced
2 green (bell) peppers, thinly sliced
2 garlic cloves, crushed
6 large tomatoes, skinned, seeded and
*   chopped*
Salt and freshly ground black pepper

Heat the oil and fry (sauté) the onions until soft. Add the peppers and garlic and simmer for 15 minutes until soft and tender. Stir in the tomatoes and cook for another 30 minutes until the mixture has thickened. Season with the salt and pepper. Turn into a serving dish and leave to cool.

Sfogliata di Patate

Potato Puffs
Serves 4

900 g/2 lb potatoes, cut into slices
Oil for deep-frying
Salt

Fill two large saucepans one-third full with oil. Heat the oil in one pan until a small cube of stale bread dropped into the oil turns golden in one minute. Heat the oil in the second pan until another piece of bread turns golden in 30 seconds. Put the potato slices into the first pan and deep-fry for 4 minutes. Using a slotted spoon, transfer the slices to the second pan and deep-fry for 2 minutes until they puff up. Remove from the oil and drain on kitchen paper. Sprinkle liberally with salt and serve.

Verdure Pollo in Cartoccio

Italian Vegetable Parcels
Serves 4

45 ml/3 tbsp olive oil
2 garlic cloves, crushed
10 ml/2 tsp chopped fresh herbs
4 chicken breasts
450 g/1 lb courgettes (zucchini), thinly
*   sliced*
1 aubergine (eggplant), diced
1 red onion, sliced
1 small green (bell) pepper, chopped
2 tomatoes, chopped
Salt and freshly ground black pepper

Blend the oil and garlic together with the chopped herbs in a bowl. Cut the chicken into 1 cm/½ in strips and add to the marinade. Allow to marinate while preparing the remaining ingredients. Divide the courgettes, aubergine, onion, green pepper and tomatoes between four large foil squares. Divide the chicken among the four portions and pour over the marinade. Season with the salt and pepper and wrap up tightly. Cook for 20 minutes in a preheated oven at 200°C/400°F/gas mark 6. Place on warm plates, open and serve.

Peperoni di Predappio

Predappio Peppers
Serves 4

4 green (bell) peppers
60 ml/4 tbsp olive oil
2 shallots, chopped
2 garlic cloves, crushed
450 g/1 lb tomatoes, skinned and
* chopped*
15 ml/1 tbsp tomato purée (paste)
10 ml/2 tsp chopped fresh basil
5 ml/1 tsp chopped fresh oregano
Salt and freshly ground black pepper
425 g/15 oz/1 large can tuna, drained
* and flaked*
4 canned anchovy fillets, drained and
* chopped*
4 black olives, stoned (pitted) and
* chopped*
5 ml/1 tsp capers
4 slices Mozzarella cheese

Slice the top off each pepper and remove the seeds. Dice the green tops from the peppers, discarding the stalks. Heat half the olive oil in a pan and fry (sauté) the shallots, garlic and diced peppers for 5 minutes. Add the chopped tomatoes, tomato purée, basil, oregano, salt and pepper. Cover the pan and cook rapidly for 5 minutes. Remove the lid and cook for 15 minutes, stirring from time to time, until the mixture has thickened. Stir in the tuna, anchovy fillets, olives and capers and cook for a further 5 minutes. Spoon into the peppers and fill to within 1 cm/½ in of the top. Oil a baking tin (pan) and carefully place the peppers on to it. Bake in a preheated oven at 160°C/325°F/gas mark 3 for 40 minutes, basting occasionally with the oil. Lay the cheese slices over and bake for a further 10 minutes.

Piperade Alla Svelta

Quick Piperade
Serves 4

2 red (bell) peppers
2 yellow (bell) peppers
1 red onion, finely sliced
30 ml/2 tbsp olive oil
6 eggs, beaten and strained
15 ml/1 tbsp chopped fresh sage
1.5 ml/¼ tsp freshly ground black
* pepper*

Place the peppers under a preheated grill (broiler) until the skins blacken, turning occasionally, then put them in a brown paper bag to soften the skins. Peel off the skins and finely slice. Heat the oil in a frying pan (skillet) and cook the onion until soft. Stir in the peppers and cook for 5 minutes. Pour in the beaten eggs and stir until cooked. Season with the sage and pepper and serve.

Aglio Arrostito con Finocchio

Roast Garlic and Fennel
Serves 6

3 garlic bulbs
2 fennel bulbs, sliced
1 shallot, chopped
15 ml/1 tbsp olive oil

Separate the garlic bulbs and peel. Place the garlic cloves and the sliced fennel on to a large piece of foil. Add the chopped shallot and pour over the olive oil. Wrap up in a parcel and roast in a preheated oven at 180°C/350°F/gas mark 4 for 30 minutes. Serve with grilled fish or meat.

Pezzi di Patata al Rosmarino

Rosemary Potato Chunks
Serves 4

450 g/1 lb potatoes
30 ml/2 tbsp olive oil
1 large onion, sliced
3 rashers (slices) bacon, rinded and
*   chopped*
5 ml/1 tsp fresh rosemary
50 g/2 oz/½ cup Parmesan cheese,
*   grated*

Peel the potatoes and cut into small chunks. Place the oil in a frying pan (skillet) and fry (sauté) the potatoes, onion and bacon for 8 minutes until they are browned. Spoon into an ovenproof dish, sprinkle over the rosemary and Parmesan cheese and bake in a preheated oven at 180°C/350°F/gas mark 4 for 15 minutes.

Salame con Fagioli

Salami with Beans
Serves 4–6

30 ml/2 tbsp olive oil
2 onions, sliced
2 garlic cloves, chopped
Salt and freshly ground black pepper
10 ml/2 tsp chopped fresh sage
10 ml/2 tsp chopped fresh coriander
*   (cilantro)*
300 ml/½ pt/1¼ cups vegetable or
*   chicken stock*
225 g/8 oz/1⅓ cups red lentils
225 g/8 oz shelled broad (lima) beans
45 ml/3 tbsp tomato purée (paste)
75 g/3 oz Italian salami, cut into strips
Small sprigs of fresh sage, to garnish

Heat the olive oil in an ovenproof casserole (Dutch oven) and fry (sauté) the onions and garlic for 2 minutes. Season with the salt and pepper and stir in the sage, coriander, stock and red lentils. Cover and cook for 20 minutes until the lentils are tender. Add the beans and tomato purée and continue cooking for 10 minutes until the beans are soft. Pour in more stock if necessary. Stir in the salami and heat through. Spoon on to serving plates and garnish with sprigs of sage.

Peperoni Arrostiti

Roasted Peppers
Serves 4

3 orange (bell) peppers, quartered
3 tomatoes, skinned
45 ml/3 tbsp grated Parmesan cheese
2 garlic cloves, finely chopped
12 olives
30 ml/2 tbsp virgin olive oil
Salt and freshly ground black pepper
30 ml/2 tbsp chopped fresh parsley
Crusty bread, to serve

Arrange the peppers in an oiled, shallow, ovenproof dish, cut side up. Divide the tomatoes between the peppers. Scatter over the Parmesan cheese and sprinkle with the garlic. Place an olive on each piece of pepper and drizzle over the olive oil. Season with the salt and pepper and cook for 30 minutes in a preheated oven at 200°C/400°F/gas mark 6. Scatter over the parsley and serve warm with plenty of crusty bread.

Fagioli in Antipasto

Savoury Haricot Beans

Serves 4

350 g/12 oz/2 cups dried haricot
(navy) beans
15 g/½ oz/1 tbsp butter
1 onion, chopped
1 garlic clove, chopped
400 g/14 oz/1 large can chopped
tomatoes
300 ml/½ pt/1¼ cups vegetable or
chicken stock
15 g/1 tbsp chopped fresh parsley
Salt and freshly ground black pepper

Soak the haricot beans overnight. Boil rapidly in water for 10 minutes then simmer gently for 1½ hours or until tender. Heat the butter in a frying pan (skillet) and cook the onion and garlic for 5 minutes until browned. Stir in the tomatoes, stock and parsley. Bring to the boil and cook for 2 minutes. Lower the heat, season to taste and simmer for 45 minutes, stirring occasionally, until the sauce has reduced and thickened. Drain the beans and add to the sauce. Stir well and serve.

Fette di Salame

Salami Slices

Serves 6

1 large Ciabatta loaf
75 ml/5 tbsp olive oil
1 garlic clove, cut in half
200 g/7 oz/good 1 cup olives
225 g/8 oz Italian salami, thinly sliced
225 g/8 oz Mozzarella cheese, sliced
Fresh herbs, to garnish

Cut the bread into slices about 2.5 cm/ 1 in thick. Brush the olive oil over both sides of the bread. Bake in a preheated oven at 190°C/375°F/gas mark 5 for 5 minutes or toast under a moderate grill (broiler). Rub garlic over one side of each piece of toast. Arrange the olives, salami and slices of Mozzarella on the toast and bake or grill (broil) until the cheese has melted.

Frittatine Imbottite

Spicy Italian Pancakes

Serves 4

450 g/1 lb/4 cups minced (ground) beef
1 onion, chopped
1 garlic clove, crushed
2.5 ml/½ tsp chilli powder
15 ml/1 tbsp tomato purée (paste)
150 ml/¼ pt/⅔ cup beef stock
Salt and freshly ground black pepper
8 cooked pancakes or:

75 g/3 oz/¾ cup plain (all-purpose)
flour
1 egg, beaten
90 ml/6 tbsp milk
60 ml/4 tbsp oil

Place the mince and the onion in a saucepan and fry (sauté) until brown. Stir in the crushed garlic, chilli and tomato purée. Add the stock and bring to the boil. Season with the salt and pepper and cover with a lid. Simmer for 25 minutes. To make the pancakes: beat the flour, egg and milk together. Allow to stand for 10 minutes then beat again. Heat a little of the oil in a frying pan (skillet) and pour in enough mixture to coat the base of the pan. Cook for 2 minutes on each side and slide on to a warm plate. Continue cooking the remaining pancakes. Spoon a little of the spicy filling into the centre of each pancake and fold over. Serve at once.

Fritelle di Acetoselle e Zucchini

Sorrel and Courgette Fritters
Serves 6

2 large courgettes (zucchini)
10 ml/2 tsp salt
75 g/3 oz/¾ cup plain (all-purpose)
*   flour*
2 eggs
30 ml/2 tbsp single (light) cream
50 g/2 oz fresh sorrel, shredded
4 spring onions (scallions), chopped
30 ml/2 tbsp milk
Freshly ground black pepper
Oil for frying

Grate the courgettes and place them in a bowl. Sprinkle with salt and leave to stand for 30 minutes. Squeeze out the moisture from the courgettes and drain on kitchen paper. Beat the flour, eggs and cream together and stir in the courgettes, sorrel and spring onions. Thin with a little milk to obtain the consistency of thick cream. Season with the pepper. Heat the oil and drop tablespoons of the batter into the pan. Cook for 4 minutes, turning once until the fritters are golden. Drain on kitchen paper. Serve hot.

Pasticcio di Spinaci e Acciughe

Spinach and Anchovy Pâté
Serves 4

350 g/12 oz spinach leaves
50 g/2 oz/1 small can anchovy fillets
1 small onion, finely chopped
2.5 ml/½ tsp pepper
3 eggs
100 g/4 oz/2 cups fresh breadcrumbs
Lemon slices, to garnish
Buttered crackers, to serve

Wash the spinach leaves and shake off excess water. Cook in a covered pan until wilted. Drain thoroughly. Drain the oil from the can of anchovies into a pan with the onion and cook over a high heat for 3 minutes. Blend all the ingredients to a paste in a blender or food processor. Divide the mixture between 6 individual ramekins (custard cups). Place them in a pan half-filled with boiling water and cook in a preheated oven at 180°C/350°F/gas mark 4 for 30 minutes until set. Garnish with the lemon slices. Serve with buttered crackers.

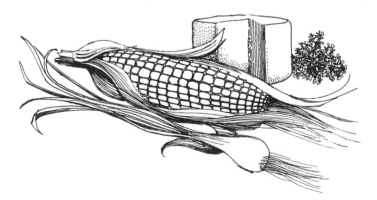

Frittelle di Foglie di Spinaci

Spinach Leaf Fritters
Makes 30 fritters

450 g/1 lb fresh spinach leaves
100 g/4 oz/1 cup plain (all-purpose)
* flour*
2.5 ml/½ tsp salt
1 egg
90 ml/6 tbsp milk
2.5 ml/½ tsp bicarbonate of soda
* (baking soda)*
45 ml/3 tbsp lemon juice
15 ml/1 tbsp olive oil
Salt and freshly ground black pepper
Oil for deep-frying

Remove the stalks from the spinach. Place the flour and salt in a bowl and beat in the egg, milk and bicarbonate of soda. Place the lemon juice, olive oil, salt and pepper in a bowl. Dip the spinach leaves in this mixture and press 4 leaves together. Drain on kitchen paper and dip in the batter. Heat the oil for frying. Quickly drop each bundle of battered leaves into the hot oil and deep-fry for 1 minute until golden. Drain on kitchen paper and keep hot while cooking the remainder. Season with salt and pepper and serve with the marinade.

Finocchio Ripieno con Olive

Stuffed Fennel with Olives
Serves 4

4 fennel bulbs
45 ml/3 tbsp olive oil
1 onion, finely chopped
2 garlic cloves, finely chopped
2 eggs, hard-boiled (hard-cooked) and
* chopped*
100 g/4 oz/2 cups breadcrumbs
15 ml/1 tbsp chopped fresh mint
15 ml/1 tbsp chopped fresh coriander
* (cilantro)*
Salt and freshly ground black pepper
75 g/3 oz/¾ cup Parmesan cheese,
* grated*
8 black olives, stoned (pitted)

Trim the feathery tops from the fennel and reserve. Cut the fennel in half lengthways and place in a pan of boiling salted water for 2 minutes. Drain, cool and scoop out the centre layers with a sharp knife. Chop the scooped-out flesh and set aside. Heat 15 ml/1 tbsp oil in a frying pan (skillet) and cook the onion for 5 minutes until golden. Add the reserved chopped fennel and the garlic and cook for 2 minutes. Stir in the eggs, breadcrumbs, mint and coriander. Season with salt and pepper and fill the fennel shells with the mixture. Place in an oiled baking dish and sprinkle with the Parmesan cheese. Drizzle over the remaining oil and cook in a preheated oven at 200°C/400°F/gas mark 6 for 30 minutes. Garnish with the fennel tops and the olives.

Cipolle Ripiene

Stuffed Onions
Serves 4

4 large onions
Salt and freshly ground black pepper
50 g/2 oz/¼ cup butter
100 g/4 oz mushrooms, chopped
50 g/2 oz/¼ cup arborio rice
300 ml/½ pt/1¼ cups water

Simmer the onions in a pan of boiling salted water for 20 minutes and drain. Remove the centres and chop roughly. Melt half the butter in a frying pan (skillet) and fry (sauté) the mushrooms. Add the rice and cook, stirring occasionally until the fat has been absorbed. Pile the stuffing into the onion cases and top with the remaining butter. Place in a baking dish, pour the water around cover with foil and cook in a preheated oven for 1 hour at 180°C/350°F/gas mark 4.

Melanzane Ripiene con Prosciutto

Stuffed Aubergines with Ham
Serves 4

2 aubergines (eggplants)
50 g/2 oz/¼ cup butter
1 onion, chopped
100 g/4 oz mushrooms, chopped
2 tomatoes, skinned, seeded and
*   chopped*
25 g/1 oz/½ cup breadcrumbs
Salt and freshly ground black pepper
100 g/4 oz ham, chopped

Cut the aubergines in halves and scoop out the centres. Heat half of the butter in a large pan and fry (sauté) the onion and mushrooms for 4 minutes. Add the tomatoes and cook for 5 minutes, stirring. Sprinkle over the breadcrumbs and season with the salt and pepper. Stir in the ham and the chopped flesh from the centre of the aubergines. Pile the mixture into the aubergine cases, dot with the remaining butter and bake for 1 hour in a preheated oven at 180°C/350°F/gas mark 4.

Peperoni Ripieni

Stuffed Peppers
Serves 4

4 green (bell) peppers
1 garlic clove, chopped
30 ml/2 tbsp oil
4 tomatoes, chopped
100 g/4 oz/1 cup cooked long-grain
*   rice*
15 ml/1 tbsp chopped fresh basil
Salt and freshly ground black pepper
Chunky Tomato Sauce (see page 357),
*   to serve*

Cut the tops off the peppers and remove the cores and seeds, reserving the tops. Place the peppers in a pan of boiling, salted water, cook for 5 minutes then drain well. Fry (sauté) the chopped garlic in the oil and add the chopped tomatoes. Cook for 5 minutes, stirring. Stir in the rice, basil, salt and pepper. Fill the peppers with the mixture, replace the lids and put into a greased pie dish. Cover with greased foil and bake in a preheated oven at 200°C/400°F/gas mark 6 for 25 minutes. Serve with Chunky Tomato Sauce.

Soffi di Olive Ripiene

Stuffed Olive Puffs
Makes 25

100 g/4 oz/½ cup margarine, softened
225 g/8 oz/2 cups hard cheese, grated
350g/12 oz/3 cups self-raising (self-
*   rising) flour*
5 ml/1 tsp paprika
25 stuffed olives, drained and dried

Cream the margarine and cheese together.
Add the flour and mix in with the hands. Stir
in the paprika and add enough water to form
a soft dough. Chill the dough for 10 to 20
minutes. Mould a small piece of pastry
around each dry olive. Chill overnight. Bake
in a preheated oven at 200°C/400°F/gas
mark 6 for 10 to 12 minutes.

Carote in Agrodolce

Sweet-and-sour Carrots
Serves 4

4 carrots, grated
1 onion, chopped
15 g/½ oz/1 tbsp unsalted (sweet) butter
25 g/1 oz/¼ cup plain (all-purpose) flour
10 ml/2 tsp sugar
Salt and freshly ground black pepper
15 ml/1 tbsp wine or tarragon vinegar
15 ml/1 tbsp chopped fresh parsley

Cook the carrots and onions in boiling,
salted water for 15 minutes. Drain, keep
warm and reserve the liquid. Heat the butter in a saucepan, blend in the flour and
cook for 1 minute. Gradually add enough
of the carrot liquid to blend to a smooth
sauce, stirring all the time. Stir in the sugar,
pepper and vinegar. Arrange the carrots
and onions on a dish, pour over the sauce
and garnish with the chopped parsley.

Peperoni Dolci con Bagna Cauda

Sweet Peppers with Bagna Cauda
Serves 4

2 red (bell) peppers, cut into strips
2 green (bell) peppers, cut into strips
2 yellow (bell) peppers, cut into strips

Bagna Cauda
50 g/2 oz/¼ cup unsalted (sweet) butter
60 ml/4 tbsp olive oil
30 ml/2 tbsp walnut oil
3 garlic cloves, crushed
50 g/2 oz/1 small can anchovy fillets
45 ml/3 tbsp double (heavy) cream
*   (optional)*

Arrange the peppers on a large serving
platter and set aside. Heat the butter and
oil in a pan and cook the garlic and
anchovies for 10 minutes, stirring until
smooth. Blend in the cream (if using) and
transfer to a warm bowl. Serve immediately with the vegetables.

Melanzane alla Parmigiana

Baked Aubergines Parmesan-style

Serves 4

2 large aubergines (eggplants)
5 ml/1 tsp salt
45 ml/3 tbsp olive oil
100 g/4 oz Mozzarella cheese, grated
30 ml/2 tbsp chopped fresh basil
45 ml/3 tbsp passata (sieved tomatoes)
50 g/2 oz/½ cup Parmesan cheese,
    grated

Cut the aubergines into 1 cm/½ in thick slices lengthways. Lay them on a flat dish and sprinkle with the salt. Allow the aubergines to stand for 30 minutes. Wash, drain and wipe thoroughly on kitchen paper. Heat the oil in a frying pan (skillet) and fry (sauté) a few slices at a time until golden brown on either side. Cover the base of an ovenproof dish with the aubergine slices. Sprinkle with a layer of Mozzarella cheese, basil and then passata. Continue to layer the ingredients in this manner, finishing with a layer of cheese. Sprinkle with the Parmesan. Bake in a pre-heated oven at 180°C/350°F/gas mark 4 for 20 minutes.

Fiche con Prosciutto

Figs with Ham

Serves 4

8 fresh figs, wiped clean
8 thin slices prosciutto
5 ml/1 tsp chopped fresh basil
15 ml/1 tbsp olive oil

Make a cut in each fig downwards but do not cut through. Roll up the ham slices and place one curled roll in each cut fig. Blend the basil and oil together and sprinkle over the figs. Chill for 30 minutes before serving.

Peperoni Tarantini

Taranto Peppers

Serves 4

25 g/1 oz/2 tbsp unsalted (sweet) butter
30 ml/2 tbsp olive oil
1 large onion, thinly sliced
2 garlic cloves, crushed
3 red (bell) peppers, sliced thinly
5 ml/1 tsp chopped fresh basil
Salt and freshly ground black pepper
2.5 ml/½ tsp cayenne
1 bay leaf

Heat the butter and oil in a saucepan and fry (sauté) the onion and garlic for 5 minutes. Add the red peppers, cover the pan with foil or a lid and reduce the heat. Cook gently for 12 minutes and stir in the remaining ingredients. Simmer, uncovered, for a further 20 minutes.

Formaggio di Capra Tostato

Toasted Goats' Cheese

Serves 4–5

175 g/6 oz goats' cheese
10 ml/2 tsp olive oil
5 ml/1 tsp made mustard
Salt and freshly ground black pepper
Radicchio leaves

Cut the goats' cheese into 10 thin slices. Lay on a baking sheet. Blend the oil with the mustard and brush over the cheese. Cook under the grill (broiler) until the cheese is bubbling and brown. Sprinkle over the salt and pepper and serve on the radicchio.

Vasetti di Fegatini di Pollo

Chicken Liver Ramekins
Serves 4

100 g/4 oz/1 cup chicken livers
15 ml/1 tbsp olive oil
1 large onion, chopped
1.5 ml/¼ tsp cayenne
150 ml/¼ pt/⅔ cup single (light) cream
15 ml/1 tbsp chopped fresh parsley
Fresh bread, to serve

Chop the liver into 2.5 cm/1 in pieces. Fry (sauté) the liver in the oil for 3 minutes. Add the chopped onion and continue cooking until the onion is translucent but not brown. Put the liver and onion through a mincer (grinder) and place in a bowl. Beat in the cayenne and the cream. Spoon into small ramekin dishes (custard cups), sprinkle with parsley and serve with chunks of fresh, home-made bread.

Acciughe e Aglio

Anchovies and Garlic
Serves 4

3 garlic cloves, quartered
30 ml/2 tbsp wine vinegar
50 g/2 oz/1 small can anchovy fillets, drained
90 ml/6 tbsp olive oil
2.5 ml/½ tsp salt
2.5 ml/½ tsp freshly ground black pepper
Lettuce leaves, to serve

Chop the anchovies into 1 cm/½ in pieces. Put the garlic pieces and vinegar into a bowl, stir well, and allow to stand for at least 1 hour. Press the garlic pieces against the side of the bowl with the back of a spoon, and discard them. Add the anchovies, oil, salt and pepper. Toss. Serve on a bed of lettuce.

Funghi con Ripieno di Formaggio

Cheese Stuffed Mushrooms
Serves 4

15 ml/1 tbsp olive oil
8 large mushrooms, peeled
225 g/8 oz Pecorino cheese, in one piece
50 g/2 oz/¼ cup unsalted (sweet) butter
1 garlic clove, crushed
225 g/8 oz/4 cups fresh breadcrumbs
15 ml/1 tbsp chopped fresh coriander (cilantro)

Brush oil over the mushrooms and place in an ovenproof dish. Cut the cheese into 8 slices and put a slice into the centre of each mushroom. Melt the butter and fry (sauté) the garlic for 1 minute. Stir in the breadcrumbs and coriander and remove from the heat. Spoon the mixture over the cheese and press down firmly. Cook for 10–12 minutes in a preheated oven at 220°C/425°F/gas mark 7 and serve hot.

Salsetta di Gorgonzola

Gorgonzola Dip
Makes 250 ml/8 fl oz/1 cup

100 g/4 oz/1 cup Gorgonzola cheese
75 g/3 oz/⅓ cup cream cheese
30 ml/2 tbsp single (light) cream
30 ml/2 tbsp brandy
15 ml/1 tbsp finely chopped fresh chives
Fresh vegetable sticks or grissini

Cream the Gorgonzola until soft and blend in the cream cheese and the single cream a little at a time. Mix in the brandy and stir in the chives. Spoon into a small bowl and chill before serving with fresh vegetable sticks or grissini.

Salsetta di Aglio

Garlic Dip
Makes 175 g/6 oz/1½ cups

175 g/6 oz/¾ cup Ricotta cheese
3 garlic cloves, crushed
15 ml/1 tbsp double (heavy) cream
5 ml/1 tsp salt
2.5 ml/½ tsp freshly ground black
  pepper
15 ml/1 tbsp snipped fresh chives
Raw vegetable sticks, to serve

Blend all the ingredients in a bowl and
spoon into a shallow serving dish. Chill for
30 minutes. Serve with raw vegetable
sticks.

Salsa Acciughe

Anchovy Dip
Serves 4

12 salted anchovies
4 garlic cloves, crushed
30 ml/2 tbsp olive oil
75 g/3 oz/⅓ cup unsalted (sweet) butter
Gorgonzola Savouries (see page 291),
  to serve

Wash and drain the anchovies and remove
any bones. Chop. Put the anchovies in a
saucepan with the garlic and slowly add
the oil. Cook for 15 minutes over a low
heat. Stir in the butter and blend well.
Serve hot with Gorgonzola Savouries.

Salsetta di Pomodoro Secco

Sun-dried Dip
Serves 6–8

400 g/14 oz/1 large can pimientos,
  drained
100 g/4 oz sun-dried tomatoes in oil
2 garlic cloves, crushed
15 ml/1 tbsp lemon juice
15 ml/1 tbsp chopped fresh parsley
300 ml/½ pt/1¼ cups single (light)
  cream
Salt and freshly ground black pepper
Raw vegetable sticks, to serve

Purée the pimientos, tomatoes and garlic
in a blender or food processor. Blend in the
remaining ingredients. Serve with raw
vegetable sticks.

Uova al Forno con Parmigiano

Baked Eggs with Parmesan
Serves 4

25 g/1 oz/2 tbsp unsalted (sweet) butter
50 g/2 oz/½ cup Parmesan cheese,
  grated
4 eggs
Salt and freshly ground black pepper
Black Olive Bread (see page 283)

Grease 4 small ramekin dishes (custard cups) with half the butter. Sprinkle with the Parmesan cheese and break an egg into each dish. Add a small knob of butter and season with the salt and pepper. Place on a baking sheet and bake in a preheated oven at 180°C/350°F/gas mark 4 for 10 minutes. Serve immediately with slices of Black Olive Bread.

Uova con Ripieno di Olive

Olive-stuffed Eggs
Serves 4

4 hard-boiled (hard-cooked) eggs,
  halved
25 g/1 oz/2 tbsp unsalted (sweet)
  butter, softened
30 ml/2 tbsp mayonnaise
15 ml/1 tbsp Ricotta or cream cheese
5 ml/1 tsp chopped fresh basil
10 black olives, stoned (pitted) and
  chopped
Salt and freshly ground black pepper
8 small pickled gherkins (cornichons)

Remove the yolks from each egg half and place the yolks in a mixing bowl. Beat in the butter, mayonnaise, Ricotta, basil, black olives, salt and pepper until the mixture forms a smooth paste. Spoon equal amounts of the paste into each egg white and top with a pickled gherkin. Place the eggs on a plate and chill for 30 minutes.

Pasta d'Olive e Acciughe

Olive and Anchovy Paste
Serves 4

100 g/4 oz green olives, stoned (pitted)
30 ml/2 tbsp capers, chopped
50 g/2 oz/1 small can anchovies in oil
Freshly ground black pepper
Ciabatta bread, to serve

Place the olives and capers in a blender or food processor and blend until smooth. Drain the anchovies and add to the paste. Slowly blend in the anchovy oil, a little at a time until the paste forms a soft texture. Season to taste with the pepper. Serve with Ciabatta bread.

Uova con Ripieno d'Aglio

Garlic Stuffed Eggs

Serves 4

8 hard-boiled (hard-cooked) eggs
1 garlic clove, crushed
50 g/2 oz/¼ cup unsalted (sweet)
   butter, softened
60 ml/4 tbsp double (heavy) cream
Salt and freshly ground black pepper
5 ml/1 tsp chopped fresh sage
Lettuce leaves

Cut the tops off each egg and set aside. Trim the bases so the eggs will stand up. Scoop out the egg yolks and place in a bowl. Add the garlic and butter and mash together until they form a paste. Mash in the cream, salt, pepper and sage. Spoon equal amounts into the hollowed out eggs and press the tops back on to the eggs. Serve chilled on a bed of lettuce.

Fonduta all' Italiana

Fondue Italienne

Serves 4

1 garlic clove, halved
300 ml/½ pt/1¼ cups milk
225 g/8 oz/2 cups Mozzarella cheese,
   grated
225 g/8 oz/2 cups Dolcelatte cheese,
   chopped
50 g/2 oz/½ cup Parmesan cheese,
   grated
10 ml/2 tsp cornflour (cornstarch)
45 ml/3 tbsp dry white wine
2 large apples, peeled, cored and
   quartered
175 g/6 oz salami, thinly sliced
Crusty bread, cut in chunks

Rub the inside of a fondue pot with the cut clove of garlic. Add the milk and heat until bubbling. Stir in all the cheeses and continue to heat until melted, stirring all the time. Blend the cornflour with the wine and stir into the cheese mixture. Cook for 4 minutes, until thick and creamy. Serve with apple quarters, slices of rolled up salami and chunks of bread to dip in.

Uova e Fegato

Eggs and Liver

Serves 3–4

6 chicken livers
Salt and freshly ground black pepper
30 ml/2 tbsp olive oil
90 ml/6 tbsp white wine
1 small onion, chopped
45 ml/3 tbsp tomato purée (paste)
4 eggs
Focaccia Bread (see page 285), to
   serve

Cut the chicken livers into small pieces and season with salt and pepper. Heat the olive oil in a saucepan and cook the chicken livers for 4 minutes. Remove the livers and pour in the wine. Add the onion and simmer for 3 minutes. Add the tomato purée and cook for 5 minutes. Return the livers to the sauce, break the eggs into the pan and cover with a lid. Cook for 4 minutes. Carefully lift out the eggs with a fish slice and place on warm plates. Spoon over the sauce and serve with Focaccia.

Mozzarella e Odori in Conserva

Preserved Mozzarella and Herbs

Serves 4

225 g/8 oz Mozzarella cheese, cut into
* 1 cm/½ in cubes*
1 red (bell) pepper, halved
1 green (bell) pepper, halved
15 ml/1 tbsp peppercorns
2 garlic cloves, peeled
2 sprigs of rosemary
600 ml/1 pt/2½ cups olive oil
Italian bread, to serve

Place the peppers skin-sides up under the grill (broiler) until the skins blacken. Peel off the skins and slice into thin strips. Place the cheese, peppers, peppercorns and whole garlic in a sterilised wide-necked jar. Carefully put in the rosemary sprigs and top up with the olive oil. Replace the lid securely and leave for a week before serving. To serve, arrange the cheese and peppers on individual plates and accompany with bread. Use the remaining oil as a salad dressing or for cooking chicken.

Peperoni in Conserva

Preserved Peppers

Makes 750 g/1½ lb

4 large red (bell) peppers, halved
900 ml/1½ pts/3¾ cups white wine
* vinegar*
2.5 ml/½ tsp salt
6 black peppercorns
4 sprigs of parsley
2 sprigs of thyme
1 bay leaf
60 ml/4 tbsp olive oil

Grill the peppers for 5 minutes, skin sides up, until the skin is charred. Peel off the black skin. Slice the peppers and pack into sterilised jars. Set aside. Bring the remaining ingredients, except the oil, to the boil in a saucepan and strain the vinegar into the jars. Allow to cool and add the olive oil on the top of each jar. Seal and store in a cool, dark place.

Affettato Misto

Mixed Cured Meats

Serves 4

350 g/12 oz mixed cooked Italian
* meats (Milano salami, salsiccia,*
* capicolla, prosciutto, mortadella)*
50 g/2 oz/⅓ cup mixed black and green
* olives*
15 ml/1 tbsp capers
Grissini or warm Ciabatta bread, to
* serve*

Lay the meats attractively on one large or four small serving plates. Scatter the olives and capers over. Serve with grissini or warm Ciabatta bread.

Gnocchi alla Romana

Roman-style Gnocchi
Serves 6

900 ml/1½ pts/3¾ cups milk
1 sprig of rosemary
225 g/8 oz/1⅓ cups semolina (cream of
wheat)
100 g/4 oz/½ cup unsalted (sweet)
butter
175 g/6 oz/1½ cups Parmesan cheese,
freshly grated
Salt and freshly ground black pepper
3 large eggs, beaten
Flour, for dusting
Freshly grated nutmeg

Put the milk in a saucepan with the rosemary. Bring to the boil, remove from the
heat and leave to infuse for 15 minutes.
Remove the rosemary. Stir in the semolina,
bring to the boil and cook for 5 minutes,
stirring all the time. Remove from the heat
and stir in half the butter and 100 g/4 oz/1
cup of the cheese. Season well with salt
and pepper. Gradually beat the eggs into
the mixture. Turn into a greased shallow
baking tin (pan) and chill for 2 hours until
firm. Cut into squares, then roll into wal-
nut-sized balls with lightly floured hands.
Use a little of the remaining butter to
grease an ovenproof dish. Arrange the
gnocchi in a single layer in the dish.
Sprinkle with a little more salt and pepper
and some grated nutmeg. Melt the remaining butter and drizzle over the surface.
Sprinkle with the remaining cheese and
bake in a preheated oven at 180°C/350°F/,
gas mark 4 for about 40 minutes until
golden brown. Serve straight away.

Gnocchi Verdi

Green Gnocchi
Serves 4–6

450 g/1 lb spinach
100 g/4 oz/½ cup unsalted (sweet)
butter
175 g/6 oz/¾ cup curd (smooth
cottage) cheese
45 ml/3 tbsp plain (all-purpose) flour
30 ml/2 tbsp double (heavy) cream
2 eggs, beaten
Salt and freshly ground black pepper
2.5 ml/½ tsp freshly grated nutmeg
100 g/4 oz/1 cup Parmesan cheese,
freshly grated
A little extra flour

Wash the spinach in several changes of
water. Put in a saucepan with no extra
water, cover and cook for 5 minutes.
Drain, squeeze out all excess moisture
then finely chop. Melt half the butter in a
saucepan. Add the spinach and curd
cheese and cook, stirring, for 3–4 minutes.
Remove from the heat, stir in the flour,
cream, eggs, some salt and pepper, the nutmeg and 25 g/1 oz/¼ cup of the Parmesan
cheese. Mix thoroughly, then turn the mixture into a large shallow dish and chill for
2 hours until firm. With floured hands,
shape the gnocchi into small balls. Drop a
few at a time into a pan of boiling water
and cook until they puff up and rise to the
surface. Remove with a draining spoon
and arrange in a buttered flameproof dish.
Melt the remaining butter and drizzle over
the gnocchi. Sprinkle with the remaining
cheese and grill (broil) until the top is
golden brown. Serve straight away.

Gnocchi di Patate

Potato Gnocchi
Serves 4–6

750 g/1½ lb potatoes, cut in even pieces
Salt and freshly ground black pepper
225 g/8 oz/2 cups plain (all-purpose) flour
1 egg
15 g/½ oz/1 tbsp butter
75 g/3 oz/¾ cup Parmesan cheese, grated

Boil the potatoes in salted water for 12 minutes until just tender. Pass through a sieve (strainer) and season. Blend with the flour, egg and butter. Form into small balls. Cook in boiling salted water for 3–4 minutes or until they rise to the surface. Remove from the pan with a draining spoon and sprinkle with the Parmesan cheese.

Gnocchi di Semolina

Semolina Dumplings
Makes 24 dumplings

300 ml/½ pt/1¼ cups milk
15 g/½ oz/1 tbsp unsalted (sweet) butter
2.5 ml/½ tsp salt
100 g/4 oz/⅓ cup semolina (cream of wheat)
2 eggs, beaten
5 ml/1 tsp ground cinnamon
Butter, to taste (optional)
Parmesan cheese, to taste (optional)

Heat the milk in a large saucepan and stir in the butter and salt. Bring to the boil and add the semolina, stirring constantly. Reduce the heat and gently simmer for 5 minutes. Remove from the heat and beat in the eggs and cinnamon. Allow the semolina mixture to cool for 30 minutes.

Shape into 24 small nut-sized balls and set aside. Half fill a large saucepan with water and bring to the boil. Reduce the heat and drop the balls into the water, a few at a time. Cook for 5 minutes until they rise to the surface. Remove from the pan with a draining spoon and keep warm until required. Drizzle with melted butter and sprinkle with Parmesan cheese or serve in soup.

Caponata Siciliana

Sicilian-style Aubergine and Olive Antipasto

Serves 4–6

2 aubergines (eggplants), diced
Salt
100 ml/3½ fl oz/6½ tbsp olive oil
1 large red onion, finely chopped
200 g/7 oz/1 small can pimiento caps,
  drained and sliced
4 ripe tomatoes, seeded and cut in
  eighths
30 ml/2 tbsp capers
75 g/3 oz/½ cup green olives, stoned
  (pitted)
1 celery stick, finely chopped
15 ml/1 tbsp granulated sugar
60 ml/4 tbsp red wine vinegar
30 ml/2 tbsp pine nuts
15 ml/1 tbsp chopped fresh parsley
Ciabatta bread, to serve

Place the diced aubergines in a colander and sprinkle with salt. Leave to stand for 30 minutes then rinse with cold water and dry on kitchen paper. Heat half the oil in a large frying pan (skillet) and fry (sauté) the aubergines until soft and golden, stirring frequently. Meanwhile, heat the remaining oil in a saucepan, add the onion, pimientos, tomatoes, olives and celery. Cook over a gentle heat for 10 minutes then stir in the sugar and vinegar. Simmer for 2–3 minutes, remove from the heat then stir in the aubergines. Turn into a serving dish, sprinkle with the pine nuts and parsley and serve warm or cold with Ciabatta.

Soups

Most comforting, hearty Italian soups are substantial enough for a main course in themselves. Ideal for lunch or supper, the soups need only fresh, hot bread to accompany them. They should be served directly from the saucepan into soup bowls with a touch of olive oil added at the last moment.

In Italy, every family, village, town and region has a favourite recipe and a heavy soup would be followed by a delicate fish course. Most of the vegetable soups have the advantage that they improve when they are made in advance and heated a day or two later.

Zuppa d'Autunno

Autumn Soup

Serves 6

1 onion, finely chopped
25 g/1 oz/2 tbsp unsalted (sweet) butter
2 courgettes (zucchini), coarsely chopped
1 yellow (bell) pepper, chopped
2 large carrots, chopped
500 ml/17 fl oz/2¼ cups chicken stock
150 g/5 oz/scant 1 cup red lentils
2.5 ml/½ tsp curry powder
250 ml/8 fl oz/1 cup thick (heavy) cream
Salt and freshly ground black pepper

Cook the onion in the butter until soft and golden. Add the vegetables and cook for 8 minutes, stirring. Pour in the chicken stock and lentils. Bring to the boil and simmer, covered, for 30 minutes. Allow the mixture to cool slightly. Transfer to a blender or food processor and purée until smooth. Return to the saucepan. Add the remaining ingredients and reheat. Do not allow to boil.

Zuppa Mandorle

Almond Soup

Serves 4

25 g/1 oz/2 tbsp unsalted (sweet) butter
1 onion, minced
100 g/4 oz/1 cup ground almonds
250 ml/8 fl oz/1 cup water
250 ml/8 fl oz/1 cup single (light) cream
¼ cucumber, cut in small cubes and steamed
Salt and freshly ground black pepper

Heat the butter in a frying pan (skillet) and cook the onion for 2 minutes. Stir in the almonds and cook until slightly browned. Add the water and cream. Simmer for 15 minutes and add the cucumber cubes. Season and serve.

Zuppa di Cozze

Mussel Soup
Serves 6

225 g/8 oz/1⅓ cups dried white
* cannellini beans*
1 large onion
5 ml/1 tsp olive oil
1 garlic clove, crushed
1.2 litres/2 pts/5 cups stock
225 g/8 oz mussels, scrubbed and
* beards removed*
1 bay leaf
3 carrots, chopped
100 g/4 oz fresh or frozen peas
4 leaves of fresh parsley, chopped
4 tomatoes, skinned, seeded and diced
3 celery sticks, chopped
Salt and freshly ground black pepper

Place the beans in a large bowl, cover with cold water and soak overnight. Drain. Place in a large saucepan. Cover with cold water. Bring to the boil and boil rapidly for 10 minutes. Reduce the heat and simmer for 1 hour. Drain. Chop the onion and place in the saucepan with the oil and garlic. Cook until they are translucent. Pour in the stock, add the mussels and the bay leaf and simmer for about 10 minutes. Skim the surface of the soup if necessary. Add the remaining ingredients and the cannellini beans and cook, uncovered, for 10 minutes. Remove any mussels that have not opened and discard. Remove the bay leaf before serving.

Sostanzioso Minestrone di Verdura

Big Vegetable Minestrone
Serves 4–6

5 ml/1 tsp olive oil
225 g/8 oz salt belly pork, rinded and
* diced*
1 garlic clove, finely chopped
1 onion, chopped
5 ml/1 tsp chopped fresh parsley
5 ml/1 tsp chopped fresh oregano
2.5 ml/½ tsp freshly ground black
* pepper*
15 ml/1 tbsp tomato purée (paste)
1.2 litres/2 pts/5 cups vegetable or
* chicken stock*
2 carrots, finely diced
3 celery sticks, chopped
2 potatoes, diced
225 g/8 oz/2 cups cooked haricot
* (navy) beans (or 2 x 425 g/*
* 2 x 15 oz/2 large cans, drained)*
100 g/4 oz fresh or frozen peas
4 tomatoes, skinned and chopped
100 g/4 oz fine noodles
30 ml/2 tbsp grated Parmesan cheese

Place the oil in a large pan and add the meat, garlic, onion, parsley, oregano, and pepper. Cook for 10 minutes until the ingredients begin to brown. Add the tomato purée and 120 ml/4 fl oz/½ cup of the stock. Cook for a further 5 minutes. Add all the vegetables and the beans and the remaining stock, then simmer for 45 minutes. Add the noodles and cook for 10 minutes. Turn into a hot tureen and sprinkle with the grated cheese.

Zuppa di Castagne

Chestnut Soup
Serves 4–6

450 g/1 lb chestnuts
25 g/1 oz/2 tbsp butter
1 small onion, minced
25 g/1 oz/¼ cup plain (all-purpose)
  flour
600 ml/1 pt/2½ cups milk
Salt and freshly ground black pepper
2.5 ml/½ tsp grated nutmeg
150 ml/¼ pt/⅔ cup single (light) cream
5 ml/1 tsp chopped fresh parsley

Slit the chestnuts and boil them until they are soft. Remove the outer shell and the inner skin. Blend or rub through a sieve. Heat the butter in a saucepan and cook the onion. Sprinkle over the flour and stir. Gradually stir in the milk and bring to the boil. Stir until the sauce has thickened and there are no lumps. Blend in the chestnut purée. Season with the salt, pepper and nutmeg and cook for 8–10 minutes, stirring all the time. Remove from the heat and stir in half the cream. Serve hot with some of the remaining cream poured in the centre of each dish and garnish with the parsley.

Zuppa di Agrumi

Citrus Soup
Serves 4

450 g/1 lb frozen lemon sorbet
20 ml/4 tsp vodka
Thin strips of lemon rind
Sprigs of mint, to garnish

Put 4 soup plates in the freezer for 10 minutes. Allow the sorbet to soften in the fridge for 20 minutes and purée for 20 seconds in a food processor or blender, adding the vodka halfway through. Pour into the soup bowls. Sprinkle over the lemon rind and garnish with the mint.

Zuppa di Sedani

Cream of Celery Soup
Serves 4

1 head celery, roughly chopped
1 small onion, chopped
15 ml/1 tbsp olive oil
250 ml/8 fl oz/1 cup double (heavy)
  cream
250 ml/8 fl oz/1 cup milk
Salt and freshly ground black pepper

Put the celery in a saucepan with 600 ml/ 1 pint/2½ cups water and bring to the boil until soft. Fry (sauté) the onion in the olive oil for 5 minutes. Put the celery with its liquid and onion through a sieve (strainer), blender or food processor and return to the saucepan. Add the cream and milk and season well with the salt and pepper. Serve very hot.

Zuppa di Pollo e Sedano

Chicken and Celery Soup
Serves 6

6 celery sticks
30 ml/2 tbsp oil
1 onion, finely chopped
450 g/1 lb chicken, finely chopped
900 ml/1½ pts/3¾ cups chicken stock
30 ml/2 tbsp chopped fresh oregano
100 g/4 oz fine macaroni
Salt and freshly ground black pepper

Chop the celery into 1 cm/½ in pieces. Heat the oil in a large saucepan and cook the celery and onion for 1 minute. Add the chicken and cook for 5 minutes, stirring all the time. Add the stock and oregano and bring to the boil. Lower the heat and simmer for 40 minutes, stirring occasionally. Stir the macaroni into the broth and season well with the salt and pepper. Continue cooking for 20 minutes, stirring from time to time, then serve very hot.

Zuppa di Pesce

Fish Soup
Serves 4–6

450 g/1 lb clams
15 ml/1 tbsp olive oil
2 garlic cloves, chopped
1 onion, chopped
225 g/8 oz monkfish, skinned and cut into 1 cm/½ in cubes
225 g/8 oz raw prawns (shrimp), shelled
600 ml/1 pt/2½ cups fish or chicken stock
Salt and freshly ground black pepper
15 ml/1 tbsp chopped fresh sage
Focaccia Bread (see page 285), to serve

Soak the clams, then drain and cook in 45 ml/3 tbsp water until they open. Strain the cooking liquid and discard any shells that have not opened. Remove the clams from their shells if liked. Heat the oil in a frying pan (skillet) and cook the garlic and onion for 3 minutes. Add the monkfish and prawns and fry (sauté) for 5 minutes. Blend in the stock and cook for 20 minutes, stirring occasionally. Season with the salt and pepper and add the clams and sage. Stir well and serve very hot with Focaccia Bread.

Zuppa di Ciliege

Cherry Soup
Serves 6

50 g/2 oz/⅓ cup semolina (cream of wheat)
900 g/2 lb cherries, stoned (pitted)
900 ml/1½ pts/3¾ cups water
100 g/4 oz/½ cup sugar
3 cinnamon sticks
Juice of ½ lemon
3 egg yolks

Place the semolina in a saucepan with 150 ml/¼ pt/⅔ cup hot water and bring to the boil. Cook gently until thick, stirring. Put the cherries into a large saucepan with the remaining water, sugar, cinnamon sticks and lemon juice. Simmer for 15 minutes. Stir in the cooked semolina and simmer for two more minutes, discard the cinnamon sticks. Beat the egg yolks in a large bowl and whisk in the soup. Stir then cool thoroughly before serving.

Zuppa Rustica di Verdura

Country Vegetable Soup
Serves 4

2 leeks
225 g/8 oz parsnips
225 g/8 oz carrots
1 large onion
2 celery sticks
2 garlic cloves
275 g/10 oz courgettes (zucchini)
450 g/1 lb tomatoes
450 g/1 lb green cabbage
225 g/8 oz broccoli
30 ml/2 tbsp chopped fresh parsley
2.5 ml/½ tsp chopped fresh thyme
2.5 ml/½ tsp chopped fresh basil
2 bay leaves
Salt and freshly ground black pepper

Roughly chop the vegetables and the parsley. Place in a stock pot and cover with 1.25 litres/2¼ pts/5½ cups water. Bring to the boil over a high heat. Reduce the heat and add the herbs. Cover with a lid and simmer for 1 hour. Discard the bay leaves before serving.

Zuppa di Vongole e Gamberetti

Clam and Shrimp Soup
Serves 4–6

450 g/1 lb clams
15 ml/1 tbsp olive oil
2 garlic cloves, chopped
1 onion, chopped
75 g/3 oz prosciutto, chopped
2 tomatoes, skinned and finely
chopped
600 ml/1 pt/2½ cups fish or chicken
stock
Salt and freshly ground black pepper
225 g/8 oz cooked peeled prawns
(shrimp)
15 ml/1 tbsp chopped fresh sage
Focaccia Bread (see page 285), to
serve

Soak the clams, then drain and cook in 45 ml/3 tbsp water until they open. Strain the cooking liquid and discard any shells that have not opened. Remove the clams from their shells. Heat the oil in a frying pan (skillet) and cook the garlic and onion for 3 minutes. Stir in the chopped prosciutto and cook, stirring, for 2 minutes. Add the tomatoes and fry (sauté) for 5 minutes. Blend in the stock and cook for 20 minutes, stirring occasionally. Season with the salt and pepper and add the prawns and clams with the sage. Stir well and serve very hot with Focaccia bread.

Zuppa di Gamberi

Crayfish Soup
Serves 6

24 large crayfish or Dublin Bay Prawns
1.2 litres/2 pts/5 cups water
25 g/1 oz/2 tbsp butter
2 onions, chopped
150 ml/¼ pt/⅔ cup brandy
25g/1 oz/2 tbsp long-grain rice
5 ml/1 tsp tomato purée (paste)
2 tomatoes, chopped
2 egg yolks
45 ml/3 tbsp single (light) cream
15 ml/1 tbsp chopped fresh parsley

Place the crayfish in a large saucepan with the water and bring to the boil. Reduce the heat and simmer for 20 minutes. Drain and reserve the liquid. Shell the crayfish and roughly chop. Meanwhile, heat the butter in a saucepan and fry (sauté) the onions. Add the stock from the crayfish with the brandy, rice, tomato purée and tomatoes and bring to the boil. Simmer for 20 minutes. Add the crayfish. Stir in the egg yolks and the cream. Blend and reheat gently, but do not boil. Sprinkle with the parsley and serve.

Zuppa con Latte

Milk Soup
Serves 4

1.5 litres/2½ pts/6 cups milk
100 g/4 oz/½ cup arborio rice
15 g/½ oz/1 tbsp unsalted (sweet) butter
Salt, to taste

Bring the milk to the boil. Add the rice and simmer gently for 15–20 minutes until tender. Stir in the butter and salt.

Minestra di Lattuga

Cream of Lettuce Soup
Serves 4

450 g/1 lb lettuce or endive, chopped
600 ml/1 pt/2½ cups Celery Soup (see page 43)
2.5 ml/½ tsp celery salt
250 ml/8 fl oz/1 cup single (light) cream

Place the lettuce in a saucepan with the celery soup and simmer for 20 minutes until soft. Put through a sieve (strainer), or purée in a blender or food processor and return to the saucepan. Cook gently for 30 minutes to reduce and thicken the soup. Stir in the celery salt and add the cream. Reheat for 2 minutes.

Minestra di Funghi

Mushroom Soup
Serves 4

450 g/1 lb mushrooms, cut in halves
15 g/½ oz/1 tbsp butter
250 ml/8 fl oz/1 cup vegetable stock
250 ml/8 fl oz/1 cup single (light) cream
2.5 ml/½ tsp paprika

Cook the mushrooms in the butter for 5 minutes and stir in the vegetable stock. Simmer for 20 minutes until the mushrooms are tender. Rub through a coarse sieve (strainer) or purée in a blender or food processor. Stir in the cream. Sprinkle lightly with the paprika.

Zuppa di Zucchini e Patate

Courgette and Potato Soup
Serves 4–6

25 g/1 oz/2 tbsp unsalted (sweet) butter
15 ml/1 tbsp olive oil
1 large onion, finely chopped
450 g/1 lb potatoes, diced
300 ml/½ pt/ 1¼ cups milk
300 ml/½ pt/1¼ cups vegetable stock
5 ml/1 tsp grated nutmeg
25 g/1 oz/¼ cup Parmesan cheese,
* grated*
2.5 ml/½ tsp paprika
30 ml/2 tbsp fresh snipped chives
225 g/8 oz courgettes (zucchini),
* grated*

Melt the butter and oil in a saucepan and cook the onion for 2 minutes. Add the potatoes and cook for a further 5 minutes, stirring occasionally. Stir in the milk, stock and nutmeg and bring to the boil. Simmer for 12 minutes. Blend the Parmesan and paprika together. Snip the chives into small pieces with scissors and mix into the Parmesan. Allow the soup to cool slightly and purée in a blender or food processor until smooth. Return to the pan and stir in the courgettes. Cover and simmer for 8 minutes until the courgettes are cooked. Spoon into bowls and scatter over the Parmesan mixture.

Anatra e Zuppa di Fagioli

Duck and Bean Soup
Serves 4

30 ml/2 tbsp oil
2 duck legs
100 g/4 oz/⅔ cup dried haricot (navy)
* beans, soaked overnight, then*
* boiled rapidly for 10 minutes and*
* drained*
1 onion, sliced
2 carrots, sliced
1 celery stick, chopped
1 garlic clove, crushed
15 ml/1 tbsp fresh coriander (cilantro),
* chopped*
Salt and freshly ground black pepper
1.2 litres/2 pts/5 cups water
300 ml/½ pt/1¼ cups red wine
Black Olive Bread (see page 283), to
* serve*

Heat the oil and fry (sauté) the duck legs for 5 minutes until browned all over. Put the duck with the remaining ingredients in a large casserole dish (Dutch oven). Cover with a lid and place in a preheated oven to cook gently for 2 hours at 180°C/350°F/ gas mark 4. Remove the skin and bones from the duck legs. Chop the meat and return to the soup. Serve with Black Olive Bread.

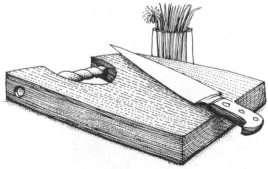

Zuppa di Anguille

Eel Soup
Serves 6

2 onions, sliced
2 carrots, chopped
2 celery sticks, chopped
300 ml/½ pt/1¼ cups red wine
Salt and freshly ground black pepper
2 garlic cloves, sliced
Large bunch of mixed herbs
150 ml/¼ pt/⅔ cup chicken stock
1 kg/2¼ lb eel, cut into 5 cm/2 in pieces
15 g/½ oz/1 tbsp unsalted (sweet) butter

Put the onions, carrots, celery, wine, salt and pepper, garlic and herbs into a saucepan with the stock and bring to the boil. Simmer for 10 minutes. Lay the eel pieces in a shallow pan and strain over the hot stock until it covers the fish. Cover with a lid and bring to the boil. Simmer for 12–15 minutes until the fish flakes easily. Transfer the fish to a serving dish and keep warm. Bring the liquid to the boil and whisk in the butter. Simmer for a few moments and pour over the fish. Serve at once.

Zuppa di Pomodoro e Basilico

Tomato and Basil Soup
Serves 4

3 beefsteak tomatoes, skinned and chopped
1.2 litres/2 pts/5 cups chicken stock
10 ml/2 tsp tomato purée (paste)
15 g/½ oz/1 tbsp unsalted (sweet) butter
100 g/4 oz/½ cup arborio rice
4 basil leaves, chopped
Salt and freshly ground black pepper

Put the tomatoes in a pan with the stock, tomato purée and butter. Bring to the boil. Add the rice, reduce the heat and simmer for 15–20 minutes until the rice is just tender but still has texture. Stir in the basil and season to taste. Serve straight away.

Zuppa di Finocchio

Fennel Soup
Serves 4

2 fennel bulbs, with the feathery fronds
1.2 litres/2 pts/5 cups vegetable or chicken stock
2.5 ml/½ tsp salt
2.5 ml/½ tsp freshly ground black pepper
2 egg yolks
15 ml/1 tbsp lemon juice

Wash the fennel and slice into 1 cm/½ in lengths. Finely chop the fronds and reserve 30 ml/2 tbsp. Place the pieces of fennel in a large saucepan and pour in the stock, salt and pepper. Bring to the boil, lower the heat and simmer for 25 minutes, until the fennel is soft. Remove the pan from the heat and allow to cool for 2 minutes. Purée in a blender or food processor until smooth. Blend the egg yolks and lemon juice together and beat in 60 ml/4 tbsp of the fennel purée. Return the egg yolks to the purée and cook, stirring, for 2 minutes to heat the soup, but do not boil. Spoon into warmed soup plates and sprinkle with the reserved chopped fennel fronds.

Zuppa d'Aglio

Garlic Soup

Serves 4

1.2 litres/2 pts/5 cups vegetable stock
175 g/6 oz potatoes, diced
3 onions, chopped
4 tomatoes, skinned and chopped
2 carrots, chopped
450 g/1 lb French (green) beans, chopped
Salt and freshly ground black pepper
4 garlic cloves, crushed
5 ml/1 tsp chopped fresh basil
30 ml/2 tbsp olive oil

Put the stock into a saucepan and bring to the boil. Add the vegetables and simmer for 15 minutes, stirring occasionally. Stir in the salt and pepper. Add the garlic, basil and olive oil, continue cooking for a further 10 minutes and serve.

Zuppa Gelata di Pomodoro e Finnochio

Iced Tomato and Fennel Soup

Serves 6

2 onions, finely chopped
600 ml/1 pt/2½ cups vegetable stock
450 g/1 lb ripe tomatoes, quartered
1 potato, peeled and cubed
1 fennel bulb, thinly sliced, fronds reserved
10 ml/2 tsp brown sugar
30 ml/2 tbsp tomato purée (paste)
Salt and freshly ground black pepper

Soften the onions in a little stock. Add the remaining ingredients and simmer for 20 minutes until tender. Pour the soup into a blender or food processor and blend until smooth. Cool then chill. Ladle into soup bowls and garnish with the fennel fronds just before serving.

Zuppa Sostanziosa di Fagioli

Filling Bean Soup

Serves 6

225 g/8 oz/1⅓ cups dried white cannellini beans
1 large onion
5 ml/1 tsp olive oil
1 garlic clove, chopped
1.2 litres/2 pts/5 cups vegetable or chicken stock
1 bay leaf
3 celery sticks, chopped
3 carrots, chopped
3 potatoes, diced
4 tomatoes, skinned, seeded and diced
100 g/4 oz fresh or frozen peas
4 fresh basil leaves, chopped
Salt and freshly ground black pepper

Place the beans in a large bowl, cover with cold water and soak overnight, drain. Chop the onion and place in a large saucepan with the oil. Cook until the onion is translucent. Add the garlic and the cannellini beans. Pour in the stock and the bay leaf. Bring to the boil and boil rapidly for 10 minutes then reduce the heat. Cover and simmer for 1 hour. Skim the surface of the soup if necessary. Add the remaining ingredients and cook, uncovered, until the beans are tender. Remove the bay leaf before serving.

Zuppa di Limone e Riso

Lemon and Rice Soup
Serves 4

900 ml/1½ pts/3¾ cups chicken stock
100 g/4 oz/½ cup long-grain rice
3 egg yolks
75 g/3 oz/¾ cup Parmesan cheese, grated
Juice of ½ lemon

Heat the stock until boiling then pour in the rice. Cook for 20 minutes. Allow to cool for 5 minutes. Beat the egg yolks in a bowl and stir in the cheese and lemon juice. Stir this mixture into the soup immediately before serving.

Minestrone alla Microonda

Microwave Minestrone
Serves 4

300 ml/½ pt/1¼ cups vegetable stock
300 ml/½ pt/1¼ cups boiling water
150 g/5 oz/1 small can baked beans in tomato sauce
2 carrots, finely diced
1 leek, cut into 2.5 cm/1 in rings
50 g/2 oz quick-cook macaroni
225g/8 oz/1 small can tomatoes
1 garlic clove, crushed
1 celery stick, sliced
1 onion, chopped
Salt and freshly ground black pepper
15 ml/1 tbsp grated Parmesan cheese

Combine all the ingredients except the Parmesan cheese in a bowl. Cover with clingfilm (plastic wrap), pierce once or twice and microwave on full for 8 minutes. Stir well and cook again for 10 minutes. Leave to stand for 5 minutes. Serve in individual bowls and sprinkle with the Parmesan cheese.

Minestrone alla Milanese

Minestrone
Serves 4

5 ml/1 tsp olive oil
1 garlic clove, finely chopped
1 onion, chopped
5 ml/1 tsp fresh chopped parsley
5 ml/1 tsp fresh chopped oregano
2.5 ml/½ tsp freshly ground black pepper
15 ml/1 tbsp tomato purée (paste)
1.2 litres/2 pts/5 cups vegetable stock
2 carrots, finely diced
3 celery sticks, chopped
2 potatoes, diced
225 g/8 oz/2 cups cooked haricot (navy) beans (or 2 × 425 g/ 2 × 15 oz/2 large cans, drained)
100 g/4 oz fresh or frozen peas
4 tomatoes, skinned and chopped
100 g/4 oz fine taglioni pasta
1 quantity Pesto (see page 366)
30 ml/2 tbsp Parmesan cheese, grated

Place the oil in a large pan and add the garlic, onion, parsley, oregano, and pepper. Cook for 5 minutes until the ingredients begin to brown. Add the tomato purée and 120 ml/4 fl oz/½ cup stock. Cook for a further 5 minutes. Add all the vegetables and the remaining stock and simmer for 45 minutes. Add the taglioni and cook for 10 minutes. Remove from the heat and blend in the Pesto. Sprinkle over grated Parmesan cheese.

Zuppa Rustica

Peasant Soup
Serves 4

4 carrots, chopped
1 small cabbage, chopped
2 onions, chopped
225 g/8 oz fresh or frozen peas
225 g/8 oz fresh or frozen broad (lima)
  beans
4 leeks, chopped
3 potatoes, chopped
225 g/8 oz bacon, rinded and chopped
1.2 litres/2 pts/5 cups chicken or
  vegetable stock
6 small Italian sausages, halved
Salt and freshly ground black pepper
Fresh bread, to serve

Put the vegetables into a saucepan with the chopped bacon. Add the stock and bring to the boil. Reduce heat and simmer for 1 hour. Add the sausages and cook for 15 minutes. Season and serve in large bowls with fresh bread.

Minestra di Zucca Gialla

Pumpkin Soup
Serves 3–4

200 ml/7 fl oz/scant 1 cup water
350 g/12 oz pumpkin, diced
15 ml/1 tbsp sugar
15 g/½ oz/1 tbsp unsalted (sweet)
  butter
450 ml/¾ pt/2 cups milk
1.5 ml/¼ tsp salt
Salt and freshly ground black pepper
Croûtons, to serve

Mix the water, pumpkin, sugar and butter in a saucepan and cook very slowly for 15 minutes until the pumpkin is tender. Remove from the heat and purée in a blender or food processor or press through a sieve (strainer). Bring the milk to boiling point. Add the pumpkin purée and the salt. Taste and adjust the seasoning, reheat and serve hot, garnished with croûtons.

Zuppa di Patate

Potato Soup
Serves 4

2 leeks
50 g/2 oz/¼ cup butter
900 g/2 lb potatoes, thinly sliced
25 g/1 oz/¼ cup plain (all-purpose)
  flour
600 ml/1 pt/2½ cups milk
2.5 ml/½ tsp grated nutmeg
Salt and freshly ground black pepper
1 bouquet garni sachet

Split the leeks in half and chop into chunks. Place the butter in a large saucepan and heat until melted. Add the leeks and potatoes to the butter and cook until they are soft. Sprinkle the flour over the vegetables and cook for 1 minute, stirring all the time. Pour in the milk and bring to the boil, stirring. Season to taste with the nutmeg, salt and pepper and bouquet garni. Cover the pan, lower the heat and cook for a further 15 minutes, stirring occasionally. Remove the bouquet garni before serving.

Zuppa Densa di Salame

Thick Salami Soup

Serves 4

15 g/½ oz/1 tbsp butter
2 large potatoes, diced
3 carrots, diced
1 onion, chopped
400 g/14 oz/1 large can chopped
    tomatoes
10 ml/2 tsp chopped fresh herbs
30 ml/2 tbsp tomato purée (paste)
300 ml/½ pt/1¼ cups chicken stock
Salt and freshly ground black pepper
50 g/2 oz salami, skinned and diced
400 g/14 oz/1 large can cannellini
    beans, drained

Melt the butter in a saucepan and fry
(sauté) the potatoes, carrots and onion for
5 minutes until soft. Stir in the tomatoes, 5
ml/1 tsp of the herbs, the tomato purée and
stock. Bring to the boil, lower the heat and
simmer for 30 minutes. Stir in the salami
and the beans. Season to taste and heat for
5 minutes. Sprinkle the remaining herbs
over and serve.

Minestra di Zucchini Alla Svelta

Quick Courgette Soup

Serves 4

350 g/12 oz firm courgettes (zucchini),
    cut into chunks
3 tomatoes, skinned and quartered
450 ml/¾ pt/2 cups milk
1.5 ml/¼ tsp cayenne
Salt and freshly ground black pepper
45 ml/3 tbsp single (light) cream
5 ml/1 tsp snipped fresh chives

Mix all the ingredients except the cream

and chives and simmer for 15 minutes.
Purée in a blender or food processor or
press through a sieve (strainer). Reheat.
Pour the soup into individual bowls. Add a
swirl of cream and sprinkle with chives
before serving.

Zuppa di Riso e Piselli

Soup with Rice and Peas

Serves 6

225 g/8 oz/1 cup long-grain rice
10 ml/2 tsp olive oil
2 onions, chopped
2 garlic cloves, chopped
1.2 litres/2 pts/5 cups chicken stock or
    water
225 g/8 oz ham, diced
4 tomatoes, skinned and chopped
2 celery sticks, chopped
225 g/8 oz fresh or frozen peas
5 ml/1 tsp chopped fresh basil
Salt and freshly ground black pepper

Soak the rice for 10 minutes in cold water.
Drain the rice and place in a saucepan with
the oil and chopped onions and garlic.
Cook, stirring, for 2 minutes. Add the
stock and ham to the saucepan and bring to
the boil. Skim off the top if necessary.
Simmer for 30 minutes. Add the vegetables and basil and cook for 10 minutes,
stirring occasionally. Stir in the salt and
pepper. Continue cooking for a further 10
minutes.

Zuppa di Pomodoro e Crema

Cream of Tomato Soup
Serves 4

2 onions, chopped
5 ml/1 tsp olive oil
25 g/1 oz/¼ cup plain (all-purpose)
* flour*
1 kg/2¼ lb tomatoes, skinned and
* chopped*
2.5 ml/½ tsp sugar
Salt and freshly ground black pepper
1.2 litres/2 pts/5 cups chicken or
* vegetable stock*
150 ml/¼ pt/⅔ cup single (light) cream

Place the onions in a frying pan (skillet) with the oil. Cook until translucent and soft and sprinkle over the flour. Cook for 2 minutes. Stir in the tomatoes and sugar. Season with the salt and pepper. Pour in the stock and cook for 15 minutes. Purée in a blender or food processor or rub through a sieve (strainer). Stir in the cream just before serving.

Il Brodo

Beef Tea
Serves 4

350 g/12 oz shin of beef
1.2 litres/2 pts/5 cups cold water
1.5 ml/¼ tsp salt
2 cloves
1 onion
2 celery sticks
2 carrots, roughly chopped
Bunch of fresh herbs, such as parsley,
* tarragon and basil*

Place the meat in a large saucepan and cover with the cold water. Add the salt, cover and bring to the boil. Skim the surface with a slotted spoon to remove the foam. Push the cloves into the onion and add to the pan with the other vegetables and herbs. Stir and cover. Simmer for 1¼ hours, remove from the heat and allow to cool for 10 minutes. Strain the broth through a muslin cloth (cheesecloth). Allow to cool completely and strain again. Reheat before serving. This is also good with a little cooked rice or soup pasta added.

Zuppa di Pomodoro e Acciughe

Tomato Anchovy Soup
Serves 4

50 g/2 oz/¼ cup butter
50 g/2 oz/1 small can anchovy fillets in
* oil*
450 g/1 lb ripe tomatoes, skinned,
* seeded and finely chopped*
2 garlic cloves, crushed
5 ml/1 tsp caster (superfine) sugar
1.2 litres/2 pts/5 cups chicken or
* vegetable stock*
Salt and freshly ground black pepper
450 g/1 lb courgettes (zucchini), cut
* into thin slices*
15 fresh basil leaves, torn into small
* pieces*
Ciabatta Bread, to serve

Melt the butter in a large saucepan and add the anchovies Cook over a low heat until the anchovies have dissolved into a purée. Stir in the tomatoes, garlic, sugar and stock. Bring to the boil and simmer for 30 minutes. Season to taste and stir in the courgettes. Boil for 2 minutes and pour into a soup tureen. Sprinkle over the basil leaves. Serve hot with Ciabatta bread.

Gnocchi di Semolina in Brodo

Semolina Dumplings in Hot Soup
Serves 4

25 g/1 oz/2 tbsp butter
2 eggs
Salt and freshly ground black pepper
2.5 ml/½ tsp grated nutmeg
50 g/2 oz/⅓ cup semolina (cream of wheat)
750 ml/1¼ pts/3 cups chicken stock

Cream the butter and eggs together until light and fluffy. Season with salt, pepper and nutmeg. Gradually blend in the semolina. Fill a large saucepan with boiling water and carefully drop very small spoonfuls of the semolina mixture into it. The semolina will swell and resemble small eggs. Cook for 2 minutes until they rise to the surface. Drain and place in a saucepan of the simmering stock. Cook for a further 2 minutes before serving.

Minestra di Maltagliati

'Badly cut' Pasta Soup
Serves 6

3 eggs
275 g/10 oz/2½ cups plain (all-purpose) flour
Salt
1.25 litres/2¼ pts/5½ cups chicken stock
150 ml/¼ pt/⅔ cup white wine

Put the eggs, flour and a pinch of salt into a large bowl and blend to a firm dough. Roll out very thinly and allow to stand for 35 minutes to dry. Cut the dough into small triangles, about the size of a thumbnail. Place the stock and wine in a saucepan and bring to the boil. Lower the heat and simmer. Add the pasta to the stock. Cook for 4 minutes or until the pasta is tender and serve hot.

Zuppa di Spattenna

Tuscan Bean Broth
Serves 4

30 ml/2 tbsp oil
1 onion, sliced
2 garlic cloves, crushed
1 celery stick, chopped
2 carrots, chopped
100 g/4 oz/⅔ cup haricot (navy) beans, soaked overnight
100 g/4 oz/⅔ cup borlotti beans, soaked overnight
100 g/4 oz/⅔ cup lentils
1.2 litres/2 pts/5 cups vegetable stock
Salt and freshly ground black pepper
15 ml/1 tbsp fresh chopped parsley
Black Olive Bread (see page 283), to serve

Heat the oil and fry (sauté) the onion, garlic, celery and carrots in a large flameproof casserole dish (Dutch oven) for 5–6 minutes until browned all over. Add the remaining ingredients except the parsley. Bring to the boil, cover with a lid and place in a preheated oven to cook gently for 2½ hours at 180°C/350°F/gas mark 4. Sprinkle with chopped parsley and serve with Black Olive Bread.

Zuppa Spessa di Pesce con Vermicelli

Thick Fish Soup with Noodles
Serves 4–6

10 ml/2 tbsp olive oil
2 onions, sliced
2 garlic cloves, chopped
3 tomatoes, chopped
1.2 litres/2 pts/5 cups water
900 g/2 lb mixed fish fillets, e.g.
  whiting, sole, mullet, cod, hake,
  mackerel, chopped
300 ml/½ pt/1¼ cups white wine
100 g/4 oz vermicelli, broken in pieces
Salt and freshly ground black pepper

Heat the oil in a large pan and fry (sauté) the sliced onions for 2 minutes. Stir in the garlic and tomatoes and cook until soft. Stir in the water and the fish. Bring to the boil, lower the heat and simmer for about 10 minutes. Remove the fish carefully and place in a dish. Keep warm. Stir the white wine into the stock and vegetables, bring to the boil and add the vermicelli. Cook for 5–10 minutes, then pour over the fish and season to taste.

Zuppa di Pomodori e Funghi

Tomato and Mushroom Soup
Serves 4

450 g/1 lb wild mushrooms
45 ml/3 tbsp olive oil
1 onion, chopped
1 garlic clove, crushed
Salt and freshly ground black pepper
225 g/8 oz tomatoes, skinned and
  chopped
Salt and freshly ground black pepper
30 ml/2 tbsp grated Parmesan cheese

Slice the mushrooms. Heat the oil and fry (sauté) the onion and garlic for 1 minute. Add the mushrooms and season with the salt and pepper. Cook for 15 minutes, stirring occasionally and add the tomatoes. Stir in 600 ml/1 pt/2½ cups boiling water and allow to simmer for 15 minutes. Season to taste. Pour into a soup tureen and sprinkle over the Parmesan cheese.

Jota

Barley and Sauerkraut Soup
Serves 6

175 g/6 oz/1 cup white cannellini or
  borlotti beans, soaked overnight in
  cold water
25 g/1 oz/2 tbsp unsalted (sweet) butter
100 g/4 oz smoked pancetta or streaky
  bacon, rinded and cut in very small
  dice
2 slices fat belly pork, rinded and cut
  in small dice
1 red onion, finely chopped
3 garlic cloves, crushed
45 ml/3 tbsp chopped fresh parsley
15 ml/1 tbsp chopped fresh sage
175 g/6 oz/scant 1 cup pearl barley,
  soaked overnight in cold water and
  drained
2 litres/3½ pts/8½ cups pork or beef
  stock
Salt and freshly ground black pepper
2 potatoes, diced
175 g/6 oz sauerkraut, drained

Drain the beans, place in a pan, cover with
cold water and bring to the boil. Boil
rapidly for 10 minutes then drain. Melt the
butter in a large saucepan. Add the
pancetta, pork, onion and garlic and fry
(sauté), stirring, for 3–4 minutes until
lightly browned. Add the herbs, drained
beans, barley and stock. Bring to the boil,
skim the surface then reduce the heat, part-
cover and simmer gently for 2 hours until
the beans, pork and barley are really tender. Add the potatoes and some salt and
pepper and continue to cook for a further
15 minutes. Stir in the sauerkraut, taste
and re-season if necessary. Heat through
then serve straight away.

Zuppa di Aragosta

Lobster Soup
Serves 6

1 cooked lobster
1 garlic clove, crushed
1 large onion, finely chopped
60 ml/4 tbsp olive oil
45 ml/3 tbsp brandy
1 wineglass dry white wine
450 g/1 lb tomatoes, skinned, seeded
  and chopped
1 litre/1¾ pts/4¼ cups fish stock
250 ml/8 fl oz/1 cup double (heavy)
  cream
15 ml/1 tbsp chopped fresh parsley
10 ml/2 tsp chopped fresh tarragon
Salt and freshly ground black pepper
30 ml/2 tbsp cornflour (cornstarch)
45 ml/3 tbsp water

Cut the lobster in quarters and remove the
stomach sac from behind its head and the
black thread running the length of its body.
Fry (sauté) the garlic and onion in the oil
in a large saucepan for 2 minutes, stirring.
Add the lobster and pour over the brandy.
Ignite and shake the pan until the flames
die down. Add the wine and simmer for 3
minutes. Add the tomatoes, stock and
cream. Bring to the boil, reduce the heat,
part-cover and simmer gently for 35 minutes. Lift out the lobster pieces and when
cool enough to handle, remove all the meat
from the shell. Chop and return the meat to
the saucepan with the herbs and seasoning
to taste. Blend the cornflour with the water
and stir into the soup. Bring to the boil,
reduce the heat and simmer for 2 minutes,
stirring. Serve hot.

Zuppa di Cavolo

Cabbage Soup
Serves 6

1 small savoy cabbage, shredded
1.2 litres/2 pts/5 cups chicken or
vegetable stock
175 g/6 oz stale white bread, diced and
crusts removed
175 g/6 oz/1½ cups Fontina cheese,
grated
100 g/4 oz/1 cup Mozzarella cheese,
grated
40 g/1½ oz/3 tbsp unsalted (sweet)
butter
15 ml/1 tbsp chopped fresh parsley

Boil the cabbage in the stock until tender, about 5 minutes. Drain thoroughly, reserving the stock. Put a layer of cabbage in the base of a flameproof casserole (Dutch oven). Add a layer of bread, then some of each type of cheese. Repeat the layers until all the ingredients are used. Press down gently. Bring the reserved stock back to the boil and pour over the layers. Place over a very gentle heat for 5 minutes to soak. Melt the butter in a small pan and add the parsley. When foaming, pour over the soup and serve straight away.

Zuppa di Riso e Spinaci

Rice and Spinach Soup
Serves 4

275 g/10 oz/1 carton frozen chopped
spinach, thawed
1.2 litres/2 pts/5 cups chicken or
vegetable stock
15 g/½ oz/1 tbsp unsalted (sweet)
butter
100 g/4 oz/½ cup arborio rice
Salt and freshly ground black pepper
Freshly grated Parmesan cheese

Place the spinach in a pan with the stock and butter. Bring to the boil. Add the rice, reduce the heat and simmer for 15–20 minutes until the rice is just tender. Season to taste, ladle into soup bowls and serve with the Parmesan cheese.

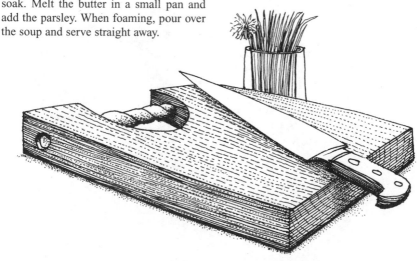

Zuppa di Cozze allo Zafferano

Mussel Soup with Saffron
Serves 6

*2 kg/4½ lb fresh mussels, scrubbed and
  beards removed*
1 wineglass dry white wine
1 large onion, finely chopped
25 g/1 oz/2 tbsp unsalted (sweet) butter
*450 g/1 lb tomatoes, skinned, seeded
  and chopped*
1 litre/1¾ pts/4¼ cups fish stock
*150 ml/¼ pt/⅔ cup double (heavy)
  cream*
5 ml/1 tsp saffron powder
15 ml/1 tbsp chopped fresh parsley
Salt and freshly ground black pepper
Croûtons, to garnish

Discard any mussels that are broken or
open. Place the remainder in a large
saucepan with the wine. Bring to the boil,
cover and cook for a few minutes, shaking
the pan occasionally until the shells open.
Remove the opened mussels from their
shells and reserve. Strain the cooking liquid and reserve. Fry (sauté) the onion in
the butter in a large clean saucepan for 3
minutes to soften. Add the tomatoes and
stock, bring to the boil, reduce the heat and
simmer for 10 minutes. Add the mussels,
the strained mussel cooking liquid, the
cream, saffron and parsley. Simmer for a
further 10 minutes. Season to taste then
ladle into warm soup bowls and garnish
with croûtons before serving.

Zuppa di Fave

Broad Bean Soup
Serves 4

30 ml/2 tbsp oil
1 onion, sliced
1 celery stick, chopped
1 garlic clove, crushed
*450 g/1 lb fresh or frozen broad (lima)
  beans*
15 ml/1 tbsp chopped fresh parsley
Salt and freshly ground black pepper
1.2 litres/2 pts/5 cups chicken stock

Heat the oil in a saucepan. Add the onion,
celery and garlic and fry (sauté) for 3 minutes. Add the remaining ingredients, bring
to the boil, reduce the heat, cover and simmer gently for 20 minutes. Purée in a
blender or food processor. Return to the
pan, heat through and serve.

Snacks and Light Meals

If you fancy a light bite that is tempting and sumptuous, yet not too filling, then look no further. In this chapter you will find Italian specialities which will make you drool!

Tramezzini alle Albicocche

Apricot Sandwiches
Serves 4

450 g/1 lb fresh apricots
8 thick slices of bread
75 ml/5 tbsp caster (superfine) sugar
10 ml/2 tsp ground cinnamon
5 ml/1 tsp grated nutmeg
150 ml/1¼ pt/⅔ cup milk
2 eggs, lightly beaten
50 g/2 oz/¼ cup butter

Place the apricots in a basin of boiling water and leave for 1 minute. Drain, peel off the skins, discard the stones (pits) and slice thinly. Remove the crusts from the bread. Divide the apricots between half the bread. Mix half the sugar, the cinnamon and nutmeg together. Sprinkle a little of this mixture over the apricots reserving the rest. Top with the remaining slices of bread. Mix the remaining sugar, milk and eggs together in a shallow plate.

Heat the butter in a frying pan (skillet). Dip the apricot sandwiches in the egg mixture and fry (sauté) on both sides until golden brown. Remove from the pan and cut each sandwich in half. Sprinkle over the remaining sugar and spice mix and serve immediately.

Infornate all'Acciuga

Anchovy Bakes
Serves 4

8 thick slices bread
75 ml/5 tbsp olive oil
1 garlic clove, cut in half
50 g/2 oz/1 small can anchovies
225 g/8 oz Mozzarella cheese, sliced
200 g/7 oz/good 1 cup olives, stoned (pitted)
Fresh parsley, to garnish

Brush both sides of the bread with olive oil. Bake in a preheated oven at 190°C/375°F/gas mark 5 for 5 minutes or toast under a moderate grill (broiler). Cut the garlic in half and rub over one side of each piece of bread. Drain the anchovies and separate them gently. Arrange on the bread and cover with slices of Mozzarella. Add the olives and bake or grill (broil) until the cheese has melted. Garnish with the fresh parsley.

Fritelle di Gamberette alla Avellino

Avellino Prawn Fritters

Serves 4

100 g/4 oz/1 cup plain (all-purpose)
flour
1 egg
150 ml/¼ pt/⅔ cup milk
15 ml/1 tbsp chopped fresh parsley
5 ml/1 tsp bicarbonate of soda (baking
soda)
Salt and freshly ground black pepper
450 g/1 lb king prawns (jumbo
shrimp), peeled
Oil for deep-frying
Napoli Sauce (see page 358), to serve

Sift the flour into a bowl and beat in the egg, milk, parsley, bicarbonate of soda, salt and pepper until the mixture is smooth and thick. Dry the prawns on kitchen paper and dip several at a time in the batter until well coated. Lower the battered prawns into the hot oil and deep-fry for 3 minutes until golden brown. Drain on kitchen paper and serve with Napoli Sauce.

Calzone con Parmigiano

Cheese Popovers

Makes 8

100 g/4 oz/1 cup plain (all-purpose)
flour
45 ml/3 tbsp grated Parmesan cheese
5 ml/1 tsp salt
2 eggs, lightly beaten
250 ml/8 fl oz/1 cup milk
15 ml/1 tbsp melted butter
15 ml/1 tbsp oil

Preheat oven to 220°C/425°F/gas mark 7. Blend together the flour, cheese and salt in a mixing bowl. In a separate bowl, combine the eggs and the milk. Gradually add to the flour mix, stirring well. Pour in the melted butter and blend thoroughly. Divide the oil between 8 bun tins (muffin pans) and heat in the oven for 1 minute.

Divide the batter evenly in the bun tins. Bake for 10 minutes. Reduce the heat to 180°C/350°F/gas mark 4 and bake for 25 minutes until golden brown. Remove from the tins and serve immediately.

Pane con Erbe

Crisp Herb Slices

Serves 4

75 g/3 oz/⅓ cup butter
5 ml/1 tsp lemon juice
5 ml/1 tsp chopped fresh chervil
2.5 ml/½ tsp chopped fresh sage
2.5 ml/½ tsp chopped fresh thyme
2.5 ml/½ tsp chopped fresh parsley
1 garlic clove, crushed
12 thin slices Sicilian Bread (see page
289)
Bagna Cauda (see Peperoni Dolce con
Bagna Cauda page 31)

Cream the butter until soft and stir in the lemon juice and herbs. Beat in the garlic and spread the butter over the bread slices. Place on a baking sheet and bake for 15–20 minutes in a preheated oven at 180°C/350°F/gas mark 4 until golden brown and crisp. Remove from the oven and serve with Bagna Cauda.

Pane con Granchio e Gamberetti

Crab and Prawn Bread
Serves 4

150 g/5 oz crabmeat
100 g/4 oz peeled prawns (shrimp)
45 ml/3 tbsp mayonnaise
Grated rind of ½ lime
Salt and freshly ground black pepper
1 loaf of Sicilian Bread (see page 289)
50 g/2 oz/¼ cup butter

Put the crabmeat in a bowl and break into flakes. Chop the prawns and add to the bowl with the mayonnaise and grated lime rind. Season with the salt and pepper. Slice the bread thickly and spread with butter. Spread the crab and prawn mix thickly over the slices, sandwiching two together, and serve immediately.

Focaccia di Funghi

Focaccia Mushrooms
Serves 4–6

225 g/8 oz field mushrooms
225 g/8 oz large flat mushrooms
225 g/8 oz button mushrooms
75 ml/5 tbsp olive oil
50 g/2 oz/¼ cup unsalted (sweet) butter
2 garlic cloves, chopped
2 sprigs of rosemary
1 Rosemary Focaccia Loaf (see page 287)
45 ml/3 tbsp chopped fresh parsley
Salt and freshly ground black pepper

Peel and slice large flat mushrooms thickly and halve the smaller ones. Remove any stalks and chop. Heat the oil and butter and fry (sauté) the garlic for 1 minute with the mushrooms and rosemary. Slice the bread and brush with hot oil from the mushroom pan. Heat another frying pan (skillet) and sear the bread on both sides. Sprinkle the parsley over the mushrooms and serve piled on the slices of bread.

Pane con Vaniglia

Fried Vanilla Bread
Serves 4

150 ml/¼ pt/⅔ cup milk
45 ml/3 tbsp sugar
8 slices bread
2 eggs, beaten
10 ml/2 tsp vanilla essence (extract)
75 g/3 oz/⅓ cup butter
A little icing (confectioners') sugar
Fresh apricots, to serve

Pour the milk and sugar into a bowl and stir. Add the bread and allow to soak for 10 minutes. Beat the eggs and vanilla together in a shallow dish. Carefully remove the slices from the milk and transfer to the egg mixture. Heat the butter in a frying pan (skillet) and fry (sauté) each slice of bread until brown on both sides. Dust with icing sugar if desired and serve with fresh apricots.

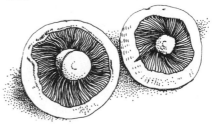

Bruschetta al Formaggio e Pomodoro

Cheese and Tomato Bread
Serves 4

60 ml/4 tbsp olive oil
1 small onion, finely chopped
3 garlic cloves
4 plum tomatoes, diced
10 ml/2 tsp chopped fresh oregano
10 ml/2 tsp chopped fresh basil
Freshly ground black pepper
15 ml/1 tbsp balsamic vinegar
12 slices Italian-style country bread,
*   cut into 1 cm/½ in thick slices*
10 ml/2 tsp grated Parmesan cheese

Heat 30 ml/2 tbsp oil in pan and fry (sauté) the onion and 2 crushed garlic cloves until tender. Add the diced tomatoes and herbs and season to taste. Stir and heat thoroughly. Remove from the heat and add the balsamic vinegar. Toast the bread on both sides. Rub one side of the hot toast with cut garlic. Drizzle the remaining olive oil evenly over the bread pieces. Spoon tomato mixture over the hot toast and sprinkle with the cheese. Grill (broil) for 30 seconds and serve immediately.

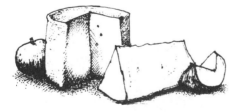

Bruschetta al Pomodoro

Italian Tomato Bread
Serves 4

1 Ciabatta loaf
1 garlic clove, crushed
5 tomatoes, skinned and chopped
5 ml/1 tsp chopped fresh sage
5 ml/1 tsp olive oil
Salt and freshly ground black pepper

Cut the ciabatta loaf in half making two long slices. Cut in half again widthways and toast lightly. Spread the cut side of the bread with the garlic. Blend the tomatoes, sage and olive oil together and spread over the bread. Sprinkle with the salt and pepper and serve at once.

Fette di Prosciutto Crudo e Pesto

Italian Ham and Pesto Slice
Serves 4

1 Pugliese round crusty loaf
40 ml/8 tsp passata (sieved tomatoes)
40 ml/8 tsp Pesto (see page 366)
8 thin slices prosciutto
100 g/4 oz Mozzarella, sliced
8 tomatoes, sliced
5 ml/1 tsp freshly ground black pepper
10 ml/2 tsp chopped fresh basil

Cut the loaf into 8 thick rounds and toast one side. Top with passata then pesto. Lay over the prosciutto, then the Mozzarella and tomato slices. Sprinkle with the pepper. Grill (broil) until the cheese melts. Sprinkle with the chopped basil.

Crostatine Mediterranea

Mediterranean Tartlets
Serves 6

Pastry:
225g/8 oz/2 cups plain (all-purpose)
   flour
1.5 ml/¼ tsp salt
5 ml/1 tsp paprika
75g/3 oz/⅓ cup butter or margarine

Filling:
45 ml/3 tbsp virgin olive oil
2 large onions, sliced
2 garlic cloves, crushed
75 g/3 oz sun-dried tomatoes, chopped
1 orange (bell) pepper
30 ml/2 tbsp chopped fresh basil
Salt and freshly ground black pepper
100 g/4 oz/1 cup Pecorino cheese,
   grated
75 g/3 oz/½ cup black olives, stoned
   (pitted)

Sift the flour, salt and paprika into a bowl. Rub in the butter or margarine until the mixture resembles fine breadcrumbs. Add enough water to mix to a firm dough and knead the pastry for 1 minute. Wrap in clingfilm (plastic wrap) and chill for 30 minutes. Preheat the oven to 200°C/400°F/gas mark 6. Roll out the pastry on a floured board and use to line six 10 cm/4 in fluted tartlet tins (patty pans). Line each pastry case with greaseproof (waxed) paper and fill with baking beans. Bake blind for 15 minutes. Remove from the oven and allow to cool for 2 minutes. Remove the paper and beans. Heat the oil in a frying pan (skillet) and cook the onions and garlic for 4 minutes until soft. Add the tomatoes, pepper, basil, salt and pepper. Cook for 5 minutes and stir in the cheese. Spoon into the cooked pastry cases and top with the olives.

Fritelle di Funghi e Fegato

Mushroom and Liver Fritters
Makes 30 fritters

25 g/1 oz/2 tbsp butter
100 g/4 oz mushrooms, halved
225 g/8 oz/2 cups chicken livers,
   chopped
Salt and freshly ground black pepper
75 ml/5 tbsp Basic White Sauce
   (see page 357)
Oil for deep-frying

Melt the butter in a frying pan (skillet) and add the mushrooms, chicken livers, salt and pepper. Fry (sauté) for 5 minutes, stirring frequently, until the chicken livers are brown. Remove the pan from the heat. Drain off any liquid. Stir the chicken livers and mushrooms into the white sauce and mix well. Leave to one side until the mixture is cold and set. Heat a pan of oil until a cube of bread sizzles and browns in a few seconds. Dip a tablespoon in cold water and take spoonfuls of the sauce mixture and place on a plate. Dip a fondue fork or skewer into each spoonful of mixture and deep-fry each for 3–4 minutes until completely golden brown. Remove from the oil with a draining spoon. Drain on kitchen paper and keep warm while you cook the remainder. Serve with a green salad.

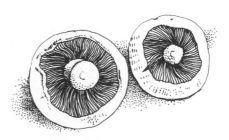

Fritelle con Ripieno di Uova sode di Tonno

Pancakes Filled with Eggs and Tuna

Serves 4

Pancakes:
50 g/2 oz/½ cup plain (all-purpose) flour
1 egg
1.5 ml/¼ tsp salt
90 ml/6 tbsp milk
25 g/1 oz/2 tbsp butter
30 ml/2 tbsp oil

Filling:
185 g/6½ oz/1 small can tuna, drained
4 eggs, hard-boiled (hard-cooked) and chopped
1.5 ml/¼ tsp cayenne
60 ml/4 tbsp double (heavy) cream
15 ml/1 tbsp finely chopped fresh basil

Put the flour in a large bowl and add the egg, salt and milk. Beat well and leave to stand for 5 minutes. Heat a small amount of the butter and oil in a frying pan (skillet). Beat the batter again and pour a little into the pan. Rotate and tilt the pan to ensure even cooking and cook for 1 minute until the pancake has set. Turn over with a spatula and cook until the underside has turned brown. Transfer to a warmed serving dish while the remaining pancakes are cooked. Mix the tuna and eggs in a small pan. Season with the cayenne and blend in the cream and basil. Heat through. Place a pancake on a plate and spread with a little of the filling. Repeat with the remainder and roll up. Serve immediately.

Pizza Rustica

Rustic Pizza

Serves 4

225 g/8 oz shortcrust pastry (basic pie crust)
3 egg yolks
350 g/12 oz/1½ cups Ricotta cheese
100 g/4 oz Mozzarella cheese, cut in small pieces
175 ml/6 fl oz/¾ cup milk
Salt and freshly ground black pepper
1.5 ml/¼ tsp cayenne
Chunky Tomato Sauce (see page 357), to serve

Roll out the pastry and use to line a 23 cm/9 in flan tin (pie pan). Fill with greaseproof (waxed) paper and baking beans and bake in a preheated oven at 190°C/375°F/gas mark 5 for 10 minutes. Take the pastry from the oven and remove the paper and baking beans. Beat the egg yolks and Ricotta together with the Mozzarella. Stir in the milk and season with the salt, pepper and cayenne. Pour into the pastry case and bake at 180°C/350°F/gas mark 4 for 40 minutes. Serve with Chunky Tomato Sauce.

Fritelle con Ripieno di Peperoni Rosso

Pancakes with Red Pepper Filling
Serves 4

1 quantity pancake batter (see page 64)
Filling:
15 ml/1 tbsp oil
1 small onion, chopped
3 red (bell) peppers, sliced
5 ml/1 tsp made mustard
Salt and freshly ground black pepper

Prepare the pancakes. Make the filling. Heat the oil in a pan and cook the onion for 2 minutes. Stir in the red peppers and the mustard and season with the salt and pepper. Cook for 4–5 minutes until soft. Place 2 pancakes on each plate, spoon over the peppers and roll up lightly. Serve at once.

Patate con Zucchini e Olive

Fried Potatoes with Courgettes and Olives
Serves 4

15 ml/1 tbsp olive oil
15 g/½ oz/1 tbsp butter
900 g/2 lb potatoes, thinly sliced
1 large leek, sliced
2 garlic cloves, crushed
Salt and freshly ground black pepper
2 large courgettes (zucchini), sliced
30 ml/2 tbsp green olives, halved and stoned (pitted)
15 ml/1 tbsp chopped fresh basil

Heat the olive oil and butter in a large saucepan and add the potatoes, sliced leek, garlic, salt and pepper. Cook, stirring frequently, for 10 minutes until the potatoes are brown on the edges. Add the courgettes and continue cooking for 15 minutes. Stir in the olives and basil and cook for a further 5 minutes before serving.

Polenta Parmigiano

Parmesan Polenta
Makes 24 round discs

600 ml/1 pt/2½ cups milk
25 g/1 oz/2 tbsp butter
175 g/6 oz/1½ cups pre-cooked cornmeal
75 g/3 oz/¾ cup Parmesan cheese, finely grated
15 ml/1 tbsp chopped fresh mint
Salt and freshly ground black pepper
Flour for dusting
Oil for deep-frying

Heat the milk and butter together in a saucepan until not quite boiling. Whisk in the cornmeal and beat over a moderate heat with a wooden spoon until the mixture thickens. Allow to cool slightly and add the Parmesan, mint, salt and pepper. Leave to cool. Roll out the polenta on a floured board to 1 cm/½ in thick and cut out rounds with pastry cutters. Deep-fry for 2–3 minutes until golden brown and drain on kitchen paper. The discs can be topped with fish, meat or vegetables.

Variation: Rosemary or thyme can be used instead of mint if preferred.

Variation: 5 ml/1 tsp paprika can be added instead of the mint for a spicy-flavoured polenta.

Oristano Crostini

Garlic, Ham and Tomato Slice
Serves 4

15 ml/1 tbsp olive oil
1 garlic clove, crushed
120 ml/4 fl oz/½ cup passata (sieved
  tomatoes)
1 Italian Flat Bread loaf (see page
  289)
4 slices cooked ham, cut into small
  strips
4 black olives, stoned (pitted) and
  chopped

Heat the oil and cook the garlic for 2 minutes. Add the passata and cook uncovered for 5 minutes to reduce the mixture. Slice the bread into 8 pieces and spread one side with the tomato mixture. Place on a baking sheet and cook in a preheated oven at 220°C/425°F/gas mark 7 for 8 minutes. Remove from the oven and arrange the ham and olives on the top before serving.

Pasticcio di Spinaci e Mozzarella

Spinach and Mozzarella Pastry
Serves 4–6

150 g/5 oz/1¼ cups plain (all-purpose)
  flour
50 g/2 oz/¼ cup butter
1 egg yolk
Salt and freshly ground black pepper
1 large tomato, thinly sliced
400 g/14 oz spinach, cooked and
  drained
2 whole eggs
75 ml/5 tbsp double (heavy) cream
50 g/2 oz/1 small can anchovy fillets
75 g/3 oz Mozzarella cheese, sliced

Put the flour in a large bowl and rub in the butter until the mixture resembles breadcrumbs. Blend in the egg yolk, salt and pepper and 45 ml/3 tbsp cold water to form a stiff dough. Roll out the pastry and use to line a 20 cm/8 in flan tin (pie pan). Place the tomato slices over the base and spoon over the cooked and drained spinach. Whisk the whole eggs and cream together and season with salt and pepper. Drain the anchovies and lay over the spinach. Place slices of Mozzarella over the anchovies and pour over the cream mixture. Bake in a preheated oven at 190°C/375°F/gas mark 5 for 30 minutes until set and golden. Serve hot or cold.

Sformato di Patate

Potato Flan
Serves 4

225 g/8oz shortcrust pastry (basic pie
  crust)
450 g/1 lb potatoes, boiled and sliced
3 bacon rashers (slices), rinded and
  chopped
2 onions, chopped
Salt and freshly ground black pepper
2 eggs
30 ml/2 tbsp single (light) cream

Line a 23 cm/9 in flan tin (pie pan) with pastry. Cover the base with a layer of the sliced potatoes, bacon and onion and continue to add in layers until the pastry is almost filled. Season with salt and pepper. Beat the eggs and cream together and pour over the potato mix. Bake in a preheated oven at 190°C/375°F/gas mark 5 for 20–25 minutes until set and golden.

Crostini alla Svelta

Quick Crostini
Serves 6

1 long Ciabatta loaf
30 ml/2 tbsp olive oil
45 ml/3 tbsp vegetable oil
1 garlic clove
450 g/1 lb tomatoes
225 g/8 oz Mozzarella cheese, sliced
200 g/7 oz/good 1 cup olives, stoned
(pitted)
Fresh dill (dill weed), to garnish

Cut the bread into slices about 2.5 cm/
1 in thick. Blend the olive oil and vegetable
oil together and brush over both sides of the
bread. Bake in a preheated oven at
190°C/375°F/gas mark 5 for 5 minutes or
toast under a moderate grill (broiler). Cut
the garlic in half and rub over one side of
each piece of bread. Cut the tomatoes into
slices and arrange on the bread. Lay over
the slices of Mozzarella. Add the olives and
bake for a further 8 minutes until the cheese
has melted. Garnish with the fresh dill.

Rotelle di Polenta con Salvio

Sage Polenta Discs
Makes 24

600 ml/1 pt/2½ cups milk
25 g/1 oz/2 tbsp butter
175 g/6 oz/1½ cups pre-cooked cornmeal
50 g/2 oz/½ cup Parmesan cheese,
grated
30 ml/2 tbsp finely chopped fresh sage
Salt and freshly ground black pepper
15 ml/1 tbsp plain (all-purpose) flour
100 g/4 oz goats' cheese, diced
10 ml/2 tsp chopped fresh oregano

Heat the milk and butter together in a
saucepan until almost boiling. Whisk in
the cornmeal and beat over a moderate
heat with a wooden spoon until thick.
Cool for 1 minute and add the Parmesan,
sage, salt and pepper. Cool for 5 minutes.
Roll the polenta out on a floured board to
1 cm/½ in thick and cut out 24 round discs.
Grill (broil) until golden. Serve garnished
with goats' cheese and oregano.

Bruschetta con Fegato di Pollo

Chicken Liver Toasts
Serves 4

450 g/1 lb/4 cups chicken livers,
trimmed
15 ml/1 tbsp olive oil
25 g/1 oz/2 tbsp unsalted (sweet) butter
2 onions, finely chopped
Salt and freshly ground black pepper
50 g/2 oz/⅓ cup black olives, stoned
(pitted) and chopped
30 ml/2 tbsp chopped fresh basil
8 slices bread, toasted and buttered
15 ml/1 tbsp chopped fresh coriander
(cilantro)

Heat the oil and butter together in a frying
pan (skillet) and fry (sauté) the onions for
3 minutes. Add the chicken livers and stir
well. Cook for 6–7 minutes, until the livers
are cooked but still slightly pink in the centre. Season well with salt and pepper and
stir in the olives. Cook for a further 2 minutes. Remove from the heat. Stir in the
basil and mash well until combined. Spread
the mixture on to the toast and serve garnished with the chopped coriander.

Crespelle Allo Zafferano con Ripieno di Cozze

Saffron Pancakes with Mussels
Serves 4

2.5 ml/½ tsp saffron powder
225 g/8 oz/2 cups plain (all-purpose) flour
2.5 ml/½ tsp salt
2 eggs, beaten
450 ml/¾ pt/2 cups milk
150 ml/¼ pt/⅔ cup water
50 g/2 oz/¼ cup butter, melted
15 ml/1 tbsp oil
1 small onion, chopped
120 ml/4 fl oz/½ cup white wine
1 kg/2¼ lb mussels, scrubbed and beards removed
150 ml/¼ pt/⅔ cup double (heavy) cream
5 ml/1 tsp made mustard
Salt and freshly ground black pepper

Put the saffron in 45 ml/3 tbsp hot water for 10 minutes. Sift the flour into a bowl and add the salt. Pour in the beaten eggs and gradually incorporate into the flour. Stir in the milk a little at a time and beat to a smooth batter. Whisk in the saffron water and the measured water. Stir in half the melted butter. Heat the remaining butter in a frying pan (skillet) and pour in enough batter to lightly coat the base of the pan. Cook for 1 minute on each side. Continue until the batter is used. Stack the pancakes on a plate and cover to keep warm. Heat the oil in a pan and cook the onion for 2 minutes. Stir in the wine. Bring to the boil and add the cleaned mussels. Cover with a lid and cook for 5 minutes, shaking the pan occasionally. Check the mussels and discard any shells that are unopened. Shell the mussels and set aside. Strain the liquid and return to the pan. Boil rapidly for 5 minutes to reduce, lower the heat and blend in the cream and mustard. Season with the salt and pepper and return the mussels to the pan. Lay 2 pancakes on each plate, spoon over the mussels and roll up lightly. Serve at once.

Polenta con Funghi

Polenta with Mushrooms
Serves 4

5 ml/1 tsp salt
1.2 litres/2 pts/5 cups water
275 g/10 oz/2½ cups coarse yellow cornmeal
30 ml/2 tbsp olive oil
225 g/8 oz mushrooms, sliced
150 ml/¼ pt/⅔ cup double (heavy) cream

Bring a large pan of the salted measured water to the boil and pour in the cornmeal. Whisk continuously and reduce the heat. Simmer for 30 minutes, stirring occasionally, until the cornmeal is thick and pulls away from the side of the pan. Heat the oil in a frying pan (skillet) and cook the mushrooms for 5 minutes. Add the cream and bring to the boil. Add salt to taste. Spoon the polenta on to a heated plate and cover with the mushroom sauce. Serve immediately.

Fritelle di Pollo e Melanzane

Chicken and Aubergine Fritters

Serves 4–6

2 eggs, beaten
50 g/2 oz/½ cup plain (all-purpose)
  flour
Salt
5 ml/1 tsp cayenne
5 ml/1 tsp capers
5 ml/1 tsp tomato purée (paste)
175 g/6 oz/1½ cups cooked chicken,
  finely chopped
1 small aubergine (eggplant), chopped
Oil for frying

Place the eggs and flour in a bowl and beat well. Season with the salt and cayenne. Mix in the capers and tomato purée and gradually beat in the chopped chicken. Stir in the chopped aubergine. Heat the oil in a shallow frying pan (skillet) and gently fry (sauté) tablespoons of the mixture for 2 minutes on each side until golden brown. Drain on kitchen paper.

Piatto Appetitoso di Fegatini di Pollo

Chicken Liver Savoury

Serves 4

5 ml/1 tsp olive oil
4 large, round crusty rolls
25 g/1 oz/2 tbsp unsalted (sweet) butter
1 large onion, chopped
1 garlic clove, crushed
100 g/4 oz/1 cup chicken livers,
  chopped
1 egg, beaten
30 ml/2 tbsp chopped fresh oregano
Freshly ground black pepper
75 g/3 oz/¾ cup Mozzarella cheese,
  chopped
1 tomato, sliced in four

Lightly oil a baking sheet. Cut a small slice from the top of each roll and carefully hollow out the centre of the bread with a teaspoon. Place the top and inside of the rolls into a food processor and blend to make breadcrumbs. Empty into a bowl and set aside. Heat the butter and fry (sauté) the onion and garlic for 3 minutes. Add the chicken livers and fry for a further 3–4 minutes until browned on the outside and pink in the centre. Add to the breadcrumbs and blend in the egg and oregano. Season with the pepper. Add half the cheese and spoon the stuffing into the rolls. Top with a slice of tomato and the remaining cheese. Bake in a preheated oven at 200°C/400°F/ gas mark 6 for 10 minutes until the tops are brown.

Frittata di Pollo

Chicken Omelette

Serves 4

30 ml/2 tbsp olive oil
1 large onion, sliced
3 potatoes, cooked and cut into
  1 cm/½ in dice
1 garlic clove, chopped
1 small green (bell) pepper, chopped
1 small red (bell) pepper, chopped
100 g/4 oz/1 cup cooked chicken, diced
6 eggs
Salt and freshly ground black pepper

Heat the oil and fry (sauté) the onion, potatoes, garlic, peppers and chicken, stirring occasionally, for 10 minutes. Beat and season the eggs. Pour into the pan and cook over a low heat for about 4 minutes. Place under a hot grill (broiler) until set and the surface is golden brown. Serve at once, cut into large wedges.

Pomodori con Ripieno di Pollo

Chicken in Tomato Cases

Serves 4

4 large tomatoes
5 ml/1 tbsp olive oil
½ onion, chopped
1 garlic clove, crushed
75 ml/5 tbsp cooked rice
10 ml/2 tsp chopped fresh parsley
25 g/1 oz/½ cup fresh breadcrumbs
Salt and freshly ground black pepper
100 g/4 oz/1 cup cooked chicken
  breast, chopped
Knob of unsalted (sweet) butter

Cut the tops off the tomatoes and scoop out the centres. Place the tomatoes in an ovenproof dish. Heat the oil in a frying pan (skillet) and fry (sauté) the onion and garlic. Add the cooked rice. Stir in the parsley and breadcrumbs. Season to taste and stir in the cooked chicken. Spoon into the tomatoes. Dot with tiny amounts of butter and replace the lids. Bake in a preheated oven at 200°C/400°F/gas mark 6 for 12 minutes.

Fritelle di Prosciutto e Mandorle

Ham and Almond Fritters

Serves 4

120 ml/4 fl oz/½ cup water
50 g/2 oz/¼ cup unsalted (sweet) butter
2.5 ml/½ tsp salt
1.5 ml/¼ tsp freshly ground black
  pepper
75 g/3 oz/¾ cup plain (all-purpose)
  flour
2 eggs
75 g/3 oz/¾ cup flaked (slivered)
  almonds
100 g/4 oz cooked ham, chopped
Oil for deep-frying

Bring the water to the boil and add the butter, salt and pepper. Remove from the heat when the butter has melted and beat in the flour. Continue beating until the mixture comes away from the sides of the pan. Beat in the eggs, one at a time and fold in the almonds and ham. Allow to cool for 10 minutes. Deep-fry teaspoons of the mixture for 3–4 minutes until golden brown. Remove from the pan and drain on kitchen paper. Keep warm while the rest of the fritters are cooking. Serve hot.

Mortadella Ciabatta

Mortadella Rolls
Serves 4

*4 large green (bell) peppers, halved
and seeded*
2.5 ml/½ tsp salt
2.5 ml/½ tsp chopped fresh marjoram
10 ml/2 tsp olive oil
4 Ciabatta rolls, halved
8 slices mortadella sausage
*50 g/2 oz/½ cup Parmesan cheese,
grated*

Arrange the halved green peppers skin side up on a grill (broiler) rack and grill (broil) for 10 minutes on each side until the peppers are light brown. Transfer the peppers to an ovenproof dish and sprinkle over the salt and marjoram and keep warm. Warm the oil in a saucepan. Place the rolls, cut sides up on the grill rack. Top with a slice of sausage and half a pepper. Sprinkle with Parmesan cheese and spoon over a little olive oil. Place under the grill for 3–4 minutes until golden.

Crostini alla Siciliana

Sicilian Toast
Serves 4–6

100 g/4 oz/1 cup calves' liver
15 ml/1 tbsp olive oil
1 onion, chopped
1 egg
Freshly ground black pepper
*150 ml/¼ pt/⅔ cup double (heavy)
cream*
4 slices bread
15 ml/1 tbsp chopped fresh parsley

Fry (sauté) the liver in the oil for 5 minutes. Add the chopped onion and continue cooking until the onion is translucent. Hard-boil (hard-cook) the egg, peel and chop. Put the liver and onion through a mincer (grinder) and mix with the egg, pepper and cream. Toast the bread and remove the crusts. Cut into shapes and place on a platter. Spoon the liver and onion mixture into the centre of each toasted shape and sprinkle with the parsley.

Vasetti di Peperone Rosso

Red Pepper Pots
Serves 4

*4 red (bell) peppers, seeded and
quartered*
2 garlic cloves, finely chopped
4 tomatoes, halved
30 ml/2 tbsp virgin olive oil
Salt and freshly ground black pepper
100 g/4 oz/½ cup cream cheese
15 ml/1 tbsp chopped fresh parsley
*4 black olives, stoned (pitted) and
chopped*
Crusty bread, to serve

Put the peppers, garlic and tomatoes in a shallow ovenproof dish and sprinkle with olive oil. Season with the salt and pepper. Cook in a preheated oven for 45 minutes at 200°C/400°F/gas mark 6. Purée in a blender or food processor. Leave to cool slightly then blend in the cream cheese. Season to taste and divide between four individual dishes. Scatter over the parsley and chopped black olives. Serve straight away with plenty of crusty bread.

Prosciutto e Acciughe Arrotolate

Ham and Anchovy Rolls

Serves 4

5 ml/1 tsp olive oil
4 large round crusty rolls
25 g/1 oz/2 tbsp unsalted (sweet) butter
1 small onion, chopped
50 g/2 oz mushrooms, chopped
100 g/4 oz prosciutto, chopped
25 g/1 oz/½ small can anchovy fillets,
    drained and chopped
1 egg beaten
30 ml/2 tbsp chopped fresh parsley
Freshly ground black pepper
75 g/3 oz Mozzarella cheese, chopped
1 tomato, sliced in four

Lightly oil a baking sheet. Cut a small slice from the top of each roll and carefully hollow out the centre of the bread with a teaspoon. Place the top and inside of the rolls into a food processor and blend to make breadcrumbs. Remove to a bowl and set aside. Heat the butter and fry (sauté) the onion for 3 minutes. Add the mushrooms and fry for a further 3 minutes. Transfer to a bowl and add the prosciutto and anchovy fillets. Blend in the egg and parsley and season with the pepper. Add half the cheese and spoon the stuffing into the rolls. Top with a slice of tomato and the remaining cheese. Bake in a preheated oven at 200°C/400°F/gas mark 6 for 10 minutes until the tops are brown.

Formaggio Rinascimento

Renaissance Cheese

Serves 4

5 ml/1 tsp unsalted (sweet) butter
3 egg yolks
100 g/4 oz/1 cup Fontina or Gruyère
    (Swiss) cheese, grated
Freshly ground black pepper
2.5 ml/½ tsp chopped fresh oregano
4 slices of bread, fried

Put the butter and egg yolks in a basin over hot water and beat well. Stir in the cheese and continue stirring until the cheese has melted. Stir in pepper to taste and the oregano. Remove from the heat and serve on the fried bread.

Carote Frittata

Carrot Omelette

Serves 4

45 ml/3 tbsp olive oil
1 small onion, chopped
4 eggs
6 carrots, grated
30 ml/2 tbsp grated Parmesan cheese
Salt and freshly ground black pepper

Heat the oil in a frying pan (skillet) and add the onion. Cook for 1 minute to soften. Whisk the eggs in a bowl and stir in the grated carrots, Parmesan and seasoning. Pour the egg mixture over the onion and cook over a low heat until the base of the frittata is a golden colour. Put the pan under a hot grill (broiler) to cook the surface. Cut the frittata into wedges and serve hot or cold.

Bruschetta con Bresaola

Lombardy Bread
Serves 6

6 slices Italian bread, 2.5 cm/1 in thick
75 ml/5 tbsp olive oil
1 garlic clove, cut in half
225 g/8 oz bresaola (naturally cured
beef), thinly sliced
225 g/8 oz Mozzarella cheese, sliced
200 g/7 oz/good 1 cup olives
Fresh parsley, to garnish

Brush the olive oil over both sides of the
bread slices. Bake in a preheated oven at
190°C/375°F/gas mark 5 for 5 minutes or
toast under a moderate grill (broiler). Cut
the garlic in half and rub over one side of
each piece of bread. Arrange the bresaola
and slices of Mozzarella on the bread. Add
the olives and bake for a further 8 minutes
until the cheese has melted. Garnish with
the fresh parsley.

Uova con Piselli e Pomodori

Eggs with Peas and Tomatoes
Serves 4

25 g/1 oz/2 tbsp unsalted (sweet) butter
2 garlic cloves
8 slices of bread
4 tomatoes, chopped
50 ml/2 fl oz/3½ tbsp red wine
1 bouquet garni sachet
Salt and freshly ground black pepper
8 eggs
100 g/4 oz fresh or frozen peas, cooked

Heat the butter in a frying pan (skillet).
Add the garlic. Fry (sauté) the bread slices
until they are golden and crisp. Keep
warm. Put the tomatoes, wine and herbs in
a saucepan and bring to the boil. Season
with the salt and pepper and boil for 3
minutes. Remove the bouquet garni. Poach
the eggs in the tomatoes and wine mixture
until the whites are set. Remove each egg
with a draining spoon and place carefully
on a slice of bread. Surround with the peas
and serve at once.

Pasticcio all' Asparago

Asparagus in Pastry
Serves 4

100 g/4 oz/½ cup unsalted (sweet)
butter
16 asparagus spears
16 sheets filo pastry
75 g/3 oz/⅓ cup cream cheese
Salt and freshly ground black pepper

Melt the butter in a saucepan. Trim the
ends of the asparagus spears. Brush the
surface of a sheet of filo pastry with the
melted butter. Spoon over a little of the
cream cheese and top with an asparagus
spear. Season to taste. Fold the ends then
roll up the pastry and brush the surface
with more butter. Make the remaining rolls
in the same way. Place on the a buttered
baking sheet and cook in a preheated oven
at 180°C/350°F/ gas mark 4 for 15 minutes.

Frittata di Carciofi

Artichoke Omelette
Serves 4

50 g/2 oz/¼ cup unsalted (sweet) butter
400 g/14 oz/1 large can artichoke
hearts, drained and chopped
30 ml/2 tbsp single (light) cream
Salt and freshly ground black pepper
6 eggs

Heat the butter in a saucepan and add the artichoke hearts. Sauté for 2–3 minutes. Add the cream and season with the salt and pepper. Keep hot. Heat the remaining butter in a frying pan (skillet). Beat the eggs, season with salt and pepper and pour into the pan. Cook for 3 minutes until nearly set and add the artichoke mixture. Fold the omelette over and cook for 1 minute to make sure the omelette is firm. Turn out on to a heated serving dish and serve immediately.

Formaggio al Forno

Cheese on Toast
Serves 4

100 g/4 oz hard cheese, chopped
75 ml/5 tbsp white wine
30 ml/2 tbsp chopped fresh basil
Freshly ground black pepper
4 thick slices bread
5 ml/1 tsp unsalted (sweet) butter

Place the cheese in an ovenproof dish. Blend the wine with the chopped basil. Pour the wine over the cheese and season generously with the pepper. Place in a pre-heated oven at 200°C/400°F/gas mark 6 for 10 minutes until golden and bubbling. Meanwhile, remove the crusts from the bread, toast and butter the slices. Spoon the cooked cheese on to each slice of toast.

Uova al Forno con Gorgonzola

Eggs Baked with Gorgonzola
Serves 4

5 ml/1 tsp unsalted (sweet) butter
4 eggs
50 g/2 oz Gorgonzola, crumbled
2.5 ml/½ tsp freshly ground black pepper
2.5 ml/½ tsp grated nutmeg
50 g/2 oz/1 cup fresh breadcrumbs

Butter a pie dish. Break the eggs into the dish. Mix the Gorgonzola with the pepper, nutmeg and breadcrumbs and spoon over the eggs. Bake in a preheated oven at 200°C/400°F/gas mark 6 for 8 minutes until the eggs are just set and the breadcrumbs are golden.

Fonduta

Melted Cheese with Egg Yolks
Serves 4

5 ml/1 tsp unsalted (sweet) butter, melted
3 egg yolks
100 g/4 oz Fontina or Gruyère (Swiss)
cheese, grated
2.5 ml/½ tsp freshly ground black
pepper
2.5 ml/½ tsp grated nutmeg
4 slices of bread, fried in unsalted
(sweet) butter

Put the butter and egg yolks in a basin over hot water and beat well. Stir in the cheese and continue stirring until the cheese has melted. Stir in the pepper and nutmeg. Remove from the heat and serve spoonfuls on individual plates with fingers of fried bread.

Uova alla Francescana

Franciscan Eggs
Serves 2

4 small potatoes
300 ml/½ pt/1¼ cups milk
2 eggs, hard-boiled (hard-cooked), halved
25 g/1 oz/2 tbsp unsalted (sweet) butter
25 g/1 oz/¼ cup plain (all-purpose) flour
1 garlic clove, crushed
50 g/2 oz/½ cup hard cheese, grated
30 ml/2 tbsp capers

Boil the potatoes in the milk for 12 minutes until soft. Drain and reserve the milk. Place the eggs in an ovenproof dish. Put the butter in a saucepan and cook with the flour for 1 minute. Gradually blend in the reserved milk and add the crushed garlic. Cut each potato into four and add to the eggs. Pour over the sauce and sprinkle over the cheese and capers. Place under a grill (broiler) until brown and serve.

Frittata di Piselli

Pea Frittata
Serves 4

225 g/8 oz fresh shelled peas
45 ml/3 tbsp olive oil
2 spring onions (scallions), chopped
4 eggs
30 ml/2 tbsp grated Parmesan cheese
Salt and freshly ground black pepper

Steam the peas for 15 minutes until they are just tender. Heat the oil in a frying pan (skillet) and add the chopped spring onions. Cook until browned. Stir in the peas and cook for 1 minute. Whisk the eggs in a bowl and stir in the Parmesan and seasoning. Pour the egg mixture over the peas and spring onions and cook over a low heat until the base of the frittata is a golden colour. Put the pan under a hot grill (broiler) to cook the surface. Cut the frittata into wedges and serve hot or cold.

Sformato di Pancetta e Uova

Bacon and Egg Flan
Serves 6

225 g/8 oz shortcrust pastry (basic pie crust)
25 g/1 oz/2 tbsp unsalted (sweet) butter
100 g/4 oz pancetta, diced small
1 small onion, chopped
4 eggs
300 ml/½ pt/1¼ cups single (light) cream
Salt and freshly ground black pepper

Grease a 20 cm/8 in flan tin (pie pan). Roll the pastry out on a floured board and line the flan tin. Line with greaseproof (waxed) paper and baking beans and bake blind in a preheated oven for 8 minutes at 200°C/400°F/gas mark 6. Melt the butter in a saucepan. Add the pancetta and fry (sauté) in the butter with the chopped onion for 3 minutes. Drain. Spread the onion and bacon evenly over the bottom of the pastry. Beat the eggs and cream together and season with the salt and pepper. Pour into the flan case and bake at 190°C/375°F/gas mark 5 for 20 minutes until set and golden.

Focaccia all' Acciuga

Anchovy Bread
Makes 1 loaf

225 g/8 oz/1 cup unsalted (sweet)
butter, softened
1 garlic clove, crushed
6 anchovies, finely chopped
2.5 ml/½ tsp salt
Rosemary Focaccia bread (see page
287)

Cream the butter, garlic and anchovies together. Slice the bread crosswise to within 5 mm/¼ in of the bottom. Spread the butter mixture generously on one side of each of the slices. Wrap the loaf in foil and place on a baking sheet in the oven. Bake in a preheated oven at 200°C/400°F/gas mark 6 for 15 minutes. Remove from the foil and serve while still warm. This is also good served with soup.

Frittata con Tonno

Open Tuna Omelette
Serves 4

30 ml/2 tbsp olive oil
1 onion, chopped
185 g/6½ oz/1 small can tuna, drained
8 eggs, lightly beaten
Salt and freshly ground black pepper
15 ml/1 tbsp finely chopped fresh basil

Heat the oil and fry (sauté) the onion for 4–5 minutes until soft but not brown. Add the tuna and season with the salt and pepper. Pour in the eggs and stir well for 3–4 minutes until the eggs are set. Sprinkle with basil just before serving.

Crostata di Mozzarella

Mozzarella Tart
Serves 4

1 quantity Yeast Pastry (paste) (see
page 283)
100 g/4 oz Mozzarella cheese, sliced
3 bacon rashers (slices), rinded and
chopped
3 large tomatoes, sliced
50 g/2 oz/½ cup Parmesan cheese,
grated
2 eggs
Salt and freshly ground black pepper

Roll out the yeast pastry and line a 20 cm/8 in flan tin (pie pan). Cover with thin slices of Mozzarella. Place the bacon in a frying pan (skillet) and cook for 3 minutes, stirring. Spoon over the cheese and add the sliced tomatoes. Sprinkle with the Parmesan cheese. Beat the eggs with the salt and pepper until frothy and pour the mixture over the Parmesan. Bake in a preheated oven at 190°C/375°F/gas mark 5 for 35–40 minutes until golden and set.

Pasticcio di Cipolle

Onion Flan
Serves 6

225 g/8 oz shortcrust pastry (basic pie crust)
15 ml/1 tbsp oil
450 g/1 lb large onions, chopped
2 garlic cloves, chopped
20 anchovy fillets
20 olives, stoned (pitted) and halved

Roll out and line a shallow, 23 cm/9 in flan tin (pie pan) with the pastry. Prick the bottom of the pastry with a fork. Heat the oil in a frying pan (skillet). Add the onions and garlic and fry (sauté), stirring occasionally for 5 minutes. Arrange the onion mixture in the pastry case (pie shell). Place the anchovies in a lattice pattern over the surface of the onions. Press the olives into the surface of the onions and bake for 20 minutes in a preheated oven at 190°C/375°F/gas mark 5 until the pastry is golden.

Sciatt

Cheese Fritters
Serves 4

175 g/6 oz/1½ cups rye flour
150 g/5 oz/1¼ cups plain (all-purpose) flour
Salt
250 ml/8 fl oz/1 cup cold water
150 g/5 oz Mozzarella, cut in cubes
15 ml/1 tbsp Grappa or brandy
Oil for deep-frying

Sift the flours and salt into a bowl. Make a well in the centre and gradually whisk in enough of the water to form a smooth batter. Leave to stand for at least 30 minutes. Stir in the cheese and Grappa or brandy. Heat the oil until a cube of day-old bread browns in 30 seconds. Add spoonfuls of the batter and cheese and fry until golden and puffy. Lift out with a draining spoon, drain on kitchen paper and serve straight away.

Sciatt con Basilico

Cheese Fritters with Basil
Serves 4

Prepare as for Sciatt (above) but add 30 ml/2 tbsp chopped fresh basil to the batter mixture.

Crespelle del Buongustaio

Gourmet Pancakes
Serves 6

Batter:
150 g/5 oz/1¼ cups plain (all-purpose)
  flour
Salt
6 eggs
200 ml/7 fl oz/scant 1 cup milk
30 ml/2 tbsp chopped fresh parsley
Oil for frying

Filling:
100 g/4 oz frozen chopped spinach,
  thawed
150 g/5 oz/⅔ cup Ricotta cheese
50 g/2 oz/½ cup walnuts, very finely
  chopped
50 g/2 oz Mozzarella cheese, chopped
50 g/2 oz/½ cup Parmesan cheese, grated
Freshly ground black pepper
1 quantity Tomato Sauce (see page 358)

Sift the flour in a bowl with a good pinch of salt. Make a well in the centre and add the eggs. Beat well with enough of the milk to form a smooth batter. Stir in the parsley. Heat a little oil in a frying pan (skillet) and add enough of the batter to make a thin pancake. Fry (sauté) until golden underneath and set. Flip over and brown the other side. Repeat with the remaining batter to form 12 pancakes. Make the filling. Squeeze out all excess moisture from the spinach and place in a bowl. Beat in the Ricotta cheese, nuts, Mozzarella and Parmesan. Season with salt and pepper. Use this mixture to fill the pancakes, roll up and pack in a single layer in an oiled large, shallow ovenproof dish. Spoon over the tomato sauce and bake in a preheated oven at 180°C/350°F/gas mark 4 for about 20 minutes until piping hot through.

Frittata di Basilico e Prezzemolo

Parsley and Basil Omelette
Serves 2–4

4 large eggs
30 ml/2 tbsp single (light) cream
30 ml/2 tbsp chopped fresh parsley
30 ml/2 tbsp chopped fresh basil
Salt and freshly ground black pepper
45 ml/3 tbsp olive oil

Break the eggs into a bowl. Add the cream and lightly beat until blended. Beat in the herbs and a little salt and pepper. Heat the oil in a frying pan (skillet). Add the egg mixture and fry (sauté), lifting and stirring until the base begins to set, then cook until golden underneath and set. Invert on to a plate then slide back in the pan and cook the other side for 2–3 minutes until golden. Serve warm or cold.

Formaggio Fritto

Fried Cheese with Eggs
Serves 4

350 g/12 oz hard cheese, cut into fingers
60 ml/4 tbsp polenta
75 g/3 oz/⅓ cup unsalted (sweet) butter
30 ml/2 tbsp olive oil
4 large eggs
Rosemary Focaccia Bread (see page
  287), to serve

Roll the cheese in the polenta to coat completely. Melt the butter and oil in a frying pan (skillet). Fry (sauté) the cheese fingers until turning golden on all sides. Meanwhile, heat the oil in a separate frying pan and fry the eggs until set. Slide the cheese and eggs on to warm plates and serve with Rosemary Focaccia.

Meat

Meat in Italy can range from a very plain chop to an extravagant creation. Many meat dishes are browned and then simmered until tender with plenty of vegetables to provide a rich sauce. Chicken and game appear on many tables across the country with rabbit being a speciality. Offal is also commonly used, and liver is a great favourite with Italians. Meatballs or meat sauces are often served with pasta – a staple part of the Italian diet.

Beef

Fette di Manzo in Salsa di Arancia

Beef Slices in Orange Sauce

Serves 4

1 orange
45 g/1½ oz/3 tbsp unsalted (sweet) butter
4 spring onions (scallions) chopped
2 celery sticks, chopped
5 ml/1 tsp chopped fresh oregano
Freshly ground black pepper
25 g/1 oz/½ cup breadcrumbs
60 ml/4 tbsp Marsala
50 g/2 oz/½ cup pine nuts
Salt
6 thin slices braising beef
6 thin slices prosciutto
30 ml/2 tbsp olive oil
1 litre/1¾ pts/4¼ cups beef stock
Salt and freshly ground black pepper
Plain boiled rice, to serve

Thinly pare the rind from half the orange and cut into thin strips. Grate the remainder. Squeeze the juice. Heat 15 g/½ oz/ 1 tbsp butter and add the spring onions, celery, oregano and pepper to taste. Cook, stirring, until the onions become pale yellow. Place the breadcrumbs into a mixing bowl, and add the onion mixture and grated orange rind. Add 30 ml/2 tbsp of the Marsala, the pine nuts and salt to taste. Blend well. Spoon equal amounts on to the beef slices, pressing it down with your fingers to help it adhere. Place a slice of prosciutto on top of each beef slice. Roll up the meat, beginning with the narrower end, and secure each roll with a cocktail stick (toothpick) or tie with string. Heat the remaining butter and the olive oil and brown the beef on all sides for 6–8 minutes. Pour off the fat. Add the remaining Marsala, the stock and the orange juice. Season to taste. Cover tightly, and simmer for 1 hour or longer, until the beef is tender. Remove the meat and boil the sauce rapidly to reduce slightly. Discard the cocktail sticks or string from the meat and return to the sauce. Serve piping hot with plain boiled rice.

Filleto Adrano

Adrano Fillet of Beef
Serves 4

1 kg/2¼ lb beef fillet
60 ml/4 tbsp olive oil
225 g/8 oz mushrooms, sliced
2 shallots, chopped
15 g/½ oz/1 tbsp butter
30 ml/2 tbsp plain (all-purpose) flour
250 ml/8 fl oz/1 cup beef stock
90 ml/6 tbsp sherry
2.5 ml/½ tsp green peppercorns
Grated rind and juice of ½ lemon
120 ml/4 fl oz/½ cup double (heavy)
*   cream*

Cut the beef into thin slices. In a large frying pan (skillet), heat the oil and cook the slices quickly for 1 minute on each side. Remove and keep warm. Add the mushrooms to the pan and cook for 5 minutes. Transfer to a small bowl, and set aside. In the same pan melt the butter, add the shallots and cook for 2 minutes. Stir in the flour, blending well with a small wire whisk. Slowly add the stock, and keep stirring. Cook for 3–4 minutes until the sauce thickens. Stir in the sherry, green peppercorns, lemon rind and juice, cream and salt. Mix well, and simmer for 2 minutes. Place the beef slices and mushrooms in the sauce and bring to the boil over a high heat. Immediately remove from the heat and serve.

Manzo alla Perugina

Chuck Steak in Red Wine
Serves 4–6

1 onion, chopped
50 g/2 oz/¼ cup unsalted (sweet) butter
1 kg/2¼ lb chuck steak (or rump)
30 ml/2 tbsp plain (all-purpose) flour
90 ml/6 tbsp red wine
45 ml/3 tbsp red wine vinegar
250 ml/8 fl oz/1 cup beef stock
15 ml/1 tbsp capers, chopped
Salt and freshly ground black pepper
250 ml/8 fl oz/1 cup single (light)
*   cream*

In a frying pan (skillet), cook the onion in the butter for 5 minutes. Remove with a draining spoon and set aside. Cut the meat into 2.5 cm/1 in cubes and coat with the flour. Fry (sauté) in the butter to seal on all sides. When the steak is brown, pour over the red wine and red wine vinegar and cook rapidly until the liquid has evaporated. Pour in the stock, lower the heat and simmer. Add the capers. Return the onion to the pan and stir well. Season with salt and pepper and cover with a lid. Simmer for 2½ hours until the meat is tender, adding a little water or stock if the stew becomes too dry. Add the cream, stir and season to taste. Serve very hot.

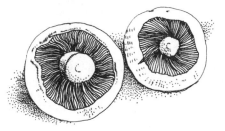

Rolle di Manzo con Verdura

Beef Roll with Vegetables
Serves 4

4 slices white bread
250 ml/8 fl oz/1 cup milk
30 ml/2 tbsp olive oil
25 g/1 oz/2 tbsp butter
2 large onions, finely chopped
2 carrots, grated
3 celery sticks, finely chopped
2 garlic cloves, finely chopped
45 ml/3 tbsp chopped fresh parsley
100 g/4 oz/1 cup Parmesan cheese,
  grated
5 ml/1 tsp chopped fresh oregano
1 egg
Salt and freshly ground black pepper
750 g/1½ lb top rump steak
15 ml/1 tbsp olive oil
15 g/½ oz/1 tbsp butter
60 ml/4 tbsp brandy
120 ml/4 fl oz/½ cup dry red wine
250 ml/8 fl oz/1 cup beef stock
45 ml/3 tbsp tomato purée (paste)
5 ml/1 tsp chopped fresh oregano
Plain boiled potatoes, to serve

Soak the bread in the milk. In a frying pan (skillet), heat the oil and butter. Add the onions, carrots and celery and cook for 5 minutes, until the onions begin to turn brown. Add the garlic and cook for 1 minute. Transfer to a large bowl. Squeeze the bread to remove some of the milk. Break into small pieces, and add to vegetable mixture. Blend in the parsley, cheese, oregano, and egg. Add 2.5 ml/½ tsp salt, and sprinkle liberally with freshly ground pepper. Mix well, and set aside. Spread out the steak on a flat surface. Pound it with a mallet to achieve the desired thinness (approximately 5 mm/¼ in thick). Season liberally, and spread as evenly as you can with the vegetable and bread mixture. Beginning with the smaller or narrower end, roll up the steak and secure it with a string, cocktail sticks (toothpicks) or small skewers. In a large, saucepan, heat the oil and butter, and brown the beef roll on all sides. Remove the pan from the heat and quickly add the brandy. Ignite it, and allow to flame for a few seconds. Return the pan to the heat. Add the wine, stock, tomato purée and oregano and simmer, uncovered, for 5 minutes. Cover the pan, and cook for 50 minutes. Baste the beef roll every 10 minutes. To serve, place the beef roll on a large serving platter, remove the string or skewers, and slice carefully. Serve with potatoes.

Manzo alla Pizzaiola

Pizzaiola Steak
Serves 4

450 g/1 lb rump or sirloin steak, thinly
  sliced
60 ml/4 tbsp olive oil
2 garlic cloves, crushed
450 g/1 lb tomatoes, skinned and
  chopped
30 ml/2 tbsp chopped fresh parsley
30 ml/2 tbsp chopped fresh basil
Salt and freshly ground black pepper

Place the slices of meat between two sheets of greaseproof (waxed) paper or clingfilm (plastic wrap) and flatten with a mallet until very thin. Heat the oil in a large frying pan (skillet) and gently fry (sauté) the steak for 2–3 minutes. Add the garlic, tomatoes and herbs and bring to the boil. Cook over a high heat for 5 minutes. Season with salt and pepper and serve at once.

Polpettine

Italian Meatballs

Serves 4

450 g/1 lb/4 cups lean minced
(ground) beef
1 large onion, finely chopped
50 g/2 oz/1 cup fresh breadcrumbs
1 egg, beaten
15 ml/1 tbsp chopped fresh herbs
50 g/2 oz/½ cup sage and onion
stuffing
Salt and freshly ground black pepper
Piquant Chinese Sauce (see page 365),
to serve

Combine all the ingredients together in a large mixing bowl. Shape the mixture firmly into 18 balls. Put the meatballs in a greased ovenproof dish and cook in a preheated oven at 190°C/375°F/gas mark 5 for 25 minutes until browned. Serve with Piquant Chinese Sauce.

Peperoni con Ripieno di Manzo

Beef-stuffed Peppers

Serves 4

4 green (bell) peppers
300 g/11 oz/2¾ cups lean minced
(ground) beef
1 garlic clove, crushed
1 onion, finely chopped
100 g/4 oz mushrooms, chopped
5 ml/1 tsp chopped fresh herbs
Salt and freshly ground black pepper
250 ml/8 fl oz/1 cup tomato juice

Slice the tops off the stalk end of the peppers and reserve them to use as lids. Remove and discard the seeds and the white pith from inside each pepper. Mix together the beef, garlic, onion, mush-rooms, herbs and seasoning. Spoon the mixture into the peppers and cover with the reserved tops. Arrange the peppers upright in a large saucepan and pour over the tomato juice. Cover with a lid and simmer gently for 40 minutes. Serve hot surrounded by the cooking liquid.

Arrosto in Casseruola All'Italiana

Italian-style Pot Roast

Serves 4

Salt and freshly ground black pepper
30 ml/2 tbsp plain (all-purpose) flour
1.25 kg/2¼ lb beef topside
15 ml/1 tbsp olive oil
15 g/½ oz/1 tbsp unsalted (sweet) butter
2 garlic cloves, chopped
1 onion, chopped
450 ml/¾ pt/2 cups dry red wine
4 tomatoes, skinned, seeded and
chopped
250 ml/8 fl oz/1 cup passata (sieved
tomatoes)
2.5 ml/½ tsp chopped fresh sage
2.5 ml/½ tsp chopped fresh oregano
2.5 ml/½ tsp chopped fresh thyme
2 bay leaves
30 ml/2 tbsp chopped fresh parsley

Season the flour and liberally pat all over the beef. Heat the oil and butter in a large flameproof casserole (Dutch oven) and brown the meat well on all sides. Add the garlic and onion, and cook for 2 minutes, stirring. Add the wine and allow to cook, uncovered, for 10 minutes. Stir in the tomatoes, passata, sage, oregano, thyme, and bay leaves. Cover the casserole, and simmer for 2½ hours. To serve, remove the meat from the casserole, and set on a plate. Pour the sauce over it, and sprinkle the roast with the chopped parsley.

Polpette alla Corsica

Corsican Meatballs
Serves 4

100 g/4 oz/1 cup fine cracked wheat
150 ml/¼ pt/⅔ cup boiling water
2 eggs, beaten
Plain (all-purpose) flour, for dusting
400 g/14 oz/3½ cups minced (ground)
 beef
2 onions, finely chopped
1 garlic clove, crushed
5 ml/1 tsp cayenne
Salt and freshly ground black pepper
Oil for shallow-frying

Add the cracked wheat to the boiling water, stir and cook for 20 minutes. Leave to cool for 8–10 minutes and blend in the eggs. Dust the hands with a little flour and divide the mixture into 8 balls. Flatten each ball to form a round and set aside. Combine the beef, onions, garlic and cayenne and season with the salt and pepper. Form into 8 balls slightly smaller than the cracked wheat balls. Flatten each one to form rounds in the same manner. Place a meat round in the centre of each cracked wheat round and roll up into a sausage shape. Roll each one in a little flour. Heat a little oil in a shallow pan and fry (sauté) the rolls for 6–8 minutes until they are golden and cooked through. Drain on kitchen paper and serve.

Carbonata alla Val d'Aosta

Rich Beef in Red Wine
Serves 4

750 g/1½ lb chuck steak, cubed
45 ml/3 tbsp red wine vinegar
15 ml/1 tbsp sugar
1 garlic clove, crushed
45 ml/3 tbsp plain (all-purpose) flour
50 g/2 oz/¼ cup butter
1 large onion, thickly sliced
About ¾ bottle full-bodied red wine
Salt and freshly ground black pepper
Hot polenta, to serve

Place the cubes of steak in a large bowl and sprinkle with the vinegar and sugar. Stir in the crushed garlic, cover and allow to marinate in the fridge for at least 2 hours, stirring occasionally. Lift out the meat, reserving the marinade, and dry on kitchen paper. Toss the meat in the flour. Place the butter in a large pan and fry (sauté) the meat quickly until browned on all sides. Remove the meat and keep aside. Fry the onion in the butter until soft, then return the meat to the pan. Add half of the wine and cook until it has been absorbed into the meat. Season with salt and pepper. Pour in the remaining wine and cook again in this way. Return the reserved marinade to the pan and cook gently, stirring until the gravy thickens. Serve with hot polenta.

Sbriciolato di Carne Tritata

Minced Beef Crumble

Serves 4–6

450 g/1 lb/4 cups minced (ground)
beef
1 onion, chopped
175 g/6 oz/1½ cups plain (all-purpose)
flour
4 large tomatoes, skinned and chopped
2.5 ml/½ tsp dry mustard
Salt and freshly ground black pepper
75 g/3 oz/⅓ cup margarine

Place the beef in a saucepan with the onion and cook, stirring for 5 minutes. Sprinkle over 15 ml/1 tbsp flour and add the chopped tomatoes. Stir well and cook for 1 minute. Place in a greased pie dish. Put the remaining flour, mustard, salt and pepper in a large bowl and rub in the margarine. Sprinkle the mixture over the beef and bake in a preheated oven at 200°C/400°F/ gas mark 6 for 35 minutes until the topping is golden brown.

Pasticcini di Carne alla Parmigiano

Cheeseburgers

Serves 4

450 g/1 lb/4 cups lean minced
(ground) beef
2 shallots, finely chopped
75 g/3 oz sun-dried tomatoes in oil,
drained and chopped
25 g/1 oz/¼ cup Parmesan cheese,
grated
45 ml/3 tbsp chopped fresh basil
Salt and freshly ground black pepper

Mix the meat, chopped shallots, tomatoes, cheese, basil and seasoning together. Divide into four and shape into thick rounds. Place on a lightly greased baking sheet, season again and grill (broil) under a high heat for 5 minutes, turning once, until cooked through.

Bistecca Milanese

Milanese Steak

Serves 6

6 rump or sirloin steaks
Salt and freshly ground black pepper
15 ml/1 tbsp plain (all-purpose) flour
30 ml/2 tbsp olive oil
25 g/1 oz/2 tbsp unsalted (sweet) butter
1 onion, chopped
6 large tomatoes, skinned and sliced
10 ml/2 tsp chopped fresh parsley
1.5 ml/¼ tsp fennel seeds

Pound the steaks out thinly and dip them in well-seasoned flour. Heat the olive oil in a frying pan (skillet) with the butter. Add the onion and cook for 1 minute. Brown the steaks on both sides and cover them with the sliced tomatoes. Simmer for 5 minutes and add the parsley and the fennel seeds. Cook for 8–10 minutes until the meat is tender.

Pasticcio di Lenticchie Rosso

Red Lentil Pie
Serves 4

2 onions, sliced
400 g/1 lb/4 cups minced (ground) beef
150 g/5 oz/⅔ cup margarine
100 g/4 oz/⅔ cup red lentils
2 garlic cloves, crushed
200 g/7 oz/1 small can tomatoes
5 ml/1 tsp chopped fresh thyme
90 ml/6 tbsp beef stock
100 g/4 oz/1 cup hard cheese, grated
1 egg, beaten
225 g/8 oz/2 cups plain (all-purpose) flour
Salt and freshly ground black pepper

Cook the onions and minced beef in 15 g/½ oz/1 tbsp of the margarine for 5 minutes and add the lentils and garlic. Add the canned tomatoes, fresh thyme and stock and bring to the boil. Simmer for 20 minutes. Continue cooking over a high heat to evaporate the liquid. Remove the pan from the heat and allow to cool, stirring in the cheese and half the egg. Season to taste. Put the flour into a bowl and work in the remaining margarine until the mixture resembles breadcrumbs. Season and add about 45 ml/3 tbsp water. Form into a soft dough and chill for 30 minutes. Preheat the oven to 200°C/400°F/gas mark 6. Roll out half the pastry and line a 20 cm/8 in pie dish. Spoon in the beef mixture and cover with the remaining pastry. Seal the edges of the pie and glaze with the remaining egg. Bake for 35 minutes until the pastry is golden brown.

Pebronata

Rump Steak, Tomatoes and Peppers
Serves 4

800 g/1¾ lb rump steak
60 ml/4 tbsp oil
1 onion, chopped
1 garlic clove, crushed
450 g/1 lb tomatoes, skinned and chopped
75 ml/5 tbsp white wine
15 ml/1 tbsp chopped fresh parsley
15 ml/1 tbsp chopped fresh thyme
Salt and freshly ground black pepper
6 juniper berries
1 bay leaf
2 large red (bell) peppers, seeded

Cut the steak into 6 cm/2½ in pieces and fry (sauté) in a frying pan (skillet) in half the oil, turning occasionally, until browned on all sides. Transfer to a warm casserole dish (Dutch oven). Place in an oven preheated to 180°C/350°F/gas mark 4 and cook for 25 minutes. Fry the onion and garlic in the frying pan until the onion is brown and crispy. Add the tomatoes. Pour in the wine and add the parsley, thyme and a little seasoning. Grind the juniper berries or pound in a mortar and add to the wine and seasonings with the bay leaf. Simmer for 5 minutes and pour over the cooked beef. Return to the oven and continue cooking for a further 35 minutes. Heat the remaining oil in the frying pan. Cut the red peppers into thin 5 mm/¼ in strips and fry in the oil. Remove the beef from the oven and stir in the fried red peppers. Remove the bay leaf and serve immediately.

Bistecca alla Salsa di Basilico

Steak with Basil Sauce
Serves 2–3

450 g/1 lb rump or fillet steak
Freshly ground black pepper
100 g/4 oz shallots (or 1 onion),
chopped
60 ml/4 tbsp water
350 g/12 oz courgettes (zucchini),
trimmed and grated
15 ml/1 tbsp oil
15 ml/1 tbsp capers, drained and
chopped
60 ml/4 tbsp chopped fresh basil
15 g/½ oz/1 tbsp butter

Cut the steak into two or three thick pieces. Remove any excess fat. Sprinkle with the freshly ground black pepper and leave aside. Place the shallots in a saucepan with the water. Bring to the boil and cook until they are translucent and the water has reduced by half. Stir in the courgettes and oil. Cover and cook over a low heat for 10 minutes, stirring frequently, until the courgettes are soft and pulpy. Pass the vegetables through a sieve (strainer) or purée in a blender or food processor. Stir in the capers and basil and season with pepper. Heat a frying pan (skillet) and sear the steak over a high heat for 30 seconds on each side. lower the heat and cook the meat for 8–10 minutes (for medium rare), turning once or twice. Cook for 3–4 minutes more on each side if you prefer the steak well done. Reheat the basil sauce and stir in the butter. Cut the steak downwards and slanting into thin slices and spoon over the sauce.

Manzo alla Napoletano

Neapolitan Beef
Serves 4

15 ml/1 tbsp oil
2 onions, chopped
2 garlic cloves, crushed
750 g/1½ lb braising steak, cubed
400 g/14 oz/1 large can chopped
tomatoes
300 ml/½ pt/1¼ cups red wine
150 ml/¼ pt/⅔ cup beef stock
30 ml/2 tbsp tomato purée (paste)
Salt and freshly ground black pepper
15 ml/1 tbsp chopped fresh oregano
1 red (bell) pepper, diced
1 courgette (zucchini), sliced
1 small aubergine (eggplant), cut into
chunks

Heat the oil in a flameproof casserole (Dutch oven). Add the onions and cook until softened. Stir in the garlic and beef and cook until browned. Add the tomatoes, wine, stock, tomato purée, salt and pepper and bring to the boil. Cover with a lid or foil and place in a preheated oven at 180°C/350°F/gas mark 4 for 1½ hours. Remove the dish from the oven and stir in the red pepper, courgette and aubergine. Cover and return the casserole dish to the oven for a further 30 minutes.

Scaloppine alla Sanremese

Sanremo-style Escalopes
Serves 4

8 thin slices of tender beef
4 anchovy fillets, drained
15 ml/1 tbsp capers
1 garlic clove, peeled
15 ml/1 tbsp pine nuts
6 fresh basil leaves
30 ml/2 tbsp olive oil
Salt and freshly ground black pepper
Grated rind and juice of ½ lemon

Flatten the meat as much as possible between two sheets of greaseproof (waxed) paper or clingfilm (plastic wrap). Chop the anchovies, capers, garlic, pine nuts and basil leaves. Pour the oil into a frying pan (skillet) and add the anchovy mixture. Lay the meat on the top, season with the salt and pepper and sprinkle over the lemon juice. Fry (sauté) for 6 minutes on each side and serve with the anchovy mixture spread over.

Polpettone con Mozzarella

Mozzarella Meat Loaf
Serves 4

450 g/1 lb Italian sausages
75 g/3 oz Mozzarella cheese
5 pieces Italian bread
175 ml/6 fl oz/¾ cup milk
900 g/2 lb/8 cups minced (ground) beef
2 eggs beaten
2 onions, chopped
30 ml/2 tbsp chopped fresh parsley
1 garlic clove, chopped
50 g/2 oz/½ cup Parmesan cheese, grated
45 ml/3 tbsp passata (sieved tomatoes)
Salt and freshly ground black pepper
50 g/2 oz/1 cup fresh breadcrumbs

Remove the sausages from their casings and crumble into a bowl. Cut the Mozzarella into cubes. Soak the bread in milk for 5 minutes and squeeze dry. In a large bowl, combine the minced beef with the sausage. Add the eggs, onions, parsley, garlic, Parmesan cheese, Mozzarella, bread and passata. Add salt and pepper to taste. On a flat surface, shape the mixture into a loaf shape, roll in the breadcrumbs, and place in an oiled baking dish. Bake in a preheated oven at 180°C/350°F/gas mark 4 for 1½ hours. Remove from the oven, and transfer the meat loaf to a warm serving plate. Serve sliced.

Polpettone Piccante

Savoury Meat Loaf
Serves 4

15 g/½ oz/1 tbsp unsalted (sweet) butter
50 g/2 oz/1 cup breadcrumbs
350 g/12 oz/3 cups minced (ground) beef
50 g/2 oz/¼ cup ground rice
2 large onions, finely chopped
Salt and freshly ground black pepper
30 ml/2 tbsp chopped fresh mixed herbs
45 ml/3 tbsp tomato purée (paste)
1 egg, beaten

Preheat the oven to 190°C/375°F/gas mark 5. Grease a 450 g/1 lb loaf tin with the butter and coat with half the breadcrumbs. Put the remaining ingredients in a large bowl and mix thoroughly. Pack the mixture into the loaf tin and place in the oven. Bake for 1¼ hours.

Arrosto in Casseruola con Zucchini

Pot Roast with Courgettes
Serves 4

50 g/2 oz/¼ cup butter
1.25 kg/2¾ lb pot roast beef
2 large onions, chopped
600 ml/1 pt/2½ cups beef stock
450 g/1 lb tomatoes, skinned, seeded
*   and chopped*
15 ml/1 tbsp tomato purée (paste)
2 garlic cloves, crushed
Salt and freshly ground black pepper
350 g/12 oz courgettes (zucchini),
*   chopped*
30 ml/2 tbsp chopped fresh herbs
Pasta, to serve

Melt the butter in a large pan. Place the beef in the pan with the onions and cook over a moderate heat until the beef is browned on all sides. Pour in the stock and bring to the boil. Lower the heat and add the tomatoes and tomato purée. Stir in the crushed garlic. Season with salt and pepper and cover the pan. Simmer for 1½ hours. Stir in the chopped courgettes and continue cooking for 20 minutes. Sprinkle with the fresh herbs and serve with pasta.

Bistecca alla Fiorentina

Florentine Steak
Serves 2

2 large sirloin or rump steaks
5 ml/1 tsp olive oil
15 ml/1 tbsp chopped fresh oregano
2 large tomatoes, skinned, seeded and
*   chopped*
Salt and freshly ground black pepper

Heat the grill (broiler) and brush the steaks with the oil. Lay the steaks on the rack and cook for 3 minutes on one side until the meat is sealed. Meanwhile, simmer the oregano and tomatoes together in a saucepan. Turn over the meat and season well. Cook the meat for 3 minutes. Remove from the grill, pour over the sauce and serve immediately. The meat can also be cooked on a barbecue.

Brasato al Chianti

Braised Beef with Chianti
Serves 4–6

1 kg/2¼ lb piece of roasting beef
1 onion, sliced
2 carrots, chopped
1 celery stick, chopped
1 bay leaf
15 ml/1 tbsp juniper berries, lightly
*   crushed*
Salt and freshly ground black pepper
15 ml/1 tbsp chopped fresh oregano
½ bottle Chianti
250 ml/8 fl oz/1 cup beef stock
5 ml/1 tsp olive oil

Trim any fat from the meat. Put all the remaining ingredients, except the oil, in a large bowl and stir well. Add the piece of beef and allow to marinate, preferably overnight. Drain the meat, reserving the marinade. Heat the oil in a flameproof casserole dish (Dutch oven) and sear the meat thoroughly on all sides. When the meat is well browned, pour over the vegetables and marinade. Cover with a lid and cook in a preheated oven at 180ºC/350ºF/gas mark 4 for 2½ hours. Remove the meat and keep warm. Purée the sauce in a blender or food processor then return to the pan with the meat. Cover and cook for a further 30 minutes. Slice the meat before serving.

Stracotto

Pot Roast
Serves 4–6

1.5 kg/3 lb piece brisket
2–3 garlic cloves, cut into strips
75 g/3 oz/⅓ cup butter
1 onion, chopped
1 carrot, chopped
1 celery stick, chopped
50 g/2 oz fat bacon, chopped
1 litre/1¾ pts/4¼ cups beef stock
Salt and freshly ground black pepper
15 ml/1 tbsp tomato purée (paste)

Pierce the meat at intervals with the point of a sharp knife and insert the strips of garlic into the holes, adjusting the amount to suit your taste. Melt the butter in a heavy-based flameproof casserole (Dutch oven) and fry (sauté) the onion, carrot, celery and bacon for about 5 minutes until softened. Place the meat on top and fry until browned on all sides. Pour in about one-third of the stock, season with salt and pepper, stir in the tomato purée and bring to the boil. Cover and simmer over a very low heat for about 4 hours until the meat is very tender, adding a little more stock occasionally to prevent the dish from drying out. Remove the meat from the casserole, place on a warmed serving plate and slice it thickly. If you prefer a thicker gravy, rub the cooked vegetables through a sieve (strainer) or purée in a blender or food processor, then return them to the casserole to heat through before pouring over the meat.

Polpette Nella Foglia

Tomato Sauce Balls
Serves 6

450 g/1 lb/4 cups minced (ground) beef
225 g/8 oz/2 cups minced (ground) pork
2 onions, finely chopped
2 thick slices white bread
Cold water to soak
1 egg, beaten
2.5 ml/½ tsp salt
5 ml/1 tsp chopped fresh sage
5 ml/1 tsp chopped fresh marjoram
5 ml/1 tsp freshly ground black pepper
30 ml/2 tbsp vegetable oil
450 g/1 lb tomatoes, skinned and chopped
15 ml/1 tbsp tomato purée (paste)
1 garlic clove, crushed
2.5 ml/½ tsp dried thyme
2.5 ml/½ tsp dried coriander (cilantro)
8 lemon or vine leaves

In a large bowl mix together the beef and pork and one of the finely chopped onions. Soak the bread in the cold water and squeeze dry. Crumble the bread and mix into the meat. Stir in the egg and the salt, sage, marjoram and pepper. Shape the meat into small balls the size of walnuts. Fry (sauté) the meat balls in the oil until they are brown. Remove with a draining spoon and set aside. Put the remaining onion into the pan and fry until golden brown. Add the tomatoes and the remaining ingredients except for the lemon or vine leaves, and cook, covered, for 20 minutes over a low heat, stirring occasionally. Return the meatballs to the sauce and continue to simmer for a further 20 minutes. Season with salt and pepper if necessary and serve on the lemon or vine leaves.

Bistecca con Ripieno di Melanzane

Steak filled with Aubergine
Serves 4

1 large aubergine (eggplant)
75 g/3 oz/⅓ cup unsalted (sweet) butter
90 ml/6 tbsp olive oil
1 onion, chopped
1 garlic clove, chopped
2 celery sticks, chopped
2.5 ml/½ tsp chopped fresh oregano
15 ml/1 tbsp chopped fresh parsley
5 ml/1 tsp salt
2.5 ml/½ tsp black pepper
100 g/4 oz/2 cups breadcrumbs
2 eggs
1 kg/2¼ lb top rump steak in one piece
2 carrots, sliced
1 onion, chopped
4 tomatoes, skinned and chopped
375 ml/13 fl oz/1½ cups dry red wine
1.5 ml/¼ tsp chopped fresh oregano
Salt and freshly ground black pepper

Peel and cut the aubergine into 1 cm/½ in cubes. In a large frying pan (skillet), heat half the butter and oil, and fry (sauté) the aubergine for 10 minutes. Add the onion, garlic, celery, oregano, parsley, salt and pepper to taste, and cook for a further 5 minutes. Remove the pan from the heat, and transfer its contents to a large bowl. Add the breadcrumbs and blend well. Beat the eggs lightly and add to the mixture. mix well, and set aside. Lay the steak on a flat surface and spread with the stuffing. Roll gently and secure with a large metal skewer or with string. Heat the remaining butter and oil in a large, flameproof casserole (Dutch oven). Cook the steak on all sides for approximately 10 minutes until browned. Add the carrots, onions, and tomatoes, and cook for 10 minutes on low heat. Add the wine, oregano, salt and pepper to taste, and cover the casserole. Simmer for 1½ hours until the meat is tender. Cut in thick slices, removing the skewer or string. Serve with the vegetables and sauce spooned over.

Braciole con Salsa di Pepe Verde

Steak with Green Peppercorn Sauce
Serves 4

45 g/1½ oz/3 tbsp butter
4 rump or sirloin steaks
75 ml/5 tbsp white wine
30 ml/2 tbsp green peppercorns
120 ml/4 fl oz/½ cup double (heavy) cream
30 ml/2 tbsp mustard
15 ml/1 tbsp chopped fresh parsley

In a large frying pan (skillet) heat the butter and add the steaks. Cook until browned on both sides and cooked to your liking. Remove the steaks to a warm plate, and keep warm. Season to taste with salt. Pour off excess fat. Return the pan to the heat and pour in the wine. Cook for 3–4 minutes over a high heat, then add the peppercorns and cook for 1 minute. Lower the heat and stir in the cream and mustard. Place a steak in the centre of each plate and top with a sprinkling of chopped parsley and spoon the sauce around the steaks. Serve immediately.

Filetto di Manzo alla Paprika

Fillet of Beef with Paprika
Serves 4

25 g/1 oz/2 tbsp unsalted (sweet) butter
4 fillet steaks
Salt and freshly ground black pepper
1 wineglass red wine
5 ml/1 tsp paprika
150 ml/¼ pt/⅔ cup double (heavy) cream
15 ml/1 tbsp chopped fresh parsley

Melt the butter in a frying pan (skillet). Add the steaks and season with salt and pepper. Fry (sauté) until golden brown on both sides and cooked to your liking. Remove from the pan and keep warm. Add the wine to the pan juices and boil for 2 minutes. Stir in the paprika and cream. Simmer until thickened and slightly reduced. Stir in the parsley, taste and re-season, if necessary. Spoon over the steaks and serve straight away.

Stracotto di Manzo alla Toscana

Tuscan Braised Beef
Serves 4

900 g/2 lb braising steak
2 garlic cloves, cut in halves
Salt and freshly ground black pepper
10 ml/2 tsp chopped fresh sage
10 ml/2 tsp chopped fresh thyme
30 ml/2 tbsp olive oil
25 g/1 oz/2 tbsp unsalted (sweet) butter
2 onions, sliced
2 carrots, chopped
150 ml/¼ pt/⅔ cup beef stock
Coarsely grated rind of ½ lemon
45 ml/3 tbsp tomato purée (paste)
150 ml/¼ pt/⅔ cup red wine

Rub the steak with the garlic cloves and sprinkle with salt, pepper, sage and thyme. Heat the olive oil in a flameproof casserole (Dutch oven) and add the butter. Brown the meat all over and add the onions and carrots. Brown the vegetables and blend in the stock, lemon rind, tomato purée and red wine. Place in a preheated oven at 190°C/375°F/gas mark 5 for 2½ hours until the sauce is thick and the meat almost falls apart. Slice the meat and spoon over the vegetables and sauce.

Manzo con Guarnizione al Pomodoro

Tomato Topped Beef
Serves 4

30 ml/2 tbsp oil
450 g/1 lb cabbage, shredded
2 garlic cloves, crushed
450 g/1 lb/4 cups lean minced (ground) beef
15 ml/1 tbsp tomato purée (paste)
10 ml/2 tsp fresh orange juice
30 ml/2 tbsp water
5 ml/1 tsp fresh chopped marjoram
Salt and freshly ground black pepper
4 tomatoes, sliced

Heat the oil in a frying pan (skillet) and fry (sauté) the cabbage and garlic together for 5 minutes. Stir in the minced beef and continue cooking for a further 10 minutes. Blend the tomato purée, orange juice, water and marjoram together and pour over the mince. Stir well and continue cooking for 5 minutes. Season. Arrange the slices of tomato on top of the cabbage and beef mixture. Cover with a lid and cook for a further 10 minutes. Serve straight from the pan.

Poultry and Game

Pollo Alla Valdarno

Arno Valley Chicken

Serves 4

Grated rind and juice of 2 limes
2 garlic cloves, crushed
10 ml/2 tsp grated fresh root ginger
5 ml/1 tsp peppercorns
30 ml/2 tbsp Amaretto
4 boneless chicken breasts
15 ml/1 tbsp olive oil
1 onion, chopped
400 g/14 oz/1 large can chopped
*   tomatoes*
30 ml/2 tbsp black treacle (molasses)
30 ml/2 tbsp chopped fresh oregano

Blend the rind and juice of the limes together with the garlic, ginger, peppercorns and Amaretto. Discard any skin from the chicken breasts then place them in a deep dish. Coat with the marinade, cover and chill for at least 3 hours, turning occasionally. Remove the chicken from the marinade, reserving the liquid. Heat the oil in a frying pan (skillet) and brown the chicken over a high heat for 3 minutes on each side. Remove from the pan and set aside. Cook the onion in the oil until softened. Stir in the marinade and the tomatoes, black treacle and oregano. Return the chicken to the pan and bring to the boil. Reduce the heat and simmer the chicken, uncovered, for 20 minutes. Transfer the chicken breasts with a draining spoon on to a heated serving dish, cover and keep hot. Boil the sauce for 5 minutes to thicken it. Pour the sauce over the chicken and serve.

Parmigiana di Asparagi e Pollo

Chicken and Asparagus with Parmesan Sauce

Serves 4

450 g/1 lb asparagus
15 ml/1 tbsp unsalted (sweet) butter
2 egg yolks
15 ml/1 tbsp vinegar
Salt and freshly ground black pepper
4 boneless chicken breasts
15 ml/1 tbsp olive oil
50 g/2 oz/½ cup Parmesan cheese,
*   grated*

Cut the asparagus into even-sized 6 cm/ 2½ in lengths. Cook the asparagus in boiling salted water for 5 minutes or until tender. Drain well. Place on a warmed serving plate and pile up in the shape of a pyramid. Keep warm. Place the butter in a saucepan and beat in the two egg yolks. Add the vinegar and season with salt and pepper. Cook until thickened, stirring all the time. Do not boil. Cut the chicken breasts into strips. Heat the oil in a frying pan (skillet) and fry (sauté) the chicken strips for 5 minutes until the edges of the meat begin to turn brown. Pile on top of the asparagus spears. Pour over the sauce, sprinkle with the Parmesan cheese and serve at once.

Pollo al Cognac

Brandied Chicken

Serves 4

1 large onion, chopped
4 chicken breast fillets, thickly sliced
50 g/2 oz/¼ cup unsalted (sweet) butter
30 ml/2 tbsp brandy
300 ml/½ pt/1¼ cups red wine
1 garlic clove, chopped
225 g/8 oz mushrooms, thinly sliced
Freshly ground black pepper
4 eggs

Brown the onion and chicken in the butter in a large frying pan (skillet). Pour over the brandy. Set light to the brandy immediately and give the pan a shake until the flames have died down. Pour in the red wine and leave over a low heat. Stir in the chopped garlic and mushrooms and season with pepper. Simmer for 5 minutes. Stir well. Break the eggs into the pan and leave for 3–4 minutes until the eggs are cooked but soft. Serve straight from the pan.

Pollo con Sherry Aceto e Dragonella

Chicken with Sherry Vinegar and Tarragon

Serves 4

30 ml/2 tbsp tomato purée (paste)
60 ml/4 tbsp sherry vinegar
60 ml/4 tbsp sherry
10 ml/2 tsp made mustard
30 ml/2 tbsp olive oil
4 chicken portions
30 ml/2 tbsp chopped fresh tarragon

In a small bowl blend the tomato purée with the sherry vinegar, sherry and mustard. Beat in the olive oil. Place the meat on foil on a grill (broiler) rack and brush the sauce over the chicken pieces. Grill (broil) the chicken for 10 minutes on each side, remove from the heat and brush over another layer of the sauce. Return to the grill and cook for a further 10–15 minutes on each side. Sprinkle over the tarragon leaves and serve immediately.

Pollo alla Cacciatora

Hunter-style Chicken

Serves 4

4 chicken portions
30 ml/2 tbsp olive oil
75 ml/5 tbsp tomato purée (paste)
30 ml/2 tbsp capers
2 canned anchovy fillets, finely
* chopped*
1 garlic clove, chopped
1 large sprig of rosemary
90 ml/6 tbsp dry white wine
150 ml/¼ pt/⅔ cup chicken stock
Grated rind and juice of ½ lemon
Salt and freshly ground black pepper
4 slices Ciabatta bread, fried in olive
* oil, to garnish*

Wipe the chicken and brown in the oil in a flameproof casserole (Dutch oven). Add the remaining ingredients except the fried Ciabatta bread. Bring to the boil, reduce the heat, cover and simmer very gently for 40 minutes or until the chicken is tender. Carefully lift the chicken out on to a serving dish. Spoon off any excess oil from the cooking juices. Discard the rosemary. Boil rapidly for 1 minute to thicken, if necessary, then taste and re-season. Spoon over the chicken and garnish with the fried bread.

Cupola di Pollo

Chicken Dome
Serves 4–6

100 g/4 oz/½ cup unsalted (sweet)
butter
1 carrot, finely chopped
1 onion, finely chopped
2.5 ml/½ tsp chopped fresh thyme
100 g/4 oz lean bacon rashers (slices),
rinded and cut into strips
50 g/2 oz button mushrooms, sliced
350 g/12 oz raw chicken meat, finely
chopped
100 ml/3½ fl oz/6½ tbsp dry white wine
Salt and freshly ground black pepper
450 g/1 lb penne pasta
50 g/2 oz/½ cup plain (all-purpose)
flour
400 ml/14 fl oz/1¾ cups milk
A little oil for greasing
40 g/1½ oz/¾ cup breadcrumbs
100 g/4 oz/1 cup Parmesan cheese,
grated

Melt half the butter in a large saucepan
and add the carrot, onion and thyme. Cook
for 5 minutes and stir in the bacon. Add the
mushrooms to the pan and continue to fry
(sauté) for 5 minutes. Stir in the chicken
meat and fry until brown. Stir in the wine
and season with the salt and pepper. Cover
with a lid and cook for 15 minutes until the
chicken is tender. Bring a pan of salted
water to the boil and add the penne. Bring
to the boil. Lower the heat and simmer for
10 minutes until tender but firm. Drain.
Melt the remaining butter in a saucepan
and sprinkle in the flour. Cook for 1
minute and gradually stir in the milk. Cook
until the sauce is thick and smooth. Season
with salt and pepper and remove from the
heat. Grease a large soufflé or casserole
dish (Dutch oven) with a little oil and
sprinkle in half the breadcrumbs. Mix the
chicken mixture with the pasta, sauce and
Parmesan cheese. Turn into the soufflé
dish and top with the remaining breadcrumbs. Cover with foil and cook in a preheated oven at 200°C/400°F/gas mark 6 for
25 minutes.

Coscia di Pollo Ripieno

Stuffed Chicken Thighs
Serves 4

75 ml/5 tbsp Pesto (see page 366)
5 ml/1 tsp paprika
8 chicken thighs, boned
60 ml/4 tbsp olive oil
1 red onion, chopped
1 onion, chopped
400 g/14 oz/1 large can chopped
tomatoes
15 ml/1 tbsp tomato purée (paste)
7 fresh basil leaves, chopped
150 ml/¼ pt/⅔ cup white wine
1 red (bell) pepper, sliced
1 green (bell) pepper, sliced
1 orange (bell) pepper, sliced

Blend the pesto with the paprika and
spread a little of the mixture under the skin
of each chicken thigh. Heat half the oil in
a frying pan (skillet) and cook the chicken
for 10 minutes until browned all over.
Remove from the pan. Add the onions to
the pan and cook for 3 minutes. Stir in the
tomatoes, tomato purée and the basil
leaves. Add the chicken thighs and stir in
the white wine and simmer for 5 minutes.
Put the peppers and the remaining oil in a
separate frying pan and cook for 5 minutes. Pour over the chicken thighs and
place in a preheated oven at 190°C/375°F/
gas mark 5 for 20 minutes.

Pasticcio di Pollo e Zucchini

Chicken and Courgette Pie
Serves 4–6

225 g/8 oz courgettes (zucchini)
Salt and freshly ground black pepper
15 g/½ oz/2 tbsp plain (all-purpose) flour
30 ml/2 tbsp olive oil
225 g/8 oz/2 cups cooked chicken breast, minced
175 g/6 oz/1½ cups Padano cheese, grated
1 quantity Caper and Tomato Sauce (see page 358)
1 egg, beaten
250 ml/8 fl oz/1 cup single (light) cream
15 ml/1 tbsp chopped fresh parsley

Slice the courgettes into 1 cm/½ in rounds. Layer the courgettes in a dish and sprinkle salt between each layer. Leave to stand for 1 hour to remove the bitter juice. Rinse thoroughly and drain well. Pat the courgettes with kitchen paper to remove any excess liquid. Dust with flour lightly. Heat the oil in a frying pan (skillet) and cook on both sides, one layer at a time. Leave to one side. Oil an ovenproof dish and put a layer of fried courgettes on the base. Cover with a layer of half the chicken, a layer of a third of the cheese and a layer of half the sauce. Repeat and season with the salt and pepper. Beat the egg into the cream and pour over the sauce. Sprinkle over the remaining cheese and bake in a preheated oven at 180°C/350°F/gas mark 4 for 40 minutes. Garnish with chopped parsley.

Mousse di Pollo e Prosciutto

Chicken and Prosciutto Mousse
Serves 6–8

2 garlic cloves, crushed
50 g/2 oz/¼ cup unsalted (sweet) butter
30 ml/2 tbsp oil
4 boneless chicken breasts
275 g/10 oz/2½ cups chicken livers
1 large onion, chopped
75 g/3 oz prosciutto
3 eggs, separated
100 ml/3½ fl oz/6½ tbsp double (heavy) cream
30 ml/2 tbsp brandy
Salt and freshly ground black pepper
Thinly buttered toast, to serve

Butter a mould (mold) with a little of the garlic butter made by beating the butter and crushed garlic cloves together. Heat the oil and fry (sauté) the chicken breasts for 3 minutes on either side. Remove from the pan and leave to one side. Add the chicken livers and chopped onion to the pan and fry, stirring for 3–4 minutes. Add to the chicken breasts. Briefly mince or process the chicken breasts with the chicken livers, onion and prosciutto. Spoon into a bowl. Beat three egg yolks and one whisked egg white into the chicken mixture. Gradually beat in the cream and mix to a paste. Beat the two remaining egg whites until stiff and fold into the mixture with the brandy. Season lightly. Turn into the buttered mould. Cover with buttered greased paper and foil and steam for 30 minutes. Remove from the steamer, cool and chill. Turn out the chicken and ham mousse on to a flat dish, and garnish with piped rosettes of the remaining garlic butter. Chill until required and serve with thinly buttered toast.

Pollo e Carote

Chicken and Carrots
Serves 4

30 ml/2 tbsp oil
4 chicken portions
450 g/1 lb carrots, chopped
1 garlic clove, crushed
1 onion, chopped
15 ml/1 tbsp plain (all-purpose) flour
600 ml/1 pt/2½ cups chicken stock
450 g/1 lb potatoes, cut into chunks

Heat the oil in a flameproof casserole dish (Dutch oven). Brown the chicken on all sides and transfer to a plate. Brown the carrots, garlic and onion and sprinkle with the flour. Cook for 1 minute and gradually stir in the stock. Heat for 2 minutes, stirring until the gravy thickens. Stir in the potatoes. Return the meat to the pan, cover with a lid and cook in a preheated oven at 160°C/325°F/gas mark 3 for 2½ hours.

Pollo Marengo

Chicken Marengo
Serves 4

1.5 kg/3 lb oven-ready chicken
30 ml/2 tbsp oil
4 tomatoes
15 ml/1 tbsp tomato purée (paste)
15 ml/1 tbsp plain (all-purpose) flour
90 ml/6 tbsp white wine
90 ml/6 tbsp chicken stock
10 g/¼ oz/2 tsp butter
12 button mushrooms
12 small shallots, peeled
1 garlic clove, finely sliced
Salt and freshly ground black pepper
30 ml/2 tbsp sherry
30 ml/2 tbsp chopped fresh parsley
Croûtons (optional)

Joint the chicken. Heat the oil in a saucepan and add the chicken pieces. Cook until the chicken is golden brown all over. Chop the tomatoes roughly and add to the chicken with the tomato purée. Sprinkle the joints with the flour and stir well until the flour browns. Pour in the white wine and stock. Heat the butter in a pan and stir in the mushrooms. Add the peeled shallots and cook until brown. Stir in the sliced garlic and season with the salt and pepper. Add to the chicken and simmer for 1½ hours. Remove the chicken pieces to a hot dish and garnish with the mushrooms and shallots. Keep warm. Add the sherry to the sauce and simmer for 1 minute. Pour over the chicken and sprinkle with parsley and croûtons if liked.

Pollo al Marsala

Chicken in Marsala Sauce
Serves 4

30 ml/2 tbsp oil
4 chicken joints
3 celery sticks, cut into chunks
1 garlic clove, crushed
1 onion, chopped
25 g/1 oz/¼ cup plain (all-purpose) flour
600 ml/1 pt/2½ cups chicken stock
60 ml/4 tbsp Marsala

Heat the oil in a large saucepan and brown the chicken on all sides. Remove to a plate. Brown the celery, garlic and onion and sprinkle over the flour. Cook for 1 minute and gradually stir in the stock. Heat for 2 minutes, stirring until the sauce thickens and stir in the Marsala. Return the meat to the pan, cover with a lid, reduce the heat and cook for 1 hour, stirring occasionally.

Photograph opposite: **Tuscan Bean Broth (page 54)**

Classico Sformato Italiano

Classic Italian Casserole
Serves 4

50 g/2 oz/¼ cup unsalted (sweet) butter
4 chicken portions
2 large onions, chopped
600 ml/1 pt/2½ cups chicken stock
450 g/1 lb fresh tomatoes, skinned,
    seeded and chopped
15 ml/1 tbsp tomato purée (paste)
2 garlic cloves, crushed
Salt and freshly ground black pepper
30 ml/2 tbsp chopped fresh herbs
Pasta, to serve

Melt the butter in a large pan. Place the chicken in the pan with the onions and cook over a moderate heat until the chicken is browned on all sides and the onions are translucent. Pour in the stock and bring to the boil. Lower the heat and add the tomatoes and tomato purée. Stir in the crushed garlic. Season with the salt and pepper and cover the pan. Simmer for 50 minutes. Sprinkle with the fresh herbs and serve with pasta.

Pollo con Finocchio Avellino

Avellino Chicken and Fennel
Serves 4–6

30 ml/2 tbsp olive oil
8 chicken thighs
2 large fennel bulbs, trimmed
30 ml/2 tbsp tomato purée (paste)
1 bay leaf
15 ml/1 tbsp chopped fresh basil
300 ml/½ pt/1¼ cups white wine
15 ml/1 tbsp chopped fresh parsley

Photograph opposite: **Focaccia Mushrooms (page 61)**

Put 15 ml/1 tbsp olive oil into a saucepan and add the chicken thighs. Cook over a high heat until lightly browned. Chop each fennel bulb into thin slices. Place in the saucepan with the chicken thighs, the remaining oil and the tomato purée. Add the bay leaf and sprinkle over the basil. Pour in the white wine and simmer for 30 minutes. Remove the fennel and chicken thighs and place in a serving dish. Keep warm. Bring the sauce back to the boil and reduce the liquid by simmering until it has thickened. Remove the bay leaf and pour the sauce over the chicken and fennel. Sprinkle with the parsley and serve.

Pollo con Mele e Salmoriglio

Chicken with Apples and Lemon Sauce
Serves 4

3 apples, cored and quartered
30 ml/2 tbsp lemon juice
4 skinless chicken breasts
30 ml/2 tbsp olive oil
30 ml/2 tbsp honey
45 ml/3 tbsp water
5 ml/1 tsp ground cinnamon
1 quantity Lemon Sauce (see page 360)

Put the apples in a bowl with the lemon juice. Fry (sauté) the chicken in the olive oil for 6 minutes on each side and place in an ovenproof dish. Add the apples to the chicken and pour over the honey and water. Sprinkle with the cinnamon and place in a preheated oven at 180°C/350°F/gas mark 4 for 10 minutes, stirring halfway through cooking. Serve with Lemon Sauce.

Pollo con Limone e Mandorle

Chicken with Lemon and Almonds

Serves 4

4 skinless chicken breasts
450 ml/¾ pt/2 cups water
90 ml/6 tbsp chicken stock
Salt and freshly ground black pepper
1 bay leaf
25 g/1 oz/2 tbsp unsalted (sweet) butter
25 g/1 oz/¼ cup plain (all-purpose) flour
30 ml/2 tbsp lemon juice
50 g/2 oz/½ cup toasted flaked (slivered) almonds
Lemon slices and dill (dill weed), to garnish

Place the chicken breasts in a saucepan with the water, stock, salt, pepper and bay leaf and bring to the boil. Lower the heat and simmer for 25 minutes. Remove the chicken from the pan, keep warm, and strain the stock. Return the stock to the saucepan and boil for 10 minutes to reduce the volume. Melt the butter in a saucepan and stir in the flour. Cook for a few minutes and gradually blend in the stock. Stir in the lemon juice and cook until the sauce thickens. Add the flaked almonds and pour over the chicken. Garnish with the lemon and dill before serving.

Pollo con Salsa di Dragonella e Besciamella al Formaggio

Chicken with Tarragon and Cheese Sauce

Serves 4

75 g/3 oz/⅓ cup butter
4 chicken breasts, skin removed
150 g/5 oz/1¼ cups Parmesan cheese, grated
15 g/½ oz/1 tbsp plain (all-purpose) flour
250 ml/8 fl oz/1 cup chicken stock
30 ml/2 tbsp white wine
5 ml/1 tsp mustard
30 ml/2 tbsp chopped fresh tarragon
150 ml/¼ pt/⅔ cup single (light) cream
Salt and freshly ground black pepper

Melt half the butter and fry (sauté) the chicken for 10 minutes until golden brown. Slit each chicken breast down the length to form a pocket opening and place 15 ml/1 tbsp cheese into each. Place in an ovenproof dish. Melt the remaining butter and add the flour. Cook for 1 minute and remove from the heat. Gradually stir in the stock and white wine and bring to the boil. Simmer until the sauce thickens and stir in the mustard, tarragon and remaining cheese. Remove from the heat and stir in the cream. Pour the sauce over the chicken breasts and place in a preheated oven at 190°C/ 375°F/gas mark 5 for 20 minutes. Serve immediately.

Pollo con Ripieno di Fichi

Chicken with Fig Stuffing
Serves 4–6

Stuffing:
1 onion, chopped
1 garlic clove, crushed
1 carrot, finely diced
10 ml/2 tsp chopped fresh thyme
Grated rind and juice of 1 lime
50 g/2 oz/¼ cup risotto rice
175 g/6 oz fresh figs, chopped
600 ml/1 pt/2½ cups chicken stock
Freshly ground black pepper

2 kg/4½ lb oven-ready chicken
45 ml/3 tbsp water
Small bunch of fresh herbs
Fresh figs, to garnish

Put the chopped onion, garlic, carrot, thyme, lime, rice and chopped figs into a large saucepan and pour in the stock. Season with the pepper. Bring to the boil, reduce the heat and cover with a tight fitting lid. Simmer for 30 minutes until the rice has absorbed all the stock. Remove from the heat. Spoon the rice mixture into the neck end of the bird. Put any remaining stuffing in a separate greased dish. Tie the legs of the chicken together with clean string and place on a rack in a roasting tin (pan). Put the water and bunch of herbs into the tin. Roast the chicken in a preheated oven at 200°C/400°F/gas mark 6 for 1 hour. Baste the chicken and continue cooking for a further 40 minutes. Lift the cooked chicken on to a warmed serving plate. Cover it loosely with foil and allow to rest for 10 minutes. Garnish the chicken with wedges of fresh figs and carve at the table.

Pollo alla Veneziana

Venetian-style Chicken
Serves 4

120 ml/4 fl oz/½ cup olive oil
1.5 kg/3 lb oven-ready chicken, jointed
(or 4 chicken portions)
45 ml/3 tbsp plain (all-purpose) flour
Salt and freshly ground black pepper
3 large tomatoes, seeded and chopped
30 ml/2 tbsp chopped fresh basil
200 ml/7 fl oz/scant 1 cup dry white wine
2 garlic cloves, crushed
1 green (bell) pepper, sliced
100 g/4 oz mushrooms, sliced
4 slices white bread, crusts removed
4 eggs
Juice of 1 lemon

Heat half the oil in a large pan. Flour the chicken joints and season with salt and pepper. Cook in the oil until brown all over. Add the tomatoes, basil, wine, garlic and sliced pepper to the chicken. Cover and cook for 20–30 minutes. Add the mushrooms, return the lid and cook for a further 15 minutes until the chicken is cooked through. Heat the remaining oil in a separate frying pan (skillet) and fry (sauté) the bread until crisp and golden brown. Remove and keep warm. Fry the eggs in the oil. Remove the chicken and arrange on a large plate with the sauce and fried bread. Place an egg on top of each piece of bread. Drizzle over the lemon juice and serve immediately.

Pollo Colosseo

Coliseum Chicken
Serves 4

1.5 kg/3 lb oven-ready chicken
Salt and freshly ground black pepper
30 ml/2 tbsp oil
4 rashers (slices) bacon, rinded and
*   diced*
1 large onion, chopped
2 garlic cloves, sliced
10 ml/2 tsp chopped fresh rosemary
300 ml/½ pt/1¼ cups white wine
45 ml/3 tbsp tomato purée (paste)
600 ml/1 pt/2½ cups chicken stock

Joint the chicken, season with the salt and pepper and brush with oil. Heat the oil in a deep saucepan and fry (sauté) the bacon, onion and garlic for 1 minute, stirring. Add the chicken pieces and fry until they are golden brown, turning frequently. Sprinkle with the chopped rosemary and pour in the wine. Simmer for 5 minutes. Stir in the tomato purée and gradually add the stock. Cook for 50 minutes and serve with the sauce.

Pollo Alla Diavola

Devilled Chicken
Serves 4

450 g/1 lb cold cooked chicken
30 ml/2 tbsp tomato purée (paste)
30 ml/2 tbsp white wine vinegar
2.5 ml/½ tsp cayenne
10 ml/2 tsp made mustard
5 ml/1 tsp chopped fresh sage
30 ml/2 tbsp olive oil

Cut the chicken into 5 cm/2 in pieces. In a small bowl blend the tomato purée with the white wine vinegar, cayenne, ready-made mustard and sage. Beat in the olive oil. Lay the meat on a baking sheet and brush the sauce over the chicken pieces. Grill (broil) the chicken for 5 minutes on each side, remove from the heat and brush over another layer of the sauce. Return to the grill (broiler) and cook for a further minute on each side.

Pollo con Barbabietolle e Salsa di Aglio

Chicken with Beetroot and Garlic Sauce
Serves 4

75 g/3 oz/⅓ cup unsalted (sweet) butter
4 chicken breasts, skin removed
3 garlic cloves, crushed
275 g/10 oz cooked beetroot, finely
*   chopped*
Salt and freshly ground black pepper
250 ml/8 fl oz/1 cup chicken stock
75 ml/5 tbsp single (light) cream
Pasta, to serve

Melt half the butter in a frying pan (skillet) and fry (sauté) the chicken for 10 minutes until golden and cooked through. Remove the chicken from the pan and place in an ovenproof dish, keep warm. Melt the remaining butter in the pan and fry the garlic. Add the chopped beetroot and fry for 5 minutes. Season with salt and pepper and add the stock. Cook for 3 minutes and remove the pan from the heat. Allow the beetroot to cool and purée in a blender or food processor or pass through a sieve (strainer). Stir in the single cream and blend well. Pour over the chicken breasts and serve with pasta.

Pollo con Agrumi

Citrus Chicken

Serves 4

15 ml/1 tbsp olive oil
1 large onion, cut into rings
8 chicken thighs
150 ml/¼ pt/⅔ cup chicken stock
30 ml/2 tbsp chopped fresh basil
Juice and rind of 1 lemon
5 ml/1 tsp peppercorns, lightly crushed
15 ml/1 tbsp water
5 ml/1 tsp cornflour (cornstarch)
15 ml/1 tbsp chopped fresh chives

Heat the oil and fry (sauté) the onion. Add the chicken thighs and cook for 5 minutes, turning them until they are lightly brown all over. Pour the stock into the frying pan (skillet) and add the basil. Bring to the boil, cook for 3 minutes until the liquid is reduced by half. Lower the heat and add the lemon juice and rind. Add the peppercorns with the chicken and cover with a lid. Cook for 30 minutes. Blend the water and cornflour together and stir into the sauce. Cook for 1 minute. Arrange on a hot serving dish and garnish with chopped chives.

Coscette di Pollo alla Griglia

Grilled Chicken Thighs

Serves 4–6

12 skinless chicken thighs
3 garlic cloves, crushed
5 ml/1 tsp chilli powder
60 ml/4 tbsp Worcestershire sauce
45 ml/3 tbsp olive oil
45 ml/3 tbsp tomato purée (paste)
Lime slices, to garnish

Make two shallow slits horizontally across the surface of the thighs. Blend the remaining ingredients together and pour over the chicken. Leave to marinate for at least 2 hours, turning over occasionally. Grill (broil) under a moderate grill (broiler) for 15 minutes, turning frequently to avoid burning. Serve garnished with slices of lime.

Pollo Alla Romana

Roman Chicken

Serves 4

1.25 kg/2¾ lb oven-ready chicken
Salt and freshly ground black pepper
30 ml/2 tbsp oil
4 rashers (slices) bacon, rinded and diced
1 large onion, chopped
2 garlic cloves, sliced
10 ml/2 tsp chopped fresh rosemary
300 ml/½ pt/1¼ cups white wine
45 ml/3 tbsp tomato purée (paste)
600 ml/1 pt/2½ cups chicken stock
Noodles, to serve

Joint the chicken, season with salt and pepper and brush with some of the oil. Heat the oil in a deep saucepan and fry (sauté) the bacon, onion and garlic for 1 minute, stirring. Add the chicken pieces and fry until they are golden brown, turning frequently. Sprinkle with the chopped rosemary and pour in the wine. Simmer for 5 minutes. Stir in the tomato purée and gradually add the stock. Cook for 40 minutes and serve with noodles.

Gnochetti Croccanti

Crispy Quenelles
Serves 4

275 g/10 oz/2½ cups cooked chicken
25 g/1 oz/2 tbsp unsalted (sweet) butter
25 g/1 oz/¼ cup plain (all-purpose)
  flour
150 ml/¼ pt/⅔ cup milk
Salt and freshly ground black pepper
1 egg, beaten
50 g/2 oz/1 cup fresh breadcrumbs
4 rashers (slices) bacon, rinded
Oil
30 ml/2 tbsp chopped fresh parsley

Put the cooked chicken through a mincer or chop briefly in a food processor. Heat the butter in a saucepan and stir in the flour. Cook for 1 minute and gradually add the milk. Bring to the boil, stirring all the time, until the sauce thickens. Leave to cool and season with salt and pepper. Stir in the chicken, half the egg and half the breadcrumbs. Form into 8 small oval shapes with two spoons. Halve each rasher of bacon and wrap 1 piece of bacon round each oval. Dip each oval in the remaining egg and coat thoroughly in the remaining breadcrumbs until well-coated. Heat the oil in a frying pan (skillet) and fry (sauté) the quenelles until crisp and brown. Continue cooking slowly for 3–4 minutes. Remove to a serving plate and sprinkle with the chopped parsley.

Pollo con Peperoni Rossi e Dragonella

Chicken with Red Pepper and Tarragon
Serves 4

75 g/3 oz/⅓ cup unsalted (sweet) butter
4 chicken breasts, skin removed
2 red (bell) peppers, thinly sliced
15 g/½ oz/1 tbsp plain (all-purpose)
  flour
250 ml/8 fl oz/1 cup chicken stock
30 ml/2 tbsp white wine
5 ml/1 tsp mustard
30 ml/2 tbsp chopped fresh tarragon
150 ml/¼ pt/⅔ single (light) cream
Salt and freshly ground black pepper

Melt half the butter in a frying pan (skillet) and fry (sauté) the chicken for 10 minutes until golden brown. Remove the breasts from the pan and place in an ovenproof dish. Add the red peppers to the frying pan and continue cooking for 5 minutes. Add to the chicken. Melt the remaining butter and add the flour. Cook for 1 minute and remove from the heat. Gradually stir in the stock and white wine return to the heat and bring to the boil, stirring. Simmer until the sauce thickens and then stir in the mustard and tarragon. Remove from the heat and stir in the cream. Pour the sauce over the chicken breasts and peppers and cook in a preheated oven at 190°C/375°F/gas mark 5 for 20 minutes.

Pollo con Erbette, Aglio e Limone

Herb, Garlic and Lemon Chicken
Serves 6

1.25 kg/2¾ lb oven-ready chicken
Salt and freshly ground black pepper
1 lemon, sliced
2 garlic cloves, chopped

Marinade:
Juice of 1 lemon
75 ml/5 tbsp olive oil
60 ml/4 tbsp red wine
2 garlic cloves, crushed
1 onion, sliced

Stuffing:
85 g/3½ oz/1 packet lemon and parsley
* stuffing mix*
½ onion, chopped
30 ml/2 tbsp chopped fresh oregano
15 ml/1 tbsp chopped fresh coriander
* (cilantro)*
25 g/1 oz/2 tbsp unsalted (sweet) butter
2 onions, cut in wedges
6 courgettes (zucchini), sliced
* lengthways*

Season the inside of the chicken with the salt and pepper and push the lemon slices and garlic inside the cavity. Place in a shallow dish. Blend the marinade ingredients together and pour over the chicken. Allow to marinate for 4 hours or as long as possible, turning occasionally.

Make up the stuffing mix as directed on the packet and stir in the chopped onion, oregano and coriander. Fill the cavity of the bird. Place in a roasting tin (pan). Pour over the marinade. Dot the butter over the skin of the bird and cook in a preheated oven at 200°C/400°F/gas mark 6 for 1 hour 5 mins. Remove the dish from the oven.

Place the onions and courgettes around the chicken then return to the oven. Cook for 25 minutes or until the vegetables are tender.

Pollo al Lumia

Lime Chicken
Serves 4

Grated rind and juice of 2 limes
2 garlic cloves, crushed
30 ml/2 tbsp Amaretto
10 ml/2 tsp grated fresh root ginger
4 boneless chicken breasts
15 ml/1 tbsp olive oil
1 onion, chopped
400 g/14 oz/1 large can chopped
* tomatoes*
30 ml/2 tbsp black treacle (molasses)
30 ml/2 tbsp chopped fresh oregano

Blend the rind and juice of the limes with the garlic, Amaretto and ginger. Remove any skin from the chicken breasts and lay in a deep dish. Coat with the marinade, cover and chill for at least 3 hours, turning occasionally. Remove the chicken from the marinade, reserving the liquid. Heat the oil in a frying pan (skillet) and brown the chicken over a high heat for 3 minutes on each side. Remove from the pan and set aside. Cook the onion in the same pan until softened. Stir in the marinade and the tomatoes, black treacle and oregano. Return the chicken to the pan and bring to the boil. Reduce the heat and simmer the chicken, uncovered, for 20 minutes. Remove the chicken breasts on to a heated serving dish with a draining spoon, cover and keep hot. Boil the sauce for 5 minutes to reduce it. Pour the sauce over the chicken.

Pollo Mediterraneo

Mediterranean Chicken
Serves 4–6

50 g/2 oz/½ cup chicken livers, minced
100 g/4 oz/2 cups fresh breadcrumbs
2 large onions, chopped
1 garlic clove, crushed
60 ml/4 tbsp finely chopped fresh sage
1 egg, beaten
1.75 kg/4 lb oven-ready chicken
50 g/2 oz/¼ cup butter

Boil the chicken livers in a little water for 3–4 minutes. Place in a basin. Mix the breadcrumbs with the livers and stir in the onion, garlic and chopped sage. Blend in the beaten egg. Use this mixture to stuff the neck of the chicken. Place the bird in a baking tin (pan) and prick the skin with a sharp knife. Dot with the butter. Bake in a preheated oven at 200°C/400°F/gas mark 6 for 30 minutes. Baste the chicken and lower the heat to 180°C/350°F/gas mark 4 for 1½ hours, until the juices run clear when the thigh is pierced with a skewer. Should the breast of the bird appear to be too brown cover with foil for the remainder of the cooking period.

Pollo con Mozzarella

Mozzarella Chicken
Serves 4

4 chicken breasts, cubed
100 g/4 oz Mozzarella cheese, cut into cubes
75 ml/5 tbsp white wine
30 ml/2 tbsp chopped fresh basil
Freshly ground black pepper
225 g/8 oz pasta spirals
15 g/½ oz/1 tbsp unsalted (sweet) butter

Place the cubes of chicken and cheese in an ovenproof dish. Blend the wine with the chopped basil. Pour the wine over the cheese and chicken and season generously with the pepper. Place in a preheated oven at 200°C/400°F/gas mark 6 for 20 minutes until golden and bubbling. Meanwhile, cook the pasta in boiling salted water until it is firm but cooked. Drain, stir in the butter and pour into a deep dish. Spoon over the cooked chicken and cheese and serve immediately.

Funghi e Pollo Assisi

Mushroom and Chicken Assisi
Serves 4

1.25 kg/2¾ lb oven-ready chicken
50 g/2 oz/¼ cup unsalted (sweet) butter
225 g/8 oz mushrooms, chopped
1 onion, chopped
1 garlic clove, chopped
15 ml/1 tbsp olive oil
3 tomatoes, skinned and chopped
Salt and freshly ground black pepper
Chopped fresh herbs (optional)

Joint the chicken into 8 pieces. Heat half the butter in a frying pan (skillet) and cook the mushrooms. Add the onion and chopped garlic and cook until the onion is slightly golden. Remove from the pan and set aside. Lay the chicken joints in the pan, add the remaining butter and the oil and cook until the pieces are a rich golden brown. Return the mushrooms and onions to the pan and stir in the chopped tomatoes. Season with the salt and pepper and simmer gently for 45 minutes. Place the pieces of chicken on a hot dish, pour over the sauce and garnish with freshly chopped herbs if liked.

Pollo Palermo

Palermo Chicken
Serves 4

1.25 kg/2¾ lb oven-ready chicken
30 ml/2 tbsp oil
15 ml/1 tbsp tomato purée (paste)
15 ml/1 tbsp plain (all-purpose) flour
90 ml/6 tbsp white wine
90 ml/6 tbsp chicken stock
6 tomatoes, roughly chopped
1 garlic clove, finely sliced
Salt and freshly ground black pepper
Small knob of unsalted (sweet) butter
2 red (bell) peppers, thinly sliced
4 shallots, sliced
30 ml/2 tbsp sherry
30 ml/2 tbsp chopped fresh parsley
Croûtons, optional

Joint the chicken into 8 pieces. Heat the oil in a saucepan and add the chicken pieces. Cook until the chicken is golden brown on all sides. Sprinkle the joints with the flour and stir well until the flour browns. Pour in the white wine and stock. Stir in the tomatoes, tomato purée and sliced garlic and season with salt and pepper. Cover and simmer for 1½ hours. Heat the butter in a pan and fry (sauté) the sliced peppers and shallots. Remove the chicken pieces to a hot dish and garnish with the peppers and shallots. Keep warm. Add the sherry to the sauce and simmer for 1 minute. Pour over the chicken and sprinkle with parsley and croûtons of fried bread if using.

Torta di Spinaci e Pollo

Genoese Spinach and Chicken Pie
Serves 4–6

5 ml/1 tsp melted unsalted (sweet) butter
450 g/1 lb fresh or frozen spinach, cooked and drained
4 eggs
50 g/2 oz/½ cup Parmesan cheese, grated
100 g/4 oz/½ cup Ricotta cheese
2.5 ml/½ tsp grated nutmeg
225 g/8 oz/2 cups cooked chicken, minced (ground)
350 g/12 oz shortcrust pastry (basic pie crust)
30 ml/2 tbsp milk
Salt and freshly ground black pepper

Preheat the oven to 180°C/350°F/gas mark 4. Lightly butter a 25 cm/10 in flan dish (pie pan). Squeeze the spinach dry and chop coarsely. Place in a bowl and beat in the eggs and Parmesan cheese. Mix in the Ricotta and nutmeg. Stir in the minced chicken and season well. Roll out just over half of the pastry and line the dish. Spoon the spinach and chicken mixture into the pastry. Brush the edges of the pastry with the milk and roll out the remaining pastry to use as a lid. Trim, seal the edges with the prongs of a fork or crimp between finger and thumb. Decorate with pastry trimmings and make a hole in the centre to allow steam to escape. Brush over with the remaining milk and bake for 45 minutes until golden brown.

Pollo con Pesche alla Reggio

Royal Peach Chicken
Serves 4

450 g/1 lb chicken breasts
50 g/2 oz/¼ cup unsalted (sweet) butter
Salt and freshly ground black pepper
4 peaches, stoned (pitted) and sliced
1 onion, cut into rings
1 bay leaf
250 ml/8 fl oz/1 cup white wine

Cut the chicken into slices. Place in an ovenproof dish, dot with butter and season with salt and pepper. Cover with the peach slices and onion rings. Add the bay leaf to the dish. Pour over the white wine, cover with a lid or foil and bake in a preheated oven at 190°C/375°F/gas mark 5 for 35 minutes.

Stufato di Acetoselle e Pollo

Sorrel and Chicken Stew
Serves 4

45 g/1½ oz/3 tbsp unsalted (sweet)
butter
30 ml/2 tbsp plain (all purpose) flour
900 ml/1½ pts/3¾ cups chicken stock
225 g/8 oz/2 cups cooked chicken,
chopped
2 carrots, chopped
2 leeks, chopped
50 g/2 oz/¼ cup long-grain rice
Salt and freshly ground black pepper
300 ml/½ pt/1¼ cups single (light)
cream
6 sorrel leaves, torn

Heat half the butter in a saucepan and blend in the flour. Cook for 1 minute and gradually stir in the stock. Bring to the boil and add the chicken, carrots, leeks and rice. Season with salt and pepper and simmer for 40 minutes. Remove from the heat and blend in the cream. Add the sorrel leaves and return to a low heat. Simmer for 2 minutes, season and serve hot.

Pollo all'Italiano con Salsa al Basilico

Italian Chicken with Basil Sauce
Serves 4

4 chicken breast fillets, skinned
Freshly ground black pepper
100 g/4 oz shallots (or 1 large onion),
chopped
60 ml/4 tbsp water
350 g/12 oz courgettes (zucchini), grated
30 ml/2 tbsp oil
15 ml/1 tbsp capers, chopped
60 ml/4 tbsp chopped fresh basil
15 g/½ oz/1 tbsp butter

Sprinkle the chicken with freshly ground black pepper. Place the shallots in a saucepan with the water. Bring to the boil and cook until they are translucent and the water has reduced by half. Stir in the courgettes and half of the oil. Cover and cook over a low heat for 10 minutes, stirring frequently, until the courgettes are soft and pulpy. Pass the vegetables through a food mill, sieve (strainer) or blend in a food processor. Stir in the capers and basil and season with pepper. Heat the remaining oil in a frying pan (skillet) and sear the chicken over a high heat for 30 seconds on each side. Lower the heat and cook the meat for 10–12 minutes, turning it once or twice. Reheat the basil sauce and stir in the butter. Cut the chicken diagonally into thin slices and spoon over the sauce.

Zucchini e Pollo Milanese

Milan-style Chicken and Courgettes
Serves 3

6 large courgettes (zucchini), thickly
sliced
Oil for frying
1 garlic clove, crushed
3 boneless chicken breasts, sliced
thinly
2 eggs, beaten
50 g/2 oz/1 cup fresh breadcrumbs
Salt and freshly ground black pepper

Cook the courgettes in boiling, salted water for 5 minutes. Drain. Heat a little oil in a shallow pan. Add the crushed garlic and the chicken. Cook for 10 minutes, turning once. Remove to a warm serving plate and keep warm. Dip each courgette slice into the beaten egg and then into the breadcrumbs. Fry (sauté) the courgettes for two minutes until brown on both sides and serve while still hot with the chicken slices.

Polpette di Carne di Pollo Alla Veronese

Verona Chickenmeat Balls
Serves 4

350 g/12 oz/3 cups minced (ground)
chicken
30 ml/2 tbsp chopped fresh oregano
15 ml/1 tbsp chopped fresh basil
2 eggs
30 ml/2 tbsp unsalted (sweet) butter
100 g/4 oz/2 cups breadcrumbs
30 ml/2 tbsp double (heavy) cream
Salt and freshly ground black pepper
600 ml/1 pt/2½ cups chicken stock
Tomato Sauce (see page 358), to serve

Blend the chicken with the oregano and basil. Mix in the eggs and butter. Stir in the breadcrumbs and beat in the cream, salt and pepper until the mixture binds together. Take teaspoons of the mixture and roll into balls. Heat the stock until boiling. Add the meatballs and simmer for 8 minutes. Remove with a draining spoon and serve with Tomato Sauce.

Tostati di Petti di Piccione

Pigeon Breasts on Toast
Serves 4

4 pigeons, halved lengthways
1 carrot, chopped
1 onion, chopped
1 bay leaf
450 ml/¾ pt/2 cups chicken stock
1 wineglass sherry
50 g/2 oz/¼ cup unsalted (sweet) butter
8 slices of bread

Place the pigeons in a large saucepan with the carrot, onion and bay leaf and cover with the stock. Bring to the boil and cook for 15 minutes. Remove and drain the meat. Add the sherry and continue boiling the stock until it is reduced by half. Cut the breast and wing from the pigeon. Heat half the butter in a frying pan (skillet) and fry (sauté) the pigeons for 3 minutes, turning once during cooking. Keep warm. Remove the crusts from the bread. Toast and butter the slices. Strain the stock and keep warm. Arrange the toasted bread on a heated dish, top with the pigeon breasts and pour over the sauce. Serve at once.

Anatra col Pien

Venetian Boiled Duck
Serves 6–8

2 kg/4½ lb oven-ready duck
1 onion, chopped
2 carrots, chopped
1 celery stick, chopped
45 ml/3 tbsp chopped fresh parsley
Salt and freshly ground black pepper
1.75 litres/3 pts/7½ cups cold water
2 garlic cloves, sliced
100 g/4 oz/1 cup duck or chicken livers
2 bacon rashers (slices), rinded and chopped
60 ml/4 tbsp fresh breadcrumbs
1 egg, beaten

Wash and dry the duck. Put the onion, carrots, celery and half the parsley into a large saucepan with the cold water and bring slowly to the boil. Lower the heat and simmer. Blend the remaining parsley, garlic, duck or chicken livers, bacon rashers and breadcrumbs together with the egg in a small bowl. Season with salt and pepper. Spoon the liver and breadcrumb mix into the duck and sew up the bird with fine string. Place the bird in the saucepan of stock and simmer for 2½ hours until the bird is tender. Remove the duck from the water and undo the stitching. Slide out the stuffing, slice and lay on a warm plate. Joint the bird and slice the breast. Lay the meat on the stuffing and serve immediately.

Anatroccolo al Limone

Lemon Duckling
Serves 4

1.75 kg/4 lb oven-ready duckling
2 lemons, sliced
Salt and freshly ground black pepper
Grated rind and juice of 1 orange
50 g/2 oz/¼ cup sugar
5 ml/1 tsp ground cinnamon
5 ml/1 tsp chopped fresh oregano
5 ml/1 tsp chopped fresh sage
60 ml/4 tbsp Marsala

Season the duck and stuff with three-quarters of the lemon slices. Prick the duck breast with a sharp knife and put on a rack in a roasting tin (pan) in a preheated oven at 200°C/400°F/gas mark 6 for 25 minutes. Pour away the excess fat and place the duck in the roasting tin. Place the rind and juice of the orange in a saucepan with the sugar and cinnamon and bring to the boil. Chop the remaining lemon slices and add to the liquid. Simmer until the liquid has reduced by half and stir in the oregano, sage and Marsala. Pour over the duck and return to the oven for 1 hour 30 minutes, basting the duck with the juices every 30 minutes. Remove the duck from the oven and transfer to a warmed serving plate. Skim the fat from the pan juices and boil the sauce rapidly to reduce. Serve separately.

Coniglio Rustico

Farmer's Rabbit
Serves 4

1 large rabbit
45 ml/3 tbsp oil
1 garlic bulb, separated into cloves and
  peeled
90 ml/6 tbsp chicken stock
60 ml/4 tbsp red wine
15 ml/1 tbsp chopped fresh parsley
2 bay leaves
Salt and freshly ground black pepper

Joint the rabbit and fry (sauté) in a flame-proof casserole (Dutch oven) in the oil with the garlic. Cook the meat quickly to brown and seal the juices. Add the separated garlic cloves and cook for 5 minutes. Pour in the stock and red wine and sprinkle in the parsley. Add the bay leaves and seasoning, cover and bake in a preheated oven at 190°C/375°F/gas mark 5 for 1¼ hours.

Coniglio in Pentola

Rabbit in a Pot
Serves 4

30 ml/2 tbsp oil
1 large rabbit, cut into 4 joints
450 g/1 lb carrots, sliced thickly
2 garlic cloves, crushed
1 onion, chopped
25 g/1 oz/¼ cup plain (all-purpose) flour
600 ml/1 pt/2½ cups chicken stock
100 g/4 oz/1 cup borlotti beans, soaked
  overnight, boiled rapidly for 10
  minutes and drained

Heat the oil in a flameproof casserole dish (Dutch oven). Brown the rabbit on all sides and remove to a plate. Brown the carrots, garlic and onion and sprinkle over the flour. Cook for 1 minute and gradually stir in the stock. Heat for 2 minutes, stirring until the gravy thickens. Add the drained beans. Return the meat to the pan, cover with a lid and cook in a preheated oven at 150°C/300°F/gas mark 2 for 2–3 hours until the beans and rabbit are both tender.

Arrosto Ripieno

Roast Stuffed Turkey Roll
Serves 4

3 eggs, beaten
90 g/3½ oz/scant 1 cup Parmesan
  cheese, grated
Salt and freshly ground black pepper
60 ml/4 tbsp olive oil
750 g/1½ lb spinach, chopped
100 g/4 oz/½ cup unsalted (sweet) butter
1 kg/2¼ lb boned turkey breast
100 g/4 oz pancetta or bacon, thinly
  sliced

Blend the eggs, half the cheese and a sprinkling of salt and pepper. Pour 5 ml/1 tsp of oil into a pan and cook the eggs to make an omelette. Allow to cool. Place the spinach and butter in a large saucepan and cook for 8 minutes until soft. Stir in the remaining cheese and season with salt and pepper. Set aside. Lay the turkey on a board and flatten with a mallet to 1 cm/½ in thickness. Lay the pancetta over the turkey and cover with the spinach. Lay the omelette over the spinach. Roll up like a Swiss (jelly) roll to enclose all the ingredients and sew up with fine string. Tie in muslin cloth (cheesecloth). Heat the remaining oil in a large ovenproof dish and pour in 250 ml/8 fl oz/1 cup cold water. Add to the turkey, cover with a lid and bake in a preheated oven at 180°C/350°F/gas mark 4 for 1¼ hours, adding more water if necessary. Discard the muslin and string and slice thickly.

Tacchino alla Sanremese

Turkey Breast Sanremo
Serves 4

4 slices turkey breast
3 canned anchovies
50 g/2 oz prosciutto
10 ml/2 tsp capers
1 garlic clove, sliced
15 ml/1 tbsp pine nuts
30 ml/2 tbsp olive oil
45 ml/3 tbsp fresh breadcrumbs
2 large tomatoes, skinned, seeded and chopped
Salt and freshly ground black pepper

Flatten the turkey between two sheets of greaseproof (waxed) paper or clingfilm (plastic wrap). Chop and mix together the anchovies, prosciutto, capers, garlic and pine nuts. Heat the olive oil in a large frying pan (skillet) and cook the mixed ingredients for 5 minutes. Stir in the breadcrumbs. Place the meat on top and cook for 5 minutes on each side or until the turkey is cooked through. Arrange the meat on individual plates and spoon the contents of the pan over. Serve at once.

Petti di Tacchino di Prosciutto

Turkey Breasts with Prosciutto
Serves 4

4 thin turkey breasts
10 ml/2 tsp plain (all-purpose) flour
2.5 ml/½ tsp paprika
Salt
75 g/3 oz/⅓ cup unsalted (sweet) butter
4 slices prosciutto
4 slices Mozzarella cheese
30 ml/2 tbsp chopped fresh basil

Flatten the turkey breasts with a meat mallet. Blend the flour, paprika and salt together and coat the turkey breasts. Melt the butter in a frying pan (skillet) and add the turkey. Fry (sauté) on both sides to seal. Cover each slice of turkey with a slice of prosciutto and place a slice of Mozzarella on the top. Cover the pan with a lid. Increase the heat and cook for 3–5 minutes, or until the cheese has melted slightly. Transfer to a warm dish and sprinkle over the basil. Serve as soon as possible.

Faraona con Mela

Guinea Fowl with Apple
Serves 2–4

1 guinea fowl
2 eating (dessert) apples
10 ml/2 tsp grated lemon rind
1 garlic clove, chopped
45 ml/3 tbsp breadcrumbs
5 ml/1 tsp chopped fresh sage
Salt and freshly ground black pepper
45g/1½ oz/3 tbsp butter
60 ml/4 tbsp chicken stock

Wash and dry the guinea fowl and spread the outside skin with the butter. Peel, core and chop the apples and mix in a bowl with the lemon rind, garlic, breadcrumbs, sage, salt and pepper. Pack loosely into the bird. Place the bird on a rack in a roasting tin (pan). Pour over the stock and roast in a preheated oven at 190°C/375°F/gas mark 5 for about 1 hour or until the juices run clear. Serve with crispy roast potatoes.

Pernici con Lenticchie

Partridge and Lentil Casserole

If partridge is unavailable, poussins or chicken breasts can be used.

Serves 4

200 g/7 oz/good 1 cup green lentils, soaked overnight in cold water
75 ml/5 tbsp olive oil
1 large onion, chopped
2 partridges
30 ml/2 tbsp tomato purée (paste)
1 bay leaf
1 sprig of fresh rosemary
Salt and freshly ground black pepper
Tagliatelle, to serve

Drain and rinse the lentils. Place in a large pan of cold water and bring to the boil. Lower the heat and simmer for 40 minutes or until tender. Drain, reserving the cooking liquid. Pour the oil into a large saucepan and fry (sauté) the onion until lightly brown. Add the partridges and brown all over. Add the lentils and half the reserved cooking liquid. Stir in the tomato purée and add the bay leaf and rosemary. Simmer, uncovered, for 45 minutes, stirring from time to time. Add additional reserved liquid as necessary and season with salt and pepper. Serve very hot with tagliatelle.

Quaglia con Lamponi

Quail with Raspberries
Serves 2

2 apples
2 oven-ready quails
45 g/1½ oz/3 tbsp unsalted (sweet) butter
Salt and freshly ground black pepper
45 ml/3 tbsp sugar
250 ml/8 fl oz/1 cup water
120 ml/4 fl oz/½ cup Madeira
250 ml/8 fl oz/1 cup chicken stock
30 ml/2 tbsp brandy
15 ml/1 tbsp finely grated orange rind
225 g/8 oz raspberries

Wipe, quarter, core and pare apples. Truss the wings of the quails. Melt the butter in a large, heavy saucepan. Brown the birds on all sides, add salt and pepper to taste. Arrange the apples in a shallow baking dish, and sprinkle over the sugar. Add the quails, water and Madeira. Cover and cook in a pre-heated oven at 190°C/375°F/gas mark 5 for 30 minutes basting the birds frequently. Remove the pan from the oven and transfer the quails and apples to a large, warm serving dish. Keep warm. Add the stock, brandy and orange rind to the pan. Bring to the boil, reduce the heat, and simmer for approximately 15 minutes, stirring frequently. Add the fresh raspberries and stir well. Cook for 1 minute. Lift out the raspberries with a draining spoon and place around the quails. Pour the sauce over the birds and serve immediately.

Lamb

Agnello All'Albicocca

Apricot Lamb
Serves 4

8 potatoes
8 lamb shoulder chops
45 ml/3 tbsp olive oil
5 ml/1 tsp chopped fresh oregano
5 ml/1 tsp chopped fresh basil
5 ml/1 tsp chopped fresh parsley
1 garlic clove, chopped
Salt and freshly ground black pepper
8 fresh apricots, stoned
100 g/4 oz peas, cooked

Peel and cut the potatoes into slices. Cut away any excess fat from the chops. Pour the oil in a roasting tin (pan) and place the chops in the pan. Sprinkle over the oregano, basil, parsley and garlic. Add the potatoes to the pan around the chops. Season with salt and pepper. Turn over in the oil Bake in a preheated oven at 180°C/350°F/gas mark 4 for 35–40 minutes. Drain the fat from the pan and add the apricots and peas. Continue cooking for 10 minutes and serve immediately.

Arrosto di Agnello al Miele

Honeyed Roast Lamb
Serves 6–8

90 ml/6 tbsp honey
30 ml/2 tbsp white wine vinegar
30 ml/2 tbsp finely chopped fresh root ginger
250 ml/8 fl oz/1 cup orange juice
1.5 kg/3 lb loin of lamb

Combine the first four ingredients in a large bowl and add the lamb. Chill for at least 4 hours, turning from time to time. Place the lamb in a roasting tin (pan) and pour the marinade over the meat. Bake in a preheated oven at 180°C/350°F/gas mark 4 for 2 hours, basting with the marinade from time to time.

Coscia Di Agnello con Vino

Wined Leg of Lamb
Serves 4–6

1.5 kg/3 lb leg of lamb
30 ml/2 tbsp oil
250 ml/8 fl oz/1 cup red wine
Salt and freshly ground black pepper
2 garlic cloves, sliced
1 red chilli, seeded and finely chopped
100 g/4 oz/⅔ cup black olives, stoned (pitted)
75 g/3 oz/¾ cup Pecorino cheese, grated

Trim the meat of any excess fat. Pour the oil into a flameproof casserole dish (Dutch oven) and add the leg of lamb. Cook over a high heat to seal in the juices. Add the wine, allowing the alcohol fumes to evaporate for 3 minutes. Sprinkle well with salt, pepper, sliced garlic, finely chopped chilli and the olives. Stir well and cover with a lid. Transfer to a preheated oven and cook at 180°C/350°F/gas mark 4 for 1¼ hours. Remove and sprinkle the Pecorino cheese thickly over the meat. Return to the oven and cook, uncovered, until the cheese has browned. Serve immediately.

Melanzane con Agnello

Aubergine with Lamb
Serves 4

1 large onion, chopped
2 garlic cloves, crushed
1 green (bell) pepper, chopped
15 ml/1 tbsp oil
1 large aubergine (eggplant), chopped
450 g/1 lb/4 cups minced (ground)
*   lamb*
400 g/14 oz/1 large can chopped
*   tomatoes*
Salt and freshly ground black pepper

Fry (sauté) the onion, garlic and green pepper in the hot oil and transfer to a casserole dish (Dutch oven). Mix well. Fry the aubergine and add to the dish. Crumble in the lamb and pour over the tomatoes. Season with the salt and pepper and cook in a preheated oven for 30 minutes at 180°C/350°F/gas mark 4.

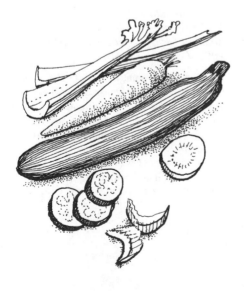

Agnello all'Italiano

Italian Lamb
Serves 4

1 aubergine, (eggplant) sliced
Freshly ground black pepper
45 ml/3 tbsp olive oil
15 g/½ oz/1 tbsp unsalted (sweet)
*   butter*
1 garlic clove, crushed
4 courgettes (zucchini), sliced
1 green (bell) pepper, sliced
4 tomatoes, skinned, seeded and
*   chopped*
30 ml/2 tbsp tomato purée (paste)
5 ml/1 tsp chopped fresh oregano
1 bay leaf
900 g/2 lb lamb chops
Grated rind and juice of 1 lime

Sprinkle the aubergine with salt and leave for 30 minutes. Rinse and dry on kitchen paper. Rub salt and pepper over the lamb. Heat half the oil in a frying pan (skillet) and cook the aubergine slices for 3 minutes on each side until they are browned. Remove from the pan and drain on kitchen paper. Melt the butter in a saucepan and fry (sauté) the garlic. Add the courgettes and cook for 3 minutes, stirring all the time. Add the aubergine slices, green pepper, tomatoes, tomato purée, oregano and the bay leaf. Season with salt and pepper. Reduce the heat to low and cook the vegetables for 5 minutes. Add the remaining oil to the frying pan and cook the lamb chops for 6 minutes on each side. Remove from the pan and keep warm. Stir the lime rind and juice into the vegetables and bring to the boil. Remove the bay leaf and pour the vegetables over the chops.

Agnello, Fagioli e Gnocchi

Lamb, Beans and Gnocchi

Serves 4–6

Gnocchi:
600 ml/1 pt/2½ cups milk
100 g/4 oz/⅔ cup semolina (cream of wheat)
75 g/3 oz/¾ cup Asiago or other hard cheese, grated
50 g/2 oz/½ cup Parmesan cheese, grated
2.5 ml/½ tsp grated nutmeg
1 egg
Salt and freshly ground black pepper

Lamb:
1 large onion, peeled and chopped
60 ml/4 tbsp olive oil
1 kg/2¼ lb boned shoulder lamb
150 ml/¼ pt/⅔ cup tarragon vinegar
1 bay leaf
2 sprigs of rosemary
400 g/14 oz/1 large can borlotti beans, rinsed and drained
450 g/1 lb French (green) beans, halved
25 g/1 oz/2 tbsp butter

Bring the milk to the boil, turn down the heat and pour in the semolina, stirring all the time. Cook for 3 minutes, stirring, until the mixture thickens. Beat in the grated Asiago cheese and half the Parmesan cheese. Cook for a further 2 minutes then beat in the nutmeg and egg. Season well with salt and pepper and spread the mixture in a baking dish. Level the top and cool and chill for 1 hour. Preheat the oven to 190°C/375°F/gas mark 5. Fry (sauté) the onion in the olive oil for 5 minutes until it starts to brown and remove from the pan. Cut the lamb into 5 cm/2 in cubes and fry in the oil until browned all over. Return the onion to the pan and season well. Pour in the vinegar and add the bay leaf and sprigs of rosemary. Cook for 1 minute and transfer to a casserole dish (Dutch oven). Cover with a lid and cook in the oven for 1 hour. Add the borlotti beans and green beans to the dish after 30 minutes. Cut the gnocchi into 4 cm/1½ in cubes. Butter a large ovenproof dish and place the cubes of gnocchi in it. Cover with the remaining Parmesan and dot with butter. Bake for 25 minutes at the top of the oven.

Agnello Brasato All'Italiano

Italian Braised Lamb

Serves 4

8 potatoes
45 ml/3 tbsp olive oil
1 onion, cut in quarters
1 garlic clove, chopped
1.5 kg/3 lb shoulder of lamb
600 ml/1 pt/2½ cups lamb or chicken stock
4 large tomatoes, chopped
5 ml/1 tsp chopped fresh oregano
Salt and freshly ground black pepper
100 g/4 oz peas, cooked

Peel and cut the potatoes into chunks. Pour the oil into a large saucepan and fry (sauté) the onion and garlic for 2 minutes. Brown the meat on all sides and stir in the stock, tomatoes, oregano, salt and pepper. Bring to the boil, lower the heat and cook for 2 hours, stirring occasionally. Add the potatoes and continue cooking for 20 minutes. Stir in the peas and heat through.

Agnello in Salsa di Funghi

Lamb in Mushroom Sauce
Serves 4

225 g/8 oz button mushrooms
15 ml/1 tbsp lemon juice
15 g/½ oz/1 tbsp unsalted (sweet)
  butter
15 ml/1 tbsp oil
1 large onion, chopped
4 boned lamb cutlets, flattened
15 ml/1 tbsp plain (all-purpose) flour
5 ml/1 tsp chopped fresh sage
150 ml/¼ pt/⅔ cup chicken stock
150 ml/¼ pt/⅔ cup dry white wine
300 ml/½ pt/1¼ cups single (light)
  cream
Salt and freshly ground black pepper
Pasta, to serve

Cook the mushrooms in the lemon juice for 5 minutes. Remove from the heat. Melt the butter and oil in a frying pan (skillet) and fry (sauté) the onion until translucent. Add the lamb cutlets and fry for 8 minutes until cooked and browned on both sides. Remove from the pan and keep warm. Stir in the flour and cook for 1 minute. Add the sage and stir in the stock and wine. Cook for 3 minutes, stirring all the time. Return the meat to the pan, stir in the cream and mushrooms with their liquid and heat through. Season with salt and pepper and serve with pasta.

Costolette di Agnello e Capperi

Lamb Cutlets and Capers
Serves 4

4 lamb cutlets
Oil for greasing
1 shallot, finely chopped
450 g/1 lb tomatoes, skinned and
  chopped
Salt and freshly ground black pepper
15 g/½ oz/1 tbsp unsalted (sweet)
  butter
15 g/1 tbsp plain (all-purpose) flour
15 ml/1 tbsp chopped fresh parsley
10 ml/2 tsp tomato purée (paste)
15 ml/1 tbsp capers, chopped

Arrange the cutlets in a greased ovenproof dish. Scatter over the chopped shallot and add the chopped tomatoes. Season with salt and pepper and dot with the butter. Cover and bake in a preheated oven at 190°C/375°F/gas mark 5 for 35 minutes. Transfer to a warmed serving dish and keep hot. Spoon the cooking liquid into a saucepan and blend in the flour, parsley and tomato purée. Bring to the boil, lower the heat and simmer for 2 minutes. Stir in the chopped capers and pour the sauce over the cutlets.

Agnello Catanese

Lamb Catania
Serves 4

30 ml/2 tbsp olive oil
1 large red onion, chopped
4 lamb cutlets
4 ripe tomatoes, skinned, seeded and
* chopped*
30 ml/2 tbsp lemon juice
60 ml/4 tbsp chopped fresh coriander
* (cilantro)*
1 green chilli, seeded and chopped
Salt and freshly ground black pepper

Place the oil in a frying pan (skillet) and add the onion. Cook for 1 minute and add the lamb cutlets. Brown quickly all over, remove from the pan and place in an oven-proof dish. Add the tomatoes, lemon juice and coriander to the oil in the pan and cook for 5 minutes until the liquid has reduced. Pour over the lamb and add the chilli, salt and pepper. Place in a preheated oven at 200°C/400°F/gas mark 6 for 40 minutes.

Agnello con Salsa di Rosmarino e Lamponi

Lamb with Rosemary and Raspberry Sauce
Serves 4

45 ml/3 tbsp olive oil
1.5 kg/3 lb shoulder lamb
5 ml/1 tsp chopped fresh oregano
5 ml/1 tsp chopped fresh parsley
Salt and freshly ground black pepper
4 garlic cloves, peeled but left whole
Rosemary and Raspberry Sauce (see
* page 366)*

Pour the oil into a roasting tin (pan) and place the meat in the tin. Sprinkle over the oregano and parsley. Season with salt and pepper and add the garlic cloves to the pan. Bake in a preheated oven at 180°C/350°F/gas mark 4 for 1½ hours. Drain the fat from the pan and continue cooking for 10 minutes. Place on a carving dish with the garlic cloves. Meanwhile make the Rosemary and Raspberry Sauce and stir in any meat juices from the roasting tin. Carve the lamb and pour over the sauce.

Agnello Pisticci

Pisticci Lamb
Serves 4–6

1 large onion, peeled and chopped
30 ml/2 tbsp olive oil
1 kg/2¼ lb boned shoulder lamb
25 g/1 oz/2 tbsp unsalted (sweet) butter
Salt and freshly ground black pepper
6 tomatoes, skinned and chopped
1 bay leaf
450 g/1 lb French (green) beans,
* halved*
250 g/14 oz/1 large can red kidney
* beans, rinsed and drained*

Fry (sauté) the onion in the olive oil in a flameproof casserole (Dutch oven) for 5 minutes until it starts to brown and remove from the pan. Cut the lamb into 5 cm/2 in cubes and fry in the oil and butter until browned all over. Return the onion to the pan and season well. Add the tomatoes, bay leaf and green beans. Cook on high for 1 minute. Adjust the seasoning and stir in the red kidney beans. Cover with a lid and cook in a preheated oven at 190°C/375°F/gas mark 5 for 1 hour.

Agnello con Prugne

Lamb with Prunes
Serves 6

50 g/2 oz/¼ cup unsalted (sweet) butter
1.5 kg/3 lb leg of lamb
Salt and freshly ground black pepper
1 garlic clove, sliced
2 celery sticks, chopped
15 ml/1 tbsp chopped fresh rosemary
60 ml/1 tbsp tomato purée (paste)
450 g/1 lb tomatoes, skinned and
*   chopped*
90 ml/6 tbsp lamb or chicken stock
12 ready-to-eat prunes

Melt the butter in a large flameproof casserole dish (Dutch oven) and add the lamb. Cook for 10 minutes to brown the lamb, turning regularly. Add the remaining ingredients except the prunes and seal with a lid. Cook for 1 hour over a gentle heat. Remove the lamb to a heated serving dish and add the prunes to the sauce. Cook for 5 minutes and spoon over the lamb.

Agnello alla Dragonella

Tarragon Lamb
Serves 4–6

3 garlic cloves, halved
15 ml/1 tbsp chopped fresh tarragon
15 ml/1 tbsp chopped fresh basil
90 ml/6 tbsp dry white wine
2 racks of lamb
6 large potatoes
1 onion, chopped
4 carrots, chopped
2 celery sticks, chopped
2 bay leaves
Salt and freshly ground black pepper

Put the garlic, tarragon, basil and wine in a bowl and blend together. Place the racks of lamb in a dish and pour the mixture over the meat. Allow to marinate for 4 hours, covered, in the fridge. Peel the potatoes and cut into chunks. Transfer the lamb to a roasting tin (pan), fat side up, and roast in a preheated oven at 200°C/400°F/gas mark 6 for 25 minutes. Remove the pan from the oven and add the potatoes, chopped onion, carrots, and celery to the pan. Spoon the marinade over the meat and vegetables. Add the bay leaves and season with salt and pepper. Reduce the oven to 180°C/350°F/gas mark 4 and roast for 1 hour.

Agnello con Salsa di Rosmarino e Arance

Lamb with Rosemary and Orange Sauce
Serves 6–8

1.5 kg/3 lb loin of lamb
2 garlic cloves, sliced
30 ml/2 tbsp olive oil
250 ml/8 fl oz/1 cup orange juice
60 ml/4 tbsp chopped fresh rosemary
30 ml/2 tbsp grated orange rind
30 ml/2 tbsp brown sugar
60 ml/4 tbsp lamb or chicken stock

Place the lamb in a roasting tin (pan) and score the skin. Insert slices of the garlic into the slits and pour the olive oil over the meat. Roast in a preheated oven at 180°C/350°F/gas mark 4 for 2 hours. Blend the remaining ingredients together and use to baste the meat every 20 minutes during cooking. Transfer the meat to a carving dish. Spoon off any fat in the roasting tin. Stir in any remaining baste and bring to the boil. Serve with the lamb.

Costolette di Agnello con Spinaci

Spinach Lamb Cutlets

Serves 4

25 g/1 oz/2 tbsp unsalted (sweet) butter
900 g/2 lb lamb cutlets
Salt and freshly ground black pepper
60 ml/4 tbsp red wine
30 ml/2 tbsp tomato purée (paste)
225 g/8 oz spinach
4 tomatoes, halved
Salt and freshly ground black pepper

Heat the butter in a frying pan (skillet). Rub the cutlets with salt and pepper and add to the pan. Brown them on both sides. Pour over the wine and simmer for 15 minutes until the wine has almost evaporated. Stir in the tomato purée. Wash the spinach and place in a saucepan with 15 ml/1 tbsp water. Cook for 10 minutes until the spinach has softened. Drain well. Grill (broil) the tomatoes. Place the spinach in a heated serving dish and top with the cutlets. Top with the grilled tomatoes.

Agnello Trebbiano

Trebbiano Lamb

Serves 4

Marinade:
75 ml/5 tbsp wine vinegar
3 garlic cloves, crushed
75 ml/5 tbsp dry white wine
30 ml/2 tbsp olive oil
1 onion, chopped

1 kg/2¼ lb lean shoulder of lamb
45 ml/3 tbsp oil
90 ml/6 tbsp lamb or chicken stock
Salt and freshly ground black pepper
10 ml/2 tsp grated lemon rind
15 ml/1 tbsp chopped fresh basil
2 bay leaves

Blend the marinade ingredients together. Put the meat into a bowl and pour over the marinade. Cover the bowl and leave for a minimum of 2 hours, turning once or twice. Heat the oil in a flameproof casserole (Dutch oven) and add the lamb. Cook the meat until it browns all over. Pour over the marinade with the stock, salt and pepper. Add the lemon rind, basil and bay leaves and bake in a preheated oven at 190°/375°F/gas mark 5 for 1¼ hours.

Pork, Ham and Sausage

Stufato alla Calabroso

Calabrian Casserole

Serves 4

30 ml/2 tbsp olive oil
3 onions, sliced
3 garlic cloves, crushed
2 pork knuckles
225 g/8 oz carrots, diced
Salt and freshly ground black pepper
275 g/10 oz/1⅓ cups flageolot beans,
*   soaked overnight*
250 ml/8 fl oz/1 cup dry white wine
5 ml/1 tsp chopped fresh oregano
1 bay leaf
900 ml/1½ pints/3¾ cups chicken or
*   pork stock or water*
15g/½ oz/1 tbsp unsalted (sweet) butter
100 g/4 oz Parma ham slices, diced
2 sprigs of thyme, chopped
5 ml/1 tsp paprika
15 ml/1 tbsp white wine vinegar

Heat the oil in a saucepan and fry (sauté) the onions and garlic for 5 minutes over a high heat. Add the knuckles of pork and fry for 5 minutes, turning occasionally. Add the carrots and season with the salt and pepper. Fry for 3 minutes and stir in the beans, wine, oregano and bay leaf and bring to the boil. Pour in the stock or water and bring to the boil. Boil rapidly for 10 minutes. Reduce the heat and cook for 2 hours. Remove the pork knuckles from the pan and allow to cool for 5 minutes. Remove the meat from the bones and set aside. Heat the butter in a saucepan and stir in the Parma ham. Fry for 1 minute until tender and add the chopped thyme.

Add the meat from the bones and stir in the paprika and the vinegar. Cook for 1 minute, stirring and add to the beans. Heat through and serve.

Frittelle di Salsicce

Sausage Fritters

Serves 4

100 g/4 oz salami, cut into
*   5 mm/¼ in slices*
225 g/8 oz garlic sausage, in one piece
100 g/4 oz/1 cup plain (all-purpose)
*   flour*
2.5 ml/½ tsp salt
5 ml/1 tsp chopped fresh oregano
30 ml/2 tbsp olive oil
1 egg
175 ml/6 fl oz/¾ cup warm water
Oil for frying
Piquant Chinese Sauce (see page 365),
*   to serve*

Cut the salami slices in quarters. Cut the garlic sausage in half lengthways and cut again into 1 cm/½ in slices. Put 15 ml/1 tbsp of the flour in a polythene bag and add the salami and garlic sausages. Shake well until they are evenly coated and set aside. Place the remaining flour in a bowl and stir in the salt, oregano and oil. Beat in the egg and water and continue beating to form a smooth batter. Heat the oil in a frying pan (skillet) and dip the sausages in the batter. Fry (sauté) 4 or 5 pieces at a time until they are golden brown. Drain on kitchen paper and serve with Piquant Chinese Sauce.

Proscuitto e Piselli Verdi

Ham and Green Peas
Serves 4

450 g/1 lb fresh shelled green peas
5 ml/1 tsp salt
50 g/2 oz/¼ cup unsalted (sweet) butter
1 onion, sliced
8 thick slices prosciutto, cut in strips
15 ml/1 tbsp chopped fresh basil
Freshly ground black pepper

Put the peas into a large saucepan with the salt and add enough water to just cover. Bring to the boil, reduce the heat and cook for 8 minutes until tender. Melt the butter in a frying pan (skillet) and cook the onion for 5 minutes. Add the prosciutto and basil and season with the pepper. Stir well and cook for 10 minutes. Drain the peas and stir into the ham mixture. Transfer to a heated serving dish.

Pancetta e Fagioli

Bacon and Beans
Serves 4–6

15 ml/1 tbsp olive oil
2 onions, sliced
350 g/12 oz pancetta
2 garlic cloves, crushed
450 g/1 lb fresh or frozen broad (lima) beans
90 ml/6 tbsp white wine
Salt and freshly ground black pepper
15 ml/1 tbsp chopped fresh sage
15 ml/1 tbsp chopped fresh thyme
2.5 ml/½ tsp paprika (optional)

Heat the oil in a pan and fry (sauté) the onions for 3 minutes. Dice the pancetta and add to the pan with the crushed garlic. Fry for 5 minutes until browned and stir in the broad beans, wine, salt and pepper. Cook for 10 minutes until the beans are tender and stir in the sage and thyme. Transfer to a warmed serving dish and sprinkle with the paprika if required.

Pagnotta di Olive

Olive Loaf
Serves 6

350 g/12 oz/3 cups minced (ground) pork
275 g/10 oz lean bacon rashers (slices), rinded and minced
50 g/2 oz/1 cup breadcrumbs
2.5 ml/½ tsp chopped fresh sage
5 ml/1 tsp chopped fresh basil
Salt and freshly ground black pepper
1 egg beaten
10 olives, stoned (pitted) and sliced
3 hard-boiled (hard-cooked) eggs
2 slices Prosciutto

Mix the pork, minced bacon, breadcrumbs, sage, basil, salt and pepper in a large bowl and stir in the egg and olives. Knead the mixture together and spoon half of the meat into a loaf tin (pan). Slice the hard-boiled eggs and arrange in a row on the top. Cover with the remaining meat mixture and press down firmly with the back of a spoon. Lay the ham slices over the top. Cover with foil and place the tin in a large roasting tin half-filled with hot water. Bake at 180°C/350°F/gas mark 4 for 1 hour. Remove the tin from the oven and pour off the fat from the meat loaf. Remove the foil and return to the oven for 10 minutes to brown the top. Remove the tin from the oven and again cover the loaf with the foil. Allow to cool. Chill for 1 hour before slicing.

Carne di Maiale, Mele e Bacche di Ginepro

Pork with Apple and Juniper Berries

Serves 4

450 g/1 lb boneless pork
60 ml/4 tbsp olive oil
1 small onion, finely chopped
120 ml/4 fl oz/½ cup white wine
120 ml/4 fl oz/½ cup pork or chicken
 stock
2.5 ml/½ tsp chopped fresh thyme
1 bay leaf
15 juniper berries, crushed lightly
2 eating (dessert) apples, cored and
 peeled
Salt and freshly ground black pepper

Cut the meat into 2.5 cm/1 in cubes. Put the oil and onion and pork in a frying pan (skillet) and cook for 5 minutes to ensure all the meat is browned. Stir in the wine and cook for 2 minutes. Add the stock, thyme, bay leaf and juniper berries. Cut each apple into 8 segments, add to the frying pan and season with salt and pepper. Cover with a lid and simmer gently for 1½ hours until the meat is tender.

Carne di Maiale, Funghi e Bacche di Ginepro

Pork with Mushrooms and Juniper Berries

Serves 4

Prepare as for Pork with Apple and Juniper Berries (above) but omit the apple and add 100 g/4 oz wild sliced mushrooms instead.

Proscuitto di Montagna

Mountain Ham

Serves 4

30 ml/2 tbsp olive oil
2 onions, sliced
2 garlic cloves, crushed
100 g/4 oz mushrooms, sliced
Salt and freshly ground black pepper
450 g/1 lb tomatoes, skinned and
 chopped
250 ml/8 fl oz/1 cup dry white wine
5 ml/1 tsp chopped fresh oregano
5 ml/1 tsp mustard
275 g/10 oz Parma ham slices
15 ml/1 tbsp unsalted (sweet) butter
15 ml/1 tbsp capers, chopped
2 sprigs of parsley, chopped

Heat the oil in a saucepan and fry (sauté) the onions and garlic for 5 minutes. Add the mushrooms and season with salt and pepper. Fry for 3 minutes and stir in the tomatoes, wine, oregano and mustard and bring to the boil. Reduce the heat and cook for 35 minutes. Cut the Parma ham into strips and fry in the butter. Place the meat in the ovenproof dish and pour over the sauce. Cover loosely with foil and bake for 15 minutes at 180°C/350°F/gas mark 4. Remove the foil, stir in the capers and serve garnished with the parsley.

Cotoletta di Maiale con Mele

Pork Chops with Apples

Serves 4

15 ml/1 tbsp olive oil
4 pork chops
90 ml/6 tbsp white wine
5 ml/1 tsp mustard
Salt and freshly ground black pepper
2 large eating (dessert) apples
5 ml/1 tsp lemon juice

Heat the oil in a frying pan (skillet) and brown the chops for 3 minutes on each side. Add the wine and mustard and season with the salt and pepper. Peel, core and slice the apples and soak the rings in the lemon juice. Add the apple rings to the pan and cook for 10–15 minutes.

Carne di Maiale e Verdura

Pork and Vegetables

Serves 6

60 ml/4 tbsp olive oil
900 g/2 lb boneless pork
1 onion, finely chopped
100 g/4 oz carrots, sliced
450 g/1 lb potatoes, roughly chopped
2 large parsnips, chopped
120 ml/4 fl oz/½ cup white wine
120 ml/4 fl oz/½ cup pork or chicken stock
2.5 ml/½ tsp chopped fresh thyme
1 bay leaf
2 sprigs of rosemary, lightly crushed
Salt and freshly ground black pepper
Pasta, to serve

Put the oil in a flameproof casserole dish (Dutch oven) and brown the meat all over for 12–15 minutes. Remove and keep warm. Add the onion to the dish and cook for 5 minutes. Add the carrots, potatoes and parsnips and cook until browned. Stir in the wine and cook for 2 minutes. Add the stock, thyme, bay leaf and rosemary. Season with salt and pepper and cover with a lid. Simmer for 1½ hours until the meat is tender, remove the bay leaf and serve with a large bowl of hot pasta.

Carbonata di Maiale Originale

Original Rich Pork Stew

Serves 4

30 ml/2 tbsp olive oil
450 g/1 lb boneless pork, cut into cubes
1 onion, chopped
10 ml/2 tsp chopped fresh sage
2 bay leaves
15 ml/1 tbsp chopped fresh parsley
15 ml/1 tbsp chopped fennel leaves
5 ml/1 tsp chopped fresh thyme
Salt and freshly ground black pepper
600 ml/1 pt/2½ cups dry white wine
30 ml/2 tbsp vermouth or sherry
15 ml/1 tbsp capers
Polenta, to serve

Heat the oil in a pan and fry (sauté) the pork quickly until browned all over. Lower the heat and add the onions, herbs, salt and pepper. Stir in the white wine and cover with a lid or foil. Cook over a low heat for 1½ hours. Remove the meat to a heated dish and keep warm. Add the vermouth or sherry to the pan and boil rapidly for 2 minutes. Stir in the capers and return the meat. Cook for 5 minutes, remove the bay leaves and serve hot with polenta.

Braciole di Maiale in Salsa Verde

Pork Chops in Green Sauce
Serves 4

4 pork loin chops
Salt and freshly ground black pepper
45 ml/3 tbsp oil
2 garlic cloves, crushed
5 ml/1 tsp chopped fresh basil
5 ml/1 tsp chopped fresh thyme
1 bay leaf
120 ml/4 fl oz/½ cup Chianti
450 g/1 lb tomatoes, skinned, seeded
*   and chopped*
30 ml/2 tbsp tomato purée (paste)
25 g/1 oz/2 tbsp unsalted (sweet) butter
2 large green (bell) peppers, finely
*   chopped*
1 large onion, sliced
225 g/8 oz button mushrooms,
*   quartered*
10 ml/2 tsp cornflour (cornstarch),
*   dissolved in 15 ml/1 tbsp water*
15 ml/1 tbsp chopped fresh parsley

Sprinkle the chops with salt and pepper on each side. Heat the oil in a frying pan (skillet) and cook the chops for 3 minutes until browned, turning once. Transfer to a warm dish. Add the garlic, basil, thyme and bay leaf and cook for 1 minute. Stir in the wine and tomatoes. Bring to the boil and add the tomato purée. Return the pork chops to the pan and baste them with the sauce. Reduce the heat to low and cook for 40 minutes, turning regularly. Melt the butter in a saucepan and fry (sauté) the green peppers and onion for 8 minutes, stirring. Add the mushrooms and cook for a further 5 minutes. Add to the pork chops and simmer for 15 minutes. Arrange the chops on a warm serving dish and stir the cornflour into the vegetables. Cook, stir-

ring, for 3 minutes. Discard the bay leaf and pour the sauce over the chops. Garnish with the parsley and serve immediately.

Maiale con Latte

Pork with Milk
Serves 4

900 g/2 lb loin of pork, boned
2 sprigs of fresh thyme, chopped
Salt and freshly ground black pepper
75 g/3 oz/⅓ cup unsalted (sweet) butter
1 celery stick, diced
2 leeks, finely chopped
1 litre/1¾ pts/4¼ cups milk

Place the pork on a board and sprinkle with the thyme. Roll up the pork with the thyme inside, tie it with string and rub the pork with salt and pepper. Melt the butter in a large flameproof casserole (Dutch oven) and brown the pork all over. Add the celery and leeks and cook for a few minutes until softened. Season with salt and pepper, then pour in the milk. Cover and cook in a preheated oven at 180°C/350°F/ gas mark 4 for about 2 hours, or until the meat is tender. Check occasionally to make sure the milk does not burn. If the meat seems to be drying out, add a few tablespoons of hot water. To serve, slice the meat thickly, strain any remaining liquid and pour over.

Pasticcio di Prosciutto e Pollo

Ham and Chicken in Pastry
Serves 4–6

Pastry (paste):
150 g/5 oz/1¼ cups plain (all-purpose) flour
75 g/3 oz/⅓ cup unsalted (sweet) butter
5 ml/1 tsp lemon juice
15 ml/1 tbsp water

Filling:
25 g/1 oz/2 tbsp margarine
15 g/½ oz/2 tbsp plain (all-purpose) flour
300 ml/½ pt/1¼ cups chicken stock
100 g/4 oz/1 cup cooked chicken, chopped
100 g/4 oz ham, finely chopped
30 ml/2 tbsp chopped fresh oregano
Salt and freshly ground black pepper

Put the flour into a bowl and rub in the butter until the mixture resembles fine breadcrumbs. Add the lemon juice and water and blend to make a stiff dough. Wrap the pastry in clingfilm (plastic wrap) and chill for 30 minutes. Heat the oven to 200°C/400°F/gas mark 6. Grease small tartlet tins (patty pans). Roll out the dough thinly and line the tins. Lay buttered paper in each of the pastry cases and pour in baking beans. Bake blind for 8–10 minutes, until the pastry cases are a pale biscuit colour. Remove the paper and the beans and return the cases briefly to the oven to dry out. Place the margarine in a saucepan with the flour and cook for 1 minute. Gradually stir in the chicken stock and cook until the sauce thickens. Blend in the cooked, chopped chicken and the ham. Season well with the oregano, salt and pepper. Fill the pastry cases with the chicken and ham mixture and heap into peaks.

Crostata di Salame e Capperi

Salami and Caper Tart
Serves 4–6

100 g/4 oz/1 cup plain (all-purpose) flour
50 g/2 oz/¼ cup margarine or butter
3 eggs
175 g/6 oz/¾ cup Ricotta cheese
100 g/4 oz piece salami, skinned and chopped
30 ml/2 tbsp capers, drained and chopped
Salt and freshly ground black pepper

Place the flour and margarine or butter in a bowl and work to fine breadcrumbs. Stir in 1.5 ml/¼ tsp salt and blend in 30 ml/2 tbsp water. Mix to a soft dough and roll out the pastry on a lightly floured surface. Line an 18 cm/7 in loose-bottomed flan tin (pie pan) with pastry and prick with a fork. Line with greaseproof (waxed) paper and weight down with baking beans. Bake blind in a preheated oven at 200°C/400°F/gas mark 6 for 10 minutes. Remove the beans and paper and brush over the inside of the pastry case with a little beaten egg. Return to the oven for 5 minutes. Beat the eggs into the Ricotta cheese and add the salami and capers. Season with pepper. Spoon the filling into the pastry case (shell) and return to the oven at 180°C/350°F/gas mark 4 for 25 minutes until set. Serve hot or cold.

Salsicce e Prosciutto con Patate

Sausage and Prosciutto with Potato
Serves 4

450 g/1 lb Italian sausages
750 g/1½ lb potatoes, cut in small
even-sized pieces
450 ml/¾ pt/2 cups water
Salt and freshly ground black pepper
15 g/½ oz/1 tbsp margarine or butter
100 g/4 oz/1 cup prosciutto, chopped
finely
2.5 ml/½ tsp made mustard

Remove the sausagemeat from the skins and roll the meat into tiny balls. Flatten each ball out in the palm of your hand. Boil the potatoes for 20 minutes in the water, strain and save the potato liquid. Mash and season the potatoes with the salt and pepper and beat in the margarine or butter. Beat in a little of the potato water until the mashed potatoes are soft. Make a thick layer with this potato in the bottom of a greased ovenproof dish. Sprinkle over the chopped prosciutto. Spread the mustard on one side of each round of sausage and arrange, mustard side down on the mashed potato. Cook in a preheated oven at 180°C/350°F/gas mark 4 for 20 minutes until the sausagemeat is golden brown.

Salsicce in Vino

Sausages in Wine
Serves 6

450 g/1 lb small Italian sausages
250 ml/8 fl oz/1 cup white wine
Large bunch of rosemary
3 eating (dessert) apples
Juice of ½ lemon

Prick each sausage and place in a casserole dish (Dutch oven). Cover with the wine and the rosemary. Place a lid on the casserole and cook in a preheated oven at 180°C/350°F/gas mark 4 for 35 minutes until the wine is absorbed and the sausages are browned. Remove the sausages from the dish and allow to cool. Peel and core the apples and cut into quarters. Place in a bowl and sprinkle over the lemon juice. Place the sausages and apple quarters alternately on the wooden skewers and serve as soon as possible.

Carne di Maiale con Pomodori e Cipolle

Pork with Tomatoes and Onions
Serves 4

4 pork cutlets
60 ml/4 tbsp olive oil
175 g/6 oz shallots, halved
15 ml/1 tbsp brown sugar
100 g/4 oz cherry tomatoes, halved
400 g/14 oz/1 large can of chopped
tomatoes
5 ml/1 tsp chopped fresh basil
Salt and freshly ground black pepper

Place the pork cutlets in a frying pan (skillet) with the oil and cook for 12 minutes until tender. Remove to a warm serving dish. Add the shallots to the pan with the sugar and cook on high for 5 minutes, stirring occasionally. Add both sorts of tomatoes and fry (sauté) for another minute. Spoon the shallots and tomatoes over the chops, sprinkle over the basil and salt and pepper and serve.

Prosciutto Torinese

Torino Ham
Serves 4

4 aubergines (eggplants)
50 g/2 oz/¼ cup unsalted (sweet) butter
1 onion, chopped
100 g/4 oz mushrooms, chopped
2 tomatoes, skinned, seeded and
*   chopped*
25 g/1 oz/½ cup breadcrumbs
Salt and freshly ground black pepper
100 g/4 oz prosciutto, chopped
5 ml/1 tsp fresh chopped basil

Cut the aubergines in half and scoop out the centres. Chop the scooped out flesh. Heat the butter in a large pan and fry (sauté) the onion and mushrooms for 4 minutes. Add the tomatoes and chopped aubergines and cook for 3 minutes, stirring. Sprinkle over the breadcrumbs and season with the salt and pepper. Stir in the prosciutto. Pile the mixture into the aubergine cases and bake in a preheated oven for 30 minutes at 180°C/350°F/gas mark 4. Sprinkle over the basil before serving.

Salsicce e Fagioli

Sausages with Beans
Serves 4

450 g/1 lb/2⅔ cups dried white
*   cannellini beans, soaked overnight*
*   in cold water*
5 ml/½ tsp salt
5 garlic cloves
8 Italian pork sausages
60 ml/4 tbsp olive oil
4 fresh sage leaves
15 ml/1 tbsp tomato purée (paste)

Drain the beans, then place in a large pan and just cover with fresh water. Bring to the boil, boil rapidly for 10 minutes, then cover and simmer for about 1½ hours until tender. Add the salt and 3 of the garlic cloves and simmer for a further 20 minutes. Add the sausages and cook for a further 15 minutes. Heat the oil in a large frying pan. Crush the remaining garlic and fry (sauté) for about 5 minutes until golden. Remove the sausages from the beans, place in the frying pan and fry for a few minutes until browned. Drain the beans and add them to the frying pan with the sage and the tomato purée. Cover and simmer for 15 minutes before serving.

Salsicce di Lenticchie e Aglio

Lentils and Garlic Sausage
Serves 4–6

15 ml/1 tbsp olive oil
2 onions, sliced
2 garlic cloves, crushed
225 g/8 oz/1⅓ cups green lentils,
*   soaked for 2 hours and drained*
450 g/1 lb tomatoes, skinned and
*   chopped*
600 ml/1 pt/2½ cups pork or chicken
*   stock*
Salt and freshly ground black pepper
450 g/1 lb Italian sausages
30 ml/2 tbsp chopped fresh parsley

Heat the oil in a pan and fry (sauté) the onions for 3 minutes. Stir in the garlic and lentils and cook for 1 minute. Add the tomatoes and stock and season with salt and pepper. Cover with a lid and simmer for 40 minutes, stirring occasionally until the lentils are tender. Grill (broil) the sausages 10 minutes before the end of cooking. Pour the lentils into a serving dish, place the sausages on top and garnish with the chopped parsley.

Rognoni in Salsa di Vino Rosso

Kidneys in Red Wine Sauce

Serves 4–6

450 g/1 lb lambs' kidneys, skinned and
*   cored*
25 g/1 oz/2 tbsp unsalted (sweet) butter
15 ml/1 tbsp oil
3 shallots, finely chopped
15 ml/1 tbsp plain (all-purpose) flour
250 ml/8 fl oz/1 cup beef stock
90 ml/6 tbsp red wine
5 ml/1 tsp chopped fresh rosemary
Salt and freshly ground black pepper

Chop the kidneys into 1 cm/½ in cubes and place in a bowl of cold water. Set the bowl aside for 2 hours. Drain the kidney pieces and place them in a saucepan. Cover with water and bring to the boil. As soon as the water comes to the boil, remove the pan from the heat and drain the kidney pieces. Discard the water. Melt the butter and oil in a frying pan (skillet) and add the shallots. Cook, stirring occasionally, for 4 minutes. Add the kidney pieces and cook for a further 4 minutes. Sprinkle over the flour and stir well. Pour in the stock and red wine. Bring the liquid to the boil, lower the heat and cook until the gravy thickens. Season with the rosemary and the salt and pepper. Remove the pan from the heat and pour into an ovenproof dish. Place the dish to cook in a preheated oven at 180°C/350°F/gas mark 4 for 20 minutes.

Mousse di Fegato

Liver Soufflé

Serves 4–6

45 g/1½ oz/3 tbsp unsalted (sweet)
*   butter*
1 onion, finely chopped
2 garlic cloves, crushed
450 g/1 lb calves' liver, trimmed
250 ml/8 fl oz/1 cup Basic White Sauce
*   (see page 357)*
3 eggs, separated
30 ml/2 tbsp fresh breadcrumbs
Salt and freshly ground black pepper
15 ml/1 tbsp chopped fresh parsley
45 ml/3 tbsp sherry

Melt the butter in a frying pan (skillet) and add the onion and garlic. Fry (sauté) until the onion is soft and translucent but not brown. Add the calves' liver and fry, stirring continuously, for 4–5 minutes until lightly browned. Purée in a blender or food processor. Heat the white sauce gently and stir in the egg yolks. Stir the sauce into the liver mixture. Stir in the breadcrumbs, salt and pepper and beat well. Add the parsley and sherry and blend again. Whisk the egg whites until stiff. Fold the egg whites carefully into the liver mixture and pour into a 1.2 litre/2 pt/5 cup greased soufflé or ovenproof dish. Cover the dish with foil and place the dish in a roasting tin (pan) half-filled with hot water. Place in the oven at 160°C/325°F/gas mark 3 for 1 hour or until the soufflé is risen and firm to the touch.

Fegatelli di Maiale

Pigs' Liver Brochettes
Serves 4

15 ml/1 tbsp fennel seeds
Salt and freshly ground black pepper
8 rashers (slices) bacon, rinded and
  halved
450 g/1 lb pigs' liver, cut into about 16
  cubes
4 thick pieces Italian bread, cut into
  chunks
60 ml/4 tbsp olive oil
A handful of fresh sage leaves

Crush the fennel seeds in a mortar with the salt and pepper. Wrap a piece of bacon around each cube of liver. Dip the bread into the olive oil. Thread the liver on to 4 skewers, alternately with sage leaves and chunks of bread. Grill (broil) the kebabs for 10 minutes under a hot grill until cooked to your liking, turning frequently and basting with a little more oil if necessary. Garnish with sage leaves and serve.

Rognoni in Crema

Kidneys in Cream
Serves 4

15 ml/1 tbsp olive oil
1 small onion, chopped
100 g/4 oz lambs' kidneys, skinned
  and cored
2 eggs, hard-boiled (hard cooked) and
  shelled
150 ml/¼ pt/⅔ cup double (heavy)
  cream
15 ml/1 tbsp chopped fresh sage
Salt and freshly ground black pepper
Plain boiled rice, to serve

Heat the oil, add the chopped onion and cook until the onion is translucent. Cut the kidneys into 1 cm/½ in pieces and add to the pan. Cook for 5 minutes, stirring. Chop the egg and add to the kidneys with the cream and mix well. Add the sage and season with the salt and pepper. Serve on a bed of rice.

Fegato in Vino Bianco

Liver in White Wine
Serves 4

50 g/2 oz/½ cup plain (all-purpose)
  flour
Salt and freshly ground black pepper
550 g/1¼ lb calves' liver
40 g/1½ oz/3 tbsp unsalted (sweet)
  butter
250 ml/8 fl oz/1 cup dry white wine
60 ml/4 tbsp single (light) cream

Season the flour with the salt and pepper and place on a large plate. Cut the liver into 5 mm/¼ in slices and dip each piece in the flour to coat well. Melt the butter in a frying pan (skillet). Add the liver slices and cook them for 1 minute on each side. Pour in the wine and heat until boiling. Reduce the heat to low and simmer the liver for 3 minutes. Transfer the liver slices to a heated serving dish with a draining spoon and keep hot. Stir the cream into the frying pan and blend well. Add more seasoning if required. Heat the sauce but do not allow to boil. Pour the sauce over the liver slices and serve immediately.

Photograph opposite: **Chicken and Asparagus with Parmesan Sauce (page 92)**

Fegata alla Veneziata

Venetian Liver
Serves 4

30 ml/2 tbsp oil
450 g/1 lb large onions, thinly sliced
2 garlic cloves, crushed
45 ml/3 tbsp chopped fresh parsley
450 g/1 lb calves' liver, very thinly sliced
75 ml/5 tbsp white wine
15 g/½ oz/1 tbsp unsalted (sweet) butter

Heat the oil in a frying pan (skillet) and slowly cook the onions, garlic and parsley for 20 minutes until soft. Transfer to warm serving plates. Increase the heat and fry (sauté) the liver for 2 minutes on each side. Remove from the pan and arrange on top of the onions. Pour the wine into the pan and allow it to boil. Stir in the butter and spoon the sauce over the liver.

Fegato alla Fabriano

Fabriano Liver
Serves 4

30 ml/2 tbsp olive oil
2 large onions, thinly sliced
25 g/1 oz/¼ cup plain (all-purpose) flour
Salt and freshly ground black pepper
450 g/1 lb calves' liver, cut into 1 cm/½ in slices
60 ml/4 tbsp dry white wine
Grated rind and juice of 1 lemon
15 ml/1 tbsp chopped fresh sage
Grilled (broiled) tomatoes, to serve

Heat the olive oil and fry (sauté) the onions for 5 minutes until light brown. Spread the flour on a plate and season with the salt and pepper. Dip the liver slices in the flour and coat well. Add the liver slices to the cooked onion in the pan and cook, uncovered for 4 minutes on each side or until tender. Transfer the onions and liver to a serving dish and keep warm. Sprinkle the reserved flour into the pan and stir with a spoon. Gradually add the wine, lemon rind and juice and stir in the sage. Bring to the boil, reduce the heat and simmer for 2 minutes. Pour over the liver and serve with grilled tomatoes.

Rognone in Umido

Roman Kidneys
Serves 4

450 g/1 lb lambs' kidneys, skinned and cored
15 g/½ oz/1 tbsp unsalted (sweet) butter
2 strips of belly pork, rinded and cubed
1 large onion, sliced
400 g/14 oz/1 large can chopped tomatoes
45 ml/3 tbsp dry white wine
Salt and freshly ground black pepper
45 ml/3 tbsp chopped fresh parsley

Slice the kidneys. Place in a large frying pan (skillet) with the butter and fry (sauté), stirring, over a moderate heat until brown and the juices run. Remove from the pan. Add the belly pork and onion to the pan and fry gently for about 8 minutes or until the onion is golden. Add the tomatoes and wine and cook for 15 minutes. Stir in the kidneys and simmer for 5 minutes. Season generously with salt and pepper and transfer to a warmed platter. Sprinkle with chopped parsley and serve immediately.

Photograph opposite: **Guinea Fowl with Apple (page 110)**

Fegato di Agnello con Verdura Tagliuzzata

Lambs' Liver with Chopped Vegetables
Serves 4

45 ml/3 tbsp olive oil
1 small onion, chopped
1 garlic clove, chopped
1 celery stick, chopped
225 g/8 oz lambs' liver
30 ml/2 tbsp white wine
30 ml/2 tbsp tomato purée (paste)
15 ml/1 tbsp capers, chopped

Heat the oil and fry (sauté) the onion, garlic and celery stick for 2 minutes. Slice the lambs' liver thinly and add to the vegetables. Cook for 5 minutes and stir in the wine, tomato purée and capers. Cook for 1 minute until the mixture has thickened.

Rognoni con Crema Acida

Kidneys with Soured Cream
Serves 4

450 g/1 lb lambs' kidneys, skinned and cored
1 egg, lightly beaten
50 g/2 oz/1 cup fresh breadcrumbs
25 g/1 oz/2 tbsp unsalted (sweet) butter
15 ml/1 tbsp oil
2 onions, thinly sliced
5 ml/1 tsp chopped fresh marjoram
250 ml/8 fl oz/1 cup soured (dairy sour) cream

Thickly slice the kidneys and place in a small saucepan. Cover with water and bring to the boil. Reduce the heat and cook very gently for 5 minutes. Drain the kidney slices, dry them on kitchen paper and set aside. Place the egg in a small dish and the breadcrumbs on a plate. Dip each piece of sliced kidney into the egg and then the breadcrumbs, coating well on each side. Melt the butter and oil in a large frying pan (skillet) and add the kidney slices. Cook for 4 minutes on each side until they are brown. Transfer to a warmed serving dish with a slotted spoon and keep warm. Add the onion slices to the pan and fry (sauté), stirring, for 5 minutes until brown. Remove the onions from the pan and place on top of the kidneys. Pour off the fat from the pan and return it to the heat. Stir in the marjoram and sour cream and heat, stirring occasionally. Pour the sauce over the kidney and onions and serve immediately.

Fegato di Vitello con Funghi, Pomodori e Cipolle

Calves' Liver with Mushrooms, Tomatoes and Onions
Serves 4

1 large onion, sliced
2 garlic cloves, crushed
5 ml/1 tsp chopped fresh basil
5 ml/1 tsp chopped fresh thyme
1 bay leaf
15 ml/1 tbsp oil
Salt and freshly ground black pepper
120 ml/4 fl oz/½ cup Chianti
450 g/1 lb tomatoes, skinned and chopped
30 ml/2 tbsp tomato purée (paste)
25 g/1 oz/2 tbsp unsalted (sweet) butter
450 g/1 lb calves' liver, thinly sliced
225 g/8 oz button mushrooms, quartered
10 ml/2 tsp cornflour (cornstarch), dissolved in 15 ml/1 tbsp water

Place the onion, garlic, basil, thyme, bay leaf and oil in a frying pan (skillet) and cook for 3 minutes. Season with the salt and pepper and stir in the Chianti and tomatoes. Bring to the boil and add the tomato purée. Reduce the heat and cook gently for 30 minutes, stirring occasionally. Melt the butter in a frying pan (skillet) and fry (sauté) the calves' liver for 3 minutes on each side. Remove the liver to a warm serving dish. Add the mushrooms to the pan and cook for 5 minutes, stirring occasionally. Spoon over the liver. Pour the tomato sauce into the frying pan and stir in the cornflour. Cook, stirring, for 3 minutes. Discard the bay leaf and pour the sauce over the liver.

Fegato di Vitello con Parmigiano

Calves' Liver with Parmesan Cheese
Serves 4

8 thin slices calves' liver
2.5 ml/½ tsp salt
2.5 ml/½ tsp freshly ground black pepper
50 g/2 oz/¼ cup unsalted (sweet) butter
15 ml/1 tbsp oil
1 large onion, thinly sliced
5 ml/1 tsp chopped fresh basil
30 ml/2 tbsp breadcrumbs
50 g/2 oz/½ cup Parmesan cheese, grated
8 slices prosciutto

Sprinkle the liver with the salt and pepper. Melt the butter and oil in a frying pan (skillet) and fry (sauté) the onion for 6 minutes until it is golden brown. Stir in the basil. Add the liver slices and fry for 3 minutes on each side. Remove with a draining spoon and keep warm. In a small bowl combine the breadcrumbs and cheese. Turn the liver into a shallow oven-proof dish and spoon over the onion. Lay the slices of prosciutto on the liver and spoon over the breadcrumb mixture. Place under a hot grill (broiler) for 4–5 minutes until the top is golden.

Fegato e Pancetta

Liver and Bacon
Serves 4

450 g/1 lb calves' liver
15 ml/1 tbsp lemon juice
50 g/2 oz/½ cup unsalted (sweet) butter
2 small courgettes (zucchini), sliced
50 g/2 oz/½ cup plain (all-purpose) flour
2.5 ml/½ tsp cayenne
2.5 ml/½ tsp salt
2 onions, thinly sliced
8 lean rashers (slices) back bacon, rinded and chopped
15 ml/1 tbsp chopped fresh parsley

Cut the liver into 5 mm/¼ in slices and sprinkle with the lemon juice. Set aside for 15 minutes. Melt half of the butter in a frying pan (skillet) and add the courgettes. Fry (sauté) for 1 minute on each side and transfer to a heated serving dish. Blend the flour with the cayenne and salt in a shallow dish. Dip the liver slices in the seasoned flour and shake off any excess. Fry the liver for 3 minutes on each side until the pieces are tender. Transfer to the serving dish with a draining spoon and keep warm. Fry the onion slices in the remaining butter until translucent. Add the bacon and fry until the bacon and onions are crisp and brown. Arrange around the liver slices and sprinkle over the parsley. Serve at once.

Fegato in Burro e Aglio

Liver in Garlic Butter
Serves 4

50 g/2 oz/¼ cup unsalted (sweet) butter
3 garlic cloves, crushed
225 g/8 oz calves' liver
15 ml/1 tbsp chopped fresh thyme
1 egg, beaten
25 g/1 oz/½ cup breadcrumbs

Heat the butter in a frying pan (skillet) and cook the garlic for 1 minute, stirring. Slice the liver thinly. Beat the thyme into the egg and dip the liver slices into it. Place the breadcrumbs on a plate and coat the liver thoroughly. Cook for 4 minutes in the garlic butter, turning once.

Fegatini di Pollo con Salvia e Pancetta

Chicken Liver with Sage and Bacon
Serves 4

450 g/1 lb/4 cups chicken livers, cleaned
15 ml/1 tbsp chopped fresh sage
Salt and freshly ground black pepper
25 g/1 oz/2 tbsp unsalted (sweet) butter
6 bacon rashers (slices), rinded and chopped
45 ml/3 tbsp white wine

Sprinkle the liver with the sage, salt and pepper and set aside. Place the butter in a frying pan (skillet) and cook the bacon pieces. Add the chicken livers to the pan and cook, stirring for 6 minutes. Pour in the wine and simmer for 5 minutes. Remove from the pan and serve at once.

Rognone di Manzo con Mostarda

Ox Kidney with Mustard
Serves 4

50 g/2 oz/¼ cup unsalted (sweet) butter
450 g/1 lb ox kidney, skinned and cored
4 shallots, finely chopped
10 ml/2 tsp French mustard
300 ml/½ pt/1¼ cups dry white wine
15 ml/1 tbsp chopped fresh herbs
75 g/3 oz/⅓ cup unsalted (sweet) butter
Freshly ground black pepper
2.5 ml/½ tsp lemon juice

Melt the butter in a large frying pan (skillet). Cut the kidney in 2.5 cm/1 in pieces. Add to the pan and fry (sauté) them, uncovered, until they are lighter in colour on all sides and tender. Remove from the pan and keep warm. Add the chopped shallots to the pan and cook for 3 minutes. Stir in the mustard, pour in the wine and bring to the boil, stirring all the time. Allow to boil rapidly for 5 minutes until the liquid is reduced to about half. Stir in the chopped herbs. Remove the pan from the heat. Whisk the remaining butter with the pepper into the reduced sauce. Return the kidneys to the pan, stir in the lemon juice and cook over a low heat for 2–3 minutes to heat through.

Veal

Orvietto Vitello

Orvietto Veal

Serves 4–6

Salt and freshly ground black pepper
50 g/2 oz/½ cup plain (all-purpose)
* flour*
900 g/2 lb veal knuckle, chopped into
* 7.5 cm/3 in chunks*
75 g/3 oz/⅓ cup unsalted (sweet) butter
1 large onion, sliced
2 garlic cloves, crushed
450 g/1 lb tomatoes, skinned and
* chopped*
15 ml/1 tbsp tomato purée (paste)
75 ml/6 tbsp Orvieto wine
15 ml/1 tbsp grated lemon rind
30 ml/2 tbsp chopped fresh sage
Green tagliatelle, to serve

Place the seasoned flour on a large plate
and dip in the veal pieces. Melt the butter
in a flameproof casserole (Dutch oven) and
fry (sauté) the veal for 5 minutes until
browned on all sides. Transfer to a plate
and set aside. Add the onion and crushed
garlic to the butter and cook for 5 minutes.
Stir in the tomatoes and the tomato purée
and cook for 5 minutes. Stir in the wine
and season with salt and pepper. Return
the veal pieces to the casserole, reduce the
heat to low and cover with a lid. Simmer
for 2 hours until the meat is tender. Stir in
the lemon rind and sage. Serve with Green
Tagliatelle.

Filetti di Vitello e Patate al Forno

Baked Fillet of Veal and Potatoes

Serves 4

450 g/1 lb fillet of veal
25 g/1 oz/¼ cup plain (all-purpose)
* flour*
50 g/2 oz/¼ cup unsalted (sweet) butter
450 g/1 lb carrots, roughly chopped
60 ml/4 tbsp chicken stock
1 garlic clove, crushed
1 bay leaf
Salt and pepper
8 potatoes, cut in quarters

Coat the veal with the flour. Melt the butter in a flameproof casserole (Dutch oven)
and fry (sauté) the veal until well browned
on both sides. Add the carrots and cook for
5 minutes. Add the stock, garlic clove, bay
leaf, salt and pepper. Bring to the boil,
reduce the heat, cover and simmer for 1
hour. Add the potatoes and place in a preheated oven, uncovered at 190°C/375°F/
gas mark 5 for 45 minutes. Remove the
meat and slice it thinly. Arrange on a serving dish surrounded with the potatoes and
carrots. Pour over the juices from the pan.

Arrosto di Vitello con Salsa di Sedano

Roast Veal and Celery Sauce
Serves 4-6

50 g/2 oz/¼ cup unsalted (sweet) butter
1 kg/2¼ lb boneless veal shoulder
Freshly ground black pepper
175 ml/6 fl oz/¾ cup beef stock
400 g/14 oz/1 large can celery soup
1 onion, chopped
4 carrots, sliced·
1 bay leaf
5 ml/1 tsp chopped fresh marjoram

Soften the butter and spread over the veal. Sprinkle the veal with pepper and place in an ovenproof dish. Blend the stock and celery soup together and pour around the meat. Add the onion, carrots and bay leaf to the sauce. Sprinkle over the chopped marjoram and cook in a preheated oven at 180°C/350°C/gas mark 4 for 1½ hours.

Vitello con Mozzarella

Mozzarella Veal
Serves 4

4 veal escalopes, flattened
Salt and freshly ground black pepper
25 g/1 oz/¼ cup plain (all-purpose)
  flour
15 g/½ oz/1 tbsp unsalted (sweet)
  butter
15 ml/1 tbsp oil
15 ml/1 tbsp tomato purée (paste)
4 large tomatoes, skinned, seeded and
  chopped
5 ml/1 tsp chopped fresh oregano
5 ml/1 tsp chopped fresh thyme
100 g/4 oz Mozzarella cheese, sliced
4 black olives, stoned (pitted)

Season the veal with the salt and pepper and toss in the flour. Melt the butter and oil in a frying pan (skillet) and fry (sauté) the veal until brown on both sides. Stir the tomato purée into the chopped tomatoes and pour over the veal. Bring to the boil Sprinkle over the oregano and thyme and top with the cheese slices. Place an olive on the top of each slice of veal and place under a hot grill (broiler) until the cheese softens. Serve at once.

Osso Buco

Osso Buco
Serves 6

40 g/1½ oz/3 tbsp unsalted (sweet) butter
6 slices shin of veal
300 ml/½ pt/1¼ cups dry white wine
400 g/14 oz/1 large can tomatoes
300 ml/½ pt/1¼ cups chicken stock or
  water
Salt and freshly ground black pepper
25 g/1 oz chopped fresh parsley
1 garlic clove, finely chopped
10 ml/2 tsp finely grated lemon rind
Risotto alla Milanese (see page 258),
  to serve

Melt the butter in a heavy flameproof casserole (Dutch oven). Add the veal and fry (sauté) until browned on all sides. Arrange the veal in a single layer in the base of the casserole, then add the wine and boil until reduced by about one third. Add the tomatoes and cook for 5 minutes. Add the stock or water, bring to the boil, and season with salt and pepper. Cover and cook in a preheated oven at 120°C/250°F/gas mark ½ for 2–3 hours until the veal is tender. Mix together the parsley, garlic and lemon rind. Sprinkle the mixture over the casserole just before serving with Risotto alla Milanese.

Involtini di Vitello all'Italiana

Italian Veal Rolls

Serves 4

450 g/1 lb veal, cut into 8 thin slices
15 ml/1 tbsp mustard
4 thin slices cooked ham
100 g/4 oz Mozzarella, cut into 8 sticks
25 g/1 oz/2 tbsp unsalted (sweet) butter
15 ml/1 tbsp olive oil
1 onion, chopped
1 garlic clove, crushed
100 g/4 oz mushrooms, chopped
450 g/1 lb tomatoes, skinned, seeded and chopped
60 ml/4 tbsp beef or chicken stock
5 ml/1 tsp chopped fresh oregano
1 bay leaf
Salt and freshly ground black pepper
15 ml/1 tbsp chopped fresh sage

Place the veal pieces between 2 sheets of greaseproof (waxed) paper and pound with a rolling pin to flatten. Cover each with mustard and a ham slice. Place a cheese stick at one end of the veal and ham and roll up. Tie the rolls at both ends with fine string. Heat the butter and oil in a large frying pan (skillet) and cook the veal rolls for 5–6 minutes to brown all over. Remove the rolls and place in an ovenproof dish. Fry (sauté) the onion and garlic in the oil and butter for 5 minutes until the onion is soft. Stir in the mushrooms and cook for 3 minutes. Add the tomatoes. Stir in the remaining ingredients except the sage, seasoning to taste. Bring to the boil, lower the heat and allow to simmer for 5 minutes, stirring occasionally. Pour the sauce over the veal and cook in a preheated oven at 200°C/ 400°F/gas mark 6 for 15 minutes. Discard the bay leaf before serving, and sprinkle with the chopped sage.

Fette di Vitello Farato

Stuffed Veal Slices

Serves 4

2 large veal escalopes, flattened
50 g/2 oz/¼ cup butter
1 onion, finely chopped
75 g/3 oz mushrooms, chopped
175 g/6 oz/1½ cups chicken livers
60 ml/4 tbsp breadcrumbs
5 ml/1 tsp chopped fresh sage
Salt and freshly ground black pepper
120 ml/4 fl oz/½ cup dry white wine
120 ml/4 fl oz/½ cup beef or chicken stock
120 ml/4 fl oz/½ cup double (heavy) cream
Plain boiled rice, to serve

Cut the veal into long thin strips. Heat half the butter in a frying pan (skillet) and cook the onion for 3 minutes. Add the mushrooms and cook for a further 5 minutes. Stir in the chicken livers and cook until brown but slightly pink inside. Remove from the pan and transfer to a chopping board. Chop the chicken livers finely and transfer to a bowl with the mushrooms and onions. Add the breadcrumbs, sage, salt and pepper and blend the ingredients together. Spread a layer of the liver over each slice of veal and roll up. Secure with fine string. Melt the remaining butter and fry (sauté) the veal rolls for 8 minutes, turning to brown all sides. Arrange the rolls in a flameproof casserole dish (Dutch oven). Pour over the wine and stock and bake in a preheated oven at 180°C/350°F/ gas mark 4 for 40 minutes. Remove the rolls to a serving plate and boil the liquid in the casserole dish to reduce it. When the liquid thickens, lower the heat and stir in the cream. Pour over the veal and serve immediately with plain boiled rice.

Vitello con Gorgonzola

Veal with Gorgonzola
Serves 4

50 g/2 oz/¼ cup unsalted (sweet) butter
50 g/2 oz Gorgonzola cheese, crumbled
4 veal escalopes
50 g/2 oz/½ cup plain (all-purpose) flour
2.5 ml/½ tsp cayenne
Salt and freshly ground black pepper
1 egg, beaten
50 g/2 oz/1 cup fresh breadcrumbs
45 ml/3 tbsp oil

Soften the butter and blend with the Gorgonzola. Spread the cheese and butter mixture over both sides of the escalopes. Put the flour into a large bowl and season with the cayenne, salt and pepper. Coat the veal in the seasoned flour, then the egg and finally the breadcrumbs. Chill for 1 hour. Heat the oil in a frying pan (skillet). Fry (sauté) the escalopes for 3–4 minutes on each side or until they are golden brown and cooked through. Serve immediately.

Costolette di Vitello alla Parmigiana

Parmesan Veal Cutlets
Serves 4

450 g/1 lb very thin veal cutlets
15 g/½ oz/1 tbsp unsalted (sweet) butter, melted
225 g/8 oz Mozzarella cheese, thinly sliced
175 ml/6 fl oz/¾ cup Tomato Sauce (see page 358)
5 ml/1 tsp chopped fresh thyme
50 g/2 oz/½ cup Parmesan cheese, grated

Brush the cutlets with the melted butter and place under a moderate grill (broiler) for 3 minutes on each side. Brush with butter again and add a thin slice of Mozzarella to each cutlet. Grill (broil) until the cheese is brown. Place in a hot dish and top with the tomato sauce. Sprinkle over the thyme and Parmesan and bake in a preheated oven at 190°C/375°F/ gas mark 5 for 15 minutes.

Spalla di Vitello Farato

Stuffed Shoulder of Veal
Serves 6–8

1.5 kg/3 lb shoulder of veal, boned, rolled and trimmed of fat
10 g/¼ oz/2 tsp unsalted (sweet) butter
1 onion, chopped
1 garlic clove, crushed
100 g/4 oz/1 cup sausagemeat
2.5 ml/½ tsp chopped fresh thyme
15 ml/1 tbsp snipped fresh chives
50 g/2 oz/½ cup chopped almonds
Salt and freshly ground black pepper
25 g/1 oz/½ cup breadcrumbs
150 ml/¼ pt/⅔ cup beef or chicken stock
75 ml/5 tbsp white wine
30 ml/2 tbsp orange juice
1 bay leaf

Melt the butter in a saucepan and fry (sauté) the onion and garlic for 3 minutes. Add the sausagemeat and fry for 5 minutes, stirring. Add the thyme, chives and almonds. Season with salt and pepper and cook for 10 minutes. Stir in the breadcrumbs and set aside. Spread the stuffing over the meat and roll up. Tie the rolled veal with string and place in a deep-sided roasting tin (pan). Combine the stock, wine and orange juice and pour round the meat. Add the bay leaf and cover with foil. Place in a preheated oven at 180°C/350°F/gas mark 4 and bake for 1½ hours, basting occasionally. Remove the bay leaf and serve with the gravy.

Stufatino Di Vitello

Tuscan Veal Stew
Serves 4–6

60 ml/4 tbsp olive oil
2 garlic cloves, crushed
1 small red chilli, seeded and chopped
Plain (all-purpose) flour for dusting
Salt and freshly ground black pepper
750 g/1½ lb lean veal, cubed
120 ml/4 fl oz/½ cup white wine
2 large ripe tomatoes, skinned, seeded and chopped
45 ml/3 tbsp chopped fresh parsley

Heat the oil in a large, heavy-based pan and fry (sauté) the garlic and chilli until browned. Season the flour with salt and pepper, then dust the veal with the flour. Add the veal to the pan and fry until browned on all sides. Add the wine and cook for a few minutes until almost all the wine has evaporated. Add the tomatoes and season to taste with salt and pepper. Cover the pan and cook over a low heat for about 1 hour until the veal is tender. Stir in the parsley just before serving.

Petto di Vitello Ripieno

Stuffed Breast of Veal
Serves 6–8

1.5 kg/3 lb breast of veal, boned
75 g/3 oz/¾ cup hard cheese, grated
1 onion, chopped
3 eggs
175 g/6 oz/3 cups fresh breadcrumbs
45 ml/3 tbsp chopped fresh parsley
15 ml/1 tbsp chopped fresh oregano
45 ml/3 tbsp olive oil
1 garlic clove, crushed
Salt and freshly ground black pepper
Sprig of fresh rosemary

Make a pocket down the centre of the veal. Blend the grated cheese, onion and eggs together and stir in the breadcrumbs, parsley and oregano. Pack the mixture into the veal pocket and sew the edges together. Mix the oil with the garlic and brush the meat. Place in a roasting tin (pan) with the salt and pepper and the rosemary. Pour over any remaining garlic oil and bake in a preheated oven at 180°C/350°F/gas mark 4 for 1¼ hours.

Stirico di Vitello al Sedano

Veal in Soured Cream and Celery
Serves 4

50 g/2 oz/¼ cup unsalted (sweet) butter
450 g/1 lb breast of veal, boned and rolled
2 large onions, sliced
2 celery sticks, sliced
2 garlic cloves, crushed
3 tomatoes, skinned and chopped
75 ml/5 tbsp beef stock
Salt and freshly ground black pepper
2.5 ml/½ tsp paprika
150 ml/¼ pt/⅔ cup soured (dairy sour) cream
30 ml/2 tbsp chopped fresh herbs

Melt the butter in a flameproof casserole (Dutch oven) and add the veal. Fry (sauté) for 5 minutes until it is evenly browned all over. Add the onions, celery and crushed garlic and cook for 2 minutes. Add the tomatoes to the casserole dish. Pour in the stock and season with salt, pepper and the paprika. Cover with a lid. Place the casserole dish in a preheated oven at 180°C/350°F/gas mark 4 for 50 minutes. Just before serving top with the soured cream and sprinkle over the freshly chopped herbs.

Vitello Bellagio

Veal Bellagio
Serves 4

45 ml/3 tbsp plain (all-purpose) flour
Salt and freshly ground black pepper
450 g/1 lb leg veal, cubed
10 ml/2 tsp grated lemon rind
100 g/4 oz/2 cups breadcrumbs
3 eggs, beaten
30 ml/2 tbsp olive oil
1 onion, chopped
2 garlic cloves, crushed
3 tomatoes, skinned and chopped
75 ml/5 tbsp dry white wine
15 ml/1 tbsp chopped fresh basil

Season the flour with the salt and pepper and toss the veal until well covered. Blend the lemon rind with the breadcrumbs and place the beaten eggs in a bowl. Dip the veal cubes in the beaten egg and coat in the breadcrumbs. Heat the oil in a saucepan and fry (sauté) the onion and garlic for 5 minutes. Remove from the pan. Fry the veal for 6–10 minutes until browned all over. Remove from the pan and keep warm. Pour the tomatoes into the saucepan, add the onions and garlic, the wine and season with salt and pepper. Simmer for 30 minutes. Purée the sauce in a blender or food processor and stir in the basil. Reheat the sauce and serve with the hot veal.

Vitello alla Dragonella

Tarragon Veal
Serves 6

750 g/1½ lb veal steaks, cubed
Salt and freshly ground black pepper
50 g/2 oz/¼ cup unsalted (sweet) butter
15 ml/1 tbsp oil
225 g/8 oz mushrooms, thinly sliced
30 ml/2 tbsp chopped fresh tarragon
300 ml/½ pt/1¼ cups single (light)
cream
75 g/3 oz Mozzarella cheese, sliced
2 tarragon sprigs, to garnish

Season the veal with salt and pepper. Melt the butter and oil in a frying pan (skillet) and fry (sauté) the veal for about 10 minutes until browned all over. Transfer to a flameproof dish and keep warm. Add the mushrooms to the pan and fry for 5 minutes until soft. Stir in the chopped tarragon and fry for a further 3 minutes. Add to the veal. Stir the cream into the pan and bring to the boil, stirring. Pour the sauce over the meat and top with the Mozzarella cheese. Place under a hot grill (broiler) and melt the cheese. Serve garnished with the tarragon sprigs.

Vitello Tonnato

Veal in Tuna Sauce
Serves 4

300 ml/½ pt/1¼ cups olive oil
750 g/1½ lb roasting veal in a single piece
150 ml/¼ pt/⅔ cup dry white wine
Salt and freshly ground black pepper
2 bay leaves
1 garlic clove
8 celery leaves
2 egg yolks
Juice of ½ lemon
15 ml/2 tbsp white wine vinegar
30 ml/2 tbsp capers, finely chopped
185 g/6½ oz/1 small can tuna in oil, drained and flaked
2 salted anchovies, cleaned, boned and finely chopped or 4 canned anchovy fillets, drained and finely chopped
A few olives and fresh parsley sprigs, to garnish

Heat 60 ml/4 tbsp of the oil in a large frying pan (skillet) and fry (sauté) the meat until browned on all sides. Remove the meat from the pan and place in a roasting tin (pan) with the wine, salt, pepper, bay leaves, garlic and celery leaves. Roast in a preheated oven at 180°C/350°F/gas mark 4 for 45 minutes, basting occasionally. Remove the meat from the roasting tin and allow to cool completely. Whisk together the egg yolks and lemon juice, then gradually whisk in the remaining oil a little at a time until the mayonnaise thickens. Stir in the wine vinegar. Alternatively use 300 ml/ ½ pt/1¼ cups ready-made mayonnaise. Stir in the capers, tuna and anchovies and season to taste with salt and pepper. Thinly slice the meat and arrange on a serving platter. Spoon over the mayonnaise to cover the meat. Garnish with olives and parsley and chill before serving.

Vitello in Salsa Cremosa di Funghi

Veal in Creamy Mushroom Sauce
Serves 4

225 g/8 oz button mushrooms
15 ml/1 tbsp lemon juice
15 g/½ oz/1 tbsp unsalted (sweet) butter
15 ml/1 tbsp oil
1 large onion, chopped
4 veal escalopes, flattened
15 ml/1 tbsp plain (all-purpose) flour
5 ml/1 tsp chopped fresh oregano
150 ml/¼ pt/⅔ cup chicken stock
150 ml/¼ pt/⅔ cup dry white wine
300 ml/½ pt/1¼ cups single (light) cream
Salt and freshly ground black pepper

Cook the mushrooms in the lemon juice for 1 minute. Remove from the pan and keep warm. Reserve the cooking liquid. Melt the butter and oil in the frying pan (skillet) and fry (sauté) the onion until translucent. Add the veal and fry until browned on both sides. Remove from the pan and keep warm. Stir in the flour and cook for 1 minute. Add the oregano and stir in the stock, wine and mushroom liquid. Cook for 3 minutes, stirring all the time. Stir in the cream, mushrooms and veal and heat through. Season with salt and pepper and serve at once.

Tortini di Vitello in Salsa di Vino

Veal Patties in Wine Sauce

Serves 4

450 g/1 lb lean veal
1 large onion
1 garlic clove, crushed
Salt and freshly ground black pepper
50 g/2 oz/1 cup breadcrumbs
1 egg, lightly beaten
45 ml/3 tbsp chopped fresh oregano
45 ml/3 tbsp plain (all-purpose) flour
50 g/2 oz/¼ cup unsalted (sweet) butter
90 ml/6 tbsp dry white wine
150 ml/¼ pt/⅔ cup double (heavy) cream

Mince (grind) the veal with the onion and place in a large bowl. Stir in the garlic, salt and pepper and stir in the breadcrumbs and egg. Add half of the oregano and blend well. Shape the mixture into 8 patties and coat with the flour. Melt the butter and fry (sauté) the patties for 8 minutes on each side. Transfer to a warmed serving dish and keep hot. Pour the wine into the pan and bring to the boil. Reduce the heat and stir in the cream. Bring back to the boil and cook for 2 minutes until the sauce is hot and has thickened. Pour the sauce over the patties and serve at once.

Vitello e Funghi

Veal and Mushrooms

Serves 4

50 g/2 oz/¼ cup unsalted (sweet) butter
4 veal chops
2 rashers (slices) streaky bacon, rinded and chopped
4 shallots, chopped
100 g/4 oz button mushrooms, sliced
15 ml/1 tbsp plain (all-purpose) flour
120 ml/4 fl oz/½ cup white wine
250 ml/8 fl oz/1 cup veal stock
1 bay leaf
10 ml/2 tsp fresh chopped herbs
Salt and freshly ground black pepper
120 ml/4 fl oz/½ cup single (light) cream

Melt the butter in a saucepan and add the chops. Fry (sauté) on both sides until brown. Transfer to a warmed dish. Add the bacon to the pan with the shallots and mushrooms. Cook for 4–5 minutes until the bacon is crisp. Stir in the flour and cook for 30 seconds. Add the wine, stock, bay leaf and fresh herbs. Season with the salt and pepper and bring to the boil. Return the chops to the pan and simmer for 35 minutes until the chops are tender. Stir in the cream and serve at once.

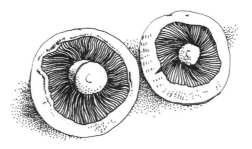

Vitello in Salsa Crema

Veal in a Cream Sauce
Serves 4

600 ml/1 pt/2½ cups water, beef or chicken stock
2 large onions, chopped
450 g/1 lb carrots, chopped
1 bouquet garni sachet
Salt and freshly ground black pepper
45 g/1½ oz/3 tbsp unsalted (sweet) butter
4 veal chops
45 g/1½ oz/⅓ cup plain (all-purpose) flour
2 egg yolks
150 ml/¼ pt/⅔ cup single (light) cream

Put the water or stock into a saucepan. Bring to the boil. Add the onions and carrots with the bouquet garni and seasoning. Boil rapidly, reduce the heat and cook for 15–20 minutes until the carrots are soft. Drain and keep warm, reserving the cooking liquid. Put half the butter into a frying pan (skillet) and fry (sauté) the veal chops for 5–8 minutes on each side. Reduce the heat and cook gently for a further 2 minutes. Remove to a warmed serving dish and keep warm. Put the remaining butter into the pan, stir in the flour and cook for 1 minute. Gradually blend in enough of the reserved stock until the sauce has thickened. Remove from the heat, cool for 1 minute and beat in the egg yolks and cream. Taste and reseason if necessary. Pour the sauce over the meat and serve at once.

Vitello e Pasticcio di Ginepro

Veal and Juniper Pie
Serves 4

45 ml/3 tablespoons oil
2 leeks, sliced
225g/8 oz button mushrooms, roughly chopped
275g/10 oz veal
30 ml/2 tbsp plain (all-purpose) flour
2.5 ml/½ tsp juniper berries, roughly crushed
15 ml/1 tbsp tomato purée (paste)
300ml/½ pt/1¼ cups beef stock
Salt and freshly ground black pepper
2 potatoes, diced
225g/8 oz packet puff pastry (paste)
Beaten egg, to glaze

Heat the oil in a flameproof casserole (Dutch oven). Add the leeks and mushrooms and fry (sauté) gently for 3 minutes. Remove and set aside. Cut the veal into 2.5 cm/1 in cubes. Add the veal to the juices in the casserole and fry until evenly browned. Stir in half the flour and cook for 1 minute. Add the juniper berries, tomato purée, beef stock and seasoning. Bring to the boil, cover and cook in a preheated oven at 200°C/400°F/gas mark 6. for 30 minutes. Remove from the oven. Stir the leeks, mushrooms and potatoes into the veal. Spoon the ingredients into a large pie dish with a rim. Roll out the pastry on a lightly floured surface. Wet the edges of the dish. Cover the filling with the pastry, pressing the edges tightly to seal. Use the pastry trimmings to decorate and make a hole in the centre to allow steam to escape. Brush the pastry top with the beaten egg and stand on a baking sheet. Return to the oven for 35 minutes until the pastry is golden brown.

Vitello con Pomodori

Veal with Tomatoes
Serves 4

15 ml/1 tbsp oil
2 garlic cloves, chopped
4 veal escalopes, flattened
250 ml/8 fl oz/1 cup white wine
4 large tomatoes, skinned, seeded and
* chopped*
30 ml/2 tbsp tomato purée (paste)
5 ml/1 tsp chopped fresh oregano
5 ml/1 tsp chopped fresh rosemary
Salt and freshly ground black pepper

Heat the oil and fry (sauté) the garlic for 1 minute. Add the veal escalopes and fry until browned on both sides. Stir in the wine and tomatoes and bring to the boil. Simmer for 5 minutes and stir in the tomato purée, oregano, rosemary and season to taste with the salt and pepper. Simmer for a further 5 minutes before serving.

Vitello con Mostarda e Formaggio

Veal with Mustard and Cheese
Serves 4

75 g/3 oz/⅓ cup unsalted (sweet) butter
4 veal escalopes, flattened
15 ml/1 tbsp plain (all-purpose) flour
250 ml/8 fl oz/1 cup chicken stock
30 ml/2 tbsp white wine
5 ml/1 tsp made mustard
50 g/2 oz/½ cup Parmesan cheese,
* grated*
150 ml/¼ pt/⅔ cup single (light) cream
Salt and freshly ground black pepper
75 g/3 oz/1½ cups breadcrumbs

Melt half the butter and fry (sauté) the veal escalopes for 2 minutes on each side until golden brown. Place in an ovenproof dish. Melt the remaining butter and add the flour. Cook for 1 minute and remove from the heat. Gradually stir in the stock and white wine and bring to the boil. Simmer until the sauce thickens and stir in the mustard and half the cheese. Remove from the heat and stir in the cream. Season to taste. Pour the sauce over the veal, scatter with the remaining cheese and the breadcrumbs and place in a preheated oven at 190°C/375°F/gas mark 5 for 12–15 minutes.

Costolette di Vitello

Veal Cutlets
Serves 4

4 boneless veal cutlets
100 g/4 oz cooked ham
4 slices Gruyère (Swiss) cheese
50 g/2 oz/¼ cup unsalted (sweet) butter
250 ml/8 fl oz/1 cup dry white wine
Freshly ground black pepper
12 stoned (pitted) olives, sliced

Pound the cutlets until 5 mm/¼ in thick. Shred the ham into thin slices. Arrange over the cutlets. Place a slice of cheese over each cutlet and roll up so that the cheese is on the inside of the veal. Melt the butter in an ovenproof dish and put in the veal cutlets. Pour over the wine and sprinkle with the pepper. Place in a preheated oven at 190°C/375°F/gas mark 5 for 25–30 minutes. Scatter the olives over and serve.

Braciole al Vino

Wine Chops
Serves 4

45 ml/3 tbsp plain (all-purpose) flour
Salt and freshly ground black pepper
5 ml/1 tsp chopped fresh thyme
4 thick veal chops
60 ml/4 tbsp olive oil
100 g/4 oz mushrooms, sliced
1 onion, sliced
250 ml/8 fl oz/1 cup white wine

Season the flour with salt, pepper and thyme. Use to coat the veal chops. Heat the oil and brown the chops on both sides. Remove to a casserole dish (Dutch oven). Add the mushrooms and onion to the frying pan (skillet) and cook for 3 minutes. Add to the casserole. Pour the wine into the pan, simmer for 5 minutes then pour over the chops. Cover and cook in a pre-heated oven at 200°C/400°F/gas mark 6 for 40 minutes.

Scaloppine con Limone e Capperi

Veal with Lemon and Capers
Serves 4

30 ml/1 tbsp plain (all-purpose) flour
Salt and freshly ground black pepper
1.5 ml/¼ tsp cayenne
4 veal escalopes, flattened
25 g/1 oz/2 tbsp unsalted (sweet) butter
15 ml/1 tbsp olive oil
Juice of 1 lemon
75 ml/5 tbsp dry white wine
15 ml/1 tbsp capers, chopped

Mix the flour, salt, pepper and cayenne and coat the veal. Heat the butter and oil and fry (sauté) the escalopes for 2–3 minutes until golden. Transfer to a dish and keep warm. Heat the lemon juice and wine in the pan for 1 minute. Add the capers and seasoning, heat for 1 minute and pour over the veal.

Vitello con Riso

Veal with Rice
Serves 4–6

100 g/4 oz/1 cup chicken livers,
* chopped*
1 small onion, chopped
150 g/5 oz/1¼ cups cooked rice
Salt and freshly ground black pepper
1 kg/2¼ lb breast or shoulder of veal,
* boned*
50 g/2 oz/¼ cup unsalted (sweet) butter

Chop the chicken livers and blend with the chopped onion and rice. Season with the salt and pepper. Open out the meat and stuff with the mixture. Tie into shape with string. Place in a roasting tin (pan) and dot with the butter. Cook the meat in a pre-heated oven at 180°C/350°F/gas mark 4 for 2 hours, basting occasionally with the juices in the pan.

Scaloppa di Vitello alla Milanese

Milanese-style Veal Escalope
Serves 4

4 veal escalopes
Plain (all-purpose) flour
Salt and freshly ground black pepper
1 large egg, beaten
75 g/3 oz./1½ cups fresh breadcrumbs
100 g/4 oz/½ cup unsalted (sweet) butter
Lemon wedges and parsley sprigs, to garnish

Put a veal escalope between two sheets of clingfilm (plastic wrap) and flatten with a meat mallet or rolling pin. Repeat with the remaining escalopes. Dust with flour then sprinkle with salt and pepper. Dip in the beaten egg then breadcrumbs to coat completely. Fry (sauté) in the butter until golden brown on both sides and cooked through. Drain on kitchen paper. Serve garnished with lemon wedges and parsley sprigs.

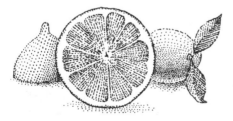

Lombetto di Vitello alla Valdostana

Loin of Veal Valdostana-style
Serves 4

8 small slices veal loin
Plain (all-purpose) flour
Salt and freshly ground black pepper
1 egg, beaten
25 g/1 oz/2 tbsp unsalted (sweet) butter
15 ml/1 tbsp olive oil
8 thin slices prosciutto
8 thin slices Fontina cheese
75 ml/5 tbsp dry white wine
75 ml/5 tbsp chicken stock
50 g/2 oz/1 cup fresh breadcrumbs

Place a slice of veal between two sheets of clingfilm (plastic wrap) and beat until flattened with a rolling pin or meat mallet. Repeat with the remaining veal slices. Dust with flour, season with salt and pepper and dip in beaten egg. Melt three-quarters of the butter in a large frying pan (skillet) with the oil. Fry (sauté) the veal until golden brown on both sides. Transfer to a large, shallow baking dish. Lay a slice of prosciutto on top of each veal slice and top with a slice of cheese. Add the wine and stock to the juices in the pan and bring to the boil, stirring. Pour over the meat. Sprinkle the breadcrumbs over, season with a little salt and pepper and dot with the remaining butter. Bake in a preheated oven at 200°C/400°F/gas mark 6 for 15–20 minutes until golden on top. Serve straight away.

Saltimbocca alla Romana

Roman-style Veal Escalopes

Serves 4

8 small veal escalopes
8 thin slices prosciutto
8 sage leaves
Salt and freshly ground black pepper
25 g/1 oz/2 tbsp unsalted (sweet) butter
1 wineglass dry white wine
150 ml/¼ pt/⅔ cup chicken stock
15 ml/1 tbsp plain (all-purpose) flour
30 ml/2 tbsp water

Place an escalope between two sheets of clingfilm (plastic wrap) and beat with a rolling pin or meat mallet to flatten. Repeat with the remaining escalopes. Lay a slice of prosciutto and a sage leaf on each. Season with salt and pepper and roll up. Secure with cocktails sticks (toothpicks). Melt the butter in a flameproof casserole (Dutch oven). Add the veal and brown on all sides. Add the wine and stock, bring to the boil, reduce the heat, cover and poach until the veal is tender. Lift out the meat, remove the cocktail sticks and arrange on a warm dish. Keep warm. Blend the flour with the water and stir into the cooking liquid. Bring to the boil and cook for 2 minutes, stirring all the time. Taste and re-season if necessary. Spoon over the veal and serve straight away.

Galantina di Vitello agli Spinaci

Galantine of Veal with Spinach

Serves 6

350 g/12 oz spinach
25 g/1 oz/2 tbsp unsalted (sweet) butter
4 eggs, beaten
100 g/4 oz/1 cup Parmesan cheese, grated
Salt and freshly ground black pepper
2.5 ml/½ tsp grated nutmeg
900 g/2 lb breast of veal, boned
Vegetable stock

Shred the spinach, discarding any thick stalks. Melt the butter in a saucepan. Add the spinach, cover and cook gently until tender, about 5 minutes, stirring occasionally. Remove the lid and cook rapidly until all the liquid has evaporated. Remove from the heat and leave to cool slightly. Snip finely with scissors. Beat in the eggs, cheese, a little salt and pepper and the nutmeg. Lay the veal on a board, boned side up. Make a pocket in the meat with a sharp knife and fill with some of the spinach mixture. Spread the remaining mixture over the boned side of the meat. Roll up and tie securely with string. Season with a little more salt and pepper. Wrap in foil. Place in a large flameproof casserole (Dutch oven) and pour over enough hot vegetable stock to cover. Bring to the boil, reduce the heat, cover and simmer gently for 2 hours. Leave to cool in the liquid then chill. Unwrap, remove the string and serve sliced. *Note:* this dish is equally good made with lamb.

Fish

All seafood is popular in Italy and the Italians have created the most fantastic range of local specialities. From anchovies to tuna, red mullet to lobster — there are sumptuous dishes for every occasion.

Filetti al Forno con Sugo al Vino

Baked Fillets in Wine Sauce

Serves 4

5 shallots, chopped
100 g/4 oz mushrooms, sliced
75 g/3 oz/⅓ cup unsalted (sweet) butter
30 ml/2 tbsp chopped fresh parsley
225 g/8 oz sole or plaice fillets, skinned
150 ml/¼ pt/⅔ cup white wine
150 ml/¼ pt/⅔ cup fish or chicken stock
½ lemon
25 g/1 oz/¼ cup plain (all-purpose) flour
Salt and freshly ground black pepper

Fry (sauté) the shallots and mushrooms in half the butter until soft and brown. Stir in the parsley and spread over the base of an ovenproof dish. Roll up the sole fillets from the tail to the head and secure each with a cocktail stick. Place on top of the shallots. Pour over the wine and stock. Squeeze the lemon and pour the juice over the sole. Season well. Bake in a preheated oven at 180°C/350°F/gas mark 4 for 15 minutes. Drain and lay on a warm serving dish. Keep hot. Heat the remaining butter in a saucepan and add the flour. Cook for 1 minute. Strain the cooking liquid from the fish and gradually add to the butter and flour mix, stirring until the sauce thickens. Simmer for 2 minutes. Pour over the fish. Spoon the mushrooms and shallots around the fish. Serve hot.

Passerino con Sherry al Forno

Baked Flatfish with Sherry Butter

Serves 6

6 flatfish fillets, skinned
45 g/1½ oz/3 tbsp unsalted (sweet) butter
30 ml/2 tbsp lemon juice
1 onion, chopped
1 garlic clove, chopped
2 celery sticks, finely chopped
60 ml/4 tbsp dry sherry
25 g/1 oz/¼ cup plain (all-purpose) flour
Salt and freshly ground black pepper
60 ml/4 tbsp milk
60 ml/4 tbsp double (heavy) cream

Wash the fillets and dry on kitchen paper. Use two-thirds of the butter to grease a shallow baking dish. Arrange the fillets in the dish. Blend the lemon juice, onion and garlic together and pour over the fish. Cover with foil and bake in a preheated oven at 180°C/350°F/gas mark 4 for 15 minutes. Melt the remaining butter in a saucepan and fry (sauté) the celery for 3 minutes. Pour in the sherry and season with salt and pepper. Cover with a lid and cook slowly for 10–15 minutes. Add the flour and stir well. Stir in the juices from the fish dish and slowly add the milk. Bring to the boil and cook for two minutes, stirring. Blend in the cream. Pour the sauce over the fish and serve at once.

Trota alla Mandoria

Almond Trout
Serves 4

50 g/2 oz/¼ cup unsalted (sweet) butter
4 trout, about 225 g/8 oz each, cleaned
15 ml/1 tbsp plain (all-purpose) flour
5 ml/1 tsp salt
Freshly ground black pepper
75 g/3 oz/¾ cup flaked (slivered)
*   almonds*
30 ml/1 tbsp lemon juice

Melt the butter in a large frying pan (skillet). Dust the trout with flour, salt and pepper. Fry (sauté) the floured fish over a moderate heat for 10 minutes, turn and cook for 8 minutes. When golden brown, transfer to a warmed serving dish. Add the almonds and lemon juice to the pan juices. Cook for 3–5 minutes until the almonds are golden. Pour over the hot trout.

Pesce Rombo al Forno con Pomidori

Baked Turbot with Tomatoes
Serves 4

1 kg/2¼ lb turbot fillets
25 g/1 oz/2 tbsp unsalted (sweet) butter
1 egg
60 ml/4 tbsp double (heavy) cream
30 ml/2 tbsp white wine
Salt and freshly ground black pepper
30 ml/2 tbsp chopped fresh parsley
4 tomatoes, sliced

Fry (sauté) the fish in the butter for 5 minutes. Place in a large ovenproof dish. Combine the egg, cream, wine, salt, a grinding of pepper and the parsley. Pour over the sauce and lay the sliced tomatoes around the edge of the dish. Place in a preheated oven at 180°C/350°F/gas mark 4 for 20 minutes.

Spigola con Aneto

Baked Bass with Dill
Serves 4–6

1.75 kg/4 lb whole striped bass,
*   cleaned*
Grated rind and juice of 1 lemon
1 carrot, diced
6 shallots, chopped
30 ml/2 tbsp chopped fresh dill (dill
*   weed)*
Salt and freshly ground black pepper
25 g/1 oz/2 tbsp unsalted (sweet) butter
45 ml/3 tbsp plain (all-purpose) flour
300 ml/½ pt/1¼ cups fish stock
90 ml/6 tbsp dry white wine

Wash the bass several times in cold water. Pat dry and lay on a baking sheet covered with foil. Sprinkle the lemon juice inside and out. Place the lemon rind, carrot, shallots and dill inside the fish and season with the salt and pepper. Fold the foil over the fish to enclose it and cook for 30 minutes in a preheated oven at 180°C/350°F/gas mark 4 or until the fish flakes easily with a fork. Melt the butter in a saucepan and stir in the flour. Beat constantly and stir in the stock and wine. Blend well and cook over a low heat for 10 minutes, stirring all the time. Serve with the fish.

Spigola Arrosto alla Brace

Roast Sea Bass
Serves 6

2 x 750–900 g/1½–2 lb sea bass, cleaned
45 ml/3 tbsp olive oil
60 ml/4 tbsp water
Salt and freshly ground black pepper
1 garlic clove, chopped
1 sprig of fresh rosemary, chopped
2 sprigs of fresh thyme, chopped
Lemon juice
6 slices of lemon, to garnish

Brush each sea bass with a little oil and place in a large roasting tin (pan). Cook in a preheated oven at 180°C/350°F/gas mark 4 for 30 minutes or until cooked through. Meanwhile, prepare the dressing. Mix the water, salt, pepper, garlic and remaining oil together in a small pan and add the herbs. Spike with lemon juice and bring to the boil. Arrange the fish on a serving dish and pour the dressing over. Serve garnished with lemon slices.

Filetto di Sogliola al Forno con Salsa di Gamberetti

Baked Fillet of Sole with Prawn Sauce
Serves 6

1 small onion, diced
15 g/½ oz/1 tbsp unsalted (sweet) butter
225 g/8 oz cooked peeled prawns (shrimp)
30 ml/2 tbsp dry sherry
450 ml/¾ pt/2 cups Mushroom Soup (see page 46), or a large can
6 sole fillets, skinned
Salt and freshly ground black pepper

Fry (sauté) the onion in the butter and add the prawns and sherry. Cook for 5 minutes and mix in the mushroom soup. Continue cooking for 1 minute. Lay the fillets of sole in a large dish and pour over the prawn sauce. Season with the salt and pepper. Bake in a preheated oven at 180°C/350°F/gas mark 4 for 25 minutes.

Capperi, Pomodori e Triglie

Capers, Tomatoes and Mullet
Serves 4

10 g/¼ oz/2 tsp unsalted (sweet) butter
5 ml/1 tsp salt
4 small red mullet, cleaned and scaled
30 ml/2 tbsp olive oil
2 onions, sliced
2 garlic cloves, crushed
3 tomatoes, skinned and chopped
250 ml/8 fl oz/1 cup dry white wine
5 ml/1 tsp chopped fresh oregano
5 ml/1 tsp made mustard
Salt and freshly ground black pepper
30 ml/2 tbsp capers
2 sprigs of parsley

Lightly grease a large ovenproof dish with the butter and set aside. Sprinkle the salt over the fish and make 3 or 4 diagonal cuts across each fish. Place in the dish. Heat the oil in a saucepan and fry (sauté) the onions and garlic for 5 minutes. Stir in the tomatoes, wine, oregano and mustard and bring to the boil. Reduce the heat and cook for 35 minutes. Season with the salt and pepper. Pour the sauce over the fish. Cover loosely with foil and bake for 35 minutes in a preheated oven at 180°C/350°F/gas mark 4. Remove the foil, sprinkle over the capers and continue baking for a further 10 minutes to brown the top of the fish. Remove from the dish and garnish with the parsley.

Crespelle alle Vongole e Formaggio

Clam and Cheese Pancakes
Serves 4

Filling:
225 g/8 oz fresh clams in shells
100 g/4 oz/½ cup cream cheese
90 ml/6 tbsp double (heavy) cream
2.5 ml/½ tsp chopped fresh parsley
Salt and freshly ground black pepper

Pancakes:
50 g/2 oz/½ cup plain (all-purpose) flour
1 egg
1.5 ml/¼ tsp salt
90 ml/6 tbsp milk
25 g/1 oz/2 tbsp unsalted (sweet) butter

Put the clams in a large pan of boiling salted water and cook for 8 minutes. Drain and remove the clams from their shells. Beat the cream cheese with the cream and parsley and stir in the clams. Season with the salt and pepper. For the pancakes, put the flour in a large bowl and add the egg, salt and milk. Beat well and leave to stand for 5 minutes. Heat a small amount of the butter in a large pan. Beat the pancake mixture again and pour a little into the pan. Rotate and tilt the pan to ensure an even coating of the batter and fry (sauté) for 1 minute until the pancake has set. Turn over with a palette knife and cook until the underside has turned brown. Transfer to a warmed serving dish while cooking the remaining pancakes. Place the pancakes on plates and spread with the filling. Roll up and serve immediately.

Sedano con Triglie

Celery with Mullet
Serves 4

1.5 kg/3 lb grey mullet, cleaned, scaled and filleted
5 ml/1 tsp salt
Freshly ground black pepper
25 g/1 oz/2 tbsp unsalted (sweet) butter
15 ml/1 tbsp olive oil
1 onion, sliced
3 celery sticks, cleaned and chopped
100 g/4 oz mushrooms, cleaned and quartered
250 ml/8 fl oz/1 cup white wine
150 ml/¼ pt/⅔ cup fish stock
450 ml/¾ pt/2 cups Basic White Sauce (see page 357)
15 ml/1 tbsp chopped fresh marjoram

Sprinkle the fish with the salt and pepper and set aside. Melt half of the butter with the olive oil in a large saucepan and fry (sauté) the onion and celery for 4 minutes. Arrange the fish over the vegetables. Melt the remaining butter in a frying pan (skillet) and fry the mushrooms for 3 minutes. Spoon over the fish. Pour over the wine and fish stock and cover the pan with a lid or foil, allowing the steam to escape. Cook over a low heat and poach the fish for 15 minutes. Remove the fish and transfer to a heated serving dish. Keep warm. Increase the heat under the saucepan and boil for 5 minutes until the liquid is reduced by half. Reduce the heat and stir in the white sauce. Cook, stirring, for 5 minutes. Pour over the fish and sprinkle with the marjoram.

Aragosta con Salsa alla Diavola

Lobster with Devilled Sauce
Serves 4

2 large lobsters, cooked
15 g/½ oz/1 tbsp unsalted (sweet) butter
15 ml/1 tbsp olive oil
1 onion, chopped
4 large tomatoes, chopped
15 ml/1 tbsp clear honey
Juice of 1 lemon
15 ml/1 tbsp chopped fresh oregano

Halve the lobsters and crack the claws. Remove the gills, the green sac behind the head and the black vein along the body. Place the lobsters in a casserole dish (Dutch oven). Melt the butter in a saucepan and stir in the oil. Fry (sauté) the onion and add the tomatoes, honey and lemon juice. Stir in the oregano and cook for 1 minute, stirring. Pour the sauce over the lobsters and bake in a preheated oven at 180°C/350°F/gas mark 4 for 15 minutes.

Calamari Ripieni

Stuffed Squid
Serves 4

6 squid, cleaned thoroughly and skinned
45 ml/3 tbsp breadcrumbs
15 ml/1 tbsp grated lime rind
30 ml/2 tbsp chopped fresh parsley
90 ml/6 tbsp grated Parmesan cheese
1 garlic clove, crushed
1 egg, lightly beaten
15 ml/1 tbsp olive oil
Salt and freshly ground black pepper
25 g/1 oz/2 tbsp unsalted (sweet) butter
30 ml/2 tbsp white wine
4 tomatoes, chopped

Chop the tentacles off the squid. Place in a large bowl with the breadcrumbs, lime rind, parsley, cheese, garlic, egg, olive oil and seasoning and mix well. Divide the mixture between the squid and fill the body sacs. Sew up the opening of each squid. Heat the butter in a frying pan (skillet) and cook the squid for 5 minutes until browned on all sides. Pour in the wine and add the chopped tomatoes. Season and simmer very gently for 25 minutes. Lift out the squid and discard the sewing thread. Slice the squid thickly on the serving plate and spoon the sauce around.

Capesante alla Champagne

Champagne Scallops
Serves 4

50 g/2 oz/¼ cup unsalted (sweet) butter
2 shallots, finely chopped
300 ml/½ pt/1¼ cups pink Champagne
*   or rosé wine*
15 ml/1 tbsp chopped fresh sage
Salt and freshly ground black pepper
16 scallops, shelled
Sprigs of parsley, to garnish

Put half of the butter into a pan and cooked the chopped shallots until soft. Add the Champagne or wine and stir in the chopped sage and seasoning. Bring to the boil, reduce the heat and simmer for 10–15 minutes until the liquid has reduced by about half. Add the scallops to the pan and cook for 2 minutes. Lift out the scallops and place them on individual heated dishes. Keep warm. Increase the heat and whisk the remaining butter into the sauce, a little at a time. Pour the sauce over the scallops and garnish with sprigs of parsley.

Filetto di Merlizzo con Salsa di Capperi

Cod Fillet in Caper Sauce

Serves 4

5 ml/1 tsp cornflour (cornstarch)
150 ml/¼ pt/⅔ cup dry white wine
8 small cod fillets, skinned
300 ml/½ pt/1¼ cups fish stock
1.5 ml/¼ tsp salt
1.5 ml/¼ tsp freshly ground black pepper
8 raw king prawns (jumbo shrimp), peeled
1.5 ml/¼ tsp cayenne
150 ml/¼ pt/⅔ cup double (heavy) cream
30 ml/2 tbsp capers

Mix the cornflour with 15 ml/1 tbsp of the white wine in a basin and set aside. Roll up the cod fillets and fasten each with a cocktail stick (toothpick). Place the rolled fillets in a saucepan and pour over the stock, white wine, salt and pepper. Bring to the boil, reduce the heat, cover and simmer for 20 minutes, add the prawns for the last 5 minutes. Remove the fish fillets and prawns and arrange in a warmed serving dish. Keep hot. Bring the liquid to the boil and boil rapidly for 8 minutes to reduce. Stir in the dissolved cornflour and the cayenne. Reduce the heat and simmer, stirring all the time, for 2 minutes. Remove from the heat and stir in the cream and capers. Pour the sauce over the fish. Serve immediately.

Gamberetti con Crema

Creamed Prawns

Serves 4

75 g/3 oz/⅓ cup unsalted (sweet) butter
100 g/4 oz mushrooms, sliced
45 ml/3 tbsp plain (all-purpose) flour
250 ml/8 fl oz/1 cup milk
150 ml/¼ pt/⅔ cup white wine
450 g/1 lb cooked peeled prawns (shrimp)
100 g/4 oz peas, cooked
60 ml/4 tbsp breadcrumbs
45 ml/3 tbsp grated Parmesan cheese
15 ml/1 tbsp chopped fresh parsley

Grease an ovenproof baking dish with 5 ml/1 tsp of the butter and set aside. Melt half of the remaining butter and fry (sauté) the mushrooms for 2 minutes. Remove the mushrooms from the pan and set aside. Add the remaining butter to the pan and stir in the flour. Cook for 1 minute and gradually stir in the milk and wine. Cook, stirring constantly, for 3–4 minutes until the sauce is smooth. Stir in the mushrooms, prawns and peas and simmer for 5 minutes. Pour the mixture into the greased baking dish. Mix the breadcrumbs and cheese together and sprinkle over the top of the shrimps. Grill (broil) for 5 minutes until brown on top. Sprinkle over the chopped parsley and serve immediately.

Vongole, Pesto e Spaghetti

Clams, Pesto and Spaghetti
Serves 4

2 garlic cloves, peeled
15 ml/1 tbsp olive oil
1 small onion, chopped
90 ml/6 tbsp white wine
150 ml/¼ pt/⅔ cup fish or chicken
  stock
450 g/1 lb baby clams in shells
275 g/10 oz spaghetti
75 ml/5 tbsp Red Pesto Sauce
  (see page 366)

Crush the garlic cloves and fry (sauté) in the oil with the onion for 1 minute. Pour in the wine and stock and bring to the boil. Add the clams and cover with a lid. Cook for 3 minutes to open the clams. Discard any clams which have not opened. Bring a large pan of salted water to the boil and cook the spaghetti for 5 minutes until tender. Drain and pour into a warmed serving dish. Add the clams. Heat the Red Pesto Sauce in a saucepan for 1 minute. Pour over the pasta and clams. Toss and serve.

Frutti di Mare Gratinati

Grilled Seafood
Serves 4

16 large fresh mussels, in shells
8 large oysters, in shells
4 fresh razor shells
20 large fresh clams, in shells
4 scallops, shelled
60 ml/4 tbsp fresh breadcrumbs
60 ml/4 tbsp Pecorino or Parmesan
  cheese, grated
3 garlic cloves, finely chopped
45 ml/3 tbsp chopped fresh parsley
75 ml/5 tbsp olive oil

Carefully clean and scrub all the shellfish, discarding any which are not closed. Place them in a large pan with just enough water to cover the base of the pan. Place over a high heat, cover and steam for 5–8 minutes until the shellfish open. Discard any which remain closed. Remove from the pan and allow to cool quickly. Remove them from their shells and arrange in a single layer in a shallow flameproof dish. Mix together all the other ingredients except the olive oil, cover the top of each piece of seafood with this mixture, then drizzle the olive oil over the top. Grill (broil) the seafood under a moderate grill (broiler) for 5 minutes, then serve at once.

Baccala

Salt Cod
Serves 4

450 g/1 lb salt cod
15 ml/1 tbsp olive oil
4 tomatoes
50 g/2 oz/1 small can anchovies
Small bunch of fresh, mixed herbs
150 ml/¼ pt/⅔ cup white wine
15 ml/1 tbsp brandy

Soak the cod in cold water for 24 hours, changing the water several times. Drain well, cut the cod into slices and fry (sauté) in the oil for 2 minutes on each side. Chop the tomatoes and add to the pan with the anchovies, herbs and wine. Simmer for 15 minutes. Remove the herbs and stir in the brandy.

Pesce Incartocciato

Foiled Fish
Serves 4

Italian sauce:
4 garlic cloves, crushed
120 ml/4 fl oz/½ cup olive oil
400 g/14 oz/1 large can of chopped
  tomatoes
30 ml/2 tbsp chopped fresh parsley
Large bunch of fresh basil
Salt and freshly ground black pepper

Fish:
30 ml/2 tbsp olive oil
750 g/1½ lb fillets of red mullet or any
  large white fish – bass, haddock or
  cod
450 g/1 lb mussels in their shells,
  scrubbed and beards removed
12 rings of baby squid (optional)
8 large raw prawns (jumbo shrimp)
  (optional)
2 garlic cloves, finely chopped
45 ml/3 tbsp chopped fresh basil
45 ml/3 tbsp dry white wine

Make the sauce. Fry (sauté) the garlic in
the oil for 1 minute. Stir in the canned
tomatoes and simmer for 10 minutes. Add
the parsley and basil, season with salt and
pepper and cook for 2 minutes, stirring.
Blend the sauce to a purée in a blender or
food processor. Place a large piece of foil
on an ovenproof baking sheet and brush
with the olive oil. Place the fish in the centre of the foil. Cover with the mussels,
squid and prawns, if using, the garlic and
basil. Close the foil and bake in a preheated oven at 180°C/350°F/gas mark 4 for 15
minutes. Remove from the oven and open
the parcel. Pour in the wine and the sauce.
Return to the oven for a further 5 minutes
with the foil open. Serve.

Rana Pescatrice con Granchio e Gamberetti

Monkfish with Crab and Shrimp
Serves 6

100 g/4 oz/½ cup unsalted (sweet)
  butter
100 g/4 oz crabmeat, flaked
225 g/8 oz cooked shrimps (miniature
  shrimp), shelled
30 ml/2 tbsp plain (all-purpose) flour
250 ml/8 fl oz/1 cup fish stock
60 ml/4 tbsp double (heavy) cream
60 ml/4 tbsp white wine
100 g/4 oz mushrooms, chopped
1 green (bell) pepper, chopped
50 g/2 oz/½ cup cooked rice
Salt and freshly ground black pepper
1 kg/2 lb monkfish tail, skinned, boned
  and opened out flat

Butter a shallow ovenproof dish and set
aside. Heat half the remaining butter. Add
the crabmeat and shrimps to the pan. Coat
with the butter and stir in the flour. Pour in
the fish stock, cream and wine, stirring
constantly. Add the mushrooms, green
pepper, rice, salt and pepper and continue
cooking for 2 minutes. Remove the pan
from the heat and spoon as much crab and
shrimp mix over the monkfish as possible.
Fold the monkfish over the stuffing. Spread
the rest of the mixture over the bottom of
the ovenproof dish. Place the stuffed fish
on top. Melt the remaining butter and pour
over. Cover the dish with foil and bake in a
preheated oven at 180°C/350°F/gas mark 4
for 35 minutes. Remove the dish from the
oven and serve at once.

Gamberetti alla Venezina

Venetian Prawns

Serves 4

150 ml/¼ pt/⅔ cup olive oil
900 g/2 lb whole king prawns (jumbo shrimp)
15 ml/1 tbsp chopped fresh parsley
1 bay leaf
5 garlic cloves, chopped
150 ml/¼ pt/⅔ cup dry white wine
Salt and freshly ground black pepper
Juice of 1 lemon

Heat the oil in a pan and add the prawns, parsley, bay leaf and garlic. Reduce the heat and cook for 5 minutes. Add the white wine and boil rapidly for a further 5 minutes until reduced. Season with salt and pepper, sprinkle with the lemon juice and place on a warmed serving plate.

Frutti di Mare con Guarnizione Friabile

Crumbly Topped Seafood

Serves 6

30 ml/2 tbsp olive oil
2 garlic cloves, crushed
100 g/4 oz mushrooms, quartered
350 g/12 oz white fish fillets, skinned
Salt and freshly ground black pepper
175 g/6 oz squid, cut into small pieces
225 g/8 oz cooked, peeled prawns (shrimp)
75 ml/5 tbsp dry white wine
90 ml/6 tbsp single (light) cream
90 ml/6 tbsp breadcrumbs
15 ml/1 tbsp chopped fresh parsley

Heat the oil in a large frying pan (skillet) and cook the garlic for 1 minute. Stir in the mushrooms and cook for 3 minutes. Cut the fish into 4 cm/1½ in pieces and add to the oil. Cook, stirring for 3 minutes and season with the salt and pepper. Stir in the squid and prawns. Pour in the wine and simmer for 1 minute. Gradually blend in the cream then transfer the mixture to an ovenproof dish. Sprinkle over the breadcrumbs and bake in a preheated oven at 190°C/375°F/gas mark 5 for 10 minutes. Serve sprinkled with the chopped parsley.

Stufato di Pesce

Fish Stew

Serves 4

450 g/1 lb white fish, skinned and boned
25 g/1 oz/2 tbsp unsalted (sweet) butter
1 onion, chopped
2 celery sticks, finely chopped
4 carrots, chopped
Grated rind and juice of 1 lemon
Salt and freshly ground black pepper
30 ml/2 tbsp plain (all-purpose) flour
15 ml/1 tbsp chopped fresh parsley
300 ml/½ pt/1¼ cups fish stock
2 bay leaves
6 large tomatoes, skinned and chopped

Cut the fish into 4 cm/1½ in squares. Melt the butter in a deep frying pan (skillet) and fry (sauté) the chopped onion, celery and carrot for 5 minutes. Add the fish and cook gently for 2 minutes. Remove the pan from the heat and add the rind and juice of the lemon. Season with salt and pepper. Sprinkle over the flour and parsley and cook for 1 minute, stirring. Pour in the fish stock and the bay leaves. Cook, stirring, for 2 minutes until the sauce thickens. Add the tomatoes to the pan. Cover with a lid and cook for 5 minutes.

Anguilla e Piselli Verdi

Eel and Green Peas
Serves 4

100 g/4 oz pancetta, diced
900 g/2 lb eel, skinned and sliced
300 ml/½ pt/1¼ cups Chunky Tomato
 Sauce (see page 357)
450 g/1 lb fresh or frozen peas
Salt and freshly ground black pepper

Fry (sauté) the pancetta for 3 minutes. Add the sliced eel and cook until lightly browned. Stir in the tomato sauce and peas and simmer for 20 minutes. Season with the salt and pepper.

Pesce e Fagottini di Finocchio

Fish and Fennel Parcels
Serves 4

25 g/1 oz/2 tbsp unsalted (sweet) butter
1 fennel bulb, trimmed and chopped
Grated rind and juice of 1 lemon
Salt and freshly ground black pepper
45 ml/3 tbsp chopped fresh parsley
8 small white fish fillets, skinned
6 large tomatoes, skinned and sliced

Melt the butter in a frying pan (skillet) and add the chopped fennel. Cook gently for 8 minutes. Remove the pan from the heat and add the lemon rind and juice. Season with the salt and pepper. Sprinkle the parsley over the fish fillets and roll them up, starting from the thick end. Lightly oil 4 large sheets of foil or baking parchment. Divide the tomato slices between the sheets. Spread the fennel on top and place two fish rolls on each. Seal the parcels tightly and place in a roasting tin (pan). Bake in a preheated oven at 190°C/375°F/gas mark 5 for 20 minutes. Serve one parcel per person.

Gamberetti per Cena Festiva

Dinner Party Prawns
Serves 4

350 g/12 oz/1½ cups Italian rice
2.5 ml/½ tsp salt
30 ml/2 tbsp olive oil
2 garlic cloves, crushed
900 g/2 lb large raw prawns (jumbo
 shrimp), peeled
1 large red (bell) pepper, chopped
2.5 ml/½ tsp cayenne
30 ml/2 tbsp light brown sugar
Salt and freshly ground black pepper
10 ml/2 tsp cornflour (cornstarch)
250 ml/8 fl oz/1 cup red wine
15 ml/1 tbsp chopped fresh basil

Place the rice in a large saucepan and cover with water. Add the salt and bring to the boil. Reduce to a simmer and cook for 10–15 minutes until just tender. Drain. Transfer to a warmed serving dish and keep warm. Place half the oil in a large frying pan (skillet) and cook the garlic and prawns for 10 minutes. Remove and place on top of the rice. Keep warm. Add the red pepper and remaining oil. Cook, stirring, for 3 minutes until soft. Stir in the cayenne, brown sugar and season with salt and pepper. Dissolve the cornflour in a little of the red wine and add to the peppers with the remaining wine and basil. Bring to the boil and cook for 1 minute, stirring. Pour over the prawns and serve.

Anguilla del Pescatore

Fisherman's Eel

Serves 4

450 g/1 lb eels, skinned
Salt and freshly ground black pepper
30 ml/2 tbsp plain (all-purpose) flour
25 g/1 oz/2 tbsp unsalted (sweet) butter
225 g/8 oz peaches, halved and stoned
** (pitted)**
150 ml/¼ pt/⅔ cup brandy
Boiled potatoes, to serve

Wash the eels and dry them on kitchen paper. Rub the outside with salt and pepper and cut into 6 cm/2½ in pieces. Roll the eel chunks in flour. Heat the butter in a frying pan (skillet). Cook the eel in the butter for 12 minutes. Add the peach halves and continue cooking for 2 minutes, turning once. Pour in the brandy and ignite. Allow the flames to die down and serve immediately with boiled potatoes.

Pesce, Cipolla e Fagottini di Carote

Fish, Onion and Carrot Parcels

Serves 4

25 g/1 oz/2 tbsp unsalted (sweet) butter
1 onion, trimmed and chopped
4 carrots, thinly sliced
Grated rind and juice of 1 lemon
Salt and freshly ground black pepper
15 ml/1 tbsp chopped fresh thyme
8 small white fish fillets, skinned
6 large tomatoes, skinned and sliced

Melt the butter in a frying pan (skillet) and add the chopped onion and carrot. Cook gently for 2 minutes. Remove the pan from the heat and add the lemon rind and juice.

Season with the salt and pepper. Sprinkle the thyme over the fish fillets and roll up, starting from the thick end. Lightly oil four large sheets of foil or non-stick baking parchment. Divide the tomatoes between the sheets. Spread the onion and carrots on top and place two fish rolls on each. Seal the parcels tightly and place in a roasting tin (pan). Bake in a preheated oven at 190°C/375°F/gas mark 5 for 20 minutes. Serve one parcel per person.

Filetti di Pesce con Capperi

Fish Fillets and Capers

Serves 4

4 white fish fillets, skinned
1 shallot, finely chopped
3 tomatoes, skinned and chopped
Salt and freshly ground black pepper
15g/½ oz/1 tbsp unsalted (sweet) butter
15 ml/1 tbsp plain (all-purpose) flour
15 ml/1 tbsp chopped fresh sage
10 ml/2 tsp tomato purée (paste)
15 ml/1 tbsp capers, chopped
Oil for greasing

Cut each fillet in half lengthways and arrange in an ovenproof dish. Scatter over the shallot and add the tomatoes. Season with salt and pepper and dot with the butter. Cover the fish with foil and bake in a preheated oven at 190°C/375°F/gas mark 5 for 25 minutes. Transfer the fish fillets to a warmed serving dish and keep hot. Spoon any cooking liquid into a saucepan and blend in the flour, sage and tomato purée. Bring to the boil, reduce the heat and simmer for 2 minutes. Stir in the chopped capers and pour the sauce over the fish fillets. Serve immediately.

Scampi Fritti

Battered Prawns
Serves 2

20 raw whole king prawns (jumbo
  shrimp)
1 egg
150 ml/¼ pt/⅔ cup milk
25 g/1 oz/¼ cup plain (all-purpose)
  flour
Salt and freshly ground black pepper
Oil for deep-frying
Lemon wedges, to serve

Shell the prawns. Beat the egg into the
milk in a shallow dish. Season the flour.
Dip the prawns in the milk then into the
seasoned flour. Heat the oil and deep-fry
the prawns until golden brown. Arrange on
a dish or in a basket and serve hot with
lemon wedges.

Triglie alla Griglia

Grilled Red Mullet
Serves 4

4 red mullet, cleaned and scaled
60 ml/4 tbsp olive oil
2 bay leaves
15 ml/1 tbsp vinegar
Salt and freshly ground black pepper

Split the fish down the centre. Place on a
grill (broiler) pan. Put the olive oil in a
saucepan with the bay leaves and simmer
for 4–5 minutes. Stir in the vinegar and
salt and pepper. Brush a little of the sauce
over the mullet and grill (broil) slowly for
8–10 minutes or until the flesh flakes easily when tested with a fork, brushing frequently with the baste.

Capesante alla Griglia

Grilled Scallops
Serves 4

8 scallops, shelled
50 g/2 oz/¼ cup unsalted (sweet)
  butter, melted
1 onion, finely chopped
1 garlic clove, crushed
2.5 ml/½ tsp chopped fresh parsley

Clean and dry the scallops on kitchen
paper and place on foil on a grill pan
(broiler). Brush with a little of the butter.
Grill (broil) under a moderate heat for 4
minutes. Transfer to a hot dish. Mix the
onion, garlic and parsley in the remaining
butter and cook for 2 minutes. Pour the
mixture over the scallops and serve.

Stratti di Pesce Arrostito

Layered Fish Roast
Serves 4

25 g/1 oz/2 tbsp unsalted (sweet) butter
1 onion, finely chopped
75 g/3 oz/1½ cups breadcrumbs
30 ml/2 tbsp chopped fresh dill (dill
  weed)
30 ml/2 tbsp snipped fresh chives
120 ml/4 fl oz/½ cup soured (dairy
  sour) cream
1 egg, beaten
900 g/2 lb white fish fillets, such as
  haddock, monkfish and sole, skinned

Melt the butter in a saucepan. Remove
from the heat and stir in the remaining
ingredients, except the fish. Layer the fish
and filling in an ovenproof dish and bake
in a preheated oven at 180°C/350°F/gas
mark 4 for 45 minutes. Remove from the
oven and allow to rest for 5 minutes. Cut in
small pieces and serve.

Pesce Fritto all' Italiano

Italian Fried Fish

Serves 4

100 g/4 oz/1 cup plain (all-purpose)
flour
Salt and freshly ground black pepper
1 egg
150 ml/¼ pt/⅔ cup milk
450 g/1 lb assorted white fish, skinned,
boned and cut into small pieces
8 raw king prawns (jumbo shrimp),
shelled
100 g/4 oz tiny octopus, cooked and
cut into rings
Oil for deep-frying
Lemon wedges, to serve

Sift the flour and salt and pepper into a
bowl. Beat in the egg and milk until the
mixture is smooth and thick. Dip the fish
in the batter to coat and deep-fry until
crisp and golden brown in the hot oil.
Drain on kitchen paper. Serve with lemon
wedges.

Cozze Alla Toscana

Mussels Tuscany Style

Serves 4

1 small onion
450 g/1 lb mussels, scrubbed and
beards removed
150 ml/¼ pt/⅔ cup white wine
2 sprigs of thyme
Salt and freshly ground black pepper
300 ml/½ pt/1¼ cups stock or water
15 ml/1 tbsp oil
3 tomatoes, peeled and chopped
30 ml/2 tbsp tomato purée (paste)

Chop the onion and place in a large pan
with the mussels, wine, thyme, salt and
pepper and stock or water. Cover and heat
rapidly until the mussels open. Drain the
mussels reserving the liquid. Remove the
mussels from their shells. Discard any
unopened ones. Heat the oil in a pan, add
the tomatoes and simmer until they are
soft. Add the mussels and simmer for two
minutes. Stir in the tomato purée and serve
immediately.

Cozze Fritte

Fried Mussels

Serves 4

100 g/4 oz/1 cup plain (all-purpose)
flour
Salt and freshly ground black pepper
1 egg
150 ml/¼ pt/⅔ cup milk
900 g/2 lb mussels, scrubbed and
beards removed
Oil for frying
Creamy Garlic Sauce (see page 361),
to serve

Sift the flour and salt and pepper into a
bowl. Beat in the egg and milk until the
mixture is smooth and thick. Immerse the
mussels in a pan of boiling salted water
and cook for 3 minutes. Remove the mussels from the shells, discarding any that do
not open. Dip the mussels in the batter to
coat and fry (sauté) for 1 minute in hot oil
until the batter is crisp and golden brown.
Serve with Creamy Garlic Sauce.

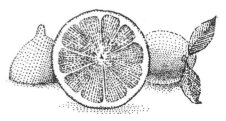

Calamari e Aragosta

Squid and Crayfish
Serves 2

15 ml/1 tbsp olive oil
25 g/1 oz/2 tbsp unsalted (sweet) butter
1 onion, chopped
1 garlic clove, crushed
45 ml/3 tbsp chopped fresh parsley
200 g/7 oz small squid, sliced in rings
225 g/8 oz/1 cup long-grain rice
45 ml/3 tbsp brandy
150 ml/¼ pt/⅔ cup fish or chicken stock
Salt and freshly ground black pepper
2 crayfish, cleaned and cooked

Heat the oil and butter and fry (sauté) the onion, garlic, parsley, squid and rice for 3 minutes. Add the brandy and ignite. Allow the flames to die down then pour in the stock. Bring to the boil, stirring and lower the heat. Simmer for 15 minutes until the rice is cooked. Season with the salt and pepper and add the cooked crayfish. Leave to heat for 3–4 minutes, stirring occasionally.

Triglie Messinese

Messina Mullet
Serves 4

60 ml/4 tbsp olive oil
5 ml/1 tsp salt
4 small grey mullet, cleaned
4 shallots, sliced
4 tomatoes, peeled and sliced
1 carrot, scraped and cut into strips
250 ml/8 fl oz/1 cup dry white wine
5 ml/1 tsp chopped fresh oregano
Lemon quarters, to garnish

Lightly oil a large baking dish and set aside. Sprinkle the salt over the fish and make 3 or 4 diagonal cuts across each fish. Arrange the sliced shallots in the base of the baking dish. Top with the tomato slices and carrot strips. Lay the fish over the vegetables and pour over the remaining olive oil and the white wine. Sprinkle with the oregano and cover loosely with foil. Bake for 35 minutes in a preheated oven at 180°C/350°F/gas mark 4. Remove the foil and continue baking for a further 10 minutes to brown the top of the fish. Remove from the dish and garnish with the lemon.

Triglie con Funghi

Mushroom Mullet
Serves 4

45 ml/3 tbsp olive oil
1 garlic clove, crushed
1 onion, finely chopped
225 g/8 oz mushrooms, chopped
Salt and freshly ground black pepper
15 ml/1 tbsp chopped fresh parsley
50 g/2 oz/1 cup breadcrumbs
4 red mullet, cleaned and scaled

Grease a shallow ovenproof dish with a little of the oil. Place the remaining oil in a frying pan (skillet) and add the garlic and onion. Fry (sauté) for 5 minutes until the onion is translucent. Add the mushrooms. Season with the salt and pepper and blend in half of the parsley. Stir in the breadcrumbs and continue cooking for 3 minutes. Spoon into the dish and arrange the red mullet on top. Cover with greaseproof (waxed) paper or foil and bake in a preheated oven for 10 minutes at 180°C/350°F /gas mark 4. Remove the paper and bake for a further 10 minutes until the fish is cooked through and tinged with brown. Sprinkle with the remaining parsley.

Aragosta con Parmigiano

Lobster with Parmesan
Serves 4

2 large lobsters, cooked
15 g/½ oz/1 tbsp unsalted (sweet)
butter
15 ml/1 tbsp plain (all-purpose) flour
300 ml/½ pt/1¼ cups milk
Salt and freshly ground black pepper
100 g/4 oz/1 cup Parmesan cheese,
grated
15 ml/1 tbsp chopped fresh parsley

Halve the lobsters and crack the claws. Remove the gills, green sac behind the head and the long black vein down the body. Place the lobsters in a casserole dish (Dutch oven). Melt the butter in a saucepan and stir in the flour. Cook for 1 minute and gradually stir in the milk. Season with the salt and pepper and cook, stirring until the sauce thickens. Add half the cheese and continue cooking for 1 minute. Pour the sauce over the lobsters and sprinkle with the remaining cheese. Bake in a preheated oven at 180°C/ 350°F/gas mark 4 for 20 minutes. Garnish with chopped parsley and serve.

Involtini di Prosciutto con Gamberetti

Prawns in Prosciutto
Serves 4

8 cooked king prawns (jumbo shrimp),
shelled, keeping the tails intact
16 thin slices of prosciutto
15 ml/1 tbsp lemon juice
30 ml/2 tbsp finely chopped fresh parsley

Wrap the prawns in the prosciutto and place on foil on the grill (broiler) rack. Grill (broil) under a high heat for 1 minute on each side. Transfer to serving plates and sprinkle with the lemon juice and parsley.

Tonno Jonico

Ionian Tuna
Serves 4

1 aubergine (eggplant), roughly
chopped
1 kg/2¼ lb fresh tuna
2 onions, chopped
45 ml/3 tbsp olive oil
2 tomatoes, skinned, seeded and
chopped
8 black olives, stoned (pitted)
2 garlic cloves, chopped
15 ml/1 tbsp chopped fresh oregano
Salt and freshly ground black pepper
300 ml/½ pt/1¼ cups fish stock

Boil the aubergine in salted water for 3 minutes. Drain. Skin the tuna fish and cut into 2.5 cm/1 in cubes. Place the fish in a casserole dish (Dutch oven) and add the aubergine, chopped onions, oil, tomatoes, olives, garlic, oregano and salt and pepper. Pour over the fish stock. Season and cover with a lid or foil. Bake in a preheated oven at 190°C/375°F/gas mark 5 for 25 minutes.

***Photograph opposite:** Lamb with Rosemary and Orange Sauce (page 117)*

Rana Pescatrice in Salsa di Zafferano

Monkfish in Saffron Sauce
Serves 4

4 garlic cloves, peeled and chopped
450 g/1 lb mussels, cleaned and beards removed
1.5 ml/¼ tsp saffron powder
450 g/1 lb monkfish, skinned
225 g/8 oz tomatoes, skinned, seeded and chopped
30 ml/2 tbsp olive oil
1 onion, chopped
15 g/½ oz/1 tbsp unsalted (sweet) butter
100 ml/3½ fl oz/6½ tbsp white wine
30 ml/2 tbsp chopped fresh parsley
Salt and freshly ground black pepper

Bring 150 ml/¼ pt/⅔ cup water to the boil and add 3 of the garlic cloves. Put in the mussels and cook until they open. Remove the mussels from the water with a draining spoon and remove them from the shells. Discard any unopened ones. Put the shelled mussels in a bowl and strain the liquid through a sieve (strainer). Add the saffron to the liquid, stir well and set aside. Cut the monkfish into 3 cm/1¼ in chunks. Put the tomatoes in a small saucepan and cook over a low heat for 10 minutes, stirring occasionally. Fry (sauté) the remaining garlic in the oil, adding the onion and butter. Cook for 1 minute and stir in the monkfish. Cook for 3 minutes, stirring occasionally. Pour in the wine and allow the fish to cook for 10 minutes. Add the mussels and parsley. Stir in the tomatoes and the saffron and mussel liquid. Season with salt and pepper and continue cooking for a further 7–8 minutes.

***Photograph opposite:* Calves' Liver with Mushrooms, Tomatoes and Onions (page 130)**

Fritelle di Gamberetti e Mozzarella

Prawn and Mozzarella Fritters
Serves 4

120 ml/4 fl oz/½ cup water
50 g/2 oz/¼ cup unsalted (sweet) butter
2.5 ml/½ tsp salt
1.5 ml/¼ tsp freshly ground black pepper
5 ml/1 tsp chopped fresh basil
75 g/3 oz/¾ cup plain (all-purpose) flour
2 eggs
100 g/4 oz (preferably raw) peeled prawns (shrimp), chopped
100 g/4 oz/1 cup Mozzarella cheese, grated
Oil for deep-frying

Bring the water to the boil and add the butter, salt, pepper and basil. Remove from the heat when the butter has melted and beat in the flour. Continue beating until the mixture comes away from the sides of the pan. Beat in the eggs, one at a time and fold in the prawns and Mozzarella. Allow to cool for 10 minutes. Deep-fry teaspoons of the mixture in hot oil for 3–4 minutes until golden brown. Remove from the pan with a draining spoon and drain on kitchen paper. Keep warm while the rest of the fritters are cooking. Serve hot.

Pesce al Forno con Mostarda e Odori

Baked Mustard and Herb Fish

Serves 4

Oil for greasing
450 g/1 lb thick white fish fillets,
skinned
45 ml/3 tbsp double (heavy) cream or
crème fraîche
15 ml/1 tbsp made mustard
30 ml/2 tbsp chopped fresh herbs
1.5 ml/¼ tsp chopped fresh root ginger
Salt and freshly ground black pepper

Brush an ovenproof dish with the oil and add the fish fillets. Blend the cream, mustard, fresh herbs and ginger together in a bowl. Season the cod fillets with salt and pepper and spread with the cream mixture. Bake in a preheated oven at 180°C/350°F/gas mark 4 for 25 minutes.

Triglie Nella Papillote

Red Mullet Baked in Paper

Serves 4

175 g/6 oz mushrooms
4 red mullet, cleaned and scaled
50 g/2 oz/¼ cup unsalted (sweet) butter
Salt
Cayenne
30 ml/2 tbsp lemon juice
4 sprigs of fresh rosemary

Slice the mushrooms and place on a large piece of greaseproof (waxed) paper on a baking sheet. Place the cleaned mullet in a single layer on the mushrooms. Dot with pieces of the butter and sprinkle with the salt and a dash of cayenne. Sprinkle over the lemon juice. Place a sprig of fresh

rosemary on top of each mullet. Fold the paper over the fish and twist and fold the edges to seal. Bake in a preheated oven at 190°C/375°F/gas mark 5 for 20 minutes. Remove the fish from the parcel and place on a warmed plate. Pour the sauce from the paper over the fish and garnish if desired.

Triglie e Pomodori

Red Mullet and Tomatoes

Serves 6

45 ml/3 tbsp olive oil
30 ml/2 tbsp chopped fresh fennel fronds
or dill (dill weed)
6 small red mullet, cleaned and scaled
1 bay leaf
Salt and freshly ground black pepper
6 tomatoes, cut into wedges

Blend the oil and fennel. Place the fish in a large dish and pour over the oil. Season with the bay leaf and salt and pepper. Allow to marinate for 1 hour. Lift the fish out of the marinade and grill (broil) for about 6 minutes on each side, depending on the size of the fish. Baste once or twice while grilling with the marinade. Add the tomato wedges to the grill (broiler) pan for the last minute of cooking. Serve at once.

Arrosto di Rana Pescatrice con Salsa Maggiorana

Roast Monkfish with Bacon and Marjoram Sauce

Serves 4

5 ml/1 tsp chopped fresh sage
450 g/1 lb monkfish tail, trimmed of all membrane
Salt and freshly ground black pepper
6 thin rashers (slices) streaky bacon, rinded
30 ml/2 tbsp olive oil
45 ml/3 tbsp dry white wine
30 ml/2 tbsp white wine vinegar
1 small shallot, chopped
15 ml/1 tbsp double (heavy) cream
15 ml/1 tbsp chopped fresh marjoram
150g/5 oz/⅔ cup unsalted (sweet) butter

Sprinkle half the sage over the monkfish tail and season with the salt and pepper. Stretch the bacon rashers with a knife and wrap around the fish, overlapping slightly. Place in an ovenproof dish. Drizzle over the olive oil, cover and chill for 15 minutes. Roast the fish for 25 minutes in a preheated oven at 220°C/425°F/gas mark 7 until the bacon is crispy. Place the white wine, vinegar and chopped shallot in a saucepan and boil for 4 minutes to reduce the liquid. Remove from the heat and stir in the cream and marjoram. Whisk the butter into the sauce in small pieces until the sauce is thickened. Keep warm. Place the fish on a heated dish and pour over the marjoram sauce.

Pasticcio di Salmone e Peperoni

Salmon and Pepper Pie

Serves 4

225 g/8 oz shortcrust pastry (basic pie crust)
150 ml/¼ pt/⅔ cup double (heavy) cream or crème fraîche
3 eggs, beaten
Salt and freshly ground black pepper
100 g/4 oz salmon fillet
1 bay leaf
1 sprig of rosemary
2 lemon slices
2 red (bell) peppers, sliced thinly
A few parsley sprigs, to garnish

Roll out the pastry and use to line a 25 cm/10 in pizza tin (pan). Trim round the edge and turn the edge of the pastry under so that it is thicker around the edge. Prick the base lightly with a fork and chill for 15 minutes. Beat together the cream or crème fraîche with the eggs and season with the salt and pepper. Place the salmon in a saucepan with the bay leaf, rosemary and lemon slices. Season with the salt and pepper and bring to the boil. Simmer gently for 5 minutes and allow to cool for 5 minutes. Break the salmon into flakes, discarding the skin and bones. Arrange the sliced peppers and salmon over the top of the pastry, pour over the egg mixture. Bake in a preheated oven at 190°C/375°F/gas mark 5 for 35 minutes until the pastry is cooked and the egg mixture is brown and set. Garnish with parsley and serve.

Patate con Salsa di Gamberetti

Potatoes with Prawn Sauce
Serves 4

6 potatoes, sliced
½ onion, diced
25 g/1 oz/2 tbsp unsalted (sweet) butter
225 g/8 oz cooked peeled prawns (shrimp), chopped
30 ml/2 tbsp dry sherry
250 ml/8 fl oz/1 cup single (light) cream
Salt and freshly ground black pepper

Boil the potatoes in salted water for 4 minutes. Drain. Fry (sauté) the onion in 15 g/ ½ oz/1 tbsp butter and add the prawns and sherry. Fry for 5 minutes and mix in the cream. Continue cooking for 1 minute. Lay the potatoes in a large dish, dot with the remaining butter and pour over the prawn sauce. Season with the salt and pepper. Bake in a preheated oven at 180°C/ 350°F/gas mark 4 for 25 minutes until golden and cooked through.

Triglie all Livornese

Red Mullet Leghorn Style
Serves 4

4 red mullet, cleaned and scaled
150 ml/¼ pt/⅔ cup white wine
600 ml/1 pt/2½ cups water
3 sprigs of thyme
Salt and freshly ground black pepper
15 ml/1 tbsp oil
2 large onions, chopped
3 egg yolks
30 ml/2 tbsp single (light) cream
1 garlic clove, crushed
5 ml/1 tsp chopped fresh parsley

Put the cleaned fish in a pan with the wine, water and thyme. Season with the salt and pepper and poach gently for 10 minutes. Drain the fish and reserve the liquid. Set aside. Heat the oil in a saucepan and cook the onions until brown. Strain in half the fish stock and boil very fast to reduce the quantity. Remove from the heat and allow to cool. Place the fish on a large platter. Whisk the egg yolks into the sauce and blend in the cream and crushed garlic. Pour over the fish, sprinkle with chopped parsley and serve immediately.

Involtini di Foglie di Vite con Sardino

Sardines in Vine Leaves
Serves 4

12 vine leaves
50 g/2 oz/¼ cup unsalted (sweet) butter, softened
12 fresh sardines, as small as possible, cleaned and scaled if necessary
1.5 ml/¼ tsp freshly ground black pepper
15 ml/1 tbsp lemon juice
1.5 ml/¼ tsp chopped fresh sage
2 garlic cloves, crushed

Brush each vine leaf with the softened butter and place a sardine in the centre of each leaf. Blend the remaining butter with the pepper, lemon juice, sage and crushed garlic and dot over each sardine. Wrap up the vine leaf and secure with a cocktail stick (toothpick) or tie with fine string. Preheat the grill (broiler) and place the vine leaf parcels on the rack. Grill (broil) for 3 minutes, depending on the size of each sardine, allowing 1 minute per 2.5 cm/1 in of fish, until the edges of each leaf turn black. Place on a warmed serving dish.

Scardine di Mare Mediterraneo

Mediterranean Sea Bream
Serves 4

30 ml/2 tbsp chopped fresh thyme
15 ml/1 tbsp chopped fresh coriander
(cilantro)
4 × 225 g/8 oz sea bream, cleaned and
scaled
25 g/1 oz/2 tbsp unsalted (sweet) butter
Salt and freshly ground black pepper
120 ml/4 fl oz/½ cup white wine
15 ml/1 tbsp olive oil
3 tomatoes, sliced
Small new potatoes, boiled, to serve

Blend the chopped thyme and coriander together. Make two deep incisions along the back of the fish and insert some of the herbs. Place the butter inside the fish and sprinkle with the salt and pepper. Place the fish on a rack in a large roasting tin (pan). Pour over the wine, olive oil and remaining herbs. Arrange the tomato slices on top. Bake in a preheated oven at 180°C/350°F/gas mark 4 for 20 minutes. Remove from the oven and baste the fish with the juices. Continue cooking for a further 10 minutes and serve with new potatoes.

Sardine e Salsa di Coriandolo

Sardines and Coriander Sauce
Serves 4

12–16 sardines, cleaned and scaled
Salt and freshly ground black pepper
5 ml/1 tsp paprika
3 red (bell) peppers, halved
45 ml/3 tbsp olive oil
45 ml/3 tbsp chopped fresh coriander
(cilantro)
1 red onion, chopped

Sprinkle the sardines with salt, pepper and paprika. Place the peppers, skin side up, under a hot grill (broiler) until the skin is charred. Strip off the skin when cool. Roughly chop the peppers and place in a blender with the oil, coriander and onion. Blend until smooth. Season the sauce with salt and pepper. Grill (broil) the sardines for 4 minutes on each side and serve hot with the sauce.

Triglie Condita

Seasoned Red Mullet
Serves 4

4 red mullet, cleaned and scaled
Salt and freshly ground black pepper
1 orange, sliced
45 ml/3 tbsp chopped fresh oregano
1 onion, sliced
Grated rind and juice of 1 lemon
30 ml/2 tbsp chopped fresh mint
5 ml/1 tsp paprika
60 ml/4 tbsp plain yoghurt

Season the mullet with salt and pepper. Place the orange slices, oregano and onion in a large frying pan (skillet) and place the fish on the top. Sprinkle over the lemon rind and juice and pour over 150 ml/¼ pt/⅔ cup water. Bring to the boil. Cover with a lid or foil and cook gently for 20 minutes. Blend the mint, paprika and yoghurt together and season with the salt and pepper and serve with the fish.

Frutti di Mare con Mostardo e Salsa al Formaggio

Seafood with Mustard and Cheese Sauce

Serves 4

75 g/3 oz/⅓ cup unsalted (sweet) butter
225 g/8 oz shelled scallops
225 g/8 oz raw peeled prawns (shrimp)
15 g/½ oz/1 tbsp plain (all-purpose) flour
250 ml/8 fl oz/1 cup chicken stock
30 ml/2 tbsp white wine
5 ml/1 tsp made mustard
50 g/2 oz/½ cup Parmesan cheese, grated
150 ml/¼ pt/⅔ cup single (light) cream
Salt and freshly ground black pepper

Melt half the butter and fry (sauté) the seafood for 3 minutes until golden brown. Place in an ovenproof dish. Melt the remaining butter and add the flour. Cook for 1 minute and remove from the heat. Gradually stir in the stock and white wine and bring to the boil. Simmer until the sauce thickens and stir in the mustard and half the cheese. Remove from the heat and stir in the cream. Pour the sauce over the seafood, scatter with the remaining cheese and place in a preheated oven at 190°C/375°F/gas mark 5 for 15 minutes. Serve immediately.

Pasticchio di Frutta di Mare

Seafood Pie
Serves 4

225 g/8 oz shortcrust pastry (basic pie crust)
25 g/1 oz/2 tbsp unsalted (sweet) butter
1 large onion, chopped
100 g/4 oz mushrooms, sliced
300 ml/½ pt/1¼ cups Basic White Sauce (see page 357)
150 ml/¼ pt/⅔ cup double (heavy) cream
Salt and freshly ground black pepper
15 ml/1 tbsp lemon juice
225 g/8 oz cooked peeled prawns (shrimp)
225 g/8 oz white fish, cooked and flaked
30 ml/2 tbsp chopped fresh parsley
100 g/4 oz/1 cup hard cheese, grated

Roll out the pastry and line a 23 cm/9 in pie dish. Prick the pastry with a fork and line with greaseproof (waxed) paper and baking beans. Bake in a preheated oven at 190°C/375°F/gas mark 5 for 10 minutes. Remove the paper and beans and continue baking for 5 minutes. Remove from the oven and set aside. Melt the butter and cook the onion for 5 minutes. Add the mushrooms and cook for a further 5 minutes. Drain off any excess liquid. Blend the white sauce, cream, salt, pepper and lemon juice and stir in the onion and mushrooms, prawns, flaked white fish and parsley. Pour into the pastry case (pie shell) and sprinkle over the grated cheese. Return the pie to the oven and bake for 15–20 minutes until brown on top and piping hot.

Gamberetti al Naturale

Simple Prawns

Serves 4

600 ml/1 pt/2½ cups water
300 ml/½ pt/1¼ cups white wine
15 ml/1 tbsp red wine vinegar
1 large onion, cut in half
2 cloves
3 carrots, sliced
Large bunch of fresh herbs
½ lemon, sliced
16 raw king prawns (jumbo shrimp),
  peeled
Cream of Fennel Sauce (see page
  362), to serve

Simmer all the ingredients except the prawns together in a large saucepan for 30 minutes and strain. Discard the vegetables. Return the stock to the heat and boil for 5 minutes to reduce. Add the prawns, lower the heat and poach for 5–6 minutes. Remove from the liquid with a slotted spoon and reserve the liquid for stock or soup the next day. Serve with Cream of Fennel Sauce.

Capesante alla Veneziana

Venetian Scallops

Serves 3–4

450 g/1 lb potatoes
Salt
60 ml/4 tbsp milk
25 g/1 oz/2 tbsp unsalted (sweet) butter
12 large shelled scallops
75 ml/5 tbsp olive oil
1 garlic clove, peeled and chopped
5 sprigs of fresh parsley, chopped
Salt and freshly ground black pepper
Juice of 1 lemon (optional)

Chop the potatoes roughly and place in a pan of salted water. Cook for 15–20 minutes until soft. Drain and mash, adding the milk and butter. Pipe the potatoes around the edge of an ovenproof dish and place under a hot grill (broiler) for 2–3 minutes until browned on the edges. Place the scallops in a large saucepan with the oil, garlic and parsley. Season with a little salt. Cover with a lid and cook for 5 minutes. Spoon the scallops into the centre of the potatoes and serve immediately, sprinkled with lemon juice if liked.

Tonno alla Griglia

Grilled Tuna

Serves 4

15 ml/1 tbsp olive oil
4 tuna steaks
Salt and freshly ground black pepper
10 ml/2 tsp chopped fresh tarragon
3 canned anchovy fillets
25 g/1 oz/2 tbsp unsalted (sweet)
  butter, softened
2.5 ml/½ tsp lemon juice
120 ml/4 fl oz/½ cup Tomato Sauce
  (see page 358)
Sprigs of parsley

Drizzle oil over the tuna in a shallow dish and season with salt and pepper. Sprinkle over half the tarragon and leave to marinate. Pound the anchovies and blend in the softened butter. Stir in the lemon juice and shape into a roll. Wrap in kitchen foil and chill. Heat the tomato sauce slowly. Place the tuna pieces on foil on a grill (broiler) rack. Top with slices of the anchovy butter and grill (broil) for 3 minutes on each side. Spoon over the sauce and garnish with the parsley.

Filetti di Sogliola in Salsa di Limetta

Sole Fillets in Lime Sauce
Serves 6

25 g/1 oz/2 tbsp unsalted (sweet) butter
2 celery sticks, finely chopped
50 g/2 oz/1 cup breadcrumbs
2.5 ml/½ tsp chopped fresh oregano
Finely grated rind and juice of 1 lime
6 sole fillets
15 ml/1 tbsp olive oil
Salt and freshly ground black pepper
250 ml/8 fl oz/1 cup fish stock
15 ml/1 tbsp cornflour (cornstarch)
100 g/4 oz white grapes, halved and seeded

Heat 15 ml/1 tbsp butter and add the celery and cook, stirring, for 5 minutes. Place the breadcrumbs into a mixing bowl and add the celery, oregano and lime rind. Blend well. Spoon equal amounts on to one side of each of the sole fillets, pressing it down with your fingers to help it adhere. Roll up the fish, beginning with the narrow end, and skewer each roll with a cocktail stick (toothpick). Heat the remaining butter with the olive oil in a frying pan (skillet) and cook the sole rolls for 6–8 minutes. Place the fish in a casserole dish (Dutch oven) and season with salt and pepper. Blend a little of the stock with the cornflour and pour into the frying pan. Add the remaining stock and the lime juice and bring to the boil, stirring, until thickened. Pour over the fish. Add the halved grapes and bake in a preheated oven at 180°C/ 350°F/gas mark 4 for 12 minutes.

Sforma di Acciughe

Anchovy Mousse
Serves 6–8

5 ml/1 tsp olive oil for greasing
15 g/½ oz/1 tbsp gelatine
120 ml/4 fl oz/½ cup white wine
2 egg yolks
Salt and freshly ground black pepper
2.5 ml/½ tsp dry mustard
120 ml/4 fl oz/½ cup olive oil
15 ml/1 tbsp lemon juice
50 g/2 oz/1 small can anchovies, drained and chopped
15 ml/1 tbsp snipped fresh chives
15 ml/1 tbsp chopped fresh parsley
8 hard-boiled (hard-cooked) eggs, chopped
250 ml/8 fl oz/1 cup Basic White Sauce (see page 357)
175 ml/6 fl oz/¾ cup double (heavy) cream, lightly whipped
2.5 ml/½ tsp cayenne
Thin slices cucumber, to garnish

Oil a mould (mold) and set aside. Place the gelatine in a small bowl and add the wine. Place the bowl over a saucepan of simmering water until the gelatine dissolves then remove from the heat. Place the egg yolks, salt, pepper and mustard in a bowl and whisk until they are blended. Gradually add the oil, whisking all the time. Whisk in the lemon juice a little at a time. Stir in the anchovies, chives, parsley, hard-boiled eggs and gelatine. Fold in the white sauce, cream, cayenne and season with salt and pepper. Pour the mixture into the mould and chill until set. Turn out on to a serving dish and garnish with the cucumber.

Tonno con Mandorle

Tuna Fish with Almonds
Serves 4

4 tuna steaks
Salt and freshly ground black pepper
15 ml/1 tbsp olive oil
50 g/2 oz/1 small can anchovy fillets,
drained
15 ml/1 tbsp oregano, chopped
50 g/2 oz/½ cup flaked (slivered) almonds

Place the tuna in a greased, shallow, flame-proof dish and season with salt and pepper. Pour over the oil and arrange the anchovies on top. Sprinkle over the oregano and almonds and cover with foil. Bake in a pre-heated oven at 190°C/375°F/gas mark 5 for 25 minutes.

Sogliola e Salsa Madera

Sole and Madeira Sauce
Serves 4

1 egg
60 ml/4 tbsp double (heavy) cream
30 ml/2 tbsp Madeira
Salt and freshly ground black pepper
30 ml/2 tbsp chopped fresh parsley
4 sole fillets
Butter for greasing
1 lemon, cut into wedges

Combine the egg, cream, Madeira, salt, a dash of pepper and the parsley. Place the sole fillets in a large buttered casserole dish (Dutch oven). Pour over the egg mixture and leave to stand, covered, for 1½ hours. Cook the fish and marinade in a pre-heated oven at 180°C/350°F/gas mark 4 for 20 minutes and serve with the lemon wedges.

Sogliola con Aglio e Pomodori

Sole with Garlic and Tomatoes
Serves 4

30 ml/2 tbsp olive oil
3 garlic cloves, crushed
3 tomatoes, skinned, seeded and
chopped
60 ml/4 tbsp tomato purée (paste)
15 ml/1 tbsp chopped fresh oregano
2.5 ml/½ tsp salt
Freshly ground black pepper
45 ml/3 tbsp plain (all-purpose) flour
4 sole fillets
25 g/1 oz/2 tbsp unsalted (sweet) butter

Heat the oil and fry (sauté) the garlic for 1 minute. Add the tomatoes, tomato purée, oregano, half the salt and some pepper. Stir well and reduce the heat to simmering. Cover the pan and cook for 30 minutes, stirring occasionally, until the sauce has thickened. Blend the flour and remaining salt on a plate. Dip the sole fillets in the flour to coat them and shake off any excess. Melt the butter in a frying pan (skillet) and add the fish fillets. Reduce the heat to moderate and fry (sauté) for 3 minutes on each side. Transfer the fillets to an ovenproof dish and pour over the sauce. Place in a preheated oven at 180°C/350°F/gas mark 4 for 20 minutes.

Rombo al Finocchi

Turbot with Fennel

Serves 4

1 fennel bulb, thinly sliced, reserving
  the green fronds for garnish
1 large onion, thinly sliced
50 g/2 oz/¼ cup unsalted (sweet) butter
1 chicken turbot, about 1.5 kg/3 lb
1 wineglass dry white wine
1 wineglass dry vermouth
Salt and freshly ground black pepper
300 ml/½ pt/1¼ cups double (heavy)
  cream
2 tomatoes, skinned, seeded and finely
  chopped

Fry (sauté) the fennel and onion in the butter for 5 minutes until softened and slightly golden in a large flameproof casserole (Dutch oven). Lay the turbot on top and pour over the wine and vermouth. Season with salt and pepper. Cover and transfer to a preheated oven at 200°C/400°F/gas mark 6 for about 30 minutes or until the turbot is tender. Carefully lift the fish out on to a warm serving plate. Keep warm. Stir the cream in to the pan with the tomatoes. Bring to the boil and boil rapidly, stirring, for 5 minutes until thickened. Season to taste. Carefully peel off the skin from the top of the turbot. Spoon the sauce over and serve.

Medaglioni di Cernia Calabresella

Calabrian-style Grouper Fillets

Serves 6

1 small aubergine (eggplant), finely
  diced
Salt
6 fillets Mediterranean grouper or sea
  bass, about 150 g/5 oz each
Plain (all-purpose) flour
Freshly ground black pepper
30 ml/2 tbsp olive oil
75 g/3 oz/⅓ cup unsalted (sweet) butter
50 g/2 oz/⅓ cup black olives, stoned
  (pitted) and sliced
3 tomatoes, skinned, seeded and
  chopped
15 ml/1 tbsp capers, chopped
75 ml/5 tbsp dry vermouth

Sprinkle the aubergine with salt in a colander and leave to stand for 30 minutes. Rinse with cold water, drain and dry on kitchen paper. Toss the fish in flour, seasoned with a little salt and pepper. Heat half the oil and butter in a large frying pan (skillet) and fry (sauté) the fish on both sides until golden and cooked through. Transfer to a warm serving dish and keep warm. Heat the remaining oil and butter in the frying pan. Add the aubergines and fry for 2 minutes, stirring. Add the remaining ingredients and simmer until the aubergine is tender and most of the liquid has evaporated. Season to taste. Spoon over the fish and serve straight away.

Vegetable Dishes

Italians set great store by the freshness of their vegetables, even to the extent of growing them in pots on their balconies. Aubergines, peppers, artichokes, courgettes – all kinds of wonderful produce are used in a vast array of dishes and thick vegetable sauces are used over pasta and on top of pizza.

Although not strictly a vegetable, the tomato plays an important part in Italian cookery. In the Vucceria market of Palermo, tomatoes are crushed, cooked and then dried in the sun. This turns them into a dark red solid paste called Estratto di Pomodoro. This is an ideal method of preserving the tomato for use throughout the year, and the technique is still used by some Southern Italian farmers today. This product, known as Conserva di Pomodor, started to be commercialised in the 1840s and sold in the markets where it is cut in slices and served on fresh fig leaves.

Whole or halved sun-dried tomatoes have become increasingly popular and are widely used as a condiment. They are available in packs or ready-soaked in jars of olive oil. Passata (sieved tomatoes) too is readily available in jars.

The wonderful thing about all Italian vegetable dishes is that they are bursting with colour and flavour.

Sformato di Asparagi

Asparagus Casserole

Serves 4

4 hard-boiled (hard-cooked) eggs
400 g/14 oz/1 large can asparagus spears
100 g/4 oz fresh or frozen peas
Salt and freshly ground black pepper
15 g/½ oz/1 tbsp unsalted (sweet) butter
295 g/10½ oz/1 large can condensed mushroom soup
50 g/2 oz/½ cup dry breadcrumbs

Slice the eggs. Drain the asparagus and put a layer in a casserole dish (Dutch oven). Add a layer of peas and a layer of sliced eggs. Sprinkle with salt and pepper. Dot with butter. Repeat until casserole is full. Spread over the mushroom soup and top with a layer of breadcrumbs. Bake in a preheated oven at 200°C/400°F/gas mark 6 for 25–30 minutes until brown.

Melanzane al Forno

Aubergine Bake
Serves 4–6

4 aubergines (eggplants), thinly sliced
10 ml/2 tsp salt
75 ml/5 tbsp olive oil
1 onion, chopped
900 g/2 lb spinach, chopped
5 ml/1 tsp grated nutmeg
450 g/1 lb courgettes (zucchini), sliced
*   and blanched*
25 g/1 oz/2 tbsp unsalted (sweet) butter
30 ml/2 tbsp plain (all-purpose) flour
450 ml/¾ pt/2 cups milk
50 g/2 oz/½ cup Parmesan cheese, grated
30 ml/2 tbsp chopped fresh parsley
Salt and freshly ground black pepper

Arrange the sliced aubergines on a large plate and sprinkle liberally with salt. Leave for 30 minutes, drain and rinse under cold water. Drain again and dry with kitchen paper. Fry (sauté) in half the oil until golden and drain on kitchen paper. Heat the remaining oil in a pan and cook the onion until translucent. Add the spinach and cook for 3 minutes, stirring occasionally. Strain off any excess liquid and season with the nutmeg. Place a layer of aubergine slices in the base of a greased casserole dish (Dutch oven) and cover with half the spinach and half the courgettes. Add a further layer of each vegetable finishing with a layer of aubergine. Melt the butter in a pan and stir in the flour. Cook for 1 minute and gradually blend in the milk, stirring continuously. Bring to the boil and simmer for 1 minute. Reduce the heat, add the Parmesan and parsley. Season to taste and pour over the vegetables. Cook in a preheated oven at 180°C/350°F/gas mark 4 for 30 minutes until brown and cooked through.

Carciofa con Zucchini con Ripieno di Mandorle

Almond Stuffed Courgettes
Serves 6

6 courgettes (zucchini), trimmed and
*   blanched*
60 ml/4 tbsp unsalted (sweet) butter,
*   melted*
15 ml/1 tbsp oil
1 large onion, chopped
75 g/3 oz/¾ cup ground almonds
120 ml/4 fl oz/½ cup double (heavy)
*   cream*
75 g/3 oz/1½ cups fresh breadcrumbs
75 g/3 oz/¾ cup hard cheese, grated
15 ml/1 tbsp chopped fresh oregano
Salt and freshly ground black pepper

Cut the courgettes in half lengthways and hollow out the flesh from the centres. Chop the flesh and allow to drain to extract as much juice as possible. Set aside. Grease an ovenproof dish with butter and add the courgettes in a single layer. Heat the oil and fry (sauté) the onion until soft but not brown. Stir in the courgette flesh and cook for 5 minutes. Remove from the heat and add the almonds, cream and half of the breadcrumbs. Blend the ingredients thoroughly. Stir in three-quarters of the cheese and the oregano. Season with salt and pepper and fill the courgette shells. Sprinkle over the remaining cheese and breadcrumbs and bake in a preheated oven at 200°C/400°F/gas mark 6 for 30 minutes until cooked through and brown on top.

Ripieno di Formaggio

Artichokes Stuffed with Cheese
Serves 4

50 g/2 oz/¼ cup Ricotta cheese
175 g/6 oz/1½ cups fine dry
*   breadcrumbs*
1 egg
2.5 ml/½ tsp chopped fresh oregano
Salt and freshly ground black pepper
4 globe artichokes
3 tomatoes, coarsely chopped
4 sprigs of fresh parsley

Blend the Ricotta cheese, breadcrumbs, egg and oregano together and season with salt and pepper. Remove the stems from the artichokes. Cut each artichoke in half crosswise, about 5 cm/2 in from the base. With a sharp knife scrape out and remove the hairy choke. Pack the prepared filling mixture tightly into the hollowed-out artichoke. Place the stuffed artichokes in a baking dish with 45 ml/3 tbsp water. Top with the chopped tomatoes and cook in a preheated oven at 180°C/350°F/gas mark 4 for 40 minutes or until the artichokes are tender and the leaves pull out easily. Garnish with the parsley.

Asparago con Panna Piccante

Asparagus with Pepper Cream
Serves 4

450 g/1 lb asparagus, cleaned
25 g/1 oz/2 tbsp unsalted (sweet)
*   butter, melted*
1.5 ml/¼ tsp cayenne
60 ml/4 tbsp single (light) cream
Salt and freshly ground black pepper
50 g/2 oz/½ cup Parmesan cheese,
*   grated*

Pour sufficient water into a frying pan (skillet) to give a depth of 2 cm/¾ in. Add a pinch of salt and bring to the boil. Add the asparagus spears and cook for 4–5 minutes until almost tender and drain, reserving the cooking liquid for further use as vegetable stock. Melt the butter in a saucepan and add the cayenne and the cream. Season with the salt and pepper. Pour over the asparagus and sprinkle over the Parmesan. Place under a hot grill (broiler) to brown.

Pasticcio di Asparagi e Pomodori

Asparagus and Tomato Pie
Serves 4

3 eggs
75 g/3 oz/1½ cups fresh breadcrumbs
175 ml/6 fl oz/¾ cup boiling milk
75 g/3 oz/¾ cup hard cheese, grated
25 g/1 oz/2 tbsp margarine, melted
45 ml/3 tbsp chopped fresh oregano
Salt and freshly ground black pepper
400 g/14 oz/1 large can of asparagus,
*   well-drained*
2 tomatoes, sliced

Separate the eggs and set aside. Place the breadcrumbs in a bowl and pour over the boiling milk. Leave to soak for 30 minutes. Add the cheese, margarine, oregano, egg yolks and seasoning. Beat the egg whites until stiff and fold into the mixture. Pour into an ovenproof pie dish or casserole (Dutch oven). Arrange the asparagus over the top and garnish with the sliced tomatoes. Bake for 25–30 minutes in a preheated oven at 200°C/400°F/gas mark 6. Serve hot or cold.

Finocchio Aromatizzato

Aromatic Fennel

Serves 4

2 fennel bulbs
12 small onions
2 garlic cloves, crushed
5 ml/1 tsp chopped fresh basil
5 ml/1 tsp chopped fresh thyme
1 bay leaf
15 ml/1 tbsp oil
Salt and freshly ground black pepper
90 ml/6 tbsp Chianti
3 tomatoes, skinned, peeled and
  chopped
30 ml/2 tbsp tomato purée (paste)
10 ml/2 tsp cornflour (cornstarch)
  blended with 15ml/1 tbsp water

Cut the fennel bulbs into quarters. Place the onions, garlic, basil, thyme, bay leaf and oil in a frying pan (skillet) and cook for 3 minutes. Add the fennel pieces and season with the salt and pepper. Stir in the chianti and tomatoes. Bring to the boil and add the tomato purée. Reduce the heat to low and cook for 30 minutes, stirring occasionally. Stir in the blended cornflour and cook, stirring, for 3 minutes to thicken the sauce. Discard the bay leaf and serve.

Pomodori al Burro

Buttered Tomatoes

Serves 4

4 beefsteak tomatoes
50 g/2 oz/¼ cup unsalted (sweet) butter
Salt and freshly ground black pepper
10 ml/2 tsp chopped fresh basil

Halve the tomatoes and place them in an ovenproof dish. Melt the butter and brush over the tomatoes. Season with the salt and freshly ground pepper. Grill (broil) for 2 minutes, brush again with butter, grill for a further 2 minutes. Sprinkle again with the pepper and garnish with the basil.

Melanzane con Fagioli e Formaggio

Aubergine and Haricot Beans with Cheese

Serves 4

100 g/4 oz/⅔ cup dried haricot (navy)
  beans, soaked overnight
2 aubergines (eggplants)
5 ml/1 tsp salt
45 ml/3 tbsp olive oil
100 g/4 oz Mozzarella cheese, grated
30 ml/2 tbsp chopped fresh basil
45 ml/3 tbsp passata (sieved tomatoes)
30 ml/2 tbsp Parmesan cheese, grated
2.5 ml/½ tsp cayenne

Soak the haricot beans overnight. Next day boil rapidly in plenty of water for 10 minutes then simmer until soft. Drain. Cut the aubergines crossways into 1 cm/½ in thick slices. Place on a flat dish and sprinkle with salt. Allow the aubergines to stand for 30 minutes. Wash, drain and dry thoroughly on kitchen paper. Heat the oil in a frying pan (skillet) and fry (sauté) a few slices at a time until golden brown on either side. Cover the base of an ovenproof dish with the aubergine slices. Add a layer of the drained haricot beans and cover with a layer of Mozzarella cheese, basil and then passata. Repeat the layers finishing with a layer of cheese. Sprinkle over the Parmesan cheese and dust with the cayenne. Bake in a preheated oven at 180°C/350°F/gas mark 4 for 20 minutes.

Torta di Asparagi

Asparagus Gateaux
Serves 6

2 × 400 g/2 × 14 oz/2 large cans
  asparagus spears
5 eggs
300 ml/½ pt/1¼ cups single (light) cream
100 g/4 oz/1 cup Gruyère (Swiss)
  cheese, grated
2.5 ml/½ tsp grated nutmeg
Salt and freshly ground black pepper
25 g/1 oz/2 tbsp unsalted (sweet) butter

Drain the cans of asparagus spears and cut
the tips off each spear. Reserve as a garnish. Place the remainder of the asparagus
in a blender or pound in a mortar. Stir in
the eggs, cream, cheese and nutmeg.
Season with the salt and pepper. Butter 6
ramekin dishes (custard cups) and divide
the mixture evenly among them. Place the
dishes in a baking tin (pan) and surround
with a little boiling water. Bake for 20
minutes in a preheated oven at 220°C/
425°F/gas mark 7 until set. Turn out on a
large platter and decorate with the
reserved asparagus spears.

Broccoli al Forno

Broccoli Bake
Serves 4

3 eggs
120 ml/4 fl oz/½ cup milk
120 ml/4 fl oz/½ cup single (light)
  cream
100 g/4 oz/1 cup hard cheese, grated
100 g/4 oz Mozzarella cheese, chopped
1 onion, chopped
275 g/10 oz frozen broccoli, thawed
  and chopped
25 cm/10 in pastry case (pie shell)

Beat the eggs, milk, cream, cheeses, and
onion together and blend with the chopped
broccoli. Pour into the unbaked pastry case
and cook in a preheated oven at 190°C/
375°F/gas mark 5 for 45 minutes until set
and golden. Allow to stand 5 minutes
before serving.

Carciofi in Salsa al Formaggio

Artichokes in Cheese Sauce
Serves 4

450 g/1 lb Jerusalem artichokes,
  scrubbed or scraped
15 ml/1 tbsp lemon juice
25 g/1 oz/2 tbsp unsalted (sweet) butter
30 ml/2 tbsp plain (all-purpose) flour
250 ml/8 fl oz/1 cup milk
120 ml/4 fl oz/½ cup single (light) cream
Salt and freshly ground black pepper
50 g/2 oz/½ cup hard cheese, grated
15 ml/1 tbsp breadcrumbs
30 ml/2 tbsp Parmesan cheese, grated

Cut the artichokes into chunks. Place in a
pan of cold water and stir in the lemon
juice. Bring to the boil and cook for 8 minutes or until tender. Drain and transfer to
an ovenproof dish. Melt the butter and stir
in the flour. Gradually stir in the milk until
smooth. Bring to the boil and cook gently
for 2 minutes, stirring all the time. Stir in
the cream, salt and pepper. Cook, stirring,
for 1 minute and add the hard cheese. Pour
the sauce over the artichokes and sprinkle
over the breadcrumbs and Parmesan
cheese. Bake in a preheated oven for 25
minutes at 180°C/350°F/gas mark 4.

Pasticcio di Melanzane

Aubergine Pie

Serves 4–6

4 aubergines (eggplants)
225 g/8 oz courgettes (zucchini)
5 ml/1 tsp salt
30 ml/2 tbsp plain (all-purpose) flour
60 ml/4 tbsp olive oil
30 ml/2 tbsp nut oil, such as walnut
3 tomatoes, skinned, seeded and
   chopped
30 ml/2 tbsp tomato purée (paste)
Salt and freshly ground black pepper
175 g/6 oz/1½ cups Padano cheese,
   grated
1 egg, beaten
250 ml/8 fl oz/1 cup single (light)
   cream
15 ml/1 tbsp chopped fresh parsley

Slice the aubergines and courgettes into
1 cm/½ in rounds. Layer the vegetables on
a dish and sprinkle salt between each layer.
Leave to stand for 30 minutes to remove
the bitterness. Rinse thoroughly and drain
well. Pat the vegetables with kitchen paper
to remove any excess liquid. Dust lightly
with flour. Heat a little of both oils in a frying pan (skillet) and cook the vegetables
on both sides, one layer at a time. Add
more oils as necessary. Leave to one side.
Place the tomatoes and tomato purée in a
saucepan and cook for 8 minutes, stirring
occasionally. Oil an ovenproof dish and
put a layer of vegetables on the base. Cover
with a layer of cheese and a layer of the
tomato. Repeat and season with the salt
and pepper. Beat the egg into the cream
and pour over the tomato. Sprinkle over
remaining cheese and bake in a preheated
oven at 180°C/350°F/gas mark 4 for 40
minutes. Garnish with chopped parsley.

Strati di Melanzane e Formaggio

Aubergine and Cheese Layer

Serves 4

1 large aubergine (eggplant), trimmed
   and cut into 8 slices
10 ml/2 tsp salt
30 ml/2 tbsp olive oil
2 shallots, chopped
3 tomatoes, skinned and chopped
45 ml/3 tbsp tomato purée (paste)
30 ml/2 tbsp chopped fresh basil
Freshly ground black pepper
275 g/10 oz Mozzarella cheese, sliced

Put the aubergine slices on a baking sheet
and sprinkle over the salt. Allow to stand
for 30 minutes, rinse and pat dry on
kitchen paper. Heat 15 ml/1 tbsp oil and
fry (sauté) the shallots for 2 minutes. Stir
in the tomatoes, tomato purée, chopped
basil and season with the pepper. Simmer
for 10 minutes. Brush the remaining oil
over the aubergine slices and grill (broil)
for 5 minutes, turning. Layer two slices of
aubergine and 2 slices of cheese to make 4
stacks, finishing with a cheese layer. Put
each mound on foil in the grill pan and
grill until the cheese is melting and just
turning brown. Transfer to warm plates
and spoon the sauce over. Serve straight
away.

Crostata di Verdure al Forno

Baked Vegetable Tart
Serves 4–6

1 red (bell) pepper, cut in thin strips
1 yellow (bell) pepper, cut in thin strips
2 courgettes (zucchini), cut in thin strips
2 carrots, cut in thin strips
100 g/4 oz thin asparagus spears
45 ml/3 tbsp olive oil
Salt and freshly ground black pepper
3 garlic cloves, peeled and finely chopped
225 g/8 oz puff pastry (paste)
15 ml/1 tbsp chopped sun-dried tomatoes in oil

Place all the vegetables on the base of a pizza tin (pan). Brush with oil, season and sprinkle with the chopped garlic. Heat the grill (broiler) and cook under a moderate heat for 15 minutes, turning occasionally. Allow to cool. Roll out the pastry to fit the pizza tin and spread with the sun-dried tomatoes. Place the pastry, tomato side down, on top of the vegetables and brush with a little oil. Bake in a preheated oven at 230°C/450°F/gas mark 8 for 15–20 minutes until the pastry is puffed and brown. Turn out of the tin so that the vegetables are on the top of the pizza and serve in wedges.

Broccoli con Salsa di Azuchi Rossi

Broccoli with Red Bean Sauce
Serves 4

225 g/8 oz broccoli florets
30 ml/2 tbsp oil
1 red (bell) pepper, chopped
3 spring onions (scallions), chopped
75 g/3 oz/³⁄₄ cup cooked aduki beans or a 425 g/15 oz/large can, drained
175 ml/6 fl oz/³⁄₄ cup vegetable stock
10 ml/2 tsp cornflour (cornstarch)

Steam the broccoli for 8 minutes and transfer to a warmed serving dish. Heat the oil in a large pan and fry (sauté) the pepper and spring onions until soft. Add the red beans and stock and cook for 3 minutes, stirring. Blend the cornflour with 15 ml/ 1 tbsp of water and add to the pan. Cook for 1 minute. Pour the sauce over the broccoli and serve at once.

Cavolo con Salsa all'Italiana

Cabbage with Italian Sauce
Serves 4

30 ml/2 tbsp oil
2 onions, chopped
1 small cabbage, shredded
5 ml/1 tsp paprika
Salt and freshly ground black pepper
400 g/14 oz/1 large can chopped
tomatoes

Heat the oil in a large frying pan (skillet) and fry (sauté) the onions and cabbage together. Season to taste with the paprika, salt and pepper and stir in the tomatoes. Cover with a lid and simmer for 20 minutes.

Carote con Salsa Piccante

Carrots with a Spicy Sauce
Serves 4

450 g/1 lb carrots, thinly sliced
30 ml/2 tbsp olive oil
1 small onion, finely chopped
15 ml/1 tbsp plain (all-purpose) flour
300 ml/½ pt/1¼ cups vegetable stock
Freshly ground black pepper
5 canned anchovy fillets, chopped
30 ml/2 tbsp tomato purée (paste)
2.5 ml/½ tsp chopped fresh basil
3 capers, chopped
1.5 ml/¼ tsp cayenne
Salt

Boil a pan of salted water and add the carrots. Cook for 8 minutes until tender. Melt the oil in a saucepan and fry (sauté) the onion. Stir in the flour and cook for 1 minute. Gradually stir in the stock. Season

well with the pepper and add the chopped anchovies, tomato purée and basil. Simmer for 5 minutes until the sauce is well blended and stir in the chopped capers and cayenne. Taste and season with salt if necessary. Drain the cooked carrots and spoon into a warmed serving dish. Pour the sauce into a jug and serve separately.

Zucchini al Forno con Melanzane

Courgettes Baked with Aubergines
Serves 4–6

2 aubergines (eggplants) halved
Salt and freshly ground black pepper
6 large courgettes (zucchini)
60 ml/4 tbsp vegetable oil
1 small onion, chopped
1 garlic clove, chopped
60 ml/4 tbsp tomato purée (paste)
150 ml/¼ pt/⅔ cup vegetable stock
15 ml/1 tbsp breadcrumbs, toasted

Sprinkle the aubergines with salt. Place them, cut sides down, on kitchen paper to drain for 30 minutes. Cut into thick slices, lengthways, and set aside. Cut the courgettes into 1 cm/½ in chunks and set aside. Pour half the oil in a large pan and fry (sauté) the aubergine slices for 3 minutes. Place in an ovenproof dish and sprinkle with salt and pepper. Repeat the process with the courgettes. Fry the onion and garlic together and arrange over the courgettes. Blend the tomato purée and stock together, season with salt and pepper and pour over the courgettes. Sprinkle with the breadcrumbs and bake in a preheated oven at 180°C/350°F/gas mark 4 for 30 minutes, until the topping is crisp and golden.

Crostata di Zucchini

Courgette Tart
Serves 4

Pastry (paste):
2.5 ml/½ tsp cumin seeds
2.5 ml/½ tsp coriander (cilantro) seeds
2.5 ml/½ tsp poppy seeds
225 g/8 oz/2 cups plain (all-purpose)
  flour
Pinch of salt
Pinch of paprika
100 g/4 oz/½ cup margarine

Filling:
30 ml/2 tbsp oil
225 g/8 oz courgettes (zucchini), thinly
  sliced in long strips
100 g/4 oz streaky bacon, rinded and
  diced
2 eggs
15 ml/1 tbsp made mustard
250 ml/8 fl oz/1 cup milk

Roughly grind the cumin, coriander and poppy seeds. Put the flour in a bowl and add the salt, ground spices and paprika. Rub in the margarine until the mixture resembles breadcrumbs. Add enough water to mix to a firm dough. Knead for 1 minute. Wrap in clingfilm (plastic wrap) and chill for 30 minutes. Roll out the pastry and line a 20 cm/8 in square flan tin (pie pan). Line with greaseproof (waxed) paper and baking beans and bake in a preheated oven at 200°C/400°F/gas mark 6 for 15 minutes. Remove the paper and beans and return to the oven for 5 minutes. Reduce the oven heat to 180°C/350°F/gas mark 4. Heat the oil in a frying pan (skillet) and fry (sauté) the courgettes and bacon for 2 minutes. Arrange in the pastry case (pie shell). Beat the eggs and mustard together. Blend in the milk and pour the mixture over the courgettes and bacon. Bake for 30 minutes until set.

Rape alla Trentina

Trentino Turnips
Serves 4

1 kg/2¼ lb small turnips, peeled but
  left whole
Salt and freshly ground black pepper
60 ml/4 tbsp olive oil
10 ml/2 tsp sugar

Place the turnips in a pan and just cover with water. Add a little salt, bring to the boil and simmer gently for about 10 minutes or until tender. Drain and leave to cool, then slice the turnips into thin strips. Heat the oil in a separate pan, then add the sugar and cook gently until it begins to colour slightly. Do not allow it to burn or become too dark. Add the turnips, stir well to coat with the sugar and season with pepper. Cook gently for a further 10 minutes then serve at once.

Corona di Carote

Carrot Ring
Serves 4

450 g/1 lb carrots, sliced and cooked
1 small onion, finely chopped
45 ml/3 tbsp milk
5 ml/1 tsp salt
3 eggs, well beaten
15 ml/1 tbsp melted butter

Mix the carrots, onion, milk and salt together and beat in the eggs. Butter a deep ring mould (mold) and set in a shallow pan of water. Spoon the carrot mixture into the mould and bake in a preheated oven for 40 minutes at 180°C/350°F/gas mark 4.

Pasticcio di Formaggio e Pomodori

Cheese and Tomato Pie

Serves 4

3 eggs
25g/1 oz/2 tbsp margarine
75 g/3 oz/1½ cups breadcrumbs
150 ml/¼ pt/⅔ cup boiling milk
400 g/14 oz/1 large can chopped
*   tomatoes*
25 g/1 oz/2 tbsp hard cheese, grated
45 ml/3 tbsp chopped fresh parsley
Salt and freshly ground black pepper
2 tomatoes, sliced

Separate the eggs and set aside. Place the margarine and breadcrumbs in a bowl and pour over the boiling milk. Leave to soak for 30 minutes. Add the chopped tomatoes, cheese, parsley, egg yolks and seasoning and mix thoroughly. Whisk the egg whites until stiff and fold into the mixture. Pour into a greased soufflé dish. Garnish with the sliced tomatoes and bake in a preheated oven at 200°C/400°F/gas mark 6 for 25–30 minutes. Serve hot when set and the top is brown.

Radicchio, Cacio e Uova

Radicchio, Cheese and Eggs

Serves 4–6

4 radicchio heads, each halved
1 large onion, chopped
45 ml/3 tbsp olive oil
2 large celery sticks, chopped
3 carrots, finely chopped
Salt and freshly ground black pepper
2 eggs, beaten
50 g/2 oz/½ cup Parmesan cheese,
*   grated*
30 ml/2 tbsp chopped fresh basil

Place the radicchio in a large pan of boiling, salted water and cook for 8–10 minutes. Fry (sauté) the chopped onion in the oil with the celery and carrots. Cook, stirring, for 5 minutes. Drain the radicchio and squeeze out the excess water. Roughly chop and add to the carrots and celery. Cook for 3 minutes. Beat the eggs, cheese and basil together, season with salt and pepper and pour over the vegetables. Mix together and cook gently until scrambled. Serve hot.

Zucchini con Zenzero e Mandorle

Courgettes with Ginger and Almonds

Serves 4

15 ml/1 tbsp vegetable oil
45 ml/3 tbsp blanched almonds
1 small onion, chopped
5 ml/1 tsp finely chopped fresh root
*   ginger*
450 g/1 lb courgettes (zucchini), sliced
*   thinly*
30 ml/2 tbsp lemon juice
15 ml/1 tbsp chopped fresh oregano

Heat the oil and add the almonds. Cook for 2 minutes until just turning brown. Drain and set aside. Add the onion and ginger to the pan and cook for 4 minutes to soften the onions. Add the courgettes with the lemon juice and cook for 5 minutes, stirring. Return the almonds to the pan and blend in the oregano. Cook for 2 minutes and serve.

Crostata di Zucchini e Pomodori

Courgette and Tomato Tart

Serves 4

30 ml/2 tbsp olive oil
2 onions, sliced
15 ml/1 tbsp caster (superfine) sugar
3 large tomatoes, thinly sliced
2 courgettes (zucchini), thinly sliced
10 ml/2 tsp chopped fresh oregano
Salt and freshly ground black pepper
A few oregano leaves, to garnish
175 g/6 oz shortcrust pastry (basic pie crust)

Heat the oil in a saucepan and fry (sauté) the onions for 3 minutes until translucent and beginning to brown. Sprinkle with sugar and add 45 ml/3 tbsp water. Simmer until tender. Spoon the onion mixture into a shallow 20 cm/8 in round sandwich tin. Arrange the sliced tomatoes and sliced courgettes in an overlapping layer. Season with the salt and pepper and sprinkle with the chopped oregano. Roll out the pastry to a 25 cm/10 in round and place over the vegetables. Fold the edges over the side of the tin and trim to fit. Place the sandwich tin on a baking sheet and cook in a pre-heated oven at 200°C/400°F/gas mark 6 for 25 minutes until the pastry is brown. Turn the tart out on to a serving dish and scatter over the oregano leaves. The tart can be served hot or cold.

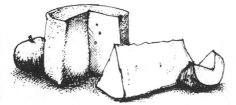

Patate al Formaggio

Cheese Potatoes

Serves 4

5 large potatoes, scrubbed
75 ml/5 tbsp hot milk
25 g/1 oz/2 tbsp unsalted (sweet) butter
Salt and freshly ground black pepper
100 g/4 oz/1 cup hard cheese, grated

Cook the potatoes in a large pan of boiling water. Peel the cooked potatoes and, while still very hot, cut into chunks and place in a large bowl. Add the milk, butter and seasoning and mash together. Add the grated cheese and spoon the mixture into an ovenproof dish. Bake in a preheated oven at 190°C/375°F/gas mark 5 for 20 minutes.

Verdure Misto Cotte

Cooked Mixed Vegetables

Serves 4

15 g/½ oz/1 tbsp unsalted (sweet) butter
900 g/2 lb carrots, diced
2 celery sticks, diced
2 potatoes, diced
1 onion, finely chopped
1 bay leaf
30 ml/2 tbsp sherry
Large bunch of fresh herbs

Place the butter in a saucepan and when hot fry (sauté) the vegetables for 3 minutes. Add the remaining ingredients and continue cooking until tender. Remove the bunch of herbs and bay leaf before serving.

Zucchini con Mostarda Piccante

Courgettes with Spicy Mustard

Serves 4

450g/1 lb courgettes (zucchini)
30 ml/2 tbsp tomato purée (paste)
15 ml/1 tbsp lemon juice
30 ml/2 tbsp white wine vinegar
2.5 ml/½ tsp cayenne
10 ml/2 tsp made mustard
5 ml/1 tsp chopped fresh sage
30 ml/2 tbsp olive oil

Trim and cut the courgettes into 5 cm/ 2 in pieces. In a small bowl blend the tomato purée with the lemon juice, white wine vinegar, cayenne, ready-made mustard and sage. Beat in the olive oil. Arrange the courgette pieces in a shallow ovenproof dish and brush over with the sauce. Cover with foil and place in a preheated oven for 15 minutes at 190°C/ 375°F/gas mark 5.

Zucca Fritta

Fried Pumpkin

Serves 4–6

550 g/1¼ lb pumpkin, peeled, seeded and sliced
Salt
500 ml/17 fl oz/2¼ cups milk
2 eggs, beaten
100 g/4 oz/½ cup unsalted (sweet) butter
30 ml/2 tbsp oil
45 ml/3 tbsp plain (all-purpose) flour
60 ml/4 tbsp stale breadcrumbs

Place the pumpkin slices in a pan, sprinkle with salt, cover with milk and bring to the boil. Simmer for about 10 minutes until tender, then drain and leave to cool. Season the eggs with salt. Heat the butter and oil in a heavy-based pan. Quickly dip each slice of pumpkin into the flour, then into the egg, then into the breadcrumbs, and fry (sauté) until crisp and brown on both sides. Drain on kitchen paper and serve at once.

Patate Arrostite con Crema

Creamy Potato Bake

Serves 4

900 g/2 lb potatoes, sliced
600 ml/1 pt/2½ cups salted water
2 garlic cloves, crushed
75 g/3 oz Mozzarella cheese, diced
Salt and freshly ground black pepper
150 ml/¼ pt/⅔ cup double (heavy) cream
150 ml/¼ pt/⅔ cup milk
50 g/2 oz/½ cup hard cheese, grated

Boil the sliced potatoes for 8 minutes in the salted water. Drain and layer in an ovenproof dish. Sprinkle over the crushed garlic and the Mozzarella cheese. Season with the salt and pepper. Blend the cream and milk together and pour over the potatoes. Sprinkle with the grated cheese and bake in a preheated oven for 45 minutes at 190°C/375°F/gas mark 5 until set and brown on the top.

Finocchio in Vino Bianco

Fennel in White Wine
Serves 4–6

2 large fennel bulbs, trimmed
½ bottle white wine
30 ml/2 tbsp olive oil
30 ml/2 tbsp tomato purée (paste)
1 bay leaf
5 ml/1 tsp chopped fresh basil
15 ml/1 tbsp chopped fresh parsley

Cut each fennel bulb into thin slices. Combine all the ingredients except the parsley in a saucepan and bring to the boil. Simmer for 12 minutes. Remove the fennel, place in a serving dish and keep warm Bring the sauce back to the boil and reduce the liquid by simmering until it has thickened. Pour the sauce over the fennel. Sprinkle with the parsley and serve.

Finocchio al Forno

Baked Fennel
Serves 4

4 fennel bulbs
225 g/8 oz courgettes (zucchini), sliced
1 green (bell) pepper, sliced
30ml/2 tbsp olive oil
15 ml/1 tbsp chopped fresh sage
30 ml/2 tbsp lemon juice
1 garlic clove, crushed
Salt and freshly ground black pepper

Slice each fennel bulb, reserving the green fronds for garnishing, and place in an ovenproof dish. Add the sliced courgettes and pepper. Blend the oil, sage, lemon juice and garlic and brush over the vegetables. Season with the salt and pepper and bake in a preheated oven, uncovered, at 200°C/400°F/gas mark 6 for 35 minutes. Garnish with the fennel fronds and serve.

Patate con Origano e Olive

Oregano and Olive Potatoes
Serves 4

15 g/½ oz/1 tbsp unsalted (sweet)
butter
15 ml/1 tbsp olive oil
900 g/2 lb potatoes, thinly sliced
1 large onion, sliced
2 garlic cloves, crushed
Salt and freshly ground black pepper
1 red (bell) pepper, diced
1 green (bell) pepper, diced
30 ml/2 tbsp black olives, halved and
stoned (pitted)
15 ml/1 tbsp chopped fresh oregano

Melt the butter and oil in a large saucepan and add the potatoes, onions, garlic, salt and pepper. Cook, stirring frequently, for 15 minutes until the potatoes are brown on the edges. Add the red and green peppers and continue cooking for 8–10 minutes. Stir in the olives and cook for a further 5 minutes. Remove from the heat, sprinkle over the chopped oregano and serve.

Finocchio e Pomodori al Forno

Fennel and Tomato Bake
Serves 4–6

900 g/2 lb potatoes, thinly sliced
1 fennel bulb with fronds
3 tomatoes, skinned and chopped
1 garlic clove, crushed
150 ml/¼ pt/⅔ cup vegetable or
*   chicken stock*
Salt and freshly ground black pepper

Cook the sliced potatoes in boiling water for 3 minutes. Thinly slice the fennel and add to the water. Continue cooking for 2 minutes and drain well. Blend the tomatoes, garlic, stock and seasoning together. Layer the blanched vegetables in a large shallow dish and pour over the stock mixture. Cover with foil. Cook in a preheated oven at 180°C/350°F/gas mark 4 for 1¼ hours. Remove the foil and garnish with the fennel fronds.

Patate con Zafferano e Finocchio al Forno

Baked Potatoes with Saffron and Fennel
Serves 4–6

900 g/2 lb potatoes
2 fennel bulbs
45 ml/3 tbsp olive oil
5 ml/1 tsp fennel seeds, lightly crushed
5 garlic cloves, peeled but left whole
Salt and freshly ground black pepper
2.5 ml/½ tsp saffron powder
45 ml/3 tbsp vegetable stock
30 ml/2 tbsp red wine

Cut the potatoes into 5 cm/2 in pieces. Trim the feathery tops from the fennel and chop finely. Cut each bulb into thick slices. Put the oil and fennel seeds into a baking tin (pan) and add the potatoes, fennel and garlic cloves. Season with salt and pepper. Stir the saffron into the stock and wine. Pour into the tin. Cover with foil and bake in a preheated oven at 200°C/400°F/gas mark 6 for 30 minutes. Remove the foil and cook, uncovered, for a further 30 minutes until brown. Sprinkle with the chopped fennel fronds before serving.

Patate al Parmigiano

Parmesan Potatoes
Serves 4

4 potatoes, sliced thinly
Salt
100 g/4 oz/½ cup Ricotta cheese
15 ml/1 tbsp chopped fresh parsley
2.5 ml/½ tsp grated nutmeg
45 ml/3 tbsp Parmesan cheese, grated
1 egg yolk, beaten

Put the sliced potatoes in a pan of salted water and boil for 6 minutes. Drain and leave to cool. Place the Ricotta cheese, parsley, nutmeg and Parmesan cheese in a bowl with the beaten egg yolk. Blend to a stiff paste. Arrange the potatoes in an ovenproof dish. Spread with the cheese and egg mixture and cook in a preheated oven at 190°C/375°F/gas mark 5 for 25 minutes.

Pizza di Patate

Pizza Potatoes
Serves 2

2 large potatoes, scrubbed
400 g/14 oz/1 large can chopped
   tomatoes
1 small green (bell) pepper, thinly
   sliced
100 g/4 oz Mozzarella cheese, cut in
   slices

Cut the potatoes in half and then into quarters, then eighths. Cook the wedges in boiling, salted water for 8 minutes or until tender. Arrange the wedges in an ovenproof dish. Pour over the tomatoes and add the green pepper slices. Top with the Mozzarella slices and place under a hot grill (broiler) for 5 minutes until the cheese has melted.

Zucchini in Agrodolce

Sweet-and-sour Courgettes
Serves 6

900 g/2 lb courgettes (zucchini), sliced
Salt and freshly ground black pepper
75 ml/5 tbsp olive oil
1.5 ml/¼ tsp ground cinnamon
60 ml/4 tbsp white wine vinegar
30 ml/2 tbsp sugar

Place the courgettes in a colander, sprinkle with salt and leave for 30 minutes. Rinse, then pat dry with kitchen paper. Heat the oil in a large pan and cook the courgettes over a low heat until almost tender. Add the cinnamon, wine vinegar and sugar and season generously with pepper. Continue to cook, stirring frequently, until most of the sauce has evaporated. Season to taste with salt and pepper before serving.

Gnocchi con Spinaci

Spinach Gnocchi
Serves 4

450 g/1 lb spinach
5 ml/1 tsp salt
50 g/2 oz/¼ cup unsalted (sweet) butter
1 onion, very finely chopped
225 g/8 oz/1 cup Ricotta cheese
2.5 ml/½ tsp freshly ground black
   pepper
2 eggs
60 ml/4 tbsp grated Parmesan cheese
100 g/4 oz/1 cup plain (all-purpose)
   flour
50 g/2 oz/¼ cup butter, melted

Wash the spinach, shake off excess water and place in a large saucepan with 2.5 ml/½ tsp salt. Cover with a lid. Cook gently for 8 minutes. Remove the pan from the heat and drain. Transfer the spinach to a chopping board and chop finely. Melt the butter in a large saucepan and cook the onion, stirring occasionally, for 5 minutes. Add the chopped spinach, Ricotta, the remaining salt and the pepper. Reduce the heat to very low and cook for 5 minutes, stirring. Remove from the heat and beat in the eggs, half the Parmesan and the flour. Cool, then chill for 2 hours. Turn the mixture on to a floured board and roll small teaspoonfuls into balls. Pour 15 ml/1 tbsp melted butter into a shallow dish and sprinkle with 15 ml/1 tbsp of the remaining Parmesan cheese. Bring a large pan of salted water to the boil and simmer the gnocchi a few at a time until they rise to the surface. Drain and place in the prepared dish. Pour the remaining melted butter and cheese over the gnocchi and grill (broil) for 5 minutes until brown.

Finocchio Roti

Roasted Fennel
Serves 4

4 fennel bulbs
30ml/2 tbsp olive oil
30 ml/2 tbsp lemon juice
1 garlic clove, crushed
Salt and freshly ground black pepper
15 ml/1 tbsp chopped fresh parsley

Trim the fennel, saving the fronds for garnish. Cut each bulb in half lengthwise and place in an ovenproof dish . Mix together the oil, lemon juice and garlic and brush over the fennel. Season with the salt and pepper and bake, uncovered, in a preheated oven at 200°C/400°F/gas mark 6 for 35 minutes. Sprinkle with the parsley before serving.

Verdure in Salsa Verde

Vegetables in Green Sauce
Serves 4

45 ml/3 tbsp oil
4 large carrots, chopped
450 g/1 lb potatoes, chopped
2 onions, chopped
2 large green (bell) peppers, finely
*   chopped*
2 garlic cloves, crushed
15 ml/1 tbsp chopped fresh basil
1 bay leaf
120 ml/4 fl oz/½ cup white wine
Salt and freshly ground black pepper
25 g/1 oz/2 tbsp unsalted (sweet) butter
10 ml/2 tsp cornflour (cornstarch)
*   dissolved in 15 ml/1 tbsp water*
15 ml/1 tbsp chopped fresh parsley

Heat the oil in a frying pan (skillet) and cook the carrots and potatoes for 5 minutes until browned, turning occasionally. Remove from the pan. Add the onions, green peppers, garlic, basil and bay leaf to the pan and cook for 2 minutes. Stir in the wine and bring to the boil. Return the carrots and potatoes to the pan and baste them with the sauce. Reduce the heat, add seasoning and cook gently for 30 minutes, turning regularly. Add the butter to the pan and stir in the blended cornflour. Cook, stirring for 3 minutes. Discard the bay leaf, sprinkle the parsley over and serve.

Pomodori Ripieni

Stuffed Tomatoes
Serves 4

4 large tomatoes
15 ml/1 tbsp olive oil
1 onion, chopped
1 garlic clove, crushed
75 ml/5 tbsp cooked rice
15 ml/1 tbsp chopped fresh parsley
75 g/3 oz/1½ cups fresh breadcrumbs
Salt and freshly ground black pepper
15 g/½ oz/1 tbsp unsalted (sweet)
*   butter*

Cut the top off the tomatoes and scoop out the centres. Place the shells in an ovenproof dish. Heat the oil in a frying pan (skillet) and fry (sauté) the onion and garlic. Add the cooked rice and the scooped out tomato flesh. Stir in the parsley and breadcrumbs. Season to taste and spoon into the tomatoes. Dot with tiny amounts of butter and replace the lids. Bake in a preheated oven at 200°C/400°F/gas mark 6 for 12–15 minutes.

Verdure alla Siciliana

Sicilian Vegetables

Serves 4

60 ml/4 tbsp olive oil
2 large onions, sliced
2 garlic cloves, crushed
1 red (bell) pepper, cut in strips
1 green (bell) pepper cut in strips
1 aubergine (eggplant), cut in strips
2 courgettes (zucchini), sliced
3 tomatoes, skinned and roughly
*   chopped*
Salt and freshly ground black pepper

Heat the oil in a large pan and fry (sauté) the onions until translucent. Add the crushed garlic and the red and green peppers. Cook for 10 minutes. Add the remaining ingredients to the pan, cover and simmer for 15–20 minutes, stirring occasionally. Season to taste.

Carote Piccante

Spiced Carrots

Serves 4

4 carrots, grated
1 onion, chopped
Salt
15 g/½ oz/1 tbsp unsalted (sweet)
*   butter*
25 g/1 oz/¼ cup plain (all-purpose)
*   flour*
10 ml/2 tsp sugar
1.5 ml/¼ tsp cayenne
15 ml/1 tbsp wine or tarragon vinegar
15 ml/1 tbsp chopped fresh parsley

Cook the carrots and onion in boiling, salted water for 5 minutes. Drain, turn into a warm dish, keep warm and reserve the liquid. Heat the butter in a saucepan, blend in the flour and cook for 1 minute. Gradually add enough of the carrot liquid to make a smooth sauce, stirring all the time. Stir in the sugar, cayenne and vinegar. Pour over the carrots and onion and garnish with the chopped parsley.

Patate con Olive

Potatoes with Olives

Serves 4

15 ml/1 tbsp olive oil
15 g/½ oz/1 tbsp unsalted (sweet)
*   butter*
2 garlic cloves, crushed
900 g/2 lb potatoes, roughly chopped
5 ml/1 tsp salt
2.5 ml/½ tsp freshly ground black
*   pepper*
120 ml/4 fl oz/½ cup vegetable stock
15 ml/1 tbsp chopped fresh oregano
12 stoned (pitted) olives, halved

Heat the oil and butter in a large saucepan and fry (sauté) the crushed garlic. Add the potatoes to the pan with the salt, pepper, stock and oregano. Blend well, bring to the boil and reduce the heat. Simmer for 30 minutes until the sauce is thick. Cool for 5 minutes. Pour into a blender and blend until smooth. Stir in the olives before serving.

Cavolo Rosso

Red Cabbage
Serves 4–6

30 ml/2 tbsp olive oil
1 large onion, thinly sliced
75 g/3 oz prosciutto
1 kg/2¼ lb red cabbage, shredded
60 ml/4 tbsp red wine
2.5 ml/½ tsp grated nutmeg
Salt and freshly ground black pepper

Heat the olive oil in a large saucepan and fry (sauté) the onion for 1 minute. Stir in the prosciutto and cook for 2 minutes. Add the red cabbage and cook, stirring frequently, for 3 minutes. Pour in the red wine and add the nutmeg, salt and pepper. Cover with a lid and cook slowly for 30 minutes.

Corona di Spinaci

Spinach Ring
Serves 4

275 g/10 oz spinach
250 ml/8 fl oz/1 cup milk
5 eggs, lightly beaten
1.5 ml/¼ tsp grated nutmeg
1.5 ml/¼ tsp salt
1.5 ml/¼ tsp freshly ground black pepper
5 ml/1 tsp butter for greasing
Carrots and peas, to serve

Wash the spinach well, drain and chop. Heat the milk until almost boiling and pour slowly over the beaten eggs. Stir in the nutmeg, salt and pepper. Stir in the spinach. Pour into a greased ring mould (mold) in a pan of hot water. Bake in a preheated oven at 180°C/350°F/gas mark 4 for 30 minutes, or until firm. Loosen around the edges and turn out. Fill the centre with freshly cooked carrots and peas.

Verdure in Intingolo

Italian Vegetables
Serves 4

100 g/4 oz/½ cup unsalted (sweet)
*   butter*
45 ml/3 tbsp vegetable oil
4 onions, sliced
3 large yellow and red (bell) peppers,
*   cut into strips*
1 large courgette (zucchini), peeled
*   and cut into thin rounds*
400 g/14 oz/1 large can tomatoes,
*   drained and coarsely chopped*
1 celery stick, chopped
60 ml/4 tbsp white wine vinegar
Salt and freshly ground black pepper

Heat the butter and oil and fry (sauté) the onions until soft but not brown. Add the peppers, courgette, tomatoes, celery and wine vinegar, stir well and season with salt and pepper. Bring to the boil, cover and simmer very gently for 40 minutes, stirring frequently and adding a little water if the mixture becomes too dry. Serve piping hot.

Pomodori in Umido

Tomato Stew

Serves 4

25 g/1 oz/2 tbsp unsalted (sweet) butter
30 ml/2 tbsp olive oil
1 large onion, thinly sliced
2 garlic cloves, crushed
3 red (bell) peppers, sliced thinly
3 tomatoes, skinned, seeded and
*   roughly chopped*
5 ml/1 tsp chopped fresh basil
Salt and freshly ground black pepper
2.5 ml/½ tsp cayenne
1 bay leaf

Heat the butter and oil in a saucepan and fry (sauté) the onion and garlic for 5 minutes. Add the red peppers and tomatoes, cover the pan with foil or a lid and reduce the heat. Simmer gently for 12 minutes and stir in the remaining ingredients. Simmer, uncovered, for a further 20 minutes.

Verdura con Gliodori

Herb Vegetables

Serves 4

900 g/2 lb carrots, diced
2 celery sticks, diced
2 potatoes, diced
1 onion, finely chopped
15 g/½ oz/1 tbsp unsalted (sweet) butter
1 bay leaf
30 ml/2 tbsp dry sherry
Large bunch of mixed herbs

Fry (sauté) the vegetables in the butter for 5 minutes, stirring. Add the remaining ingredients, cover and continue cooking until tender, stirring occasionally. Remove all the herbs before serving.

Funghi con Spinaci

Spinach Mushrooms

Serves 4

12 large open cap mushrooms, peeled
*   if necessary*
350 g/12 oz leaf spinach
15 ml/1 tbsp olive oil
1 small red onion, chopped
1 garlic clove, chopped
225 g/8 oz/2 cups mature Grana
*   Padano, Pecorino or Cacietto*
*   cheese, grated*
2.5 ml/½ tsp chopped fresh sage
1 yellow (bell) pepper, cut in chunks
1 red (bell) pepper, cut in chunks
1 green (bell) pepper, cut in chunks
5 ml/1 tsp unsalted (sweet) butter
Chopped parsley, to garnish

Remove the stalks from the mushrooms, chop finely and leave to one side. Put the spinach in a large saucepan. Cover with boiling water and allow to stand for 2 minutes. Drain the leaves, squeezing out as much moisture as you can. Finely chop the leaves and set aside. Heat the oil in a pan and fry (sauté) the onion and garlic for 3–4 minutes until brown. Add the mushroom stalks and spinach. Stir in the cheese and sage and blend well. Cook for 1 minute. Divide the mixture between the mushroom caps. Grease an ovenproof dish with the butter and put in the chunks of peppers. Arrange the mushrooms over the top and cover with kitchen foil. Bake in a preheated oven at 200°C/400°F/gas mark 6 for 20 minutes until the vegetables are tender. Garnish with parsley and serve.

Fagiolini al Burro

Buttered French Beans

Serves 4

Salt
450 g/1 lb French (green) beans,
trimmed
15 g/½ oz/1 tbsp butter
1 onion, chopped
1 garlic clove, chopped
15 g/1 tbsp chopped fresh parsley
15 ml/1 tbsp grated Parmesan cheese

Bring a pan of salted water to the boil and add the French beans. Lower the heat and simmer gently for 6 minutes or until tender. Heat the butter in a frying pan (skillet) and cook the onion and garlic for 5 minutes until browned. Lower the heat, season to taste and stir in the parsley. Drain the beans and place in a hot dish. Pour over the melted butter and onions and sprinkle with the Parmesan cheese. Place under a hot grill (broiler) for 2 minutes.

Fagioli al Gorgonzola

Gorgonzola Beans

Serves 8

30 ml/2 tbsp olive oil
1 onion, chopped
2 garlic cloves, crushed
425 g/15 oz/1 large can cannellini
beans, drained
425 g/15 oz/1 large can butter beans,
drained
4 large potatoes, sliced
225 g/8 oz Gorgonzola cheese,
crumbled
90 ml/6 tbsp double (heavy) cream
Salt and freshly ground black pepper

Heat half of the oil in a large pan and cook the onion and crushed garlic for 5 minutes. Stir in the beans and season to taste. Heat through and pour into an ovenproof dish. Meanwhile, boil the potatoes until just tender. Drain and arrange on top of the casserole. Blend the Gorgonzola with the cream, season and pour over the surface of the potatoes. Bake in a preheated oven at 200°C/400°F/ gas mark 6 for 25 minutes.

Gnocchi di Patate con Salsa alla Microonda

Potato Gnocchi with Microwave Sauce

Serves 4–6

3 large potatoes, cut in chunks
Salt and freshly ground black pepper
225 g/8 oz/2 cups plain (all-purpose)
flour
1 egg, beaten
15 g/½ oz/1 tbsp unsalted (sweet) butter
75 g/3 oz/¾ cup Parmesan cheese, grated

Sauce:
400 g/14 oz/1 large can chopped
tomatoes
10 ml/2 tsp brown sugar
2 garlic cloves, chopped
15 ml/1 tbsp tomato purée (paste)
15 ml/1 tbsp chopped fresh oregano
5 ml/1 tsp paprika

Boil the potatoes in salted water for 12 minutes until just tender. Pass through a sieve (strainer) and blend with the flour, egg and butter. Form into balls and cook in boiling salted water for 10 minutes. Drain and sprinkle with the Parmesan cheese. Meanwhile, mix all the sauce ingredients in a bowl, cover and microwave on full for 8 minutes. Stir well and leave to stand for 5 minutes. Serve with the gnocchi.

Zucchini al Limone e Origano

Lemon and Oregano Courgettes
Serves 4

8 courgettes (zucchini)
25 g/1 oz/2 tbsp butter
15 ml/1 tbsp oil
45 ml/3 tbsp lemon juice
30 ml/2 tbsp chopped fresh oregano
Salt and freshly ground black pepper

Slice the courgettes in half, lengthways and place in a large pan with half the butter. Add the olive oil and cook for 8–10 minutes, turning once. Add the lemon juice and stir in the remaining butter and oregano. Transfer to a warmed serving dish, season and serve immediately.

Zucchini Rosolati con Salvia

Sage Sautéed Courgettes
Serves 4

450 g/1 lb small courgettes (zucchini), topped and tailed
25 g/1 oz/2 tbsp unsalted (sweet) butter
1 garlic clove, finely chopped
15 ml/1 tbsp chopped fresh sage
15 ml/1 tbsp chopped fresh parsley
Salt and freshly ground black pepper
10 ml/2 tsp white wine vinegar

Slice the courgettes into 1 cm/½ in rounds. Melt the butter in a frying pan (skillet) and add the garlic, courgettes and sage. Stir until the courgettes are evenly coated with the butter and cook for 10 minutes until they are browned. Spoon into a serving bowl and sprinkle with the parsley. Season with the salt and pepper and sprinkle over the vinegar. Toss gently before serving.

Fagioli e Verdura al Forno

Bean and Vegetable Loaf
Serves 6

Oil for greasing
40 g/1½ oz/3 tbsp unsalted (sweet) butter
1 onion, very finely chopped
175 g/6 oz carrots, finely grated
400 g/14 oz/1 large can cannellini beans, well drained
2 eggs
30 ml/2 tbsp double (heavy) cream
75 g/3 oz/1½ cups breadcrumbs
45 ml/3 tbsp coriander (cilantro), chopped
15 ml/1 tbsp snipped fresh chives
15 ml/1 tbsp chopped fresh basil
15 ml/1 tbsp chopped fresh thyme
4 olives, stoned (pitted) and chopped
Salt and freshly ground black pepper

Oil a 900 g/2 lb loaf tin and line the base with greaseproof (waxed) paper. Oil the paper thoroughly. Melt the butter in a frying pan (skillet) and cook the onion and carrots for 5 minutes until the onion is translucent. Set the pan aside. Pour the beans into a bowl and mash with a fork. Beat in the eggs. Stir in the onion and carrots and add the remaining ingredients. Blend well and season to taste. Spoon the mixture into the prepared loaf tin and level off the surface. Cover with foil and bake in a preheated oven at 200°C/400°F/gas mark 6 for 1 hour 10 minutes until firm to the touch. Remove from the oven and allow to cool before slicing.

Fagioli Italiani

Italian Beans
Serves 4–6

450 g/1 lb/2⅔ cups dried white beans,
soaked overnight
2 garlic cloves, crushed
30 ml/2 tbsp chopped fresh basil
2.5 ml/½ tsp salt
1.5 ml/¼ tsp freshly ground black
pepper
6 bacon rashers (slices), rinded and
chopped
600 ml/1 pt/2½ cups water

Place the beans, garlic, basil, salt and pepper in a large flameproof casserole (Dutch oven) and stir well. Add the bacon and cover with the water. Bring to the boil and boil rapidly for 10 minutes. Cover and bake in a preheated oven at 150°C/300°F/ gas mark 2 for 3 hours until the beans are tender. Remove from the oven, strain off any excess liquid and serve at once.

Fagioli Sostanziosi

Hearty Beans
Serves 8

30 ml/2 tbsp olive oil
1 onion, chopped
2 garlic cloves, crushed
400 g/14 oz/1 large can chopped
tomatoes
30 ml/2 tbsp tomato purée (paste)
425 g/15 oz/1 large can cannellini
beans
425 g/15 oz/1 large can red kidney
beans
425 g/15 oz/1 large can butter beans
Salt and freshly ground black pepper
4 large potatoes, sliced

Heat half the oil in a large pan and cook the onion and crushed garlic for 5 minutes. Stir in the tomatoes and tomato purée. Drain the beans, add to the pan and season to taste. Bring to the boil and pour into a casserole dish (Dutch oven). Cook the potatoes in a pan of boiling water for 5 minutes until just tender. Drain and arrange on top of the casserole. Brush over with the remaining oil and bake in a pre-heated oven at 200°C/400°F/gas mark 6 for 25 minutes.

Finocchi all' Acciuga

Fennel in Anchovy Sauce
Serves 4

4 fennel bulbs
30 ml/2 tbsp olive oil
4 anchovy fillets in oil, drained
175 ml/6 fl oz/¾ cup double (heavy)
cream
Salt and freshly ground black pepper
50 g/2 oz/½ cup Parmesan cheese,
grated

Bring a large pan of salted water to the boil and add the fennel. Simmer for 5 minutes. Drain and place in a large bowl of iced water. The iced water prevents discolouring. Remove the stems and root end from the bulbs. Drain again and slice lengthways. Heat the oil in a pan and add the anchovies. Fry (sauté) for 2 minutes until the anchovies melt. Stir in the cream and add the fennel. Cover with a lid and cook over a very low heat for 10 minutes. Arrange on a serving dish and sprinkle over the salt, pepper and Parmesan cheese.

Photograph opposite: **Veal with Lemon and Capers (page 143)**

Pasticcio con Spinaci

Spinach Flan
Serves 4

225 g/8 oz shortcrust pastry (basic pie crust)
350 g/12 oz spinach
3 eggs
250 ml/8 fl oz/1 cup milk
Salt and freshly ground black pepper
1.5 ml/¼ tsp cayenne

Roll out the pastry and line a 23 cm/9 in flan tin (pie pan). Line with greaseproof (waxed) paper and baking beans and bake in a preheated oven at 190°C/375°F/gas mark 5 for 10 minutes. Remove the paper and baking beans. Place the spinach in a saucepan with 15 ml/1 tbsp water and cover with a lid. Cook for 8 minutes, drain and allow to cool. Beat the eggs into the spinach. Stir in the milk and season with the salt, pepper and cayenne. Pour into the pastry case and bake in a preheated oven at 180°C/350°F/gas mark 4 for 40 minutes until set.

Melanzane e Formaggio al Forno

Cheese and Aubergine Bake
Serves 4

2 large aubergines (eggplants)
15 g/½ oz/1 tbsp unsalted (sweet) butter
45 ml/3 tbsp olive oil
1 large onion, sliced
225 g/8 oz mushrooms, quartered
2.5 ml/½ tsp grated nutmeg
1.5 ml/¼ tsp cayenne
100 g/4 oz/1 cup hard cheese, grated
100 g/4 oz lean cooked ham, diced
250 ml/8 fl oz/1 cup Basic White Sauce (see page 357)

Cut the aubergines into thin slices. Lightly grease an ovenproof casserole dish (Dutch oven) with butter and set aside. Heat 15 ml/1 tbsp oil in a frying pan (skillet) and cook the aubergine slices for 7–8 minutes, turning occasionally, until they are browned on both sides. Remove and keep warm. Add the remaining oil and butter to the pan and fry (sauté) the onion and mushrooms for 5 minutes. Set aside. Blend the nutmeg, cayenne and 2.5 ml/½ tsp salt together. Arrange a layer of aubergine slices in the casserole dish. Sprinkle with a little of the seasoning. Add a layer of onions and mushrooms and continue layering until the ingredients have been used. Stir the cheese, ham and sauce together. Pour over the vegetables and bake in a preheated oven at 180°C/350°F/gas mark 4 for 30 minutes.

Funghi con Formaggio

Mushrooms with Cheese
Serves 4–6

450 g/1 lb mushrooms
25 g/1 oz/2 tbsp unsalted (sweet) butter
300 ml/½ pt/1¼ cups Basic White Sauce (see page 357)
50 g/2 oz/½ cup Parmesan cheese, grated

Remove the mushroom stalks. Using half the butter, grease an ovenproof dish and add the mushrooms. Dot with the remaining butter and bake in a preheated oven at 190°C/375°F/gas mark 5 for 8–10 minutes. Pour over the white sauce and sprinkle with the Parmesan. Return to the oven for 10–15 minutes to brown.

Photograph opposite: **Roast Monkfish with Bacon and Marjoram Sauce (page 163)**

Tortini di Patate

Potato Cakes

Serves 4

4 large baking potatoes
75 ml/3 tbsp olive oil
Salt and freshly ground black pepper
15 ml/1 tbsp chopped fresh basil

Thinly slice the potatoes and brush each slice with olive oil. Arrange the potato slices on a baking sheet, slightly overlapping each slice. Sprinkle with the salt and pepper. Bake in a preheated oven at 180°C/350°F/gas mark 4 for 10 minutes until the edges are golden brown. Serve hot. Sprinkle over the chopped basil before serving. The potato cakes can be made in advance so are good for dinner parties when they can be reheated for 2–3 minutes.

Pomodori con Formaggio

Cheesy Tomatoes

Serves 4

8 large tomatoes
Salt and freshly ground black pepper
225 g/8 oz hard cheese, grated
25 g/1 oz Mozzarella cheese, chopped
30 ml/2 tbsp chopped fresh basil
45 ml/3 tbsp soured (dairy sour) cream

Slice the lid from the top of each tomato and set aside. Scoop out the flesh and seeds and set aside for further use. Season the inside of the tomatoes with the salt and pepper. Stand the tomatoes in a large ovenproof dish. Mix the cheeses in a bowl with the basil. Stir in the soured cream and spoon the mixture back into the tomato shells. Replace the lids and bake in a preheated oven at 200°C/400°F/gas mark 6 for 15 minutes. Serve immediately.

Zucchine con Formaggio e Salame

Cheese and Salami Courgettes

Serves 4

2 large courgettes (zucchini), halved
75 g/3 oz/⅓ cup hard cheese, grated
2 hard-boiled (hard-cooked) eggs, chopped
5 ml/1 tsp chopped fresh parsley
Salt and freshly ground black pepper
50 g/2 oz salami, chopped

Scoop out the centres of the courgettes, chop and place in a bowl. Arrange the shells in a shallow ovenproof dish. Mix half the cheese, eggs and parsley with the courgette flesh and season with the salt and pepper. Spoon into the courgette shells and top with the salami. Sprinkle over the remaining cheese and bake in a preheated oven at 190°C/375°F/gas mark 5 for 35 minutes until brown and cooked through.

Patate e Porri in Besciamella

Potato and Leeks in White Sauce

Serves 4

2 leeks, halved and sliced
50 g/2 oz/¼ cup unsalted (sweet) butter
900 g/2 lb potatoes, thinly sliced
25 g/1 oz/¼ cup plain (all-purpose)
flour
600 ml/1 pt/2½ cups milk
2.5 ml/½ tsp grated nutmeg
Salt and freshly ground black pepper
Bouquet garni sachet

Melt the butter in a large saucepan. Add the leeks and potatoes and cook for approximately 10 minutes until they are soft. Sprinkle the flour over the vegetables and cook for 1 minute, stirring all the time. Pour in the milk and bring to the boil, stirring. Season to taste with the nutmeg, salt and pepper and bouquet garni. Cover the pan, reduce the heat and simmer very gently for a further 15 minutes, stirring occasionally. Remove the bouquet garni before serving.

Sedano e Pomodoro Brasati

Braised Celery and Tomato

Serves 4

2 large celery heads, trimmed
25 g/1 oz/2 tbsp unsalted (sweet) butter
1 onion, chopped
450 g/1 lb tomatoes, skinned, seeded
and roughly chopped
Salt and freshly ground black pepper
30 ml/2 tbsp chopped fresh basil
8 olives, to garnish (optional)

Bring a pan of salted water to the boil. Cut the celery into 9 cm/3½ in pieces and add to the boiling water. Simmer for 3 minutes and drain. Melt the butter and fry (sauté) the chopped onion for 3 minutes. Add the celery and tomatoes and season with the salt, pepper and basil. Cover the pan with a lid and simmer for 10 minutes. Turn into a heated serving dish and garnish with the olives, if using.

Papate Brasate al Forno

Braised Oven-cooked Potatoes

Serves 6

2 large onions, roughly cut up
900 g/2 lb potatoes, scrubbed and
thickly sliced
15 ml/1 tbsp chopped fresh parsley
15 ml/1 tbsp chopped fresh basil
10 ml/2 tsp chopped fresh sage
15 ml/1 tbsp chopped fresh oregano
4 ripe tomatoes, skinned, seeded and
roughly chopped
Salt and freshly ground black pepper
60 ml/4 tbsp olive oil
2.5 ml/½ tsp caster (superfine) sugar
Coarse sea salt

Put all the ingredients in a roasting tin (pan) except the sea salt and toss gently but thoroughly until well blended. Bake in a preheated oven at 230°C/450°F/gas mark 8 for about 1 hour until the potatoes are tender and turning golden. Sprinkle with a little coarse sea salt and serve straight from the pan.

Pasta

There are over 600 different Italian pasta shapes in a variety of colours and flavours. They are all interchangable with any sauce or topping – with the exception of lasagne and cannelloni of course! There is no difference in the cooking method for dried or fresh pasta – the only rule being that fresh pasta takes much less time to cook. Always drain as soon as it is cooked, pour the topping or sauce over and serve at once. Likewise, baked pasta dishes are best served as soon as they are ready, or the pasta continues to absorb any liquid in the sauce and the dish can become dry.

Pasta all'Uova

Basic Fresh Egg Pasta

Serves 4

225 g/8 oz/2 cups plain (all-purpose)
*   flour*
1.5 ml/¼ tsp salt
2 eggs, beaten
5 ml/1 tsp olive oil
Cold water

Sift the flour and salt in a bowl and blend in the eggs and olive oil. Use your hands to mix to a dough adding a little water if necessary. Using the palm of the hand knead the dough strongly until smooth, dusting with a little flour to prevent sticking. Roll and re-roll the dough thinly and cut into strips to produce noodles, or wider strips for lasagne depending on the type of pasta you wish to make. Hang up to dry or lay a clean cloth over the back of a chair and put the strips of pasta over this. The pasta can be stored an airtight container in the fridge for several days. Cook in plenty of boiling, salted water for 3–5 minutes, depending on thickness until just tender but still with some texture. Drain and use as required.

Pasta Nera (1)

Black Pasta

Makes approx 550 g/1¼ lb

450 g/1 lb/4 cups plain (all-purpose)
*   flour*
1.5 ml/¼ tsp salt
4 eggs, beaten
15 ml/1 tbsp cuttlefish ink

Sift the flour and salt in a bowl and blend in the eggs and cuttlefish ink. Knead very thoroughly until smooth. Cover the bowl with a cloth and leave to rest for 30 minutes. Roll out the dough thinly and cut into strips for noodles, or wider strips for lasagne. Hang up to dry or lay a clean cloth over the back of a chair and put the strips of pasta over this. The pasta can be stored in an airtight container in the fridge for several days. Cook in plenty of boiling, salted water for 3–5 minutes, depending on thickness until just tender but still with some texture. Drain and use as required.

Pasta Nera (2)

Black Pasta
Makes approx 550 g/1¼ lb

2 large flat mushrooms, peeled and
sliced
15 ml/1 tbsp olive oil
15 ml/1 tbsp water
450 g/1 lb/4 cups plain (all-purpose)
flour
1.5 ml/¼ tsp salt
4 eggs, beaten
A little extra flour

Fry (sauté) the mushrooms in the oil for 1 minute, stirring. Add the water, cover and cook gently for about 5 minutes until the mushrooms are tender. Purée in a blender or food processor. Sift the flour and salt into a large bowl. Make a well in the centre and add the mushroom purée and eggs. Gradually work in the flour until the mixture forms a soft but not sticky dough. Add a little more flour, if necessary. Knead gently on a lightly floured surface. Return to the bowl, cover with clingfilm (plastic wrap) and leave to stand for 30 minutes. Roll out to paper thinness and cut into thin strips. Lay a clean cloth over the back of a chair and put the strips of pasta over it to dry. The pasta can be stored in an airtight container in the fridge for several days. Cook in plenty of boiling, salted water for 3–5 minutes, depending on thickness until just tender but still with some texture. Drain and use as required.

Tagliatelle Verde

Green Pasta
Serves 4

100 g/4 oz spinach, washed
450 g/1 lb/4 cups plain (all-purpose)
flour
1.5 ml/¼ tsp salt
4 eggs, beaten

Place the spinach in a saucepan and cook, covered for 8–10 minutes until cooked. Chop finely or purée until smooth. Drain thoroughly. Sift the flour and salt in a bowl and blend in the eggs and spinach. The green colour can be altered by the quantity of spinach included in the recipe. Knead very thoroughly until smooth. Cover the bowl with a cloth and leave to rest for 30 minutes. Roll out the dough thinly and cut into strips to make noodles. Hang up to dry or place on a clean cloth over the back of a chair. The pasta can be stored in an airtight container in the fridge for several days. Cook in plenty of boiling, salted water for 3–5 minutes, depending on thickness until just tender but still with some texture. Drain and use as required.

Pasta Rossa

Red Pasta

Serves 4

450 g/1 lb/4 cups plain (all-purpose)
  flour
1.5 ml/¼ tsp salt
4 eggs, beaten
45 ml/3 tbsp tomato purée (paste)

Sift the flour and salt in a bowl and blend in the eggs and tomato purée. The red colour can be altered by the quantity of tomato purée included in the recipe. Knead very thoroughly until smooth. Cover the bowl with a cloth and leave to stand for 30 minutes. Roll out the dough thinly and cut into strips to make noodles. Hang up to dry or place on a clean cloth over the back of a chair. The pasta can be stored in an airtight container in the fridge for several days. Cook in plenty of boiling, salted water for 3–5 minutes, depending on thickness until just tender but still with some texture. Drain and use as required.

Pappardelle

Thick Ribbon Pasta

Serves 4

450 g/1 lb/4 cups plain (all-purpose)
  flour
5 eggs, beaten
2.5 ml/½ tsp salt
Water

Put the flour in a mound on a pastry board and make a well in the centre. Break the eggs into the well and add a little water. Pour over the salt. Fold the flour over the eggs and water gently and keep turning it with the fingers until the liquid is absorbed, adding a little more water if the pastry is too dry. The pastry should have a smooth consistency. Knead well with floured hands for 10 minutes. Roll into a large square. Fold up and roll out again. Cover and leave to rest for 30 minutes. Repeat this process twice more. Roll the pastry again thinly and allow to dry out for 30 minutes. Cut into 2 cm/¾ in wide ribbons and dry over a cloth on the back of a chair. Store in airtight containers in the fridge and use within 3–4 days. Cook in plenty of boiling, salted water for 3–5 minutes, depending on thickness, until just tender but still with some texture. Drain and use as required.

Tagliarini

Tagliarini Pasta

Serves 4

450 g/1 lb/4 cups plain (all-purpose)
  flour
1.5 ml/¼ tsp salt
4 eggs, beaten
30 ml/2 tbsp milk or single (light)
  cream

Sift the flour and salt in a bowl and blend in the eggs and cream. Knead very thoroughly until smooth. Cover the bowl with a cloth. Leave to stand for 30 minutes. Roll out the dough thinly and cut into very fine strips to produce tagliarini. Hang up to dry or place on a clean cloth over the back of a chair. The pasta can be stored in an airtight container in the fridge. Cook in plenty of boiling, salted water for 3–5 minutes, depending on thickness until just tender but still with some texture. Drain and use as required.

Ripieno di Formaggio per Pasta

Cheese Filling for Pasta
Makes about 300 g/11 oz

225 g/8 oz/1 cup Ricotta cheese
75 g/3 oz/¾ cup hard cheese, grated
2 eggs
2.5 ml/½ tsp sugar
Salt and freshly ground black pepper
15 ml/1 tbsp chopped fresh parsley

Combine all the ingredients in a blender and blend on a low speed until smooth and creamy. Use as a filling for large cannelloni or manicotti.

Pasta con Salsa di Manzo

Pasta with Meat Sauce
Serves 4

2 large onions, chopped
2 garlic cloves, chopped
15 ml/1 tbsp oil
225 g/8 oz/2 cups lean minced
  (ground) beef
600 ml/1 pt/2½ cups beef stock
400 g/14 oz/1 large can chopped
  tomatoes
15 ml/1 tbsp chopped fresh parsley
Salt and freshly ground black pepper
275 g/10 oz pasta shells
Grated cheese (optional), to serve

Fry (sauté) the onions and garlic in the oil until translucent but not brown. Add the beef and cook for 3–4 minutes, stirring. Blend in the remaining ingredients and cook uncovered for 10 minutes, stirring occasionally. Cover and simmer for 40 minutes and season to taste. Bring a large pan of salted water to the boil and cook the pasta for 10–12 minutes until *al dente*. Drain and pour into a hot serving dish. Pour over the beef sauce and serve immediately with grated cheese, if liked.

Maccheroni al Forno

Baked Macaroni
Serves 4

15 g/½ oz/1 tbsp unsalted (sweet) butter
15 ml/1 tbsp olive oil
100 g/4 oz mushrooms, chopped
4 large tomatoes, sliced
30 ml/2 tbsp chopped fresh parsley
225 g/8 oz large macaroni
175 ml/6 fl oz/¾ cup Basic White
  Sauce (see page 357)
75 g/3 oz/¾ cup Pecorino cheese, grated
Salt and freshly ground black pepper

Heat half the butter with the oil in a pan and cook the mushrooms for 5 minutes until browned. Add the tomatoes and parsley. Stir in 120 ml/4 fl oz/½ cup water and simmer for 3 minutes. Cook the macaroni in a large pan of boiling, salted water until *al dente*. Drain. Butter an ovenproof dish and turn the macaroni into it. Pour over the white sauce and then the mushroom mixture. Sprinkle over the cheese and season with the salt and pepper. Bake in a preheated oven at 180°C/350°F/gas mark 4 for 30 minutes.

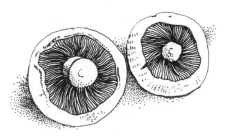

Crema di Asparagi con Pasta

Asparagus Cream with Pasta
Serves 6

450 g/1 lb asparagus
300 ml/½ pt/1¼ cups single (light)
  cream
Salt and freshly ground black pepper
450 g/1 lb fresh pasta
15 ml/1 tbsp Parmesan cheese, grated

Trim the asparagus and cut off the tips to use for decoration. Cook the asparagus for 10 minutes until tender. Drain and reserve the cooking liquid. Purée the stalks with the cream in a blender or food processor and return to a clean saucepan. Reheat gently and season with the salt and pepper. Place the pasta in a large saucepan of boiling, salted water and cook for 3–4 minutes until *al dente*. Drain well. Spoon the pasta on to 6 hot plates and pour the sauce over the pasta. Arrange the asparagus tips on top. Sprinkle with the Parmesan and serve immediately.

Maccheroni e Manzo al Forno

Beef and Macaroni Bake
Serves 4

450g/1 lb minced (ground) beef
2 onions, chopped
2 garlic cloves, crushed
15 ml/1 tbsp plain (all-purpose) flour
300 ml/½ pt/1¼ cups beef stock
100g/4 oz mushrooms, sliced
10 ml/2 tsp chopped fresh mixed
  herbs
Salt and freshly ground black pepper
1 bay leaf
175 g/6 oz macaroni
50 g/2 oz/½ cup Parmesan, grated

Place the minced beef, onions and crushed garlic in a frying pan (skillet) or deep saucepan and cook until browned. Blend in the flour. Gradually stir in the beef stock and add the mushrooms, herbs and bay leaf. Season to taste. Bring to the boil, reduce the heat and simmer for 15 minutes. Cook the pasta in boiling salted water for 12 minutes until *al dente*. Remove the bay leaf from the meat and transfer the meat to a large ovenproof dish. Drain the pasta and place over the top of the meat. Sprinkle over the grated cheese. Bake in a preheated oven at 200°C/400°F/gas mark 6 for 20 minutes.

Sformato di Pollo e Maccheroni

Chicken and Macaroni Casserole
Serves 4

225 g/8 oz elbow macaroni
Oil for greasing
4 carrots, diced
1 onion, chopped
225 g/8 oz/2 cups cooked chicken, diced
1 green (bell) pepper, diced
Salt and freshly ground black pepper
2 eggs
300 ml/½ pt/1¼ cups milk

Bring a large pan of salted water to the boil and cook the macaroni for 15 minutes until tender. Drain and place in an oiled casserole dish (Dutch oven). Add the carrots, onion, chicken, green pepper, salt and pepper. Beat the eggs and milk together in a bowl and pour over the vegetables. Place the casserole dish in a roasting tin (pan) of hot water and bake in a preheated oven at 180°C/350°F/gas mark 4 for 1 hour. Serve immediately.

Eliche al Formaggio

Cheese Pasta Twists

Serves 4

350 g/12 oz pasta twists
1 garlic clove, chopped
15 ml/1 tbsp olive oil
275 g/10 oz/2½ cups Pecorino cheese,
grated

Cook the pasta in a large saucepan of boiling, salted water for 8 minutes. Drain and pour into a warmed serving dish. Cook the garlic in the oil and add the cheese. Pour over the pasta. Toss and serve.

Carciofi e Pasta di Olive

Artichoke and Olive Pasta

Serves 4

400 g/14 oz/1 large can artichoke
hearts, drained
50 g/2 oz/1 small can anchovy fillets,
drained
50 g/2 oz/⅓ cup black olives, stoned
(pitted)
1 dried chilli, finely chopped
10 ml/2 tsp chopped fresh oregano
15 ml/1 tbsp olive oil
400 g/14 oz/1 large can chopped
tomatoes
15 ml/1 tbsp tomato purée (paste)
350 g/12 oz tagliatelle
15 ml/1 tbsp capers

Quarter the artichoke hearts and set aside. Place the drained anchovy fillets in a bowl of warm water and allow to stand. Chop the olives. Put the chopped chilli, oregano and olive oil in a frying pan (skillet) and cook for 1 minute. Stir in the chopped tomatoes, tomato purée and olives. Bring to the boil, reduce the heat and simmer for 10 minutes. Bring a large pan of salted water to the boil and add the pasta. Cook for 8 minutes, then add the artichoke hearts. Cook for a further 2 minutes and drain. Drain the anchovies, chop and add to the tomato sauce with the capers. Drain the pasta and artichokes and serve on warm plates. Pour over the sauce and serve hot.

Penne al Bel Paese

Bel Paese Quills

Serves 4

15 ml/1 tbsp olive oil
1 garlic clove, crushed
1 celery stick, chopped
15 ml/1 tbsp tomato purée (paste)
3 tomatoes, skinned and chopped
Salt and freshly ground black pepper
225 g/8 oz Italian sausages, thinly
sliced
350 g/12 oz penne
225 g/8 oz Bel Paese cheese, sliced

Heat half the oil and add the garlic and celery. Cook for 2 minutes, stirring. Add the tomato purée, reduce the heat and stir in the tomatoes. Season with the salt and pepper and simmer for 30 minutes. Set aside. Heat the remaining oil and fry (sauté) the sausages until brown. Bring a large pan of salted water to the boil and cook the pasta for 8–10 minutes until *al dente*. Drain well. Spoon the penne into an ovenproof dish and add the sausages. Pour over the sauce and top with the cheese slices. Bake in a preheated oven at 180°C/350°F/gas mark 4 for 20 minutes.

Frittata di Pollo e Pasta

Chicken Omelette and Pasta

Serves 4

60 ml/4 tbsp olive oil
2 carrots, diced
1 onion, chopped
225 g/8 oz/2 cups cooked chicken, diced
1 red (bell) pepper, diced
Salt and freshly ground black pepper
2 eggs
300 ml/½ pt/1¼ cups milk
225 g/8 oz pasta spirals

Place half the oil, the carrots, onion, chicken, red pepper and a little salt and pepper in a frying pan (skillet) and cook rapidly for 5 minutes. Beat the eggs and milk together in a bowl and pour into the frying pan. Cook gently for 15 minutes until set. Bring a large pan of salted water to the boil and cook the pasta spirals for 10 minutes until tender. Drain and place in a warmed serving dish. Toss in the remaining oil and a good grinding of pepper. Cut the frittata into wedges and serve with the pasta.

Fettuccine a Tre Colori

Three-colour Fettucine

Serves 2

225 g/8 oz tricolour fettucine
60 ml/4 tbsp olive oil
25 g/1 oz/2 tbsp unsalted (sweet) butter
5 ml/1 tsp lemon rind
Salt and freshly ground black pepper
45 ml/3 tbsp chopped fresh herbs
4 tomatoes, skinned and chopped
Slivers of Parmesan cheese

Bring a large pan of salted water to the boil and cook the fettucine for 10 minutes until firm but tender. Heat the olive oil and butter in a frying pan (skillet) and add the lemon rind and seasoning. Stir in the herbs and tomatoes and cook thoroughly for 5 minutes. Drain the pasta and turn into a warm serving bowl. Pour over the sauce and serve immediately with the Parmesan cheese.

Pollo alla Bolognese

Chicken Bolognese

Serves 4

2 large onions, chopped
25 g/1 oz/2 tbsp unsalted (sweet) butter
2 garlic cloves, crushed
450 g/1 lb boneless chicken breasts,
*   finely chopped*
Salt and freshly ground black pepper
50 ml/2 fl oz/3½ tbsp white wine
400 g/14 oz/1 large can chopped
*   tomatoes*
5 ml/1 tsp chopped fresh oregano
350 g/12 oz spaghetti
30 ml/2 tbsp olive oil
Salt and freshly ground black pepper
75 g/3 oz/¾ cup Parmesan cheese,
*   grated*

Fry (sauté) the onions in the butter until they are translucent then stir in the garlic and chicken. Season well with the salt and pepper. Cook, stirring, for 3 minutes. Blend in the white wine, tomatoes and oregano and stir thoroughly. Simmer for 20 minutes, stirring regularly. Bring a pan of salted water to the boil and cook the spaghetti for 8–10 minutes or until tender but firm. Drain the spaghetti, return to the saucepan and add the oil. Toss the spaghetti in the oil, season with salt and pepper and add half the grated cheese and the chicken sauce. Toss over a gentle heat and serve immediately, sprinkled with the remaining cheese.

Tagliatelle con Pollo e Noci

Chicken and Walnut Tagliatelle

Serves 4–6

350 g/12 oz tagliatelle
225 g/8 oz/2 cups cooked chicken
  meat, cut in small strips
60 ml/4 tbsp Mascarpone cheese
2.5 ml/½ tsp grated nutmeg
100 g/4 oz/1 cup walnuts, roughly
  chopped
Salt and freshly ground black pepper

Bring a large pan of salted water to the boil
and cook the tagliatelle for 8–10 minutes
until tender. Drain and return to the pan.
Gently mix in the Mascarpone and nutmeg
and toss well over a gentle heat. Add the
chicken and chopped nuts and toss to heat
through. Transfer to a flameproof dish.
Season well. Place under a hot grill (broiler) for 6–8 minutes until piping hot and
glazed on top.

Pasta Cremosa

Creamy Pasta

Serves 6

350 g/12 oz pasta shells
Salt and freshly ground black pepper
25 g/1 oz/2 tbsp unsalted (sweet) butter
100 g/4 oz mushrooms, sliced
225 g/8 oz/2 cups cooked chicken
  breast, cut into strips
150 ml/¼ pt/⅔ cup double (heavy)
  cream
100 g/4 oz/1 cup hard cheese, grated
15 ml/1 tbsp chopped fresh parsley
15 ml/1 tbsp chopped fresh thyme
50 g/2 oz/½ cup Parmesan cheese,
  grated

Cook the pasta in boiling salted water until
just tender. Drain. Meanwhile, melt the
butter and add the mushrooms. Fry (sauté)
for 2 minutes and stir in the chicken. Cook
for 5 minutes and stir in the pasta. Lower
the heat and blend in the cream, grated hard
cheese, parsley and thyme. Season with
salt and pepper and when piping hot turn
into a warmed serving dish. Sprinkle with
the Parmesan cheese and serve at once.

Fettuccine con Panna

Fettuccine with Cream

Serves 4

1.2 litres/2 pts/5 cups water
10 ml/2 tsp salt
350 g/12 oz fettuccine
25 g/1 oz/2 tbsp unsalted (sweet) butter
250 ml/8 fl oz/1 cup double (heavy)
  cream
100 g/4 oz/1 cup Parmesan cheese,
  grated
Freshly ground black pepper

Bring a pan of salted water to the boil and
drop the fettuccine into the water. Reduce
the heat to simmering and cook the fettuccine for 7–8 minutes until tender but still
firm. Remove from the heat and drain well.
Transfer to a warm serving dish. Warm the
butter, cream, cheese and pepper in a
saucepan for 1 minute and pour over the
fettuccine. Toss and add more seasoning if
required.

Cannelloni con Pollo

Chicken Cannelloni
Serves 4–6

350 g/12 oz/3 cups plain (all-purpose)
* flour*
Salt and freshly ground black pepper
2 eggs
225 g/8 oz boneless chicken breasts
1 large onion
15 ml/1 tbsp chopped fresh oregano
Tomato Sauce (see page 358), to serve

Put the flour and a little salt and pepper
into a bowl. Beat the eggs and mix into the
flour. Mix with enough cold water to form
a firm dough. Knead well. Roll out on a
floured board and cut into thin rounds the
size of a saucer. Mince (grind) the chicken
breasts and onion together and blend with
the oregano. Season with the salt and pepper. Spread a little mixture on each round
of dough and wet the edges of the dough
with water. Roll up firmly. Place each cannelloni carefully into a pan of boiling
water and boil for 8–10 minutes. Drain
well and serve with Tomato Sauce.

Farfalle con Salsa di Pomodoro

Pasta Bows with Tomato Sauce
Serves 4

15 ml/1 tbsp oil
1 onion, chopped
400 g/14 oz/1 large can of chopped
* tomatoes*
Salt and freshly ground black pepper
350 g/12 oz pasta bows
100 g/4 oz Mozzarella cheese, chopped
5 ml/1 tsp chopped fresh basil
Pecorino cheese, grated, to serve

Heat the oil and cook the onion for 5 minutes until soft. Add the tomatoes and cook
slowly for 15 minutes. Bring a large pan of
salted water to the boil and cook the far-
falle for 8 minutes. Drain and return to the
saucepan. Pour over the tomato sauce and
stir in the Mozzarella cheese. Toss gently.
Turn on to warm plates. Sprinkle over the
basil and some Pecorino cheese and serve
straight away.

Farfalle con Salsa di Peperoni Rosso

Pasta Bows with Red Pepper Sauce
Serves 4

15 ml/1 tbsp oil
1 onion, cut into chunks
1 carrot, chopped
2 red (bell) peppers, chopped
1 celery stick, chopped
400 g/14 oz/1 large can of chopped
* tomatoes*
5 ml/1 tsp chopped fresh marjoram
Salt and freshly ground black pepper
350 g/12 oz pasta bows

Heat the oil and cook the onion, carrot,
peppers and celery for 5 minutes until soft.
Add the tomatoes, marjoram and seasoning and cook slowly for 15 minutes. Bring
a large pan of salted water to the boil and
cook the pasta for 8–10 minutes. Drain
and return to the saucepan. Pour over the
sauce, toss and serve immediately.

Pasta con Ricotta

Pasta with Ricotta
Serves 4

350 g/12 oz pasta spirals
Grated rind of 2 lemons
175 g/6 oz/¾ cup Ricotta cheese
10 g/¼ oz/2 tsp unsalted (sweet) butter
Salt and freshly ground black pepper
50 g/2 oz/½ cup Parmesan cheese,
*   grated*

Place the pasta in a large pan of boiling, salted water and cook for 5 minutes. Stir the lemon rind into the Ricotta cheese. Drain the pasta and stir in the butter, Ricotta cheese and seasoning. Place in an ovenproof dish and sprinkle over the Parmesan cheese. Bake in a preheated oven at 190°C/375°F/gas mark 5 for 10 minutes until brown.

Farfalle con Verdure Arrostite

Pasta Bows with Roasted Vegetables
Serves 4

1 red onion, cut into chunks
2 beefsteak tomatoes, cut into chunks
3 courgettes (zucchini), cut into
*   1 cm/½ in slices*
2 garlic cloves, crushed
90 ml/6 tbsp olive oil
Salt and freshly ground black pepper
50 g/2 oz/½ cup pine nuts
350 g/12 oz pasta bows
Few sprigs of basil, torn into small
*   pieces*
225 g/8 oz/2 cups Mozzarella cheese,
*   grated*
50 g/2 oz/½ cup Pecorino cheese,
*   grated*

Place the onion, tomatoes, courgettes and garlic in a large roasting tin (pan). Drizzle over the olive oil and season with the salt and pepper. Roast in a preheated oven at 220°C/425°F/gas mark 7 for 30 minutes. Stir halfway through cooking. Add the pine nuts for the last 10 minutes of cooking time. Cook the pasta bows in a large pan of boiling salted water until *al dente*. Drain and toss with the vegetables. Stir in the basil, Mozzarella and Pecorino cheeses and serve immediately.

Pasta con Funghi Misti

Pasta with Mixed Mushrooms
Serves 4–6

90 ml/6 tbsp milk
25 g/1 oz dried porcini mushrooms
15 ml/1 tbsp olive oil
225 g/8 oz button mushrooms
225 g/8 oz brown-cap mushrooms
2.5 ml/½ tsp cornflour (cornstarch)
225 g/8 oz papardelle (wide ribbon
*   noodles)*
Salt and freshly ground black pepper

Warm the milk in a saucepan and add the porcini mushrooms. Allow to stand for 30 minutes. Meanwhile, place the olive oil in a frying pan (skillet) and cook the button mushrooms over a high heat. Add the brown-cap mushrooms to the button mushrooms and cook, stirring for 3–4 minutes. Drain the porcini mushrooms reserving the milk. Place the cornflour in a small bowl with 30 ml/2 tbsp water. Stir well and blend into the milk then add to the brown-cap and button mushrooms with the porcini and allow to simmer for 5 minutes, stirring continuously. Bring a large pan of salted water to the boil and cook the pasta for 10 minutes until tender. Drain. Stir in the mushroom mixture. Season to taste and serve immediately.

Cannelloni Ripieni

Filled Cannelloni

Serves 4

Sauce:
15 ml/1 tbsp olive oil
1 onion, finely chopped
900 g/2 lb tomatoes, skinned and
    chopped
5 ml/1 tsp chopped fresh oregano
5 ml/1 tsp chopped fresh thyme
Salt and freshly ground black pepper

Filling:·
225 g/8 oz pancetta, finely minced
    (ground)
5 ml/1 tsp chopped fresh parsley
2 garlic cloves, finely chopped
30 ml/2 tbsp olive oil
1 egg, beaten
450 g/1 lb no-need-to-precook
    cannelloni
15 ml/1 tbsp olive oil
100 g/4 oz/1 cup Parmesan cheese,
    grated

Make the sauce. Heat the olive oil and fry (sauté) the onion for 5 minutes until soft but not brown. Add the chopped tomatoes, oregano and thyme. Season with the salt and pepper and simmer for 20 minutes, stirring occasionally. Make the filling. Blend the pancetta with the parsley and garlic. Heat the oil in a frying pan (skillet) and add the ham mixture. Fry for 5 minutes, stirring continually with a wooden spoon to brown evenly. Turn into a bowl, allow to cool and beat in the egg. Using a small teaspoon carefully stuff the cannelloni with the meat mixture. Lay in an oiled ovenproof dish. Pour the hot sauce over the pasta and sprinkle with the Parmesan cheese. Bake in a preheated oven at 190°C/375°F/gas mark 5 for 35 minutes until the cannelloni are tender.

Pasta con Burro di Acciughe

Pasta with Anchovy Butter

Serves 6

225 g/8 oz/2 cups plain (all-purpose)
    flour
1.5 ml/¼ tsp salt
2 eggs
5 ml/1 tsp olive oil
Cold water
6 canned anchovy fillets, rinsed and
    dried
100 g/4 oz/½ cup unsalted (sweet)
    butter
5 ml/1 tsp lemon juice
15 ml/1 tbsp capers, chopped
15 ml/1 tbsp chopped fresh parsley
Freshly ground black pepper

Sift the flour and salt in a bowl and blend in the eggs and olive oil. Mix with the hands adding a little water as necessary to form a firm dough. Using the palm of the hand knead the dough firmly until smooth, dusting with a little flour to prevent sticking. Roll and re-roll out the dough thinly and cut into strips to make noodles. Hang up to dry or place on a clean cloth over the back of a chair for 15 minutes. Cook in boiling, salted water for 3–4 minutes until tender. Drain and return to the saucepan. Meanwhile, mash the anchovy fillets to a paste and put into a saucepan with 15 g/½ oz/1 tbsp of the butter. Stir in the lemon juice and the capers. Cook for 5 minutes, stirring. Lower the heat and whisk in the remaining butter, a little at a time. Do not allow the sauce to boil. Remove the saucepan from the heat and mix in the parsley. Season well with pepper, spoon over the pasta, toss and serve straight away.

Fusilli con Funghi

Pasta Spirals with Mushrooms
Serves 4

30 ml/2 tbsp olive oil
1 onion, chopped
1 garlic clove, crushed
450 g/1 lb mushrooms, chopped
100 g/4 oz Parma ham, chopped
60 ml/4 tbsp dry white wine
Salt and freshly ground black pepper
350 g/12 oz pasta spirals
*50 g/2 oz/½ cup Pecorino cheese,
  grated*
30 ml/2 tbsp chopped fresh sage

Heat the oil and fry (sauté) the onion and
garlic for 1 minute. Stir in the mushrooms
and cook until they are beginning to
brown. Add the ham, wine, salt and pepper
and continue cooking for 5 minutes. Place
the pasta in a pan of boiling, salted water
and cook for 8–10 minutes, until tender,
but still firm. Drain well. Mix the pasta
with the mushroom sauce, sprinkle with
the cheese and sage and serve.

Linguini con Carciofi

Linguini with Artichokes
Serves 4

*400 g/14 oz/1 large can artichoke
  hearts, drained*
185 g/6½ oz/1 small can tuna, drained
350 g/12 oz linguini
15 ml/1 tbsp virgin olive oil
1 red (bell) pepper, sliced
15 ml/1 tbsp lemon juice
Salt and freshly ground black pepper

Coarsely chop the artichoke hearts and
roughly flake the tuna. Bring a large pan of
salted water to the boil and cook the linguini for 5–6 minutes. Heat the olive oil in
a frying pan (skillet) and fry (sauté) the red
pepper for 2 minutes. Stir in the lemon
juice. Drain the pasta and return to the pan.
Add the artichokes, tuna and the pepper
mixture. Toss over a gentle heat. Season to
taste and serve at once.

Tagliatelle Porcini al Cognac

Noodles with Porcini and Cognac
Serves 4

25 g/1 oz dried porcini mushrooms
250 ml/8 fl oz/1 cup brandy
75 g/3 oz/⅓ cup unsalted (sweet) butter
5 shallots, finely chopped
5 garlic cloves, finely chopped
*750 ml/1¼ pts/3 cups double (heavy)
  cream*
350 g/12 oz tagliatelle
Salt and freshly ground black pepper
45 ml/3 tbsp snipped fresh chives

Soak the mushrooms in the brandy for
about 10 minutes until soft. Drain the
mushrooms, reserving the brandy, and
coarsely chop. Melt the butter in a large
pan and fry (sauté) the shallots and garlic
until soft. Add the mushrooms and fry for
a further 2 minutes. Add the brandy and
simmer for 2 minutes. Stir in the cream
and simmer for about 20 minutes until the
sauce has reduced by half. Meanwhile,
cook the pasta in a large pan of boiling,
salted water until tender but still firm.
Drain well. Pour the sauce over the cooked
pasta and season generously with salt and
pepper. Serve sprinkled with the chives.

Maccheroni con Carne al Forno

Baked Macaroni with Meat

Serves 4

450g/1 lb minced (ground) beef
1 onion, chopped
1 garlic clove, crushed
15 ml/1 tbsp plain (all-purpose) flour
300 ml/½ pt/1¼ cups beef stock
1 red (bell) pepper, finely chopped
10 ml/2 tsp chopped fresh sage
1 bay leaf
175g/6 oz macaroni
50g/2 oz/½ cup hard cheese, grated

Place the minced beef, onion and crushed garlic in a frying pan (skillet) or saucepan and cook, stirring, until browned. Blend in the flour. Gradually stir in the beef stock and add the red pepper, sage and bay leaf. Bring to the boil, reduce the heat and simmer for 15 minutes. Cook the pasta in boiling, salted water for 12 minutes. Drain. Remove the bay leaf from the meat and stir in the macaroni. Transfer to a large ovenproof dish. Sprinkle over the grated cheese. Bake in a preheated oven at 200°C/400°F/gas mark 6 for 20 minutes and serve hot.

Spaghetti in Salsa Napoletana

Spaghetti in Neapolitan Sauce

Serves 4

2 garlic cloves, crushed
5 ml/1 tsp chopped fresh basil
5 ml/1 tsp chopped fresh thyme
1 bay leaf
15 ml/1 tbsp oil
90 ml/6 tbsp red wine
3 tomatoes, skinned and chopped
30 ml/2 tbsp tomato purée (paste)
25 g/1 oz/2 tbsp unsalted (sweet) butter
3 large green (bell) peppers, finely chopped
1 large onion, sliced
225 g/8 oz button mushrooms, quartered
10 ml/2 tsp cornflour (cornstarch), dissolved in 15 ml/1 tbsp water
Salt and freshly ground black pepper
350 g/12 oz spaghetti
15 ml/1 tbsp chopped fresh parsley

Place the garlic, basil, thyme, bay leaf and oil in a saucepan and cook for 1 minute. Stir in the wine and tomatoes. Bring to the boil and add the tomato purée. Reduce the heat and simmer gently for 30 minutes, stirring occasionally. Melt half the butter and fry (sauté) the green peppers and onion. Cook for 10 minutes, stirring. Add the mushrooms and cook for a further 5 minutes. Stir in the tomato mixture and the blended cornflour. Season to taste and cook, stirring, for 3 minutes. Discard the bay leaf. Meanwhile, bring a pan of salted water to the boil and add the spaghetti. Cook for 8–10 minutes until tender but still firm. Drain and toss in the remaining butter. Pour the sauce over the spaghetti. Garnish with the parsley and serve immediately.

Linguini al Aglio e Parmigiano

Linguini with Garlic and Parmesan
Serves 4

350 g/12 oz linguini
350 g/12 oz/1½ cups unsalted (sweet) butter, diced
175 g/6 oz/1½ cups dried breadcrumbs
6 garlic cloves, finely chopped
100 g/4 oz/1 cup Parmesan cheese, freshly grated
45 ml/3 tbsp chopped fresh parsley

Cook the linguini in a large pan of boiling, salted water until just tender but still firm. Drain well. Meanwhile, melt the butter until it foams, then stir in the breadcrumbs. Cook over a low heat, stirring continuously, until golden brown. Add the garlic and cook for a further 2 minutes. Stir in the Parmesan and parsley. Pour over the cooked pasta and toss together well before serving.

Pasta con Ceci

Noodles with Chick Peas
Serves 4

225 g/8 oz/1⅓ cup dried chick peas (garbanzos), soaked overnight
60 ml/4 tbsp olive oil
50 g/2 oz Pancetta or bacon, rinded and chopped
15 ml/1 tbsp chopped fresh oregano
1 garlic clove, chopped
1.5 litres/2½ pts/6 cups stock
225 g/8 oz fettuccine
Salt and freshly ground black pepper

Drain the chick peas and pour into a large saucepan. Add enough water to cover and 15 ml/1 tbsp oil. Cover with a lid, bring to the boil and boil rapidly for 10 minutes, then reduce the heat and simmer for 3 hours until tender. Remove from the heat and drain. Heat 30 ml/2 tbsp olive oil and fry (sauté) the pancetta, oregano and garlic for 5 minutes. Pour in the stock and the drained chick peas. Cook for 10 minutes, stirring. Add the fettuccine and boil rapidly until tender. Season with the salt and pepper and pour into a serving dish.

Maccheroni alla Neapoletana

Neapolitan Macaroni
Serves 4–6

Oil for frying
100 g/4 oz/⅔ cup bacon, rinded and diced
1 onion, chopped
2 celery sticks, chopped
2 carrots, chopped
Salt and freshly ground black pepper
15 ml/1 tbsp chopped fresh basil
15 ml/1 tbsp chopped fresh tarragon
3 tomatoes, skinned and sliced
25 g/1 oz/2 tbsp unsalted (sweet) butter
225 g/8 oz macaroni
75 g/3 oz/¾ cup Parmesan cheese, grated

Heat the oil and fry (sauté) the bacon, then brown the onion, celery and carrots. Add the salt, pepper, basil and tarragon. Stir in the tomatoes and simmer for 5 minutes. Pour in enough water just to cover the mixture and continue to simmer for 40 minutes. Stir in the butter. Bring a pan of salted water to the boil and add the macaroni. Cook for 10–15 minutes until tender but still firm. Drain and turn into a deep serving dish. Pour over the sauce. Serve with the Parmesan cheese.

Salmone Tegame con Pasta

Pan-fried Salmon and Pasta

Serves 4

225 g/8 oz salmon fillet, skinned
15 ml/1 tbsp olive oil
15 ml/1 tbsp plain (all-purpose) flour
300 ml/½ pt/1¼ cups milk
15 g/½ oz/1 tbsp unsalted (sweet)
* butter*
Salt and freshly ground black pepper
15 ml/1 tbsp capers, chopped
15 ml/1 tbsp chopped fresh parsley
175 g/6 oz rigatoni

Cut the salmon into slices 2.5 cm/1 in thick. Heat the oil in a frying pan (skillet) and fry (sauté) the salmon for 4–5 minutes, turning once. Blend the flour to a paste with 45 ml/3 tbsp of milk and place in a saucepan with the remaining milk. Add the butter. Bring to the boil, slowly, stirring until thickened. Season with the salt and pepper and simmer for 2 minutes. Stir in the capers and parsley. Bring a large pan of salted water to the boil and cook the pasta for 10 minutes. Drain. Place the pasta on a serving dish. Place the salmon pieces on top and spoon over the sauce.

Fettuccine con Salvia

Fettuccine with Sage

Serves 4

15 g/½ oz/1 tbsp unsalted (sweet)
* butter*
1 onion, chopped
Salt and freshly ground black pepper
350 g/12 oz fettuccine
45 ml/3 tbsp chopped fresh sage
50 g/2 oz/½ cup Pecorino cheese,
* grated*

Heat the butter and cook the onion for 5 minutes until soft. Bring a large pan of salted water to the boil and cook the fettuccine for 8 minutes. Drain and return to the saucepan. Pour over the butter and onion and stir in the sage. Spoon into a heated serving dish and sprinkle over the Pecorino cheese.

Pasta alla Salsa Verde

Pasta with Green Sauce

Serves 4

15 ml/1 tbsp olive oil
1 onion, chopped
4 rashers (slices) bacon, rinded and
* chopped*
5 ml/1 tsp chopped fresh basil
2.5 ml/½ tsp salt
Freshly ground black pepper
350 g/12 oz fresh or frozen peas
175 ml/6 fl oz/¾ cup water
120 ml/4 fl oz/½ cup single (light)
* cream*
350 g/12 oz pasta twists
25 g/1 oz/2 tbsp unsalted (sweet) butter
75 g/3 oz/¾ cup Parmesan cheese,
* grated*

Heat the oil and fry (sauté) the onion and bacon for 3 minutes. Stir in the basil, salt, pepper and peas. Pour in the water and bring to the boil. Reduce the heat to low and simmer for 12 minutes until the peas are soft. Remove the pan from the heat and purée the contents. Return the sauce to the pan and stir in the cream over a very low heat. Keep warm. Add the pasta to a large saucepan of boiling water and cook for 10 minutes until tender but firm. Drain and return to the pan. Add the butter and toss well. Place in a warmed serving dish, pour over the green sauce and sprinkle with the Parmesan.

Vermicelli alla Noce

Nutty Vermicelli
Serves 4

350 g/12 oz vermicelli
90 ml/6 tbsp virgin olive oil
3 garlic cloves, chopped
Salt and freshly ground black pepper
14 walnuts, shelled, peeled and finely
chopped
75 g/3 oz/¾ cup Parmesan cheese,
grated
15 ml/1 tbsp chopped fresh parsley

Add the pasta to a large saucepan of boiling water and cook for 5–6 minutes. Drain and return to the saucepan. Heat the oil and add the garlic. Cook for 1 minute and stir in the nuts. Place the pasta in a warmed serving dish and pour over the sauce. Sprinkle with the cheese and parsley and serve immediately. Note: use fresh walnuts if possible.

Pappardelle con Spinaci e Salvia

Pasta with Spinach and Sage
Serves 4

15 g/½ oz/1 tbsp unsalted (sweet)
butter
1 onion, chopped
350 g/12 oz spinach, roughly chopped
350 g/12 oz pappardelle (wide pasta
noodles)
45 ml/3 tbsp chopped fresh sage
Salt and freshly ground black pepper
50 g/2 oz/½ cup Pecorino cheese,
grated

Heat the butter in a saucepan and cook the onion for 5 minutes until soft. Add the spinach, cover and cook gently for 5 minutes. Cook the pappardelle in salted water for 10 minutes. Drain and return to the saucepan. Pour over the butter, the onion, the spinach and the sage. Toss and season well. Spoon into a heated serving dish. Sprinkle over the Pecorino cheese and serve.

Pappardelle al Forno con Sugo di Carne

Baked Pasta Ribbons in Meat Sauce
Serves 4–6

450 g/1 lb/4 cups plain (all-purpose)
flour
1.5 ml/¼ tsp salt
4 eggs
30 ml/2 tbsp milk
175 ml/6 fl oz/¾ cup Meat Sauce (see
page 356)
175 g/6 oz Mozzarella cheese, sliced
thinly
Salt and freshly ground black pepper
50 g/2 oz/½ cup Parmesan cheese,
grated

Sift the flour and salt in a bowl and blend in the eggs and milk. Knead very thoroughly until smooth. Cover the bowl with a cloth and leave to rest for 30 minutes. Roll out the dough thinly and cut into long strips about 2 cm/¾ in wide. Hang up to dry or place over a clean cloth on the back of a chair for 15 minutes. Cook in boiling, salted water for 4–5 minutes until tender. Drain and put a layer of half the pasta into a buttered ovenproof dish. Add a layer of meat sauce and cover with all the cheese slices. Season with salt and pepper and repeat the layers, ending with the Parmesan cheese. Bake for 20 minutes in a preheated oven at 200°C/400°F/gas mark 6.

Pollo con Pasta

Pasta Chicken
Serves 4

350 g/12 oz pasta shapes
175 g/6 oz broccoli florets
225 g/8 oz/2 cups cooked chicken,
chopped
400 g/14 oz/1 large can chopped
tomatoes
15 ml/1 tbsp tomato purée (paste)
15 ml/1 tbsp chopped fresh oregano

Cook the pasta and broccoli in separate pans for 10 minutes or until just tender. Drain. Simmer the chopped chicken, tomatoes, tomato purée and oregano for 5 minutes. Add the pasta and broccoli and serve.

Pasta con Zafferano e Capesante

Pasta with Saffron and Scallops
Serves 4

25 g/1 oz/2 tbsp unsalted (sweet) butter
1 small onion, finely chopped
1 garlic clove, chopped
1 large yellow (bell) pepper, chopped
1 large red (bell) pepper, chopped
15 ml/1 tbsp chopped fresh parsley
Salt and freshly ground black pepper
12 shelled scallops
150 ml/¼ pt/⅔ cup white wine
2.5 ml/½ tsp saffron powder
15 ml/1 tbsp olive oil
25 g/1 oz/2 tbsp unsalted (sweet) butter
450 g/1 lb fresh tagliarini

Heat the butter in a frying pan (skillet) and add the onion and garlic. Cook for 3 minutes and add the peppers and parsley.

Season with salt and pepper and stir in the scallops. Cook for 4–5 minutes and stir in the wine and saffron. Bring a large pan of salted water to the boil and stir in the olive oil. Add the tagliarini and cook for 5 minutes until the pasta is tender but still firm. Drain and return to the pan with the butter. Heat and pour in the scallop and saffron sauce. Toss gently and serve.

Pasta con Gamberetti e Crema

Pasta with Prawns and Cream
Serves 4

350 g/12 oz tagliatelle
25 g/1 oz/2 tbsp unsalted (sweet) butter
15 ml/1 tbsp olive oil
1 onion, chopped
5 ml/1 tsp chopped fresh basil
2.5 ml/½ tsp salt
2.5 ml/½ tsp freshly ground black
pepper
120 ml/4 fl oz/½ cup white wine
175 ml/6 fl oz/¾ cup double (heavy)
cream
450 g/1 lb cooked, peeled prawns
(shrimp)
30 ml/2 tbsp chopped fresh parsley

Add the pasta to a large saucepan of boiling water and cook for 8–10 minutes. Drain and return to the saucepan with the butter. Heat the oil and fry (sauté) the onion for 3 minutes. Stir in the basil, salt, pepper and wine. Pour in the cream and just bring to the boil. Add the prawns and cover with a lid. Cook for 4 minutes. Place the pasta in a warmed serving dish and pour over the sauce. Sprinkle with the parsley and serve immediately.

Pasta con Cozze

Pasta with Mussels
Serves 4

15 ml/1 tbsp olive oil
1 onion, chopped
5 ml/1 tsp chopped fresh parsley
2.5 ml/½ tsp salt
2.5 ml/½ tsp freshly ground black
  pepper
120 ml/4 fl oz/½ cup white wine
175 ml/6 fl oz/¾ cup water
900 g/2 lb mussels in shells, scrubbed
  and beards removed
350 g/12 oz spaghetti
25 g/1 oz/2 tbsp unsalted (sweet) butter
30 ml/2 tbsp chopped fresh parsley

Heat the oil and fry (sauté) the onion for 3 minutes. Stir in the parsley, salt, pepper and wine. Pour in the water and bring to the boil. Add the mussels and cover with a lid. Cook for 4 minutes. Discard any mussels that have not opened. Add the pasta to a large saucepan of boiling water and cook for 10 minutes until tender but firm. Drain and return to the pan. Add the butter and toss well. Place in a warmed serving dish, spoon over the mussels. Sprinkle with the parsley and serve immediately.

Pasta con Peperoni Arrostiti

Pasta with Grilled Peppers
Serves 4

4 red, yellow and green (bell) peppers,
  halved
3 garlic cloves, crushed
15 ml/1 tbsp balsamic vinegar
5 ml/1 tsp paprika
350 g/12 oz tagliatelle
60 ml/4 tbsp olive oil

Place the peppers and garlic on a grill (broiler) pan and cook on high for 15–20 minutes until the peppers are blistered all over. Allow to cool for 1 minute. Peel the peppers and remove the core and seeds. Slice the peppers and mix with the garlic, vinegar and paprika. Place the pasta in a large pan of boiling, salted water and cook for 8–10 minutes. Drain and add the olive oil. Spoon over the pepper mixture and serve immediately.

Spaghetti con Frutti di Mare

Pasta with Seafood Topping
Serves 4–6

2 onions, chopped
30 ml/2 tbsp olive oil
150 ml/¼ pt/⅔ cup white wine
225 g/8 oz shelled small scallops
225 g/8 oz peeled prawns (shrimp)
Salt and freshly ground black pepper
15 ml/1 tbsp chopped fresh parsley
450 g/1 lb spaghetti

Fry (sauté) the chopped onions in the oil for 5 minutes. Heat the white wine in a saucepan and add the scallops. Poach for 3 minutes and add the prawns. Continue cooking for 3 minutes, stirring continuously. Stir in the onions and season with the salt, pepper and parsley and heat through. Bring a large pan of salted water to the boil and pour in the pasta. Cook for 10 minutes, drain and serve with the seafood mixture.

Penne Arrabiata

Fiery Pasta Quills
Serves 4–6

30 ml/2 tbsp olive oil
1 onion, chopped
1 garlic clove, crushed
3 tomatoes, skinned and chopped
15 ml/1 tbsp tomato purée (paste)
1 red chilli, seeded and finely chopped
Salt and freshly ground black pepper
350 g/12 oz penne
30 ml/2 tbsp chopped fresh basil

Heat the oil in a large pan and fry (sauté) the onion and garlic until soft. Add the tomatoes, tomato purée and chilli and season with the salt and pepper. Bring a large pan of salted water to the boil and cook the pasta for 8–10 minutes until tender but still firm. Drain the pasta and toss into the hot sauce. Sprinkle with the basil.

Spaghetti con Peperoni Mandorle e Frutti di Mare

Pepper and Almond Spaghetti with Seafood
Serves 4

1 red (bell) pepper
1 red chilli
75 g/3 oz/¾ cup blanched almonds, toasted
3 garlic cloves, crushed
30 ml/2 tbsp red wine vinegar
300 ml/½ pt/1¼ cups tomato juice
450 g/1 lb mixed cooked seafood, such as mussels, squid and prawns (shrimp)
350 g/12 oz spaghetti
30 ml/2 tbsp chopped fresh parsley
Salt and freshly ground black pepper

Place the pepper and chilli under a hot grill (broiler) and cook until the skins blacken. Cool for 1 minute and remove the skins. Halve, discard the seeds and purée in a blender or food processor. Add the nuts, garlic, vinegar and tomato juice and blend until smooth. Transfer to a saucepan and bring to the boil. Reduce the heat, add the prepared seafood and simmer gently for 5 minutes. Bring a large pan of salted water to the boil and add the spaghetti. Cook for 8–10 minutes until just tender but firm and drain. Toss in the parsley and pour into a heated serving dish. Pour over the sauce and season to taste.

Patate e Tagliatelle con Salsa all' Aglio

Potatoes and Noodles with Garlic Sauce
Serves 4

450 g/1 lb small new potatoes
Salt and freshly ground black pepper
350 g/12 oz tagliatelle
250 ml/8 fl oz/1 cup Creamy Garlic Sauce (see page 361)
A few sprigs of basil, torn into small pieces
50 g/2 oz/½ cup Pecorino cheese, grated

Boil the potatoes in their skins for 10–15 minutes until tender. Drain, cool and cut thickly into rounds. Bring 600 ml/1 pt/ 2½ cups salted water to the boil. Cook the tagliatelle rapidly for 8 minutes. Drain and mix with the sliced potatoes. Heat the Creamy Garlic Sauce and pour over the potatoes and noodles. Sprinkle with the basil and grated cheese and serve immediately.

Pasta all' Amatriciana

Pasta with Bacon Sauce
Serves 4

350 g/12 oz macaroni or bucatini
Salt
8 streaky bacon rashers (slices),
  rinded
15 ml/1 tbsp olive oil
1 small onion, chopped
45 ml/3 tbsp grated Pecorino cheese
30 ml/2 tbsp chopped fresh basil

Cook the pasta in a large pan of boiling, salted water. Grill (broil) the bacon until crisp, crumble into pieces and set aside. Heat the oil in a frying pan (skillet) and fry (sauté) the onion for 5 minutes. Add the bacon and cheese to the pan and keep the mixture warm. Drain the pasta and transfer to a bowl. Pour over the sauce, toss well and sprinkle with the basil.

Salsicce e Conchiglie

Sausage and Pasta Shells
Serves 4

10 ml/2 tsp olive oil
75 g/3 oz fresh or frozen peas
225 g/8 oz garlic sausage, skinned and
  cubed
1 red (bell) pepper, cut into strips
1 green (bell) pepper, cut into strips
175 g/6 oz large pasta shells
150 ml/¼ pt/⅔ cup single (light) cream
30 ml/2 tbsp chopped fresh basil
Salt and freshly ground black pepper

Heat the oil and add the peas, diced sausage and red and green peppers and cook for 5 minutes. Bring a large pan of salted water to the boil. Cook the pasta until tender and drain. Return the pasta to the pan and stir in the cream with the peas, sausage and peppers. Toss over a gentle heat until piping hot. Transfer to a warmed dish. Sprinkle over the basil and season with salt and pepper.

Pasticcio di Spaghetti con Carne

Spaghetti Meat Pie
Serves 4

450 g/1 lb stewing beef, trimmed of
  excess fat
1 onion, halved
75 g/3 oz Bel Paese cheese, diced
15 ml/1 tbsp chopped fresh basil
2 eggs
225 g/8 oz spaghetti
Salt and freshly ground black pepper
25 g/1 oz/2 tbsp unsalted (sweet) butter

Put the meat and onion through a mincer (grinder). Spoon into a bowl and add the cheese, basil and eggs. Bring a pan of salted water to the boil and add the spaghetti. Cook for 10 minutes until tender but still firm. Drain and stir in the meat and onion mixture. Season well. Turn into a greased, ovenproof dish and dot with pieces of butter. Bake in a preheated oven at 180°C/350°F/gas mark 4 for 25 minutes.

Gomiti in Crema

Elbow Pasta
Serves 4

15 ml/1 tbsp olive oil
450 g/1 lb elbow pasta
150 g/5 oz/⅔ cup unsalted (sweet)
   butter
100 g/4 oz button mushrooms, sliced
150 ml/¼ pt/⅔ cup single (light) cream
2 egg yolks
75 g/3 oz/¾ cup Caciocavallo or
   Parmesan cheese, grated
Salt and freshly ground black pepper
100 g/4 oz peas, cooked

Bring a large pan of salted water to the boil and add the olive oil and the pasta. Lower the heat and simmer for 10–12 minutes until tender. Meanwhile, melt half the butter in a pan and fry (sauté) the mushrooms for 5 minutes. Mix the cream, egg yolks and grated cheese together and season with the salt and pepper. Melt the remaining butter in a pan and pour in the cream and egg yolk mixture. Drain the cooked pasta and add to the cream sauce with the peas. Stir until heated and spoon into a warmed serving dish.

Fettucine con Frutti di Mare e Mascarpone

Seafood and Mascarpone Fettucine
Serves 4

150 ml/¼ pt/⅔ cup passata (sieved
   tomatoes)
100 g/4 oz/½ cup Mascarpone cheese
350 g/12 oz frozen seafood cocktail,
   thawed
450 g/1 lb fettucine
Salt and freshly ground black pepper

Heat the passata with the Mascarpone over a low heat until they are very hot and well blended. Stir in the seafood and simmer for 5 minutes. Bring a large pan of salted water to the boil and add the fettucine. Cook for 10 minutes until tender. Drain thoroughly and pour into a serving dish. Pour over the hot seafood and season well.

Spaghetti alla Bolognese

Spaghetti Bolognese
Serves 4

2 large onions
25 g/1 oz/2 tbsp unsalted (sweet) butter
450 g/1 lb/4 cups minced (ground) beef
Salt and freshly ground black pepper
50 ml/2 fl oz/3½ tbsp red wine
400 g/14 oz/1 large can chopped
   tomatoes
15 ml/1 tbsp tomato purée (paste)
2 garlic cloves, crushed
1 bay leaf
450 g/1 lb spaghetti
15 ml/1 tbsp olive oil
75 g/3 oz/¾ cup Parmesan cheese, grated

Chop the onions and fry (sauté) them in the butter until they are translucent. Add the meat and season with the salt and pepper. Blend in the red wine, tomatoes and tomato purée. Stir in the crushed garlic and bay leaf. Cook for 20 minutes, stirring regularly, discard the bay leaf. Cook the spaghetti in a large pan of boiling, salted water for 8–10 minutes. Drain the spaghetti, return to the saucepan and add the oil. Toss the spaghetti in the oil, season with salt and pepper and add the grated cheese and Bolognese sauce. Toss over a gentle heat and serve immediately.

Spaghetti alla Carbonara

Spaghetti with Bacon and Eggs
Serves 4

15 ml/1 tbsp olive oil
25 g/1 oz/2 tbsp unsalted (sweet) butter
1 onion, chopped
1 garlic clove, crushed
175 g/6 oz bacon, rinded and chopped
90 ml/6 tbsp dry white wine
350 g/12 oz spaghetti
2 eggs
1 egg yolk
75 g/3 oz/¾ cup Parmesan cheese,
   grated
15 ml/1 tbsp chopped fresh parsley
Salt and freshly ground black pepper

Heat the oil and butter and fry (sauté) the onion and garlic until soft. Add the bacon. Fry for 2 minutes and pour in the wine. Bring to the boil, lower the heat and simmer until the wine has evaporated. Cook the spaghetti in boiling salted water for 8–10 minutes until tender, but still firm. Drain. Beat the eggs and egg yolk with the cheese and parsley and season to taste. Toss the spaghetti with the egg mixture then mix in the bacon mixture. Return to the pan for 30 seconds until the eggs are creamy and serve immediately.

Spaghetti con Burro all' Aglio

Spaghetti with Garlic Butter
Serves 4

75g/3 oz/⅓ cup unsalted (sweet) butter
4 garlic cloves, crushed
90 ml/6 tbsp chopped fresh parsley
350 g/12 oz spaghetti
Salt and freshly ground black pepper
75 g/3 oz/¾ cup Pecorino cheese,
   grated

Melt the butter and add the garlic. Stir in the parsley and cook over a low heat for 2 minutes. Cook the spaghetti in boiling salted water for 8–10 minutes until tender, but still firm. Drain. Toss the spaghetti in the garlic butter, season to taste with the salt and pepper and turn into a warmed serving dish. Serve sprinkled with the cheese.

Spaghetti alla Siciliani

Sicilian Spaghetti
Serves 4

15 ml/1 tbsp oil
1 onion, chopped
2 garlic cloves, chopped
1 red (bell) pepper, chopped
2 celery sticks, chopped
400 g/14 oz/1 large can of chopped
   tomatoes
5 ml/1 tsp chopped fresh tarragon
350 g/12 oz spaghetti
Salt and freshly ground black pepper
50 g/2 oz/½ cup Parmesan cheese,
   grated

Heat the oil and cook the onion, garlic, pepper and celery for 5 minutes until soft. Add the tomatoes and tarragon, and cook slowly for 15 minutes. Bring a large pan of salted water to the boil and cook the spaghetti for 8 minutes. Drain and return to the saucepan. Pour over the sauce, season and serve immediately with the Parmesan cheese sprinkled over.

Lasagne Verde al Forno

Baked Green Lasagne
Serves 6

50 g/2 oz/¼ cup unsalted (sweet) butter
50 g/2 oz pancetta, finely diced
1 small onion, finely chopped
1 carrot, finely diced
50 g/2 oz button mushrooms, finely
  sliced
225 g/8 oz/2 cups minced (ground)
  beef
100 g/4 oz/1 cup chicken livers, finely
  chopped
15 ml/1 tbsp tomato purée (paste)
150 ml/¼ pt/⅔ cup dry white wine
300 ml/½ pt/1¼ cups beef stock
5 ml/1 tsp caster (superfine) sugar
Salt and freshly ground black pepper
450 ml/¾ pt/2 cups milk
25 g/1 oz/¼ cup plain (all-purpose)
  flour
1 bay leaf
8 sheets no-need-to-precook green
  lasagne
50 g/2 oz/½ cup Parmesan cheese,
  grated

Melt a quarter of the butter in a large saucepan. Fry (sauté) the pancetta, onion and carrot for 3 minutes. Add the mushrooms and cook for 1 minute. Add the beef and chicken livers and cook, stirring, until brown and all the grains are separate. Stir in the tomato purée, wine, stock, sugar and a little salt and pepper. Bring to the boil, reduce the heat and simmer gently for 30 minutes until a rich sauce is formed, stirring occasionally. Meanwhile, blend the milk with the flour in a saucepan. Add 25 g/1 oz/2 tbsp of the remaining butter and the bay leaf. Bring to the boil and cook for 2 minutes, stirring all the time until thickened. Season to taste. Discard the bay leaf. Put a thin layer of the meat mixture in the base of a large shallow ovenproof dish, greased with the remaining butter. Top with a layer of white sauce, then a layer of lasagne sheets. Repeat the layers until all the ingredients are used, finishing with a layer of white sauce. Sprinkle the top with Parmesan and bake in a preheated oven at 190°C/375°F/gas mark 5 for 40 minutes until cooked through and golden brown.

Spaghetti alla Mediterraneo

Mediterranean Spaghetti
Serves 4

15 ml/1 tbsp olive oil
1 garlic clove, crushed
1 onion, roughly chopped
2 red (bell) peppers, sliced
1 yellow (bell) pepper, sliced
1 aubergine (eggplant), diced
1 courgette (zucchini), diced
3 tomatoes, skinned and chopped
30 ml/2 tbsp tomato purée (paste)
Salt and freshly ground black pepper
15 ml/1 tbsp chopped fresh basil or
  oregano
350 g/12 oz spaghetti

Heat the oil in a frying pan (skillet) and cook the garlic and onion for 2 minutes. Add the peppers, aubergine and courgette and fry (sauté) for 3 minutes. Blend in the tomatoes and tomato purée. Season well with the salt and pepper and blend in the basil. Reduce the heat and cook for 10 minutes, stirring occasionally. Bring a large pan of salted water to the boil and add the spaghetti. Cook for 8–10 minutes. Drain well and return the pasta to the pan. Pour in the hot sauce and heat before serving.

Penne con Melazzane

Pasta Quills with Aubergine

Serves 4

45 ml/3 tbsp olive oil
2 large onions, finely chopped
2 garlic cloves, crushed
2 large aubergines (eggplants),
  chopped
150 ml/¼ pt/⅔ cup white wine
150 ml/¼ pt/⅔ cup double (heavy)
  cream
Salt and freshly ground black pepper
350 g/12 oz pasta quills
15 ml/1 tbsp chopped fresh marjoram

Heat the oil in a saucepan and cook the onions and garlic until softened. Add the aubergines and cook for 4 minutes. Stir in the wine, cream, salt and pepper. Bring to the boil, reduce the heat and simmer for 5 minutes until the mixture is pulpy. Bring a large pan of salted water to the boil and cook the pasta for 8–10 minutes. Drain well. Season to taste with the salt and pepper and divide between the serving dishes. Spoon over the aubergine mixture. Garnish with the chopped marjoram and serve at once.

Crespelle di Spaghetti

Spaghetti Pancakes

Serves 4

150 g/5 oz spaghetti
5 eggs
1.5 ml/¼ tsp cayenne
50 g/2 oz/½ cup Parmesan cheese,
  grated
Salt
60 ml/4 tbsp oil
Chunky Tomato Sauce (see page 357),
  to serve

Break the spaghetti roughly into 5 cm/ 2 in lengths and cook in boiling salted water for 8–10 minutes until just tender. Drain. Beat the eggs with the cayenne and cheese and season with the salt. Stir in the hot spaghetti. Heat 15 ml/1 tbsp of the oil in a frying pan (skillet) and fry (sauté) a quarter of the spaghetti mixture for 1 minute. Turn and fry on the other side for a further minute. Remove from the heat and keep warm while the remaining 3 portions of the mixture are cooked. Serve with Chunky Tomato Sauce.

Pasta Piccante con Broccolo

Spicy Broccoli Pasta

Serves 4

350 g/12 oz broccoli florets
450 g/1 lb pasta shells
60 ml/4 tbsp olive oil
1 red onion, finely chopped
75 g/3 oz/¾ cup flaked almonds
225 g/8 oz pepperoni, sliced
15 ml/1 tbsp chopped fresh basil
15 ml/1 tbsp Pesto (see page 366)
Salt and freshly ground black pepper
50 g/2 oz/½ cup Bagozza (or other
  hard) cheese, grated
2.5 ml/½ tsp paprika

Cook the broccoli florets in boiling, salted water for 8 minutes, until just tender. Drain well. Cook the pasta in a separate pan of boiling, salted water for 10 minutes until just tender. Drain well. Heat the oil in a frying pan (skillet) and cook the onion until translucent. Stir in the almonds and cook quickly, until golden. Reduce the heat and add the pepperoni. Cook for 1 minute and stir in the broccoli, pasta, basil and pesto sauce. Season to taste and stir in the cheese. Toss well to mix and sprinkle with the paprika before serving.

Spaghetti e Spinaci al Forno

Spaghetti and Spinach Bake
Serves 4

25 g/1 oz/2 tbsp unsalted (sweet) butter
1 large onion, chopped
2 garlic cloves, crushed
900 g/2 lb spinach
350 g/12 oz spaghetti
250 ml/8 fl oz/1 cup Basic White
* Sauce (see page 357)*
5 ml/1 tsp chopped fresh basil
75 g/3 oz/¾ cup Parmesan cheese, grated

Melt the butter in a large frying pan (skillet) and cook the onion and garlic for 5 minutes. Place the washed spinach in a saucepan and cover with a lid. Cook for 5 minutes, stirring occasionally. Remove the lid and continue cooking for 5 minutes to evaporate the moisture. Drain and stir into the onion and garlic and continue cooking for 2 minutes. Spoon into a serving dish. Meanwhile, cook the spaghetti in boiling, salted water for 10 minutes until the spaghetti is firm but tender. Drain well and blend with the white sauce. Pour over the spinach. Sprinkle with the basil and Parmesan cheese and bake in a preheated oven at 190°C/375°F/gas mark 5 for 20 minutes until brown on the top.

Capellini Aromatici

Aromatic Angel Hair
Serves 4–6

225 g/8 oz capellini
200 ml/7 fl oz./scant 1 cup olive oil
4 garlic cloves, chopped
25 ml/1½ tbsp grated fresh root ginger
8 basil leaves, torn
Freshly grated Parmesan cheese

Cook the pasta. Drain. Heat the oil in a saucepan. Add the garlic and ginger and cook for 2–3 minutes until lightly golden. Pile the pasta on warm plates and drizzle over the fragrant oil. Sprinkle over the basil and lots of Parmesan cheese.

Spaghetti con Funghi

Spaghetti with Oyster Mushrooms
Serves 4

45 ml/3 tbsp olive oil
2 large onions, finely chopped
2 garlic cloves, crushed
350 g/12 oz oyster mushrooms,
* roughly chopped*
150 ml/¼ pt/⅔ cup white wine
150 ml/¼ pt/⅔ cup double (heavy)
* cream*
Salt and freshly ground black pepper
350 g/12 oz spaghetti
15 ml/1 tbsp chopped fresh marjoram

Heat the oil in a saucepan and cook the onions and garlic until softened. Stir in the mushrooms and cook for 4 minutes. Stir in the wine, cream, salt and pepper. Bring to the boil, reduce the heat and simmer for 5 minutes until the mixture is thick and creamy. Bring a large pan of salted water to the boil and cook the spaghetti until just tender. Drain well. Season to taste with the salt and pepper and divide between four serving dishes. Spoon over the mushroom mixture. Garnish with the chopped marjoram and serve at once.

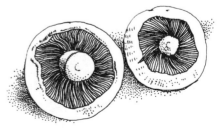

Spaghetti con Maiale, Acciughe e Pomodori

Spaghetti with Pork, Anchovies & Tomato

Serves 3–4

15 ml/1 tbsp olive oil
1 garlic clove, peeled but left whole
1 onion, sliced
225 g/8 oz/2 cups cooked pork minced (ground)
3 tomatoes, skinned and chopped
1 red (bell) pepper, sliced
25 g/1 oz/½ small can anchovies, drained and chopped
2 bay leaves
150 ml/¼ pt/⅔ cup pork or vegetable stock
Salt and freshly ground black pepper
225 g/8 oz spaghetti
60 ml/4 tbsp grated Pecorino cheese

Heat the oil in a pan and brown the garlic, onion and minced pork. Remove the garlic and add the chopped tomatoes, sliced red peppers, anchovies and bay leaves. Cook for 5 minutes and stir in the stock. Season with the salt and pepper and simmer for 30 minutes. Remove the bay leaves. Bring a pan of salted boiling water to the boil and add the spaghetti. Cook for 10 minutes until tender but still firm and drain well. Pile into a serving dish, pour over the sauce and serve, sprinkled with the cheese.

Spaghetti al Aglio e Olio

Spaghetti with Garlic and Oil

Serves 4–6

450 g/1 lb spaghetti
375 ml/13 fl oz/1½ cups olive oil
10 garlic cloves, coarsely chopped
45 ml/3 tbsp finely chopped fresh root ginger
50 g/2 oz/½ cup Parmesan cheese, freshly grated

Cook the spaghetti in a large pan of boiling, salted water until just tender but still firm. Drain well. Meanwhile, heat the oil and fry (sauté) the garlic and ginger for a few minutes until golden brown, stirring continuously. Pour over the cooked pasta and toss together well. Serve sprinkled with the Parmesan.

Tagliarini con Burro e Tartufo

Pasta with Butter and Truffle

Serves 4

350 g/12 oz tagliarini
50 g/2 oz/¼ cup unsalted (sweet) butter
Salt and freshly ground black pepper
15 ml/1 tbsp chopped fresh parsley
1 white truffle, shaved into fine slivers

Add the pasta to a large saucepan of boiling water and cook until just tender. Drain and return to the saucepan. Heat the butter, season and add the parsley. Spoon the pasta into a warmed serving dish and pour over the butter. Sprinkle with the truffle and serve immediately.

Ravioli di Spinaci e Uova

Spinach and Egg Ravioli
Serves 4–6

450 g/1 lb/4 cups plain (all-purpose)
 flour
1.5 ml/¼ tsp salt
3 eggs, beaten
30 ml/2 tbsp milk or single (light)
 cream
225 g/8 oz spinach, cooked and
 chopped
2 eggs, beaten
15 ml/1 tbsp chopped fresh basil
50 g/2 oz/½ cup Mozzarella cheese,
 grated
Salt and freshly ground black pepper
Tomato Sauce (see page 358), to serve

Sift the flour and salt in a bowl and blend
in the eggs and cream. Knead very thoroughly until smooth. Cover the bowl with
a cloth and leave for 30 minutes. Roll out
the dough thinly and cut in half. Hang up
to dry or place on a clean cloth over the
back of a chairs. Leave for 10 minutes.
Purée the spinach and place in a saucepan.
Heat for 1 minute, stirring and beat in the
eggs, basil and grated Mozzarella. Remove
from the heat and beat again. Season with
the salt and pepper. Put teaspoonfuls of the
filling at regular intervals in rows on one
half of the pasta and brush all round the
filling with water. Lay the other half on
top. Press gently round each mound of filling and cut between the filling down the
length then across the width to form little
cushions of filled pasta. Drop into a pan of
rapidly boiling salted water and cook for 8
minutes. Remove with a slotted spoon and
serve at once with Tomato Sauce.

Lasagne al Tonno

Tuna Lasagne
Serves 4

15 ml/1 tbsp virgin olive oil
1 onion, chopped
1 garlic clove, crushed
100 g/4 oz bacon, rinded and cut into
 thin strips
150 g/5 oz mushrooms, chopped
30 ml/2 tbsp capers, chopped
30 ml/2 tbsp chopped fresh basil
400 g/14 oz/1 large can of tomatoes,
 chopped
30 ml/2 tbsp tomato purée (paste)
370 g/13 oz/1 large can tuna, drained
Salt and freshly ground black pepper
50 g/2 oz/¼ cup unsalted (sweet) butter
50 g/2 oz/½ cup plain (all-purpose)
 flour
600 ml/1 pt/2½ cups milk
9 sheets of no-need-to-cook lasagne
50 g/2 oz/½ cup Parmesan cheese,
 grated

Heat the oil in a saucepan and fry (sauté)
the onion and garlic for 2 minutes. Stir in
the bacon and mushrooms. Cook for a further 2 minutes and add the capers, basil,
tomatoes and tomato purée. Simmer for 8
minutes. Flake the tuna and stir into the
sauce. Season with the salt and pepper.
Melt the butter in a separate saucepan.
Blend in the flour and stir for 1 minute.
Remove from the heat and whisk in the
milk. Return to the heat, whisking until the
sauce comes to the boil. Season to taste.
Place one third of the tuna mix in an ovenproof dish. Cover with 3 sheets of lasagne.
Repeat twice more. Pour over the white
sauce and sprinkle over the Parmesan
cheese. Bake in a preheated oven for 45
minutes at 190°C/375°F/gas mark 5.

Tagliatelle con Dolcelatte e Broccolo

Tagliatelle with Cheese and Broccoli

Serves 4–6

225 g/8 oz broccoli, cut in small florets
350 g/12 oz tagliatelle
60 ml/4 tbsp Mascarpone cheese
100 g/4 oz Dolcelatte cheese, cubed
2.5 ml/½ tsp grated nutmeg
Salt and freshly ground black pepper
50 g/2 oz/½ cup walnuts, chopped

Bring a large pan of salted water to the boil and cook the broccoli for 4 minutes until tender. Drain and set aside. Bring the pasta to the boil a large pan of salted water and cook for 8–10 minutes until tender. Drain and return to the pan. Gently mix in the Mascarpone, Dolcelatte and nutmeg and toss well. Add the broccoli, seasoning and chopped nuts and transfer to an ovenproof dish. Bake in a preheated oven at 200°C/400°F/gas mark 6 for 10 minutes.

Fettuccine con Spinaci e Prosciutto

Spinach and Ham Fettuccine

Serves 4

Salt
175 g/6 oz fettuccine
225 g/8 oz fresh spinach, shredded
300 ml/½ pt/1¼ cups Parmesan Sauce
  (see page 361)
5 ml/1 tsp made mustard
15 ml/1 tbsp chopped fresh parsley
75 g/3 oz prosciutto, thinly sliced
15 g/½ oz/2 tbsp Parmesan cheese, grated
25 g/1 oz/½ cup fresh breadcrumbs

Bring a large pan of salted water to the boil and cook the pasta for 10 minutes until just tender. Drain thoroughly and return to the saucepan. Add the spinach, Parmesan sauce, mustard and parsley and toss gently. Spoon into an ovenproof dish. Cover with the slices of prosciutto and sprinkle over the cheese and breadcrumbs. Bake in a preheated oven at 200°C/400°F/gas mark 6 for about 15 minutes until brown on top.

Spaghetti all' Alsaziana

Spaghetti Alsacienne

Serves 4

350 g/12 oz spaghetti
50 g/2 oz/¼ cup unsalted (sweet) butter
Salt and freshly ground black pepper
100 g/4 oz Bel Paese cheese, cut into chunks
5 ml/1 tsp chopped fresh basil
100 g/4 oz lean ham, chopped
400 ml/14 fl oz/1¾ cups Tomato Sauce (see page 358)

Bring a pan of salted water to the boil and add the spaghetti. Cook for 10 minutes until tender but still firm. Drain and add the butter. Return the pan to the heat for a few seconds and season with the salt and pepper. Stir in the cheese, basil and ham. Pile into a serving dish and pour over the hot Tomato Sauce.

Tagliarini con Noci, Funghi e Formaggio

Walnut, Mushroom and Cheese Pasta

Serves 4

30 ml/2 tbsp olive oil
1 small onion, finely chopped
1 garlic clove, chopped
100 g/4 oz mushrooms, thinly sliced
75 g/3 oz/¾ cup walnut pieces
Salt and freshly ground black pepper
400 g/1 lb tagliarini
100 g/4 oz/1 cup goats' cheese,
* crumbled*
30 ml/2 tbsp chopped fresh sage

Heat the oil in a frying pan (skillet), cook the onion and garlic and add the mushrooms. Cook until the mushrooms are soft and add the walnuts, salt and pepper. Cook for a further 3 minutes. Bring a large pan of salted water to the boil and cook the tagliarini for 5 minutes until the pasta is firm but tender. Drain. Spoon the sauce over the pasta. Crumble the goats' cheese with the chopped sage and sprinkle over the pasta.

Tagliarini con Piselli

Tagliarini with Peas

Serves 4

175 g/6 oz fresh or frozen peas
40 g/1½ oz/5 tbsp unsalted (sweet)
* butter*
90 ml/6 tbsp double (heavy) cream
Salt and freshly ground black pepper
350 g/12 oz tagliarini
15 ml/1 tbsp chopped fresh basil
50 g/2 oz/½ cup Pecorino cheese,
* grated*

Cook the peas, drain and purée in a blender or food processor. Stir in the butter and cream. Season to taste and heat through. Bring a large pan of salted water to the boil and cook the tagliarini until just tender. Drain and return to the saucepan. Pour over the pea sauce, season with salt and pepper and sprinkle over the basil and Pecorino cheese.

Tagliatelle con Pomodori Secchi e Crema

Tagliatelle with Sun-dried Tomatoes and Cream

Serves 4

45 ml/3 tbsp olive oil
1 large onion, finely chopped
2 garlic cloves, crushed
50 g/2 oz sun-dried tomatoes,
* in oil, drained and roughly chopped*
225 g/8 oz oyster mushrooms, sliced
150 ml/¼ pt/⅔ cup white wine
150 ml/¼ pt/⅔ cup double (heavy)
* cream*
Salt and freshly ground black pepper
350 g/12 oz tagliatelle
15 ml/1 tbsp chopped fresh marjoram

Heat the oil in a saucepan and cook the onion and garlic until softened. Stir in the tomatoes and mushrooms and cook for 4 minutes. Stir in the wine, cream, salt and pepper. Bring to the boil, reduce the heat and simmer for 5 minutes until the mixture is thick and creamy. Bring a large pan of salted water to the boil and cook the tagliatelle until just tender. Drain well. Season to taste with the salt and pepper and divide between four serving dishes. Spoon over the mushroom mixture. Garnish with the chopped marjoram and serve at once.

***Photograph opposite:* Oregano and Olive Potatoes (page 183)**

Pasta con Pomodori Secchi

Sun-dried Tomato Pasta

Serves 4

30 ml/2 tbsp chopped fresh coriander
  (cilantro)
75 g/3 oz/¾ cup Parmesan cheese,
  grated
60 ml/4 tbsp Ricotta cheese
Salt and freshly ground black pepper
50 g/2 oz sun-dried tomatoes, drained
  and chopped
75 ml/5 tbsp olive oil
350 g/12 oz pasta spirals

Purée the coriander with the Parmesan, Ricotta cheese, salt, pepper, sun-dried tomatoes and olive oil in a blender or food processor until smooth. Cook the pasta in plenty of salted, boiling water for 10 minutes until firm but cooked. Drain and return the pasta to the pan. Pour over the dressing and toss together over a low heat. Serve immediately.

Tagliatelle con Pomodoro e Cipolla

Tomato and Onion Tagliatelle

Serves 4

175 g/6 oz button (pearl) onions,
  quartered
60 ml/4 tbsp olive oil
15 ml/1 tbsp brown sugar
100 g/4 oz small cherry tomatoes,
  halved
350 g/12 oz tagliatelle
25 g/1 oz/2 tbsp unsalted (sweet) butter
Salt and freshly ground black pepper
5 ml/1 tsp chopped fresh sage

Photograph opposite: **Spinach and Egg Ravioli (page 222)**

Place the onions in a frying pan (skillet) with the oil and sugar and cook on high for 5 minutes, stirring occasionally. Add the tomatoes and fry (sauté) for 1 minute. Place the pasta in a large pan of boiling, salted water and cook until just tender. Drain and return to the pan. Add the butter and pour into a warmed serving dish. Spoon over the onions and tomatoes, season and sprinkle over the sage.

Tortellini con Salsa di Pomodoro, Cappero e Cipolla

Tortellini with Tomato, Caper and Onion Sauce

Serves 4

30 ml/2 tbsp olive oil
2 onions, chopped
1 garlic clove, chopped
5 large tomatoes, skinned, seeded and
  chopped
60 ml/4 tbsp vegetable stock
30 ml/2 tbsp capers, chopped
Salt and freshly ground black pepper
350 g/12 oz tortellini
75 g/3 oz/¾ cup Parmesan cheese,
  grated

Heat the oil in a saucepan and fry (sauté) the onions and garlic. Stir in the tomatoes and stock. Bring to the boil, reduce the heat and simmer for 10 minutes. Add the capers and season with the salt and pepper. Cook a further 10 minutes until the sauce is pulpy. Bring a large pan of salted water to the boil and cook the pasta for 10 minutes. Drain. Spoon the sauce over the cooked pasta. Sprinkle with Parmesan cheese and serve immediately.

Conchiglie con Verdura

Pasta Shells with Vegetables
Serves 4

30 ml/2 tbsp olive oil
1 aubergine (eggplant), chopped,
  salted and drained
1 garlic clove, crushed
2 large courgettes (zucchini), sliced
1 green (bell) pepper, sliced
1 red (bell) pepper, sliced
1 yellow (bell) pepper, sliced
400 g/14 oz/1 large can chopped tomatoes
30 ml/2 tbsp tomato purée (paste)
Salt and freshly ground black pepper
350 g/12 oz pasta shells
30 ml/2 tbsp chopped fresh oregano
50 g/2 oz/½ cup Parmesan cheese, grated

Heat the oil in a pan and cook the aubergine, garlic and courgettes for 4 minutes. Stir in the sliced peppers, tomatoes and tomato purée and cook for 10 minutes. Season with the salt and pepper. Cook the pasta shells in boiling salted water for 10 minutes until firm but tender. Drain the pasta and transfer to a large bowl. Pour over the sauce and sprinkle over the oregano and Parmesan cheese.

Maccheroni al Forno con Pomodori

Tomato-baked Macaroni
Serves 4

2.5 ml/½ tsp salt
225 g/8 oz macaroni
25 g/1 oz/2 tbsp unsalted (sweet) butter
3 tomatoes, skinned and sliced
30 ml/2 tbsp olive oil
Salt and freshly ground black pepper
100 g/4 oz/1 cup Parmesan cheese,
  grated

Bring a large pan of salted water to the boil and cook the macaroni for 10 minutes. Drain well and pour into a casserole dish (Dutch oven). Dot with small pieces of butter. Place the sliced tomatoes over the macaroni and pour the oil over the tomatoes. Season well. Bake at 190°C/375°F/gas mark 5 for 15 minutes. Sprinkle with the grated cheese and return to the oven for 10 minutes. Serve at once.

Vermicelli con Peperoni

Vermicelli with Peppers
Serves 4

15 ml/1 tbsp olive oil
1 red onion, sliced
1 red (bell) pepper, sliced
1 green (bell) pepper, sliced
1 yellow (bell) pepper, sliced
15 ml/1 tbsp red wine
15 ml/1 tbsp wine vinegar
3 tomatoes, skinned, seeded and
  chopped
5 ml/1 tsp sugar
Salt and freshly ground black pepper
350 g/12 oz vermicelli
15 ml/1 tbsp chopped fresh parsley

Heat the oil and fry (sauté) the onion and peppers until soft. Stir in the wine and vinegar and heat until the liquid has evaporated. Stir in the tomatoes, sugar, salt and pepper and simmer for 20 minutes. Cook the vermicelli in boiling water for 8 minutes until tender but still firm. Drain, and turn into a warmed serving dish. Pour over the pepper sauce and serve sprinkled with the parsley.

Tuscany Pappardelle

Tuscan Pappardelle
Serves 4

2 large onions, chopped
25 g/1 oz/2 tbsp unsalted (sweet) butter
450 g/1 lb/4 cups minced (ground) beef
Salt and freshly ground black pepper
50 ml/2 fl oz/3½ tbsp red wine
400 g/14 oz/1 large can chopped
* tomatoes*
2 garlic cloves, crushed
15 ml/1 tbsp chopped stoned (pitted)
* green olives*
450 g/1 lb pappardelle
15 ml/1 tbsp olive oil
75 g/3 oz/¾ cup Parmesan cheese,
* grated*

Fry (sauté) the onions in the butter until they are translucent. Add the meat and season with the salt and pepper. Cook for 10 minutes stirring until the grains of meat are brown and separate. Blend in the red wine and chopped tomatoes. Stir in the crushed garlic and olives. Cook for a further 10 minutes. Bring a large pan of salted water to the boil and add the pappardelle. Boil for 6–8 minutes until tender but firm. Drain the pasta, return to the saucepan and toss with the oil. Season with salt and pepper and add the grated cheese and meat sauce. Serve immediately.

Penne alla Noce e Asparagi

Walnut and Asparagus Penne
Serves 4

60 ml/4 tbsp walnut oil
50 g/2 oz/1 cup breadcrumbs made
* from nut bread*
350 g/12 oz asparagus, cut into
* 1 cm/½ in pieces*
5 ml/1 tsp salt
350 g/12 oz penne
2 garlic cloves, chopped
1 small red (bell) pepper, seeded and
* finely chopped*
10 ml/2 tsp chopped fresh thyme
50 g/2 oz/½ cup olives, stoned (pitted)
* and halved*
8 walnuts, chopped

Heat half the walnut oil in a frying pan (skillet) and fry (sauté) the breadcrumbs for 5 minutes until brown. Drain on kitchen paper and set aside. Put the asparagus in boiling water for 2 minutes. Drain and refresh under cold running water. Pat dry on kitchen paper. Bring a large pan of water to the boil, add salt and cook the pasta for 10 minutes until firm but cooked. Put the remaining oil in the frying pan and cook the garlic, pepper and thyme for 1 minute. Add the asparagus and cook for 2 minutes over a high heat. Drain the pasta and stir into the asparagus. Add the olives and chopped walnuts. Season if desired and serve immediately.

Cannelloni con Carne di Manzo

Beef Cannelloni

Serves 4
50 g/2 oz/¼ cup unsalted (sweet) butter
2 carrots, finely chopped
1 onion, finely chopped
1 garlic clove, crushed
450 g/1 lb/4 cups minced (ground)
* beef*
Salt and freshly ground black pepper
15 ml/1 tbsp plain (all-purpose) flour
120 ml/4 fl oz/½ cup dry white wine
450 g/1 lb tomatoes, skinned and
* chopped*
5 ml/1 tsp chopped fresh oregano
5 ml/1 tsp butter for greasing
12 cannelloni tubes

Sauce:
100 g/4 oz/½ cup unsalted (sweet)
* butter*
50 g/2 oz/½ cup plain (all-purpose)
* flour*
400 ml/14 fl oz/1¾ cups milk
50 g/2 oz/½ cup Parmesan cheese,
* grated*

Melt the butter in a saucepan, add the carrot, onion, garlic and fry (sauté) for 5 minutes until the onion is translucent. Add the beef and fry until the meat is brown. Season with the salt and pepper. Lower the heat, sprinkle in the flour and cook for 1 minute. Remove from the heat and blend in the wine, tomatoes and oregano. Return to the heat and bring to the boil. Lower the heat and simmer for 20 minutes, stirring occasionally. Adjust the seasoning and leave to cool. Grease a large shallow ovenproof dish. Stuff the cannelloni with the filling mixture and cover the bottom of the dish with the filled tubes. Make the sauce. Melt half the butter in a saucepan and add the flour. Cook for 1 minute and gradually blend in the milk. Cook for 3 minutes, stirring until thick and smooth and season with salt and pepper. Pour over the white sauce. Dot with the remaining butter and sprinkle over the Parmesan cheese. Bake in a preheated oven at 200°C/400°F/gas mark 6 for 30 minutes or until the cannelloni is tender.

Cannelloni

Filled Pasta Tubes
Serves 4–6

350 g/12 oz/3 cups plain (all-purpose)
* flour*
Salt and freshly ground black pepper
2 eggs
225 g/8 oz/2 cups lean minced (ground)
* beef*
1 large onion, minced
5 ml/1 tsp dried oregano
Tomato Sauce (see page 358), to serve

Put the flour with a little salt and pepper in a bowl. Beat the eggs and mix into the flour. Mix with enough cold water to form a firm dough. Knead well. Roll out on a floured board and cut into rectangles about 7.5 × 10 cm/3 × 4 in. Mix together the minced beef and onion and blend with the oregano. Season with the salt and pepper. Spread a little of the mixture on each piece of dough and wet the edges of the pastry with water. Roll up like a sausage roll. Place the cannelloni carefully into a pan of boiling water and boil for 8–10 minutes. Drain well and serve with Tomato Sauce.

Piatto Affumicato con Spaghettini

Smoked Platter with Spaghettini
Serves 4

225 g/8 oz Parma ham/salami/dried salt beef slices, mixed
275 g/10 oz spaghettini (very thin spaghetti)
175 g/6 oz sun-dried tomatoes in oil
Salt and freshly ground black pepper
90 ml/6 tbsp olive oil
30 ml/2 tbsp chopped fresh basil
175 g/6 oz/³⁄₄ cup creamy, soft goats' cheese
75 g/3 oz/³⁄₄ cup Parmesan cheese, grated

Divide the sliced meats between individual serving plates. Bring a large pan of salted water to the boil and add the spaghettini. Cook until just tender. Drain the sun-dried tomatoes, reserving the oil, and chop roughly. Drain the spaghettini. Return to the saucepan and toss in the tomatoes, olive oil and basil. Add the reserved tomato oil if desired. Stir in the goats' cheese and cook over a low heat. Add the grated Parmesan and cook for 2–3 minutes. Serve the pasta with the sliced meat.

Manzo con Pasta

Steak with Pasta
Serves 4

15 ml/1 tbsp oil
1 onion, chopped
1 garlic clove, crushed
100 g/4 oz Parma ham, chopped
175 g/6 oz top rump steak, diced
100 g/4 oz mushrooms, sliced
60 ml/4 tbsp white wine
175 ml/6 fl oz/³⁄₄ cup beef stock
5 ml/1 tsp chopped fresh thyme
Salt and freshly ground black pepper
30 ml/2 tbsp double (heavy) cream
350 g/12 oz conchiglie

Heat the oil in a frying pan (skillet) and cook the onion and garlic for 1 minute. Add the Parma ham and cook for a further 2 minutes. Add the steak and fry (sauté) until browned. Stir in the mushrooms and cook for 15 minutes. Pour in the wine and bring to the boil. Cook until the liquid has reduced by three-quarters. Stir in the stock, thyme, salt and pepper. Simmer over a low heat for 40 minutes. Remove from the heat and stir in the cream. Cook the conchiglie in boiling, salted water for 8–10 minutes until just tender, then rinse in hot water. Drain well and turn the pasta into a warmed serving dish. Pour over the steak and ham mixture.

Pasta di Pescara

Pescara Pasta
Serves 4

2 large onions, chopped
25 g/1 oz/2 tbsp unsalted (sweet) butter
450 g/1 lb/4 cups minced (ground)
  beef
Salt and freshly ground black pepper
50 ml/2 fl oz/3½ tbsp red wine
400 g/14 oz/1 large can chopped
  tomatoes
2 garlic cloves, crushed
350 g/12 oz spaghetti
15 ml/1 tbsp olive oil
75 g/3 oz/¾ cup Parmesan cheese,
  grated

Fry (sauté) the onions in the butter until they are translucent. Add the meat and season with the salt and pepper. Blend in the red wine and tomatoes. Stir in the crushed garlic. Cook for 20 minutes, stirring regularly. Place a large pan of hot water over a high heat and when boiling add the spaghetti and a large pinch of salt. Boil for 6 minutes. Drain the spaghetti, return to the saucepan and add the oil. Toss the spaghetti in this, season with salt and pepper and add the grated cheese and meat sauce. Cook together for 4-5 minutes, stirring and serve immediately.

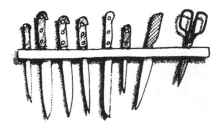

Lasagne con Pollo

Chicken Lasagne
Serves 6

30 ml/2 tbsp olive oil
2 onions, chopped
50 g/2 oz/½ cup plain (all-purpose) flour
300 ml/½ pt/1¼ cups chicken stock
420 g/14 oz/1 large can chopped
  tomatoes
450 g/1 lb/4 cups cooked chicken,
  chopped
15 ml/1 tbsp tomato purée (paste)
Salt and freshly ground black pepper
8 strips no-need-to-precook lasagne
25 g/1 oz/2 tbsp margarine
300 ml/½ pt/1¼ cups milk
100 g/4 oz/1 cup cheese, grated

Grease a shallow ovenproof dish with a little of the oil and preheat the oven to 190°C/375°F/gas mark 5. Heat the remaining oil in a pan and add the onions. Fry (sauté) until soft and sprinkle over half the flour, stirring. Cook for 1 minute and gradually stir in the stock, tomatoes, chopped chicken and tomato purée. Bring to the boil, lower the heat and simmer for 3 minutes. Season to taste. Melt the margarine in a saucepan, sprinkle in the remaining flour, season with the salt and pepper and cook for 1 minute. Gradually stir in the milk and cook until the sauce thickens. Spread a little of the chicken mixture in the bottom of the greased ovenproof dish. Place some of the lasagne on the top, breaking to fit. Spread half the remaining chicken and tomato mixture over the lasagne. Cover with a second layer of lasagne. Repeat these layers. Cover with the white sauce. Sprinkle over the grated cheese and bake for 40 minutes until cooked through and golden brown.

Stufato di Pollo e Tagliatelle

Casserole of Chicken and Noodles
Serves 4

1.5 kg/3 lb oven-ready chicken
1 onion, studded with 4 cloves
2 celery sticks, chopped
5 ml/1 tsp salt
1 bay leaf
2 carrots, chopped
400 ml/14 fl oz/1¾ cups chicken stock
50 g/2 oz/¼ cup unsalted (sweet) butter
25 g/1 oz/¼ cup plain (all-purpose) flour
1 egg yolk
30 ml/2 tbsp sherry or red wine
120 ml/4 fl oz/½ cup single (light) cream
225 g/8 oz mushrooms, sliced
225 g/8 oz tagliatelle
75 g/3 oz/¾ cup Parmesan cheese, grated

Put the chicken, onion, celery, salt, bay leaf, carrots and stock in a large saucepan and bring to the boil over a high heat. Cover with a lid, reduce the heat and simmer for 1½ hours. Remove the pan from the heat and allow the chicken to cool in the stock. Drain and place on a chopping board. Remove the skin and bones from the chicken. Strain the stock, reserve and cool. Skim off any fat. Grease a shallow ovenproof casserole dish (Dutch oven) and set aside. Bring the reserved stock to the boil in a saucepan and allow to simmer. Melt half the butter in another pan and stir in the flour. Gradually add the reserved stock and cook for one minute. Lightly beat the egg yolk in a cup and add 30 ml/ 2 tbsp of the hot stock. Return the egg yolk mixture to the saucepan and stir in the sherry, cream and chicken. Heat the remaining butter and fry (sauté) the mushrooms until they are just beginning to brown. Boil the noodles in plenty of salted water for 10 minutes until they are just tender. Drain well and place a layer in the base of the casserole dish. Lay over half the chicken mixture and half the mushrooms. Repeat this layering process and top the dish with Parmesan cheese. Place under a grill (broiler) to brown the top and serve at once.

Gnocchi al Forno con Salsa di Pomodoro

Baked Gnocchi in Tomato Sauce
Serves 4

4 egg yolks
10 ml/2 tsp sugar
50 g/2 oz/½ cup plain (all-purpose) flour
30 ml/2 tbsp cornflour (cornstarch)
Salt and freshly ground black pepper
50 g/2 oz/¼ cup unsalted (sweet) butter
100 g/4 oz/1 cup Parmesan cheese, grated
450 ml/¾ pt/2 cups milk
Tomato Sauce (see page 358), to serve

Place the egg yolks and sugar in a saucepan and beat until creamy. Sift the flour and cornflour into a mixing bowl and gradually add to the creamy mixture, beating constantly. Season to taste. Stir in half of the butter and three-quarters of the cheese. Place the pan over a low heat and gradually add the milk, stirring constantly. Cook for 3 minutes until the mixture has thickened. Remove the pan from the heat. Pour the mixture into a large flat dish and smooth out the surface. Chill for 25–30 minutes. Grease an ovenproof dish with the remaining butter. Cut the gnocchi into 4 cm/1½ in squares and overlap in the baking dish. Sprinkle them with the remaining cheese and bake in a preheated oven at 190°C/375°F/gas mark 5 for 20 minutes. Serve with the sauce poured over the top.

Tortellini e Pollo alla Carbonara

Tortellini and Chicken Carbonara
Serves 4

15 ml/1 tbsp oil
1 onion, chopped
1 garlic clove, crushed
25 g/1 oz/2 tbsp unsalted (sweet) butter
175 g/6 oz/1½ cups cooked chicken, chopped
175 g/6 oz bacon, rinded and chopped
90 ml/6 tbsp dry white wine
350 g/12 oz tortellini
3 eggs
75 g/3 oz/¾ cup Parmesan cheese, grated
15 ml/1 tbsp chopped fresh parsley
Salt and freshly ground black pepper
120 ml/4 fl oz/½ cup double (heavy) cream

Heat the oil and fry (sauté) the onion and garlic until soft. Add the butter, chicken and the bacon. Fry until golden and pour in the wine. Bring to the boil, lower the heat and simmer until the wine has evaporated. Cook the pasta in boiling salted water for 8–10 minutes or until tender, but still firm. Rinse in hot water and drain. Return to the pan. Beat the eggs with the cheese and parsley and season to taste. Add to the pasta with the egg mixture then spoon in the bacon mixture. Toss over a gentle heat for 30 seconds to cook the eggs. Stir in the cream and serve immediately.

Pollo e Maccheroni al Forno

Chicken and Macaroni Bake
Serves 4

15 ml/1 tbsp oil
2 onions, chopped
2 garlic cloves, crushed
450 g/1 lb boneless chicken breasts
25 g/1oz/¼ cup plain (all-purpose) flour
300 ml/½ pt/1¼ cups chicken stock
100 g/4 oz mushrooms, sliced
10 ml/2 tsp chopped fresh mixed herbs
1 bay leaf
175 g/6 oz macaroni
Pinch of salt
50 g/2 oz/½ cup Cheddar cheese, grated

Heat the oil in a large frying pan (skillet) or saucepan. Add the onions and crushed garlic and cook for 1 minute. Finely chop the chicken breasts and add to the frying pan. Cook for 10 minutes stirring. Blend in the flour. Gradually stir in the chicken stock and add the mushrooms, herbs and bay leaf. Bring to the boil, lower the heat and simmer for 15 minutes. Cook the pasta in boiling, salted water for 12 minutes or until just tender, stirring occasionally. Remove the bay leaf and transfer the chicken and onion mixture to a large oven-proof dish. Drain the pasta and place over the chicken. Sprinkle with the grated cheese. Bake in a preheated oven at 200°C/400°F/gas mark 6 for 20 minutes, until the cheese is melted and golden brown.

Penne con Pollo Piccante

Penne with Spicy Chicken
Serves 4–6

450 g/1 lb penne
450 g/1 lb skinless chicken breast
  fillets
30 ml/2 tbsp olive oil
1 red (bell) pepper, cut in thin strips
150 ml/¼ pt/⅔ cup white wine
15 ml/1 tbsp tomato purée (paste)
150 ml/¼ pt/⅔ cup single (light) cream
1 red chilli, seeded and finely chopped

Cook the pasta in lightly salted water for 10 minutes until firm but tender. Cut the chicken into 2 cm/¾ in cubes and fry (sauté) in the oil for 4 minutes on each side. Put the red pepper, white wine and tomato purée into a saucepan and boil, stirring occasionally, until the liquid has reduced by half. Stir in the cream and seasoning and heat gently for 1 minute. Drain the pasta and stir into the sauce with the chicken and chopped chilli. Heat through and serve.

Maniche con Pollo

Pasta with Chicken
Serves 4

225 g/8 oz broccoli florets
75 g/3 oz/⅓ cup unsalted (sweet) butter
25 g/1 oz/¼ cup plain (all-purpose)
  flour
400 ml/14 fl oz/1¾ cups chicken stock
150 ml/¼ pt/⅔ cup double (heavy) cream
5 ml/1 tsp chopped fresh sage
Salt and freshly ground black pepper
350 g/12 oz maniche or macaroni
450 g/1 lb cooked chicken, chopped
75 g/3 oz/¾ cup Parmesan cheese,
  grated

Cook the broccoli in boiling salted water until just tender. Drain well. Heat half the butter in a saucepan and stir in the flour. Cook for 1 minute then whisk in the stock. Cook, stirring, until the sauce thickens. Simmer for 5 minutes and stir in the broccoli. Reduce the heat to very low and add the cream, sage, salt and pepper. Bring a pan of salted water to the boil and add the pasta. Cook for 8–10 minutes until the pasta is tender, but still firm. Drain, rinse in hot water and drain well. Add the remaining butter and spoon the pasta into an ovenproof dish. Top with the chicken and then the sauce. Sprinkle with the cheese and bake in a preheated oven at 220°C/425°F/gas mark 7 for 20 minutes.

Conchiglie di Prosciutto

Ham Pasta Shells
Serves 4

45 ml/3 tbsp olive oil
1 onion, chopped
2 garlic cloves, crushed
100 g/4 oz Parma ham, chopped
450 g/1 lb tomatoes, skinned, seeded
  and chopped
60 ml/4 tbsp dry white wine
Salt and freshly ground black pepper
350 g/12 oz pasta shells
50 g/2 oz/½ cup Pecorino cheese,
  grated
30 ml/2 tbsp chopped fresh sage

Heat the oil and fry (sauté) the onion and garlic until soft. Stir in the ham, tomatoes, wine, salt and pepper. Place the pasta shells in a pan of salted, boiling water and cook for 8–10 minutes, until tender, but still firm. Rinse in hot water and drain well. Blend the pasta with the ham sauce and serve sprinkled with the cheese and sage.

Fegattini di Pollo con Capellini

Capellini Chicken Livers
Serves 4

30 ml/2 tbsp olive oil
50 g/2 oz/¼ cup unsalted (sweet) butter
3 garlic cloves, crushed
450 g/1 lb/4 cups chicken livers,
*   trimmed and chopped*
15 ml/1 tbsp chopped fresh parsley
Salt and freshly ground black pepper
225 g/8 oz capellini

Heat half the oil and the butter and cook the crushed garlic for a few seconds. Add the chicken livers and parsley. Season with salt and pepper and cook for 2–3 minutes until pink and juicy. Remove from the heat. Add the remaining oil to the pan of boiling water and add the pasta. Cook for 8–10 minutes until tender but still firm. Drain. Return the pasta to the pan and stir in the livers and parsley. Toss until piping hot. Serve immediately.

Vitello e Spaghetti

Spaghetti Veal
Serves 4

30 ml/2 tbsp plain (all-purpose) flour
Salt and freshly ground black pepper
2.5 ml/½ tsp chopped fresh oregano
4 veal steaks
75 ml/5 tbsp olive oil
2 onions, chopped
120 ml/4 fl oz/½ cup water
75 g/3 oz/¾ cup Parmesan cheese,
*   grated*
350 g/12 oz spaghetti

Season the flour with the salt, pepper and oregano. Toss the steaks in the seasoned flour. Heat the oil in a frying pan (skillet) and brown the steaks on both sides. Place them in an ovenproof dish. Fry (sauté) the onions in the oil, drain and add to the dish with the water. Bake in a preheated oven at 180°C/350°F/gas mark 4 for 1 hour. Add the grated cheese to the oil left in the frying pan and heat gently. Bring a large pan of salted water to the boil and cook the spaghetti for 10 minutes until tender. Drain well. Lay the meat in the centre of a serving plate, surround with the spaghetti and pour the sauce over the meat.

Pancetta al Forno

Bacon Bake
Serves 4

225 g/8 oz pasta shapes
4 bacon chops
400g/14 oz/1 large can chopped
*   tomatoes*
5 ml/1 tsp chilli sauce
15 ml/1 tbsp chopped fresh oregano
225 g/8 oz fresh or frozen peas
50 g/2 oz/1 cup fresh breadcrumbs
75 g/3 oz/¾ cup hard cheese, grated
Salt and freshly ground black pepper

Bring a large pan of salted water to the boil and cook the pasta until firm but tender. Drain well. Grill the bacon chops for 4 minutes on each side and cut into chunks. Mix the tomatoes with the chilli sauce and oregano. Layer the pasta in an ovenproof dish with the tomatoes, bacon and peas, seasoning each layer. Mix together the breadcrumbs and cheese and sprinkle over the top. Bake for 25 minutes in a preheated oven at 200°C/400°F/gas mark 6 until golden brown on the top.

Penne con Grancho

Penne with Crab
Serves 4–6

225 g/8 oz crabmeat, flaked
10 ml/2 tsp olive oil
2.5 ml/½ tsp salt
450 g/1 lb fresh penne
25 g/1 oz/2 tbsp unsalted (sweet) butter
10 ml/2 tsp chopped fresh sage
5 ml/1 tsp freshly ground black
*   pepper*

Check the crabmeat to ensure there is no remaining shell. Put the oil and salt in boiling water and add the fresh penne. Boil for 3–4 minutes until the pasta is firm but cooked. Drain and return to the hot pan. Add the butter, sage, crabmeat and pepper. Toss well until piping hot and serve immediately.

Pappardelle con il Granchio Piccante

Spicy Pappardelle with Crab
Serves 4

175 g/6 oz/¾ cup unsalted (sweet)
*   butter*
350 g/12 oz crabmeat, flaked
45 ml/3 tbsp white wine
120 ml/4 fl oz/½ cup single (light)
*   cream*
2.5 ml/½ tsp cayenne
Salt
350 g/12 oz pappardelle or other
*   ribbon pasta*
30 ml/2 tbsp chopped fresh parsley

Melt half the butter in a pan over low heat and stir in the crabmeat. Add the wine, increase the heat and boil until the wine has almost evaporated. Stir in the cream and cayenne and season to taste with salt. Cook over a low heat for a few minutes, stirring. Meanwhile, bring a large pan of salted water to the boil. Add the pappardelle and boil for about 5 minutes for fresh or about 15 minutes for dried, until the pasta is just tender. Drain and transfer to a warmed serving bowl. Toss with the remaining butter. Pour the crab sauce over the pasta, sprinkle with the parsley and serve at once.

Vitello con Maccheroni

Veal with Macaroni
Serves 4

100 g/4 oz macaroni
25 g/1 oz/2 tbsp unsalted (sweet) butter
15 ml/1 tbsp oil
1 large onion, sliced
3 large tomatoes, skinned and sliced
4 slices veal, cut from loin fillet
Salt and freshly ground black pepper
1 egg, hard-boiled (hard-cooked) and
*   chopped*
15 ml/1 tbsp chopped fresh parsley

Bring a pan of salted water to the boil and add the macaroni. Cook for 10 minutes and drain. Heat the butter and oil in a frying pan (skillet) and cook the onion and tomatoes until tender. Place in a hot dish and add the drained macaroni. Keep warm. Season the fillets with the salt and pepper and fry (sauté) in the oil for 6–8 minutes on both sides until tender. Arrange the veal fillets on top of the tomato and macaroni. Blend the chopped hard-boiled egg with the parsley and sprinkle over the veal. Serve at once.

Vitello Sostanziosa con Conchiglie

Rich Veal with Pasta Shells
Serves 4

25 g/1 oz/2 tbsp unsalted (sweet) butter
15 ml/1 tbsp oil
1 onion, chopped
100 g/4 oz pie veal, chopped
100 g/4 oz mushrooms, sliced
60 ml/4 tbsp white wine
400 g/14 oz/1 large can chopped
  tomatoes
30 ml/2 tbsp tomato purée (paste)
5 ml/1 tsp chopped fresh thyme
15 ml/1 tbsp chopped fresh oregano
Salt and freshly ground black pepper
350 g/12 oz pasta shells

Heat the butter and oil together in a frying pan (skillet) and cook the onion for 1 minute. Add the veal and fry (sauté) until browned. Stir in the mushrooms and cook for 5 minutes. Pour in the wine and bring to the boil. Cook until the liquid has reduced by three-quarters. Stir in the tomatoes, tomato purée, thyme, oregano, salt and pepper. Simmer over a low heat for 30 minutes. Cook the conchiglie in boiling, salted water for 8–10 minutes until just tender, then rinse in hot water. Drain well and turn the pasta into a serving dish. Pour over the veal sauce.

Ravioli di Vitello

Veal Ravioli
Makes approx 450 g/1 lb ravioli

450 g/1 lb/4 cups plain (all-purpose)
  flour
1.5 ml/¼ tsp salt
4 eggs
30 ml/2 tbsp milk or single (light)
  cream
15 ml/1 tbsp olive oil
1 onion, chopped
225 g/8 oz cooked veal
15 ml/1 tbsp chopped fresh basil
Salt and freshly ground black pepper
Tomato Sauce (see page 358), to serve

Sift the flour and salt in a bowl and blend in the eggs and cream. Knead very thoroughly until smooth. Cover the bowl with a cloth and leave for 10 minutes. Roll out the dough to paper thinness and cut into two strips. Hang up to dry or lay a clean cloth over the back of a chair and put the strips of pasta over this. Leave for 10 minutes. Heat the oil in a frying pan (skillet) and cook the chopped onion for 2 minutes. Mince (grind) the veal and stir into the onion with the basil, salt and pepper. Place the pasta strips on to a floured working surface. Put spoonfuls of the filling on one half of the pasta and brush all round with water. Lay the other half on top. Press very firmly round the filling and cut into 2.5 cm/1 in squares, ensuring that each ravioli is firmly sealed. Drop into a pan of rapidly boiling salted water and cook for 8 minutes. Remove with a draining spoon and serve at once with the Tomato Sauce.

Gambella di Tagliatelle al Pesce

Fishy Noodle Ring
Serves 4

175 g/6 oz tagliatelle
30 ml/2 tbsp oil
4 eggs, beaten
300 ml/½ pt/1¼ cups milk
1.5 ml/¼ tsp grated nutmeg
Salt
25 g/1 oz/2 tbsp unsalted (sweet) butter, melted
1 large onion, chopped
3 tomatoes, skinned and chopped
10 ml/2 tsp chopped fresh parsley
Freshly ground black pepper
450 g/1 lb white fish fillets, skinned

Bring a large pan of salted water to the boil and add the tagliatelle and 15 ml/1 tbsp oil. Lower the heat and simmer for 10 minutes until the pasta is tender but firm. Drain. Whisk the eggs and milk together in a bowl and add the nutmeg, 1.5 ml/¼ tsp salt, and half the melted butter. Pour into a greased ring mould (mold). Drain the noodles and spoon evenly into the ring mould. Put the mould into an ovenproof dish and half-fill the dish with boiling water. Cook in a preheated oven at 180°C/350°F/gas mark 4 for 35 minutes until set. Heat the remaining oil in a pan and fry (sauté) the onion for 3 minutes. Stir in the tomatoes and cook for 20 minutes until the sauce is thick. Add the parsley and season with salt and pepper. Cut the fish into 4 cm/1½ in pieces and add to the sauce. Cook for 5–6 minutes until the fish flakes easily with a fork. Loosen the mould and turn on to a serving dish. Spoon the sauce and fish into the centre and serve.

Cannelloni al Gamberetti

Prawn Cannelloni
Serves 4–6

15 ml/1 tbsp olive oil
1 onion, chopped
3 tomatoes, skinned, seeded and chopped
100 g/4 oz mushrooms, sliced
150 ml/¼ pt/⅔ cup white wine
15 ml/1 tbsp plain (all-purpose) flour
450 g/1 lb cooked peeled prawns (shrimp)
1.5 ml/¼ tsp grated nutmeg
Salt and freshly ground black pepper
450 g/1 lb cannelloni
225 g/8 oz Mozzarella cheese, sliced

Heat the oil and fry (sauté) the onion until soft. Add the tomatoes and mushrooms. Blend the wine with the flour and stir into the pan. Bring to the boil, stirring, lower the heat and simmer for 15 minutes. Add the prawns and nutmeg and season with salt and pepper. Meanwhile, place the cannelloni in a pan of boiling salted water for 5–8 minutes until just tender. Drain and rinse in cold water. Fill the cannelloni with the prawn mixture and arrange in an oiled ovenproof dish. Pour any remaining sauce over the pasta and top with the Mozzarella cheese. Bake in a preheated oven at 200°C/400°F/gas mark 6 for 15 minutes or until piping hot. Note: If you use no-need-to-precook cannelloni, add an extra 30 ml/2 tbsp wine to the sauce and bake for 35 minutes or until the pasta is tender. Add the cheese after 15 minutes cooking.

Coriandola di Conghiglie Marina

Coriander Sea Shells

Serves 4

350 g/12 oz pasta shells
60 ml/4 tbsp chopped fresh coriander
(cilantro)
75 g/3 oz/³⁄₄ cup pine nuts
1 garlic clove, crushed
15 ml/1 tbsp lemon juice
30 ml/2 tbsp olive oil
50 g/2 oz/¹⁄₂ cup Parmesan cheese,
grated

Cook the pasta in slightly salted boiling water for 8–10 minutes until firm but cooked. Drain and return to the saucepan. Stir in the coriander and keep warm. Put the pine nuts, garlic and lemon juice in a blender and process for 10 seconds. Gradually blend in the oil. Stir the sauce into the pasta and toss well to coat. Spoon on warm plates. Sprinkle over the grated Parmesan and serve.

Spaghetti con Frutti di Mare

Seafood Spaghetti

Serves 4

225 g/8 oz cooked peeled prawns
(shrimp)
225 g/8 oz shelled scallops
150 ml/¹⁄₄ pt/²⁄₃ cup dry white wine
15 ml/1 tbsp olive oil
1 onion, chopped
3 tomatoes, skinned and finely
chopped
350 g/12 oz spaghetti
Salt and freshly ground black pepper

Poach the scallops in the white wine for 5 minutes. Lift out of the wine and cut in quarters. Heat the oil in a frying pan (skillet) and cook the onion for 2 minutes until soft. Add the tomatoes and wine from the scallops and cook rapidly for 5 minutes, reduce the heat and simmer for 20 minutes. Bring a large pan of salted water to the boil and add the spaghetti. Cook for 10 minutes until firm but tender. Drain well and place in a warmed serving dish. Stir the scallops and prawns into the tomato sauce and season well with the salt and pepper. Heat for 5 minutes and spoon over the spaghetti.

Conchiglie Puttanesca

Pasta Shells 'of Easy Virtue'

Serves 4

50 ml/2 fl oz/3¹⁄₂ tbsp olive oil
225 g/8 oz back bacon, rinded and
diced
6 garlic cloves, chopped
3 green chillies, seeded and chopped
4 red onions, chopped
2 × 400 g/2 × 14 oz/2 large cans
chopped tomatoes
5 ml/1 tsp dried oregano
5 ml/1 tsp dried basil
5 ml/1 tsp dried thyme
5 ml/1 tsp caster (superfine) sugar
Salt and freshly ground black pepper
350 g/12 oz conchiglie

Heat the oil and fry (sauté) the bacon, garlic, chillies and onions for 5 minutes, stirring. Add the tomatoes, herbs, sugar and a little salt and pepper. Simmer for 20 minutes until thick and pulpy. Meanwhile, cook the pasta according to the packet directions. Drain. Add to the sauce, toss well and serve straight away.

Salmone Affumicato con Tagliatelle Verde

Smoked Salmon with Green Noodles
Serves 4–6

100 g/4 oz spinach, washed
450 g/1 lb/4 cups plain (all-purpose)
  flour
1.5 ml/¼ tsp salt
4 eggs
300 ml/½ pt/1¼ cups double (heavy)
  cream
1.5 ml/¼ tsp cayenne
50 g/2 oz/¼ cup unsalted (sweet)
  butter, heated
225 g/8 oz smoked salmon, chopped

Place the spinach in a saucepan and cook, covered, for 8–10 minutes. Chop finely or purée until smooth. Sift the flour and salt in a bowl and blend into the eggs and spinach. The green colour can be altered by the quantity of spinach included in the recipe. Knead very thoroughly until smooth. Cover the bowl with a cloth and leave to stand for 30 minutes. Roll out the dough paper-thinly and cut into strips to produce green noodles. Hang the pasta to dry on a clean cloth over the back of a chair. Heat the cream in a basin over hot water and stir in the cayenne. Cook the noodles in plenty of boiling salted water for 3 minutes. Drain and return to the saucepan. Stir in the butter and mix in the salmon. Pour the cream over the pasta and serve immediately.

Tagliatelle con Frutte di Mare

Seafood Noodles
Serves 4–6

30 ml/2 tbsp olive oil
2 garlic cloves, crushed
15 ml/1 tbsp chopped fresh parsley
4 canned anchovy fillets, finely
  chopped
Salt and freshly ground black pepper
175 g/6 oz squid, cut into small pieces
75 ml/5 tbsp dry white wine
100 g/4 oz mushrooms, quartered
225 g/8 oz shelled mussels
225 g/8 oz shelled cockles
350 g/12 oz tagliatelle

Heat half the oil in a large frying pan (skillet) and cook the garlic, parsley and anchovies for 1 minute. Season with salt and pepper. Add the remaining oil to another pan and cook the squid for 2 minutes. Add the squid to the garlic and anchovies in the frying pan. Pour in the wine and simmer for 8 minutes. Stir in the mushrooms and cook for 2 minutes. Add the mussels and cockles and simmer for 5 minutes. Bring a large pan of salted water to the boil and add the tagliatelle. Cook for 10 minutes until firm but tender. Drain well and place in a warm dish. Spoon over the seafood and add a good grinding of black pepper.

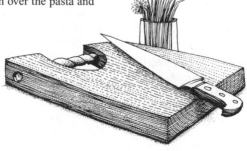

Spaghetti con Vongolette

Spaghetti with Baby Clams
Serves 4

30 ml/2 tbsp olive oil
2 garlic cloves, chopped
2.5 ml/½ tsp salt
Freshly ground black pepper
120 ml/4 fl oz/½ cup white wine
175 ml/6 fl oz/¾ cup water
1 kg/2¼ lb fresh clams in shells,
*   scrubbed*
350 g/12 oz spaghetti
25 g/1 oz/2 tbsp unsalted (sweet) butter
30 ml/2 tbsp chopped fresh parsley

Heat the oil and fry (sauté) the garlic for 5 minutes. Stir in the salt, some pepper and the wine. Pour in the water and bring to the boil. Add the clams and cover with a lid. Cook for 8 minutes, stirring occasionally. Drain, reserving the stock, and discard any clams that have not opened. Meanwhile, add the pasta to a large saucepan of boiling water and cook for 8–10 minutes until tender but firm. Drain and return to the pan. Add the butter to the stock and bring to the boil. Pour the spaghetti into a warmed serving dish and spoon over the clams. Pour over the stock and sprinkle with the parsley.

Carote Fettuccine

Carrot Pasta
Serves 4

225 g/8 oz fettuccine
15 ml/1 tbsp olive oil
450 g/1 lb carrots, grated
Salt and freshly ground black pepper
120 ml/4 fl oz/½ cup single (light) cream
15 ml/1 tbsp chopped fresh parsley
75 g/3 oz/¾ cup Parmesan cheese,
*   grated*

Cook the fettuccine in boiling, lightly salted water for 8–10 minutes until tender but firm. Drain. Meanwhile, heat the oil in a frying pan (skillet) and cook the carrots with a little salt and pepper for 1 minute to soften. Stir in the cream and add the parsley. Cook for 4 minutes. Spoon over the fettuccine and sprinkle over the Parmesan cheese. Serve immediately.

Tagliatelle con Grancho

Tagliatelle Crab
Serves 4

1 onion, finely chopped
100 g/4 oz mushrooms, chopped
15 ml/1 tbsp olive oil
225 g/8 oz cauliflower florets
450 g/1 lb tagliatelle
50 g/2 oz/¼ cup unsalted (sweet) butter
50 g/2 oz/½ cup plain (all-purpose)
*   flour*
600 ml/1 pt/2½ cups milk
30 ml/2 tbsp white wine
225 g/8 oz crabmeat, flaked
Salt and freshly ground black pepper

Fry (sauté) the onion and mushrooms in the oil and boil or steam the cauliflower for 10 minutes until just tender. Cook the pasta in boiling water until it is firm but cooked. Heat the butter in a saucepan and stir in the flour. Cook for 1 minute and gradually stir in the milk. Add the white wine, return to the heat and bring to the boil, stirring. Stir in the crab, cauliflower and the mushroom and onion mixture. Heat through and season to taste. Drain the pasta and arrange in a large serving bowl. Pour over the crab mixture and serve.

Fave e Pasta alla Crema

Broad Bean and Cream Pasta
Serves 6

15 ml/1 tbsp olive oil
25 g/1 oz/2 tbsp unsalted (sweet) butter
100 g/4 oz mushrooms, sliced
225 g/8 oz fresh or frozen broad (lima) beans
45 ml/3 tbsp water
350 g/12 oz spaghettini
150 ml/¼ pt/⅔ cup double (heavy) cream
100 g/4 oz/1 cup Mozzarella cheese, grated
15 ml/1 tbsp chopped fresh thyme
Salt and freshly ground black pepper

Heat the oil and butter in a saucepan and add the mushrooms. Fry (sauté) for 2 minutes and stir in the broad beans and water. Cover and cook for 15 minutes. Meanwhile, cook the pasta in boiling, salted water until just tender. Drain and transfer to a heated serving dish. Lower the heat under the saucepan and blend in the cream, Mozzarella, and thyme. Season with salt and pepper and spoon over the spaghettini.

Spaghettini Fritto

Crispy Fried Spaghetti
Serves 4

225 g/8 oz spaghettini
10 ml/2 tsp olive oil
Vegetable oil for deep-frying
10 ml/2 tsp salt
2.5 ml/½ tsp cayenne
60 ml/4 tbsp Parmesan cheese, grated

Cook the pasta in boiling salted water until just tender, but still firm. Drain very thoroughly, then cut into 10 cm/4 in lengths. Toss with the olive oil. Deep-fry in small batches until crisp and golden, then drain well on kitchen paper. Sprinkle with salt, cayenne and cheese. Toss together and break up any large lumps before serving.

Spaghetti con Peperoni, Acciughe e Pomodori

Spaghetti with Peppers, Anchovies and Tomato
Serves 3–4

30 ml/2 tbsp olive oil
1 garlic clove, crushed
1 onion, sliced
50 g/2 oz/1 small can anchovies, drained and chopped
3 tomatoes, skinned and chopped
2 red (bell) peppers, sliced
30 ml/2 tbsp chopped fresh parsley
150 ml/¼ pt/⅔ cup fish or chicken stock
Salt and freshly ground black pepper
225 g/8 oz spaghetti
60 ml/4 tbsp Pecorino cheese, grated

Heat the oil in a pan and fry (sauté) the garlic and onion until soft. Add the chopped anchovies and cook until 'melting'. Add the chopped tomatoes, sliced red peppers and parsley. Cook for 5 minutes and stir in the stock. Season with the salt and pepper and simmer for 30 minutes. Bring a pan of salted water to the boil and add the spaghetti. Cook for 10 minutes until tender but still firm and drain well. Blend in the grated cheese and pour into a bowl. Pour over the sauce and serve extra grated cheese if required.

Tuoni e Lampo

Thunder and Lightning
Serves 4

225 g/8 oz pasta twists
1 onion, chopped
1 garlic clove, crushed
30 ml/2 tbsp olive oil
430 g/15½ oz/1 large can chick peas (garbanzos), drained
5 ml/1 tsp dried oregano
450 g/¾ pt/2 cups passata (sieved tomatoes)
30 ml/2 tbsp tomato purée (paste)
5 ml/1 tsp caster (superfine) sugar
Salt and freshly ground black pepper
10 ml/2 tsp chopped fresh basil
75 g/3 oz/¾ cup Pecorino cheese, grated
A few green olives, stoned (pitted) and halved

Cook the pasta according to the packet directions. Drain. Meanwhile, fry (sauté) the onion and garlic in the oil for 3 minutes, stirring. Add the chick peas and oregano and cook gently for a further 5 minutes. Add to the pasta and toss well. Meanwhile, simmer the passata, tomato purée, sugar and a little salt and pepper gently for 10 minutes, stirring occasionally. Add the chopped basil and half the cheese. Pile the pasta mixture on to warm serving plates. Spoon the tomato sauce over, sprinkle with the remaining Pecorino cheese and garnish with the olives.

Rigatoni con Cavolfiore e Pollo

Cauliflower and Chicken Rigatoni
Serves 4–6

2 large onions, chopped
25 g/1 oz/2 tbsp unsalted (sweet) butter
2 garlic cloves, crushed
450 g/1 lb boneless chicken breasts, finely chopped
Salt and freshly ground black pepper
150 ml/¼ pt/⅔ cup single (light) cream
1 cauliflower, divided into small florets
450 g/1 lb rigatoni
75 g/3 oz/¾ cup Parmesan cheese, grated

Fry (sauté) the onions in the butter until they are translucent. Stir in the crushed garlic and the chicken. Season well with the salt and pepper. Cook for 20 minutes and stir in the cream. In another saucepan cook the cauliflower in boiling, salted water for 10 minutes. Place a large pan of hot water over a high heat and when boiling add the rigatoni and a pinch of salt. Boil for 6 minutes. Drain the rigatoni, and place in a heated serving dish. Drain the cauliflower and add to the pasta with the chicken. Sprinkle with the Parmesan and serve at once.

Lasagne con Funghi

Mushroom Lasagne
Serves 6

25 g/1 oz/2 tbsp unsalted (sweet) butter
2 onions, chopped
425 g/15 oz mushrooms, sliced
25 g/1 oz/2 tbsp margarine
25 g/1 oz/¼ cup plain (all-purpose) flour
300 ml/½ pt/1¼ cups milk
1 bay leaf
Salt and freshly ground black pepper
6 no-need-to-precook lasagne sheets
100 g/4 oz/1 cup Parmesan cheese,
  grated

Grease a shallow ovenproof dish with a little of the butter. Heat the remaining butter in a frying pan (skillet) and add the onions. Add the mushrooms and fry (sauté) until soft. Melt the margarine in a saucepan, then sprinkle in the flour. Cook for 1 minute and gradually stir in the milk. Add the bay leaf. Bring to the boil, reduce the heat and simmer for 3 minutes stirring. Season to taste. Spread half the sauce in the bottom of the greased ovenproof dish and sprinkle with salt and pepper. Place 3 strips of lasagne on the sauce. Spread the mushrooms over the lasagne. Cover with a second layer of lasagne. Season with salt and pepper and cover with the remaining white sauce. Sprinkle over the grated cheese and bake in a preheated oven at 190°C/375°F/gas mark 5 for 40 minutes or until the lasagne feels tender when a knife is inserted down through the centre.

Cannelloni con Fegato di Pollo e Nocciolo

Chicken Liver and Hazelnut-stuffed Cannelloni
Serves 4

45 ml/3 tbsp olive oil
1 onion, finely chopped
1 garlic clove, crushed
450 g/1 lb/4 cups chicken livers, finely
  chopped or minced (ground)
5 ml/1 tsp dried oregano
200 g/7 oz/1 small can chopped
  tomatoes
30 ml/2 tbsp tomato purée (paste)
50 g/2 oz/½ cup hazelnuts, roughly
  chopped
Salt and freshly ground black pepper
8 no-need-to-precook cannelloni tubes
1½ quantities Basic White Sauce (see
  page 357)
60 ml/4 tbsp grated Parmesan cheese

Heat the oil in a saucepan. Add the onion and garlic and fry (sauté), stirring, for 2 minutes. Add the chicken livers, oregano, tomatoes, tomato purée, nuts and a little salt and pepper. Cook gently for 5 minutes, stirring occasionally. Spoon into a piping bag fitted with a large plain tube (tip). Use to fill the cannelloni tubes (or use a teaspoon). Arrange in a single layer in a greased ovenproof dish. Pour over the white sauce and sprinkle with the Parmesan. Bake in a preheated oven at 190°C/375°F/gas mark 5 for about 35 minutes or until the cannelloni is tender and the top is golden brown.

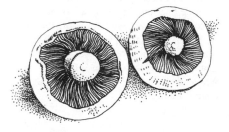

Lasagne con Pollo e Spinaci

Chicken and Spinach Lasagne
Serves 6

30 ml/2 tbsp oil
1 large onion, finely chopped
1 garlic clove, crushed
225 g/8 oz raw chicken meat, diced
200 g/7 oz/1¼ cups chicken livers,
 trimmed and chopped
100 g/4 oz button mushrooms, sliced
5 ml/1 tsp dried thyme
2.5 ml/½ tsp ground mace
65 g/2½ oz/⅔ cup plain (all-purpose)
 flour
300 ml/½ pt/1¼ cups chicken stock
225 g/8 oz/1 cup frozen chopped
 spinach, thawed
450 ml/¾ pt/2 cups milk
50 g/2 oz/¼ cup unsalted (sweet) butter
50 g/2 oz/½ cup Fontina cheese, grated
Salt and freshly ground black pepper
8 sheets no-need-to-precook lasagne
Grated Pecorino cheese

Heat the oil in a large pan. Add the onion and garlic and fry (sauté) for 2 minutes. Add the chicken and cook, stirring for 4 minutes. Stir in the chicken livers, mushrooms, thyme and mace and cook for 30 seconds. Stir in 15 ml/1 tbsp of the flour and cook for 1 minute. Blend in the stock, bring to the boil, reduce the heat, cover and simmer for 10 minutes. Squeeze out all the moisture from the spinach, stir into the chicken and season to taste. Meanwhile, whisk the milk with the remaining flour in a saucepan. Add the butter and bring to the boil, stirring all the time. Simmer for 2 minutes, stir in the Fontina cheese and season to taste. Spoon a very thin layer of the chicken mixture into a greased 2 litre/3½ pt/8½ cup ovenproof dish. Top with a layer of pasta. Add a layer of half the remaining chicken, then a third of the cheese sauce then a layer of pasta. Add the rest of the chicken, half the remaining cheese sauce and all the remaining pasta. Top with the remaining cheese sauce. Sprinkle with the Pecorino cheese and bake in a preheated oven at 180°C/350°F/gas mark 4 for 40 minutes or until the lasagne is tender when a knife is inserted down through the centre.

Vermicelli Dragonella

Vermicelli with Tarragon
Serves 4

100 g/4 oz/½ cup unsalted (sweet)
 butter, softened
30 ml/2 tbsp chopped fresh tarragon
1 garlic clove, crushed
Freshly ground black pepper
225 g/8 oz vermicelli
Olive oil
Thin slivers of fresh Parmesan cheese

Mash the butter with the tarragon, garlic and a good grinding of pepper until well blended. Shape into a roll on a sheet of greaseproof (waxed) paper or clingfilm (plastic wrap). Roll up and chill until required. Cook the pasta according to the packet directions. Drain well. *Either* unwrap the tarragon butter and cut into thin slices, toss the vermicelli in a little olive oil then pile on to plates and dot all over with the tarragon butter and garnish with the Parmesan, *or* roughly cut up the butter, add to the vermicelli and toss over a gentle heat until melted, pile on to warm plates and drizzle with olive oil then top with the Parmesan cheese. *Note:* the butter mixture is also good spread on slices of Ciabatta bread, reshaped into a loaf, wrapped in foil and baked in a moderate oven for about 20 minutes.

Ravioli al Pollo

Chicken Ravioli
Serves 6

45 ml/3 tbsp olive oil
15 g/½ oz/1 tbsp unsalted (sweet)
butter
3 garlic cloves, crushed
750 ml/1¼ pts/3 cups passata (sieved
tomatoes)
45 ml/3 tbsp tomato purée (paste)
5 ml/1 tsp dried basil
5 ml/1 tsp dried rosemary
Salt and freshly ground black pepper
100 g/4 oz/1 cup minced (ground)
pork
175 g/6 oz/1½ cups cooked chicken,
chopped
50 g/2 oz cooked ham, chopped
30 ml/2 tbsp chopped fresh parsley
3 eggs, beaten
450 g/1 lb/4 cups plain (all-purpose)
flour
250 ml/8 fl oz/1 cup water

Heat 30 ml/2 tbsp of the oil and the butter in a pan and fry (sauté) two of the garlic cloves for 1 minute. Add the passata, tomato purée, basil and rosemary. Season to taste, bring to the boil, cover and simmer gently for 30 minutes, stirring occasionally. Remove the lid after 20 minutes. Meanwhile, brown the pork with the remaining garlic, stirring until all the grains of meat are separate. Remove from the heat and mix with the remaining meats, the parsley and one of the eggs to bind. Chill until ready to use. Sift the flour with a pinch of salt into a large bowl. Make a well in the centre, add the remaining eggs and half the water to form a firm dough, adding more water as necessary. Knead gently on a lightly floured surface. Cut the dough in half. Roll out each to a large, thin square. Place spoonfuls of the filling at regular intervals over one sheet of the dough. Brush between each mound of filling with water. Top with the second sheet and press down well between the filling. Cut into squares using a pastry cutter or a sharp knife. Drop into a large pan of boiling, salted water in batches and cook for 4 minutes or until they rise to the surface. Remove with a draining spoon and keep warm while cooking the remainder. Add to the tomato sauce and simmer for 5 minutes. Serve hot.

Tortellini al Burro Nero

Tortellini in Black Butter
Serves 6

250 g/9 oz/1 packet dried or fresh
tortellini with 3 cheeses
175 g/6 oz/¾ cup unsalted (sweet)
butter
3 garlic cloves, halved
175 g/6 oz/1½ cups Parmesan cheese,
grated
Salt and freshly ground black pepper
Chopped fresh parsley

Cook the pasta according to the packet directions, drain and return to the saucepan. Meanwhile, melt the butter in a frying pan (skillet). Add the garlic and fry (sauté) until the garlic is golden and the butter nut-brown. Remove and discard the garlic. Pour the butter over the pasta with half the cheese, a little salt and pepper and half the parsley. Toss well over a gentle heat then serve immediately, garnished with the remaining parsley and the rest of the cheese handed separately.

Ravioli al Granchio

Crab Ravioli
Serves 4

225 g/8 oz/2 cups plain (all-purpose) flour
1.5 ml/¼ tsp salt
2 large eggs, beaten
75 g/3 oz/⅓ cup unsalted (sweet) butter
2 × 170 g/2 × 6 oz/2 small cans crabmeat
15 ml/1 tbsp mayonnaise
20 ml/4 tsp lemon juice
Cayenne
Salt and freshly ground black pepper
1 small egg, beaten
Flour for dusting
150 ml/¼ pt/⅔ cup milk
20 ml/4 tsp cornflour (cornstarch)
300 ml/½ pt/1¼ cups single (light) cream
15 ml/1 tbsp tomato purée (paste)
Freshly grated Parmesan cheese

Sift the flour and salt into a bowl. Make a well in the centre and add the large eggs. Melt half the butter and add to the bowl. Mix well to form a firm dough, adding a little cold water if necessary. Knead gently on a lightly floured surface until shiny and elastic. Wrap in clingfilm (plastic wrap) and leave to rest for at least 30 minutes. Meanwhile, mix the crabmeat with the mayonnaise, 5 ml/1 tsp of the lemon juice and cayenne and salt and pepper to taste. Roll out the dough on a floured surface as thinly as possible to a large square. Spoon the crab mixture at 4 cm/1½ in intervals across half the dough. Brush between the filling with beaten egg. Fold over the other half of the dough and press down between each pile of filling. Using a pastry wheel or sharp knife, cut between the filling piles to make little cushions. Dust with flour and leave to rest while making the sauce. Blend the milk and cornflour in a saucepan. Add the cream and tomato purée and bring to the boil, stirring all the time. Add the remaining lemon juice and cayenne, salt and pepper to taste. Drop the ravioli, one after the other, into a large pan of boiling, lightly salted water. When they are all in the pan, cook for about 7 minutes until just tender. Remove from the pan with a draining spoon and transfer to a warm serving dish. Spoon the hot sauce over and dust with the Parmesan before serving.

Tagliatelle alla Rustica

Rustic-style Tagliatelle
Serves 4

2 garlic cloves, crushed
90 ml/6 tbsp olive oil
50 g/2 oz/1 small can anchovies, chopped, reserving the oil
5 ml/1 tsp dried oregano
45 ml/3 tbsp chopped fresh parsley
Salt and freshly ground black pepper
225 g/8 oz tagliatelle, preferably fresh (see page 196)
Thin slivers of fresh Parmesan cheese

Fry (sauté) the garlic in the oil until golden brown. Remove from the heat and add the anchovies in their oil. Return to the heat and cook gently, stirring, until the anchovies form a paste. Stir in the oregano, parsley, a very little salt and lots of black pepper. Meanwhile, cook the tagliatelle (see page 196 if fresh, or according to the packet directions). Drain and return to the pan. Add the sauce, toss well and serve garnished with the Parmesan.

Spaghetti all'Uova

Spaghetti with Eggs
Serves 4–6

450 g/1 lb spaghetti
225 g/8 oz/1 cup unsalted (sweet)
    butter
75 g/3 oz/³⁄₄ cup Pecorino cheese,
    grated
6 eggs, beaten
Salt and freshly ground black pepper

Cook the spaghetti according to the packet directions. Drain in a colander. Cut half the butter into small pieces and place in the same saucepan. Return the spaghetti to the saucepan. Sprinkle with half the cheese, add the eggs, a little salt and lots of pepper. Toss over a very gentle heat until thoroughly blended and the eggs have just set. Turn into warm serving bowls, dot with flakes of the remaining butter and sprinkle with the remaining cheese.

Tagliatelle Primavera

Springtime Tagliatelle
Serves 4

350 g/12 oz green tagliatelle
1 bunch of spring onions (scallions),
    cut into short lengths
2 carrots, cut into matchsticks
2 leeks, cut into matchsticks
50 g/2 oz mangetout (snow peas),
    topped and tailed
100 g/4 oz asparagus tips
60 ml/4 tbsp dry vermouth
250 ml/8 fl oz/1 cup crème fraîche
Salt and freshly ground black pepper
10 ml/2 tsp chopped fresh parsley
Paprika
Freshly grated Parmesan cheese

Cook the pasta according to the packet directions. Drain and return to the pan. Meanwhile, cook the prepared vegetables in boiling, salted water for 3 minutes. Drain. Boil the vermouth and crème fraîche for about 5 minutes until reduced by half. Add the blanched vegetables, season to taste and stir in the parsley. Pour over the pasta and toss gently. Pile on to serving plates and sprinkle with paprika before serving with freshly grated Parmesan cheese.

Penne con il Tonno e Olive Nere

Penne with Tuna and Black Olives
Serves 4

60 ml/4 tbsp olive oil
1 onion, chopped
2 garlic cloves, crushed
400 g/14 oz/1 large can chopped
    tomatoes
100 g/4 oz/1 cup black olives, stoned
    (pitted)
15 ml/1 tbsp chopped fresh parsley
185 g/6½ oz/1 small can tuna, drained
    and flaked
Salt and freshly ground black pepper
350 g/12 oz penne

Heat the oil in a large pan and fry (sauté) the onion and garlic until soft but not brown. Add the tomatoes and olives and simmer for 10 minutes. Add the parsley and tuna and season to taste with salt and pepper. Simmer for about 5 minutes. Meanwhile, bring a large pan of salted water to the boil, add the pasta and boil for about 10 minutes until just tender. Drain, then transfer to a warmed serving bowl. Pour the sauce over the pasta, toss lightly together, then serve at once.

Pasta Rosso Piccante alla Milanese

Milanese Spiced Red Pasta
Serves 4

2 red onions, sliced
1 red (bell) pepper, cut into thin strips
1 red chilli, seeded and thinly sliced
1 garlic clove, crushed
45 ml/3 tbsp olive oil
400 g/14 oz/1 large can chopped
  tomatoes
15 ml/1 tbsp tomato purée (paste)
45 ml/3 tbsp water
5 ml/1 tsp dried oregano
8 stuffed green olives (optional)
50 g/2 oz Mortadella, diced
50 g/2 oz Milano salami, diced
Salt and freshly ground black pepper
350 g/12 oz red conchiglie
Grated Parmesan cheese

Fry (sauté) the onion, pepper, chilli and garlic in the oil for 3 minutes until softened but not browned. Add the tomatoes and the tomato purée blended with the water and the oregano. Bring to the boil, reduce the heat and simmer gently for about 10 minutes until pulpy. Add the olives, if using, and the diced sausages and cook for a further 2 minutes. Season to taste with salt, if necessary, and plenty of black pepper. Cook the pasta in plenty of boiling, salted water according to the packet directions. Drain and return to the pan. Add the sauce and toss well. Pile on to hot plates and serve with the Parmesan cheese.

Lasagne di Mare

Fish Lasagne
Serves 4

1 onion, finely chopped
1 garlic clove, crushed
100 g/4 oz mushrooms, finely chopped
400 g/14 oz/1 large can chopped
  tomatoes
15 ml/1 tbsp tomato purée (paste)
2.5 ml/½ tsp dried oregano
450 g/1 lb cod fillet, skinned and cubed
Salt and freshly ground black pepper
50 g/2 oz/½ cup plain (all-purpose)
  flour
50 g/2 oz/¼ cup unsalted (sweet) butter
600 ml/1 pt/2½ cups milk
100 g/4 oz/1 cup hard cheese, grated
8 sheets no-need-to-precook lasagne

Put the onion, garlic, mushrooms, tomatoes, tomato purée and oregano in a saucepan. Bring to the boil, reduce the heat and simmer for 15 minutes until pulpy. Stir in the fish and cook for a further 5 minutes. Season to taste. Meanwhile, blend the flour, butter and a little of the milk in a saucepan. Stir in the remaining milk. Bring to the boil and cook for 2´minutes, stirring until thickened. Season to taste and add half the cheese. Spoon a thin layer of the cheese sauce in the base of a 2.25 litres/4 pts/10 cups ovenproof dish. Cover with a layer of lasagne, breaking it to fit. Cover with a third of the fish sauce, then a little more cheese sauce. Repeat the layers twice more, making sure you have plenty of cheese sauce for the top. Sprinkle with the remaining cheese and bake in a preheated oven at 190ºC/375ºF/gas mark 5 for about 35–40 minutes until the pasta feels tender when a knife is inserted down through the centre.

Bucatini con Salsa di Carne e Peperoni Rosso

Bucatini with Meat and Red Pepper Sauce

Serves 4

30 ml/2 tbsp oil
2 garlic cloves, cut in half
1 onion, chopped
225 g/8 oz/2 cups minced (ground) beef
3 tomatoes, skinned and chopped
2 red (bell) peppers, sliced
30 ml/2 tbsp chopped fresh parsley
150 ml/¼ pt/⅔ cup beef stock
Salt and freshly ground black pepper
350 g/12 oz bucatini
60 ml/4 tbsp grated Parmesan cheese
Extra grated Parmesan, to serve (optional)

Heat the oil in a pan and brown the garlic, onion and minced beef. Remove the garlic and add the chopped tomatoes, sliced red peppers and parsley. Cook for 5 minutes and stir in the stock. Season with the salt and pepper and simmer for 30 minutes. Bring a pan of salted boiling water to the boil and add the pasta. Cook for 10 minutes until tender but still firm and drain well. Blend in the grated cheese and pour into a bowl. Pour over the sauce and serve extra grated cheese if liked.

Lasagne di Ricotta e Spinaci

Ricotta and Spinach Lasagne

Serves 4

1 small onion, finely chopped
1 garlic clove, crushed
30 ml/2 tbsp olive oil
225 g/8 oz frozen leaf spinach
5 ml/1 tsp dried oregano
Salt and freshly ground black pepper
A pinch of grated nutmeg
100 g/4 oz/1 cup hard cheese, grated
350 g/12 oz/1½ cups Ricotta cheese
A knob of butter for greasing
6–8 sheets no-need-to-precook lasagne
150 ml/¼ pt/⅔ cup single (light) cream
1 egg
A little grated Parmesan cheese

Fry (sauté) the onion and garlic in half the oil for 2 minutes, stirring. Add the spinach and cook until thawed. Stir in the oregano, salt and pepper and the nutmeg. Boil rapidly until all the moisture has evaporated. Remove from the heat and cool slightly. Stir half the hard cheese into the Ricotta and stir into the spinach mixture. Put a thin layer of the spinach mixture into the base of a greased ovenproof dish. Top with a layer of lasagne. Continue layering, finishing with a layer of pasta. Beat the cream and egg together with a little salt and pepper. Stir in the remaining hard cheese. Spoon on top of the pasta and sprinkle with Parmesan. Cook in a preheated oven at 190°C/375°F/gas mark 5 for about 35–40 minutes until the pasta is cooked through and the top is golden brown.

Rice

The creamy consistency of a true Italian risotto comes from using risotto rice, such as arborio. It has short, round grains which can absorb a lot of liquid without becoming too soft. Long-grain rice is also used for stuffings, salads and as a plain side dish.

Risotto di Prosciutto e Tacchino

Ham and Turkey Risotto
Serves 6

30 ml/2 tbsp oil
2 large onions, finely chopped
2 garlic cloves, crushed
350 g/12 oz/1½ cups risotto rice
900 ml/1½ pts/3¾ cups chicken stock
Salt and freshly ground black pepper
225 g/8 oz/2 cups cooked turkey, cut in strips
100 g/4 oz cooked ham, cut in strips
4 tomatoes, skinned, seeded and cut in chunks
100 g/4 oz fresh or frozen peas, thawed
100 g/4 oz/1 cup Parmesan cheese, grated

Heat the oil in a large pan and fry (sauté) the onions and garlic for 1 minute. Add the rice and cook until the oil is absorbed into the rice. Stir in the stock and simmer gently for 25 minutes until the rice is just cooked. Season with the salt and pepper and add the turkey, ham, tomatoes and drained peas. Heat through for 2 minutes, stirring all the time and season again to taste. Serve with the Parmesan cheese.

Risotto con Funghi Misto

Mixed Mushroom Risotto
Serves 4–6

25 g/1 oz/2 tbsp unsalted (sweet) butter
30 ml/2 tbsp virgin olive oil
1 small red onion, finely chopped
1 garlic clove, crushed
450 g/1 lb mixed mushrooms, finely sliced
350 g/12 oz/1½ cups risotto rice
900 ml/1½ pts/3¾ cups chicken stock
Salt and freshly ground black pepper

Heat the butter and oil in a large saucepan and fry the onion and garlic for 5 minutes. Add the mushrooms and cook for 4 minutes. Stir in the rice and cook until well coated in oil and butter. Pour in half the chicken stock and cook for approximately 10 minutes until absorbed. Stir in the remaining stock and cook for 10 minutes or until the rice is tender and has absorbed the liquid. Season with the salt and pepper and serve.

Riso con Gamberetti

Rice with Prawns
Serves 4

50 g/2 oz/¼ cup unsalted (sweet) butter
15 ml/1 tbsp olive oil
1 large onion, chopped
1 garlic clove, chopped
1 red (bell) pepper, diced
100 g/4 oz button mushrooms,
  chopped
5 ml/1 tsp chopped fresh parsley
Salt and freshly ground black pepper
225 g/8 oz/1 cup risotto rice
350 g/12 oz peeled prawns (shrimp)
750 ml/1¼ pts/3 cups fish stock
50 g/2 oz/½ cup Parmesan cheese,
  grated

Melt half the butter in a large pan and add
the oil. Stir in the onion, garlic and red
pepper and fry (sauté) for 5 minutes until
the onion is soft and translucent. Stir in the
mushrooms, parsley, salt and pepper and
cook for 5 minutes. Add the rice and cook
over a low heat for a further 5 minutes. Stir
in the shrimps and cook for 1 minute. Add
half the stock and simmer, stirring frequently, until the liquid is absorbed. Pour
in the remaining stock, a little at a time,
until the rice is tender but still firm.
Remove the pan from the heat and stir in
the remaining butter and Parmesan cheese.

Risotto con Cipolline e Zucchini

Chive and Courgette Risotto
Serves 4

50 g/2 oz/¼ cup unsalted (sweet) butter
15 ml/1 tbsp olive oil
1 onion, chopped
225 g/8 oz/1 cup risotto rice
900 ml/1½ pts/3¾ cups chicken or
  vegetable stock
450 g/1 lb courgettes (zucchini), grated
Salt and freshly ground black pepper
45 ml/3 tbsp snipped fresh chives

Heat half the butter with the olive oil and
fry (sauté) the onion for 5 minutes. Add
the rice to the pan and stir for 3 minutes.
Pour in a third of the stock and cook until
the liquid has been absorbed. Pour in
another third of the stock and continue
cooking for 10 minutes. Add the remaining stock and the courgettes and simmer
for 8–10 minutes until the rice is tender.
Season well and stir in the chives and
remaining butter.

Riso Agli Odori

Herb Rice
Serves 3–4

Salt
225 g/8 oz/1 cup risotto rice
15 ml/1 tbsp chopped fresh parsley
15 ml/1 tbsp chopped fresh oregano
15 ml/1 tbsp olive oil
Freshly ground black pepper

Bring a pan of salted water to the boil and
cook the rice for 10 minutes until soft.
Rinse and drain well. Mix in the herbs and
olive oil and season with freshly ground
black pepper.

Risotto Milanese

Risotto from Milan
Serves 3–4

25 g/1 oz/2 tbsp unsalted (sweet) butter
15 ml/1 tbsp olive oil
1 onion, chopped
225 g/8 oz/1 cup risotto rice
60 ml/4 tbsp dry white wine
750 ml/1¼ pts/3 cups chicken stock
Salt and freshly ground black pepper
2.5 ml/½ tsp saffron powder
30 ml/2 tbsp Parmesan cheese, grated
15 ml/1 tbsp chopped fresh parsley

Heat the butter and oil and fry (sauté) the onion for 5 minutes. Stir in the rice and continue cooking for 3 minutes, stirring constantly. Add the wine and continue to cook for a further 2 minutes. Stir in a little of the stock at a time and simmer until absorbed. Season with the salt and pepper. Dissolve the saffron powder in a little of the remaining stock and add to the pan. Simmer for 5 minutes. Add the remaining stock and simmer until the rice is tender and the liquid has been absorbed. Remove from the heat and stir in the Parmesan. Transfer to a warmed serving dish, sprinkle with parsley and serve immediately.

Riso al Pesto

Pesto Rice
Serves 3–4

225 g/8 oz/1 cup risotto rice
45 ml/3 tbsp Pesto (see page 366)
30 ml/2 tbsp pine nuts, lightly toasted

Heat a pan of boiling water and cook the rice for 10–12 minutes until soft. Drain, rinse and drain well. Mix in the pesto and pine nuts. Serve warm or cold with broccoli or salad.

Zucchini Ripieni con Riso

Rice-stuffed Courgettes
Serves 4

15 g/½ oz/1 tbsp unsalted (sweet)
butter
4–6 courgettes (zucchini) (depending
on size)
15 ml/1 tbsp olive oil
1 onion, finely chopped
225 g/8 oz/2 cups chicken livers,
chopped
225 g/8 oz/2 cups cooked long-grain
rice
2 tomatoes, chopped
30 ml/2 tbsp chopped fresh parsley
2.5 ml/½ tsp chopped fresh thyme
5 ml/1 tsp lemon juice
Salt and freshly ground black pepper

Grease an ovenproof dish with the butter. Cut the courgettes in halves lengthways and scoop out the seeds. Arrange in a single layer in the prepared dish. Heat the oil and fry (sauté) the onion until browned. Add the chicken livers and cook, stirring, for 2 minutes. Stir in the rice, tomatoes, parsley, thyme and lemon juice. Season with salt and pepper and fill the courgettes. Cover with foil. Bake in a preheated oven at 190°C/375°F/gas mark 5 for 30 minutes.

Riso al'Uova

Eggy Rice
Serves 4

350 g/12 oz/1½ cups arborio rice
2 large egg yolks, lightly beaten
20 g/¾ oz/1½ tbsp unsalted (sweet)
* butter*
Salt and freshly ground black pepper
50 g/2 oz/½ cup Parmesan cheese,
* grated*

Cook the rice in plenty of boiling salted water for about 16–18 minutes until just tender. Drain thoroughly. Return to the pan over a gentle heat. Pour the egg yolks over the rice and stir vigorously until well mixed and set. Stir in the butter and season with salt and pepper. Stir in the cheese and serve straight away.

Riso con Anitra e Gamberetti

Rice with Duck and Prawns
Serves 4

50 g/2 oz/¼ cup unsalted (sweet) butter
15 ml/1 tbsp olive oil
1 large onion, chopped
1 garlic clove, chopped
1 red (bell) pepper, diced
5 ml/1 tsp chopped fresh oregano
100 g/4 oz/1 cup cooked duck breast
* meat, diced*
Salt and freshly ground black pepper
225 g/8 oz/1 cup risotto rice
100 g/4 oz cooked, peeled prawns
* (shrimp)*
750 ml/1¼ pts/3 cups chicken stock

Melt half the butter in a large pan and add the oil. Stir in the onion, garlic and red pepper and fry (sauté) for 5 minutes until the onion is soft and translucent. Stir in the oregano, duck meat, salt and pepper and cook for 5 minutes until the duck is brown. Pour in the rice and cook over a gentle heat for 5 minutes. Roughly chop the prawns and add to the saucepan with half of the stock. Simmer, stirring frequently, until the liquid is absorbed. Pour in the remaining stock, a little at a time and continue cooking until the rice is tender but still firm. Remove the pan from the heat and stir in the remaining butter. Serve immediately.

Riso, Salsicce e Pomodori

Rice, Sausages and Tomatoes
Serves 2–3

600 ml/1 pt/2½ cups water
225 g/8 oz/1 cup risotto rice
15 ml/1 tbsp butter
1 large onion, chopped
1 garlic clove, crushed
400 g/14 oz/1 large can of chopped
* tomatoes*
225 g/8 oz beef sausages
15 ml/1 tbsp oil
Salt and freshly ground black pepper
½ green chilli, seeded if liked and
* finely chopped*

Bring the water to the boil in a large saucepan and add the rice. Cook for 10 minutes. Remove from the heat and drain. Rinse the rice thoroughly and drain again. Heat the butter, cook the onion and garlic until the onions are brown. Add the tomatoes to the onion. Meanwhile, fry (sauté) the sausages separately in the oil and when brown remove from the pan. Allow to cool for a few minutes and cut into chunks. Put the drained rice in a large frying pan (skillet) and add the fried onion and tomatoes. Add the sausages and mix gently with a wooden spoon. Season with the salt and pepper and mix in the finely chopped chilli. Cover the pan with a lid and simmer gently for 20 minutes, stirring frequently.

Risotto al Prosciutto

Ham Risotto

Serves 4

25 g/1 oz/2 tbsp unsalted (sweet) butter
30 ml/2 tbsp olive oil
1 onion, finely chopped
1 garlic clove, crushed
100 g/4 oz prosciutto, chopped
225 g/8 oz/1 cup risotto rice
900 ml/1½ pts/3¾ cups chicken stock
4 eggs, hard-boiled (hard-cooked),
    quartered
Salt and freshly ground black pepper

Heat the butter and oil in a large saucepan
and fry (sauté) the onion and garlic for 2
minutes. Add the chopped prosciutto and
fry for 4–5 minutes until the ham is
cooked. Stir in the rice and cook until well
coated in oil and butter. Pour in half the
chicken stock and cook for approximately
10 minutes. Stir in the remaining stock and
cook for a further 10 minutes until the rice
is tender. Add the quartered eggs and season with salt and pepper.

Risotto di Scampi

Scampi Risotto

Serves 6

1 large onion, chopped
15 g/½ oz/1 tbsp unsalted (sweet)
    butter
350 g/12 oz/1½ cups risotto rice
5 ml/1 tsp saffron powder
1.2 litres/2 pts/5 cups stock
100 g/4 oz fresh or frozen peas
30 scampi (jumbo shrimp), cleaned
    and shelled
100 g/4 oz asparagus tips
A little extra butter or grated
    Parmesan cheese, to serve

Fry (sauté) the onion in the butter. Pour in
the rice and add the saffron powder. Add
the stock, cover the saucepan and cook
very gently for 10 minutes. Add the peas
and stir. Continue cooking for a further 5
minutes. Add the scampi and asparagus
tips and cook for a further 5 minutes until
the stock has been absorbed and the rice is
tender. Turn into a serving dish and dot
with butter or a sprinkling of Parmesan
cheese, grated.

Palini di Riso

Stuffed Rice Balls

Serves 4

225 g/8 oz/1 cup risotto rice
1 egg, beaten
Salt and freshly ground black pepper
Oil for frying
350 g/12 oz/3 cups minced (ground)
    beef
15 ml/1 tbsp chopped fresh sage
2 hard-boiled (hard-cooked) eggs,
    chopped
75 g/3 oz/1½ cups breadcrumbs

Bring a pan of salted water to the boil and
add the rice. Cook for 15 minutes until just
soft. Drain and pour into a large bowl.
Beat in half the egg and season with salt
and pepper. Heat 15 ml/1 tbsp of the oil
and fry (sauté) the meat for 5 minutes, stirring. Add the chopped sage and hard-
boiled eggs. Season with salt and pepper
and allow to cool a little. Take spoonfuls of
the meat mixture and form into round
balls. Cover the meat thoroughly with rice
and form into balls. Brush with beaten egg
and roll in the breadcrumbs. Chill. Deep-
fry until crisp and brown in hot oil. Drain
on kitchen paper and serve at once.

Riso con Salame

Rice with Salami

Serves 4

50 g/2 oz/¼ cup unsalted (sweet) butter
15 ml/1 tbsp olive oil
1 large onion, chopped
225 g/8 oz Italian salami, sliced thickly
1 red (bell) pepper, diced
5 ml/1 tsp chopped fresh oregano
Salt and freshly ground black pepper
225 g/8 oz/1 cup risotto rice
750 ml/1¼ pts/3 cups stock

Melt half the butter in a large pan and add the oil. Stir in the onion, salami and red pepper and fry (sauté) for 5 minutes until the onion is soft and translucent. Stir in the oregano, salt and pepper and cook for 5 minutes until the sausage is browned. Pour in the rice and cook over a low heat for 5 minutes. Add half the stock. Simmer, stirring frequently, until the liquid is absorbed. Pour in the remaining stock, a little at a time and continue cooking, until the rice is tender but still firm. Remove the pan from the heat and stir in the remaining butter. Serve immediately.

Sformato di Spinaci e Riso

Spinach and Rice Mould

Serves 4

450 g/1 lb spinach, cooked and finely chopped
100 g/4 oz/1 cup cooked long-grain rice
25 g/1 oz/2 tbsp unsalted (sweet) butter
100 g/4 oz/1 cup Parmesan cheese, grated
5 ml/1 tsp lemon juice
Salt and freshly ground black pepper
15 ml/1 tbsp coriander (cilantro), chopped

Mix the spinach in a large bowl with the rice, butter and half of the cheese. Add the lemon juice and season with the salt and pepper. Place in a greased ovenproof dish and press down well. Sprinkle over the coriander and place the dish in a roasting tin (pan) of boiling water. Bake in a preheated oven at 180°C/350°F/gas mark 4 for 30 minutes. Sprinkle over the remaining cheese before serving.

Risotto di Funghi Selvatici

Wild Mushroom Risotto

Serves 6

6 halves sun-dried tomatoes
15 ml/1 tbsp olive oil
1 large onion, finely chopped
1 garlic clove, crushed
450 g/1 lb wild mushrooms, sliced
350 g/12 oz/1½ cups risotto rice
750 ml/1¼ pts/3 cups chicken stock
8 tomatoes, skinned, seeded and cut in chunks
Salt and freshly ground black pepper
30 ml/2 tbsp grated Parmesan cheese

Soak the sun-dried tomatoes in 250 ml/8 fl oz/1 cup hot water for 10 minutes. Strain, reserving the soaking liquid and chop the tomatoes. Heat the oil in a large pan and fry (sauté) the onion and garlic for 2 minutes. Add the mushrooms and cook for 3 minutes. Stir in the rice and cook until the oil has been absorbed into the rice. Pour in the stock and soaking liquid. Add the two types of tomatoes. Stir and simmer gently for 25 minutes until the rice is just cooked. Season with the salt and pepper. Serve with the Parmesan cheese sprinkled over.

Risotto all' Finanzierra

Rice with Chicken Livers
Serves 2

1 onion, chopped
100 g/4 oz mushrooms, sliced
8 chicken livers
50 g/2 oz/¹/₂ cup unsalted (sweet) butter
350 g/12 oz/1¹/₂ cups long-grain rice
1 red (bell) pepper, finely chopped
1.2 litres/2 pts/5 cups chicken stock
Salt and freshly ground black pepper
50 g/2 oz/¹/₂ cup Parmesan cheese,
grated

Quickly fry (sauté) the onion, mushrooms and chicken livers in the butter for 2 minutes. Add the rice and pepper and cook for 5 minutes. Pour in the stock and cook for 15 minutes until the liquid has been absorbed. Season with the salt and pepper and serve with the cheese.

Riso con Gamberetti Grandi

Tiger Prawn Rice
Serves 4

15 ml/1 tbsp olive oil
1 red onion, chopped
1 garlic clove, chopped
175 g/6 oz small button mushrooms
225 g/8 oz/1 cup risotto rice
150 ml/¹/₄ pt/²/₃ cup white wine
5 ml/1 tsp chopped fresh oregano
Salt and freshly ground black pepper
350 g/12 oz raw tiger prawns (jumbo
shrimp), peeled
750 ml/1¹/₄ pts/3 cups fish stock
15 ml/1 tbsp chopped fresh parsley
15 g/¹/₂ oz/1 tbsp unsalted (sweet)
butter
Grated Parmesan, to serve

Heat the oil and stir in the onion and garlic. Cook for 3 minutes and add the mushrooms. Fry (sauté) for 5 minutes. Stir in the rice, wine, oregano, salt and pepper and cook over a low heat for 10 minutes. Add the prawns to the saucepan with half of the stock. Simmer, stirring frequently, until the liquid is absorbed. Pour in the remaining stock, a little at a time, until the rice is tender but still firm. Remove the pan from the heat and stir in the parsley and butter. Serve immediately with a bowl of grated Parmesan cheese.

Risotto di Pollo con Piselli

Chicken Risotto with Peas
Serves 4

25 g/1 oz/2 tbsp unsalted (sweet) butter
1 onion, finely chopped
1 garlic clove, crushed
175 g/6 oz/³/₄ cup risotto rice
900 ml/1¹/₂ pts/3³/₄ cups chicken stock
Salt and freshly ground black pepper
100 g/4 oz/1 cup cooked chicken, cut
in strips
50 g/2 oz cooked ham, cut in strips
3 large tomatoes, skinned, seeded and
sliced
100 g/4 oz peas, cooked
25 g/1 oz/¹/₄ cup Parmesan cheese,
grated

Melt the butter in a large pan and fry (sauté) the onion and garlic for 2 minutes. Add the rice and cook until all the fat is absorbed. Stir in the stock and simmer for 30 minutes until the rice is just cooked. Season with the salt and pepper and stir in the chicken, ham, tomato and peas. Heat through for 2 minutes and serve immediately accompanied by the Parmesan cheese.

***Photograph opposite:* Bucatini with Meat and Red Pepper Sauce (page 249)**

Risotto con Pancetta

Bacon Risotto
Serves 4–6

25 g/1 oz/2 tbsp unsalted (sweet)
butter
30 ml/2 tbsp olive oil
2 small red onions, finely chopped
1 garlic clove, crushed
6 bacon rashers (slices), rinded and
chopped
225 g/8 oz mushrooms, finely sliced
350 g/12 oz/1½ cups risotto rice
900 ml/1½ pts/3¾ cups chicken stock
Salt and freshly ground black pepper

Heat the butter and oil in a large saucepan and fry (sauté) the onions and garlic for 2 minutes. Add the chopped bacon and fry for 4–5 minutes until the bacon is cooked. Add the mushrooms and cook for 4 minutes. Stir in the rice and cook until well coated in oil and butter. Pour in half the chicken stock and cook for approximately 10 minutes. Stir in the remaining stock and cook for 10 more minutes until the rice is tender. Season with the salt and pepper and serve.

Risotto con Gamberetti

Risotto with Prawns
Serves 6

1 large onion, chopped
15 g/½ oz/1 tbsp unsalted (sweet)
butter
450 g/1 lb/2 cups risotto rice
5 ml/1 tsp saffron powder
1.2 litres/2 pts/5 cups fish stock
100 g/4 oz fresh shelled peas
30 cooked, whole prawns (shrimp),
peeled
100 g/4 oz asparagus tips
Parmesan cheese, grated, to garnish

Fry (sauté) the onion in the butter. Pour in the rice and add the saffron powder. Add the stock, cover the saucepan and cook very gently for 10 minutes. Add the peas and stir. Continue cooking for a further 5 minutes. Add the prawns and asparagus tips and cook for a further 5 minutes until the stock has been absorbed and the rice is soft but not sticky. Turn into a bowl and sprinkle with grated Parmesan cheese to garnish.

Photograph opposite: **Wild Mushroom Risotto (page 255)**

Risotto con Latte

Milk Risotto

Serves 4

1.2 litres/2 pts/5 cups milk
450 g/1 lb/2 cups arborio rice
5 ml/1 tsp salt
30 ml/2 tbsp unsalted (sweet) butter
50 g/2 oz/½ cup Parmesan cheese,
* freshly grated*

Put the milk in a heavy-based saucepan. Add the rice and salt. Bring to the boil, reduce the heat and simmer gently for 15–20 minutes until the rice is just tender and has absorbed the milk. Stir from time to time. Stir in the butter and cheese and serve straight away.

Risotto alla Milanese

Milan-style Risotto

Serves 4

30 ml/2 tbsp olive oil
1 small onion, finely chopped
450 g/1 lb/2 cups arborio rice
1.5 ml/¼ tsp saffron powder
1.2 litres/2 pts/5 cups hot chicken
* stock*
Salt and freshly ground black pepper
30 ml/2 tbsp unsalted (sweet) butter
60 ml/4 tbsp freshly grated Parmesan
* cheese*

Heat the oil in a flameproof casserole (Dutch oven). Add the onion and fry (sauté) for 3 minutes until soft and lightly golden. Stir in the rice and cook for 1 minute. Add the saffron and 250 ml/8 fl oz/1 cup of the stock. Bring to the boil, stirring. Reduce the heat and simmer until the stock is absorbed then add another portion of stock. Continue in this way until the rice is just tender (15–20 minutes), using as much of the stock as is necessary. Season to taste. Stir in the butter and Parmesan cheese and serve straight away.

Risotto al Pollo e Funghi

Chicken and Mushroom Risotto

Serves 3–4

25 g/1 oz/2 tbsp unsalted (sweet) butter
15 ml/1 tbsp olive oil
1 onion, chopped
2 garlic cloves, crushed
225 g/8 oz mushrooms, sliced
225 g/8 oz/1 cup arborio rice
225 g/8 oz/2 cups cooked chicken,
* chopped*
60 ml/4 tbsp dry white wine
450 ml/¾ pt/2 cups hot chicken stock
2.5 ml/½ tsp saffron powder
Salt and freshly ground black pepper
15 ml/1 tbsp chopped fresh basil

Heat the butter and oil and fry (sauté) the onion and garlic for 5 minutes. Add the mushrooms and continue cooking for 5 minutes. Stir in the rice and chicken and continue cooking for 3 minutes, stirring constantly. Add the wine and continue to cook for 2 minutes more. Gradually stir in the stock a ladleful at a time, stirring until absorbed before adding more. Dissolve the saffron in a little of the stock and add to the pan. Season with salt and pepper. This will take about 20 minutes until the rice is tender and the liquid has been absorbed. Remove from the heat and stir in the chopped basil and transfer to a warmed serving dish.

Risotto con le Quaglie

Risotto with Quail
Serves 4

4 quail
Salt
4 thin slices pancetta or streaky bacon
15 ml/1 tbsp olive oil
375 ml/13 fl oz/1½ cups dry white wine
25 g/1 oz/2 tbsp unsalted (sweet) butter
1 small onion, finely chopped
450 g/1 lb/2 cups arborio rice
1.2 litres/2 pts/5 cups hot chicken
   stock
Freshly ground black pepper
100 g/4 oz/1 cup Parmesan cheese,
   freshly grated
Chopped fresh parsley

Wipe the quail inside and out with kitchen paper. Season with salt and wrap each in a slice of pancetta. Heat the oil in a large frying pan (skillet) and fry (sauté) the quail on all sides for about 15 minutes until brown and almost tender. Add the wine and simmer until it has almost evaporated. Leave in the pan and keep warm. Meanwhile, melt half the butter in a large flameproof casserole (Dutch oven). Add the onion and fry for 2 minutes. Stir in the rice and cook for 1 minute. Add about a quarter of the stock and simmer, stirring, until it has been absorbed. Repeat the process until the rice is just tender (about 15–20 minutes). Remove from the heat, stir in the remaining butter, a little salt and pepper and the cheese. Quickly pack into a large ring mould (mold) and press down firmly. Invert on to a serving plate and place the quail in the centre. Spoon any cooking juices over and sprinkle with the parsley.

Risotto Nero con Calamari

Black Risotto with Squid
Serves 4

750 g/1½ lb squid
30 ml/2 tbsp olive oil
1 garlic clove
1 small onion, finely chopped
Salt and freshly ground black pepper
375 ml/13 fl oz/1½ cups dry white wine
450 g/1 lb/2 cups arborio rice
900 ml/1½ pts/3¾ cups boiling water
15 g/½ oz/1 tbsp unsalted (sweet)
   butter
100 g/4 oz/1 cup Parmesan cheese,
   freshly grated

Ask the fishmonger to clean the squid for you, reserving the ink sacs. Empty the ink sacs into a bowl. Wash the squid well, pat dry, slice the bodies into rings and cut the tentacles into short lengths. Heat the oil in a large flameproof casserole (Dutch oven). Add the garlic clove and the onion and fry (sauté) for 3 minutes until golden. Remove the garlic and discard. Add the squid to the pan and fry for 2 minutes, stirring. Season with salt and pepper, add the wine and simmer very gently for about 20 minutes until the squid is tender. Add the rice and stir for 1 minute. Stir in a quarter of the water and simmer, stirring occasionally until it has been absorbed. Add the ink and some more water and simmer, stirring until absorbed. Repeat this process until the rice is just tender (about 15–20 minutes). Remove from the heat and stir in the butter and cheese. Serve straight away.

Risotto Bianco

Risotto with Butter
Serves 4–6

75 g/3 oz/⅓ cup unsalted (sweet) butter
15 ml/1 tbsp olive oil
1 onion, finely chopped
1 garlic clove, crushed
225 g/8 oz/1 cup arborio rice
900 ml/1½ pts/3¾ cups hot chicken
  stock
Salt and freshly ground black pepper
100 g/4 oz/1 cup Pecorino cheese, grated

Heat 50 g/2 oz/¼ cup of the butter in a
large saucepan with the oil. Add the onion
and garlic and fry (sauté) for 3 minutes
until softened and lightly golden. Stir in
the rice and cook, stirring, for 1 minute
until glistening with the oil and butter. Add
a third of the stock. Bring to the boil.
Reduce the heat, cover and simmer until
the stock has been absorbed. Gradually stir
in the remaining stock, bring to the boil,
reduce the heat, re-cover and simmer gently for about 15 minutes until all the stock
has been absorbed and the rice is creamy.
Boil rapidly, if necessary, to evaporate any
remaining stock. Season well with salt and
lots of pepper. Spoon into a warm serving
dish and sprinkle with the Pecorino cheese
before serving.

Risotto Bianco di Napoli

Naples-style Risotto with Butter
Serves 4

Prepare as for Risotto Bianco (above), but
stir in 100 g/4 oz/1 cup grated Mozzarella
cheese just before serving and garnish
with green olives. Omit the Pecorino
cheese if preferred.

Arancini Siciliani

Sicilian Oranges –
rice balls with a savoury filling
Serves 6

225 g/8 oz/1 cup arborio rice
50 g/2 oz/½ cup Parmesan cheese,
  grated
2 eggs, beaten
300 ml/½ pt/1¼ cups passata (sieved
  tomatoes)
Salt and freshly ground black pepper
50 g/2 oz Mozzarella cheese, finely
  diced
50 g/2 oz cooked ham, finely diced
Flour for dusting
50 g/2 oz/1 cup fresh breadcrumbs
Oil for deep-frying
15 ml/1 tbsp chopped fresh basil
6 small basil sprigs

Cook the rice in plenty of boiling salted
water for 15 minutes. Drain and leave until
cold. Turn into a bowl and stir in the
Parmesan cheese, eggs, 15 ml/1 tbsp of the
passata and a little salt and pepper. Mix
well. Put the cheese and ham in a separate
bowl with another 15 ml/1 tbsp of the passata and season lightly. Divide the cold rice
mixture into 12 portions. Using well-
floured hands, shape each into a ball. Make
a hollow in the centre and add a small
spoonful of the cheese and ham mixture.
Re-shape into a ball, adding a little more
rice if necessary. Repeat with each portion
of rice. Roll each thickly in the breadcrumbs. Chill if time. Deep-fry a few at a
time until crisp and golden brown. Drain on
kitchen paper. Meanwhile, warm the
remaining passata with the chopped basil
and a little salt and pepper. When all the
arancini are cooked, spoon a little passata
on to 6 serving plates. Place 2 arancini on
each plate and top each with a basil sprig.

Risotto con Pollo e Dragonella

Chicken and Tarragon Risotto
Serves 4

45 ml/3 tbsp olive oil
2 onions, finely chopped
2 garlic cloves, crushed
2 celery sticks, chopped
1 red (bell) pepper, chopped
1 green (bell) pepper, chopped
100 g/4 oz button mushrooms,
  quartered
275 g/10 oz/1¼ cups arborio rice
750 ml/1¼ pts/3 cups chicken stock
350 g/12 oz/3 cups cooked chicken,
  diced
Salt and freshly ground black pepper
Grated rind and juice of ½ small lemon
30 ml/2 tbsp chopped fresh tarragon

Heat the oil in a large frying pan (skillet). Add the onions, garlic and celery and cook, stirring, for 2 minutes. Add the peppers and mushrooms and stir for 1 minute. Add the rice and stir until all the grains are coated in the oil. Stir in the stock, bring to the boil, reduce the heat, cover and cook gently for 15 minutes. Stir, add the chicken, a little salt and pepper, the lemon rind and juice and the tarragon. Re-cover and cook for a further 5 minutes or until the rice has absorbed all the liquid and is tender. Serve hot straight from the pan.

Risotto con Melone e Prosciutto

Risotto with Melon and Prosciutto
Serves 6

1 ripe honeydew melon
75 g/3 oz/⅓ cup unsalted (sweet) butter
1 small onion, finely chopped
450 g/1 lb/2 cups arborio rice
375 ml/13 fl oz/1½ cups dry white wine
900 ml/1½ pts/3¾ cups hot chicken
  stock
250 ml/8 fl oz/1 cup single (light)
  cream
100 g/4 oz prosciutto, thinly sliced
Salt and freshly ground black pepper
Parsley sprigs
100 g/4 oz/1 cup Parmesan cheese,
  freshly grated

Halve the melon, remove the seeds and cut away the skin. Dice the flesh and purée briefly in a blender or food processor. Heat the butter in a large flameproof casserole (Dutch oven). Add the onion and fry (sauté) for 2 minutes. Stir in the rice and cook for 1 minute. Add half the wine and simmer until it is absorbed. Repeat with the rest of the wine. Then add about 250 ml/ 8 fl oz/1 cup of the stock and simmer until it is absorbed. Repeat until the rice is just tender and creamy, about 15–20 minutes. Quickly stir in the melon, cream and ham. Season to taste. Spoon on to warmed plates, garnish with parsley sprigs and serve the cheese separately.

Riso Caldo al Prezzemolo

Warm Rice with Parsley
Serves 6

450 g/1 lb/2 cups arborio rice
15 g/½ oz/1 tbsp unsalted (sweet)
  butter
30 ml/2 tbsp olive oil
50 g/2 oz/½ cup chopped fresh parsley
1 large garlic clove
100 g/4 oz/1 cup Parmesan cheese,
  grated

Cook the rice in plenty of boiling salted water for 16–18 minutes until just tender. Drain thoroughly and turn into a hot serving dish. Meanwhile, heat the butter and oil in a large frying pan (skillet). Add the parsley and garlic and fry (sauté) for 2 minutes until the garlic begins to brown. Discard the garlic. Pour the sauce over the rice and toss well. Sprinkle the Parmesan cheese over and serve straight away.

Risotto alla Toscana con Uva Passci

Tuscan Risotto with Raisins
Serves 4

45 ml/3 tbsp seedless (pitless) raisins
45 ml/3 tbsp olive oil
1 garlic clove
450 g/1 lb/2 cups arborio rice
1.2 litres/2 pts/5 cups hot beef or
  chicken stock
50 g/2 oz/½ cup chopped fresh parsley
Salt and freshly ground black pepper
50 g/2 oz Parmesan cheese, in one
  piece

Soak the raisins in boiling water for 30 minutes. Drain and pat dry in kitchen paper. Heat the oil in a flameproof casserole (Dutch oven). Add the garlic and fry (sauté) until golden, then discard. Add the rice and cook for 1 minute. Stir in 250 ml/8 fl oz/1 cup of the stock and simmer until the stock is absorbed. Repeat twice more. Stir in the raisins and continue adding stock until the rice is just tender and the risotto creamy (15–20 minutes). Stir in the parsley and season with salt and pepper. Shave off flakes of Parmesan with a potato peeler and scatter over the surface.

Risotto al Gorgonzola

Risotto with Gorgonzola
Serves 4

25 g/1 oz/2 tbsp unsalted (sweet) butter
30 ml/2 tbsp olive oil
1 small onion, finely chopped
450 g/1 lb/2 cups arborio rice
1.2 litres/2 pts/5 cups hot beef or
  chicken stock
175 g/6 oz Gorgonzola cheese,
  crumbled
Salt and freshly ground black pepper
Grated Parmesan cheese (optional)

Heat the butter and oil in a flameproof casserole (Dutch oven). Add the onion and fry (sauté) for 2 minutes. Add the rice and cook for 1 minute. Stir in 250 ml/8 fl oz/1 cup of the hot stock. Bring to the boil and simmer until the stock is absorbed. Repeat until the rice is just tender and creamy (about 15–20 minutes). Stir in the Gorgonzola and cook gently for 2 minutes, stirring until the cheese has melted and blends with the rice. Season to taste and serve straight away with Parmesan cheese, if liked.

Riso con Peperone Rosso e Piselli

Rice with Red Pepper and Peas
Serves 6

350 g/12 oz/1½ cups arborio rice
1 red (bell) pepper, cut into thin strips
1 small onion, finely chopped
45 ml/3 tbsp olive oil
275 g/10 oz/2½ cups fresh shelled,
frozen or drained canned peas
Salt and freshly ground black pepper

Cook the rice in plenty of boiling salted water for about 18 minutes until just tender. Drain thoroughly. Spoon on to a hot serving dish. Meanwhile, fry (sauté) the pepper and onion in the oil for 3 minutes, stirring. Add the peas and cook for a further 4 minutes. Spoon over the rice, season well and serve immediately.

Risotto con Fegato di Pollo

Savoury Chicken Liver Risotto
Serves 4

40 g/1½ oz dried porcini mushrooms
45 ml/3 tbsp olive oil
1 garlic clove
50 g/2 oz/1 small can anchovies,
drained and chopped
450 g/1 lb/2 cups arborio rice
1.2 litres/2 pts/5 cups hot chicken
stock
200 g/7 oz/1¾ cups chicken livers,
trimmed and cut into pieces
Freshly ground black pepper

Soak the mushrooms in boiling water for 30 minutes. Drain, rinse thoroughly then cut into bite-sized pieces. Heat the oil in a flameproof casserole (Dutch oven). Add the garlic clove, fry (sauté) until golden then remove and discard. Stir in the mushrooms, anchovies and rice. Cook for 1 minute. Add 250 ml/8 fl oz/1 cup of the stock, bring to the boil and simmer, stirring, until the stock is absorbed. Repeat with 2 more cups of stock. Then add the chicken livers and continue adding the stock until the rice is just tender and creamy (about 15–20 minutes). Serve straight away with a good grinding of black pepper.

Risotto con Funghi Porcini

Risotto with Porcini Mushrooms
Serves 4–6

40 g/1½ oz dried porcini mushrooms
45 ml/3 tbsp olive oil
1 onion, finely chopped
450 g/1 lb/2 cups arborio rice
1.2 litres/2 pts/5 cups hot chicken
stock
30 ml/2 tbsp unsalted (sweet) butter
45 ml/3 tbsp freshly grated Parmesan
cheese
Salt and freshly ground black pepper

Soak the mushrooms in boiling water for at least 30 minutes. Drain and rinse thoroughly. Squeeze dry and cut into neat pieces. Heat the oil in a flameproof casserole (Dutch oven). Add the onion and fry (sauté) for 2 minutes. Stir in the rice and cook for 1 minute. Add 250 ml/8 fl oz/ 1 cup of the stock, bring to the boil and simmer until the stock is absorbed. Repeat twice more. Add the mushrooms and continue adding stock until the rice is just tender and creamy (about 15–20 minutes). Remove from the heat, stir in the butter and cheese and season to taste.

Riso Pecorino Romano

Roman-style Rice with Pecorino Cheese

Serves 4

350 g/12 oz/1½ cups arborio rice
6 basil leaves, finely chopped
75 ml/5 tbsp grated Pecorino cheese
30 ml/2 tbsp olive oil
Salt and freshly ground black pepper
3 tomatoes, cut in wedges
Parsley sprigs

Cook the rice in plenty of boiling salted water for 18 minutes. Drain well and return to the saucepan. Stir in the basil, cheese and oil. Season to taste. Press into a large mould (mold). Immediately turn out on to a hot serving plate, garnish with the tomatoes and parsley and serve straight away.

Risotto al Champagne Cremoso

Creamy Champagne Risotto

Serves 4

25 g/1 oz/2 tbsp unsalted (sweet) butter
1 small onion, finely chopped
450 g/1 lb/2 cups arborio rice
½ bottle dry champagne
750 ml/1¼ pts/3 cups hot beef or chicken stock
120 ml/4 fl oz/½ cup double (heavy) cream
75 ml/5 tbsp freshly grated Parmesan cheese
Salt

Melt the butter in a flameproof casserole (Dutch oven). Add the onion and fry (sauté) for 2 minutes. Stir in the rice and cook for 1 minute. Add half the champagne, bring to the boil and simmer until it has been absorbed. Add a third of the stock and simmer until it is absorbed. Repeat the process with champagne and stock until the rice is just tender and creamy (about 15–20 minutes). Warm the cream in a small saucepan. When the rice is cooked, stir in the cream and cheese and season with salt. Serve straight away.

Risotto Cremificato con Limone

Creamed Risotto with Lemon

Serves 4

30 ml/2 tbsp unsalted (sweet) butter
350 g/12 oz/1½ cups arborio rice
Grated rind and juice of 1 lemon
1 litre/1¾ pts/4¼ cups hot lamb stock
15 ml/1 tbsp plain (all-purpose) flour
Salt and freshly ground black pepper
75 ml/5 tbsp double (heavy) cream

Melt half the butter in a heavy-based pan. Add the rice and cook, stirring, for 1 minute. Add the lemon rind to the stock. Add 2 ladlefuls of the stock to the rice and simmer until it has been absorbed. Repeat the process until the rice is just tender (about 15–20 minutes). Melt the remaining butter in a saucepan. Stir in the flour, then blend in the remaining stock. Bring to the boil and cook for 2 minutes until thickened. Season to taste and stir in the lemon juice and cream. Pile the rice into a warmed serving dish, pour the sauce over, stir lightly and serve.

Risotto Cremoso con Prosciutto e Porcini

Creamy Ham and Mushroom Risotto

Serves 6

50 g/2 oz/1 cup dried porcini
mushrooms
25 g/1 oz/2 tbsp unsalted (sweet) butter
30 ml/2 tbsp olive oil
1 small onion, finely chopped
450 g/1 lb/2 cups arborio rice
1.2 litres/2 pts/5 cups hot chicken
stock
Salt and freshly ground black pepper
100 g/4 oz cooked ham, diced
120 ml/4 fl oz/½ cup single (light)
cream
Chopped fresh parsley
100 g/4 oz/1 cup Parmesan cheese,
freshly grated

Soak the mushrooms in hot water for 1 hour. Drain and wash thoroughly under running water. Pat dry on kitchen paper, then slice. Heat the butter and oil in a large flameproof casserole (Dutch oven) and fry (sauté) the onion for 2 minutes. Add the rice and mushrooms and cook for 1 minute, stirring. Add 2 ladlefuls of the stock and simmer until it is absorbed. Continue this way until the rice is just tender. Season to taste. Stir in the ham and cream. Spoon on to small warmed plates, sprinkle with the parsley and cheese and serve hot.

Suppli al Telefono

Rice Balls

Serves 6

1 onion, finely chopped
50 g/2 oz/¼ cup unsalted (sweet) butter
225 g/8 oz/1 cup arborio rice
400 g/14 oz/1 large can tomato juice
150 ml/¼ pt/1¼ cups chicken stock
30 ml/2 tbsp grated Parmesan cheese
Salt and freshly ground black pepper
1.5 ml/¼ tsp cayenne
2 large eggs, beaten
100 g/4 oz Mozzarella cheese, cut into
12 cubes
100 g/4 oz salami, finely chopped
75 g/3 oz/1½ cups fresh breadcrumbs
Oil for deep-frying

Fry (sauté) the onion in the butter for 2 minutes until softened and turning golden. Stir in the rice and cook for 1 minute. Stir in the tomato juice and stock. Bring to the boil, reduce the heat, cover and cook gently for 15–20 minutes until the rice is cooked and has absorbed all the liquid. If there is any left, boil rapidly for a few minutes, stirring all the time. Remove from the heat and stir in the Parmesan. Season with salt, pepper and the cayenne. Stir in the eggs, turn the mixture into a bowl, leave to cool, then chill until fairly firm. With floured hands, take a good spoonful of the mixture and flatten in the palm. Place a cube of cheese and a twelfth of the chopped salami in the centre. Top with another spoonful of rice and shape into a ball. Repeat with the remaining ingredients. Roll in the breadcrumbs. Chill again, if time. Deep-fry a few at a time in hot oil until crisp and golden. Drain on kitchen paper and serve straight away. *Note:* When the balls are pulled apart the cheese should stretch into long threads, like telephone wires, hence the name.

Risi e Bisi

Rice and Peas

Serves 4

50 g/2 oz/¼ cup unsalted (sweet) butter
45 ml/3 tbsp olive oil
50 g/2 oz pancetta, cut in small dice
1 small onion, finely chopped
350 g/12 oz/1½ cups arborio rice
1.2 litres/2 pts/5 cups chicken stock
450 g/1 lb fresh shelled or frozen peas
Salt and freshly ground black pepper
30 ml/2 tbsp chopped fresh parsley
50 g/2 oz Parmesan cheese, in one
  piece

Heat half the butter and 30 ml/2 tbsp of the oil in a flameproof casserole (Dutch oven). Add the pancetta and onion and fry (sauté), stirring for 4 minutes. Add the rice and cook for 1 minute, stirring. Add half the stock, bring to the boil, reduce the heat, and simmer for 10 minutes. Stir in the remaining stock and the peas and simmer for a further 10 minutes or until the rice is tender and has absorbed the liquid. Stir in the remaining butter and oil and sprinkle with parsley. Shave the Parmesan with a potato peeler and scatter over the surface.

Riso Tricolore

Three-coloured Rice

Serves 4–6

350 g/12 oz/1½ cups arborio rice
1 red (bell) pepper, cut into thin strips
40 g/1½ oz/3 tbsp unsalted (sweet)
  butter
30 ml/2 tbsp chopped pistachios
100 g/4 oz/1 cup chopped fresh parsley

Cook the rice in plenty of boiling salted water for about 18 minutes until just tender. Drain thoroughly and return to the saucepan. Meanwhile, fry (sauté) the pepper in half the butter for 1 minute until slightly softened. Add to the rice with the nuts, parsley and remaining butter. Toss over a gentle heat until thoroughly combined. Serve straight away.

Risotto alla Genovese

Genoese Rice

Serves 4

60 ml/4 tbsp olive oil
1 small onion, finely chopped
60 ml/4 tbsp chopped fresh parsley
225 g/8 oz/2 cups minced (ground)
  veal
450 g/1 lb/2 cups arborio rice
1.2 litres/2 pts/5 cups hot veal or
  chicken stock
50 g/2 oz/½ cup Parmesan cheese,
  grated
Salt

Heat the oil in a flameproof casserole (Dutch oven). Add the onion, parsley and veal and fry (sauté), stirring, for about 4 minutes until the onion is lightly golden and the grains of meat are brown and separate. Add the rice and cook for 1 minute. Add 2 ladlefuls of the stock and simmer, stirring until it is absorbed. Repeat the process until the rice is just tender and creamy (about 15–20 minutes). Remove from the heat, stir in the cheese and season with salt. Serve hot.

Risotto con Salsiccia

Sausage Risotto
Serves 4

30 ml/2 tbsp olive oil
25 g/1 oz/2 tbsp unsalted (sweet) butter
1 small onion, finely chopped
*350 g/12 oz salsiccia (sweet Italian
    sausage), cut into bite-sized pieces*
450 g/1 lb/2 cups arborio rice
1.2 litres/2 pts/5 cups hot beef stock
Salt and freshly ground black pepper

Heat the oil and butter in a flameproof
casserole (Dutch oven) and fry (sauté) the
onion and sausage for 3 minutes, stirring.
Stir in the rice and cook for 1 minute. Add
250 ml/8 fl oz/1 cup of the stock and simmer, stirring, until it is absorbed. Repeat
until the rice is just tender (about 15–20
minutes). Season to taste and serve very
hot.

Risotto alla Campagnola

Peasant-style Risotto
Serves 4

30 ml/2 tbsp olive oil
1 onion, finely chopped
1 carrot, finely chopped
1 celery stick, finely chopped
*1 salsiccia (sweet Italian sausage), cut
    into bite-sized pieces*
450 g/1 lb/2 cups arborio rice
*1.2 litres/2 pts/5 cups hot beef or
    chicken stock*
*15 g/½ oz/1 tbsp unsalted (sweet)
    butter*
*100 g/4 oz/1 cup Parmesan cheese,
    grated*

Heat the oil in a large flameproof casserole
(Dutch oven). Add the onion, carrot, celery
and sausage and fry (sauté) for 2 minutes.
Add the rice and cook, stirring, for 1
minute. Add 250 ml/8 fl oz/1 cup of the
stock. Simmer, stirring, until the liquid is
absorbed. Repeat until the rice is just tender and creamy (about 15–20 minutes).
Remove from the heat and stir in the butter
and cheese. Serve straight away.

Riso Parmigiano con Basilico

Parmesan Rice with Basil
Serves 4

30 ml/2 tbsp olive oil
1 onion, finely chopped
225 g/8 oz/1 cup arborio rice
*600 ml/1 pt/2½ cups hot chicken or
    vegetable stock*
50 g/2 oz/½ cup chopped fresh basil
50 g/2 oz/½ cup chopped fresh parsley
Salt and freshly ground black pepper
*200 g/4 oz/1 cup Parmesan cheese,
    freshly grated*

Heat the oil in a large saucepan. Add the
onion and fry (sauté) for 2 minutes. Stir in
the rice and cook for 1 minute. Add 2
ladlefuls of the stock and simmer until it is
absorbed. Repeat until the rice is tender
and creamy (about 15–20 minutes). Stir in
the herbs, some salt and pepper and half
the cheese. Pile on to a warm serving dish
and top with the remaining cheese.

Pizza

Pizza has been a popular dish in Italy for centuries and the range of varieties seems endless. In Italy today, pizza is almost always bought from a pizzeria and virtually never cooked at home. It is an established fact that the further south in Italy one travels, the thinner the pizza crust becomes. The recipes that follow give a guide to some of the different crusts and toppings available.

Impasto di Pizza

Basic Pizza Dough
Makes 1 × 25 cm/10 in pizza

Oil for greasing
225 g/8 oz/2 cups strong white (bread) flour
5 ml/1 tsp chopped fresh basil
5 ml/1 tsp chopped fresh parsley
Salt and freshly ground black pepper
5 ml/1 tsp easy-blend dried yeast
5 ml/1 tsp olive oil
150 ml/¼ pt/⅔ cup hand-hot water

Grease a large pizza tin (pan) with oil. Place the flour in a mixing bowl and stir in the herbs. Season with salt and pepper and stir in the yeast. Add the oil and blend in half the water, adding more if necessary, and mix thoroughly to form a firm dough. Knead well on a lightly floured surface until smooth and elastic. Press the dough into a 25 cm/10 in circle and put on the greased tin. Cover with clingfilm (plastic wrap) and leave in a warm place for 30 minutes until the dough has risen. The pizza base is now ready to add the topping.

Pasta di Pizza Piccante

Spicy Pizza Dough
Makes 1 × 25 cm/10 in pizza

Oil for greasing
100 g/4 oz/1 cup self-raising (self-rising) flour
100 g/4oz/1 cup plain (all-purpose) flour
5 ml/1 tsp paprika
5 ml/1 tsp cayenne
Salt and freshly ground black pepper
5 ml/1 tsp easy-blend dried yeast
5 ml/1 tsp olive oil
150 ml/¼ pt/⅔ cup hand-hot water

Grease a large pizza tin (pan) with the oil. Place the flours in a mixing bowl and stir in the paprika and cayenne. Season with salt and pepper and stir in the yeast. Add the oil and blend in half the water, adding more if necessary, and mix thoroughly to form a firm dough. Press the dough into a 25 cm/10 in circle and put in the greased tin. Cover with clingfilm (plastic wrap) and leave in a warm place for 30 minutes until the dough has risen. The pizza base is now ready to add the topping.

Pizza di Farina Integrale

Wholemeal Pizza Dough
Makes 1 × 25 cm/10 in pizza

Oil for greasing
100 g/4 oz/1 cup wholemeal flour
100 g/4oz/1 cup plain (all-purpose) flour
5 ml/1 tsp chopped fresh parsley
Salt and freshly ground black pepper
10 ml/2 tsp easy-blend dried yeast
5 ml/1 tsp olive oil
150 ml/¼ pt/⅔ cup hand-hot water

Grease a large pizza tin (pan) with the oil. Place the flours in a mixing bowl and stir in the parsley. Season with salt and pepper and stir in the yeast. Add the oil and blend in half the water, adding more if necessary, and mix thoroughly to form a stiff dough. Press the dough into a 25 cm/10 in circle and put on the greased baking sheet. Cover with clingfilm (plastic wrap) and leave in a warm place for 30 minutes until the dough has risen. The pizza base is now ready to add the topping.

Pizza alla Margherita

Cheese and Tomato Pizza
Makes 1 × 25 cm/10 in pizza

1 quantity Basic Pizza Dough (see page 268)

Topping:
100 ml/3½ fl oz/6½ tbsp passata (sieved tomatoes)
100 g/4 oz Mozzarella cheese, chopped
1.5 ml/¼ tsp dried oregano
1 large tomato, skinned, halved and cut in slices
8 basil leaves, torn in pieces
Salt and freshly ground black pepper
30 ml/2 tbsp olive oil

Prepare the pizza dough. Spread the risen pizza base with the passata to within 2 cm/¾ in of the edge all round. Sprinkle over the Mozzarella, oregano and tomato slices then scatter over the torn basil leaves. Season lightly and drizzle with the olive oil. Bake in a preheated oven at 230°C/450°F/gas mark 8 for 10–15 minutes until the pizza is crisp and golden round the edges and the cheese has melted and is just beginning to brown.

Pizza con Acciughe e Tonno

Anchovy and Tuna Pizza
Makes 1 × 25 cm/10 in pizza

1 quantity Basic Pizza Dough (see page 268)

Topping:
30 ml/2 tbsp tomato purée (paste)
85 g/3½ oz/1 small can tuna, drained
6 anchovy fillets, halved
50 g/2 oz Mozzarella cheese, sliced
5 black olives, stoned (pitted)

Prepare the pizza base and leave to rise. When risen, spread with the tomato purée and add the drained tuna. Arrange the anchovy fillets over the surface. Top with the Mozzarella and olives and bake in a preheated oven at 220°C/425°F/gas mark 7 for about 15 minutes until golden and bubbling.

Pizza Palermitano

Palermo Pizza Pie

Makes 3 × 25 cm/10 in pizzas

750 g/1½ lb/6 cups strong white
   (bread) flour
10 ml/2 tsp salt
15 g/½ oz/1 tbsp easy-blend dried yeast
450 ml/¾ pt/2 cups hand-hot water
45 ml/3 tbsp olive oil
15 ml/1 tbsp semolina (cream of
   wheat)

Topping:
50 g/2 oz/½ cup Parmesan cheese,
   grated
100 g/4 oz/1 cup Mozzarella, grated or
   finely chopped
10 ml/2 tsp olive oil
45 ml/3 tbsp tomato purée (paste)
15 ml/1 tbsp chopped fresh basil
15 ml/1 tbsp black olives, stoned
   (pitted) and chopped
Sea salt (optional)

Mix the flour, salt and yeast in a large bowl and add the oil and water. Mix to a firm dough. Turn out on to a floured board, knead for 10 minutes and return to the bowl. Cover with clingfilm (plastic wrap) and leave to rise in a warm place for 1 hour. Knead the dough again for 3–4 minutes and roll the dough very thinly into six 25 cm/10 in rounds. Place three rounds of dough on baking sheets which have been dusted with the semolina. Mix the Parmesan, Mozzarella, half the olive oil, tomato purée and basil together in a bowl. Spoon the filling equally into the centre of the three rounds of dough to within 2 cm/ ¾ in of the edge. Sprinkle over the chopped olives. Lay a round of dough over the top of the pizza and seal the edge by crimping between your fingers. Bake in a preheated oven at 220°C/425°F/gas mark 7 for 15–20 minutes until crisp and golden. Remove from the oven and brush the tops with the remaining olive oil. Sea salt can be sprinkled over the surface if liked.

Pizza agli Asparagi

Asparagus Pizza

Makes 1 × 25 cm/10 in pizza

1 quantity Basic Pizza Dough (see
   page 268)

Topping:
450 g/1 lb asparagus
Salt
25 g/1 oz/2 tbsp unsalted (sweet) butter
3 tomatoes, seeded and chopped
15 ml/1 tbsp tomato purée (paste)
50 g/2 oz/½ cup Parmesan cheese,
   grated
15 ml/1 tbsp chopped fresh oregano

Prepare the pizza dough and when rising in the pizza tin (pan) prepare the topping. Pour 2 cm/¾ in of water into a frying pan (skillet). Add a pinch of salt and bring to the boil. Add the asparagus spears and cook for 4–5 minutes until almost tender and drain. Cut the asparagus into 9 cm/ 3½ in lengths. Heat the butter in a pan, add the tomatoes and tomato purée and bring to the boil. Reduce the heat and simmer for 5 minutes until the sauce is pulpy. Spoon over the dough base. Arrange the drained asparagus over and sprinkle with the Parmesan cheese, grated and oregano. Bake in a preheated oven at 220°C/ 425°F/gas mark 7 for about 15 minutes until the base is crisp.

Pizza di Prosciutto Crudo

Pizza with Raw Ham
Makes 1 × 25 cm/10 in pizza

1 quantity Basic Pizza Dough (see
page 268)
15 ml/1 tbsp olive oil
30 ml/2 tbsp passata (sieved tomatoes)
15 ml/1 tbsp Prosciutto Crudo, chopped
15 ml/1 tbsp chopped fresh oregano
50 g/2 oz Mozzarella cheese, sliced

Press the pizza dough into a 25 cm/10 in
circle and place on a greased pizza tin
(pan). Cover with clingfilm (plastic wrap)
and leave in a warm place for 30 minutes
until the dough has risen. Brush with the
oil. Cover the pizza base with the passata
and ham. Sprinkle with the oregano and
top with the sliced Mozzarella cheese.
Bake in a preheated oven for 10–15 minutes at 230°C/450°F/gas mark 8 until gold-
en and bubbling.

Pizza con Pancetta

Bacon Pizza
Makes 1 × 25 cm/10 in pizza

1 quantity Spicy Pizza Dough (see
page 268)
Oil for greasing
60 ml/4 tbsp Basil Sauce
(see page 357)
15 ml/1 tbsp olive oil
1 onion, chopped
200 g/7 oz/1 small can chopped
tomatoes
Salt and freshly ground black pepper
100 g/4 oz Mozzarella cheese, sliced
4 bacon rashers (slices), rinded and
roughly chopped
5 ml/1 tsp chopped fresh oregano

Prepare the pizza base. Roll out to a 25
cm/10 in diameter circle on a floured surface and place on an oiled baking sheet.
Leave to rise in a warm place for 25 minutes. Spread the Basil Sauce over. Heat the
oil in a frying pan (skillet) and cook the
chopped onion for 2 minutes. Pour in the
tomatoes and cook for 10 minutes until the
juice has evaporated. Season with the salt
and pepper. Spread the tomato mixture on
to the pizza base up to 2 cm/¾ in from the
edge. Lay over the sliced Mozzarella and
the bacon. Sprinkle with oregano and bake
in a preheated oven at 220°C/425°F/gas
mark 7 for 15–20 minutes until golden and
bubbling.

Pizza Ai Carciofi

Artichoke Pizza
Makes 1 × 25 cm/10 in pizza

1 quantity Basic Pizza Dough (see
page 268)

Topping:
1 onion, chopped
2 eggs
150 ml/¼ pt/⅔ cup single (light) cream
15 ml/1 tbsp chopped fresh marjoram
400 g/14 oz/1 large can artichoke
hearts, drained and halved
2 tomatoes, thinly sliced

Prepare the pizza base and leave to rise.
Meanwhile, heat the olive oil in a pan and
cook the onion until soft. Remove from the
heat. Beat in the eggs, cream, marjoram
and salt and pepper to taste. Arrange the
artichoke hearts on the pizza base. Pour
over the herb and egg mixture and arrange
the tomato slices on the top. Bake in a preheated oven at 200°C/400°F/gas mark 6 for
15–20 minutes.

Pizza alla Melanzana

Aubergine Pizza
Makes 1 × 25 cm/10 in pizza

1 quantity Basic Pizza Dough (see page 268)

Topping:
1 large aubergine (eggplant), sliced
Salt
1 onion, chopped
3 tomatoes, seeded and chopped
15 ml/1 tbsp tomato purée (paste)
15 ml/1 tbsp olive oil
50 g/2 oz/½ cup Parmesan cheese, grated
15 ml/1 tbsp chopped fresh oregano

Prepare the pizza base and leave to rise. Meanwhile sprinkle the aubergine with salt and leave to stand for 25 minutes. Rinse and dry on kitchen paper. Place on the pizza base with the onion, tomatoes and the tomato purée. Drizzle the oil over the tomatoes and sprinkle with the grated cheese and oregano. Bake in a preheated oven at 220°C/425°F/gas mark 7 for 15–20 minutes until the base is crisp.

Pizza al Pollo

Chicken Pizza
Makes 1 large rectangular pizza

1 quantity Basic Pizza Dough (see page 268)

Topping:
2 chicken breasts, thinly sliced
15 ml/1 tbsp olive oil
30 ml/2 tbsp tomato purée (paste)
5 ml/1 tsp chopped fresh basil
100 g/4 oz Mozzarella cheese, sliced
50 g/2 oz/½ cup Parmesan cheese, grated

Prepare the dough and press into an oiled 30 × 18 cm/12 × 7 in shallow baking tin (pan). Cover with clingfilm (plastic wrap) and leave in a warm place for 30 minutes until the dough has risen. Fry (sauté) the chicken in the oil for 2 minutes. Spread the dough with the tomato purée and sprinkle with the basil. Lay the chicken slices over the top. Place the Mozzarella over the chicken. Sprinkle over the Parmesan cheese. Bake in a preheated oven at 220°C/425°F/gas mark 7 for 15 minutes.

Pizza alla Marinara

The Original Pizza
Serves 2

1 ready-made 20 cm/8 in pizza base

Topping:
120 ml/4 fl oz/½ cup passata (sieved tomatoes)
2.5 ml/½ tsp dried oregano
3 garlic cloves, finely chopped
30 ml/2 tbsp chopped fresh basil
30 ml/2 tbsp olive oil
175 g/6 oz Mozzarella cheese, sliced
Salt and freshly ground black pepper
10 black olives, stoned (pitted)

Place the pizza base on a baking sheet. Spread the passata over. Scatter over the oregano, garlic and basil. Sprinkle with the olive oil and cover with the Mozzarella. Season well with salt and pepper. Dot with the olives. Bake in a preheated oven at 240°C/475°F/gas mark 9 for 10 minutes until the crust around the edges of the pizza is crisp and the Mozzarella is melted. Serve in wedges.

Pizza con Salame

Salami Pizza

Makes 1 × 25 cm/10 in pizza

25 g/1 oz/2 tbsp unsalted (sweet) butter
plus 5 ml/1 tsp for greasing
225 g/8 oz/2 cups flour
5 ml/1 tsp baking powder
Salt and freshly ground black pepper
2.5 ml/½ tsp chopped fresh sage
5 ml/1 tsp chopped fresh basil
150 ml/¼ pt/⅔ cup milk

Topping:
15 ml/1 tbsp olive oil
1 onion, sliced
1 garlic clove, chopped
400 g/14 oz/1 large can chopped
tomatoes
5 ml/1 tsp chopped fresh oregano
Salt and freshly ground black pepper
1 bay leaf
100 g/4 oz salami, cut into thin slices
225 g/8 oz Mozzarella cheese, sliced

Grease a large baking sheet with the 5 ml/
1 tsp butter and set aside. Sift the flour,
baking powder, salt and pepper into a mixing bowl and stir in the sage and basil. Rub
in the butter until the mixture resembles
breadcrumbs. Add enough milk to form a
soft but not sticky dough. Turn the dough
out on to a floured board and knead lightly. Roll out to a 25 cm/10 in circle. Lift the
dough on to the prepared baking sheet and
prepare the filling. Heat the oil in a frying
pan (skillet) and cook the onion and garlic
for 2 minutes. Add the tomatoes and sprinkle over the oregano, salt and pepper. Add
the bay leaf. Simmer for 15 minutes, stirring occasionally until pulpy. Remove the
pan from the heat and discard the bay leaf.
Spoon the tomato sauce over the pizza.
Place the salami slices on top and cover

with the cheese. Bake in a preheated oven
for 20–25 minutes at 220°C/425°F/gas
mark 7 until golden and bubbling.

Pizza di Chieti

Chicken, Garlic and Tomato Pizza

Makes 1 × 25 cm/10 in pizza

225 g/8 oz/2 cups plain (all-purpose)
flour
5 ml/1 tsp salt
100 g/4 oz/½ cup margarine
60 ml/4 tbsp water
30 ml/2 tbsp tomato purée (paste)
15 ml/1 tbsp olive oil
1 garlic clove, crushed
1 onion, roughly chopped
100 g/4 oz/1 cup cooked chicken,
chopped
3 tomatoes, skinned and chopped
15 ml/1 tbsp chopped fresh basil
Salt and freshly ground black pepper
175 g/6 oz Mozzarella cheese, sliced
15 ml/1 tbsp black olives, stoned
(pitted)

Place the flour and salt in a bowl and rub
in the margarine until the mixture resembles breadcrumbs. Blend in enough water
to form a soft but not sticky dough. Knead
lightly on a floured surface and roll out the
dough to line an oiled 25 cm/10 in pizza
tin (pan). Prick the base of the pastry and
spread with the tomato purée. Heat the oil
in a frying pan (skillet) and cook the garlic
and onion for 2 minutes. Remove from the
heat. Mix in the chicken, tomatoes, basil,
salt and pepper. Spoon over the pastry base
and top with the Mozzarella cheese.
Garnish with the olives and bake in a preheated oven at 200°C/400°F/gas mark 6 for
15–20 minutes until golden and cooked
through.

Pizza di Cipolle e Pancetta

Onion and Ham Pizza
Makes 1 × 25 cm/10 in pizza

25 g/1 oz/2 tbsp unsalted (sweet) butter
  plus 5 ml/1 tsp for greasing
225 g/8 oz/2 cups plain (all-purpose)
  flour
5 ml/1 tsp baking powder
Salt and freshly ground black pepper
2.5 ml/½ tsp chopped fresh sage
5 ml/1 tsp chopped fresh basil
50 g/2 oz/½ cup hard cheese, grated
150 ml/¼ pt/⅔ cup milk

Topping:
5 ml/1 tsp oil
2 large onions, sliced in rings
5 ml/1 tsp chopped fresh oregano
Salt and freshly ground black pepper
50 g/2 oz Parma ham, cut in strips
225 g/8 oz Mozzarella, sliced

Grease a large baking sheet with the 5 ml/
1 tsp butter and set aside. Sift the flour,
baking powder, salt and pepper into a mixing bowl and stir in the sage and basil. Rub
in the butter until the mixture resembles
breadcrumbs. Stir in the cheese and
enough milk to form a soft dough. Turn the
dough out on to a floured board and knead
lightly. Roll out to a 25 cm/10 in circle.
Lift the dough on to the prepared baking
sheet and prepare the topping. Heat the oil
in a frying pan (skillet) and cook the onion
rings for 2 minutes. Scatter over the
oregano, salt and pepper. Add the Parma
ham strips and top with the cheese. Cook
the pizza for 15–20 minutes in a preheated
oven at 220°C/425°F/gas mark 7 until crisp
and golden.

Pizza di Modena

Olive, Anchovy and Basil Pizza
Makes 1 × 25 cm/10 in pizza

1 quantity Basic Pizza Dough (see
  page 268)

Topping:
1 quantity of Olive, Anchovy and
  Tomato Paste (see page 20)
50 g/2 oz/½ cup Parmesan cheese,
  grated

Prepare the pizza base. When risen spread
with the Olive, Anchovy and Tomato Paste
to taste, sprinkle over the Parmesan cheese
and bake in a preheated oven at 220°C/
425°F/gas mark 7 for 15 minutes until
golden and bubbling.

Pizza con Gorgonzola e Noci

Pizza with Gorgonzola and Walnuts
Makes 1 × 25 cm/10 in pizza

1 quantity Basic Pizza Dough (see
  page 268)

Topping:
30 ml/2 tbsp tomato purée (paste)
10 ml/2 tsp chopped fresh sage
100 g/4 oz Gorgonzola cheese,
  crumbled
50 g/2 oz/½ cup walnuts, chopped
10 ml/2 tsp virgin olive oil

Prepare the pizza base and leave to rise.
Spread the pizza base with the tomato
purée and sprinkle over the sage and
Gorgonzola. Top with the walnuts and
drizzle over the olive oil. Bake in a preheated oven at 200°C/400°F/gas mark 6
until the pizza is cooked through and the
cheese is bubbling.

Pizza ai Funghi

Mushroom Pizza
Makes 1 × 25 cm/10 in pizza

1 quantity Basic Pizza Dough (see
page 268)

Topping:
15 ml/1 tbsp olive oil
1 onion, finely sliced
100 g/4 oz mushrooms, sliced
400 g/14 oz/1 large can tomatoes,
drained and chopped
5 ml/1 tsp chopped fresh basil
Salt and freshly ground black pepper
175 g/6 oz Mozzarella cheese, sliced

Prepare the pizza base and leave to rise.
Prepare the topping. Heat the oil in a frying pan (skillet) and cook the onion until
translucent. Add the mushrooms and fry
(sauté) for 4–5 minutes until tender.
Arrange the tomatoes over the dough and
sprinkle with the basil. Season with the
salt and pepper and top with the onion and
mushrooms and the Mozzarella slices.
Bake in a preheated oven at 220°C/425°F/
gas mark 7 for 15–20 minutes until golden
and bubbling.

Pizza di Funghi Alla Svelta

Quick Mushroom Pizza
Makes 4 bread pizzas

2 large Focaccia bread rounds
60 ml/4 tbsp olive oil
100 g/4 oz mushrooms, sliced
2 garlic cloves, crushed
425 g/15 oz/1 large jar pizza sauce
10 ml/2 tsp chopped fresh basil
225 g/8 oz Mozzarella cheese, sliced
6 black olives, stoned (pitted)

Slice the bread rounds in half horizontally
and brush each slice with the olive oil.
Place on a baking sheet. Fry (sauté) the
mushrooms in a little oil for 5 minutes.
Spread the garlic over the bread. Spoon
over half the pizza sauce and sprinkle over
the basil. Top with the mushrooms. Place
the Mozzarella on top. Spoon over the rest
of the sauce and garnish with the black
olives. Bake in a preheated oven at
200°C/400°F gas mark 6 for 15–20 minutes until the cheese has melted.

Pizza Capri

Oregano, Mozzarella
and Caper Pizza
Makes 1 × 25 cm/10 in pizza

1 quantity Basic Pizza Dough (see
page 268)

Topping:
15 ml/1 tbsp oil
1 onion, chopped
2 garlic cloves, crushed
250 ml/8 fl oz/1 cup Tomato Sauce
(see page 358)
2.5 ml/½ tsp chopped fresh marjoram
2.5 ml/½ tsp chopped fresh oregano
Salt and freshly ground black pepper
175 g/6 oz Mozzarella cheese, sliced
30 ml/2 tbsp capers
10 black olives, halved and stoned
(pitted)

Prepare the pizza base and leave to rise.
Prepare the topping. Heat the oil in a pan
and fry (sauté) the onion and garlic for 5
minutes. Stir in the tomato sauce, marjoram, oregano, salt and pepper. Simmer for
10 minutes and spoon over the dough. Top
with Mozzarella, capers and the olives and
bake in a preheated oven at 220°C/
425°F/gas mark 7 for 15–20 minutes.

Taschine di Pizza all' Acciuga

Anchovy Pizza Pockets
Serves 4

750 g/1½ lb/6 cups strong white
(bread) flour
10 ml/2 tsp salt
15 g/½ oz/1 tbsp easy-blend dried yeast
45 ml/3 tbsp olive oil
450 ml/¾ pt/2 cups hand-hot water
15 ml/1 tbsp semolina (cream of
wheat)

Topping:
6 anchovy fillets
30 ml/2 tbsp capers
5 ml/1 tsp chopped fresh oregano
12 black olives, stoned (pitted) and
sliced
5 ml/1 tsp oil for greasing
5 ml/1 tsp sea salt

Sift the flour and salt into a large bowl and add the yeast. Stir in the oil and water. Mix to a firm dough. Turn out on to a floured board, knead for 10 minutes and return to the bowl. Cover with clingfilm (plastic wrap) and leave to rise in a warm place for 1 hour. Knead the dough again for 3–4 minutes and roll the dough very thinly into four 20 cm/8 in rounds. Place each round of dough on a baking sheet which has been dusted with the semolina. Blend the anchovies, capers, oregano and olives together in a bowl. Spoon the filling equally into the centre of the rounds of dough to within 2 cm/¾ in of the edges. Brush the edges with water, fold over the rest of the dough and seal the edges by crimping between the fingers. Transfer to an oiled baking sheet. Brush with oil and sprinkle with the sea salt. Bake in a preheated oven at 220°C/425°F/gas mark 7 for 20–25 minutes until crisp and golden.

Pizza di Salsiccia

Sausage Pizza
Makes 1 large rectangular pizza

50 g/2 oz/¼ cup unsalted (sweet)
unsalted (sweet) butter
225 g/8 oz/2 cups plain (all-purpose)
flour
5 ml/1 tsp baking powder
5 ml/1 tsp chopped fresh parsley
5 ml/1 tsp chopped fresh oregano
100 g/4 oz/1 cup hard cheese, grated
Salt and freshly ground black pepper
45 ml/3 tbsp milk
45 ml/3 tbsp water
45 ml/3 tbsp tomato purée (paste)
225 g/8 oz Italian sausages, cooked
and roughly chopped
3 large tomatoes, cut into thin wedges

Grease a 28 × 18cm/11 × 7 in baking tin (pan) with a little of the butter. Sift the flour and baking powder into a bowl and rub the butter in until the mixture resembles breadcrumbs. Add half the parsley and oregano. Stir in one third of the cheese. Season with salt and pepper. Blend the milk and water and add enough to the mixture to form a soft, but not sticky, dough. Knead lightly on a floured surface and roll out to fit the pizza tin. Spread over the tomato purée and top with the chopped sausages. Arrange the tomato wedges on the pizza and sprinkle over the remaining cheese, parsley and oregano. Season with salt and pepper and bake in a preheated oven at 220°C/425°F/gas mark 7 for 15–20 minutes. Cut into large wedges and serve hot or cold.

Pizza al Mais e Pollo

Sweetcorn and Chicken Pizza

Makes 1 large rectangular pizza

50 g/2 oz/¼ cup unsalted (sweet) butter
225 g/8 oz/2 cups plain (all-purpose)
flour
5 ml/1 tsp baking powder
5 ml/1 tsp chopped fresh oregano
25 g/1 oz/¼ cup Mozzarella cheese,
grated
5 ml/1 tsp coarsely crushed black
peppercorns
Salt and freshly ground black pepper
45 ml/3 tbsp milk
45 ml/3 tbsp water
45 ml/3 tbsp tomato purée (paste)
225 g/8 oz/2 cups cooked chicken,
roughly chopped
200 g/7 oz/1 small can sweetcorn,
drained
3 large tomatoes, cut into thin slices
100 g/4 oz Mozzarella cheese, sliced

Grease a 28 × 18 cm/11 × 7 in tin with a
little of the butter. Sift the flour and baking
powder into a bowl and rub the butter in to
resemble breadcrumbs. Add half the
oregano. Stir in the grated cheese and
peppercorns. Season with salt and pepper.
Blend the milk and water and add enough
to the mixture to form a soft, but not
sticky, dough. Knead lightly on a floured
surface and roll out to fit the pizza tin.
Spread over the tomato purée and top with
the chopped chicken, sweetcorn and the
remaining oregano. Arrange the tomato
slices and top with the Mozzarella. Season
with salt and pepper and bake in a preheated oven at 220°C/425°F/gas mark 7 for
15–20 minutes. Cut into large squares and
serve hot.

Pizze Croccanti con Formaggio

Crusty Cheese Rounds

Serves 4–6

75 g/3 oz/⅓ cup unsalted (sweet) butter
25 g/1 oz/2 tbsp sugar
5 ml/1 tsp salt
2 eggs, beaten
15 g/½ oz/1 tbsp easy-blend dried yeast
30 ml/2 tbsp warm water
450 g/1 lb/4 cups strong white (bread)
flour
50 g/2 oz/½ cup Parmesan cheese,
grated

Cream two-thirds of the butter and the
sugar and beat in the salt and beaten eggs.
Add the yeast and flour, and water if necessary to form a firm dough. Knead for 5
minutes. Cover and leave to rise in a warm
place for 1 hour. Form into two 25 cm/
10 in rounds and place on greased baking
sheets. Spread each piece of dough with
the remaining butter and sprinkle with the
cheese. Leave for 20 minutes to rise. Bake
in a preheated oven at 200°C/400°F/gas
mark 6 for 20 minutes, sprinkle with additional cheese, if liked.

Pizza di Salame e Mozzarella

Salami and Mozzarella Pizza
Makes 1 × 25 cm/10 in pizza

15 ml/1 tbsp olive oil
10 ml/2 tsp semolina (cream of wheat)
1 onion, thinly sliced
1 quantity Basic Pizza Dough (see page 268)
25 g/1 oz salami, finely diced
50 g/2 oz/½ cup Mozzarella cheese, grated

Prepare the pizza base. Oil a large pizza tin (pan) and sprinkle with the semolina. Heat the remaining oil in a frying pan (skillet) and add the onion. Cook over a high heat for 2 minutes until the onion is soft. Roll out the dough into a 25 cm/10 in round and place on the pizza tin. Cover with the onion. Sprinkle with the salami and top with the grated Mozzarella cheese. Bake for 10–15 minutes in a preheated oven at 230°C/450°F/gas mark 8.

Calzone

Stuffed Pizza
Makes 2 × 20 cm/8 in folded pizzas

1 quantity Basic Pizza Dough (see page 268)

Filling:
25 g/1 oz/½ cup breadcrumbs
45 ml/3 tbsp olive oil
1 small onion, thinly sliced
50 g/2 oz mild salami, chopped
75 g/3 oz Fontina or Mozzarella cheese, finely diced
50 g/2 oz/¼ cup Ricotta cheese

Grease a large baking sheet with a little oil. Prepare the dough. Do not shape but leave in the bowl, cover and place in a warm place to rise for 30 minutes. Knead the dough for 5 minutes and roll out two 5 mm/¼ in thin circular rounds approximately 20 cm/8 in in diameter. Sprinkle half of the breadcrumbs over each pizza base and drizzle over half of the oil. Top each with half of the chopped onion, salami, Fontina and Ricotta cheeses. Fold over and pinch the two edges together to seal. Transfer to the baking sheet. Brush the tops with a pastry brush moistened in water and bake for 15–20 minutes in a preheated oven at 200°C/400°F/gas mark 6.

Pizza alla Cipolle Caramellizate

Caramelised Onion Pizza
Makes 1 × 25 cm/10 in pizza

15 ml/1 tbsp olive oil
10 ml/2 tsp semolina (cream of wheat)
3 onions, thinly sliced
1 quantity Basic Pizza Dough (see page 268)
6 rashers (slices) bacon, rinded and chopped
15 ml/1 tbsp chopped fresh sage

Oil a baking sheet and sprinkle with the semolina. Heat the remaining oil in a frying pan (skillet) and add the onion. Cook over a low heat for 25 minutes until the onions are soft and brown. Roll out the dough into a 25 cm/10 in round and place on the baking sheet. Cover with the onions. Sprinkle with the bacon or pancetta and sage and bake in a preheated oven for 10–15 minutes at 230°C/450°F/gas mark 8.

Pizza Artimino

Artimino Pizza Pie
Makes 3 × 25 cm/10 in pizzas

750 g/1½ lb/6 cups strong white
  (bread) flour
10 ml/2 tsp salt
15 g/½ oz/1 tbsp easy-blend dried yeast
45 ml/3 tbsp olive oil
450 ml/¾ pt/2 cups lukewarm water
15 ml/1 tbsp semolina (cream of wheat)
100 g/4 oz/1 cup Mozzarella, grated or
  finely chopped
10 ml/2 tsp olive oil
45 ml/3 tbsp tomato purée (paste)
15 ml/1 tbsp chopped fresh parsley
1 red (bell) pepper, seeded and sliced
15 ml/1 tbsp green olives, stoned
  (pitted) and chopped

Sift the flour and salt into a large bowl and add the yeast. Stir in the oil. Mix with the water to a firm dough. Turn out on to a floured board, knead for 10 minutes and return to the bowl. Cover with clingfilm (plastic wrap) and leave to rise in a warm place for 1 hour. Knead the dough again for 3–4 minutes and roll the dough very thinly into six 25 cm/10 in rounds. Place three rounds of dough on baking sheets which have been dusted with the semolina. Blend the Mozzarella, half the olive oil, the tomato purée, parsley and red pepper together in a bowl. Spoon the filling equally into the centre of the three rounds of dough to within 2 cm/¾ in of the edges. Sprinkle over the olives. Brush the edges with water. Lay a round of dough over the top of each pizza and seal the edges by crimping between the fingers. Bake in a preheated oven at 220°C/425°F/gas mark 7 for 20–25 minutes until crisp and golden. Remove from the oven and brush over the tops with the remaining olive oil.

Tolentino Pizza

Rosemary and Ham Pizza
Makes 1 × 25 cm/10 in pizza

Oil for greasing
275 g/10 oz packet pizza base mix
30 ml/2 tbsp Pesto (see page 366)
15 ml/1 tbsp olive oil
1 onion, peeled and chopped
225 g/8 oz/1 small can chopped
  tomatoes
Salt and freshly ground black pepper
100 g/4 oz Mozzarella cheese, sliced
4 slices prosciutto, roughly chopped
5 ml/1 tsp chopped fresh rosemary

Grease a large pizza tin (pan) with the oil. Make up the pizza base according to the instructions on the packet adding the pesto to the mixture. Roll out to a 25 cm/ 10 in diameter circle and place in the prepared tin. Cover with clingfilm (plastic wrap) and leave in a warm place for 25 minutes to rise. Heat the olive oil in a frying pan (skillet) and cook the chopped onion for 2 minutes. Add the tomatoes and cook for 10 minutes until the juice has evaporated. Season with the salt and pepper. Spread the tomato mixture on to the pizza base to within 2 cm/¾ in of the edge. Lay over the sliced Mozzarella and the prosciutto. Sprinkle with rosemary and bake in a preheated oven at 220°C/425°F/gas mark 7 for 15–20 minutes.

Pizza Jngraticciate

Pizza Lattice Pie
Serves 4

225 g/8 oz/2 cups plain (all-purpose)
  flour
5 ml/1 tsp salt
5 ml/1 tsp mustard powder
100 g/4 oz/½ cup unsalted (sweet)
  butter
100 g/4 oz/1 cup hard cheese, grated
60 ml/4 tbsp water
30 ml/2 tbsp tomato purée (paste)
15 ml/1 tbsp olive oil
1 garlic clove, crushed
2 onions, roughly chopped
1 courgette (zucchini), diced
1 tomato, peeled and chopped
15 ml/1 tbsp sage, chopped
Salt and freshly ground black pepper
175 g/6 oz/1½ cups Mozzarella cheese,
  grated
15 ml/1 tbsp black olives, stoned (pitted)

Place the flour, salt and mustard powder in a bowl and rub in the butter until the mixture resembles breadcrumbs. Stir in the grated cheese and blend in enough water to form a soft dough. Knead lightly on a floured surface and roll out the pastry to line a 23 cm/9 in flan tin (pie pan). Prick the base of the pastry and spread with the tomato purée. Heat the oil in a frying pan (skillet) and cook the garlic and onions for 2 minutes. Place the onions in a bowl and mix in the courgette, tomato, sage, salt and pepper. Spoon into the pastry case (pie shell) and top with the Mozzarella cheese. Roll out the pastry trimmings and cut 10 thin strips. Twist the strips and place five strips crossways over the flan and five at an angle to these to form a lattice topping. Trim the edges of the pastry. Garnish with the olives. Bake in a preheated oven at 200°C/400°F/gas mark 6 for 25 minutes.

Pizza di Olive

Olive Pizza
Makes 1 × 25 cm/10 in pizza

25 g/1 oz/2 tbsp unsalted (sweet) butter
  plus 5 ml/1 tsp for greasing
225 g/8 oz/2 cups plain (all-purpose)
  flour
5 ml/1 tsp baking powder
Salt and freshly ground black pepper
2.5 ml/½ tsp chopped fresh sage
5 ml/1 tsp chopped fresh basil
50 g/2 oz/½ cup Parmesan cheese,
  grated
150 ml/¼ pt/⅔ cup milk

Topping:
4 large tomatoes, sliced
185 g/6½ oz/1 small can tuna, drained
Salt and freshly ground black pepper
100 g/4 oz/1 cup hard cheese, grated
15 stuffed olives, halved

Grease a large baking sheet with the 5 ml/ 1 tsp butter and set aside. Sift the flour, baking powder, salt and pepper into a mixing bowl and stir in the sage and basil. Rub in the butter until the mixture resembles breadcrumbs. Stir in the Parmesan cheese and enough milk to form a soft, but not sticky, dough. Turn the dough out on to a floured board and knead lightly. Roll out to a 25 cm/10 in circle. Lift the dough on to the prepared baking sheet and prepare the topping. Arrange the tomato slices around the edge of the dough and place the tuna in the centre. Sprinkle over the salt and pepper and top with the cheese. Arrange the olives on top and cook the pizza in a preheated oven for 15–20 minutes at 220°C/ 425°F/gas mark 7 until golden and bubbling.

Pizza Genovese

Garlic Pizza

Makes 1 × 25 cm/10 in pizza

1 quantity Basic Pizza Dough (see page 268)

Topping:
4 garlic cloves, crushed
1.5 ml/¼ tsp salt
30 ml/2 tbsp olive oil
50 g/2 oz/½ cup Parmesan cheese, grated

Prepare the pizza base and put to rise. Make the topping. Cook the garlic, salt and oil for 2 minutes. Spoon over the pizza base and sprinkle with the grated cheese. Bake in a preheated oven at 220°C/425°F/gas mark 7 for 15–20 minutes until the base is crisp.

Pizza di Frutta di Mare Alla Svelta

Quick Seafood Pizza
Serves 4

2 large focaccia bread rounds
60 ml/4 tbsp olive oil
425 g/15 oz/1 large jar pizza sauce with basil
10 ml/2 tsp chopped fresh basil
225 g/8 oz seafood cocktail, thawed if frozen
225 g/8 oz Mozzarella cheese, thinly sliced
50 g/2 oz/1 small can anchovies, drained
6 black olives

Slice the bread rounds in half horizontally and brush each slice with olive oil. Heat a frying pan (skillet) and add each oiled slice to seal, or flash under a hot grill (broiler). This prevents the dough from becoming soggy. Place the bread rounds on baking sheets and spoon 45 ml/3 tbsp pizza sauce on each one. Cover with the cheese, then seafood and more tomato sauce. Add the anchovies and olives and bake in a preheated oven at 200°C/400°F/gas mark 6 for 15 minutes.

Pizza alla Napoletana

Anchovy Pizza
Makes 1 × 25 cm/10 in pizza

1 quantity Basic Pizza Dough (see page 268)
100 ml/3½ fl oz/6½ tbsp passata (sieved tomatoes)
100 g/4 oz Mozzarella cheese, chopped
50 g/2 oz/1 small can anchovies, drained and roughly chopped
30 ml/2 tbsp olive oil
10 ml/2 tsp capers (optional)
Freshly ground black pepper

Prepare the pizza dough. Spread the risen pizza round with the passata to within 2 cm/¾ in of the edge all round. Sprinkle the cheese over and scatter with pieces of anchovy. Drizzle with olive oil, scatter the capers over, if using, and season with pepper. Bake in a preheated oven at 230°C/450°F/gas mark 8 for about 10–15 minutes until the edges are crisp and golden.

Pizza alle Quattro Stagioni

Four-seasons Pizza
Makes 1 × 25 cm/10 in pizza

1 quantity Basic Pizza Dough (see
page 268)
100 ml/3½ fl oz/6½ tbsp passata (sieved
tomatoes)
50 g/2 oz button mushrooms, sliced
100 g/4 oz Mozzarella cheese, chopped
60 ml/4 tbsp olive oil
2 thin slices prosciutto, chopped
1 small garlic clove, finely chopped
15 ml/1 tbsp chopped fresh parsley
1.5 ml/¼ tsp dried oregano
85 g/3½ oz/1 small can tuna, drained
2 black olives, sliced
Salt and freshly ground black pepper

Prepare the pizza dough. Spread the risen
pizza base with the passata to within
2 cm/¾ in of the edge all round. Mark the
pizza into quarters with the back of a
knife. Cover one quarter with the sliced
mushrooms. Top with half the Mozzarella
and drizzle with 15 ml/1 tbsp olive oil.
Cover the opposite quarter with the prosciutto and the remaining cheese. Drizzle
with a further 15 ml/1 tbsp of the oil.
Sprinkle the third quarter with the garlic,
parsley and oregano and drizzle with half
the remaining oil. Flake the tuna and use to
cover the last quarter. Sprinkle with the
olives and drizzle with the remaining oil.
Sprinkle all over with a little salt and a
good grinding of pepper and bake in a preheated oven at 230°C/450°F/gas mark 8 for
about 15 minutes until golden and siz-
zling. Serve straight away. *Note:* You can
ring the changes with other toppings on
each quarter if you prefer.

Pizza Fritta

Fried Pizza
Serves 4

1 quantity Basic Pizza Dough (see
page 268)
Oil for frying
1 quantity Tomato Sauce (see page
358)
50 g/2 oz/½ cup Parmesan cheese,
grated
16 basil leaves, torn
8 black olives

When the dough has been left to rise in the
bowl, re-knead and cut in 8 pieces. Flatten
into small rounds. Fry on each side in hot
oil until crisp and golden. Keep warm
while cooking the remainder. Meanwhile,
heat the tomato sauce. When the pizzas are
cooked, spread with a little of the hot
tomato sauce, sprinkle with Parmesan,
scatter a few torn basil leaves over and garnish each with an olive. Serve straight
away.

Bread and Biscuits

Italians are said to eat more bread than almost any other nationality. They like their bread as fresh as possible and a great many cooks make their own each day. Any left-over bread is used in stuffings or to thicken soups. To fully appreciate Italian bread one should sit outside in the sunshine and eat the bread with a glass of wine. There are several sweet bread recipes and lots of crisp, melting biscuits to enjoy with a cup of freshly ground coffee too!

Pane Alle Olive Nere

Black Olive Bread
Makes 1 loaf

45 ml/3 tbsp olive oil
450 g/1 lb/4 cups strong white (bread) flour
10 ml/2 tsp salt
100 g/4 oz/⅔ cup black olives, stoned (pitted) and chopped
1 large onion, finely chopped
10 ml/2 tsp easy-blend dried yeast
200 ml/7 fl oz/scant 1 cup hand-hot water

Oil a baking sheet. Mix the flour and salt in a bowl. Stir in the chopped olives. Heat 30 ml/2 tbsp oil in a pan and fry (sauté) the onion for 5 minutes until soft and translucent. Cool and add to the flour. Add the yeast to the flour and mix to a soft dough with the water. Knead for 2 minutes and cover the bowl with clingfilm (plastic wrap). Leave in a warm place for 1 hour until the dough has doubled in volume. Turn out on to a floured board and knead for 2 minutes. Form into a loaf shape and leave for 30 minutes. Place on the prepared baking sheet. Brush with the remaining olive oil and bake in a preheated oven at 200°C/ 400°F/gas mark 6 for 30 minutes or until the base sounds hollow when tapped. Turn out and cool on a wire rack before serving.

Pasta Lievitata

Yeast Pastry
Makes 225 g/8 oz

225 g/8 oz plain (all-purpose) flour
2.5 ml/½ tsp salt
2.5 ml/½ tsp sugar
5 ml/1 tsp easy-blend dried yeast
15 ml/1 tbsp olive oil or melted unsalted (sweet) butter
Hand-hot water

Mix the flour, salt, sugar and yeast in a bowl. Stir in the oil or butter. Mix with enough hot water to form a soft, but not sticky, dough. Knead gently on a lightly floured surface for 5 minutes. Return to the bowl and cover with clingfilm (plastic wrap). Leave to rise in a warm place for 45 minutes. Re-knead, roll out thinly and use as required.

Panettone (1)

Panettone Breakfast Bread
Makes 1 loaf

100 g/4 oz/½ cup unsalted (sweet)
butter, melted
450 g/1 lb/4 cups plain (all-purpose)
flour
5 ml/1 tsp salt
1 sachet easy-blend dried yeast
75 g/3 oz/⅓ cup caster (superfine)
sugar
175 ml/6 fl oz/¾ cup milk
60 ml/4 tbsp warm water
3 eggs, beaten
50 g/2 oz/½ cup chopped candied peel
175 g/6 oz/1 cup sultanas (golden raisins)
5 ml/1 tsp crushed aniseed
Grated rind of 1 orange
Honey, to serve

Grease a tall cylindrical mould (mold)
20 cm/8 in high with 15 g/½ oz/1 tbsp of
the softened butter. Line the mould with
greaseproof (waxed) paper and grease
again with the softened butter. Sift the
flour into a large bowl and add the salt,
yeast and sugar. Add the milk. Gradually
blend together, adding the warm water if
necessary to form a soft dough. Turn the
dough on to a floured board and knead for
10 minutes. Return the dough to the bowl.
Cover with a damp cloth and set aside for
1¼ hours to rise. Turn the dough out and
press into a large flat shape. Spread with
all but 25 g/1 oz/2 tbsp of the remaining
softened butter, the eggs, candied peel,
sultanas, aniseed and orange rind. Roll up
the dough and knead again for 5 minutes.
Allow to stand, covered for 1 hour. Place
the dough in the prepared mould. Melt the
remaining butter and brush over the surface of the bread. Allow to stand for a further 30 minutes. Bake in a preheated oven
at 200°C/400°F/gas mark 6 for 20 minutes,
lower the heat to 180°C/350°F/gas mark 4
for a further 30 minutes and brush the surface again with melted butter. Remove
from the oven, and allow to cool in the tin
for 10 minutes. Transfer to a wire rack to
cool and serve, sliced and spread with
honey.

Panettone (2)

Almond Tea Bread
Makes 1 loaf

75 g/3 oz/⅓ cup unsalted (sweet) butter
175 g/6 oz/¾ cup caster (superfine)
sugar
3 eggs, beaten
90 ml/6 tbsp warm milk
750 g/1½ lb/6 cups plain (all-purpose)
flour
2.5 ml/½ tsp salt
15 g/½ oz/1 tbsp easy-blend dried yeast
100 g/4 oz/⅔ cup raisins
10 ml/2 tsp grated lemon rind
45 ml/3 tbsp melted unsalted (sweet)
butter
90 ml/6 tbsp fine breadcrumbs
20 whole almonds
30 ml/2 tbsp icing (confectioners')
sugar

Cream the butter and sugar together until
light. Add the eggs and beat well. Stir in
the milk. Mix the flour, salt and yeast and
beat again. Stir in the raisins and lemon
rind. Cover and allow to rise for 1 hour
until double in size. Grease a large loaf tin
(pan). Sprinkle with the breadcrumbs and
arrange the almonds in the bottom of the
tin. Knead the dough and place in the prepared tin. Allow to rise for a further 30
minutes until it reaches the top of the tin.
Bake in a preheated oven at 180°C/350°F/
gas mark 4 for 25–30 minutes. Allow to
stand for 5 minutes before removing from
the tin. Leave to cool on a wire rack and
lightly sift icing sugar over the top.

Amaretti

Almond Macaroons
Makes 20

100 g/4 oz/1 cup ground almonds
175 g/6 oz/¾ cup caster (superfine)
  sugar
2 egg whites, whisked until stiff
A few drops almond essence (extract)
20 split almonds
Unsalted (sweet) butter, for greasing
Rice paper

Place the ground almonds and sugar in a bowl and whisk in the egg whites. Add the almond essence and form into small balls. Place on a greased baking sheet lined with rice paper. Flatten each ball slightly and place a split almond on top. Bake in a preheated oven at 180°C/350°F/gas mark 4 for 20 minutes until golden brown. Leave to cool. Cut around each macaroon with scissors and store in an airtight container.

Focaccia al Formaggio e Semi di Comino

Cheese and Caraway Bread
Makes 2 loaves

750 g/1½ lb/6 cups strong white
  (bread) flour
30 ml/2 tbsp sugar
5 ml/1 tsp salt
15 g/½ oz/1 tbsp easy-blend dried yeast
2 eggs, beaten
350 g/12 oz/3 cups hard cheese, grated
45 ml/3 tbsp caraway seeds
250 ml/8 fl oz/1 cup warm water
Melted butter, for greasing

Put the flour in a large bowl and stir in sugar, salt and yeast. Stir in the eggs, cheese and caraway seeds. Add enough water to make a soft dough. Turn out on to a floured board and knead the dough. Return to the bowl and cover with a damp cloth. Allow to rise in a warm place for about 1½ hours or until doubled in size. Knead again. Turn out on to a floured board, divide the dough and place in two greased loaf tins (pans). Brush with melted butter. Allow to rise until the dough reaches the top of the tins and bake in the preheated oven at 180°C/350°F/gas mark 4 for 35 minutes or until the loaves sound hollow when tapped.

Focaccia

Focaccia Bread
Makes 2 loaves

450 g/1 lb/4 cups strong white (bread)
  flour
5 ml/1 tsp salt
1 packet easy-blend dried yeast
30 ml/2 tbsp olive oil
150 ml/¼ pt/⅔ cup hand-hot water
Oil for greasing and glazing

Sift the flour and salt into a bowl and stir in the yeast. Stir in the oil. Mix with enough water to form a soft dough. Turn the dough on to a floured board and knead for 10 minutes. Return the dough to the bowl and cover with clingfilm (plastic wrap). Allow to rise for 2 hours in a warm place. When the dough has doubled its size, knead again for 2 minutes. Form into two round loaf shapes and place on a baking sheet. Set aside for 30 minutes. Brush with olive oil and bake in a preheated oven at 200°C/400°F/gas mark 6 for 30 minutes. Turn out and cool on a wire rack before serving.

Pana al Aglio

Garlic Bread
Makes 2 loaves

225 g/8 oz/1 cup unsalted (sweet)
butter, softened
3 garlic cloves, crushed
30 ml/2 tbsp chopped fresh parsley
2.5 ml/½ tsp salt
2 long loaves Italian Flat bread
(see page 289)

Cream the butter, garlic, parsley and salt
together. Slice the bread crossways to
within 5 mm/¼ in of the base. Spread the
butter mixture generously on one side of
each of the slices. Wrap each loaf in foil
and place on a baking sheet. Bake in a preheated oven at 200°C/400°F/gas mark 6 for
15 minutes. Remove from the foil and
serve immediately.

Biscotti Dolci di Mandorla

Sweet Almond Biscuits
Makes 24

225 g/8 oz/2 cups ground almonds
100 g/4 oz/½ cup caster (superfine)
sugar
50 g/2 oz/½ cup plain (all-purpose)
flour
1 egg, beaten
5 ml/1 tsp lemon juice
Milk if necessary
A little unsalted (sweet) butter, for
greasing

Beat together the almonds with the sugar
and mix in the flour. Beat the egg and
lemon juice into the mixture and knead to
a paste. If the dough is too stiff add a little
milk. Form the dough into small round
balls and place a little apart on a greased
baking sheet. Bake in a preheated oven at
160°C/325°F/gas mark 3 for 8 minutes
until brown and crisp.

Palline di Gnocchi

Dough Balls
Makes 48 dough balls

450 g/1 lb/4 cups strong white (bread)
flour
5 ml/1 tsp salt
1 sachet easy-blend dried yeast
30 ml/2 tbsp olive oil
150 ml/¼ pt/⅔ cup hand-hot water
Unsalted (sweet) butter for greasing

Sift the flour and salt into a bowl. Stir in
the yeast and olive oil. Mix to a soft dough
with the water. Turn the dough on to a
floured board and knead for 5 minutes.
Return the dough to the bowl and cover
with clingfilm (plastic wrap). Allow to rise
for 2 hours in a warm place. When the
dough has doubled its size, knead again for
2 minutes. Break off small marble size
pieces and place on a greased baking
sheet. Bake in a preheated oven at 220°C/
425°F/gas mark 7 for 4–5 minutes until the
dough balls have risen and are very light
brown on the surface. Remove and cool on
a wire rack. To reheat, place under a hot
grill (broiler) for 20–30 seconds.

Focaccia al Rosmarino

Rosemary Focaccia Bread
Makes 4 loaves

750 g/1½ lb/6 cups strong white
(bread) flour
10 ml/2 tsp salt
15 g/½ oz/1 tbsp easy-blend dried yeast
45 ml/3 tbsp olive oil, plus extra for
brushing
15 ml/1 tbsp finely chopped fresh
rosemary
450 ml/¾ pt/2 cups hand-hot water

Sift the flour and salt into a large bowl and add the yeast, oil and rosemary. Mix to a soft dough with the water. Turn out the dough on to a floured board. Knead for 10 minutes and return to the bowl. Cover with clingfilm (plastic wrap) and leave to rise in a warm place for 2 hours. Knead the dough again for 3–4 minutes and form into four round loaves. Place on an oiled baking sheet. Allow to stand for 10 minutes. Brush the surface of each loaf with oil, sprinkle with extra salt if desired and leave for a further 10 minutes. Bake in a pre-heated oven at 200°C/400°F/gas mark 6 for 12–15 minutes or until brown and the bases sound hollow when tapped.

Pane con Zafferano e Olive

Saffron and Olive Bread
Makes 1 loaf

450 g/1 lb/4 cups strong plain (bread)
flour
5 ml/1 tsp salt
5 ml/1 tsp chopped fresh thyme
Large pinch of saffron powder
15 g/½ oz/1 tbsp fresh yeast
5 ml/1 tsp caster (superfine) sugar
45 ml/3 tbsp olive oil
45 ml/3 tbsp black olives, pitted and
chopped

Blend the flour, salt and thyme in a bowl and set in a warm place. Add the saffron to 30 ml/2 tbsp hot water. Cream the yeast with the sugar and stir in 120 ml/4 fl oz/ ½ cup warm water. Allow to stand for 10 minutes. Add the yeast, saffron water and olive oil to the flour and mix to a soft dough. Knead for 2 minutes and cover the bowl with clingfilm (plastic wrap). Leave in a warm place for 1 hour until the dough has doubled in volume. Turn out on to a floured board and add the olives. Knead for 2 minutes. Place in a loaf tin or 2 clean, well-oiled terracotta flower-pots and set aside for 30 minutes. Bake in a preheated oven at 200°C/400°F/gas mark 6 for 30 minutes. Turn out and cool on a wire rack before serving.

Pane Genovese Dolce

Sweet Genoese Bread
Makes 2 loaves

400 ml/14 fl oz/1¾ cups milk
900 g/2 lb/8 cups plain (all-purpose) flour
5 ml/1 tsp salt
1 packet easy-blend dried yeast
175 g/6 oz/¾ cup caster (superfine) sugar
30 ml/2 tbsp orange flower water
75 g/3 oz/⅓ cup unsalted (sweet) butter, melted
100 g/4 oz/1 cup chopped almonds
175 g/6 oz/1 cup raisins, soaked in 45 ml/3 tbsp Galliano, or any other anise liqueur
5 ml/1 tsp crushed aniseed
50 g/2 oz/⅓ cup chopped candied peel
50 g/2 oz/⅓ cup glacé (candied) cherries, chopped
Grated rind of 1 lemon
Butter and honey, to serve

Warm the milk in a saucepan. Sift the flour and salt into a large bowl. Add the yeast, sugar, half the milk and the orange flower water. Add the melted butter and gradually blend together, adding extra warm milk as required to form a soft, but not sticky, dough. Turn the dough on to a floured board and knead for 10 minutes. Grease a large mixing bowl and return the dough to the bowl. Cover with a damp cloth and set aside for 1½ hours to rise. Turn the dough out and press into two large flat round shapes. Sprinkle over the nuts, raisins, aniseed, candied peel, cherries and lemon rind. Roll up the dough and knead again. Shape into oblongs and place on a large greased baking sheet. Allow to stand, covered, for 1 hour and make 2 slits on the surface of the bread. Bake in a preheated oven at 190°C/375°F/gas mark 5 for 15 minutes. Reduce the heat to 160°C/325°F/gas mark 3 for a further 50 minutes, or until the bases sound hollow when tapped. Allow to cool on a wire rack and serve, sliced with butter and honey.

Pasta di Salerno

Salerno Pastry
Serves 4

75 g/3 oz/⅓ cup unsalted (sweet) butter
1 onion, thinly sliced
100 g/4 oz/1 cup plain (all-purpose) flour
2.5 ml/½ tsp cayenne
100 g/4 oz/½ cup cooked mashed potato
Salt and freshly ground black pepper
4 ripe tomatoes, sliced
50 g/2 oz sun-dried tomatoes, finely chopped
150 g/5 oz Mozzarella cheese, sliced
25 g/1 oz black olives, stoned (pitted)

Melt 25 g/1 oz/2 tbsp of the butter in a saucepan and fry (sauté) the onion for 3 minutes until softened. Leave to cool. Put the flour and cayenne in a bowl and rub in the remaining butter until the mixture resembles breadcrumbs. Stir in the cooked onion and the mashed potato and season with salt and pepper. Mix to a soft dough adding a little water if necessary. Press the dough into a greased 23 cm/9 in flan tin (pie pan) and cover with the tomato slices. Sprinkle over the chopped tomatoes and top with the slices of cheese. Scatter over the olives and bake in a preheated oven at 200°C/400°F/gas mark 6 for 20 minutes until the cheese has melted and the top is golden. Serve hot or cold.

Photograph opposite: Oregano, Mozzarella and Caper Pizza (page 282)

Piedine

Italian Flat Bread
Makes 4 loaves

*750 g/1½ lb/6 cups strong white
(bread) flour
10 ml/2 tsp salt
15 g/½ oz/1 tbsp easy-blend dried yeast
45 ml/3 tbsp olive oil
150 ml/¼ pt/⅔ cup hand-hot milk
300 ml/½ pt/1¼ cups hand-hot water*

Sift the flour and salt into a large bowl and
stir in the yeast and oil. Mix with the milk
and enough water to form a soft dough.
Turn the dough on to a floured board.
Knead for 10 minutes and return to the
bowl. Cover with clingfilm (plastic wrap)
and leave to rise for 2 hours. Knead again
for 3–4 minutes and form into four flat
loaves on oiled baking sheets. Allow to
stand for 15 minutes. Bake in a preheated
oven at 200°C/400°F/gas mark 6 for 12–15
minutes.

Pane Siciliano

Sicilian Bread
Makes 4 loaves

*750 g/1½ lb/6 cups strong white
(bread) flour
10 ml/2 tsp salt
15 g/½ oz/1 tbsp easy-blend dried yeast
45 ml/3 tbsp olive oil
15 ml/1 tbsp chopped fresh sage
1 garlic clove, crushed
450 ml/¾ pt/2 cups hand-hot water
5 ml/1 tsp olive oil for brushing
10 ml/2 tsp sea salt*

Sift the flour and salt into a large bowl and
add the yeast, oil, sage and garlic. Mix
with enough hot water to form a soft
dough. Turn out the dough on to a floured
board, knead for 10 minutes and return to

the bowl. Cover with clingfilm (plastic
wrap) and leave to rise in a warm place for
2 hours. Knead the dough again for 3–4
minutes and form into 4 loaves. Place on
oiled baking sheets. Allow to stand for 10
minutes. Brush the surface of each loaf
with oil, sprinkle with sea salt and leave
for a further 10 minutes. Bake in a preheated oven at 200°C/400°F/gas mark 6 for
12–15 minutes or until the bases sound
hollow when tapped.

Biscotti al Formaggio e Olive Apricale

Cheese Shortbread
Serves 4

*100 g/4 oz/1 cup plain (all-purpose)
flour
100 g/4 oz/1 cup Provolone cheese,
grated
75 g/3 oz/⅓ cup unsalted (sweet) butter
1.5 ml/¼ tsp cayenne
15 ml/1 tbsp chopped fresh basil
Salt and freshly ground black pepper
30 ml/2 tbsp green olives stoned
(pitted) and chopped*

Put the flour and cheese in a food processor and blend. Gradually add the butter,
cayenne, basil, salt and pepper. Turn out of
the bowl and knead in the olives. Wrap in
clingfilm (plastic wrap). Chill for 30 minutes. Roll out the shortbread to 5 mm/¼ in
thickness and cut into shapes with a biscuit
cutter. Place on baking sheets. Bake in a
preheated oven at 190°C/375°F/gas mark 5
for 8–10 minutes until golden.

Photograph opposite: **Black Olive Bread
(page 283) Rosemary Focaccia Bread
(page 287), Garlic Bread (page 286) and
Sun-dried Tomato and Walnut Loaf
(page 293)**

Focaccia alle Olive e Rosmarino

Olive and Rosemary Bread
Makes 1 loaf

450 g/1 lb/4 cups strong plain (bread) flour
10 ml/2 tsp salt
10 ml/2 tsp easy-blend dried yeast
100 g/4 oz/1 cup green olives, stoned (pitted) and chopped
15 ml/1 tbsp chopped fresh rosemary
45 ml/3 tbsp olive oil
1 large leek, finely chopped
200 ml/7 fl oz/scant 1 cup hand-hot water

Oil a baking sheet. Blend the flour and salt in a bowl. Stir in the yeast, chopped olives and rosemary. Heat 30 ml/2 tbsp oil in a pan and fry (sauté) the leek for 5 minutes until soft and translucent. Cool and add to the flour. Mix with enough water to form a soft dough. Knead for 2 minutes and cover the bowl with clingfilm (plastic wrap). Leave in a warm place for 1 hour until the dough has doubled in volume. Turn out on to a floured board and knead for 2 minutes. Form into a loaf shape and place on an oiled baking sheet. Leave for 30 minutes. Brush with the remaining olive oil and bake in a preheated oven at 200°C/400°F/gas mark 6 for 30 minutes until the base sounds hollow when tapped. Turn out and cool before slicing.

Pane con Canella Alla Svelta

Quick Cinnamon Bread
Makes 1 loaf

450 g/1 lb/4 cups plain (all-purpose) flour
10 ml/2 tsp baking powder
2.5 ml/½ tsp salt
3 eggs, lightly beaten
225 g/8 oz/1 cup caster (superfine) sugar plus 15 ml/1 tbsp
175 g/6 oz/¾ cup unsalted (sweet) butter, melted, plus extra for greasing
10 ml/2 tsp vanilla essence (extract)
175 g/6 oz/1½ cups ground almonds
15 ml/1 tbsp vegetable oil
5 ml/1 tsp ground cinnamon

Grease a large baking sheet and set aside. Sift the flour, baking powder and salt into a large bowl. Whisk the eggs in a separate bowl and whisk in the sugar, butter and vanilla essence. Fold in the ground almonds and add this mixture to the flour. Mix to a stiff dough. Turn out and knead lightly. Form the dough into a ball and place on the baking sheet. Brush the loaf over with oil and sprinkle with the 15 ml/1 tbsp sugar and the cinnamon. Bake in a preheated oven at 180°C/350°F/gas mark 4 for 45 minutes. Transfer to a wire rack to cool before serving.

Pasticcine San Severo

San Severo Pastries
Makes approximately 40

100 g/4 oz/½ cup unsalted (sweet)
butter
100 g/4 oz/1 cup plain (all-purpose)
flour
50 g/2 oz/⅓ cup semolina (cream of
wheat)
1.5 ml/¼ tsp salt
1.5 ml/¼ tsp dry mustard
100 g/4 oz/1 cup Parmesan cheese,
grated
Olive and Basil Pâté (see page 22), to
serve

Blend the butter, flour, semolina, salt, mustard and Parmesan in a food processor until smooth. Knead on a floured board lightly sprinkled with semolina. Roll out and cut into approximately 40 shapes with a biscuit cutter. Place on a baking sheet and cook in a preheated oven at 180°C/ 350°F/gas mark 4 for 20 minutes until golden brown. Transfer to a rack and cool. Store in an airtight tin and serve with Olive and Basil Pâté.

Bastoncini alla Groviera

Gruyère Sticks
Makes approximately 40

400 g/14 oz puff pastry (paste)
45 ml/3 tbsp tomato purée (paste)
Freshly ground black pepper
30 ml/2 tbsp milk
45 ml/3 tbsp Gruyère (Swiss) cheese,
grated
15 ml/1 tbsp sea salt

Roll out the pastry to a rectangle 5 mm/ ¼ in thick. Spread the top with the tomato purée and season with the pepper. Fold the pastry in half widthways, brush with milk and sprinkle over the Gruyère cheese and half the sea salt. Fold over and roll out again. Cut the pastry into 1 cm/½ inch wide strips and gently twist each one several times. Place on a baking sheet. Bake in a pre-heated oven at 200°C/400°F/gas mark 6 for 10 minutes until crisp and golden brown. Sprinkle with the sea salt and cool on a wire rack.

Biscotti al Gorgonzola

Gorgonzola Savouries
Makes 36

50 g/2 oz/¼ cup unsalted (sweet) butter
350 g/12 oz Gorgonzola cheese,
crumbled
225 g/8 oz/2 cups plain (all-purpose)
flour, sifted
1 egg, beaten
Salt and freshly ground black pepper
15 ml/1 tbsp finely chopped fresh
rosemary
Anchovy Dip (see page 34), to serve

Cream the butter until soft and crumble in the cheese. Blend well and gradually add the flour, egg, salt, pepper and rosemary. Knead the mixture to form a soft, but not sticky, dough and roll out on a floured surface to a rectangle about 5 mm/¼ in thick. Cut the biscuits into shapes and lay on a baking sheet. Bake in a preheated oven at 220°C/425°F/gas mark 7 for 10–12 minutes until brown. Remove from the baking sheet and allow to cool before serving with Anchovy Dip.

Formaggini Attoreighati al Pesto Rosso

Parmesan Pesto Twists
Makes approximately 40

400 g/14 oz ready-made puff pastry
45 ml/3 tbsp Red Pesto (see page 366)
Freshly ground black pepper
30 ml/2 tbsp milk
45 ml/3 tbsp Parmesan cheese, grated

Roll out the pastry to a rectangle 5 mm/ ¼ in thick. Spread the top with the pesto and season with the pepper. Fold the pastry in half widthways, brush with milk and sprinkle over the Parmesan cheese, grated. Cut the pastry into 1 cm/½ in wide strips and gently twist each one several times. Place on a baking sheet. Bake in a preheated oven at 200°C/ 400°F/gas mark 6 for 10 minutes until crisp and golden brown. Cool on a wire rack and store in an airtight container.

Pasta agli Odori

Herb Pastry
Makes one 23 cm/9 in pastry case

175 g/6 oz/1½ cups plain (all-purpose) flour
1.5 ml/¼ tsp salt
75 g/3 oz/⅓ cup unsalted (sweet) butter
15 ml/1 tbsp snipped fresh chives
15 ml/1 tbsp chopped fresh parsley
5 ml/1 tsp chopped fresh thyme
2 egg yolks
45–60 ml/3–4 tbsp water

Sift the flour and salt into a large bowl. Add the butter and rub into the flour until the mixture resembles fine breadcrumbs. Stir in the herbs and egg yolks and blend in the water, a little at a time to form a soft, but not sticky, dough. Roll out the dough on a lightly floured surface and use to line a 23 cm/9 in flan dish (pie pan). Use as required.

Biscotti di Pasta Frolla alla Parmigiana

Parmesan Shortbread
Serves 4

100 g/4 oz/1 cup plain (all-purpose) flour
100 g/4 oz/1 cup Parmesan cheese, grated
75 g/3 oz/⅓ cup unsalted (sweet) butter
1.5 ml/¼ tsp cayenne
15 ml/1 tbsp chopped fresh sage
Salt and freshly ground black pepper
Mascarpone cheese, to serve

Put the flour and cheese in a food processor and blend. Add the butter, cayenne, sage, salt and pepper. Chill for 30 minutes. Roll out the shortbread to 5 mm/ ¼ in thick and cut into shapes with a biscuit cutter. Place a little apart on a baking sheet. Bake in a preheated oven at 190°C/375°F/gas mark 5 for 8–10 minutes until golden. Allow to cool and top each biscuit with mascarpone cheese before serving.

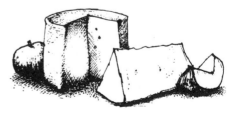

Biscotti alla Parmigiana

Parmesan Bites
Makes approximately 40

*100 g/4 oz/½ cup unsalted (sweet)
butter*
*100 g/4 oz/1 cup plain (all-purpose)
flour*
*50 g/2 oz/⅓ cup semolina (cream of
wheat)*
1.5 ml/¼ tsp salt
1.5 ml/¼ tsp dry mustard
*100 g/4 oz/1 cup Parmesan cheese,
grated*

Blend the ingredients in a food processor until smooth and knead on a floured surface. Roll out and cut into approximately 40 shapes with a biscuit cutter. Place on a baking sheet and cook in a preheated oven at 180°C/350°F/gas mark 4 for 20 minutes until golden brown. Transfer to a wire rack and cool. Store in an airtight tin.

Delizie di Noci

Walnut Delights
Serves 4

175 g/6 oz/¾ cup light brown sugar
250 ml/8 fl oz/1 cup water
5 ml/1 tsp vinegar
2 egg whites
5 ml/1 tsp vanilla essence (extract)
200 g/7 oz/1¾ cups chopped walnuts

Mix the sugar, water and vinegar together in a saucepan and cook over a moderate heat, without stirring, until a small spoonful dropped in cold water forms a hard ball. While the mixture is cooking, whisk the egg whites in a large bowl until stiff. When the hot mixture reaches the hard ball stage, remove from the heat and pour slowly over the egg whites, beating constantly. Add the vanilla essence and walnuts and continue beating until creamy and stiff. Drop teaspoonfuls on to a greased baking sheet and bake in a preheated oven at 180°C/350°F/gas mark 4 for 10–12 minutes.

Pane alla Noce con Pomodori Secchi

Sun-Dried Tomato and Walnut Loaf
Makes 1 loaf

*450 g/1 lb/4 cups strong white (bread)
flour*
5 ml/1 tsp salt
10 g/½ oz/2 tsp easy-blend dried yeast
*45 ml/3 tbsp sun-dried tomatoes in oil,
drained and chopped*
75 g/3 oz/¾ cup walnuts, chopped
1 garlic clove, crushed
150 ml/¼ pt/⅔ cup hand-hot water
5 ml/1 tsp chopped fresh thyme
15 ml/1 tbsp olive oil

Sift the flour and salt in a bowl and stir in the yeast. Add the sun-dried tomatoes, walnuts, garlic, water and thyme. Blend in the oil and mix to a soft dough, adding extra hot water if necessary. Knead for 2 minutes and cover the bowl with clingfilm (plastic wrap). Leave in a warm place for 1 hour until the dough has doubled in volume. Turn out on to a floured board and knead for 1 minute. Place in a loaf tin or 2 well-oiled terracotta plant pots and leave to rise for 30 minutes. Bake in a preheated oven at 200°C/400°F/gas mark 6 for 35 minutes. Turn out and cool on a wire rack before serving.

Biscotti a Mandorla

Almond Biscuits
Makes about 40

4 egg whites
350 g/12 oz/2 cups icing
(confectioners') sugar, sifted
5 ml/1 tsp grated nutmeg
5 ml/1 tsp ground cinnamon
450 g/1 lb/4 cups ground almonds
Juice of ½ lemon

Place the egg whites in a bowl and whisk until stiff. Gradually fold in the icing sugar with the spices. Beat well until the mixture forms a dropping consistency. Remove 90 ml/6 tbsp of the mixture and reserve. Continue to whisk the remaining mixture for 5 minutes. Stir in the ground almonds and lemon juice and mix to a smooth paste. Wrap in clingfilm (plastic wrap) and chill for 1 hour. Dust a work surface with icing sugar and roll the paste out to 5 mm/¼ in thick. Cut out shapes with biscuit cutters and place on greased baking sheets. Bake in a preheated oven at 200°C/400°F/gas mark 6 for 8 minutes until slightly browned. Remove from the oven. Loosen the biscuits but do not remove. Brush the reserved meringue mixture over the surface of the biscuits and reduce the oven temperature to 180°C/350°F/gas mark 4. Return the biscuits to the oven until the meringue has hardened without browning. If the meringue begins to brown open the oven door slightly. Cool on wire racks and store in an airtight container.

Pagnotta all' Albicocca

Apricot Loaf
Serves 8

225 g/8 oz/1 cup unsalted (sweet)
butter, softened
200 g/7 oz/scant 1 cup caster
(superfine) sugar
2 eggs, well beaten
6 ripe apricots, stoned (pitted), skinned
and mashed
300 g/11 oz/2¾ cups plain (all-
purpose) flour, sifted
1.5 ml/¼ tsp salt
5 ml/1 tsp bicarbonate of soda
(baking soda)
75 g/3 oz/¾ cup chopped almonds
5 ml/1 tsp melted butter, for greasing
2.5 ml/½ tsp plain (all-purpose) flour,
for dusting

Cream the softened butter and sugar together. Beat in the eggs and apricots. Mix together the flour, salt and bicarbonate of soda. Fold into the butter mixture with the nuts. Turn into a greased and floured loaf tin (pan). Bake in a preheated oven at 180°C/350°F/gas mark 4 for approximately 1 hour or until a skewer inserted into the centre comes out clean. Cool for 10 minutes and turn out on to a rack and leave to cool completely. Serve sliced.

Biscotti di Nocciola

Hazelnut Slices

Makes 20

175 g/6 oz/1½ cups hazelnuts
Rice paper
3 egg whites
225 g/8 oz/1 cup caster (superfine)
* sugar*
5 ml/1 tsp vanilla essence (extract)
5 ml/1 tsp ground cinnamon
5 ml/1 tsp grated lemon rind

Chop 12 hazelnuts roughly and reserve. Pound or blend the remaining hazelnuts until they are finely crushed. Line a baking sheet with rice paper and set aside. Whisk the egg whites until light and frothy. Gradually add the sugar and continue whisking until the mixture forms stiff peaks. Fold in all the hazelnuts, vanilla essence, cinnamon and lemon rind. Drop heaped teaspoons on to the lined paper and flatten out into thin strips. Sprinkle with the reserved roughly chopped hazelnuts. Leave to set for 1 hour and bake in a pre-heated oven at 180°C/350°F/gas mark 4 for 12–15 minutes until firm to the touch. Allow to cool.

Salads

Italian salads are famous throughout the world, largely I suspect, due to the wonderful olive oils used to dress them. All vegetables can be served in a salad with the traditional olive oil dressing – the dressing is an integral part of the salad and not merely an addition to it. Oranges feature in many savoury Italian salads. They are in plentiful supply and their natural affinity with chicory, spinach and fennel makes them an ideal ingredient. Although often served as a side dish, a salad of raw crunchy vegetables is the ideal antipasto if tossed well in a mixture of herbs, olive oil, freshly ground black pepper and vinegar or lemon juice.

Insalata al Fresco

Rice Salad with Olives and Tomatoes

Serves 4

225 g/8 oz/1 cup arborio rice
1 onion, thinly sliced into rings
45 ml/3 tbsp olive oil
30 ml/2 tbsp balsamic vinegar
5 ml/1 tsp caster (superfine) sugar
3 stoned (pitted) black olives, chopped
Salt and freshly ground black pepper
3 tomatoes, skinned, seeded and
*   roughly chopped*
4 mint leaves, chopped

Cook the rice in plenty of boiling salted water for 15–20 minutes until just cooked but still with texture. Drain, rinse with cold water and drain again. Turn into a bowl. Meanwhile, cook the onion in the oil gently for 3 minutes until softened. Stir in the vinegar, sugar, olives and some salt and pepper and simmer very gently for 5 minutes. Pour the hot onion mixture over the rice, add the tomatoes and mint. Toss and serve straight away.

Insalata di Barbabietola

Beetroot Salad

Serves 4

450 g/1 lb beetroot (red beets)
2 red onions, chopped
Salt and freshly ground black pepper
15 ml/1 tbsp oil
30 ml/2 tbsp tarragon or wine vinegar
5 ml/1 tsp chopped fresh parsley or
*   chervil*

Cook the beetroot in boiling water for 15 minutes or until tender. Cool, peel and cut into small cubes. Gently mix with the chopped onions. Mix the seasoning with the oil and vinegar. Pour over the beetroot and onions and arrange in a dish. Decorate with the chopped parsley or chervil.

Insalata Topinambur

Jerusalem Artichoke Salad

Serves 4

450 g/1 lb Jerusalem artichokes,
scrubbed or peeled
Salt
60 ml/4 tbsp olive oil
30 ml/2 tbsp lemon juice
Freshly ground black pepper

Wash and peel the artichokes, shaping them into a uniform size. Place immediately in a pan of water and add half the lemon juice and a pinch of salt. Boil for 10–15 minutes until tender. Drain. Mix the oil and the remaining lemon juice and toss with the artichokes. Add a good grinding of pepper.

Insalata di Fave e Dragoncella

Broad Bean and Tarragon Salad

Serves 4

225 g/8 oz fresh or frozen broad (lima)
beans
5 ml/1 tsp chopped fresh tarragon
60 ml/4 tbsp Creamy Italian Dressing
(see page 373)
Salt and freshly ground black pepper

Place the beans in a saucepan. Cover with lightly salted water and bring to the boil. Cook for 20 minutes until tender and drain. Spoon into a serving dish and sprinkle over the tarragon and Italian dressing. Season with salt and pepper and serve.

Insalata di Mele e Carote

Apple and Carrot Salad

Serves 4

2 carrots
3 apples
30 ml/2 tbsp lemon juice
Curly endive (frisée lettuce) leaves

Scrub the carrots and dry well. Slice the carrots very thinly. Cut the apples into cubes approximately 1 cm/½ in square and place in a bowl. Sprinkle the apple cubes with the lemon juice to prevent discolouration and arrange on the endive with the slices of carrot.

Insalata di Carote e Indivia

Carrot and Chicory Salad

Serves 4

2 chicory (Belgian endive) heads
2 carrots, grated
45 ml/3 tbsp virgin olive oil
½ garlic clove, crushed
15 ml/1 tbsp chopped fresh parsley
Pinch of salt

Trim the outer leaves of the chicory and cut a cone-shaped core out of the base of each. Cut the leaves in strips and place in a large bowl with the grated carrot. Blend the oil, garlic, parsley and salt together in a small bowl and pour over the salad. Toss and allow to marinate for 10 minutes before serving.

Insalata di Radicchio Rosso

Red Radicchio Salad

Serves 4–6

1 large radicchio head, shredded
1 onion, sliced
45 ml/3 tbsp olive oil
1 garlic clove, crushed
5 ml/1 tsp paprika
15 ml/1 tbsp chopped fresh parsley
15 ml/1 tbsp snipped fresh chives

Heat the oil in a saucepan. Add the onion and cook for 2 minutes. Add the radicchio and crushed garlic and cook for about 5 minutes until the radicchio is softened but not brown. Stir in the remaining ingredients and cook for 2 minutes. Transfer to a warm serving dish.

Insalata di Carote

Carrot Salad

Serves 4

4 carrots, grated
1 onion, finely chopped
30 ml/2 tbsp olive oil
15 ml/1 tbsp lemon juice
15 ml/1 tbsp chopped fresh parsley
15 ml/1 tbsp wine or tarragon vinegar
Salt and freshly ground black pepper

Mix the carrots and onion together. Blend the oil, lemon juice, parsley and vinegar together, season well and toss into the carrot and onion mixture. Arrange on plates and serve.

Insalata Genovese

Genoese Salad

Serves 2–3

½ cucumber, chopped
2 large tomatoes, thinly sliced
4 slices prosciutto
8 slices salami
2 eggs, hard-boiled (hard-cooked) and halved
45 ml/3 tbsp olive oil
15 ml/1 tbsp tarragon vinegar
Salt and freshly ground black pepper
1 garlic clove, crushed

Arrange the cucumber over the base of a serving dish with the tomato slices in the centre. Roll up the prosciutto and place over the salad with the salami and olives. Place the eggs on top of the salami. Blend the olive oil with the vinegar, salt, pepper and garlic and pour over the salad. Chill for 15 minutes before serving.

Insalata all'Indivia

Chicory Salad

Serves 4

2 chicory (Belgian endive) heads
60 ml/4 tbsp virgin olive oil
½ garlic clove, crushed
Pinch of salt
15 ml/1 tbsp chopped fresh mint

Trim the outer leaves of the chicory and cut a cone-shaped core out of the base of each. Cut the leaves in halves. Blend the oil, garlic and salt together in a small bowl and stir in the mint. Lay the chicory in a shallow dish and pour over the dressing.

Insalata di Frutti e Noci

Fruit and Nut Salad
Serves 4

2 oranges, segmented
30 ml/2 tbsp grapefruit juice
3 plums, stoned (pitted) and sliced
15 ml/1 tbsp olive oil
Iceberg lettuce leaves
120 ml/4 fl oz/½ cup double (heavy)
* cream, whipped*
15 ml/1 tbsp lemon juice
50 g/2 oz/½ cup chopped nuts

Combine the orange segments with the grapefruit juice and sliced plums. Pour over the olive oil and arrange on a bed of lettuce. Blend the whipped cream and lemon juice together and stir in the chopped nuts. Pour over the orange and plums and serve at once.

Insalata di Uva

Grape Salad
Serves 4–6

225 g/8 oz large white grapes, halved
* and seeded*
175 g/6 oz/1½ cups blanched almonds
Lettuce leaves
2 oranges, sliced and quartered
Walnut oil to sprinkle

Scatter the grapes and nuts over a bed of lettuce. Top with the orange quarter-slices and any juice. Sprinkle with walnut oil and serve.

Insalata di Apio

Celeriac Salad
Serves 4

2 eggs, hard-boiled (hard-cooked)
1 egg yolk
10 ml/2 tsp made mustard
45 ml/3 tbsp olive oil
15 ml/1 tbsp wine vinegar
1 celeriac (celery root), cut in thin
* matchsticks*
Salt and freshly ground black pepper

Blend the yolks of the hard-boiled eggs with the extra egg yolk and mustard. Whisk in the olive oil, a little at a time. Stir in the wine vinegar. Season the dressing with salt and pepper and pour over the celeriac. Leave to stand for at least an hour before serving.

Insalata di Fave

Mixed Bean Salad
Serves 4

425 g/15 oz/1 large can haricot (navy)
* beans, drained*
1 onion, chopped
5 ml/1 tsp chopped fresh tarragon
225 g/8 oz broad (lima) beans, cooked
1 garlic clove, crushed
30 ml/2 tbsp olive oil
2.5 ml/½ tsp vinegar
Salt and freshly ground black pepper

Rinse the haricot beans and drain. Place in a salad bowl. Mix in the chopped onion with the tarragon and broad beans. Blend the garlic and oil with the vinegar and mix this dressing with the beans. Season with salt and pepper and serve.

Insalata di Pasta Tiepida con Ravanelli

Warm Pasta Salad with Radishes
Serves 4

225 g/8 oz spiral pasta
50 g/2 oz fresh or frozen peas
1 bunch of radishes
5 ml/1 tsp olive oil
30 ml/2 tbsp snipped fresh chives
150 ml/¼ pt/⅔ cup single (light) cream
5 ml/1 tsp lemon juice
Salt and freshly ground black pepper

Cook the pasta in a pan of boiling salted water for 8–10 minutes and stir in the peas for the last five minutes. Cut each radish into 4 slices. Drain the pasta, stirring gently. Blend in the olive oil, chives, radishes and cream. Quickly mix in the lemon juice and season with the salt and pepper. Toss well and serve warm.

Insalata alla Romana

Roman Salad
Serves 4–6

225 g/8 oz young spinach, torn in pieces
2 large tomatoes, chopped
100 g/4 oz white button mushrooms, thinly sliced
45 ml/3 tbsp olive oil
15 ml/1 tbsp white wine vinegar
30 ml/2 tbsp chopped fresh basil
1 garlic clove, crushed
Salt and freshly ground black pepper

Toss the spinach, tomatoes and mushrooms together. Blend the olive oil, vinegar, basil, garlic, salt and pepper and pour over the salad. Toss gently and serve.

Cavolo Rosso sott' Aceto

Red Cabbage Pickle
Serves 4

1 red cabbage, finely shredded
5 ml/1 tsp salt
45 ml/3 tbsp tarragon vinegar
45 ml/3 tbsp chopped fresh chervil
45 ml/3 tbsp chopped fresh tarragon
6 radishes, sliced

Plunge the cabbage in boiling water to which the salt and half the tarragon vinegar have been added. Remove from the heat immediately. Allow to stand for 10 minutes. Drain and transfer to a deep dish. Sprinkle with the remaining vinegar, the chopped chervil and tarragon leaves. Toss well. Garnish with the radish slices.

Insalata di Riso e Scampi

Rice and Scampi Salad
Serves 4

30 ml/2 tbsp olive oil
15 ml/1 tbsp white wine vinegar
Salt and freshly ground black pepper
1.5 ml/¼ tsp grated nutmeg
1 onion, finely chopped
225 g/8 oz/2 cups cold cooked long-grain rice
100 g/4 oz cooked green peas
12 cooked scampi or king prawns (jumbo shrimp), peeled
Lettuce
45 ml/3 tbsp chopped fresh parsley

Mix the oil and vinegar in a bowl and season with the salt, pepper and nutmeg. Stir in the chopped onion and rice until thoroughly mixed. Add the peas and scampi. Serve very cold on a bed of crisp lettuce garnished with the chopped parsley.

Insalata di Frutti di Mare all' Italiana

Italian Seafood Salad
Serves 6–8

75 ml/5 tbsp virgin olive oil
45 ml/3 tbsp lemon juice
1 garlic clove, crushed
15 ml/1 tbsp chopped fresh parsley
15 ml/1 tbsp snipped fresh chives
Salt and freshly ground black pepper
450 g/1 lb cooked, whole prawns (shrimp)
450 g/1 lb cooked squid, sliced
225 g/8 oz shelled, cooked scallops
450 g/1 lb mussels, steamed, opened and removed from the shells
1 red (bell) pepper, grilled and skinned
½ cucumber, seeded and cut into 5 cm/2 in chunks
8 black olives, stoned (pitted)
30 ml/2 tbsp chopped fresh parsley

Mix the olive oil, lemon juice, crushed garlic, chopped parsley and chives together in a large bowl and season with the salt and pepper. Save a few prawns for garnishing, peel the remainder and add with the cooked squid, scallops and mussels to the bowl. Slice the red pepper thinly and add to the seafood. Season with the salt and pepper and add the cucumber and black olives. Turn gently to coat lightly in the dressing and chill for 1 hour. Just before serving, garnish with the chopped parsley and the reserved prawns.

Insalata Mediterranea

Mediterranean Salad
Serves 2

1 egg, hard-boiled (hard-cooked)
2 slices Parma ham
6 slices salami
Green salad leaves
8 black olives, stoned (pitted) and chopped
5 ml/1 tsp white wine vinegar
15 ml/1 tbsp olive oil
2.5 ml/½ tsp made mustard
5 ml/1 tsp chopped fresh basil
Salt and freshly ground black pepper

Cut the egg into quarters. Arrange the egg, Parma ham, salami and salad leaves on a serving dish. Place the chopped olives, vinegar, olive oil, mustard and basil in a bowl and whisk well. Season with the salt and pepper and pour over the salad.

Insalata di Arance alla Menta

Minted Orange Salad
Serves 4

12 mint leaves
30 ml/2 tbsp lime juice
3 oranges, segmented
2 peaches, skinned and sliced

Roughly chop the mint leaves and place in a small bowl. Blend in the lime juice. Arrange the oranges and peaches on a serving plate and pour over the lime and mint dressing.

Peperonata con Melanzane e Mozzarella

Mozzarella Salad with Ratatouille
Serves 3–4

1 aubergine (eggplant), cut in chunks
2 courgettes (zucchini), sliced
5 ml/1 tsp salt
1 orange (bell) pepper, sliced
1 onion, sliced
2 garlic cloves, crushed
45 ml/3 tbsp olive oil
Salt and freshly ground black pepper
15 ml/1 tbsp tarragon vinegar
100 g/4 oz/1 cup Mozzarella cheese, grated
15 ml/1 tbsp chopped fresh parsley
Sicilian Bread (see page 289), to serve

Place the aubergine and courgettes in a colander and sprinkle with the salt. Leave to stand for 20 minutes, then rinse and pat dry with kitchen paper. Fry (sauté) all the vegetables with the garlic in the oil for 6–8 minutes until softened. Season with the salt and pepper and stir in the vinegar. Place on a large serving dish and top with Mozzarella. Sprinkle over the parsley and serve with Sicilian Bread.

Insalata di Pesche Sport

Sporty Peach Salad
Serves 4

8 young spinach leaves, shredded
4 ripe peaches, skinned, halved and stoned (pitted)
15 ml/1 tbsp lime juice
15 ml/1 tbsp lemon juice
45 ml/3 tbsp olive oil
Freshly ground black pepper

Place the shredded spinach on four plates and top each with two peach halves. Blend the lime juice with the lemon juice and oil and sprinkle over the peaches. Sprinkle with freshly ground black pepper and serve.

Insalata di Pasta Primavera

Springtime Pasta Salad
Serves 4

Dressing:
120 ml/4 fl oz/½ cup olive oil
45 ml/3 tbsp balsamic vinegar
2 garlic cloves, crushed
2.5 ml/¼ tsp crushed, dried red chillies
45 ml/3 tbsp grated Parmesan cheese
75 g/3 oz sun-dried tomatoes, diced

225 g/8 oz spiral pasta
50 g/2 oz fresh or frozen peas
75 g/3 oz sliced spring onions (scallions)
350 g/12 oz fresh asparagus, cut into 1 cm/½ in pieces
100 g/4 oz button mushrooms, thinly sliced
2 carrots, thinly sliced
4 large lettuce leaves

Blend all the dressing ingredients and leave to stand for 1 hour. Cook the pasta in a pan of boiling water for 8–10 minutes or until tender and drain. Stir in the onions. Cook the peas, asparagus, mushrooms and carrots in boiling water for 1 minute. Drain and add to the pasta. Leave to cool. Toss in the dressing. Line four plates with the lettuce leaves and divide the pasta mixture evenly among the plates.

Insalata di Gamberetti

Prawn Salad
Serves 4

1 round lettuce, shredded
4 potatoes, boiled and sliced
4 anchovy fillets, chopped
12 cooked large prawns (jumbo
* shrimp), peeled*
15 ml/1 tbsp capers
30 ml/2 tbsp olive oil
15 ml/1 tbsp wine vinegar
30 ml/2 tbsp mayonnaise
Salt
1.5 ml/¼ tsp grated nutmeg

Line a salad bowl with the lettuce. Add the potatoes, capers, anchovies and prawns. Blend the oil, vinegar, mayonnaise, salt and nutmeg together and pour over the salad.

Insalata di Fragole, Uva e Menta

Strawberry, Grape and Mint Salad
Serves 4

350 g/12 oz white grapes, halved and
* seeded*
225 g/8 oz strawberries, halved
White cabbage, shredded
90 ml/6 tbsp Savoury Mascarpone
* Cream (see page 359)*
5 ml/1 tsp fresh chopped mint

Arrange the grapes and strawberries on a bed of white cabbage. Spoon over the Mascarpone Cream and serve, garnished with mint.

Insalata di Pere e Parmigiano

Pear and Parmesan Salad
Serves 4

30 ml/2 tbsp olive oil
15 ml/1 tbsp white wine vinegar
45 ml/3 tbsp chopped fresh parsley
Salt and freshly ground black pepper
1.5 ml/¼ tsp grated nutmeg
2 large ripe dessert pears, thinly sliced
100 g/4 oz Parmesan cheese, in one
* piece*
50 g/2 oz/½ cup walnuts, chopped
Mixed salad leaves

Put the oil, vinegar and parsley into a bowl and season with the salt, pepper and nutmeg. Blend well and add the pears. Chill. Shave the Parmesan cheese with a potato peeler. Mix the chopped walnuts with the cheese. Serve the pears and dressing on a bed of salad leaves, garnished with the walnuts and cheese.

Insalata di Peperoni Gialli

Yellow Pepper Salad
Serves 4

4 yellow (bell) peppers, cut into thin strips
1 small bunch of radishes, sliced
1 celery stick, chopped
3 tomatoes, thinly sliced
Olive oil

Place the salad vegetables in a bowl and spoon over some oil. Toss until well blended and shiny.

Insalata di Salame Piemontese

Piedmont Salami Salad
Serves 4

175 g/6 oz sliced salami
2 celery sticks, chopped
400 g/14 oz/1 large can artichoke hearts, drained
1 green (bell) pepper, cut into thin strips
100 g/4 oz button mushrooms, quartered
100 g/4 oz French (green) beans, cooked
2 large tomatoes, sliced
4 radicchio leaves
Dressing:
1 garlic clove, crushed
Salt and freshly ground black pepper
5 ml/1 tsp made mustard
45 ml/3 tbsp olive oil
15 ml/1 tbsp rosemary vinegar
Black olives, to garnish
2 eggs, hard-boiled (hard-cooked) and quartered

Place the salami in a large salad bowl with all the salad ingredients, except the radicchio. Place the radicchio in a serving dish. Whisk the garlic, salt, pepper, mustard, olive oil and vinegar in a small bowl. Pour the dressing over the salad and toss well. Garnish with the black olives and quartered eggs.

Insalata di Pasta e Verdura

Pasta and Vegetable Salad
Serves 4–6

225 g/8 oz tri-coloured pasta spirals
100 g/4 oz fresh or frozen broad (lima) beans
3 celery sticks, thinly sliced
30 ml/2 tbsp white wine vinegar
60 ml/4 tbsp olive oil
Salt and freshly ground black pepper

Cook the pasta in boiling salted water until it is tender but still firm. Drain, rinse with cold water and drain again. Allow to cool. Cook the broad beans in boiling, salted water for 5 minutes until they are tender. Drain and rinse with cold water, drain again and allow to cool. Mix the pasta and beans together with the celery and blend in the vinegar and oil. Season well with the salt and pepper.

Insalata di Albicocche

Apricot Salad
Serves 6

450 g/1 lb fresh apricots, stoned (pitted)
100 g/4 oz/1 cup fresh coconut, shredded
Shredded lettuce
1 grapefruit, cut into segments

Slice the apricots thinly and arrange on the lettuce. Cover with shredded coconut and arrange the grapefruit segments on top.

Insalata di Tonno e Peperoni

Quick Tuna and Pepper Salad
Serves 4

150 g/5 oz/⅔ cup long-grain rice
1 red (bell) pepper, thinly sliced
4 gherkins (cornichons), roughly
* chopped*
3 eggs, hard-boiled (hard-cooked) and
* quartered*
185 g/6½ oz/1 small can tuna in oil
30 ml/2 tbsp wine or herb vinegar
Salt and freshly ground black pepper
30 ml/2 tbsp chopped fresh parsley

Put the rice in a pan of boiling water and bring to the boil. Simmer for 10 minutes until tender. Drain, rinse with cold water and drain again. Turn into a salad bowl. Add the pepper and gherkins. Drain the oil from the tuna into a small bowl and stir in the vinegar. Season with the salt and pepper. Flake the fish and add to the salad. Pour over the dressing and garnish with chopped parsley.

Insalata di Arance e Susine

Orange Plum Salad
Serves 4

2 oranges, cut into segments and diced
100 g/4 oz grapes, halved and seeded
4 plums, stoned (pitted) and sliced
50 g/2 oz/½ cup chopped nuts
30 ml/2 tbsp olive oil
Lettuce leaves

Combine all the salad ingredients except the lettuce with the oil. Serve on a bed of lettuce.

Insalata di Susine

Plum Salad
Serves 4

225 g/8 oz rocket, torn into pieces
½ cucumber, seeded and cut into
* chunks*
1 small red onion, sliced into rings
350 g/12 oz red dessert plums, stoned
* (pitted) and sliced*
15 ml/1 tbsp mint leaves, torn into
* pieces*
45 ml/3 tbsp olive oil
Salt and freshly ground black pepper

Combine the rocket, cucumber, onion and plums in a bowl. Sprinkle over the mint leaves and dress with the olive oil. Season to taste.

Spinaci Conditi alla Lumia

Spinach with Lime Dressing
Serves 4

175 g/6 oz carrots, thinly sliced
45 ml/3 tbsp lime juice
15 ml/1 tbsp white wine vinegar
90 ml/6 tbsp olive oil
15 ml/1 tbsp chopped fresh dill (dill
* weed)*
5 ml/1 tsp mustard
Salt and freshly ground black pepper
30 ml/2 tbsp flaked (slivered) almonds
225 g/8 oz young spinach leaves

Place the carrots in a bowl. Blend the lime juice, vinegar, olive oil, dill and mustard together with a little salt and pepper and pour over the carrots. Allow to stand for 15 minutes. In a serving dish arrange the spinach and sprinkle over the almonds. Spoon the carrots and dressing over the spinach leaves and serve.

Insalata di Fagioli

Haricot Bean Salad
Serves 4

225 g/8 oz/1⅓ cups dried haricot (navy) beans (or use 2 × 425 g/ 2 × 15 oz/2 large cans)
1 onion, chopped
5 ml/1 tsp chopped fresh tarragon
1 garlic clove, crushed
30 ml/2 tbsp olive oil
2.5 ml/½ tsp vinegar
Salt and freshly ground black pepper

Soak the haricot beans overnight. Next day place in a large pan of water. Bring to the boil and boil rapidly for 10 minutes until soft. Alternatively, drain the canned beans, rinse and drain again. Mix the chopped onion with the tarragon, garlic and oil. Blend in the vinegar and mix with the beans. Season with salt and pepper.

Insalata di Zucchini

Courgette Salad
Serves 4–6

450 g/1 lb small courgettes (zucchini), thinly sliced
1 onion, finely chopped
45 ml/3 tbsp olive oil
1 garlic clove, crushed
15 ml/1 tbsp lemon juice
5 ml/1 tsp paprika
15 ml/1 tbsp fresh chopped parsley
15 ml/1 tbsp fresh snipped chives

Place the courgettes and onion in a salad bowl. Whisk together the remaining ingredients and pour over. Toss well before serving.

Insalata di Zucchini Caldo

Warm Courgette Salad
Serves 4–6

450 g/1 lb small courgettes, (zucchini)
1 onion
45 ml/3 tbsp olive oil
1 garlic clove, crushed
5 ml/1 tsp paprika
15 ml/1 tbsp chopped fresh parsley
15 ml/1 tbsp snipped fresh chives
Lettuce leaves

Slice the courgettes very thinly. Chop the onion finely. Heat the oil in a saucepan. Add the onion and cook for 2 minutes. Add the courgettes and crushed garlic and cook for about 5 minutes until the courgettes are soft but not brown. Stir in the remaining ingredients and cook for 2 minutes. Leave to cool slightly. Spoon on to a bed of lettuce leaves and serve warm.

Insalata di Festa Estiva

Summer Party Salad
Serves 8

1 small radicchio head
½ curly endive (frisée lettuce)
½ lollo rosso
60 ml/4 tbsp olive oil
Grated rind and juice of 1 lime
5 ml/1 tsp sugar
Salt and freshly ground black pepper
15 ml/1 tbsp chopped fresh coriander (cilantro)
100 g/4 oz/1 cup walnut pieces
225 g/8 oz button mushrooms, sliced

Tear all the salad leaves into small pieces. Arrange in a bowl. Blend the olive oil with the lime, sugar, salt and pepper and stir in the coriander. Stir in the walnut pieces and add the mushroom slices. Allow to stand for 5 minutes then spoon over the leaves.

Insalata di Capperi e Acciughi

Salad of Capers and Anchovies

Serves 3–4

8 olives, stoned (pitted) and quartered
8 radishes, sliced
4 anchovies, chopped
10 ml/2 tsp capers
1 lettuce heart, separated into leaves
Olive Oil Dressing (see page 373)

Mix the first four ingredients together. Arrange the lettuce leaves into a pyramid shape and spoon the anchovy mix over it. Pour over the olive oil dressing and serve.

Insalata Tivoli

Tivolian Salad

Serves 4

5 ml/1 tsp salt
2 aubergines (eggplants), cubed
1 green (bell) pepper, cut into strips
1 red (bell) pepper, cut into strips
1 large onion, sliced
45 ml/3 tbsp olive oil
150 ml/¼ pt/⅔ cup water
1 garlic clove, crushed
5 ml/1 tsp chopped fresh marjoram
5 ml/1 tsp chopped fresh basil
30 ml/2 tbsp white wine vinegar
Freshly ground black pepper

Sprinkle salt over the aubergines and leave to stand for 30 minutes. Rinse and drain on kitchen paper. Place the aubergines, peppers, onion, olive oil and water in a flameproof casserole dish (Dutch oven) and bring to the boil. Season with salt and stir in the garlic, marjoram and basil. Cover the casserole and bake in a preheated oven at 190°C/375°F/gas mark 5 for 1 hour until the vegetables are tender. Remove from the oven and spoon the vegetables into a warmed serving dish. Pour over the vinegar and season with the pepper. The vegetables can be served hot or cold.

Insalata di Vitello e Avocado

Veal and Avocado Salad

Serves 6

450 g/1 lb lean cooked veal
3 avocados, peeled, stoned (pitted) and sliced
1 green (bell) pepper, finely chopped
½ cucumber, peeled and chopped
175 ml/6 fl oz/¾ cup soured (dairy sour) cream
Salt and freshly ground black pepper
15 ml/1 tbsp lemon juice
1 Cos (Romaine) lettuce, chopped

Cut the veal into 1 cm/½ in cubes and place in a mixing bowl. Stir in the avocados, green pepper and cucumber cubes. Mix the soured cream, salt and pepper and lemon juice in a small bowl and pour the dressing over the meat mixture. Toss the ingredients together until they are well coated with the dressing. Arrange the chopped lettuce leaves on a large serving dish or individual plates and spoon the veal mixture in the centre. Chill before serving.

Insalata di Mare

Seafood Salad
Serves 4

20 fresh mussels in shells, scrubbed
and beards removed
40 fresh baby clams in shells,
scrubbed
1 bay leaf
1 lemon, halved
200 g/7 oz fresh or frozen squid,
cleaned and cut into rings
Salt
175 g/6 oz cooked, peeled prawns
(shrimp)
4 large cooked, peeled king prawns
(jumbo shrimp)
90 ml/6 tbsp olive oil
45 ml/3 tbsp chopped fresh parsley
Freshly ground black pepper
Crusty bread, to serve

Soak the mussels and clams overnight in a bucket of water with the bay leaf and half the lemon. Bring a pan of salted water to the boil, add the squid and simmer for 25–30 minutes until tender. Strain the mussels and clams, discarding any which are not closed. Place in a large pan with just enough fresh water to cover the base of the pan, cover and steam over a moderate heat for about 8 minutes until they open, discarding any that do not open. Remove the mussels and clams from their shells and place in a warmed bowl with the prawns and squid. Squeeze the juice from the reserved lemon over the bowl and add the oil, parsley and pepper to taste. Serve warm with plenty of crusty bread.

Insalata Verde Milanese

Milanese Green Salad
Serves 4

½ garlic clove
100 g/4 oz chicory (Belgian endive)
1 lettuce
4 tender spinach leaves
1.5 ml/¼ tsp dry mustard
45 ml/3 tbsp olive oil
15 ml/1 tbsp wine vinegar

Rub the insides of the salad bowl with the cut garlic clove. Cut a cone-shaped core out of the chicory and tear the leaves into pieces. Place in a salad bowl. Tear the lettuce and spinach leaves in to pieces and place in the bowl. Sprinkle over the dry mustard. Blend the oil and vinegar and pour this dressing over the salad leaves. Toss lightly until the dressing is absorbed. Serve with meat dishes.

Insalata di Finocchio e Cetrioli

Fennel and Cucumber Salad
Serves 4

2 fennel bulbs
5 ml/1 tsp olive oil
25 g/1 oz/¼ cup flaked (slivered)
almonds
12 small black olives
½ cucumber, sliced thinly
50 g/2 oz/½ cup Parmesan cheese in
one piece

Trim the fennel and reserve the fronds. Slice across the fennel thinly and toss in a bowl with the olive oil, almonds, olives and cucumber. Shave the Parmesan into large curls with a potato peeler and scatter over the fennel fronds.

Insalata di Pesce Bianco

White Fish Salad
Serves 4–6

150 ml/¼ pt/⅔ cup dry white wine
150 ml/¼ pt/⅔ cup water
1 onion, quartered
Juice of ½ lemon
Few sprigs of mixed fresh herbs
Salt and freshly ground black pepper
450 g/1 lb white fish fillets
1 egg yolk
5 ml/1 tsp made mustard
30 ml/2 tbsp olive oil
150 ml/¼ pt/⅔ cup single (light) cream
30 ml/2 tbsp finely snipped fresh
  chives
12 olives, to garnish

Put the wine, water, onion, lemon juice, fresh herbs, salt and pepper in a large saucepan and bring to the boil. Add the fish fillets and reduce the heat. Simmer gently for 10–12 minutes until the fish flakes easily. Lift out the fish with a fish slice. Boil the fish stock until the liquid has reduced to one-third, strain and allow to cool. Flake the fish into 1 cm/½ in pieces, discarding any skin and bones. Leave to cool. Beat the egg yolk with the mustard in a bowl until creamy. Slowly add the oil, drop by drop and gradually beat in the strained fish stock. Whisk in the cream and season to taste. Stir in the chives and fold in the fish. Spoon into a serving dish, garnish with the olives and serve with a mixed salad.

Anguille Affumicate con Insalata di Verdura

Smoked Eel and Vegetable Salad
Serves 3

1 aubergine (eggplant), cut into four
  slices lengthways
2 courgettes (zucchini), cut in half
  lengthways
1 red (bell) and 1 yellow (bell) pepper,
  quartered
1 red onion, halved
1 white onion, halved
9 asparagus tips
Oil for brushing
1 shallot, chopped
8 basil leaves, torn
60 ml/4 tbsp chopped fresh oregano
60 ml/4 tbsp olive oil
15 ml/1 tsp wine vinegar
100 g/4 oz smoked eel, thinly sliced
A few leaves of rocket or curly endive
  (frisée lettuce)

Place the vegetables on foil on a grill (broiler) rack. Brush with oil and grill (broil) until tender, turning once. Place in a dish and leave to cool. Mix the shallot with the basil, oregano, olive oil and vinegar and pour over the vegetables. Toss well to coat, cover and marinate for at least 1 hour in the fridge. Arrange the vegetables on a large dish and place the eel slices on top with the salad leaves.

Insalata di Funghi

Mixed Mushroom Salad
Serves 4–6

*750 g/1½ lb mixed mushrooms
(chanterelle, morel, shiitake, oyster
and button), trimmed and cut up if
large
90 ml/6 tbsp olive oil
1 green chilli, seeded and chopped
1 large garlic clove, finely chopped
45 ml/3 tbsp chopped fresh parsley
Freshly ground black pepper
Coarse sea salt
Lemon or lime wedges*

Plunge the mushrooms in boiling water for
30 seconds. Drain on kitchen paper. Heat
the oil in a large saucepan. Add the mushrooms, chilli and garlic and cook gently,
stirring occasionally until the mushrooms
are tender. Leave to cool. Turn into a serving dish, sprinkle with the parsley, a good
grinding of pepper and some coarse sea
salt. Serve with lemon or lime wedges to
squeeze over.

Insalata Verde di Augusta

Augusta's Vegetable Salad
Serves 4

*5 ml/1 tsp salt
2 aubergines, (eggplants) cubed
1 green (bell) pepper, cut into strips
1 red (bell) pepper, cut into strips
1 large onion, sliced
45 ml/3 tbsp olive oil
150 ml/¼ pt/⅔ cup water
1 garlic clove, crushed
5 ml/1 tsp chopped fresh marjoram
5 ml/1 tsp chopped fresh basil
30 ml/2 tbsp white wine vinegar
Freshly ground black pepper*

Sprinkle salt over the aubergine and leave
to stand for 30 minutes. Rinse and drain on
kitchen paper. Place the aubergine, peppers, onion, olive oil and water in a flameproof casserole dish (Dutch oven) and
bring to the boil. Season with salt and stir
in the garlic, marjoram and basil. Cover
the casserole and bake in a preheated oven
at 190°F/375°F/gas mark 5 for 1 hour until
the vegetables are tender. Remove from
the oven and spoon the vegetables into a
warmed serving dish. Pour over the vinegar and season with the pepper. The vegetables can be served hot or cold.

Insalata di Aragosta

Lobster Salad
Serves 2

*1 cooked lobster
1 egg
Green salad leaves
5 ml/1 tsp white wine vinegar
15 ml/1 tbsp olive oil
5 ml/1 tsp chopped fresh basil
Salt and freshly ground black pepper
100 g/4 oz peas, cooked*

Remove the meat from the lobster tail and
large claws and chop roughly, reserving
the washed, small claws for garnish. Boil
the egg for 5 minutes and rinse under cold
water. Peel, halve and slice the egg into
quarters. Arrange the boiled egg and salad
leaves on a serving dish. Add the lobster
meat. Blend the vinegar, olive oil and basil
in a bowl and beat well. Season with the
salt and pepper and pour over the lobster.
Add the green peas, garnish with the small
claws and serve.

Desserts

The rich, creamy cakes served for dessert throughout Italy are world famous. Almost every cook in Italy believes their own recipe for almond cake to be the best and I include my own version for you to try. Pastry rings are popular, as are simple fruit tarts served with freshly whipped cream. Cakes, cheesecakes, creams and mousses are all desserts that never fail to please.

Torta di Mandorla

Almond Cake
Serves 4–6

350 g/12 oz/3 cups plain (all-purpose) flour, sifted
100 g/4 oz/½ cup caster (superfine) sugar
10 ml/2 tsp baking powder
2.5 ml/½ tsp salt
1 egg
150 ml/¼ pt/⅔ cup milk
2.5 ml/½ tsp almond essence (extract)
40 g/1½ oz/3 tbsp unsalted (sweet) butter, melted
1 egg white, lightly beaten
25 g/1 oz/¼ cup chopped almonds

Mix the flour, sugar, baking powder and salt together and set aside. Place the egg in the mixing bowl, and, using an electric mixer, begin mixing on a low speed. Gradually add the milk, almond extract and melted butter. Add the dry ingredients and continue mixing until the mixture is smooth. Scrape into a greased 20 cm/8 in cake tin (pan). Brush the cake top with egg white and sprinkle with chopped almonds. Bake in a preheated oven at 220°C/425°F/ gas mark 7 for about 40 minutes until risen, golden and a skewer inserted in the centre comes out clean.

Crostate all' Albicocca

Apricot Pastry Boats
Makes 10

225 g/8 oz/2 cups plain (all-purpose) flour
100 g/4 oz/½ cup unsalted (sweet) butter
75 g/3 oz/⅓ cup caster (superfine) sugar
2 egg yolks
5 ml/1 tsp butter for greasing
90 ml/6 tbsp apricot preserve (conserve)
75 g/3 oz/¾ cup pine nuts

Place the flour in a bowl and rub in the butter until the mixture resembles breadcrumbs. Stir in the sugar and gradually blend in the egg yolks. Add 30 ml/2 tbsp water if necessary to make a soft pastry (paste). Roll out the pastry and use to line 10 greased, boat-shaped tartlet tins (patty pans). Line the pastry with greaseproof (waxed) paper and fill with baking beans. Place on a baking sheet and cook in a preheated oven at 200°C/400°F/gas mark 6 for 8–10 minutes until brown. Put the preserve in a saucepan and warm gently. Remove the beans and divide the pine nuts between each pastry case. Fill with the apricot preserve and leave to cool.

Torta di Caffè con Mandorle

Almond Coffee Torte
Serves 8

8 eggs, separated
175 g/6 oz/¾ cup caster (superfine)
  sugar
60 ml/4 tbsp very strong coffee
175 g/6 oz/1¼ cups ground almonds
45 ml/3 tbsp semolina (cream of wheat)
100 g/4 oz/1 cup plain (all-purpose)
  flour
5 ml/1 tsp unsalted (sweet) butter

Beat the egg yolks and sugar until very
thick and creamy. Add the coffee, almonds
and the semolina. Beat well and fold in the
flour. Stiffly whisk the egg whites and fold
in with a metal spoon. Pour into a greased
23 cm/9 in cake tin (pan). Bake in a preheated oven at 180°C/ 350°F/gas mark 4
for about 40–50 minutes until the centre
springs back when lightly pressed.

Tagliatelle alla Mandorle

Almond Tagliatelle
Serves 4–6

450 g/1 lb tagliatelle
450 ml/¾ pt/2 cups double (heavy)
  cream, whipped lightly
75 g/3 oz/⅓ cup unsalted (sweet) butter
450 g/1 lb/4 cups ground almonds
25 g/1 oz/¼ cup chopped almonds
60 ml/4 tbsp clear honey

Cook the tagliatelle in salted water for 10
minutes until tender. Drain well. Blend the
cream, butter and ground almonds together and mix with the tagliatelle. Heat
through. Spoon on to serving plates.
Sprinkle over the chopped almonds and
drizzle with the honey.

Sformata di Arrancia

Orange Soufflé
Serves 6–8

10 eggs, separated
225 g/8 oz/1 cup caster (superfine)
  sugar
Grated rind and juice of 1 orange
45 ml/3 tbsp fine semolina (cream of
  wheat)
Juice of 1 lemon

Beat the egg yolks and sugar until very
thick and creamy. Add the orange rind and
juice, then the semolina. Beat in the lemon
juice. Whisk the egg whites until stiff and
gently fold in with a metal spoon. Turn
into a large, greased soufflé dish and bake
in a preheated oven at 180°C/350°F/gas
mark 4 for 40–50 minutes until well risen
and just set. Serve straight away.

Fichi con Grappa

Figs in Grappa
Serves 6

12 dried figs
25 g/1 oz/2 tbsp caster (superfine)
  sugar
120 ml/4 fl oz/½ cup Grappa or brandy
12 fresh mint leaves, to decorate

Put the figs in a bowl and sprinkle over the
sugar. Allow to stand for 30 minutes and
pour over the Grappa. Cover loosely with
greaseproof (waxed) paper. Set aside at
room temperature for 14 days, stirring
occasionally. Divide the figs, among 6
plates and decorate with the mint leaves.

Torta di Formaggio con Albicocce

Apricot Cheesecake
Serves 6

100 g/4 oz/½ cup unsalted (sweet) butter plus 5 ml/1 tsp for greasing
225 g/8 oz digestive biscuits (Graham crackers), crushed
75 g/3 oz/⅓ cup caster (superfine) sugar
5 ml/1 tsp ground cinnamon
900g/2 lb/4 cups Ricotta cheese
30 ml/2 tbsp plain (all-purpose) flour
2.5 ml/½ tsp vanilla essence (extract)
Grated rind of 1 lemon
3 egg yolks
350 g/12 oz fresh apricots, halved and stoned (pitted)
50 g/2 oz/½ cup flaked (slivered) almonds, for decoration

Grease a 23 cm/9 in loose-bottomed cake tin (pan) with the 5 ml/1 tsp butter and set aside. Melt the remaining butter and stir in the biscuit crumbs, 30 ml/2 tbsp of the sugar and the cinnamon. Spoon the mixture into the prepared cake tin and spread the mixture evenly. Set aside. Place the Ricotta cheese in a bowl and add the remaining sugar, flour, vanilla essence, and lemon rind. Beat the mixture for 2 minutes and beat in the egg yolks, one at a time, until the mixture is smooth. Spoon half the mixture over the biscuit base. Spread the apricots over the Ricotta cheese mixture so that they are just touching each other and spoon over the remaining Ricotta mixture. Bake in a preheated oven at 180°C/350°F/gas mark 4 for 12–15 minutes until the filling is firm to the touch. Remove from the oven and leave until cold. Slide the cheesecake from the tin and chill for 1 hour.

Torta di Lamponi

Raspberry Cake
Serves 6–8

100 g/4 oz/½ cup unsalted (sweet) butter
225 g/8 oz/1 cup caster (superfine) sugar
2 eggs
250 ml/8 fl oz/1 cup soured (dairy sour) cream
5 ml/1 tsp vanilla essence (extract)
250 g/9 oz/2¼ cups plain (all-purpose) flour
5 ml/1 tsp baking powder
5 ml/1 tsp bicarbonate of soda (baking soda)
5 ml/1 tsp cocoa (unsweetened chocolate) powder
2.5 ml/½ tsp salt
100 g/4 oz fresh or frozen raspberries
5 ml/1 tsp melted butter for greasing
5 ml/1 tsp ground cinnamon

Cream the butter and all but 30 ml/2 tbsp of the sugar until smooth. Beat in the eggs. Add the soured cream and vanilla essence and blend well. In a bowl sift together the flour, baking powder, bicarbonate of soda, cocoa and salt. Add to the butter mixture and fold in. Fold in the raspberries. Turn into a 20 cm/8 in round cake tin (pan) that has been brushed with the melted butter. Mix together the remaining sugar and cinnamon. Sprinkle over the cake mixture. Bake in a preheated oven at 200°C/400°F/gas mark 6 for 35–40 minutes or until the top is golden brown and a skewer inserted into the centre comes out clean.

Torta di Ricotta (1)

Italian Cheesecake
Serves 4–6

Base:
25 g/1 oz/2 tbsp caster (superfine)
* sugar*
5 ml/1 tsp grated lemon rind
100 g/4 oz/1 cup plain (all-purpose)
* flour, sifted*
1.5 ml/¼ tsp vanilla essence (extract)
1 egg yolk
25 g/1 oz/2 tbsp unsalted (sweet)
* butter, softened*

Filling:
750 g/1½ lb/3 cups Ricotta cheese
225 g/8 oz/1 cup caster (superfine)
* sugar*
120 ml/4 fl oz/½ cup double (heavy)
* cream*
45 ml/3 tbsp plain (all-purpose) flour
5 ml/1 tsp vanilla essence (extract)
5 eggs, separated
150 g/5 oz soft fruit, such as
* raspberries or strawberries*

Make the base. Place the sugar, lemon rind and flour in a mixing bowl and mix well. Add the vanilla essence, egg yolk and butter. Beat until the mixture forms into a dough and the ingredients are well combined. Press half the dough mixture into a greased 23 cm/9 in springform cake tin (pan). Bake in a preheated oven at 200°C/ 400°F/gas mark 6 for 8 minutes. Remove from the oven and leave to cool, then press the remaining crust mixture on to the sides of the tin and set aside. Make the filling. Place the Ricotta cheese in a bowl and beat until creamy. Mix in the sugar, cream, flour, vanilla essence and egg yolks. Place the egg whites in a bowl and whisk until they are stiff. Gently fold the egg whites into the Ricotta cheese mixture. Pour the filling into the pastry-lined tin and bake in a preheated oven at 180°C/350°F/gas mark 4 for 1 hour. Allow the cheesecake to cool in the pan then chill. Remove from the tin and top with the fruit before serving.

Torta di Ricotta (2)

Italian Cheesecake
Serves 6–8

225 g/8 oz shortcrust pastry (basic pie
* crust)*
900 g/2 lb/4 cups Ricotta cheese
100 g/4 oz/½ cup caster (superfine)
* sugar*
30 ml/2 tbsp plain (all-purpose) flour
2.5 ml/½ tsp vanilla essence (extract)
Grated rind and juice of 1 orange
4 egg yolks
60 ml/4 tbsp raisins
30 ml/2 tbsp flaked (slivered) almonds
1 egg white, lightly beaten

Dust a pastry board with flour and roll out the pastry to line a 25 cm/10 in flan tin (pie pan). Prick the pastry all over with a fork and cover with a piece of greaseproof (waxed) paper. Fill with baking beans and bake in a preheated oven at 200°C/400°F/ gas mark 6 for 10 minutes. Remove the beans and paper and return to the oven for 5 minutes. Allow the flan case (pie shell) to cool. Place the Ricotta cheese in a bowl with the sugar, flour, vanilla essence and grated orange rind and juice. Beat in the egg yolks and stir in the raisins. Spoon the mixture into the pastry case and sprinkle over the almonds. Roll out the pastry trimmings and cut into long strips. Arrange the pastry strips over the filling in a lattice pattern. Brush the strips with beaten egg white and bake in a preheated oven for 1 hour at 180°C/350°F/gas mark 4.

Miele Croccanti

Crackled Apples
Serves 4

Juice of ½ lemon
750 g/1½ lb apples
50 g/2 oz/¼ cup unsalted (sweet) butter
75 g/3 oz/⅓ cup dark brown sugar

Pour the lemon juice into a dish. Peel, core and slice the apples into rings and place them in the lemon juice ensuring that all surfaces are coated. This helps to prevent the apples turning brown. Melt the butter in a frying pan (skillet) and fry (sauté) the apples. Arrange the apples in a flat flame-proof dish. Place under a hot grill (broiler) for 2 minutes until they are tinged with brown. Sprinkle over the dark brown sugar and replace under the grill until the sugar caramelises. Allow to cool, then chill before serving.

Nettarine Caramellate

Caramelised Nectarines
Serves 4

250 ml/8 fl oz/1 cup water
45 ml/3 tbsp clear honey
30 ml/2 tbsp light brown sugar
6 fresh nectarines
45 ml/3 tbsp Grand Marnier
Whipped cream, to serve (optional)

Pour the water, honey and brown sugar into a saucepan and bring slowly to the boil. Add the nectarines and poach for 5 minutes. Transfer to a serving dish with a draining spoon. Pour the Grand Marnier into the saucepan and boil for 3 minutes. Pour over the nectarines and serve hot or cold with whipped cream if liked.

Torta di Crema al Cioccolato e Mandorla

Chocolate Almond Cream Roll
Serves 4–6

100 g/4 oz/1 cup plain (all-purpose)
flour
2.5 ml/½ tsp baking powder
1.5 ml/¼ tsp salt
4 eggs
225 g/8 oz/1 cup caster (superfine)
sugar
5 ml/1 tsp vanilla essence (extract)
50 g/2 oz plain (semi-sweet) chocolate
1.5 ml/¼ tsp bicarbonate of soda
(baking soda)
45 ml/3 tbsp cold water
15 g/½ oz/1 tbsp butter for greasing
1 quantity Almond Cream Filling (see
page 378)

Sift the flour and add the baking powder and salt. Sift together three times. Place the eggs in a deep bowl and add three quarters of the sugar. Beat until very thick and light in colour. Add the flour all at once, stirring well. Add the vanilla essence. Melt the chocolate in a basin over boiling water. Remove from the heat. Immediately mix the remaining sugar, bicarbonate of soda and cold water in to the chocolate. Stir into the flour mixture. Transfer to a 25 cm/10 in Swiss roll tin (jelly roll pan) which has been greased, lined with grease-proof (waxed) paper, and greased again. Bake in a preheated oven at 180°C/350°F/ gas mark 4 for 15 minutes. Turn out on to a cloth, remove the paper and cover with a damp tea-towel. Cool for 5 minutes. Quickly spread the Almond Cream Filling over the sponge and roll up.

Fritelle di Castagne

Chestnut Fritters
Serves 4–6

900 g/2 lb chestnuts
150 ml/¼ pt/⅔ cup milk
100 g/4 oz/½ cup granulated sugar
5 ml/1 tsp vanilla essence (extract)
3 egg yolks
1 egg, beaten
30 ml/2 tbsp fresh breadcrumbs
Oil for frying
30 ml/2 tbsp vanilla sugar

Make a slit in the shell of each chestnut and boil for 15 minutes. Remove the outer shell and inner brown skin. Alternatively use canned chestnuts. Put in a saucepan with the milk, sugar and vanilla essence. Cook for 15 minutes until soft. Press through a sieve (strainer) or purée in a blender or food processor. Beat in the egg yolks. Leave to cool, then chill. Shape into small balls. Roll each ball in the beaten egg and then the breadcrumbs. Fry (sauté) in hot oil until brown and drain on kitchen paper. Sprinkle with the vanilla sugar and serve immediately.

Dolce al Caffè

Mocha Mousse
Serves 4–6

175 g/6 oz plain (semi-sweet)
* chocolate*
45 ml/3 tbsp strong black coffee
2 egg yolks
5 egg whites
50 g/2 oz/¼ cup caster (superfine)
* sugar*
150 ml/¼ pt/⅔ cup double (heavy)
* cream, whipped*

Grate a little of the chocolate and reserve for decoration. Break the remaining chocolate into small pieces and melt with the coffee in a bowl over a pan of hot water. Remove from the heat and beat in the egg yolks. Allow to cool for 10 minutes. Whisk the egg whites until stiff then whisk in the sugar. Carefully fold the egg whites into the chocolate mixture a little at a time. Then fold in half of the whipped cream. Spoon into a large glass bowl and chill until set. Pipe the remaining cream on the top of the mousse and decorate with the reserved chocolate.

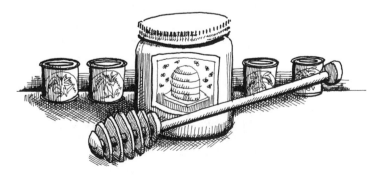

Crostata di Mele e Limone

Apple and Lemon Flan
Serves 6

2 apples, grated
Grated rind and juice of 1 lemon
225 g/8 oz shortcrust pastry (basic pie crust)
3 eggs, beaten
75 g/3 oz/⅓ cup unsalted (sweet) butter, softened
75 g/3 oz/⅓ cup caster (superfine) sugar
120 ml/4 fl oz/½ cup double (heavy) cream, whipped, to decorate

Mix the apple with the lemon rind and juice to prevent browning. Roll out the pastry and line a 25 cm/10 in flan tin (pie pan). Prick the base with a fork and place a sheet of greaseproof (waxed) paper in the pastry case. Scatter with dried peas or baking beans and bake in a preheated oven at 200°C/400°F/gas mark 6 for 10 minutes. Remove the paper and beans and bake the pastry for a further 5 minutes to dry out the base. Add the beaten eggs, butter and sugar to the apples and beat well. Pour the mixture into the pastry case and bake in the oven at 160°C/325°F/gas mark 3 for 20 minutes until set. Allow to cool. Pipe with the whipped cream to decorate.

Torta di Cioccolato

Chocolate Cake
Serves 6–8

100 g/4 oz/½ cup unsalted (sweet) butter
225 g/8 oz/1 cup light brown sugar
30 ml/2 tbsp cocoa (unsweetened chocolate) powder
3 eggs, well beaten
75 g/3 oz plain (semi-sweet) chocolate, broken into squares
150 ml/¼ pt/⅔ cup boiling water
400 g/14 oz/3½ cups plain (all-purpose) flour
5 ml/1 tsp baking powder
2.5 ml/½ tsp salt
10 ml/2 tsp vanilla essence (extract)
175 ml/6 fl oz/¾ cup single (light) cream
Chocolate Cream Topping (see page 379)

Cream the butter, sugar and cocoa powder together and add the eggs. Beat well. Melt the chocolate in the boiling water and add to the creamed mixture. Stir in the flour, baking powder and salt. Add the vanilla essence and cream and beat well. Pour into two greased 23 cm/9 in sandwich tins (pans). Bake in a preheated oven at 180°C/350°F/gas mark 4 for 25 to 30 minutes until the centres spring back when lightly pressed. Leave in the tins for 5 minutes and turn out on a wire rack to cool completely. Split the cake and fill with half of the topping, spread the remainder over the top of the cake.

Cicerchiata

Umbrian Carnival Cake
Serves 6–8

4 eggs
30 ml/2 tbsp olive oil
30 ml/2 tbsp Cointreau
Grated rind of 1 lime
350 g/12 oz/3 cups plain (all-purpose)
  flour, sifted
Oil for deep-frying
450 g/1 lb/1¼ cups thick honey
175 g/6 oz/1½ cups chopped almonds
75 g/3 oz/½ cup glacé (candied)
  cherries, chopped
Coloured sugar strands, to decorate

Beat the eggs in a large bowl and add the
olive oil. Stir in the Cointreau and lime
rind and work in the flour. Knead the
dough for 5 minutes. Roll into thin sticks.
Cut off very small pieces of the dough and
roll into balls the size of small hazelnuts.
Heat the oil and fry (sauté) the small balls
until crisp and brown. Remove and drain
on kitchen paper. Melt the honey in a
saucepan over a moderate heat for 10 minutes until the mixture thickens. Add the
dough balls, chopped almonds and cherries to the honey and stir thoroughly. Turn
the mixture out on to an oiled marble slab
or cold surface and shape into a ring.
Scatter with the sugar strands, leave to
cool, transfer to a clean plate and serve cut
in small slices.

Crostata di Fichi

Fig Tart
Serves 6

225 g/8 oz shortcrust pastry (basic pie
  crust)
1 egg, separated
6 dried figs, stalks discarded, chopped
45 ml/3 tbsp light brown sugar
2.5 ml/½ tsp ground cinnamon
1 egg yolk
1 large egg
15 ml/1 tbsp plain (all-purpose) flour
250 ml/8 fl oz/1 cup single (light)
  cream
30 ml/2 tbsp flaked (slivered) almonds

Roll out the pastry and line a 25 cm/10 in
flan tin (pie pan). Prick the base with a
fork and line with a sheet of greaseproof
(waxed) paper. Scatter with dried peas or
baking beans and bake in a preheated oven
at 200°C/400°F/gas mark 6 for 10 minutes.
Remove the paper and beans and brush the
pastry with the egg white. Bake the pastry
case for a further 10 minutes to dry out.
Put the figs, brown sugar and cinnamon in
a bowl and blend together. Cover and leave
for 15 minutes. Whisk in the egg yolk and
whole egg and then the flour. Gradually
add the cream. Pour the mixture into the
pastry case and sprinkle over the flaked
almonds. Reduce the oven to 160°C/
325°F/gas mark 3 and bake for 20 minutes
until set. Allow to cool before serving.

Crostatine alla Mandorle

Frangipane Tarlets
Makes 24

150 g/5 oz/⅔ cup unsalted (sweet)
butter
225 g/8 oz/2 cups plain (all-purpose)
flour
10 ml/2 tsp grated lemon rind
30 ml/2 tbsp lemon juice
50 g/2 oz/¼ cup caster (superfine)
sugar
1 egg, beaten
50 g/2 oz/½ cup ground almonds
100 g/4 oz/⅔ cup icing (confectioners')
sugar
15 ml/1 tbsp water
A few drops of almond essence
(extract)
Fresh cherries, to decorate

Rub 75g/3 oz/⅓ cup butter into three-quarters of the flour until the mixture resembles breadcrumbs. Mix in the lemon rind and bind with the juice until the mixture forms a soft dough. Chill for 30 minutes. Roll out and cut into rounds with a pastry cutter. Line 24 greased bun tins (muffin pans) with the rounds. Cream the remaining butter with the sugar and mix in the egg. Add the remaining flour and the ground almonds. Divide the mixture evenly between the pastry cases and bake in a preheated oven at 200°C/400°F/gas mark 6 for 15 minutes until firm. Allow to cool. Blend the icing sugar, water and almond essence together until smooth and spread over the cakes. Decorate each cake with a fresh cherry.

Pasticcio agli Agrume

Citrus Meringue Pie
Serves 4

250 ml/8 fl oz/1 cup milk
15 ml/1 tbsp cornflour (cornstarch)
2 eggs, separated
Grated rind and juice of 1 lemon or
large lime
150 g/5 oz/⅔ cup caster (superfine)
sugar
2.5 ml/½ tsp salt
20 cm/8 in baked pastry case (pie
shell)

Blend the milk and cornflour together in a saucepan. Gently cook until thickened, stirring constantly. Mix the remaining ingredients, except the egg whites and 60 ml/4 tbsp of the sugar, and stir into the thickened milk. Cook until thickened, stirring constantly. Cool the custard and put into the baked pastry case. Whisk the egg whites until stiff, adding the remaining sugar a little at a time. Spoon the meringue mixture over the citrus custard. Bake in a preheated oven at 150°C/300°F/gas mark 2 for about 15–20 minutes until crisp and just turning colour.

Torta di Noce e Cioccolato

Chocolate Nut Torta
Serves 6

175 g/6 oz/1¼ cups ground walnuts
175 g/6 oz/¾ cup caster (superfine)
  sugar
4 eggs, separated
5 ml/1 tsp vanilla essence (extract)
175 g/6 oz plain (semi-sweet)
  chocolate, grated
5 ml/1 tsp melted butter
15 ml/1 tbsp chopped walnuts

Put the nuts and sugar in a basin, beat in the egg yolks, vanilla essence and the chocolate. Whisk the egg whites very stiffly and fold carefully into the chocolate mixture. Butter an ovenproof dish and sprinkle with the chopped nuts. Pour in the mixture and bake in a preheated oven at 190°C/375°F/gas mark 5 for 25 minutes until risen and cooked through.

Budino di Limone, Riso e Mandorle

Lemon Rice Almond Pudding
Serves 4–6

1 lemon
100 g/4 oz/½ cup risotto rice
600 ml/1 pt/2½ cups milk
75 g/3 oz/¾ cup flaked (slivered)
  almonds, toasted
5 ml/1 tsp vanilla extract (essence)
75 g/3 oz/⅓ cup caster (superfine)
  sugar

Using a sharp knife peel long thin shavings of rind from the lemon. Place the rind in a saucepan with the rice and milk. Bring to the boil, reduce the heat and simmer for 15 minutes until the rice is tender. Stir in the toasted almonds, vanilla essence and sugar and cook for 5 minutes more stirring. Remove the strips of lemon. Leave to cool then chill before serving.

Crostata di Limone

Lemon Tart
Serves 4

225 g/8 oz shortcrust pastry (basic pie
  crust)
100 g/4 oz/½ cup unsalted (sweet)
  butter
4 eggs
Grated rind and juice of 2 lemons
100 g/4 oz/½ cup caster (superfine)
  sugar
250 ml/8 fl oz/1 cup double (heavy)
  cream
Mint leaves, to decorate

Roll out the pastry and use to line a 25 cm/10 in flan tin (pie pan). Prick the base with a fork and place a sheet of greaseproof (waxed) paper in the pastry case. Scatter with dried peas or baking beans and bake in a preheated oven at 200°C/400°F/gas mark 6 for 10 minutes. Remove the paper and beans and bake the pastry case for a further 5 minutes to dry out the base. Melt the butter and cool for 1 minute. Whisk the eggs in a bowl and add the grated rind and juice from the lemons. Whisk in the butter, sugar and cream. Pour the lemon mixture into the pastry case and bake at 160°C/325°F/gas mark 3 for 20 minutes until set. Allow to cool before serving. Decorate with mint leaves.

Photograph opposite: **Mediterranean Salad (page 301)**

Pasticcio di Pesche alla Fiamma

Flaming Peach Pie
Serves 4

100 g/4 oz/1 cup plain (all-purpose) flour, sifted
23 cm/9 in unbaked pastry case (pie shell)
3 fresh peaches, stoned (pitted)
50 g/2 oz/¼ cup light brown sugar
50 g/2 oz/¼ cup unsalted (sweet) butter, softened
2.5 ml/½ tsp grated nutmeg
45 ml/3 tbsp brandy

Sprinkle 5 ml/1 tsp of flour over the pastry case. Slice the peaches and layer them in the pastry case. Blend the sugar, the remaining flour, butter and nutmeg. Sprinkle over the peaches, leaving 2.5 cm/ 1 in of the outside edge uncovered. Bake in a preheated oven at 200°C/400°F/gas mark 6 for 25 minutes until the pastry and topping are crisp. Heat the brandy, ignite and pour over the fruit. Serve immediately.

Jette di Jichi

Fig Slices
Makes 16 slices

6 fresh figs, chopped
30 ml/2 tbsp clear honey
15 ml/1 tbsp lemon juice
225 g/8 oz/2 cups wholemeal flour
225 g/8 oz/2 cups rolled oats
225 g/8 oz/1 cup unsalted (sweet) butter
75 g/3 oz/⅓ cup light brown sugar

Photograph opposite: Stuffed Apricots with Mascarpone and Pistachios (page 337)

Place the figs, honey and lemon juice in a saucepan and simmer over a low heat for 5 minutes. Allow to cool slightly. Mix the flour and oats together in a bowl and rub in the butter and sugar. Press half of the mixture into a shallow greased 20 cm/8 in square tin (pan). Spread the fig mixture on top and cover with the remaining flour mixture. Press down firmly and bake in a preheated oven at 180°C/350°F/gas mark 4 for 30 minutes until golden brown. Cut into slices while still warm but leave to cool in the tin before serving.

Torta al Limone

Lemon Chiffon Cake
Serves 4

450 g/1 lb/4 cups plain (all-purpose) flour
225 g/8 oz/1 cup caster (superfine) sugar
10 ml/2 tsp baking powder
5 ml/1 tsp salt
120 ml/4 fl oz/½ cup oil
7 eggs, separated
175 ml/6 fl oz/¾ cup cold water
5 ml/1 tsp lemon juice
2.5 ml/½ tsp cream of tartar
1 quantity Lemon Topping (see page 372)

Sift the flour and place in a bowl with the sugar. Add the baking powder, salt, oil, egg yolks, cold water and lemon juice. Beat well. Whisk the egg whites with the cream of tartar until very stiff. Add to the mixture and transfer immediately to an ungreased cake tin (pan). Bake in a preheated oven at 160°C/325°F/gas mark 3 for 50–60 minutes until risen, golden and firm. Cool, and when cold loosen the sides with a spatula or knife. Remove from the tin and coat with Lemon Topping.

Crostata di Uva

Grape Tart

Serves 6

Pastry (paste):
225 g/8 oz/2 cups plain (all-purpose)
  flour
100 g/4 oz/½ cup unsalted (sweet)
  butter, plus a little for greasing
50 g/2 oz/¼ cup caster (superfine)
  sugar
1 egg yolk
15 ml/1 tbsp finely grated lemon rind
30 ml/2 tbsp milk

Filling:
2 egg yolks
50 g/2 oz/¼ cup caster (superfine)
  sugar
15 ml/1 tbsp plain (all-purpose) flour
175 ml/6 fl oz/¾ cup milk
350 g/12 oz seedless white grapes
Apricot jam (conserve), warmed

Place the flour in a bowl and rub in the measured amount of butter until the mixture resembles breadcrumbs. Stir in the sugar, egg yolk, lemon rind and milk. Mix to a soft dough and form into a ball. Wrap in clingfilm (plastic wrap) and chill for 2 hours. Grease a 25 cm/10 in flan tin (pie pan) or individual tartlet tins (patty pans) with a little butter. Roll out the dough on a floured board and line the tin. Prick the base and sides with a fork and place in a preheated oven at 180°C/350°F/gas mark 4 for 10 minutes. Remove from the oven and press the pastry down gently. Return to the oven and bake for a further 10 minutes. Allow to cool for 10 minutes. Make the filling. Blend the egg yolks with the sugar in a basin over a pan of hot water. Whisk until thick and pale. Whisk in the flour and the milk and cook, whisking, until thick

enough to coat the back of a spoon. Set aside to cool. Spoon the custard into the pastry case and top with the grapes. Brush with apricot jam and serve immediately.

Torta di Pesche e Mandorle

Peach and Almond Slice

Serves 4

225 g/8 oz/2 cups ground almonds
175 g/6 oz/¾ cup caster (superfine) sugar
1 egg
5 ml/1 tsp lemon juice
15 ml/1 tbsp Amaretto
350 g/12 oz puff pastry (paste)
4 fresh peaches, stoned (pitted)
1 egg, separated
Caster (superfine) sugar for dredging
50 g/2 oz/½ cup flaked (slivered)
  almonds

Blend the ground almonds, sugar, egg, lemon juice and Amaretto together and set aside. Roll out the pastry on a lightly floured surface to form 2 rectangles. Place 1 pastry rectangle on a baking sheet. Lightly knead the almond paste then roll out to a rectangle. Place on the pastry and arrange the peaches, cut side down, on the top. Brush the border with a little beaten egg. Fold the second pastry rectangle in half lengthways, and using a sharp knife, cut across the fold at 5 mm/¼ in intervals, leaving a border. Unfold the pastry and place over the peaches. Press down the edges and flute around the edges with the back of a knife. Chill for 30 minutes. Glaze with the egg yolk, beaten with 5 ml/1 tsp water. Bake in a preheated oven at 220°C/425°F/gas mark 7 for 20 minutes until well-risen. Brush with the egg white, dredge with caster sugar and sprinkle with the flaked almonds. Bake for a further 10 minutes until golden brown.

Fichi Maria

Figs Maria
Serves 4

100 g/4 oz macaroons
16 ripe figs
8 sponge (lady) fingers
100 g/4 oz vanilla ice cream, from a
  block
30 ml/2 tbsp Marsala or Amaretto
4 cherries

Grind the macaroons to a powder and peel
and quarter the figs. Cut the sponge fingers
in half and line small individual bowls
with them. Add a layer of ice cream and a
layer of quartered figs. Sprinkle with
Marsala wine or liqueur. Cover with
powdered macaroons and chill before
serving. Garnish with a cherry.

Pan di Spagna al Latte

Milk Sponge Cake
Serves 4

150 ml/¼ pt/⅔ cup milk
3 eggs
175 g/6 oz/¾ cup caster (superfine) sugar
5 ml/1 tsp lemon juice
350 g/12 oz/3 cups plain (all-purpose)
  flour
5 ml/1 tsp baking powder
300 ml/½ pt/1¼ cups double (heavy)
  cream, to serve

Heat the milk in a saucepan. Beat the eggs,
sugar and lemon juice until they are thick
and creamy. Add the flour and baking powder and gradually stir in the hot milk. Beat
well. Pour into a greased 20 cm/8 in cake
tin (pan) and bake in a preheated oven at
180°C/350°F/gas mark 4 for 20 minutes.
Serve with double cream.

Torta di Pesche

Peach Cake
Serves 4–6

100 g/4 oz/½ cup unsalted (sweet)
  butter
225 g/8 oz/1 cup caster (superfine)
  sugar
3 eggs, separated
450 g/1 lb/4 cups plain (all-purpose)
  flour
2.5 ml/½ tsp salt
5 ml/1 tsp bicarbonate of soda (baking
  soda)
120 ml/4 fl oz/½ cup milk
250 ml/8 fl oz/¾ cup peach jam
  (conserve)

Icing:
225 g/8 oz/1 cup granulated sugar
250 ml/8 fl oz/1 cup milk
150 g/5 oz/1 small can crushed
  pineapple, drained
100 g/4 oz/1 cup chopped mixed nuts

Cream the butter and sugar together. Beat
in the egg yolks and slowly add the flour
and salt. Stir the bicarbonate of soda into
the milk and immediately add to the flour
mixture. Lightly fold in the peach jam.
Stiffly whisk the egg whites and gently
fold into the mixture. Spoon into two lined
23 cm/9 in round cake tins (pans). Bake in
a preheated oven at 180°C/350°F/gas mark
4 for 25–30 minutes. Turn out at once on to
a cake rack. Cool completely. Cook the
sugar and milk to the hard ball stage on a
sugar thermometer or until a small spoonful of the mixture forms a hard ball when
dropped into a cup of cold water. Beat well
and stir in the coconut, pineapple and nuts.
Spread the icing between the two layers of
cake and serve sliced.

Torta di Pesche e Pere

Peach and Pear Cake
Serves 6

*175 g/6 oz/³⁄₄ cup unsalted (sweet)
    butter*
*150 g/5 oz/²⁄₃ cup caster (superfine)
    sugar*
2 eggs
75 g/3 oz/³⁄₄ cup wholemeal flour
*75 g/3 oz/³⁄₄ cup plain (all-purpose)
    flour*
10 ml/2 tsp baking powder
15 ml/1 tbsp milk
2 peaches, stoned (pitted) and chopped
2 pears, chopped
*30 ml/2 tbsp icing (confectioners')
    sugar*

Cream the butter and sugar together.
Gradually beat in the eggs. Fold in the
flours and baking powder, adding a little
milk to soften the mixture. Fold in the
chopped peaches and pears and spoon the
mixture into a greased 20 cm/8 in cake tin
(pan). Level the surface of the cake, making a slight dip in the centre to allow for
rising. Bake in a preheated oven at 190°C/
375°F/ gas mark 5 for 55 minutes to 1 hour
until firm to the touch. Remove from the
oven and allow to cool in the tin. Dust with
icing sugar. The cake will keep in an airtight container for up to 2 weeks.

Crostata di Arance e Mandorle con Crema

Orange and Frangipane Tart
Serves 6

Butter for greasing
*225 g/8 oz shortcrust pastry (basic pie
    crust)*
45 ml/3 tbsp marmalade
2.5 ml/¹⁄₂ tsp grated orange rind
*100 g/4 oz/¹⁄₂ cup unsalted (sweet)
    butter*
*100 g/4 oz/¹⁄₂ cup caster (superfine)
    sugar*
2 eggs, lightly beaten
100 g/4 oz/1 cup ground almonds

Grease a 25 cm/10 in flan tin (pie pan)
with the butter and set aside. Roll out the
pastry on a lightly floured board and line
the flan tin. Spread the base of the pastry
with the marmalade and sprinkle over the
orange rind. Beat the butter with the sugar
until pale and fluffy. Beat in the eggs and
stir in the ground almonds. Spoon the mixture into the pastry case. Bake in a preheated oven at 190°C/375°F/gas mark 5 for
35–40 minutes until the filling is set and
the top has browned. Cool in the tin for 10
minutes before serving.

Tortelli di Carnevale

Carnival Cakes
Makes about 20

300 ml/½ pt/1¼ cups milk
300 ml/½ pt/1¼ cups cold water
1.5 ml/¼ tsp salt
2.5 ml/½ tsp bicarbonate of soda
   (baking soda)
75 g/3 oz/⅓ cup caster (superfine)
   sugar
5 ml/1 tsp vanilla essence (extract)
100 g/4 oz/½ cup unsalted (sweet)
   butter
5 ml/1 tsp grated lime rind
275 g/10 oz/2½ cups plain (all-
   purpose) flour
6 eggs
2 egg yolks
30 ml/2 tbsp dark rum
Oil for deep-frying
100 g/4 oz/⅔ cup icing (confectioners')
   sugar, sifted

Put the milk, water, salt, bicarbonate of soda, sugar, vanilla essence, butter and lime rind in a saucepan and bring to the boil over a low heat. Remove the pan from the heat and pour in the flour. Beat vigorously and return to the heat for 1 minute, stirring all the time. Remove from the heat when the mixture comes away from the sides of the pan. Allow to cool for 2 minutes, stirring. Gradually add the eggs and egg yolks, beating all the time. Stir in the rum and set aside for 1 hour to cool completely. Heat the oil in a deep pan. Drop spoonfuls of the mixture into the hot oil and cook until golden. Lift out with a draining spoon and drain on kitchen paper. Dust with the sifted icing sugar. Serve at once.

Torrone al Cioccolato

Chocolate Nougat
Makes 24 shapes

400 g/14 oz/1¾ cups caster (superfine)
   sugar
90 ml/6 tbsp cold water
275 g/10 oz plain (semi-sweet) cooking
   chocolate, grated
275 g/10 oz/good ¾ cup thick honey
3 egg whites
750 g/1½ lb/6 cups chopped mixed
   nuts
Rice paper

Put 30 ml/2 tbsp of the sugar into a saucepan with half the water and cook over a high heat to reduce to a syrup. Do not allow to brown. Stir in the chocolate until it is completely melted. Keep warm over a very low heat. Put the honey into another saucepan and heat, stirring continuously, for 10 minutes. Keep warm.

Place the egg whites in a bowl over a pan of very hot water and whisk until they form peaks. Melt the remaining sugar in a saucepan with the remaining water and cook rapidly until it becomes a syrup. Pour into a large bowl and stir in the warm honey. Fold in the egg whites and chocolate. Stir in the nuts. Lay the rice paper on a baking sheet and spread the nougat mixture on the top. Smooth the surface and allow to set. Cut into shapes with a sharp knife and store in an airtight container.

Fichi Ripiene

Stuffed Figs
Serves 2

4 dried figs
25 g/1 oz/¼ cup ground almonds
16 seedless raisins, finely chopped
15 g/½ oz plain (semi-sweet) chocolate,
  grated
15 ml/1 tbsp Amaretto

Remove the stalks from the figs. Place a finger in the top of the fig and push to form a pocket. Blend the almonds, chopped raisins, chocolate and liqueur together. Fill each fig with the mixture and squeeze the tops together to seal. Place the figs in a baking tin (pan), open ends upwards and bake for 8 minutes in a preheated oven at 180°C/350°F/gas mark 4.

Dolce Margherita

Margherita Cake
Serves 4–6

4 eggs
100 g/4 oz/½ cup caster (superfine)
  sugar
50 g/2 oz/¼ cup unsalted (sweet)
  butter, softened
175 g/6 oz/1½ cups plain (all-purpose)
  flour
100 g/4 oz/1 cup potato flour
2.5 ml/½ tsp vanilla essence (extract)
5 ml/1 tsp unsalted (sweet) butter
25 g/1 oz/2 tbsp icing (confectioners')
  sugar

Separate the eggs and beat the yolks with the sugar until light and creamy. Gradually add the butter, potato flour and vanilla essence. Whisk the egg whites until stiff and fold into the cake mixture. Grease a 20 cm/8 in cake tin (pan) and pour the cake mixture into it. Bake in a preheated oven for 5 minutes at 200°C/400°F/gas mark 6. Remove the cake from the oven. Make a cross on the top of the cake and return to the oven as quickly as possible. Bake for a further 5 minutes. Lower the heat to 180°C/350°F/gas mark 4 and continue cooking for 25 minutes. Leave until cold and serve dusted with the icing sugar.

Sospiri di Monache

Nuns' Sighs
Makes 36

200 g/7 oz/1¼ cups hazelnuts
4 egg whites
275 g/10 oz/1⅔ cups icing
  (confectioners') sugar
Grated rind of 1 lime
Grated rind of 1 lemon
Fresh Apricot Sauce (see page 369), to
  serve

Spread the hazelnuts on a baking sheet and toast in a preheated oven at 180°C/350°F/gas mark 4 for 15 minutes until the skins loosen. Rub off the skins in a tea towel and chop the nuts finely. Put the egg whites and icing sugar into a bowl and whisk until the mixture forms stiff peaks. Gently fold in the chopped hazelnuts and the lime and lemon rinds. Line baking sheets with non-stick baking parchment or oiled foil and drop large spoonfuls of the meringue on to the sheets, shaping into tear shapes with the end of the spoon. Reduce the oven to 150°C/300°F/gas mark 2 and bake for 45 minutes. Allow to cool and serve with raspberry sauce.

Torta al Rum

Rum Cake
Serves 6

1 sponge cake
1 wineglass liqueur
  (about 120 ml/4 fl oz/½ cup)
Zabaglione (see page 333)
300 ml/½ pt/1¼ cups double (heavy)
  cream, whipped
10 cherries, stoned (pitted)

Cut the sponge into three thin layers and put the bottom layer in a glass bowl. Pour over one-third of the liqueur. Spread with Zabaglione and top with a sponge layer. Sprinkle over a little more liqueur. Repeat with the third sponge and use the remaining liqueur. Chill until ready to serve. Spread with the whipped cream and decorate with the cherries just before serving.

Torta Senza Cottura all' Italiana

Italian-style No-bake Cake
Serves 4

100 g/4 oz/½ cup unsalted (sweet)
  butter
175 g/6 oz plain (semi-sweet)
  chocolate
75 g/3 oz almond macaroons (see page
  285), or ready-made
175 g/6 oz/1½ cups walnuts
50 g/2 oz/½ cup pine nuts
75 g/3 oz/½ cup glacé (candied)
  cherries
30 ml/2 tbsp Grand Marnier liqueur
225 g/8 oz/1 cup Mascarpone cheese

Line a 20 cm/8 in sandwich tin (pan) with clingfilm (plastic wrap). Melt the butter and chocolate in a saucepan over hot water until softened. Remove from the heat and stir in the amaretti biscuits, nuts and cherries. Spoon the mixture into the sandwich tin and chill for approximately 1 hour until set. Turn out on to a serving plate and remove the clingfilm. Beat the Grand Marnier into the Mascarpone cheese and spread over the top of the cake.

Splendido Dessert di Noci

Luxury Nut Dessert
Serves 4

175 g/6 oz/1½ cups ground nuts
175 g/6 oz/¾ cup caster (superfine)
  sugar
175 g/6 oz plain (semi-sweet)
  chocolate, grated
4 eggs, separated
5 ml/1 tsp vanilla essence (extract)
2.5 ml/½ tsp ground cinnamon
2.5 ml/½ tsp grated nutmeg
50 g/2 oz/⅓ cup candied peel
Butter, for greasing
50 g/2 oz/½ cup chopped nuts

Blend the ground nuts, sugar and grated chocolate in a bowl and mix in the egg yolks. Add the vanilla essence, cinnamon and nutmeg and stir well. Whisk the egg whites until stiff and fold into the mixture. Gradually mix in the candied peel. Butter an ovenproof dish and sprinkle with the chopped nuts. Pour the mixture into the dish and bake in a preheated oven at 180°C/350°F/gas mark 4 for 25 minutes. Serve hot.

Crostata Genovese

Genoese Tart
Serves 4

100 g/4 oz puff pastry (paste)
50 g/2 oz/¼ cup unsalted (sweet) butter
75 g/3 oz/⅓ cup caster (superfine) sugar
75 g/3 oz/¾ cup chopped almonds
3 eggs, separated
2.5 ml/½ tsp vanilla essence (extract)
100 g/4 oz/1 cup plain (all-purpose)
   flour
100 g/4 oz/⅔ cup icing (confectioners')
   sugar
Juice of ½ lemon

Roll out the pastry and use to line a 20 cm/8 in pie dish. Cream the butter and sugar until soft and stir in the almonds, egg yolks, vanilla essence and flour. Stiffly beat the egg whites and fold into the mixture. Transfer to the lined pie dish and bake in a preheated oven at 190°C/375°F/gas mark 5 for 30 minutes. Allow to cool. Blend the icing sugar with the lemon juice and spread over the surface of the tart. Serve cold.

Budino di Pesche e Susine

Peach and Plum Pudding
Serves 6

1 sweet loaf or large brioche
2 eggs, beaten
150 ml/¼ pt/⅔ cup milk
4 peaches, stoned (pitted), skinned and
   sliced
225 g/8 oz plums, stoned (pitted) and
   sliced
60 ml/4 tbsp light brown sugar
5 ml/1 tsp ground cinnamon
10 ml/2 tsp icing (confectioners')
   sugar for dusting
Cream, to serve

Cut the loaf into 10 slices. Blend together the beaten eggs and milk and dip the slices into the mixture. Layer them in a pie dish with the peaches and plums, making sure they overlap slightly. Pour the remaining egg mixture over the fruit and sprinkle over the brown sugar and cinnamon. Bake in a preheated oven at 200°C/400°F/gas mark 6 for 15 minutes until the egg has set and the top is brown. Dust with icing sugar and serve with cream.

Le Castagnole di Cristina

Christina's Sweet Snack
Makes 12–14

2 eggs, beaten
75 ml/5 tbsp milk
90 ml/6 tbsp caster (superfine) sugar
10 ml/2 tsp baking powder
5 ml/1 tsp vanilla essence (extract)
Grated rind and juice of 1 lime
90 ml/6 tbsp oil
90 ml/6 tbsp plain (all-purpose) flour,
   sifted
Oil for deep-frying
60 ml/4 tbsp icing (confectioners')
   sugar, sifted
10 ml/2 tsp finely grated nutmeg

Beat the eggs, milk, sugar, baking powder, vanilla essence and lime rind and juice together. Add the oil and slowly stir in the flour. Dip a dessertspoon into cold water and scoop up a spoonful of the dough. Drop carefully into hot oil and deep-fry for 1–2 minutes until puffed up and golden brown. Lift from the oil with a draining spoon and drain on kitchen paper. Mix the icing sugar and nutmeg together and dust over the sweet fritters. Serve hot or cold.

Torta di Prugne

Prune Cake
Serves 10–15

Cake:
225 g/8 oz/1 cup unsalted (sweet)
butter
275 g/10 oz/1½ cups caster (superfine)
sugar
3 eggs, separated
450 g/1 lb/4 cups plain (all-purpose)
flour
5 ml/1 tsp each ground cloves, nutmeg
and cinnamon
5 ml/1 tsp bicarbonate of soda (baking
soda)
2.5 ml/½ tsp salt
5 ml/1 tsp baking powder
250 ml/8 fl oz/1 cup single (light)
cream
225 g/8 oz ready-to-eat prunes, stoned
(pitted) and chopped finely
15 ml/1 tbsp butter for greasing

Filling:
250 ml/8 fl oz/1 cup single (light)
cream
100 g/4 oz/½ cup caster (superfine)
sugar
3 egg yolks
225 g/8 oz ready-to-eat prunes, stoned
(pitted) and chopped
30 ml/2 tbsp grated orange rind
5 ml/1 tsp vanilla essence (extract)
Chopped nuts, to decorate

Make the cake. Cream the butter and sugar together and beat in the egg yolks. Stir in the flour, spices, bicarbonate of soda, salt and baking powder. Add the cream and whisked egg whites. Fold in the chopped prunes. Pour into three greased and floured 20 cm/8 in sandwich tins (pans). Bake in a preheated oven at 180°C/350°F/gas mark 4 for 25–30 minutes. Turn on to wire racks to cool. Make the filling. Mix together all the ingredients except the nuts. Place in a saucepan and cook until thickened. Use to sandwich the cake layers together and spread the remainder on top. Sprinkle with chopped nuts to decorate.

Tiramisu

Pick-Me-Up Pudding
Serves 6

4 eggs, separated
45 ml/3 tbsp caster (superfine) sugar
175 g/6 oz/¾ cup Mascarpone cheese
300 ml/½ pt/1½ cups fresh coffee
5 ml/1 tsp instant coffee powder
60 ml/4 tbsp brandy
30 ml/2 tbsp rum
35 sponge (lady) fingers
100 g/4 oz plain (semi-sweet)
chocolate, grated
60 ml/4 tbsp chopped nuts or drinking
(sweetened) chocolate powder

Whisk the egg yolks and sugar together until light and creamy. Mix in the Mascarpone cheese. Whisk the egg whites until stiff and fold them into the mixture. Mix the fresh and instant coffee with the brandy and rum. Dip each sponge finger into the coffee/brandy/rum mixture and arrange at the base and around the sides of a glass dish. Spread half the Marscapone mixture over the biscuits. Sprinkle over half the grated chocolate. Repeat the process with the biscuits, cheese and chocolate until the ingredients are used. Cover with clingfilm (plastic wrap) and chill overnight if possible. Just before serving sprinkle with the chopped nuts or drinking chocolate powder.

Pesche in Vino Bianco

Peaches in White Wine
Serves 6

6 large whole peaches
75 ml/3 tbsp caster (superfine) sugar
300 ml/½ pt/1¼ cups sweet white wine

Place the peaches in a bowl and pour boiling water over them. Leave for 20 seconds, drain and drop into iced water. The skin will peel off easily. Cut into 5 mm/¼ in slices and sprinkle with the sugar. Pour over the white wine and chill for 1 hour.

Amaretti con Lamponi

Raspberry Dessert
Serves 4

450 g/1 lb fresh raspberries
60 ml/4 tbsp caster (superfine) sugar
225 g/8 oz Almond Macaroons
  (see page 285) or ready made
250 ml/8 fl oz/1 cup crème fraîche
4 mint leaves to decorate

Wash and drain the raspberries. Place in a bowl and sprinkle over the sugar. Allow to stand for 10 minutes. Place half the raspberries in a blender or food processor with half the Almond Macaroons and the crème fraîche. Blend until smooth. Remove from the blender and stir in the remaining raspberries. Pour into a glass dish, chill until needed and serve decorated with the mint leaves and the remaining Almond Macaroons.

Zuppa Inglese

Milanese Trifle
Serves 4

25 sponge (lady) fingers
30 ml/2 tbsp Cointreau
750 ml/1¼ pts/3 cups ready-made
  custard
4 egg whites
75 ml/5 tbsp caster (superfine) sugar
300 g/11 oz Almond Macaroons (see
  page 285) or ready made, crushed

Arrange the sponge fingers in the base of an ovenproof dish. Sprinkle over the Cointreau and cover with half the custard. Beat the egg whites stiffly and fold in the sugar. Spoon on top of the custard and cover with the remaining custard. Sprinkle over the macaroons. Bake in a preheated oven at 190°C/375°F/gas mark 5 for 20 minutes until brown on top. Serve while still warm.

Fragole in Aceto Balsamico

Strawberries in Balsamic Vinegar
Serves 6

900 g/2 lb strawberries, hulled
50 g/2 oz/¼ cup caster (superfine)
  sugar
30 ml/2 tbsp balsamic vinegar
Freshly ground black pepper

Cut the strawberries in halves and place in a deep bowl. Sprinkle over the sugar and mix gently. Pour over the balsamic vinegar and sprinkle with pepper just before serving.

Semifreddo di Fragole al Torrone

Nougat and Strawberry Mousse
Serves 4–6

550 g/1¼ lb strawberries, hulled
75 g/3 oz/⅓ cup caster (superfine) sugar
60 ml/4 tbsp water
15 g/½ oz/1 tbsp gelatine
15 ml/1 tbsp sweet almond oil
350 g/12 oz/1½ cups Ricotta cheese
175 g/6 oz nougat, crushed

Purée the strawberries in a blender or food processor and pour into a bowl. Place the sugar and water in a saucepan and stir until dissolved. Heat until almost boiling. Remove from the heat and sprinkle the gelatine over. Stir until dissolved. Brush a 20 cm/8 in mould (mold) with the almond oil. Add the gelatine mixture to the strawberries. Stir in the Ricotta cheese and blend thoroughly. Stir in the nougat, reserving a little for decoration. Pour the mixture into the mould and chill for 5–6 hours. Turn out. Sprinkle the reserved nougat over before serving.

Delizia di Lamponi e Nocciole

Raspberry and Nut Dream
Serves 4

450 g/1 lb fresh raspberries
60 ml/4 tbsp caster (superfine) sugar
250 ml/8 fl oz/1 cup crème fraîche
225 g/8 oz/2 cups toasted, chopped hazelnuts
4 mint leaves, to decorate

Place the raspberries in a bowl and sprinkle with the sugar. Allow to stand for 10 minutes. Place half the raspberries in a blender or food processor with the crème fraîche. Blend until smooth. Stir in the remaining raspberries. Pour into a glass bowl, sprinkle over the hazelnuts and chill. Decorate with mint leaves.

Rolle di Cioccolato e Noci

Chocolate and Nut Roll
Serves 4–6

225 g/8 oz shortcrust pastry (basic pie crust)
175 g/6 oz plain (semi-sweet) chocolate
25 g/1 oz/2 tbsp unsalted (sweet) butter
30 ml/2 tbsp clear honey
15 ml/1 tbsp brandy
225 g/8 oz/2 cups chopped almonds
45 ml/3 tbsp ground almonds
Butter, for greasing
Icing (confectioners') sugar (optional)

Roll out the pastry to a rectangular shape. Place the chocolate and butter in a bowl over a saucepan of hot water. Heat until the chocolate has melted. Stir in the honey and brandy. Brush over the pastry until the chocolate has been used completely. Sprinkle over the chopped and ground almonds. Roll up and place on a greased baking sheet. Bake in a preheated oven at 180°C/350°F/gas mark 4 for 20–25 minutes. Cut in slices and dust with icing sugar if liked. Serve hot or cold.

Crostata di Lamponi e Mandorle

Almond Tart
Serves 6

Butter for greasing
225 g/8 oz puff pastry (paste)
45 ml/3 tbsp raspberry jam (conserve)
2.5 ml/½ tsp grated lemon rind
100 g/4 oz/½ cup unsalted (sweet)
* butter*
100 g/4 oz/½ cup caster (superfine)
* sugar*
2 eggs, lightly beaten
100 g/4 oz/1 cup ground almonds
A little icing (confectioners') sugar,
* sifted*

Grease a 25 cm/10 in flan tin (pie pan) with the butter and set aside. Roll out the pastry on a lightly floured surface and line the tin. Spread the base of the pastry with the raspberry jam and sprinkle over the lemon rind. Beat the butter with the sugar until pale and fluffy. Beat in the eggs and stir in the ground almonds. Spoon the mixture into the pastry case. Bake in a preheated oven at 190°C/375°F/gas mark 5 for 35–40 minutes until the filling is set and the top has browned. Cool in the tin for 10 minutes. Sprinkle with icing sugar before serving.

Fragole in Vino

Strawberries in Wine
Serves 4

450 g/1 lb strawberries, hulled
60 ml/4 tbsp white wine
60 ml/4 tbsp caster (superfine) sugar
300 ml/½ pt/1¼ cups double (heavy)
* cream, whipped*

Cut each strawberry in half lengthways and place in a glass bowl. Sprinkle with the wine and then the caster sugar. Leave to chill for at least 15 minutes and serve with the whipped cream.

Flan

Crème Caramel
Serves 4

100 g/4 oz/½ cup granulated sugar
15 ml/1 tbsp water
4 eggs
40 g/1½ oz/3 tbsp light brown sugar
Vanilla essence (extract)
150 ml/¼ pt/⅔ cup milk
300 ml/½ pt/1¼ cups single (light)
* cream*

Heat the sugar in a saucepan; the sugar will darken as it melts. Stir and continue to cook until it becomes a dark liquid syrup. Remove the pan from the heat, carefully add the water and stir until dissolved (be careful, it will splutter). Pour the syrup into a basin or mould (mold). Whisk together the eggs, brown sugar and vanilla essence. Heat the milk and cream in a saucepan. When nearly boiling remove from the heat and pour over the egg mixture. Whisk together until blended. Strain into the basin over the syrup. Place the basin in a roasting tin (pan) half-full of water. Cook in a preheated oven at 150°C/300°F/gas mark 2 for 1 hour or until set. Remove from the oven and allow to cool. Chill for at least 2 hours, then turn out and serve.

Pasticcine ai Ciliegi

Cherry Biscuits
Serves 4

50 g/2 oz/¼ cup unsalted (sweet) butter
50 g/2 oz/¼ cup caster (superfine)
*   sugar*
2 eggs
225 g/8 oz/2 cups plain (all-purpose)
*   flour*
5 ml/1 tsp baking powder
2.5 ml/½ tsp grated nutmeg
120 ml/4 fl oz/½ cup milk
450 g/1 lb cherries, stoned (pitted) and
*   roughly chopped*
30 ml/2 tbsp brandy or Kirsch

Cream the butter with the sugar and beat in three-quarters of the eggs until the mixture is smooth. Gradually blend in most of the flour, reserving a little for rolling out and add the baking powder, nutmeg, milk, brandy or Kirsch and the cherries and mix to a stiff dough. If necessary a little cold water can be added to make the dough more manageable. Roll out thinly onto a floured board and cut in fingers. Place on a greased baking sheet and brush lightly with beaten egg. Bake in a preheated oven for 20 minutes at 180°C/350°F/gas mark 4 until golden brown. Serve hot or cold.

Zabaglione

Whipped Marsala Custard
Serves 6

6 egg yolks
90 ml/6 tbsp caster (superfine) sugar
90 ml/6 tbsp cold water
90 ml/6 tbsp Marsala
Small ratafia biscuits (almond
*   cookies), to serve*

Place all the ingredients except the biscuits into the top half of a double boiler over hot, but not boiling, water. Whisk continuously for 15–20 minutes until the mixture thickens to a smooth, foamy consistency. Remove from the heat every 5 minutes but continue whisking. Pour into decorative, stemmed glasses and serve with the ratafia biscuits. The mixture can be cooled and chilled, if preferred.

Soffi di San Giuseppe

St Joseph's Puffs
Makes 20

300 ml/½ pt/1¼ cups water
75 g/3 oz/⅓ cup unsalted (sweet) butter
1.5 ml/¼ tsp salt
175 g/6 oz/1½ cups plain (all-purpose)
*   flour*
3 egg yolks
5 ml/1 tsp baking powder
15 ml/1 tbsp grated lemon rind
100 g/4 oz/½ cup Ricotta cheese
Icing (confectioners') sugar, sifted

Heat the water, butter and salt in a saucepan and bring to the boil. Pour in the flour and stirring all the time, remove the mixture from the heat and beat well. Return to the heat and cook, stirring, for 1 minute until the mixture comes away from the pan. Allow to cool for 2 minutes. Beat the egg yolks into the mixture, one at a time. Beat in the baking powder and lemon rind. Drop large teaspoons of the mixture on to a greased baking sheet. Bake in a preheated oven at 200°C/400°F/gas mark 6 for 20–25 minutes until golden brown. Immediately cut open the centres with a sharp knife to allow the steam to escape. Fill with Ricotta cheese and dust with icing sugar before serving.

Torta Siciliana alla Noce e Cioccolato

Sicilian Nut and Chocolate Cake
Serves 6–8

Pastry (paste):
350 g/12 oz/3 cups plain (all-purpose) flour
5 ml/1 tsp salt
100 g/4 oz/½ cup unsalted (sweet) butter
45 ml/3 tbsp cold water

Chocolate sauce:
50 g/2 oz plain (semi-sweet) chocolate
120 ml/4 fl oz/½ cup water
100 g/4 oz/½ cup caster (superfine) sugar
50 g/2 oz/¼ cup unsalted (sweet) butter
5 ml/1 tsp vanilla essence (extract)

Cake:
150 g/5 oz/⅔ cup unsalted (sweet) butter
150 g/5 oz/⅔ cup caster (superfine) sugar
275 g/10 oz/2½ cups self-raising (self-rising) flour, sifted
5 ml/1 tsp baking powder
2.5 ml/½ tsp salt
120 ml/4 fl oz/½ cup milk
1 egg
5 ml/1 tsp vanilla essence (extract)
100 g/4 oz/1 cup chopped nuts

Make the pastry. Place the flour and salt in a bowl. Rub in the butter until the mixture resembles breadcrumbs. Add enough cold water to form a firm dough. Knead gently into a ball. Wrap the dough in greaseproof (waxed) paper. Chill for 15–20 minutes while the sauce is being made. Place the chocolate and water in a saucepan over a gentle heat. Stir until the chocolate has melted. Add the sugar, stirring constantly, and bring to the boil. Remove from the heat at once, add the butter and vanilla and stir until well blended. Set aside to cool. Roll the pastry on a lightly floured board to fit a 23 cm/9 in pie dish. Line the dish with the pastry, letting it extend 2.5 cm/1 in beyond the rim. Turn the edge of the pastry under to make a high, fluted rim. Make the cake. Place the butter in a mixing bowl with the sugar and beat together until light and fluffy. Add the flour, baking powder, salt, milk, egg and vanilla essence and beat thoroughly. Transfer to the pastry-lined pie dish. Pour over the chocolate sauce and sprinkle with chopped nuts. Bake in a preheated oven at 180°C/350°F/ gas mark 4 for 50–55 minutes. When the cake is cooked the sauce will form a layer between the cake and pie shell.

Rolle di Noci

Mixed Nut Roll
Serves 4–6

225 g/8 oz shortcrust pastry (basic pie crust)
45 ml/4 tbsp clear honey
15 ml/1 tbsp liqueur or sherry
50 g/2 oz/½ cup flaked (slivered) almonds
50 g/2 oz/½ cup chopped hazelnuts
100 g/4 oz/⅔ cup chopped candied peel
2.5 ml/½ tsp ground cinnamon
2.5 ml/½ tsp grated nutmeg

Roll out the pastry thinly and brush over the honey. Sprinkle over half the liqueur and then the nuts, candied peel and spices. Roll up the pastry and nuts to form a long sausage. Place on a baking sheet. Mix the beaten egg with the remaining liqueur and brush over the sausage-shaped roll. Bake in a preheated oven at 190°C/375°F/gas mark 5 for 25 minutes.

Torta al Formaggio alla Toscana

Tuscan-style Cheesecake
Serves 4

350 g/12 oz/1½ cups caster (superfine) sugar
5 ml/1 tsp grated lemon rind
150 g/5 oz/1¼ cups plain (all-purpose) flour, sifted
7.5 ml/1½ tsp vanilla essence (extract)
1 egg yolk
50 g/2 oz/¼ cup unsalted (sweet) butter
350 g/12 oz/3 cups Mascarpone cheese, softened
120 ml/4 fl oz/½ cup double (heavy) cream
5 eggs, separated

Place 50 g/2 oz/¼ cup of the sugar, lemon rind and 100 g/4 oz/1 cup of the flour in a mixing bowl. Beat for a few seconds until well combined. Add 5 ml/1 tsp of the vanilla essence, egg yolk and the butter. Mix until the mixture forms a dough and the ingredients are well combined. Press half the dough into a 23 cm/9 in springform tin (pan). Bake in a preheated oven at 200°C/ 400°F/gas mark 6 for 8 minutes. Remove from the oven, leave to cool for 10 minutes, then press the remaining crust mixture onto the sides of the tin. Set aside. Place the softened cheese in a bowl. Blend in the remaining sugar, cream, remaining flour, vanilla essence and the egg yolks. Continue mixing until the mixture is smooth and creamy. Whisk the egg whites until stiff but not too dry. Gently fold the egg whites into the cheese mixture. Pour the filling into the crust. Bake in a preheated oven at 180°C/350°F/gas mark 4 for 1 hour. Allow the cheesecake to cool in the tin for at least 2 hours then remove from the tin and chill until ready to serve.

Crostatine di Noci alla Vaniglia

Vanilla Nut Tartlets
Serves 4

Pastry:
275 g/10 oz/2½ cups plain (all-purpose) flour
5 ml/1 tsp baking powder
100 g/4 oz/½ cup caster (superfine) sugar
25 g/1 oz/2 tbsp unsalted (sweet) butter
1 egg, lightly beaten
120 ml/4 oz/½ cup milk
5 ml/1 tsp butter for greasing

Filling:
2 eggs, well beaten
5 ml/1 tsp water
50 g/2 oz/¼ cup caster (superfine) sugar
5 ml/1 tsp vanilla essence (extract)
30 ml/2 tbsp milk or single (light) cream
50 g/2 oz/½ cup chopped mixed nuts

Mix the flour, baking powder and sugar together and rub in the butter. Add the lightly beaten egg to the milk and mix in gradually to form a thick paste. Roll out to 5 mm/¼ in thick. Line greased tartlet tins (patty pans) with pastry and bake in a preheated oven at 220°C/425°F/gas mark 7 for about 15 minutes. Blend all the filling ingredients in a saucepan and cook until thick, stirring constantly. Fill the cooled pastry shells two-thirds full. Return to the oven for 12–15 minutes until glossy.

Pesche Ripiene

Stuffed Peaches

Serves 4

4 peaches
75 g/3 oz/¾ cup ground almonds
40 g/1½ oz/¼ cup icing
(confectioners') sugar
15 ml/1 tbsp candied peel
15 ml/1 tbsp brandy or liqueur
6 macaroons, crushed

Scald the peaches in boiling water for 30 seconds and peel off the skins. Cut the peaches in half and remove the stones. Blend the ground almonds with the sugar, peel, brandy and crushed macaroons. Mix well and fill the centres of the peaches with the mixture. Place the two halves of the peaches together so that they look whole and fix with cocktail sticks (toothpicks). Place in a single layer in a shallow, ovenproof dish. Cover with foil. Bake in a preheated oven for 10 minutes at 190°C/375°F/gas mark 5 and serve hot.

Soufflé di Noci

Walnut Soufflé

Serves 4

50 g/2 oz/¼ cup unsalted (sweet) butter
45 ml/3 tbsp icing (confectioners')
sugar
45 ml/3 tbsp plain (all-purpose) flour
250 ml/8 fl oz/1 cup double (heavy)
cream
100 g/4 oz/½ cup caster (superfine)
sugar
4 eggs, separated
175 g/6 oz/1½ cups walnuts, ground
10 ml/2 tsp vanilla essence (extract)
30 ml/2 tbsp Grappa or brandy

Grease a 1.2 litre/2 pt/5 cup soufflé dish with 15 g/½ oz/1 tbsp of the butter. Sprinkle 15 ml/1 tbsp of the icing sugar into the dish and shake out any excess. Melt the remaining butter in a saucepan and remove from the heat. Stir in the flour and blend to a smooth paste. Add the cream and sugar and beat well. Set aside to cool for 15 minutes. Beat in the egg yolks, one at a time. Stir in the ground walnuts, vanilla essence and Grappa, beating constantly until the mixture is smooth. Whisk the egg whites until stiff and fold into the walnut mixture. Spoon into the prepared soufflé dish. Place in a preheated oven at 180°C/350°F/gas mark 4 for 35 minutes until risen and lightly browned. Remove from the oven and sprinkle with the remaining sifted icing sugar. Serve immediately.

Montebianco

Mont Blanc

Serves 4

450 g/1 lb chestnuts
300 ml/½ pt/1¼ cups milk
100 g/4 oz/½ cup caster (superfine)
sugar
300 ml/½ pt/1¼ cups whipping cream
2.5 ml/½ tsp vanilla essence (extract)

Slit the outer skin of the chestnuts and roast or boil for 20 minutes. Remove the outer and inner brown skins. Break the softened chestnuts and place in a saucepan Pour in the milk and sugar. Cook, stirring all the time until the mixture has thickened. Press through a sieve (strainer) into a glass bowl. Whip the cream, add the vanilla essence, and spoon over the top of the chestnut mixture.

Pan di Spagne Ravenna

Ravenna Sponge Cake
Serves 4–6

*60 ml/4 tbsp instant coffee granules or
powder
175 g/6 oz/¾ cup caster (superfine)
sugar
350 g/12 oz/3 cups plain (all-purpose)
flour
10 ml/2 tsp baking powder
6 eggs, separated
A little butter for greasing*

Dissolve the coffee in 300 ml/½ pt/1¼ cups
of water and allow to cool. Mix the sugar,
flour and baking powder together with the
egg yolks. Stir in the coffee. Whisk the egg
whites until stiff and fold into the mixture.
Pour into a greased 23 cm/ 9 in cake tin
(pan). Bake in a preheated oven at 180°C/
350°F/gas mark 4 for about 35–40 minutes
until risen and golden and the centre
springs back when pressed.

Albicocche Ripiene con Mascarpone e Pistachio

Stuffed Apricots with
Mascarpone and Pistachios
Serves 4–6

*6 ripe apricots
100 g/4 oz/½ cup Mascarpone cheese
15 ml/1 tbsp apricot jam (conserve)
30 ml/2 tbsp pistachio nuts, chopped
100 g/4 oz raspberries
15 ml/1 tbsp icing (confectioners')
sugar*

Cut the apricots in half and remove the
stones. Place the fruit on a baking sheet,
skin sides down. Blend the Mascarpone
cheese and jam together and spoon into the
apricot halves. Sprinkle with the nuts.
Purée the raspberries and icing sugar in a
blender or food processor and then pass
through a sieve (strainer) to remove the
seeds. Cook the apricots under a hot grill
(broiler) for 2 minutes and serve immediately with the raspberry sauce.

Palline Fritte di Pasta Dolce

Sweet Fried Pastry Balls
Makes 10

*225 g/8 oz/2 cups plain (all-purpose)
flour
300 ml/½ pt/1¼ cups water
45 ml/3 tbsp brandy
Oil for deep-frying
75 ml/5 tbsp icing (confectioners') sugar*

Place the flour into a saucepan and stir in
the water and brandy. Cook slowly for 8
minutes stirring, until the mixture comes
away from the sides of the saucepan.
Remove from the heat. When cool enough
to handle, knead the dough until it is soft
and roll it into a long sausage shape. Take
small pieces of the dough and form each
into a ball. Deep-fry the dough balls in the
hot oil for 2–3 minutes until they are
brown. Remove from the pan with a draining spoon and drain on kitchen paper. Roll
in icing sugar and serve hot.

Dolce di Castagne e Cioccolata

Chestnut and Chocolate Dessert

Serves 6

*100 g/4 oz plain (semi-sweet) cooking
chocolate*
150 ml/¼ pt/⅔ cup milk
*75 g/3 oz/⅓ cup caster (superfine)
sugar*
*15 g/½ oz/1 tbsp gelatine, softened in
30 ml/2 tbsp warm water*
*165 g/5½ oz/1 small can unsweetened
chestnut purée (paste)*
*300 ml/½ pt/1¼ cups double (heavy)
cream*
*150 g/5 oz/1 small can preserved
chestnuts, drained and roughly
chopped*

Grate half of the chocolate for decoration.
Line the bottom of a 1.2 litre/2 pt/
5 cup mould (mold) with a circle of
greaseproof (waxed) paper and set aside.
Melt the remaining chocolate in a small
bowl over a pan of hot water. Put the milk
and sugar in a saucepan and add the gelatine mixture. Cook gently, stirring until the
sugar and gelatine have dissolved. Slowly
stir in the chestnut purée and the melted
chocolate. Mix well and pour into a bowl.
Chill for 15 minutes. Beat the cream until
thick and beat into the gelatine mixture.
Add the preserved chestnuts to the cream.
Spoon into the lined mould. Cover with
greaseproof paper and chill for at least 6
hours. Remove the paper and place a serving plate on the top of the mould, invert the
plate and mould and shake gently. The
dessert should slide out easily. Decorate
with the reserved grated chocolate before
serving.

Panna al Marsala

Sweet Marsala Cream Cheese

Makes 750 ml/1¼ pts/3 cups

*600 ml/1 pt/2½ cups double (heavy)
cream*
*50 g/2 oz/⅓ cup icing (confectioners')
sugar*
Juice of 2 lemons
30 ml/2 tbsp Marsala wine
Fresh fruit, to serve

Whisk the cream until it forms soft peaks.
Gradually whisk in the sugar. Strain the
lemon juice into the cream with the
Marsala and mix well. Put the cream into a
muslin cloth (cheesecloth) and hang over a
bowl for 24 hours to allow any liquid to
soak through. Serve the cheese with fresh
fruit.

Bevuta all' Albicocca e Fichi

Apricot and Fig Cordial

Makes 1.2 litres/2 pts/5 cups

*450 g/1 lb ripe apricots, stoned (pitted)
and chopped*
100 g/4 oz fresh figs, chopped
1.2 litres/2 pts/5 cups boiling water
75 g/3 oz/⅓ cup light brown sugar
Grated rind of 1 lemon
*Sweet Almond Biscuits (see page 286),
to serve*

Place the fruit and water in a large
saucepan and boil for 15 minutes. Add the
sugar and lemon juice and boil for a further 10 minutes. Leave until cold then
strain. Serve over crushed ice in long tall
glasses with Sweet Almond Biscuits.

Pasticcio di Mandorle

Frangipane and Strawberry Pie
Makes 6–8 slices

Butter for greasing
225 g/8 oz shortcrust pastry (basic pie crust)
45 ml/3 tbsp strawberry jam
100 g/4 oz/½ cup unsalted (sweet) butter
100 g/4 oz/½ cup caster (superfine) sugar
2 eggs, lightly beaten
15 ml/1 tbsp rum
100 g/4 oz/1¼ cups ground almonds

Grease a 20 cm/8 in flan tin (pan) with the butter and set aside. Roll out the pastry on a lightly floured board and line the flan tin. Spread the base of the pastry with the strawberry jam. Beat the butter with the sugar until pale and fluffy. Beat in the eggs and rum. Stir in the ground almonds and spoon the mixture into the pastry case. Bake in a preheated oven at 190°C/375°F/ gas mark 5 for 35–40 minutes until the filling is set and the top has browned. Cool in the tin for 10 minutes and place on a serving dish.

Pesche Royale

Peach Royale
Serves 4

4 ripe peaches, skinned, stoned (pitted), and finely sliced
25 g/1 oz/2 tbsp caster (superfine) sugar
30 ml/2 tbsp brandy
1 bottle Asti Spumanti, chilled

Place the peach slices in open champagne glasses or wine goblets. Sprinkle with the sugar and brandy. When ready to serve, top up with Asti Spumanti. Eat the fruit then sip the peach-flavoured wine.

Pasticcio di Fragole Fresche

Fresh Strawberry Tart
Serves 4

450 g/1 lb fresh whole strawberries
225 g/8 oz shortcrust pastry (basic pie crust)
15 g/½ oz/1 tbsp unsalted (sweet) butter for greasing
75 g/3 oz/⅓ cup cream cheese
45 ml/3 tbsp soured (dairy sour) cream
45 ml/3 tbsp caster (superfine) sugar
45 ml/3 tbsp cornflour (cornstarch)
120 ml/4 fl oz/½ cup water
175 ml/6 fl oz/¾ cup double (heavy) cream, whipped

Hull the strawberries. Roll out the pastry and line a greased 25 cm/10 in flan tin (pie pan). Line with greaseproof (waxed) paper and add baking beans. Bake in a preheated oven for 15 minutes at 190°C/375°F/gas mark 5. Remove the flan case (pie shell) from the oven and set aside to cool. Beat the cream cheese and soured cream until well-blended and spread over the cooled pie shell. Arrange the whole strawberries over the cream mixture, reserving 6 large strawberries. Blend the sugar, cornflour and water in a saucepan. Chop the reserved strawberries and add to the mixture and cook over a low heat until thick. Simmer for 1 minute and set aside to cool. Pour over the strawberries and chill. Top with whipped cream just before serving.

Pasticcio al Formaggio Dolce

Lemon Cheesecake
Serves 4–6

Digestive Biscuit Shell:
25 Digestive biscuits (Graham crackers), crushed
75 g/3 oz/¹⁄₃ cup caster (superfine) sugar
5 ml/1 tsp cinnamon
75 g/3 oz/¹⁄₃ cup soft unsalted (sweet) butter

Filling:
120 ml/4 fl oz/¹⁄₂ cup single (light) cream
2 eggs
250 ml/8 fl oz/1 cup Ricotta cheese
30 ml/2 tbsp lemon juice
5 ml/1 tsp vanilla essence (extract)
100 g/4 oz/¹⁄₂ cup caster (superfine) sugar
1.5 ml/¹⁄₄ tsp salt
45 ml/3 tbsp flour

Combine the pastry shell ingredients and press into a deep 20 cm/8 in pie tin (pan). Reserve 15 ml/1 tbsp of crumbs for the top of the pie. Thoroughly mix all the filling ingredients and pour into the lined pie tin. Bake in a preheated oven at 160°C/325°F/ gas mark 3 for 50 minutes or until firm. Sprinkle with the reserved crumbs.

Confettura Mandúria

Brandied Figs
Serves 4

8 fresh figs
100 g/4 oz/¹⁄₂ cup caster (superfine) sugar
300 ml/¹⁄₂ pint/1¹⁄₄ cups Mandúria or brandy

Pack the figs into a clean, wide-necked jar. Place the sugar with the Mandúria or brandy in a heavy-based pan and heat gently until the sugar has dissolved. Boil for 3 minutes. Pour the liquid over the figs and stir gently with a skewer to release any air that may be trapped in the jar. Seal and shake gently every 2 or 3 days. Leave in a cool place for 2 weeks before using.

Liquore a Ciliege

Cherry Liqueur
Makes 1.2 litres/2 pts/5 cups

750 g/1¹⁄₂ lb Morello cherries
225 g/8 oz cherry leaves
90 ml/6 tbsp rosewater
450 g/1 lb/2 cups granulated sugar
600 ml/1 pint/2¹⁄₂ cups brandy
Almond Cake (see page 311), to serve

Remove the stones from the cherries over a large-necked jar, so as not to waste any of the juice. Crack the stones with a small hammer and add the kernels to the cherries. Add the cherry leaves, rosewater and sugar. Pour in the brandy and cover with a lid or greaseproof (waxed) paper and foil. Allow to stand for 4 weeks. Strain through a paper coffee filter and rebottle. Store in a cool dark place for at least 3 months. The liqueur will improve with age. Serve in small glasses with pieces of Almond Cake.

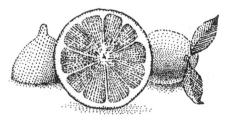

Liquore Romano Viola

Roman Violet Liqueur
Makes 500 ml/17 fl oz/2¼ cups

Rind of 1 orange, cut into strips
300 ml/½ pt/1¼ cups brandy
8 whole cloves
2.5 cm/1 in piece of cinnamon stick
1 piece star anise
50 Parma violets, stems and green
* leaves removed*
15 ml/1 tbsp orris root
½ vanilla pod
225 g/8 oz/1 cup granulated sugar
15 ml/1 tbsp violet food colouring
Vanilla Ice Cream (see page 345), to
* serve*

Place all the ingredients except the sugar and food colouring in a wide-necked jar and allow to stand for 2 weeks, shaking occasionally. Pour in the sugar and allow to stand for a further 2 weeks. Strain through a paper coffee filter and stir in the food colouring. Rebottle and use poured over Vanilla Ice Cream.

Castagne in Rum

Chestnuts in Rum
Makes 4 × 600 ml/1 pt/
2½ cup jars

1.75 litres/3 pts/7½ cups water
900 g/2 lb chestnuts
900 g/2 lb/6 cups dark brown sugar
350 ml/12 fl oz/scant 1½ cups light rum
½ orange, sliced
15 ml/1 tbsp chopped fresh root ginger
Whipped cream, to serve

Sterilise four 600 ml/1 pt/2½ cup jars. Bring 1.5 litres/2½ pts/6 cups water to the boil in a large saucepan. Add the chestnuts

and cook, covered, for 50 minutes. Drain the chestnuts, cool, and remove the skins. In another saucepan, combine the brown sugar, the remaining water, the rum, orange slices and ginger. Bring to the boil, then remove the saucepan from the heat immediately. Put the peeled chestnuts into the sterilised jars, and pour the hot syrup over them, leaving 1 cm/½ in of space at the top of each jar. Cover and seal the jars tightly. Store in a cool, dark place. Serve with whipped cream.

Fichi al Cognac

Figs in Brandy
Makes 3 × 600 ml/1 pt/2½ cup jars

1 lemon
900 g/2 lb/4 cups granulated sugar
450 ml/¾ pt/2 cups water
6 cloves
2 cinnamon sticks
30 ml/2 tbsp chopped preserved ginger
16 large fresh figs
120 ml/4 fl oz/½ cup brandy

Remove the pips and ends and slice the lemon thinly. Sterilise three 600 ml/1 pt/ 2½ cup size jars. In a large saucepan, combine the sugar, water, cloves cinnamon sticks, lemon slices and ginger pieces. Cook over a very low heat until the sugar has melted. Add the figs and continue to cook slowly for 40 minutes. Remove the figs from the saucepan and place in the jars. Divide the cloves, cinnamon sticks, lemon slices and ginger pieces equally between the jars. Boil the syrup for 5 minutes and skim the top twice. Allow to cool for 5 minutes. Add an equal quantity of brandy to each jar and fill the jars with the syrup. Cover and seal the jars. Allow to stand in a cool, dark place for at least one month before using.

Conserva di Fichi

Fig Preserve
Serves 8

*450 g/1 lb/3 cups blanched almonds,
  toasted*
750 g/1½ lb/3 cups granulated sugar
175 ml/6 fl oz/¾ cup water
15 ml/1 tbsp grated lemon rind
1.5 kg/3 lb fresh figs, sliced
½ lemon, sliced
120 ml/4 fl oz/½ cup Cognac
*Milk Sponge Cake (see page 323) and
  cream, to serve*

Combine the sugar, water and lemon rind
in a large saucepan and cook over a low
heat for 5 minutes. Add the figs and lemon
slices and simmer for 20 minutes. Allow to
stand, covered, overnight. Bring the mixture to simmering the following day and
cook for 20 minutes, until it thickens. Add
the nuts and Cognac. Cook for 1 minute
and pour into the sterilised jars and seal.
This preserve may be eaten right away or
stored for future use. Serve spooned on
Milk Sponge Cake, topped with cream, or
spread on Ciabatta bread for a snack.

Nocino

Walnut Liqueur
Makes 1 litre

10 green walnuts, quartered
1 litre/1¾ pts/4¼ cups vodka
1 cinnamon stick
10 cloves
1 star anise
350 g/12 oz/1½ cups granulated sugar
*Fresh fruit and Almond Macaroons
  (see page 285), to serve*

Put all the ingredients except the sugar in
a clean, wide-necked, screw-topped glass
jar. Seal and leave in a warm, light place
for 1–2 months. The liquid will turn a rich
brown colour. Add the sugar and stir until
completely dissolved. Strain into small,
clean bottles, cork firmly and store in a
cool, dark place. Serve in small glasses
with fresh fruit and Almond Macaroons.

Torta di Riso al Grand Marnier

Rice Cake with Grand Marnier
Makes 1 cake

1.5 litres/2½ pts/6 cups milk
A pinch of salt
350 g/12 oz/1½ cups arborio rice
Grated rind of 1 lemon
60 ml/4 tbsp caster (superfine) sugar
3 large eggs
25 g/1 oz/2 tbsp unsalted (sweet) butter
1 large egg yolk
*30 ml/2 tbsp chopped mixed (candied)
  peel*
*225 g/8 oz/2 cups toasted flaked
  (slivered) almonds*
45 ml/3 tbsp Grand Marnier
Butter for greasing
30 ml/2 tbsp dried breadcrumbs

Place the milk and salt in a heavy pan.
Bring to the boil, add the rice and lemon
rind, reduce the heat, cover and simmer for
18 minutes, stirring occasionally. Remove
from the heat. Stir in the sugar, the whole
eggs and butter and leave to cool. When
just warm, beat in the egg yolk, peel, nuts
and liqueur. Turn into a buttered 20 cm/
8 in cake tin (pan), coated in the breadcrumbs. Smooth the surface and bake in a
preheated oven at 150°C/300°F/gas mark 2
for 45 minutes or until golden and a skewer inserted in the centre comes out clean.
Leave to cool in the tin, turn out and serve
just warm.

Zuppa di Inglese

Trifle
Serves 6

4 eggs
50 g/2 oz/¼ cup caster (superfine)
*   sugar*
30 ml/2 tbsp cornflour (cornstarch)
900 ml/1½ pts/3¾ cups milk
Grated rind and juice of 1 orange
50 g/2 oz/½ cup plain (semi-sweet)
*   chocolate*
1 slab plain cake, thinly sliced
60 ml/4 tbsp medium dry sherry, or
*   half sherry and half kirsch*
Grated chocolate

Whisk together the eggs and sugtar in a saucepan. Blend the cornflour with a little of the milk. Stir in the remaining milk and add to the saucepan with the orange rind. Bring to the boil slowly over a gentle heat, stirring all the time until thickened. Do not boil rapidly or the mixture will curdle. Pour half the custard into a separate bowl. Melt the chocolate in a bowl in the microwave or over a pan of hot water and stir into the saucepan of custard. Put a layer of one-third of the cake in the base of a round glass serving dish. Mix the orange juice and sherry together and drizzle a third over the cake. Spoon over a third of the plain custard then a third of the chocolate custard. Repeat these layers, finishing with a layer of chocolate custard. Cover and chill for several hours until set. Sprinkle with grated chocolate before serving.

Tortelli di Riso

Rice Cakes
Serves 6

150 g/5 oz/⅔ cup arborio rice
300 ml/½ pt/1¼ cups milk
A pinch of salt
100 g/4 oz/½ cup caster (superfine)
*   sugar*
40 g/1½ oz/3 tbsp unsalted (sweet)
*   butter*
1 lemon
65 g/2½ oz/good ½ cup plain (all-
*   purpose) flour*
3 eggs, separated
30 ml/2 tbsp rum or Amaretto
Oil for deep-frying
10 ml/2 tsp ground cinnamon

Cook the rice in plenty of boiling water for 7 minutes. Drain, rinse with cold water, drain again and return to the pan with the milk. Bring to the boil, reduce the heat, cover and simmer for 10 minutes or until the milk has been absorbed. Remove from the heat and stir in the salt, 15 ml/1 tbsp of the sugar and the butter. Grate the rind from the lemon and add to the rice (reserve the fruit for serving). Leave to cool for 15 minutes, then stir in the flour and beat in the egg yolks and rum or liqueur. Whisk the egg whites until stiff and fold into the mixture with a metal spoon. Deep-fry spoonfuls of the mixture, a few at a time, until crisp and lightly golden. Drain on kitchen paper. Mix the remaining sugar with the cinnamon. Sprinkle over the rice cakes and serve with the lemon cut in wedges.

Fritelle di Riso

Rice Pancakes
Serves 4–6

900 ml/1½ pts/3¾ cups milk
A pinch of salt
225 g/8 oz/1 cup arborio rice
2 large eggs
15 ml/1 tbsp plain (all-purpose) flour
Grated rind of 1 orange and 1 lemon,
  reserving the fruit
Granulated sugar
Oil for shallow-frying
100 g/4 oz/½ cup icing (confectioners')
  sugar

Place the milk in a saucepan with a pinch of salt. Bring to the boil, add the rice, cover and simmer gently for 15–20 minutes, stirring occasionally until the rice is cooked and creamy, adding a little more milk if necessary. Remove from the heat and beat in the eggs, flour, orange and lemon rinds. Sweeten to taste with sugar. Heat the oil in a heavy frying pan (skillet). Drop spoonfuls of the mixture into the oil and fry (sauté) for about 4 minutes until the bases are golden. Turn over and brown the other sides. Drain on kitchen paper. Keep warm in a low oven while cooking the remainder. Sprinkle with sifted icing sugar and serve with the orange and lemon, cut into wedges, to squeeze over.

Sapajean

Lombard Zabaglione
Serves 4

4 large eggs
60 ml/4 tbsp caster (superfine) sugar
60 ml/4 tbsp red wine
Grated rind and juice of ½ lemon

Break the eggs into a bowl and add the sugar. Stand the bowl over a pan of hot, but not boiling, water. Whisk with an electric beater until the mixture is thick, pale and fluffy and doubled in bulk. Whisk in the wine a little at a time and continue whisking until the mixture is like a fluffy mousse. Whisk in the lemon juice and continue whisking for a further 5 minutes. Spoon into tall glasses and serve straight away.

Insalata di Fragole

Strawberry Salad
Serves 4

175 g/6 oz/¾ cup Mascarpone cheese
120 ml/4 fl oz/½ cup double (heavy)
  cream, whipped
225 g/8 oz strawberries, sliced
Simple Lemon Sauce (see page 370)

Mash the cheese with a fork and work to a smooth paste. Blend in the whipped cream. Stir in the sliced strawberries and shape into a roll on greaseproof (waxed) paper. Chill thoroughly and serve sliced with the sauce.

Ice Cream and Sorbets

The Italians excel at making ice creams and sorbets and it is said that they introduced these desserts to France and Britain. Italian ice cream has that special richness because it is usually made with egg custard as well as cream. Amaretti – the traditional Italian biscuits originally made from apricot-kernels – are a popular accompaniment for all ice creams and sorbets. The variety of flavours is impressive – from the well-known strawberry or lemon to the more exotic chopped glacé fruits or Maraschino.

Gelato alla Vaniglia

Vanilla Ice Cream
Serves 6

450 ml/¾ pt/2 cups single (light) cream
3 egg yolks
150 g/5 oz/⅔ cup caster (superfine) sugar
2.5 ml/½ tsp vanilla essence (extract)

Place the single cream in a saucepan and gently heat until it reaches boiling point. Remove from the heat. Beat the egg yolks and sugar in a bowl over simmering water until the mixture thickens. Whisk in the hot cream and vanilla essence and continue whisking for 4 minutes, stirring all the time, until the custard thickens and coats the back of a spoon. Cool by standing the bowl in cold water, stirring to prevent a skin from forming. Pour the mixture into a rigid freezerproof container. Cover and freeze for 1 hour. Break up the ice crystals with a fork and whisk until smooth. Return to the freezer for 45 minutes and whisk again. Freeze until firm. Remove from the freezer 10 minutes before serving.

Bombe di Lamponi

Ice Cream Bombe with Raspberries
Serves 6

100 g/4 oz raspberries
30 ml/2 tbsp raspberry liqueur
450 g/1 lb Vanilla Ice Cream (see left)
150 ml/¼ pt/⅔ cup double (heavy) cream
1 egg white

Place a bombe mould (mold) or a basin with a lid in the freezer while preparing the ice cream. Put the raspberries and the liqueur in a bowl together and allow to stand for 30 minutes. Using a spoon spread the ice cream around the inside of the mould to form a thick lining and replace in the freezer. Whip the cream and whisk the egg white until stiff. Combine together. Pass the soaked fruit through a sieve (strainer) to remove the seeds and fold the purée into the egg white and cream mixture. Fill the centre of the mould, cover with a layer of vanilla ice cream and replace in the freezer for 3 or more hours. When ready to serve, remove from the freezer. Dip the mould in hot water for 1 second and turn out on to a plate. Cut into six segments and serve immediately.

Gelato con Cioccolato in Schegge

Chocolate Chip Ice Cream
Serves 4

3 eggs, separated
75 g/3 oz/⅓ cup caster (superfine) sugar
½ vanilla pod
300 ml/½ pt/1¼ cups single (light) cream
100 g/4 oz/1 cup chocolate chips

Put the egg yolks, sugar, vanilla pod and cream into a bowl over a pan of gently simmering water and cook, whisking, until the custard is thick enough to coat the back of a wooden spoon. Do not allow the water to boil. Remove the vanilla pod and fold in the stiffly beaten egg whites. Place in a container and seal with a lid. Freeze for 2 hours then whisk with a fork to break up the ice crystals. Add the chocolate chips. Return to the freezer and freeze for a further 2 hours. Whisk again and return to the freezer until firm.

Cassata di Ciliege

Cherry Cassata
Serves 4

3 eggs, separated
75 g/3 oz/⅓ cup caster (superfine) sugar
½ vanilla pod
300 ml/½ pt/1¼ cups single (light) cream
25 g/1 oz/2 tbsp glacé (candied) cherries, chopped

Put the egg yolks, sugar, vanilla pod and cream into a bowl over a pan of gently simmering water and cook, whisking, until the custard is thick enough to coat the back of a wooden spoon. Do not allow the water to boil. Remove the vanilla pod and fold in the stiffly beaten egg whites and the cherries. Place in a container and seal with a lid. Freeze for 2 hours. Whisk with a fork to break up ice crystals. Return to the freezer and freeze for a further 2 hours. Whisk again then freeze until firm.

Gelato al Caffè

Coffee Ice Cream
Serves 6–8

15 ml/1 tbsp instant coffee granules or powder
30 ml/2 tbsp espresso coffee
30 ml/2 tbsp caster (superfine) sugar
500 ml/17 fl oz/2¼ cups thick plain yoghurt
150 ml/¼ pt/⅔ cup double (heavy) cream

Measure the instant coffee into a small saucepan. Add the espresso coffee and sugar and heat until blended. Remove from the heat, turn into a large bowl and leave until cold. Stir in the yoghurt and the cream. Turn the mixture into a freezer-proof container and cover with a lid. Freeze for 1 hour and whisk with a fork. Return to the freezer and freeze again for 1½ hours. Whisk with a fork again and freeze until required.

Gelato al Caffè e Rum

Coffee and Rum Ice Cream
Serves 6–8

15 ml/1 tbsp instant coffee granules or powder
30 ml/2 tbsp cold strong espresso coffee
30 ml/2 tbsp caster (superfine) sugar
30 ml/2 tbsp dark rum
500 ml/17 fl oz/2¼ cups thick plain yoghurt
75 g/3 oz/¾ cup walnuts, chopped
150 ml/¼ pt/⅔ cup double (heavy) cream, whipped until softly peaking

Measure the instant coffee into a small saucepan. Add the espresso coffee and sugar and heat until blended. Stir in the rum. Remove from the heat, turn into a large bowl and leave until cold. Stir in the yoghurt, chopped nuts and the cream. Turn the mixture into a freezerproof container and cover with a lid. Freeze for 1 hour and whisk with a fork. Return to the freezer and freeze again for 1½ hours. Whisk with a fork again and freeze until required.

Semifreddo al Cioccolato

Chocolate Ice Cream Cake
Serves 6

225 g/8 oz plain (semi-sweet) chocolate
45 ml/3 tbsp caster (superfine) sugar
45 ml/3 tbsp water
4 eggs, separated
30 sponge (lady) fingers
300 ml/½ pt/1¼ cups whipping cream

Melt the chocolate in a basin over hot water. Add the sugar, water, and well-beaten egg yolks. Cook slowly until thick and smooth, stirring continually. Remove the basin from the heat. Leave to cool. When cool, add the stiffly whisked egg whites. Line the bottom of a 20 cm/8 in cake tin with greaseproof (waxed) paper. Cut off the rounded ends of the sponge fingers and place close together on the sides and bottom of the tin. Cover the sponge fingers with half of the chocolate mixture. Add another layer of sponge fingers then the remaining chocolate mixture. Cover with foil and freeze until firm. When ready to serve, remove the rim of the cake tin, slip on to a decorative plate, and cover the top with the whipped cream. Leave to stand for 10 minutes before serving.

Gelato al Miele

Honey Ice Cream
Serves 6

120 ml/4 fl oz/½ cup milk
5 egg yolks
150 g/¼ pt/⅔ cup caster (superfine) sugar
450 ml/¾ pt/2 cups double (heavy) cream
120 ml/4 fl oz/½ cup clear honey

Heat the milk in a saucepan until it reaches boiling point. Remove from the heat. Whisk the egg yolks and sugar in a bowl over simmering water until the mixture thickens. Whisk in the hot milk and stir in the cream. Replace the bowl over simmering water and whisk for 5 minutes, until the custard thickens and coats the back of a spoon. Stir in the honey until dissolved, and cool by standing the bowl in cold water, stirring to prevent a skin from forming. Pour the mixture into a rigid freezerproof container. Cover and freeze for 1 hour. Remove from the freezer and whisk until smooth. Return to the freezer for 45 minutes and whisk again. Freeze until firm. Remove from the freezer 10 minutes before serving.

Gelato allo Yogurt con Arancia e Cioccolato

Orange and Chocolate Yoghurt Ice Cream
Serves 6

Juice of 3 oranges
30 ml/2 tbsp caster (superfine) sugar
500 ml/17 fl oz/2¼ cups thick plain yoghurt
150 ml/¼ pt/⅔ cup double (heavy) cream
50 g/2 oz plain (semi-sweet) chocolate, grated

Pour the orange juice into a saucepan and add the caster sugar. Heat gently until the sugar has dissolved. Allow to cool and stir in the yoghurt and the cream. Add the grated chocolate and turn the mixture into a freezerproof container. Cover with a lid. Freeze for 1 hour and whisk with a fork. Return to the freezer and freeze again for 1½ hours. Whisk with a fork again and freeze until required.

Facile Gelato alla Frutta

Easy Fruit Ice Cream
Serves 6–8

100 g/4 oz/¾ cup assorted glacé (candied) fruit, chopped
30 ml/2 tbsp sweet liqueur (any flavour)
450 g/1 lb Pistachio Ice Cream (see page 355)
150 ml/¼ pt/⅔ cup double (heavy) cream
1 egg white
100 g/4 oz/½ cup caster (superfine) sugar

Place a bombe mould (mold) or basin with a lid, in the freezer while preparing the ice cream. Put the chopped glacé fruit and the liqueur in a bowl together to soak. Using a spoon, spread the ice cream around the inside of the mould to form a thick lining. Replace in the freezer. Whip the cream and whisk the egg white with the sugar until stiff. Mix together. Add the fruit and fold into the egg white and cream mixture. Fill the centre of the mould and replace in the freezer for 3 or more hours until firm. When ready to serve, remove from the freezer. Dip the mould in hot water for 1 second and turn out on to a plate. Cut into segments and serve immediately.

Gelato al Morello

Morello Cherry Ice Cream
Serves 6–8

600 ml/1 pt/2½ cups Vanilla Ice Cream (see page 345)
300 ml/½ pt/1¼ cups single (light) cream
450 g/1 lb Morello cherries, stoned (pitted)
Grated rind of 1 orange
45 ml/3 tbsp maraschino liqueur
15 ml/1 tbsp orange juice
10 ml/2 tsp cornflour (cornstarch)

Soften the ice cream in a large bowl and beat in the cream. Place in the fridge. Put the cherries, orange rind, and maraschino liqueur into a large saucepan and bring to the boil. Cook for 3 minutes. Blend the cornflour and orange juice, and stir into the saucepan. Cook for 2 minutes and remove the pan from the heat and leave to cool for 5 minutes. Blend the mixture into the ice cream and cream. Freeze until required.

Dessert al Limone Alla Svelta

Quick Lemon Dessert
Serves 4

600 ml/1 pt/2½ cups double (heavy) cream
225 g/8 oz/1 cup caster (superfine) sugar
Juice and grated rind of 3 lemons

Bring the cream to the boil with the sugar and cook for 3 minutes, stirring. Add the lemon juice and stir in the rind. Leave to cool. Transfer to a freezerproof container and freeze for 1 hour. Break up the ice crystals with a fork and whisk for 1 minute. Return to the freezer for 45 minutes and whisk again. Freeze until firm.

Gelato all' Albicocca

Apricot Ice Cream
Serves 4

450 ml/¾ pt/2 cups single (light) cream
4 egg yolks
150 g/5 oz/⅔ cup caster (superfine) sugar
6 apricots, skinned, halved and stoned (pitted)
30 ml /2 tbsp apricot or orange liqueur

Place the cream in a saucepan and gently heat until it reaches boiling point. Remove from the heat. Whisk the egg yolks and sugar in a bowl over hot water until the mixture thickens, then whisk in the hot cream. Place the bowl over the simmering water and whisk for 5 minutes, until the custard thickens and coats the back of a spoon. Cool by standing the bowl in cold water, stirring to prevent a skin from form-ing. Place the chopped apricots in a bowl. Add the liqueur and stir in the custard. Pour the mixture into a rigid freezerproof container. Cover and freeze for 1 hour. Whisk with a fork to break up the ice crystals. Return to the freezer for 45 minutes and whisk again. Freeze until firm. Remove from the freezer 10 minutes before serving.

Spumone di Limone e Mandorle

Frozen Lemon and Almond Mousse
Serves 4–6

45 ml/3 tbsp water
2.5 ml/½ tsp gelatine
2 eggs, separated
50 g/2 oz/¼ cup caster (superfine) sugar
225 g/8 oz/1 cup cream cheese
Grated rind and juice of 2 lemons
225 g/8 oz/1 cup fromage frais
50 g/2 oz/½ cup finely chopped almonds

Put the water in a small bowl and sprinkle over the gelatine. Leave to soften for 5 minutes. Stand the bowl over a pan of hot water and stir until dissolved. Remove from the pan and leave to cool. Whisk the egg yolks and sugar together in a bowl until pale and thick. Beat in the cream cheese, rind and juice of the lemons and stir in the fromage frais. Fold the gelatine into the lemon cheese mixture. Whisk the egg whites until they form soft peaks. Fold into the soufflé mixture and spoon into a serving bowl. Freeze until firm. Decorate with the almonds just before serving.

Soufflé di Amaretti Gelato

Iced Amaretti Soufflé
Serves 6

100 g/4 oz Almond Macaroons (see
page 285) or ready made, broken
into pieces
45 ml/3 tbsp Amaretto liqueur
Grated rind and juice of 1 lemon
15 ml/1 tbsp powdered gelatine
6 eggs, separated
225 g/8 oz/1 cup light brown sugar
450 ml/³⁄₄ pt/2 cups double (heavy)
cream, lightly whipped
50 g/2 oz dark (semi-sweet) chocolate,
grated

Soak the crushed biscuits in the liqueur
and set aside. Place the lemon juice and
rind in a bowl and sprinkle over the gelatine leave for 5 minutes. Stand the bowl in
a pan of hot water and stir until the gelatine is dissolved. Whisk the egg yolks and
sugar together until pale and thick. Fold
into the biscuit mixture and stir in the gelatine and whipped cream. Whisk the egg
whites until stiff and fold into the Amaretti
mixture. Spoon the mixture into a soufflé
dish, scatter over the grated chocolate and
freeze until firm.

Granita di Limone

Lemon Granita
Serves 4

600 ml/1 pt/2½ cups water
175 g/6 oz/³⁄₄ cup granulated sugar
Grated rind and juice of 6 lemons
5 mint leaves
1 egg white, lightly beaten
15 ml/1 tbsp caster (superfine) sugar

Put the water and granulated sugar in a
saucepan. Heat gently until the sugar has
dissolved. Bring to the boil and boil for
about 5 minutes, without stirring, until a
thick syrup has formed but do not allow to
brown. Remove from the heat and set aside
to cool. Add the lemon rind and juice to
the cold syrup. Pour into a freezerproof
dish and place in the freezer compartment
for 1 hour. Remove from the freezer and
whisk to break up the ice crystals. Return
to the freezer and freeze for 3 hours, stirring every 45 minutes. Meanwhile brush
the mint leaves with the beaten egg white.
Dip the leaves into the caster sugar and
leave to dry on a rack for 1 hour before
using. Spoon the granita into individual
glass dishes and decorate with the frosted
mint leaves.

Gelato Tutti Frutti

Tutti Frutti Ice Cream
Serves 4

150 ml/¼ pt/⅔ cup double (heavy) cream
425 g/15 oz/1 large can custard
50 g/2 oz/⅓ cup glacé (candied)
cherries, chopped
15 g/½ oz/1 tbsp chopped mixed
candied peel
25 g/1 oz/2 tbsp sultanas (golden
raisins)
50 g/2 oz/½ cup chopped mixed nuts

Whip the cream until thickened and stir in
the custard. Mix until evenly combined.
Turn the mixture into a shallow freezerproof container and freeze uncovered for
1 hour. Scrape the mixture into a bowl and
beat well with a wooden spoon. Stir in the
fruit and nuts. Return the mixture to the
container, cover and freeze until firm.
Allow the ice cream to soften slightly in
the fridge before serving in individual
glass dishes.

Gelato con Mandorle e Cioccolate

Almond and Chocolate Ice Cream
Serves 6

300 ml/½ pt/1¼ cups milk
4 egg yolks
100 g/4 oz/½ cup caster (superfine) sugar
300 ml/½ pt/1¼ cups single (light) cream
100 g/4 oz/1 cup plain (semi-sweet) chocolate chips
75 g/3 oz/¾ cup toasted, chopped almonds

Place the milk in a saucepan and bring to boiling point. Remove from the heat. Whisk the egg yolks and sugar together in a bowl until pale and creamy and whisk in the hot milk. Place the bowl over a pan of simmering water and cook gently for 4 minutes, stirring constantly. When the custard thickens and lightly coats the back of a wooden spoon, remove from the heat. Cool, stirring to prevent a skin forming. Blend in the cream and pour into a rigid freezerproof container, cover and freeze for 1 hour. Whisk with a fork to break up the ice crystals. Return the mixture to the freezer for a further 40 minutes, whisk again. Fold in the chocolate chips and chopped almonds. Freeze until firm. Remove from the freezer 10 minutes before serving.

Delizia Nocciola

Hazelnut Delight
Serves 4–6

100 g/4 oz/1 cup hazelnuts
30 ml/2 tbsp cold water
15 g/½ oz/1 sachet gelatine
300 ml/½ pt/1¼ cups milk
4 egg yolks
100 g/4 oz/½ cup caster (superfine) sugar
30 ml/2 tbsp coffee granules or powder
300 ml/½ pt/1¼ cups double (heavy) cream

Coarsely crush the hazelnuts in a bowl with the end of a rolling pin or in a blender or food processor. Heat the water and sprinkle over the gelatine. Set aside. Place the nuts and milk in a saucepan and heat until simmering. Remove the pan from the heat. Whisk the egg yolks and sugar together until pale and pour the hot milk and nut mixture on to the egg yolks, stirring all the time. Return the mixture to the pan and replace over a very gentle heat. Cook, stirring constantly, for 2–3 minutes until the mixture thickens. Do not allow to boil. Remove from the heat and stir in the gelatine. Add the coffee granules, stir to mix, then pour into a mixing bowl. Leave until cold. Whip the cream until thick and stir into the cold hazelnut and coffee mixture. Pour into a soufflé dish or mould (mold) and freeze until firm.

Gelato al Maraschino

Maraschino Ice Cream
Serves 4

450 ml/¾ pt/2 cups single (light) cream
4 egg yolks
150 g/5 oz/⅔ cup caster (superfine)
  sugar
30 ml/2 tbsp Cherry Liqueur (see page
  340)
Morello cherries, to serve (optional)

Place the cream in a saucepan and gently heat until it reaches boiling point. Remove from the heat. Whisk the egg yolks and sugar in a bowl over hot water until the mixture thickens. Whisk in the hot cream and cherry liqueur. Replace over the simmering water and whisk for 5 minutes, until the custard thickens and coats the back of a spoon. Cool by standing the bowl in cold water, stirring to prevent a skin from forming. Pour the mixture into a rigid freezerproof container. Cover and freeze for 1 hour. Whisk with a fork to break up the ice crystals. Return to the freezer for 45 minutes and whisk again. Freeze until firm. Remove from the freezer 10 minutes before serving with individual bowls of morello cherries if liked.

Gelato al Limone

Lemon Ice Cream
Serves 6

120 ml/4 fl oz/½ cup milk
4 egg yolks
150 g/5 oz/⅔ cup caster (superfine)
  sugar
450 ml/¾ pt/2 cups single (light) cream
Grated rind and juice of 1 lemon

Heat the milk in a saucepan until it reaches boiling point. Remove from the heat. Whisk the egg yolks and sugar in a bowl over hot water until the mixture thickens. Whisk in the hot milk and cream. Replace over the simmering water and whisk for 5 minutes, until the custard thickens and coats the back of a spoon. Cool by standing the bowl in cold water, stirring to prevent a skin from forming. Stir in the grated rind and lemon juice and pour the mixture into a rigid freezerproof container. Cover and freeze for 1 hour. Whisk with a fork to break up the ice crystals. Return to the freezer for 45 minutes and whisk again. Freeze until firm. Remove from the freezer 10 minutes before serving.

Gelato all' Arancia

Orange Ice Cream
Serves 4

3 eggs, separated
75 g/3 oz/⅓ cup caster (superfine)
  sugar
Vanilla pod
300 ml/½ pt/1¼ cups single (light)
  cream
Grated rind and juice of 1 orange

Put the egg yolks, sugar, vanilla pod and cream into a bowl over hot water and cook, whisking, until the custard is thick enough to coat the back of a wooden spoon. Do not allow to boil. Remove the vanilla pod. Stir in the orange rind and juice. Whisk the egg whites until stiff then fold into the mixture. Place in a container and seal with a lid. Freeze for 2 hours then whisk with a fork to break up the ice crystals. Return to the freezer and freeze for a further 2 hours. Whisk again then freeze until firm.

Soufflé Caffè

Mocha Soufflé
Serves 4–6

60 ml/4 tbsp ground coffee
10 ml/2 tsp instant coffee granules or powder
150 ml/¼ pt/⅔ cup full cream milk
2 egg whites
100 g/4 oz/½ cup caster (superfine) sugar
100 g/4 oz plain (semi-sweet) chocolate
150 ml/¼ pt/⅔ cup double (heavy) cream

Heat the ground coffee, instant coffee and milk in a saucepan until just boiling and remove from the heat. Set aside for 10 minutes then strain. Whisk the egg whites in a bowl and add the sugar. Stand the bowl over a pan of simmering water and whisk for 5–6 minutes until the meringue mixture holds its shape. Remove from the heat and continue whisking for 2 minutes. Place the chocolate in a bowl and melt over a pan of hot water. Add the coffee milk and remove from the heat. Stir until the mixture cools. Whip the cream until softly peaking and blend into the coffee-chocolate mixture. Fold in the meringue mixture and turn into a freezerproof container. Cover with a lid and freeze until firm.

Crema di Lamponi

Raspberry Cream
Serves 4–6

750 g/1½ lb raspberries
75 g/3 oz/⅓ cup caster (superfine) sugar
45 ml/3 tbsp water
20 g/¾ oz/1½ tbsp gelatine
150 ml/¼ pt/⅔ cup double (heavy) cream
2 egg whites
3 mint leaves

Reserve a few whole raspberries for decoration. Put the remainder of the raspberries in a saucepan and add the sugar. Cook for 5–6 minutes until the fruit is soft and press through a nylon sieve (strainer). Put the water in a small bowl and sprinkle over the gelatine. Allow to stand for 5 minutes. Stand the bowl in a pan of simmering water and stir until the gelatine has dissolved and the liquid is clear. Pour the gelatine on to the raspberries and stir well. Allow to cool until beginning to set. Whip the cream until thick and fold into the cooled fruit. Whisk the egg whites until stiff and fold into the mixture. Pour into a serving bowl and freeze. Decorate with the reserved raspberries and mint leaves before serving.

Sorbetto al Mandarino

Tangerine Sorbet
Serves 4

4 tangerines
600 ml/1 pt/2½ cups water
175 g/6 oz/¾ cup granulated sugar
1 egg white, stiffly whisked
15 ml/1 tbsp caster (superfine) sugar

Thinly peel the rind of the tangerines with a potato peeler and place in a saucepan with the water. Bring to the boil and add the granulated sugar. Stir until the sugar has dissolved and boil for 5 minutes. Remove from the heat and set aside to cool. Squeeze the juice from the tangerines and strain into the cool syrup. Beat in the egg white and pour into a freezerproof container. Place in the freezer for 1 hour. Remove from the freezer and whisk with a fork until well blended. Return to the freezer and freeze for 3 hours, whisking every 45 minutes.

Pesche con Crema

Peaches 'n' Cream
Serves 4

450 ml/¾ pt/2 cups single (light) cream
4 egg yolks
150 g/5 oz/⅔ cup caster (superfine) sugar
2 large peaches, skinned, halved, stoned (pitted) and chopped
30 ml/2 tbsp peach liqueur

Place the cream in a saucepan and gently heat until it reaches boiling point. Remove from the heat. Whisk the egg yolks and sugar in a bowl over hot water until the mixture thickens. Whisk in the hot cream. Place the bowl over the simmering water and whisk for 5 minutes, until the custard thickens and coats the back of a spoon. Cool by standing the bowl into cold water, stirring to prevent a skin from forming. Place the chopped peaches in a bowl, add the peach liqueur and stir in the custard. Pour the mixture into a rigid freezerproof container. Cover and freeze for 1 hour. Break up the ice crystals and whisk with a fork until smooth. Return to the freezer for 45 minutes and whisk again. Freeze until firm. Remove from the freezer 10 minutes before serving.

Gelato alla Fragola

Strawberry Ice Cream
Serves 6–8

450 ml/¾ pt/2 cups milk
1 vanilla pod
5 egg yolks
50 g/2 oz/¼ cup caster (superfine) sugar
350 g/12 oz strawberries, hulled
Juice of ½ lemon
750 g/1¼ pts/3 cups double (heavy) cream

Bring the milk and vanilla pod to the boil. Whisk the egg yolks and sugar together in a bowl until pale and creamy and pour on the milk. Whisk for 1 minute. Place the mixture in a clean saucepan and stir over a low heat until the custard thickens and coats the back of the spoon. Do not allow to boil. Leave to cool. Purée the strawberries and lemon juice in a blender or food processor and pass through a sieve (strainer) to remove the small strawberry pips. Blend the strawberries, cream and custard together and place in a container in the freezer for 2 hours. Remove from the freezer and whisk with a fork for 1 minute. Refreeze and repeat the process twice more.

Gelato alla Pesca e Noci

Peach and Nut Ice Cream
Serves 4

5 peaches, halved and stoned (pitted)
300 ml/½ pt/1¼ cups water
45 ml/3 tbsp caster (superfine) sugar
5 ml/1 tsp lemon juice
300 ml/½ pt/1¼ cups single (light) cream
50 g/2 oz/½ cup almonds, chopped

Place the peach halves in a saucepan and pour in the water. Bring slowly to the boil and stir in the sugar and lemon juice. Cook until the peaches are soft then remove from the pan. Mash, or blend in a food processor. Stir in the cream and nuts. Turn into a freezerproof container. Freeze for 1 hour and whisk with a fork to break up the ice crystals. Freeze again for 2 hours and whisk again. Freeze until firm.

Gelato di Pistacchio

Pistachio Ice Cream
Serves 6

300 ml/½ pt/1¼ cups milk
4 egg yolks
100 g/4 oz/½ cup caster (superfine) sugar
1.5 ml/¼ tsp vanilla essence (extract)
300 ml/½ pt/1¼ cups single (light) cream
100 g/4 oz/1 cup pistachio nuts, chopped

Place the milk in a saucepan and bring to boiling point. Remove from the heat. Whisk the egg yolks and sugar together in a bowl until pale and creamy and whisk in the hot milk and vanilla essence. Place the bowl over a pan of simmering water and whisk for 5 minutes. When the custard thickens and lightly coats the back of a wooden spoon, remove from the heat. Cool, stirring to prevent a skin forming. Blend in the cream and pour into a rigid freezerproof container, cover and freeze for 1 hour. Break up the ice crystals with a fork and whisk for 1 minute. Return the mixture to the freezer for a further 45 minutes, then whisk again. Fold in the pistachio nuts. Freeze until firm. Remove from the freezer 10 minutes before serving.

Gelato di Pistacchio con Albicocce

Pistachio Ice Cream with Apricots
Serves 6

4 apricots, halved, stoned (pitted) and
**   chopped**
100 g/4 oz/½ cup granulated sugar
15 ml/1 tbsp water
450 g/1 lb Pistachio Ice Cream (see
**   above)**
150 ml/¼ pt/⅔ cup double (heavy) cream
1 egg white

Place a bombe mould (mold) in the freezer while preparing the ice cream. Put the chopped apricots in a saucepan with the sugar and water and cook gently, stirring, for 8–10 minutes until the apricots are soft and the sugar has dissolved. Using a spoon spread the ice cream around the inside of the mould to form a thick lining and replace in the freezer. Whip the cream and whisk the egg white until stiff. Mix together. Fold the fruit into the egg white and cream mixture. Fill the centre of the mould, cover with a layer of pistachio ice cream and replace in the freezer for 3–4 hours or until firm. When ready to serve, dip the mould in hot water for 1 second and turn out on to a plate. Cut into six segments and serve immediately.

Condiments

Sauces are used extensively in Italian cookery, to enhance the flavours of everything from meat, fish, pasta or risotto to salads, ice creams and desserts. Whether a fragrant Pesto or a sweet, sumptuous Amaretto cream, they will bring delight to your tastebuds and style to your cooking.

Sauces

Sugo di Carne

Meat Sauce

Serves 4

75 g/3 oz/⅓ cup unsalted (sweet) butter
1 large onion, finely chopped
1 celery stick, chopped
2 garlic cloves, minced
2 carrots, chopped
450 g/1 lb minced (ground) beef or lamb
4 large tomatoes, skinned, seeded and chopped
15 ml/1 tbsp chopped fresh thyme
60 ml/4 tbsp red wine
120 ml/4 fl oz/½ cup beef or lamb stock
Salt and freshly ground black pepper

Melt the butter in a saucepan and fry (sauté) the onion for 2 minutes. Stir in the celery, garlic and carrots. Cook for 5 minutes. Add the beef and cook stirring until browned and all the grains are separate. Add the tomatoes, thyme, wine and stock and reduce the heat. Simmer gently for 40 minutes. Season well with the salt and pepper and serve hot over pasta.

Salsa di Fegatini di Pollo

Chicken Liver Sauce

Serves 4

15 ml/1 tbsp olive oil
225 g/8 oz/2 cups chicken livers, chopped
2 large onions, chopped
1 garlic clove, crushed
75 g/3 oz salami, chopped
45 ml/3 tbsp white wine
400 g/14 oz/1 large can chopped tomatoes
150 ml/¼ pt/⅔ cup chicken stock
Salt and freshly ground black pepper
15 ml/1 tbsp chopped fresh rosemary

Heat the olive oil in a pan and fry (sauté) the livers until golden brown. Remove from the pan and add the onions. Fry for 4 minutes, stirring and add the garlic. Continue to cook for 1 minute. Stir in the chopped salami and the remaining ingredients. Simmer for 15 minutes and return the chicken livers to the pan. Cook for a further 2–3 minutes, adjust the seasoning and serve with pasta.

Salsa Besciamella

Basic White Sauce
Serves 4

40 g/1½ oz/3 tbsp unsalted (sweet)
  butter
25 g/1 oz/¼ cup plain (all-purpose)
  flour
300 ml/½ pt/1¼ cups milk
1 bay leaf
Salt and freshly ground black pepper

Melt the butter in a saucepan. Blend in the flour. Heat the milk and add it to the flour a little at a time, stirring well. Add the seasoning and bring to the boil, stirring all the time, until the mixture thickens. Simmer for 2 minutes. Discard the bay leaf before use.

Salsa di Basilico

Basil Sauce
Serves 4–6

150 ml/¼ pt/⅔ cup fish or chicken
  stock
250 ml/8 fl oz/1 cup double (heavy)
  cream
30 ml/2 tbsp fresh lemon juice
90 ml/6 tbsp chopped fresh basil
Salt and freshly ground black pepper

Combine the fish or chicken stock (depending on what you are serving the sauce with) and cream in a saucepan and cook for 10 minutes over a gentle heat until the liquid is reduced by half. Stir in the lemon juice and basil. Season with the salt and pepper. Serve with any seafood or chicken.

Salsa al Burro

Butter Sauce
Serves 4

60 ml/4 tbsp white wine
1 small onion, finely chopped
1 sprig of parsley, finely chopped
100 g/4 oz/½ cup unsalted (sweet)
  butter
Freshly ground black pepper

Heat the wine in a saucepan and add the onion and parsley. Simmer for 10 minutes. Cream the butter and gradually whisk it in to the mixture a bit at a time, until creamy. Do not allow the butter to burn. Season with the pepper. Serve with pasta, risotto or over grilled (broiled) fish or chicken.

Salsa di Pomodoro Densa

Chunky Tomato Sauce
Serves 4

3 tomatoes
50 g/2 oz/1 small can anchovies,
  drained
5 ml/1 tsp capers
5 ml/1 tsp olive oil
2 garlic cloves, crushed

Put the tomatoes in a large bowl of boiling water for 1 minute. Drain and remove the skins. Chop the tomatoes roughly and place in a saucepan. Pound the anchovies or chop finely and add to the tomatoes. Chop the capers and stir into the tomatoes with the olive oil and crushed garlic. Bring to the boil and simmer for 2–3 minutes until the liquid has reduced a little. Serve with pasta.

Salsa Napoli

Napoli Sauce

Serves 4

45 ml/3 tbsp olive oil
2 garlic cloves, crushed
15 ml/1 tbsp chopped fresh rosemary
4 tomatoes, skinned, seeded and
    chopped
15 ml/1 tbsp savory or thyme, chopped
45 ml/3 tbsp lime juice
Salt and freshly ground black pepper

Heat the oil in a saucepan and cook the
garlic, rosemary and tomatoes for 10 minutes until the liquid has reduced to a thick
sauce. Add the savory and lime juice and
purée in a blender if desired. Season to
taste with the salt and pepper. Serve with
pasta, fish or chicken.

Salsa di Pomodoro

Tomato Sauce

Serves 4

30 ml/2 tbsp olive oil
1 onion, chopped
1 garlic clove, chopped
3 large tomatoes, peeled, seeded and
    chopped
60 ml/4 tbsp dry white wine
15 ml/1 tbsp mustard
15 ml/1 tbsp fresh oregano, chopped
30 ml/2 tbsp chopped fresh basil
Salt and freshly ground black pepper

Heat the oil in a saucepan and fry (sauté)
the onion and garlic. Stir in the tomatoes
and white wine. Bring to the boil, lower
the heat and simmer for 10 minutes. Add
the mustard, oregano and basil and season
with the salt and pepper. Cook for a further
10 minutes until the sauce thickens.

Salsa di Pomodoro di Capperi

Caper and Tomato Sauce

Serves 4

30 ml/2 tbsp olive oil
1 onion, chopped
1 garlic clove, chopped
3 large tomatoes, skinned, seeded and
    chopped
60 ml/4 tbsp dry white wine
15 ml/1 tbsp made mustard
15 ml/1 tbsp capers, chopped
30 ml/2 tbsp chopped fresh basil
Salt and freshly ground black pepper

Heat the oil in a saucepan and fry (sauté)
the onion and garlic. Stir in the tomatoes
and white wine. Bring to the boil, reduce
the heat and simmer for 10 minutes. Add
the mustard, capers and basil and season
with the salt and pepper. Cook for a further
10 minutes until the sauce thickens. Serve
with meat, fish, pasta or risotto.

Salsa di Pomodoro e Ricotta

Tomato and Ricotta Sauce
Serves 6

450 g/1 lb/2 cups Ricotta cheese
60 ml/4 tbsp cold chicken or vegetable
stock
30 ml/2 tbsp Parmesan cheese, grated
30 ml/2 tbsp chopped fresh basil
5 large tomatoes, skinned, seeded and
chopped
Freshly ground black pepper

Blend the Ricotta cheese, stock and Parmesan cheese together in a bowl until smooth. Stir in the basil and tomatoes. Season well with the pepper and serve with cold chicken or pasta.

Salsa di Pomodoro Classico

Classic Tomato Sauce for Pasta
Serves 4

15 ml/1 tbsp olive oil
1 large onion, chopped
2 garlic cloves, crushed
8 large, ripe tomatoes, skinned, seeded
and chopped
Salt and freshly ground black pepper

Heat the oil in a large frying pan (skillet). Add the onion and sauté until soft for about 3–4 minutes. Add the garlic and cook for a further 2 minutes. Reduce the heat and stir in the tomatoes. Simmer for 10 minutes. Season well with salt and pepper and serve with pasta.

Salsa di Pomodoro con Panna

Tomato Sauce with Cream
Serves 4

75 g/3 oz/¹⁄₃ cup unsalted (sweet) butter
1 onion, chopped
2 large tomatoes, skinned, seeded and
chopped
60 ml/4 tbsp red wine
15 ml/1 tbsp chopped fresh basil
Salt and freshly ground black pepper
60 ml/4 tbsp double (heavy) cream

Heat half the butter in a saucepan and fry (sauté) the onion for 2 minutes. Stir in the tomatoes and red wine. Bring to the boil, reduce the heat and simmer for 10 minutes until the sauce is pulpy. Add the basil and season with the salt and pepper. Cook for a further 10 minutes. Remove from the heat and allow to cool for 5 minutes. Stir in the remaining butter, stirring until all the butter has been incorporated. Mix in the cream. Reheat but do not boil. Serve with chicken, veal or pasta.

Appetitosa Crema di Mascarpone

Savoury Mascarpone Cream
Serves 4

100 g/4 oz/1/2 cup Mascarpone cheese
15 ml/1 tbsp chopped fresh basil
15 ml/1 tbsp chopped fresh parsley
60 ml/4 tbsp olive oil

Place the Mascarpone cheese in a bowl and gradually blend in the remaining ingredients. Serve over pasta or as a salad dressing.

Salsetta di Limone e Menta

Lemon Mint Sauce
Serves 4

75 ml/5 tbsp chopped fresh mint
15 ml/1 tbsp chopped fresh basil
45 ml/3 tbsp grated lemon rind
250 ml/8 fl oz/1 cup Basic White Sauce
(see page 357)
60 ml/4 tbsp lemon juice

Beat the mint, basil and lemon rind into
the basic white sauce and heat through.
Gradually stir in the lemon juice and serve
hot or cold with lamb, chicken or fish.

Salsa Calda di Mente

Warm Mint Sauce
Serves 4

2 garlic cloves, minced
60 ml/4 tbsp chopped fresh parsley
75 ml/5 tbsp chopped fresh mint
250 ml/8 fl oz/1 cup Basic White Sauce
(see page 357)
Freshly ground black pepper

Beat the garlic, parsley and mint into the
white sauce and heat before serving.
Season with the pepper. Serve with any
white meat or fish.

Salmoriglio

Lemon Sauce
Serves 4

10 ml/2 tsp chopped fresh basil
45 ml/3 tbsp grated lemon rind
45 ml/3 tbsp lemon juice
5 ml/1 tsp cornflour (cornstarch)
250 ml/8 fl oz/1 cup water

Put the basil and lemon rind into a
saucepan with the lemon juice and heat for
1 minute. Blend the cornflour in a little of
the water and add to the saucepan with the
remaining water. Bring to the boil, stirring,
lower the heat and continue cooking until
the sauce thickens.

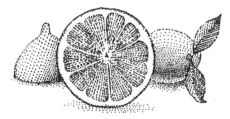

Salsa con Gli Odori

Herb Sauce
Serves 4

40 g/1½ oz/3 tbsp unsalted (sweet)
butter
2 large shallots, finely chopped
50 g/2 oz mushrooms, finely chopped
30 ml/2 tbsp plain (all-purpose) flour
250 ml/8 fl oz/1 cup chicken stock
120 ml/4 fl oz/½ cup white wine
30 ml/2 tbsp chopped fresh tarragon
15 ml/1 tbsp snipped fresh chives
15 ml/1 tbsp chopped fresh basil
30 ml/2 tbsp chopped fresh parsley
Salt and freshly ground black pepper

Melt the butter in a saucepan and stir in the
shallots and mushrooms. Cook for 5 minutes until tender. Whisk in the flour. Add
the stock and stir until smooth. Simmer
over a low heat until the sauce thickens.
Add the wine and herbs and simmer for 5
minutes. Season with the salt and pepper
and serve with white meat or fish.

Salsa Vellutata di Aglio

Creamy Garlic Sauce
Serves 4

25 g/1 oz//2 tbsp unsalted (sweet)
butter
3 garlic cloves, crushed
30 ml/2 tbsp plain (all-purpose) flour
120 ml/4 fl oz/½ cup chicken stock
30 ml/2 tbsp dry white wine
1 large egg yolk, beaten
30 ml/2 tbsp lemon juice
60 ml/4 tbsp double (heavy) cream,
whipped until stiff
Salt and freshly ground black pepper

Melt the butter in a saucepan and add the garlic. Cook for 2 minutes and stir in the flour. Blend in the stock and wine and cook for 5 minutes until thick. Whisk half of the hot sauce into the egg yolk and stir back into the sauce. Add the lemon juice and fold in the cream. Season with the salt and pepper and serve hot with pasta.

Salsa di Melanzane e Funghi

Aubergine and Mushroom Sauce
Serves 4

15 g/½ oz/1 tbsp unsalted (sweet)
butter
30 ml/2 tbsp olive oil
1 large onion, chopped
1 large aubergine (eggplant), diced
100 g/4 oz mushrooms, cut into large
pieces
4 tomatoes, skinned, seeded and
chopped
15 ml/1 tbsp chopped fresh sage
15 ml/1 tbsp chopped fresh oregano
Salt and freshly ground black pepper

Heat the butter and oil and fry (sauté) the onion for 5 minutes. Stir in the aubergine and mushrooms. Cook for 4 minutes and stir in the tomatoes. Add the sage and oregano and season. Simmer gently for 20 minutes, stirring occasionally. Serve with chops, steak or pasta.

Salsa di Parmigiano

Parmesan Sauce
Serves 4

15 g/½ oz/1 tbsp unsalted (sweet)
butter
25 g/1 oz/¼ cup plain (all-purpose)
flour
450 ml/¾ pt/2 cups milk
50 g/2 oz/½ cup Parmesan cheese,
grated
Salt and freshly ground black pepper

Melt the butter in a saucepan and stir in the flour. Cook for 30 seconds and blend in the milk, a little at a time. Bring to the boil, stirring and simmer until the sauce thickens. Stir in the cheese. Remove from the heat and season to taste. Serve with pasta, fish or meat.

Salsa di Prosciutto e Mandorle

Ham and Almond Sauce

Serves 4

25 g/1 oz/2 tbsp unsalted (sweet) butter
100 g/4 oz boiled ham, diced
15 ml/1 tbsp groundnut (peanut) oil
5 ml/1 tsp made mustard
15 ml/1 tbsp chopped fresh thyme
100 g/4 oz/1 cup toasted almonds,
  chopped
120 ml/4 fl oz/½ cup double (heavy)
  cream
Salt and freshly ground black pepper

Heat the butter in a saucepan and fry (sauté) the ham for 2 minutes. Stir in the nut oil and mustard. Cook for 2 minutes, stirring all the time. Stir in the thyme, chopped almonds, salt and pepper. Blend in the cream. Reheat and serve hot with pasta.

Salsa Vellutata di Finocchio

Cream of Fennel Sauce

Serves 4

25 g/1 oz/2 tbsp unsalted (sweet) butter
30 ml/2 tbsp plain (all-purpose) flour
250 ml/8 fl oz/1 cup single (light) cream
30 ml/2 tbsp chicken or vegetable
  stock
45 ml/3 tbsp chopped fennel leaves
Salt and freshly ground black pepper

Melt the butter and stir in the flour. Gradually stir in the cream and blend to a smooth paste. Cook gently for 2 minutes and stir in the stock, fennel leaves, salt and pepper. Cook, stirring, for 1 minute. Serve warm with fish.

Salsa al Burro con Pistacchio

Pistachio Butter Sauce

Serves 4

75 g/3 oz/⅓ cup unsalted (sweet) butter
3 spring onions (scallions), chopped
90 ml/6 tbsp dry white wine
5 ml/1 tsp lemon juice
120 ml/4 fl oz/½ cup chicken or
  vegetable stock
50 g/2 oz/½ cup pistachios, chopped
Salt and freshly ground black pepper

Melt 25 g/1 oz/2 tbsp of the butter in a saucepan over a moderate heat. Add the spring onions and cook for 2 minutes. Stir in the wine, lemon juice and stock and boil for 5 minutes until the liquid has reduced by half. Reduce the heat and whisk in the remaining butter until the sauce is smooth and creamy. Do not let the butter overheat. Stir in the pistachios and season with the salt and pepper. Serve with pasta.

Salsa di Acetoselle

Sorrel Sauce

Serves 4

225 g/8 oz sorrel leaves, washed
100 g/4 oz/½ cup sugar
150 ml/¼ pt/⅔ cup white wine vinegar
25 g/1 oz/2 tbsp unsalted (sweet) butter

Cook the sorrel leaves in as little water as possible for 8–10 minutes until soft. Stir in the sugar and white wine vinegar. Place in a blender and purée for 1 minute. Add the butter and purée again. Serve with fish or chicken.

Salsa di Funghi

Mushroom Sauce

Serves 4

30 ml/2 tbsp lemon juice
1 garlic clove, crushed
15 ml/1 tbsp chopped fresh parsley
150 ml/¼ pt/⅔ cup chicken stock
4 mushrooms, roughly chopped
25 g/1 oz/2 tbsp unsalted (sweet) butter
15 ml/1 tbsp cornflour (cornstarch)
60 ml/4 tbsp tomato purée (paste)

Put the lemon juice into a saucepan and add the crushed garlic, parsley and stock. Boil rapidly for 5 minutes. Add the mushrooms. Continue cooking for 5 minutes, reducing the heat for the last 2 minutes. Purée the sauce in a blender or food processor or rub the sauce through a sieve (strainer) into a bowl. Melt the butter, add the cornflour and add the sauce, stirring all the time until the sauce thickens. Remove from the heat and stir in the tomato purée. Serve at once.

Salsa di Funghi e Noci

Mushroom and Hazelnut Sauce

Serves 4

45 ml/3 tbsp unsalted (sweet) butter
15 ml/1 tbsp minced (ground) onion
6 large mushrooms, thinly sliced
30 ml/2 tbsp plain (all-purpose) flour
350 ml/12 fl oz/1½ cups chicken or
*   vegetable stock*
15 ml/1 tbsp made mustard
100 g/4 oz/1 cup toasted hazelnuts,
*   chopped*
Salt and freshly ground black pepper

Heat the butter in a saucepan and fry (sauté) the onion and mushrooms for 5 minutes. Stir in the flour and blend in the stock. Cook for 2 minutes, stirring all the time. Add the mustard and cook until the mixture thickens. Stir in the chopped hazelnuts and season to taste with salt and pepper. Serve with pasta, chicken or risotto.

Salsa Siciliana

Sicilian Sauce

Serves 4–6

30 ml/2 tbsp olive oil
5 garlic cloves, minced (ground)
½ onion, minced (ground)
1 small aubergine (eggplant), peeled
*   and chopped*
6 tomatoes, skinned, seeded and
*   chopped*
175 ml/6 fl oz/¾ cup passata (sieved
*   tomatoes)*
60 ml/4 tbsp red wine
30 ml/2 tbsp chopped fresh oregano
30 ml/2 tbsp chopped fresh basil
15 ml/1 tbsp chopped fresh tarragon
Salt and freshly ground black pepper

Heat the oil in a saucepan and gently fry (sauté) the garlic, onion and aubergine for 20 minutes. Stir in the remaining ingredients and simmer over a gentle heat for 25 minutes.

Salsa per Pasta Pronto

Quick Pasta Sauce

Serves 4

45 ml/3 tbsp olive oil
½ small onion, finely chopped
½ green (bell) pepper, chopped
2 garlic cloves, crushed
4 large tomatoes, skinned, seeded and
  chopped
30 ml/2 tbsp chopped fresh oregano
Freshly ground black pepper

Heat the oil in a saucepan and fry (sauté) the onion, pepper and garlic for 3–4 minutes. Stir in the tomatoes and oregano and season with the pepper.

Salsa di Dragonella

Tarragon Cream Sauce

Makes 475 ml/16 fl oz/2 cups

45 ml/3 tbsp unsalted (sweet) butter
15 ml/1 tbsp finely chopped onion
2 garlic cloves, crushed
15 ml/1 tbsp plain (all-purpose) flour
350 ml/12 fl oz/1¼ cups chicken stock
30 ml/2 tbsp lemon juice
15 ml/1 tbsp chopped fresh thyme
45 ml/3 tbsp chopped fresh tarragon
45 ml/3 tbsp double (heavy) cream

Heat the butter in a saucepan and fry (sauté) the onion and garlic for 2 minutes. Stir in the flour and cook for 2 minutes, stirring all the time. Add the stock and cook for 5 minutes until the mixture thickens. Reduce the heat and stir in the lemon juice, herbs and cream. Heat through and serve with fish, chicken or veal.

Salsa di Funghi Secchi

Dried Mushroom Sauce

Serves 4

45 ml/3 tbsp dried mushrooms
300 ml/½ pt/1¼ cups warm water
15 g/½ oz/1 tbsp unsalted (sweet) butter
15 ml/1 tbsp oil
3 bacon rashers (slices), rinded and
  chopped
1 large onion, chopped
15 ml/1 tbsp tomato purée (paste)
Salt and freshly ground black pepper

Soak the dried mushrooms for 30 minutes in the warm water. Heat the butter and oil in a saucepan. Stir in the bacon and fry (sauté) for 1 minute. Add the onion, cook until the onion is browned. Stir in the mushrooms with their liquid. Blend in the tomato purée and simmer for 30 minutes. Season with the salt and pepper and serve very hot with meat or pasta.

Salsa di Tonno

Tuna Sauce

Serves 4

185 g/6½ oz/1 small can tuna in oil,
  drained
4 anchovy fillets
10 ml/2 tsp capers
45 ml/3 tbsp lemon juice
45 ml/3 tbsp olive oil
15 ml/1 tbsp chopped fresh parsley
15 ml/1 tbsp chopped fresh tarragon
Salt and freshly ground black pepper

Place the tuna, anchovy fillets, capers, lemon juice and olive oil in a food processor and process until smooth. Stir in the parsley and tarragon and season with the salt and pepper to taste. Serve on cold, roasted veal.

Salsa Piccante Cinese

Piquant Chinese Sauce
Serves 4

15 ml/1 tbsp cornflour (cornstarch)
5 ml/1 tsp soy sauce
5 ml/1 tsp finely chopped fresh root
* ginger*
225 g/8 oz/1 small can chopped
* pineapple*
30 ml/2 tbsp brown sugar
45 ml/3 tbsp wine vinegar
2 celery sticks, finely chopped

Blend the cornflour with the soy sauce. Put the chopped ginger and the crushed pineapple into a saucepan and heat until almost boiling. Stir in the sugar, vinegar and chopped celery. Gradually mix in the blended cornflour and cook, stirring all the time until the sauce thickens. Pour over meatballs or chicken and serve at once.

Marinata di Aglio e Odori

Garlic and Herb Marinade
Serves 4

1 onion, very finely chopped
30 ml/2 tbsp lemon juice
60 ml/4 tbsp sesame oil
15 ml/1 tbsp chopped fresh chervil
2 garlic cloves, crushed
30 ml/2 tbsp clear honey
30 ml/2 tbsp chopped fresh parsley
10 ml/2 tsp chopped fresh thyme

Blend all the ingredients together and use for marinating chicken or beef.

Salsa Saporita alla Nocciola

Hazelnut Savoury Sauce
Serves 4

90 ml/6 tbsp breadcrumbs
15 ml/1 tbsp water
225 g/8 oz/2 cups ground hazelnuts
60 ml/4 tbsp olive oil
2 garlic cloves, crushed
2.5 ml/½ tsp cayenne
Salt
60 ml/4 tbsp red wine
120 ml/4 fl oz/½ cup chicken or
* vegetable stock*

Place the breadcrumbs in a bowl and sprinkle over the water. Add the hazelnuts and gradually beat in the olive oil. Stir in the garlic, cayenne, salt, wine and stock. Cover the bowl and chill until ready to serve over roast meats.

Marinata al Limone

Lemon Marinade
Serves 4

45 ml/3 tbsp olive oil
1 small onion, finely chopped
1 garlic clove, minced
30 ml/2 tbsp chopped fresh rosemary
Freshly ground black pepper
Rind and juice of 1 lemon
15 ml/1 tbsp dark brown sugar

Mix all the ingredients together and use for marinating fish or poultry.

Salsa di Noci e Basilico

Creamy Walnut and Basil Sauce
Serves 4

225 g/8 oz/2 cups shelled walnuts
1 thick slice white bread, crusts
*   removed*
60 ml/4 tbsp cold milk
1 garlic clove, crushed
Salt and freshly ground black pepper
45 ml/3 tbsp olive oil
60 ml/4 tbsp cream cheese
30 ml/2 tbsp chopped fresh basil

Place the walnuts in a bowl of boiling water for 2 minutes, drain, then dry and rub off the skins. Cover the bread with the milk and leave to soak. Grind the walnuts to a powder in a blender. Squeeze the bread as dry as possible with your hands and blend with the walnuts. Add the garlic, salt, pepper and olive oil. Blend in the cream cheese and basil and spoon into a bowl. Use as a dip for fresh vegetables or over pasta.

Pesto

Pine Nut and Basil Sauce
Serves 4

30 g/1 oz/2 tbsp fresh basil leaves
50 g/2 oz/½ cup pine nuts
30 ml/2 tbsp fresh chopped parsley
1 garlic clove, peeled
30 ml/2 tbsp olive oil
60 ml/4 tbsp Parmesan cheese, grated
Salt and freshly ground black pepper

Place the ingredients in a food processor and blend until smooth. Add the Parmesan cheese. Season to taste with the salt and pepper. Store in a clean screw-topped jar in the fridge.

Pesto Rosso

Red Pesto Sauce
Serves 4–6

2 garlic cloves, chopped
50 g/2 oz/½ cup pine nuts
25 g/1 oz basil leaves
4 sun-dried tomatoes in oil, drained
60 ml/4 tbsp olive oil
60 ml/4 tbsp Parmesan cheese, grated
Salt and freshly ground black pepper

Put the garlic in a food processor or blender with the pine nuts, basil, sun-dried tomatoes and oil. Blend well until smooth. Add the Parmesan cheese. Season to taste with the salt and pepper. Store in a clean screw-topped jar in the fridge.

Rosmarino e Salsa di Lamponi

Rosemary and Raspberry Sauce
Serves 4

275 g/10 oz raspberries
30 ml/2 tbsp water
45 ml/3 tbsp chopped fresh rosemary
45 ml/3 tbsp light brown sugar
15 ml/1 tbsp cornflour (cornstarch)
30 ml/2 tbsp red wine

Place the raspberries in a saucepan. Add the water and simmer for 5 minutes. Add the rosemary and brown sugar and heat for 1 minute. Blend the cornflour with the red wine and pour into the sauce. Cook, stirring for 2 minutes until the sauce thickens.

Pesto con Dragonella

Tarragon Pesto
Serves 4–6

100 g/4 oz/1 cup pine nuts, lightly toasted
2 garlic cloves
100 g/4 oz/1 cup Parmesan cheese, grated
30 ml/2 tbsp Ricotta cheese
5 ml/1 tsp lemon juice
60 ml/4 tbsp chopped fresh tarragon
90 ml/6 tbsp virgin olive oil

Put all the ingredients in a blender or food processor and blend together for 2 minutes. Serve with pasta and fresh bread. The pesto can be stored in the fridge in a clean screw-topped jar.

Sausse di Avije

Sauce of the Honey Bees
Serves 4

12 walnut halves
30 ml/2 tbsp boiling water
1.5 ml/¼ tsp beef extract
20 ml/4 tsp French mustard
100 g/4 oz/⅓ cup clear honey
Freshly ground black pepper

Plunge the walnuts in boiling water for 2 minutes. Drain and rub off the skins. Purée in a blender or food processor or pound with a pestle and mortar. Blend the water and beef extract together and blend into the nuts with the mustard and honey. Season well with pepper and serve with cold meats.

Salsa di Pesce

Fish Sauce
Serves 4

1 garlic clove, crushed
100 ml/3½ fl oz/6½ tbsp olive oil
15 g/½ oz/1 tbsp unsalted (sweet) butter
185 g/6½ oz/1 small can tuna. drained
50 g/2 oz/1 small can anchovies, drained
Juice of ½ lemon
Freshly ground black pepper

Crush the garlic into a saucepan and mix in the olive oil and butter. Heat for 2 minutes. Add the drained tuna fish and mash gently into the oil. Remove from the heat. Mash in the drained anchovies and beat in the lemon juice. Season with the pepper. Spoon over hot pasta and serve at once.

Agliata Piccante

Piquant Garlic Sauce
Serves 4–6

1 thick slice white bread, crusts removed
30 ml/2 tbsp white wine vinegar
4–5 garlic cloves, peeled
150 ml/¼ pt/⅔ cup olive oil
Salt and freshly ground black pepper

Break the bread into pieces and soak in the vinegar. Purée the garlic in a blender or food processor. With the machine running, add the oil a little at a time, stopping and scraping down the sides of the machine every now and then. Drop in the bread a piece at a time, blending all the time until a thin mayonnaise-like consistency is reached. Season well and serve with any type of seafood or as a dip.

Sugo Finto

Fake Meat Sauce for Pasta
Enough for 450 g/1 lb pasta

1 small onion, finely chopped
1 carrot, finely chopped
1 celery stick, finely chopped
45 ml/3 tbsp chopped fresh parsley
75 g/3 oz very fat ham or bacon, very
finely chopped
45 ml/3 tbsp tomato purée (paste)
150 ml/¼ pt/⅔ cup strong beef stock
Salt and freshly ground black pepper

Put the onion, carrot, celery, parsley and fat ham into a saucepan and fry (sauté) over a gentle heat until the fat runs and the onion is translucent, stirring all the time. Add the remaining ingredients and simmer for about 30 minutes, stirring occasionally or until thickened and the fat floats on the surface of the sauce. Add to cooked pasta, toss and serve.

Salmoriglio

Oil and Lemon Sauce
Serves 4–6

250 ml/8 fl oz/1 cup virgin olive oil
Grated rind and juice of 2 lemons
15 ml/1 tbsp chopped fresh oregano
1 large garlic clove, crushed
15 ml/1 tbsp chopped fresh parsley
Freshly ground black pepper

Put the oil in a bowl over a pan of gently simmering water. Gradually whisk in the lemon rind and juice, then the oregano, garlic and parsley. Add a good grinding of black pepper and use to brush over fish or meat as it grills (broils) or to serve drizzled over plain cooked meat or fish at the table.

Salsa Alfredo (per Pasta Fresco)

Alfred's Sauce for Fresh Pasta
Serves 4

350 g/12 oz any fresh pasta
450 ml/¾ pt/2 cups double (heavy)
cream
50 g/2 oz/¼ cup unsalted (sweet) butter
175 g/6 oz/1½ cups Parmesan cheese,
freshly grated
Freshly ground black pepper
A little crisp, crumbled pancetta or
streaky bacon (optional)

Cook the fresh pasta (see page 196 or according to packet directions). Drain. Meanwhile bring the cream and butter to the boil in a saucepan. Reduce the heat and simmer for 1 minute. Add half the cheese and some pepper and whisk until smooth. Add to the pasta with the remaining cheese and toss over a gentle heat. Pile on to warm plates add a good grinding of black pepper and serve topped with crumbled pancetta or streaky bacon, if liked.

Tocco di Noci

Ligurian Walnut Sauce
Serves 4

225 g/8 oz/2 cups walnut pieces
Thick slice of white bread, crusts
*   removed*
75 ml/5 tbsp milk
1 garlic clove, crushed
Salt and freshly ground black pepper
45 ml/3 tbsp olive oil
100 g/4 oz/½ cup Mascarpone cheese

Place the nuts in boiling water for 2 minutes. Drain and rub off the skins in a clean tea towel (dish cloth). Soak the bread in the milk. Grind the nuts to a fine powder in a blender or food processor. Squeeze out the bread and add to the nuts with the garlic and a little salt and pepper. Run the machine until the mixture is smooth. With the machine running, add the oil in a thin stream and then finally add the cheese. Add to any cooked pasta, toss and serve.

Mascarpone al Cioccolato

Chocolate Mascarpone Cream
Serves 4

150 ml/¼ pt/⅔ cup Mascarpone cheese
15 ml/1 tbsp cocoa (unsweetened
*   chocolate) powder*
15 ml/1 tbsp icing (confectioners')
*   sugar*

Beat the cheese until smooth. Stir in the cocoa powder and sifted icing sugar and beat again. Use in place of clotted cream or over hot sweet dishes.

Salsa Fresca di Albicocche

Fresh Apricot Sauce
Serves 4

250 ml/8 fl oz/1 cup water
450 g/1 lb fresh apricots, halved and
*   stoned (pitted)*
100 g/4 oz/½ cup brown sugar
30 ml/2 tbsp lemon juice
5 ml/1 tsp finely grated lemon rind
2.5 ml/½ tsp vanilla essence (extract)

Bring the water, apricots and sugar to the boil in a saucepan. Reduce the heat and simmer for 12 minutes. Allow the mixture to cool for 2 minutes and purée in a blender or food processor. Allow the sauce to cool completely before beating in the lemon juice, zest and vanilla essence. Serve with sweet pies or ice cream.

Salsa Amaretto

Amaretto Sauce
Serves 4

50 g/2 oz/¼ cup unsalted (sweet) butter
50 g/2 oz/½ cup ground almonds
50 g/2 oz/¼ cup brown sugar
60 ml/4 tbsp double (heavy) cream
60 ml/4 tbsp Amaretto liqueur

Melt the butter in a saucepan and add the ground almonds. Cook for 4 minutes until they are golden brown. Stir in the sugar and cream. Simmer over a low heat for 8 minutes, stirring two or three times. Stir in the amaretto. Heat through and serve with ice cream or a sweet soufflé.

Salsa Semplice di Limone

Simple Lemon Sauce
Serves 4

50 g/2 oz/¼ cup sugar
30 ml/2 tbsp cornflour (cornstarch)
250 ml/8 fl oz/1 cup water
60 ml/4 tbsp lemon juice
30 ml/2 tbsp grated lemon rind
25 g/1 oz/2 tbsp unsalted (sweet) butter

Place the sugar, cornflour and water in a saucepan and simmer over a low heat for 3 minutes. Stir in the lemon juice and rind and simmer for a further 3 minutes. Remove the pan from the heat and beat in the butter. Serve immediately over fruit desserts and tarts.

Salsa Dolce di Ciliege

Sweet Cherry Sauce
Serves 4

50 g/2 oz/¼ cup unsalted (sweet) butter
150 g/5 oz sweet cherries, stoned (pitted)
50 g/2 oz/¼ cup brown sugar
60 ml/4 tbsp double (heavy) cream
30 ml/2 tbsp Amaretto liqueur

Melt the butter in a saucepan and add the cherries. Cook for 4–5 minutes until they are soft and pulpy. Stir in the sugar and cream. Simmer over a low heat for 8 minutes, stirring two or three times. Stir in the Amaretto. Heat through and serve with ice cream or a sweet soufflé.

Salsa di Pesche

Peach Sauce
Serves 4

4 large peaches, skinned, stoned (pitted) and chopped
30 ml/2 tbsp water
45 ml/3 tbsp golden (light corn) syrup
45 ml/3 tbsp sugar
15 ml/1 tbsp cornflour (cornstarch)
30 ml/2 tbsp rum or brandy

Place the peaches in a saucepan. Add the water and simmer for 5 minutes. Purée in a blender or food processor and return to the saucepan. Add the syrup and sugar and heat until dissolved. Stir in the cornflour and bring to the boil over a high heat. Remove the saucepan from the heat and stir in the rum or brandy. Serve hot over ice cream.

Appetitosa Salsetta di Ciliege

Tasty Cherry Sauce
Serves 4–6

450 g/1 lb sweet cherries, stoned (pitted)
30 ml/2 tbsp sugar
30 ml/2 tbsp lemon juice
75 ml/5 tbsp white wine
1.5 ml/¼ tsp grated nutmeg
2.5 ml/½ tsp cayenne

Put the cherries, sugar, lemon juice and wine in a large saucepan. Simmer for 10 minutes. Allow the mixture to cool for 1 minute and transfer to a food processor or blender. Purée for 1 minute. Return to the saucepan and stir in the nutmeg and cayenne. Cook over a low heat for 2 minutes. Serve with duck or pork.

Budino di Crema alla Mandorla

Frangipane Custard
Serves 4–6

300 ml/½ pt/1¼ cups milk
1 vanilla pod
2 whole eggs plus 2 egg yolks
100 g/4 oz/½ cup caster (superfine) sugar
30 ml/2 tbsp plain (all-purpose) flour
40 g/1½ oz/3 tbsp butter
75 g/3 oz/¾ cup ground almonds
2.5 ml/½ tsp almond essence (extract)

Heat the milk to almost boiling point with the vanilla pod. Remove from the heat and set aside to cool. Beat the eggs, egg yolks and sugar together for 5 minutes until the mixture is pale and thick. Stir in the flour. Remove the vanilla pod from the milk and gently pour on to the egg mixture, gently stirring constantly. Pour the mixture back into the saucepan. Place over a low heat and bring the mixture to the boil and cook for 2 minutes, stirring all the time. Remove the pan from the heat and beat until smooth. Beat in the butter, ground almonds and the almond essence. The custard is now ready to use.

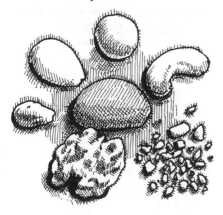

Crema Pasticcera

Egg Custard
Makes 600 ml/1 pt/2½ cups

450 ml/¾ pt/2 cups milk
5 ml/1 tsp vanilla essence (extract)
100 g/4 oz/½ cup caster (superfine) sugar
5 egg yolks
15 ml/1 tbsp cornflour (cornstarch)

Reserve 75 ml/5 tbsp of the cold milk. Slowly bring the remaining milk to the boil with the vanilla essence and sugar. Pour the egg yolks into a bowl and whisk with the cornflour until pale yellow and thick. Stir in the reserved cold milk. Pour the hot milk over the egg yolks, stirring continuously. Strain the mixture back into the saucepan and bring back to the boil, stirring all the time. Cook slowly until thickened. Use as required.

Creama

Sweet Cream
Serves 4

150 ml/¼ pt/⅔ cups double (heavy) cream
15 ml/1 tbsp icing (confectioners') sugar
15 ml/1 tbsp Amaretto liqueur
1 egg white

Whip the cream until it is thick but not stiff. Stir in the icing sugar, 5 ml/1 tsp at a time until the required sweetness is obtained. Stir in the liqueur a drop at a time. Whisk the egg white until stiff and fold into the cream.

Crema Inglese

Confectioners' Custard

Makes enough for 1 large tart or 12 small tartlets

15 ml/1 tbsp cornflour (cornstarch)
150 ml/¼ pt/⅔ cup milk
10 ml/2 tsp caster (superfine) sugar
2.5 ml/½ tsp vanilla essence (extract)
2 egg yolks
45 ml/3 tbsp double (heavy) cream, whipped

Blend the cornflour and milk together in a saucepan with the sugar and vanilla essence. Gradually bring to the boil, stirring continuously. Continue cooking until the mixture thickens. Remove from the heat and cool for a few seconds. Stir in the egg yolks and cream and return to the heat for one minute, stirring, but do not allow the mixture to boil.

Condimento Dolce di Lumia

Sweet Lime Dressing

Serves 4

30 ml/2 tbsp plain yoghurt
30 ml/2 tbsp double (heavy) cream
30 ml/2 tbsp fresh lime juice
30 ml/2 tbsp clear honey
5 ml/1 tsp grated fresh ginger
5 ml/1 tsp grated lime rind

Beat together all the ingredients in a small bowl. Chill for several hours and serve cold over fruit salad.

Crema di Limone

Lemon Topping

Serves 4

30 ml/2 tbsp plain yogurt
30 ml/2 tbsp double (heavy) cream
30 ml/2 tbsp lemon juice
15 ml/1 tbsp clear honey
5 ml/1 tsp finely grated lemon rind

Beat all the ingredients together in a small bowl. Chill for several hours and serve with fruit salad.

Crema di Limetta

Lime Topping

Serves 4

30 ml/2 tbsp plain yogurt
30 ml/2 tbsp double (heavy) cream
Rind and juice of 1 small lime
15 ml/1 tbsp clear honey

Beat all the ingredients together in a small bowl. Chill for several hours and serve with fruit salad.

Dressings

Salsa di Acciughe

Anchovy Dressing
Serves 4

50 g/2 oz/1 cup white breadcrumbs
45 ml/3 tbsp white wine
5 sprigs of parsley, chopped
1 sprig of dill (dill weed), chopped
1 garlic clove, crushed
5 anchovy fillets, chopped
60 ml/4 tbsp olive oil
Freshly ground black pepper

Soak the breadcrumbs in the white wine for 10 minutes, then squeeze out the excess moisture with your hands. Purée the crumbs for a few seconds in a blender or food processor. Add the parsley, dill and garlic. Blend for a few seconds and add the anchovy fillets. Process again and add the olive oil a little at a time. Blend until the sauce is thick and creamy. Season with the pepper and serve immediately with pasta, potatoes or a mixed green salad.

Condimento Vellutato all' Italiano

Creamy Italian Dressing
Serves 4

120 ml/4 fl oz/½ cup mayonnaise
60 ml/4 tbsp double (heavy) cream
30 ml/2 tbsp white wine vinegar
1 garlic clove, finely chopped
30 ml/2 tbsp chopped fresh oregano
Salt and freshly ground black pepper

Beat the mayonnaise and cream together and slowly add the vinegar. Stir in the garlic and oregano and season with the salt and pepper. Serve with cooked vegetables

Condimento all' Olio d'Olive

Olive Oil Dressing
Serves 6

1 garlic clove, crushed
150 ml/¼ pt/⅔ cup olive oil
Salt and freshly ground black pepper
15ml/1 tbsp chopped fresh oregano
60 ml/4 tbsp wine vinegar
Salt and freshly ground black pepper

Put all the ingredients in a screw-topped jar and shake vigorously to blend. Use as a dressing for salads.

Aceto di Rose

Rose Vinegar
Serves 4

3 or 4 handfuls of scented rose petals
600 ml/1 pt/2½ cups white wine vinegar
Fill a wide-topped jar with rose petals until it is about two-thirds full. Pour over the vinegar and fill up the jar. The flower petals should be completely covered and will sink down in 2 or 3 days. More petals can then be added if you wish. Leave the jar in the sun while the flowers are soaking, if possible. Allow the vinegar to stand for at least two weeks, strain and rebottle. Use for salad dressings.

Aceto alla Dragonella

Tarragon Vinegar
Serves 4–6

6 sprigs of fresh tarragon
6 peppercorns
600 ml/1 pt/2½ cups white wine
vinegar

Place the sprigs of tarragon and the peppercorns in a sterilised bottle. Bring the white wine vinegar to the boil. Allow to cool for 5 minutes then pour into the bottle. Seal and store in a cool, dark place. Use to enhance salad dressings, sauces and in marinades.

Olio e Odori per Cuocere alla Griglia

Herb Oil for Grilling
Makes 1 litre/1¾ pts/4¼ cups

2.5 ml/½ tsp black peppercorns
5 bay leaves
6 sage leaves
2.5 ml/½ tsp fennel seeds
2.5 ml/½ tsp coriander (cilantro) seeds
2 sprigs of rosemary
4 sprigs of thyme
3 red chillies
Virgin olive oil

Put all the ingredients except the olive oil into a clean, 1 litre/1¾ pt/4¼ cup screw-topped bottle and cover with the olive oil. Firmly screw down the lid and allow to stand for at least one week before using.

Salsa di Pomodoro Alla Svelta

Quick Tomato Sauce
Serves 4

1 large onion, finely chopped
400g/14 oz/1 large can tomatoes
2 garlic cloves, crushed
30 ml/2 tbsp tomato purée (paste)
120 ml/4 fl oz/½ cup vegetable stock
5 ml/1 tsp dried mixed herbs
Salt and freshly ground black pepper

Soften the onion in a little oil then add the remaining ingredients and simmer until soft. Blend in a blender or food processor or press through a sieve (strainer). Reheat and serve at once.

Maionese di Pomodoro Seco

Sun-dried Tomato Mayonnaise
Serves 4

1 egg yolk
45 ml/3 tbsp sun-dried tomato oil
75 g/3 oz sun-dried tomatoes in oil,
chopped
Lemon juice
30 ml/2 tbsp hot water
Salt and freshly ground black pepper

Put the egg yolk in a blender or food processor and process the yolk until creamy. Gradually add the oil from the tomatoes. Add the lemon juice to taste and process until the mixture thickens. Stir in the sun-dried tomatoes and process again. Thin down with the hot water and season to taste. Store for up to a week in a screw-topped jar in the fridge.

Marinata Piccante

Spicy Marinade
Serves 4–6

60 ml/4 tbsp dry white wine
60 ml/4 tbsp white wine vinegar
Salt and freshly ground black pepper
2 garlic cloves, crushed
2.5 ml/½ tsp chopped fresh oregano
2.5 ml/½ tsp whole black peppercorns
5 ml/1 tsp juniper berries
2.5 ml/½ tsp cayenne
30 ml/2 tbsp olive oil

Place the wine, vinegar, salt, pepper and garlic in a saucepan and bring to the boil. Allow to boil for 1 minute and remove from the heat. Stir in the oregano. Lightly crush the peppercorns and juniper berries and add to the marinade with the cayenne and olive oil. This marinade can be stored in the fridge for 2 or 3 days. Use to marinate red or white meat.

Butters

Burro al Basilico e Aglio

Basil and Garlic Butter

Serves 4–6

3 garlic cloves, crushed
100 g/4 oz/½ cup unsalted (sweet)
* butter*
60 ml/4 tbsp chopped fresh basil
5 ml/1 tsp chopped fresh mint
Freshly ground black pepper

Beat together the garlic and butter. Blend in the basil and mint and season well with the pepper. Form into a sausage roll shape and wrap in greaseproof (waxed) paper. Chill until required. Slice and serve with pasta dishes or grilled (broiled) fish and chicken.

Burro agli Odori

Herb Butter

Serves 4

100 g/4 oz/½ cup unsalted (sweet)
* butter*
30 ml/2 tbsp chopped fresh parsley
30 ml/2 tbsp chopped fresh basil
15 ml/1 tbsp chopped fresh dill (dill
* weed)*
5 ml/1 tsp chopped fresh chervil
5 ml/1 tsp chopped fresh tarragon
1 garlic clove, crushed

Cream the butter and gradually blend in the herbs and garlic. Form the mixture into a roll and wrap in greaseproof (waxed) paper. Chill until required. Use with fish and pasta.

Burro alla Dragonella

Tarragon Butter

Serves 4

20 ml/4 tsp finely chopped fresh
* tarragon*
100 g/4 oz/½ cup unsalted (sweet)
* butter, softened*
20 ml/4 tsp lemon juice

Blend the tarragon with the softened butter and gradually add the lemon juice. Serve with steamed vegetables or fish. Any leftover butter can be frozen for future use.

Burro alla Mandorla

Almond Butter

Serves 4

50 g/2 oz/½ cup blanched almonds
100 g/4 oz/½ cup unsalted (sweet)
* butter, softened*
5 ml/1 tsp grated nutmeg

Place the almonds in a blender or food processor and process for a few seconds only to chop the almonds finely. Transfer the almonds to a bowl and add the butter and nutmeg. Blend well together and form the mixture into a cylindrical, sausage shape. Wrap the roll in greaseproof (waxed) paper and chill before use.

Burro all' Acciughe

Anchovy Butter
Serves 4

6 anchovy fillets, chopped
100 g/4 oz/½ cup unsalted (sweet)
  butter
90 ml/6 tbsp sherry or brandy
5 ml/1 tsp lemon juice
15 ml/1 tbsp capers, chopped
5 ml/1 tsp chopped fresh chervil
15 ml/1 tbsp chopped fresh parsley
Freshly ground black pepper

Mash the anchovy fillets into a paste and put into a saucepan with 15 ml/1 tbsp butter. Stir in the sherry or brandy, lemon juice and the capers. Cook for 5 minutes, stirring, until the liquid has been reduced by one third. Allow to cool. Lower the heat and whisk in the remaining butter, a little at a time. Do not allow the sauce to overheat. Remove the saucepan from the heat and stir in the herbs. Season well with the pepper and serve warm with meat or fish.

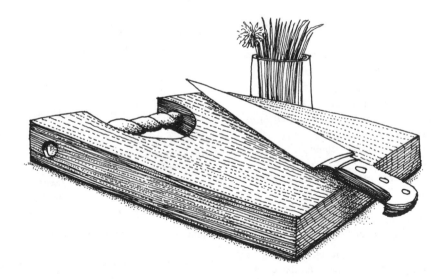

Icings, Fillings and Toppings

Glassa al Maraschino

Maraschino Icing
Makes enough for 1 cake

50 g/2 oz/¼ cup unsalted (sweet) butter
350 g/12 oz/2 cups icing
  (confectioners') sugar, sifted
1 egg
25 g/1 oz/2 tbsp chopped Maraschino
  cherries

Cream the butter and add the icing sugar and the egg. Beat until creamy. Add the cherries and beat again. The icing is now ready to use.

Crema di Caffè

Mocha Butter Icing
Makes enough to fill and
cover 1 large cake

75 g/3 oz/⅓ cup unsalted (sweet) butter
225 g/8 oz/1⅓ cups icing
  (confectioners') sugar
Pinch of salt
2.5 ml/½ tsp vanilla essence (extract)
45 ml/3 tbsp strong coffee
10 ml/2 tsp cocoa (unsweetened
  chocolate) powder
5 ml/¼ tsp instant coffee powder

Place the butter in a bowl and cream with the sugar. Add the salt, vanilla essence, coffee, cocoa and coffee powder. Beat until the icing is smooth and creamy.

Gemadi Cedio Mascarpone

Mascarpone Lime
Makes enough to fill 1 cake

Grated rind and juice of 1 lime
100 g/4 oz/½ cup Mascarpone cheese
Icing (confectioners') sugar, sifted

Gradually blend the lime rind and juice into the Mascarpone cheese. Sweeten to taste with icing sugar and use for fillings or in a cheesecake.

Ripieno di Crema alla Mandorla

Almond Cream Filling
Makes enough for 1 cake

75 g/3 oz/⅓ cup caster (superfine)
  sugar
75 g/3 oz/¾ cup plain (all-purpose)
  flour
1.5 ml/¼ tsp salt
300 ml/½ pt/1¼ cups milk
1 egg, lightly beaten
2.5 ml/½ tsp vanilla essence (extract)
2.5 ml/½ tsp almond essence (extract)
25 g/1 oz/2 tbsp unsalted (sweet) butter

Combine the sugar, flour and salt in the top of a double boiler. Blend in the milk. Place over boiling water and cook for 10 minutes, stirring thoroughly. Add small amounts of the hot mixture to the lightly beaten egg, stirring constantly. Return this mixture to the double boiler and cook for 2 minutes. Add the vanilla essence, almond essence, and butter. The cream is now ready for use.

Crema di Cioccolato

Chocolate Cream Topping
Makes enough for one large cake

100 g/4 oz/½ cup icing (confectioners')
sugar
60 ml/4 tbsp cocoa (unsweetened
chocolate) powder
300 ml/½ pt/1¼ cups whipping cream

Mix the sugar and cocoa together. Whip the cream until stiff and blend with the cocoa mixture. Spoon half of the cream on to one layer of cake, sandwich together and coat the top with the remaining cream.

Salsa di Ciliege

Cherry Topping
Serves 4

30 ml/2 tbsp water
150 g/5 oz sweet cherries, stoned
(pitted)
50 g/2 oz/⅓ cup brown sugar
60 ml/4 tbsp double (heavy) cream

Place the water and cherries in a saucepan and cook for 4–5 minutes until they are soft and pulpy. Stir in the sugar and simmer over a low heat for 8 minutes, stirring two or three times. Stir in the cream. Heat through and serve over ice cream or a sweet soufflé.

Index

Adrano fillet of beef 80
aduki beans
    broccoli with red bean sauce 177
Alfred's sauce for fresh pasta 368
almonds
    almond and chocolate ice cream 351
    almond biscuits 294
    almond butter 376
    almond cake 311
    almond coffee torte 312
    almond cream filling 378
    almond macaroons 285
    almond soup 41
    almond stuffed courgettes 172
    almond tagliatelle 312
    almond tart 332
    almond tea bread 284
    almond trout 147
    courgettes with ginger and almonds 180
    sweet almond biscuits 286
    tuna fish with almonds 169
Amaretto sauce 369
anchovies
    anchovies and garlic 33
    anchovy and tuna pizza 269
    anchovy bakes 59
    anchovy bread 76
    anchovy butter 377
    anchovy dip 34
    anchovy dressing 373
    anchovy mousse 168
    anchovy pizza 281
    anchovy pizza pockets 176
    Bologna cheese 11
    carrots with a spicy sauce 178
    fennel in anchovy sauce 192
    ham and anchovy rolls 72
    olive, anchovy and tomato paste 20
    olive and anchovy paste 35
    pasta with anchovy butter 206
    salad of capers and anchovies 307
    spinach and anchovy pâté 28
    tomato anchovy soup 53
antipasti 9–39
    see also salads; soups
antipasto platter 9
apples
    apple and carrot salad 297
    apple and lemon flan 317
    chicken with apples and lemon sauce 97
    crackled apples 315
    guinea fowl with apple 110
    pork chops with apples 122
    pork with apple and juniper berries 121

apricots
    apricot and fig cordial 338
    apricot cheesecake 313
    apricot ice cream 349
    apricot lamb 112
    apricot loaf 294
    apricot pastry boats 311
    apricot salad 304
    apricot sandwiches 59
    fresh apricot sauce 369
    stuffed apricots with Mascarpone
        and pistachios 337
Arno Valley chicken 92
aromatic angel hair 220
aromatic fennel 174
artichokes
    artichoke and olive pasta 201
    artichoke omelette 74
    artichoke pizza 271
    artichokes in cheese sauce 175
    artichokes in wine 10
    artichokes stuffed with cheese 173
    artichokes with herbs 10
    fricassee of artichokes 15
    Jerusalem artichoke salad 297
    linguini with artichokes 207
Artimino pizza pie 279
asparagus
    asparagus and tomato pie 173
    asparagus casserole 171
    asparagus cream with pasta 200
    asparagus gateaux 175
    asparagus in pastry 73
    asparagus Parmesan-style 9
    asparagus pizza 279
    asparagus with cheese 11
    asparagus with pepper cream 173
    walnut and asparagus penne 227
aubergines
    aubergine and cheese layer 176
    aubergine and haricot beans with cheese 174
    aubergine and mushroom sauce 361
    aubergine bake 172
    aubergine pie 176
    aubergine pizza 272
    aubergine with lamb 113
    baked aubergines Parmesan-style 32
    cheese and aubergine bake 195
    chicken and aubergine fritters 69
    cold aubergine antipasto 11
    courgettes baked with aubergines 178
    pasta quills with aubergine 219
    Sicilian-style aubergine and olive antipasto 40
    steak filled with aubergine 90

stuffed aubergines with ham 30
Tivolian salad 307
Augusta's vegetable salad 310
autumn soup 41
Avellino chicken and fennel 96
Avellino prawn fritters 60
bacon
    bacon and beans 120
    bacon and egg flan 75
    bacon bake 234
    bacon pizza 271
    bacon risotto 257
    chicken liver with sage and bacon 132
    liver and bacon 131
    pasta shells 'of easy virtue' 238
    pasta with bacon sauce 215
    spaghetti with bacon and eggs 217
'badly cut' pasta soup 54
baked aubergines Parmesan-style 32
baked bass with dill 147
baked eggs with Parmesan 35
baked fennel 183
baked fillet of sole with prawn sauce 148
baked fillet of veal and potatoes 133
baked fillets in wine sauce 146
baked flatfish with sherry butter 146
baked gnocchi in tomato sauce 231
baked green lasagne 218
baked macaroni 199
baked mustard and herb fish 162
baked pasta ribbons in meat sauce 211
baked turbot with tomatoes 147
baked potatoes with saffron and fennel 184
baked vegetable tart 177
barley and Sauerkraut soup 56
basic fresh egg pasta 196
basic pizza dough 268
basic white sauce 357
basil
    basil and garlic butter 376
    basil sauce 357
bass
    baked bass with dill 147
    roast sea bass 148
battered prawns 157
bean and vegetable loaf 191
beans, Italian 192
beans, mixed dried
    hearty beans 192
    mixed bean salad 299
    see also individual types e.g. haricot beans
beef
    Adrano fillet of beef 80
    beef roll with vegetables 81
    beef slices in orange sauce 79
    beef tea 53
    braised beef with Chianti 88
    cured beef starter 12
    fillet of beef with paprika 91
    Italian-style pot roast 82

Lombardy bread 73
    pot roast 89
    pot roast with courgettes 88
    Sanremo-style escalopes 87
    spaghetti meat pie 215
    Tuscan braised beef 91
    see also beef, minced; steak
beef, minced
    baked green lasagne 218
    baked macaroni with meat 208
    baked pasta ribbons in meat sauce 211
    beef and macaroni bake 200
    beef cannelloni 228
    beef-stuffed peppers 82
    bucatini with meat and red pepper sauce 249
    cheeseburgers 84
    Corsican meatballs 83
    filled pasta tubes 228
    Italian meatballs 82
    meat sauce 356
    minced beef crumble 84
    Mozzarella meat loaf 87
    pasta with meat sauce 199
    Pescara pasta 230
    red lentil pie 85
    savoury meat loaf 87
    spaghetti Bolognese 216
    stuffed rice balls 254
    tomato sauce balls 89
    tomato topped beef 91
beetroot
    beetroot salad 296
    chicken with beetroot and garlic sauce 100
Bel Paese quills 201
big vegetable minestrone 42
biscuits
    almond biscuits 294
    cherry biscuits 333
    Gorgonzola savouries 291
    hazelnut slices 295
    Parmesan bites 293
    sweet almond biscuits 286
    walnut delights 293
black olive bread 283
black pasta (1) 196
black pasta (2) 197
black risotto with squid 259
Bologna cheese 11
braised celery and tomato 195
braised oven-cooked potatoes 195
brandied chicken 93
brandied figs 340
bread
    almond tea bread 284
    apricot loaf 294
    black olive bread 283
    cheese and caraway bread 285
    dough balls 286
    focaccia bread 285
    fried vanilla bread 61

garlic bread 286
Italian flat bread 289
Italian tomato bread 62
olive and rosemary bread 290
panettone breakfast bread 284
quick cinnamon bread 290
rosemary focaccia bread 287
saffron and olive bread 287
Sicilian bread 289
sun-dried tomato and walnut loaf 293
sweet Genoese bread 288
bream
    Mediterranean sea bream 165
bresaola *see* beef
broad beans
    broad bean and cream pasta 241
    broad bean and tarragon salad 297
    broad bean soup 58
broccoli
    broccoli bake 175
    broccoli with red bean sauce 177
    spicy broccoli pasta 219
    tagliatelle with cheese and broccoli 223
bucatini with meat and red pepper sauce 249
buttered French beans 190
buttered tomatoes 174
butters
    almond butter 376
    anchovy butter 377
    basil and garlic butter 376
    butter sauce 357
    herb butter 376
    tarragon butter 376
cabbage
    cabbage soup 57
    cabbage with Italian sauce 178
    red cabbage 188
    red cabbage pickle 300
cakes
    almond cake 311
    almond coffee torte 312
    carnival cakes 325
    chocolate almond cream roll 315
    chocolate and nut roll 331
    chocolate cake 317
    chocolate ice cream cake 347
    chocolate nut torta 320
    fig slices 321
    Italian-style no-bake cake 327
    lemon chiffon cake 321
    Margherita cake 326
    milk sponge cake 323
    peach and almond slice 322
    peach and pear cake 324
    peach cake 323
    prune cake 329
    raspberry cake 313
    Ravenna sponge cake 337
    rice cake with Grand Marnier 342
    rice cakes 343

rum cake 327
    Sicilian nut and chocolate cake 334
    Umbrian carnival cake 318
Calabrian casserole 119
Calabrian-style grouper fillets 170
calves' liver with mushrooms, tomatoes
    and onions 130–31
calves' liver with Parmesan cheese 131
cannellini beans
    bean and vegetable loaf 191
    filling bean soup 49
    Gorgonzola beans 190
    sausages with beans 126
cannelloni
    beef cannelloni 228
    chicken cannelloni 204
    chicken liver and hazelnut-stuffed
        cannelloni 243
    filled cannelloni 206
    prawn cannelloni 237
capellini
    aromatic angel hair 220
    capellini chicken livers 234
capers
    caper and tomato sauce 358
    capers, tomatoes and mullet 148
    cod fillet in caper sauce 151
    lamb cutlets and capers 115
    salami and caper tart 124
    veal with lemon and capers 143
caramel
    crème caramel 332
caramelised nectarines 315
caramelised onion pizza 278
caramelised potatoes, shallots and garlic 12
carnival cakes 325
carrots
    apple and carrot salad 297
    carrot and chicory salad 297
    carrot mix 12
    carrot omelette 72
    carrot pasta 240
    carrot ring 179
    carrot salad 298
    carrots with a spicy sauce 178
    chicken and carrots 96
    spiced carrots 187
    sweet-and-sour carrots 31
casseroles
    asparagus casserole 171
    casserole of chicken and noodles 231
    partridge and lentil casserole 111
cauliflower and chicken rigatoni 242
celeriac salad 299
celery
    braised celery and tomato 195
    celery with mullet 149
    chicken and celery soup 44
    cream of celery soup 43
    veal in soured cream and celery 137

Champagne scallops 150
cheese ('hard' cheese)
   cheese and aubergine bake 195
   cheese and caraway bread 285
   cheese and salami courgettes 194
   cheese and tomato pie 180
   cheese cakes 12
   cheese on toast 74
   cheese potatoes 181
   cheese shortbread 289
   cheese stuffed mushrooms 33
   cheesy tomatoes 194
   fennel in cheese sauce 14
   fondue Italienne 36
   fried cheese with eggs 78
   gourmet pancakes 78
   see also other types e.g. Ricotta
cheeseburgers 84
cheesecakes
   apricot cheesecake 313
   Italian cheesecake (1) 314
   Italian cheesecake (2) 314
   lemon cheesecake 340
   Tuscan-style cheesecake 335
cherries
   cherry biscuits 333
   cherry cassata 346
   cherry liqueur 340
   cherry soup 44
   cherry topping 379
   Morello cherry ice cream 348
   sweet cherry sauce 370
   tasty cherry sauce 370
chestnuts
   chestnut and chocolate dessert 338
   chestnut fritters 316
   chestnut soup 43
   chestnuts in rum 341
   Mont Blanc 336
chick peas
   noodles with chick peas 209
   thunder and lightning 242
chicken
   Arno Valley chicken 92
   Avellino chicken and fennel 96
   brandied chicken 93
   casserole of chicken and noodles 231
   cauliflower and chicken rigatoni 242
   chicken and aubergine fritters 69
   chicken and carrots 96
   chicken and celery soup 44
   chicken and courgette pie 95
   chicken and macaroni bake 232
   chicken and macaroni casserole 200
   chicken and mushroom risotto 258
   chicken and prosciutto mousse 95
   chicken and spinach lasagne 244
   chicken and tarragon risotto 261
   chicken and walnut tagliatelle 203
   chicken Bolognese 202

chicken cannelloni 204
chicken dome 94
chicken, garlic and tomato pizza 273
chicken in Marsala sauce 96
chicken in tomato cases 70
chicken lasagne 230
chicken Marengo 96
chicken omelette 70
chicken omelette and pasta 202
chicken pizza 272
chicken ravioli 245
chicken risotto with peas 256
chicken with apples and lemon sauce 97
chicken with asparagus and Parmesan
   sauce 92
chicken with beetroot and garlic sauce 100
chicken with fig stuffing 99
chicken with lemon and almonds 98
chicken with red pepper and tarragon 102
chicken with sherry vinegar and tarragon 93
chicken with tarragon and cheese sauce 98
citrus chicken 101
classic Italian casserole 97
Coliseum chicken 100
creamy pasta 203
devilled chicken 100
Genoese spinach and chicken pie 105
grilled chicken thighs 101
ham and chicken in pastry 124
herb, garlic and lemon chicken 103
hunter-style chicken 93
Italian chicken with basil sauce 106
lime chicken 103
Mediterranean chicken 104
Milan-style chicken and courgettes 107
Mozzarella chicken 104
mushroom and chicken Assisi 104
Palermo chicken 105
pasta chicken 212
pasta with chicken 233
penne with chicken 233
penne with spicy chicken 233
Rimini stew 110
Roman chicken 101
royal peach chicken 106
sorrel and chicken stew 106
stuffed chicken thighs 94
sweetcorn and chicken pizza 277
tortellini and chicken carbonara 232
Venetian-style chicken 99
Verona chickenmeat balls 107
chicken livers
   capellini chicken livers 234
   chicken liver and hazelnut-stuffed
     cannelloni 243
   chicken liver ramekins 33
   chicken liver sauce 356
   chicken liver savoury 69
   chicken liver toasts 67
   chicken liver with sage and bacon 132

eggs and liver 36
mushroom and liver fritters 63
rice with chicken livers 256
savoury chicken liver risotto 263
chicory salad 298
chive and courgette risotto 251
chocolate
chestnut and chocolate dessert 338
chocolate almond cream roll 315
chocolate and nut roll 331
chocolate cake 317
chocolate chip ice cream 346
chocolate cream topping 379
chocolate ice cream cake 347
chocolate Mascarpone cream 369
chocolate nougat 325
chocolate nut torta 320
Christina's sweet snack 328
chuck steak in red wine 80
chunky tomato sauce 357
citrus chicken 101
citrus meringue pie 319
citrus soup 43
clams
clam and cheese pancakes 149
clam and shrimp soup 45
clams, pesto and spaghetti 152
spaghetti with baby clams 240
classic Italian casserole 97
classic tomato sauce for pasta 359
cod
cod fillet in caper sauce 151
fish lasagne 248
salt cod 152
coffee
coffee and rum ice cream 347
coffee ice cream 346
cold aubergine antipasto 11
Coliseum chicken 100
confectioners' custard 372
cooked mixed vegetables 181
cordial, apricot and fig 338
coriander sea shells 238
Corsican meatballs 83
country vegetable soup 45
courgettes
almond stuffed courgettes 172
aubergine pie 176
cheese and salami courgettes 194
chicken and courgette pie 95
courgette and potato soup 47
courgette and tomato tart 181
courgette fritters 13
courgette salad 306
courgette tart 179
courgettes baked with aubergines 178
courgettes in tomato sauce 13
courgettes with ginger and almonds 180
courgettes with spicy mustard 182
grilled courgettes 16

lemon and oregano courgettes 191
Milan-style chicken and courgettes 107
quick courgette soup 52
rice-stuffed courgettes 252
sage sautéed courgettes 191
sorrel and courgette fritters 28
stuffed courgettes 23
sweet-and-sour courgettes 185
warm courgette salad 306
crab
crab and prawn bread 61
crab ravioli 246
penne with crab 235
spicy pappardelle with crab 235
tagliatelle crab 240
crackled apples 315
crayfish
crayfish soup 46
squid and crayfish 159
cream cheese
sweet Marsala cream cheese 338
cream of celery soup 43
cream of fennel sauce 362
cream of lettuce soup 46
cream of tomato soup 53
cream, sweet 371
creamed prawns 151
creamed risotto with lemon 264
creamy Champagne risotto 264
creamy garlic sauce 361
creamy ham and mushroom risotto 265
creamy Italian dressing 373
creamy pasta 203
creamy potato bake 182
creamy walnut and basil sauce 366
creamy white sauce 366
crème caramel 332
crisp herb slices 60
crispy fried Mozzarella 17
crispy fried spaghetti 241
crispy quenelles 102
crostini, quick 67
crumbly topped seafood 154
crusty cheese rounds 277
cucumbers
fennel and cucumber salad 308
Florentine cucumbers 15
cured beef starter 12
custard
confectioners' custard 372
egg custard 371
frangipane custard 371
whipped Marsala custard 333
desserts
almond cake 311
almond coffee torte 312
almond tagliatelle 312
almond tart 332
apple and lemon flan 317
apricot and fig cordial 338

apricot cheesecake 313
apricot pastry boats 311
brandied figs 340
caramelised nectarines 315
carnival cakes 325
cherry biscuits 333
cherry liqueur 340
chestnut and chocolate dessert 338
chestnut fritters 316
chestnuts in rum 341
chocolate almond cream roll 315
chocolate and nut roll 331
chocolate cake 317
chocolate nougat 325
chocolate nut torta 320
Christina's sweet snack 328
citrus meringue pie 319
crackled apples 315
crème caramel 332
fig preserve 342
fig slices 321
fig tart 318
figs in brandy 341
figs in grappa 312
figs Maria 323
flaming peach pie 321
frangipane and strawberry pie 339
frangipane tartlets 319
fresh strawberry tart 339
Genoese tart 328
grape tart 322
Italian cheesecake (1) 314
Italian cheesecake (2) 314
Italian-style no-bake cake 327
lemon cheesecake 340
lemon chiffon cake 321
lemon rice almond pudding 320
lemon tart 320
Lombard zabaglione 344
luxury nut dessert 327
Margherita cake 326
Milanese trifle 330
milk sponge cake 323
mixed nut roll 334
mocha mousse 316
Mont Blanc 336
nougat and strawberry mousse 331
nuns' sighs 326
orange and frangipane tart 324
orange soufflé 312
peach and almond slice 322
peach and pear cake 324
peach and plum pudding 328
peach cake 323
peach royale 339
peaches in white wine 330
prune cake 329
raspberry and nut dream 331
raspberry cake 313
raspberry dessert 330

Ravenna sponge cake 337
rice cake with Grand Marnier 342
rice cakes 343
rice pancakes 344
Roman violet liqueur 341
rum cake 327
Sicilian nut and chocolate cake 334
St Joseph's puffs 333
strawberries in balsamic
    vinegar 330
strawberries in wine 332
stuffed apricots with Mascarpone
    and pistachios 337
stuffed figs 326
stuffed peaches 336
sweet fried pastry balls 337
sweet Marsala cream cheese 338
tiramisu 329
trifle 343
Tuscan-style cheesecake 335
Umbrian carnival cake 318
vanilla nut tartlets 335
walnut liqueur 342
walnut soufflé 336
whipped Marsala custard 333
see also ice cream; pastries
devilled chicken 100
dinner party prawns 155
dips
    anchovy dip 34
    garlic dip 34
    Gorgonzola dip 33
    sun-dried dip 34
dough balls 286
dressings
    anchovy dressing 373
    creamy Italian dressing 373
    herb oil for grilling 374
    olive oil dressing 373
    quick tomato sauce 374
    rose vinegar 373
    sun-dried tomato mayonnaise 374
    sweet lime dressing 372
    tarragon vinegar 374
dried mushroom sauce 364
duck
    duck and bean soup 47
    lemon duckling 108
    rice with duck and prawns 253
    Venetian boiled duck 108
easy fruit ice cream 348
eels
    eel and green peas 155
    eel soup 48
    fisherman's eel 156
    smoked eel and vegetable salad 309
eggs
    bacon and egg flan 75
    baked eggs with Parmesan 35
    egg and olive antipasto 13

egg custard 371
eggs and liver 36
eggs baked with Gorgonzola 74
eggs with peas and tomatoes 73
eggy rice 253
Franciscan eggs 75
garlic stuffed eggs 36
olive-stuffed eggs 35
pancakes filled with eggs and tuna 64
spaghetti with eggs 247
see also omelettes; soufflés
elbow pasta 216
Fabrino liver 129
fake meat sauce for pasta 368
farmer's rabbit 109
fennel
  aromatic fennel 174
  baked fennel 183
  cream of fennel sauce 362
  fennel and cucumber salad 308
  fennel and tomato bake 184
  fennel in anchovy sauce 192
  fennel in cheese sauce 14
  fennel in white wine 183
  fennel soup 48
  iced tomato and fennel soup 49
  roast garlic and fennel 25
  roasted fennel 186
  stuffed fennel with olives 29
  turbot with fennel 170
fettuccine
  fettuccine with cream 203
  fettuccine with sage 210
  seafood and Mascarpone fettuccine 216
  spinach and ham fettuccine 223
  three-colour fettuccine 202
fiery pasta quills 214
figs
  apricot and fig cordial 338
  brandied figs 340
  chicken with fig stuffing 99
  fig preserve 342
  fig slices 321
  fig tart 318
  figs in brandy 341
  figs in grappa 312
  figs Maria 323
  figs with ham 32
  stuffed figs 326
filled cannelloni 206
filled pasta tubes 228
fillet of beef with paprika 91
filling bean soup 49
fish
  fish and fennel parcels 155
  fish fillets and capers 156
  fish, onion and carrot parcels 156
  fish sauce 367
  fish soup 44
  fish stew 154

thick fish soup with noodles 55
see also types of fish e.g. cod; white fish
  and seafood
fisherman's eel 156
flaming peach pie 321
flans
  apple and lemon flan 317
  bacon and egg flan 75
  onion flan 77
  potato flan 66
  spinach and Mozzarella pastry 66
  spinach flan 193
flatfish
  baked flatfish with sherry butter 146
Florentine cucumbers 15
Florentine steak 88
focaccia bread 285
focaccia mushrooms 61
foiled fish 153
fondue Italienne 36
Fontina cheese
  melted cheese with egg yolks 74
  Renaissance cheese 72
four-seasons pizza 282
Franciscan eggs 75
frangipane
  frangipane and strawberry pie 339
  frangipane custard 371
  frangipane tartlets 319
  orange and frangipane tart 324
French beans
  buttered French beans 190
  nutty beans 22
fresh apricot sauce 369
fresh strawberry tart 339
fricassee of artichokes 15
fried cheese with eggs 78
fried marrow 20
fried mussels 158
fried pizza 282
fried potatoes with courgettes and olives 65
fried pumpkin 182
fried vanilla bread 61
fritters
  Avellino prawn fritters 60
  cheese fritters 77
  cheese fritters with basil 77
  chestnut fritters 316
  chicken and aubergine fritters 69
  Christina's sweet snack 328
  courgette fritters 13
  ham and almond fritters 70
  Liguria fritters 18
  mushroom and liver fritters 63
  prawn and Mozzarella fritters 161
  sausage fritters 119
  sorrel and courgette fritters 28
  spinach leaf fritters 29
frozen lemon and almond mousse 349
fruit and nut salad 299

galantine of veal with spinach 145
game *see* individual types e.g. partridge
garlic
    basil and garlic butter 376
    creamy garlic sauce 361
    garlic and herb marinade 365
    garlic and tomato peppers 24
    garlic bread 286
    garlic dip 34
    garlic, ham and tomato slice 66
    garlic pizza 281
    garlic soup 49
    garlic stuffed eggs 36
    linguini with garlic and Parmesan 209
    piquant garlic sauce 367
    roast garlic and fennel 25
    spaghetti with garlic and oil 221
    spaghetti with garlic butter 217
gateaux, asparagus 175
Genoese rice 266
Genoese salad 298
Genoese spinach and chicken pie 105
gnocchi
    baked gnocchi in tomato sauce 231
    green gnocchi 38
    lamb, beans and gnocchi 114
    potato gnocchi 39
    potato gnocchi with microwave sauce 190
    Roman-style gnocchi 38
    spinach gnocchi 185
goats' cheese
    goats' cheese antipasto 16
    toasted goats' cheese 32
Gorgonzola cheese
    eggs baked with Gorgonzola 74
    Gorgonzola beans 190
    Gorgonzola dip 33
    Gorgonzola savouries 291
    Parma ham, cheese and melon fingers 22
    pizza with Gorgonzola and walnuts 274
    risotto with Gorgonzola 262
    veal with Gorgonzola 136
gourmet pancakes 78
granita, lemon 350
grapes
    grape salad 299
    grape tart 322
green gnocchi 38
green pasta 197
grilled chicken thighs 101
grilled courgettes 16
grilled red mullet 157
grilled polenta with peppers 17
grilled scallops 157
grilled seafood 152
grilled tuna 167
grouper fillets, Calabrian-style 170
Gruyère sticks 291
guinea fowl with apple 110
ham

chicken and prosciutto mousse 95
figs with ham 32
garlic, ham and tomato slice 66
ham and almond fritters 70
ham and almond sauce 362
ham and anchovy rolls 72
ham and chicken in pastry 124
ham and green peas 120
ham and turkey risotto 250
ham pasta shells 233
ham risotto 254
Italian ham and pesto slice 62
mountain ham 121
pizza with raw ham 271
prawns in prosciutto 160
risotto with melon and prosciutto 261
sausage and prosciutto with potato 125
spaghetti Alsacienne 223
Torino ham 126
turkey breast Sanremo 110
turkey breasts with prosciutto 110
haricot beans
    aubergine and haricot beans with cheese 174
    duck and bean soup 47
    haricot bean salad 306
    savoury haricot beans 27
    Tuscan bean broth 54
hazelnuts
    hazelnut delight 351
    hazelnut savoury sauce 365
    hazelnut slices 295
    raspberry and nut dream 331
hearty beans 192
herb butter 376
herb, garlic and lemon chicken 103
herb oil for grilling 374
herb pastry 292
herb rice 251
herb sauce 360
herb vegetables 189
honey
    honey ice cream 347
    honeyed roast lamb 112
    sauce of the honey bees 367
hunter-style chicken 93
ice cream
    almond and chocolate ice cream 351
    apricot ice cream 349
    cherry cassata 346
    chocolate chip ice cream 346
    chocolate ice cream cake 347
    coffee and rum ice cream 347
    coffee ice cream 346
    easy fruit ice cream 348
    hazelnut delight 351
    honey ice cream 347
    ice cream bombe with raspberries 345
    lemon ice cream 352
    maraschino ice cream 352
    mocha soufflé 353

Morello cherry ice cream 348
orange and chocolate yoghurt ice cream 348
orange ice cream 352
peach and nut ice cream 355
peaches 'n' cream 354
pistachio ice cream 355
pistachio ice cream with apricots 355
raspberry cream 353
strawberry ice cream 354
tutti frutti ice cream 350
vanilla ice cream 345
iced Amaretti soufflé 350
iced tomato and fennel soup 49
icing
    almond cream filling 378
    cherry topping 379
    chocolate cream topping 379
    maraschino icing 378
    Mascarpone lime 378
    mocha butter icing 378
Ionan tuna 160
Italian beans 192
Italian braised lamb 114
Italian cheesecake (1) 314
Italian cheesecake (2) 314
Italian chicken with basil sauce 106
Italian flat bread 289
Italian fried fish 158
Italian ham and pesto slice 62
Italian lamb 113
Italian meatballs 82
Italian seafood salad 301
Italian-style no-bake cake 327
Italian-style pot roast 82
Italian-style potato cakes 16
Italian tomato bread 62
Italian veal rolls 135
Italian vegetable parcels 24
Italian vegetables 188
Jerusalem artichoke salad 297
kidneys, lamb
    kidneys in cream 128
    kidneys in red wine sauce 127
    kidneys with soured cream 130
    Roman kidneys 129
kidneys, ox
    ox kidney with mustard 132
lamb
    apricot lamb 112
    aubergine with lamb 113
    honeyed roast lamb 112
    Italian braised lamb 114
    Italian lamb 113
    lamb, beans and gnocchi 114
    lamb Catania 116
    lamb cutlets and capers 115
    lamb in mushroom sauce 115
    lamb with prunes 117
    lamb with rosemary and orange sauce 117
    lamb with rosemary and raspberry sauce 116

Pisticci lamb 116
spinach lamb cutlets 118
tarragon lamb 117
Trebbiano lamb 118
wined leg of lamb 112
lambs' liver with chopped vegetables 130
lasagne
    baked green lasagne 218
    chicken and spinach lasagne 244
    chicken lasagne 230
    fish lasagne 248
    mushroom lasagne 243
    Ricotta and spinach lasagne 249
    tuna lasagne 222
layered fish roast 157
layered vine leaves 18
leeks
    potato and leeks in white sauce 195
lemons
    citrus meringue pie 319
    frozen lemon and almond mousse 349
    lemon and oregano courgettes 191
    lemon and rice soup 50
    lemon cheesecake 340
    lemon chiffon cake 321
    lemon duckling 108
    lemon granita 350
    lemon ice cream 352
    lemon marinade 365
    lemon mint sauce 360
    lemon rice almond pudding 320
    lemon sauce 360
    lemon tart 320
    lemon topping 372
    quick lemon dessert 349
    simple lemon sauce 370
lentils, red
    lentils and garlic sausage 126
    partridge and lentil casserole 111
    red lentil pie 85
lettuce
    cream of lettuce soup 46
    lettuce with peas 19
Liguria fritters 18
Ligurian walnut sauce 369
lima beans
    bacon and beans 120
    salami with beans 26
limes
    lime chicken 103
    Mascarpone lime 378
    sweet lime dressing 372
    lime topping 372
linguini
    linguini with artichokes 207
    linguini with garlic and Parmesan 209
liqueurs
    cherry liqueur 340
    Roman violet liqueur 341
    walnut liqueur 343

liver, calves'
    calves' liver with mushrooms, tomatoes
       and onions 130–31
    calves' liver with Parmesan cheese 131
    Fabrino liver 129
    liver and bacon 131
    liver in garlic butter 132
    liver in white wine 128
    liver soufflé 127
    Sicilian toast 71
    Venetian liver 129
liver, lambs'
    lambs' liver with chopped vegetables 130
liver, pigs'
    pigs' liver brochettes 128
lobster
    lobster salad 310
    lobster soup 56
    lobster with devilled sauce 150
    lobster with Parmesan 160
loin of veal Valdostana-style 144
Lombard zabaglione 344
Lombardy bread 73
luxury nut dessert 327
macaroni
    baked macaroni 199
    baked macaroni with meat 208
    beef and macaroni bake 200
    chicken and macaroni bake 232
    chicken and macaroni casserole 200
    Neapolitan macaroni 209
    tomato-baked macaroni 226
    veal with macaroni 235
macaroons, almond 285
maraschino ice cream 352
maraschino icing 378
Margherita cake 326
marinades
    garlic and herb marinade 365
    lemon marinade 365
    spicy marinade 375
marinated garlic and peppers 19
marrow, fried 20
Mascarpone cheese
    chocolate Mascarpone cream 369
    Mascarpone lime 378
    savoury Mascarpone cream 359
mayonnaise, sun-dried tomato 374
meat
    fake meat sauce for pasta 368
    meat sauce 356
    mixed cured meats 37
    see also individual types e.g. lamb
meatballs
    Corsican meatballs 83
    Italian meatballs 82
    tomato sauce balls 89
Mediterranean chicken 104
Mediterranean olives 19
Mediterranean salad 301

Mediterranean sea bream 165
Mediterranean spaghetti 218
Mediterranean tartlets 63
melted cheese with egg yolks 74
meringues
    nuns' sighs 326
Messina mullet 159
metrano onions 20
microwave minestrone 50
Milan-style chicken and courgettes 107
Milan-style risotto 258
Milanese green salad 308
Milanese spiced red pasta 248
Milanese steak 84
Milanese-style veal escalope 144
Milanese trifle 330
milk
    milk risotto 258
    milk soup 46
    milk sponge cake 323
    pork with milk 123
minced beef crumble 84
minestrone
    big vegetable minestrone 42
    microwave minestrone 50
    minestrone 50
mint
    lemon mint sauce 360
    minted orange salad 301
    warm mint sauce 360
mixed bean salad 299
mixed cured meats 37
mixed mushroom risotto 250
mixed mushroom salad 310
mixed nut roll 334
mixed vegetables and olives 21
mocha butter icing 378
mocha mousse 316
mocha soufflé 353
monkfish
    monkfish in saffron sauce 161
    monkfish with crab and shrimp 153
    roast monkfish with bacon and marjoram
      sauce 163
Mont Blanc 336
mortadella sausages
    mortadella rolls 71
mountain ham 121
mousse
    anchovy mousse 168
    chicken and prosciutto mousse 95
    frozen lemon and almond mousse 349
    mocha mousse 316
    nougat and strawberry mousse 331
Mozzarella cheese
    aubergine and cheese layer 176
    cheese and tomato pizza 269
    cheese fritters 77
    cheese fritters with basil 77
    crispy fried Mozzarella 17

Mozzarella chicken 104
Mozzarella meat loaf 87
Mozzarella salad with ratatouille 302
Mozzarella tart 76
Mozzarella veal 134
preserved Mozzarella and herbs 37
spinach and Mozzarella pastry 66
mullet
capers, tomatoes and mullet 148
celery with mullet 149
grilled red mullet 157
Messina mullet 159
mushroom mullet 159
red mullet and tomatoes 162
red mullet baked in paper 162
red mullet Leghorn style 164
seasoned red mullet 165
mushrooms
cheese stuffed mushrooms 33
dried mushroom sauce 364
focaccia mushrooms 61
lamb in mushroom sauce 115
mixed mushroom risotto 250
mixed mushroom salad 310
mushroom and chicken Assisi 104
mushroom and hazelnut sauce 363
mushroom and liver fritters 63
mushroom lasagne 243
mushroom mullet 159
mushroom pizza 275
mushroom sauce 363
mushroom soup 46
mushrooms stuffed with spinach 21
mushrooms with cheese 193
noodles with porcini and Cognac 207
pasta spirals with mushrooms 207
pasta with mixed mushrooms 205
polenta with mushrooms 68
pork with mushrooms and juniper berries 121
quick mushroom pizza 275
risotto with porcini mushrooms 263
spaghetti in Neapolitan sauce 208
spaghetti with oyster mushrooms 220
spinach mushrooms 189
tomato and mushroom soup 53
veal and mushrooms 140
veal in creamy mushroom sauce 139
wild mushroom risotto 255
mussels
fried mussels 158
mussel soup 42
mussel soup with saffron 58
mussels Tuscany style 158
pasta with mussels 213
saffron pancakes with mussels 68
mustard
courgettes with spicy mustard 182
Naples-style risotto with butter 260
Napoli sauce 358
Neapolitan beef 86

Neapolitan macaroni 209
nectarines, caramelised 315
noodles
casserole of chicken and noodles 231
fishy noodle ring 237
noodles with chick peas 209
noodles with porcini and Cognac 207
potatoes and noodles with garlic sauce 214
seafood noodles 239
smoked salmon with green noodles 239
nougat
nougat and strawberry mousse 331
chocolate nougat 325
nuns' sighs 326
nuts
luxury nut dessert 327
mixed nut roll 334
nutty beans 22
nutty vermicelli 211
vanilla nut tartlets 335
see also individual types e.g. walnuts
offal see individual types e.g. kidneys
oil and lemon sauce 368
olives
egg and olive antipasto 13
Mediterranean olives 19
olive, anchovy and basil pizza 274
olive, anchovy and tomato paste 20
olive and anchovy paste 35
olive and basil pâté 22
olive and rosemary bread 290
olive loaf 120
olive oil dressing 373
olive pizza 280
olive-stuffed eggs 35
oregano and olive potatoes 183
pan-fried olives 22
potatoes with olives 187
stuffed fried olives 15
stuffed olive puffs 31
omelettes
artichoke omelette 74
carrot omelette 72
chicken omelette 70
chicken omelette and pasta 202
open tuna omelette 76
parsley and basil omelette 78
pea omelette 75
onions
caramelised onion pizza 278
metrano onions 20
onion and ham pizza 274
onion flan 77
stuffed onions 30
open tuna omelette 76
oranges
orange and chocolate yoghurt ice cream 348
orange and frangipane tart 324
orange ice cream 352
orange plum salad 305

orange soufflé 312
Sicilian oranges – rice balls with a
   savoury filling 260
oregano and olive potatoes 183
oregano, Mozzarella and caper pizza 275
the original pizza 272
original rich pork stew 122
Orvietto veal 133
osso buco 134
ox kidney with mustard 132
Palermo chicken 105
Palermo pizza pie 270
pan-fried olives 22
pan-fried salmon and pasta 210
pan-roasted radicchio 16
pancakes
   clam and cheese pancakes 149
   gourmet pancakes 78
   pancakes filled with eggs and tuna 64
   pancakes with red pepper filling 65
   rice pancakes 344
   saffron pancakes with mussels 68
   spaghetti pancakes 219
   spicy Italian pancakes 27
pancetta
   filled cannelloni 206
panettone breakfast bread 284
pappardelle
   spicy pappardelle with crab 235
   Tuscan pappardelle 227
Parma ham, cheese and melon fingers 22
Parmesan cheese
   artichokes in cheese sauce 175
   asparagus Parmesan-style 9
   asparagus with cheese 11
   cheese and tomato bread 62
   cheese popovers 60
   chicken with asparagus and Parmesan
      sauce 92
   lobster with Parmesan 160
   mushrooms with cheese 193
   Parmesan bites 293
   Parmesan pesto twists 292
   Parmesan polenta 65
   Parmesan potatoes 184
   Parmesan rice with basil 267
   Parmesan sauce 361
   Parmesan shortbread 292
   Parmesan veal cutlets 136
   radicchio, cheese and eggs 180
   veal with mustard and cheese 142
parsley and basil omelette 78
partridge and lentil casserole 111
pasta
   artichoke and olive pasta 201
   asparagus cream with pasta 200
   bacon bake 234
   'badly cut' pasta soup 54
   baked pasta ribbons in meat sauce 211
   basic fresh egg pasta 196

black pasta (1) 196
black pasta (2) 197
broad bean and cream pasta 241
carrot pasta 240
cheese filling for pasta 199
cheese pasta twists 201
chicken omelette and pasta 202
coriander sea shells 238
creamy pasta 203
elbow pasta 216
filled pasta tubes 228
green pasta 197
ham pasta shells 233
Milanese spiced red pasta 248
pan-fried salmon and pasta 210
pasta and vegetable salad 304
pasta bows with red pepper sauce 204
pasta bows with roasted vegetables 205
pasta bows with tomato sauce 204
pasta chicken 212
pasta quills with aubergine 219
pasta shells 'of easy virtue' 238
pasta shells with vegetables 226
pasta spirals with mushrooms 207
pasta with anchovy butter 206
pasta with bacon sauce 215
pasta with butter and truffle 221
pasta with chicken 233
pasta with green sauce 210
pasta with grilled peppers 213
pasta with meat sauce 199
pasta with mixed mushrooms 205
pasta with mussels 213
pasta with prawns and cream 212
pasta with Ricotta 205
pasta with saffron and scallops 212
pasta with seafood topping 213
pasta with spinach and sage 211
Pescara pasta 230
red pasta 198
rich veal with pasta shells 236
sausage and pasta shells 215
spicy broccoli pasta 219
springtime pasta salad 302
steak with pasta 229
sun-dried tomato pasta 225
tagliarini pasta 198
thick ribbon pasta 198
thunder and lightning 242
walnut, mushroom and cheese pasta 224
warm pasta salad with radishes 300
see also individual types e.g. spaghetti
pastries
   apricot pastry boats 311
   Gruyère sticks 291
   herb pastry 292
   Parmesan pesto twists 292
   Salerno pastry 288
   San Severo pastries 291
   St Joseph's puffs 333

sweet fried pastry balls 337
yeast pastry 283
see also flans, pies, tarts
pâtés
    olive and basil pâté 22
    spinach and anchovy pâté 28
peaches
    flaming peach pie 321
    peach and almond slice 322
    peach and nut ice cream 355
    peach and pear cake 324
    peach and plum pudding 328
    peach cake 323
    peach royale 339
    peach sauce 370
    peaches in white wine 330
    peaches 'n' cream 354
    sporty peach salad 302
    stuffed peaches 336
pear and Parmesan salad 303
peas
    eel and green peas 155
    eggs with peas and tomatoes 73
    ham and green peas 120
    lettuce with peas 19
    pasta with green sauce 210
    pea omelette 75
    rice and peas 266
    tagliarini with peas 224
peasant soup 51
peasant-style risotto 267
Pecorino cheese
    cheese pasta twists 201
    cheese stuffed mushrooms 33
    Roman-style rice with Pecorino cheese 264
penne
    Bel Paese quills 201
    chicken dome 94
    fiery pasta quills 214
    penne with chicken 233
    penne with crab 235
    penne with spicy chicken 233
    penne with tuna and black olives 247
    walnut and asparagus penne 227
peppers
    beef-stuffed peppers 82
    chicken with red pepper and tarragon 102
    garlic and tomato peppers 24
    pancakes with red pepper filling 65
    pasta bows with red pepper sauce 204
    pasta with grilled peppers 213
    pepper and almond spaghetti with
      seafood 214
    peppers in tomato sauce 23
    predappio peppers 25
    preserved peppers 37
    quick piperade 25
    red pepper pots 71
    rice with red pepper and peas 263
    roasted peppers 26

salmon and pepper pie 163
    spaghetti with peppers, anchovies
      and tomato 241
    stuffed peppers 30
    sweet peppers with bagna cauda 31
    Taranto peppers 32
    vermicelli with peppers 226
    yellow pepper salad 304
Pescara pasta 230
pesto
    pesto rice 252
    red pesto sauce 366
    tarragon pesto 367
pick-me-up pudding 329
Piedmont salami salad 304
pies
    asparagus in pastry 73
    flaming peach pie 321
    frangipane and strawberry pie 339
    seafood pie 166
    veal and juniper pie 141
pigeon breasts on toast 107
pigs' liver brochettes 128
pine nut and basil sauce 366
piquant Chinese sauce 365
piquant garlic sauce 367
pistachio nuts
    pistachio butter sauce 362
    pistachio ice cream 355
    pistachio ice cream with apricots 355
Pisticci lamb 116
pizzaiola steak 81
pizzas
    anchovy and tuna pizza 269
    anchovy pizza 281
    anchovy pizza pockets 176
    artichoke pizza 271
    Artimino pizza pie 279
    asparagus pizza 279
    aubergine pizza 272
    bacon pizza 271
    basic pizza dough 268
    caramelised onion pizza 278
    cheese and tomato pizza 269
    chicken, garlic and tomato pizza 273
    chicken pizza 272
    crusty cheese rounds 277
    four-seasons pizza 282
    fried pizza 282
    garlic pizza 281
    mushroom pizza 275
    olive, anchovy and basil pizza 274
    olive pizza 280
    onion and ham pizza 274
    oregano, Mozzarella and caper pizza 275
    the original pizza 272
    Palermo pizza pie 270
    pizza lattice pie 280
    pizza potatoes 185
    pizza with Gorgonzola and walnuts 274

pizza with raw ham 271
quick mushroom pizza 275
quick seafood pizza 281
rosemary and ham pizza 279
rustic pizza 64
salami and Mozzarella pizza 278
salami pizza 273
sausage pizza 276
spicy pizza dough 268
stuffed pizza 278
sweetcorn and chicken pizza 277
wholemeal pizza dough 269
plums
  peach and plum pudding 328
  plum salad 305
polenta
  grilled polenta with peppers 17
  marinated garlic and peppers 19
  Parmesan polenta 65
  polenta with mushrooms 68
  sage polenta discs 67
pork
  Calabrian casserole 119
  olive loaf 120
  original rich pork stew 122
  pork and vegetables 122
  pork chops in green sauce 123
  pork chops with apples 122
  pork with apple and juniper berries 121
  pork with milk 123
  pork with mushrooms and juniper berries 121
  pork with tomatoes and onions 125
  spaghetti with pork, anchovies and tomato 221
pot roasts
  pot roast 89
  pot roast with courgettes 88
potatoes
  baked potatoes with saffron and fennel 184
  braised oven-cooked potatoes 195
  cheese potatoes 181
  courgette and potato soup 47
  creamy potato bake 182
  fried potatoes with courgettes and olives 65
  Italian-style potato cakes 16
  oregano and olive potatoes 183
  Parmesan potatoes 184
  pizza potatoes 185
  potato and leeks in white sauce 195
  potatoes and noodles with garlic sauce 214
  potato cakes 194
  potato flan 66
  potato gnocchi 39
  potato gnocchi with microwave sauce 190
  potato puffs 24
  potato soup 51
  potatoes with olives 187
  potatoes with prawn sauce 164
  rosemary potato chunks 26

poultry *see* individual types e.g. chicken
prawns
  Avellino prawn fritters 60
  battered prawns 157
  crab and prawn bread 61
  creamed prawns 151
  dinner party prawns 155
  pasta with prawns and cream 212
  potatoes with prawn sauce 164
  prawn and Mozzarella fritters 161
  prawn cannelloni 237
  prawn salad 303
  prawns in prosciutto 160
  rice with prawns 251
  risotto with prawns 257
  simple prawns 167
  tiger prawn rice 256
  Venetian prawns 154
predappio peppers 25
preserve, fig 340
preserved Mozzarella and herbs 37
preserved peppers 37
prosciutto ham *see* ham
prunes
  lamb with prunes 117
  prune cake 329
pumpkin
  fried pumpkin 182
  pumpkin soup 51
quail
  quail with raspberries 111
  risotto with quail 259
quenelles, crispy 101
quick cinnamon bread 290
quick courgette soup 52
quick crostini 67
quick lemon dessert 349
quick mushroom pizza 275
quick pasta sauce 364
quick piperade 25
quick seafood pizza 281
quick tomato sauce 374
quick tuna and pepper salad 305
rabbit
  farmer's rabbit 109
  rabbit in a pot 109
radicchio
  pan-roasted radicchio 16
  radicchio, cheese and eggs 180
  red radicchio salad 298
raspberries
  ice cream bombe with raspberries 345
  raspberry and nut dream 331
  raspberry cake 313
  raspberry cream 353
  raspberry dessert 330
  rosemary and raspberry sauce 366
ratatouille
  Mozzarella salad with ratatouille 302

Ravenna sponge cake 337
ravioli
    chicken ravioli 245
    crab ravioli 246
    spinach and egg ravioli 222
    veal ravioli 236
red cabbage
    red cabbage 188
    red cabbage pickle 300
red lentil pie 85
red mullet *see* mullet
red pasta 198
red pepper pots 71
red pesto sauce 366
red radicchio salad 298
Renaissance cheese 72
rice
    eggy rice 253
    Genoese rice 266
    herb rice 251
    lemon and rice soup 50
    lemon rice almond pudding 320
    Parmesan rice with basil 267
    pesto rice 252
    rice and peas 266
    rice and scampi salad 300
    rice and spinach soup 57
    rice balls 265
    rice cake with Grand Marnier 342
    rice cakes 343
    rice pancakes 344
    rice salad with olives and tomatoes 296
    rice, sausages and tomatoes 253
    rice-stuffed courgettes 252
    rice with chicken livers 256
    rice with duck and prawns 253
    rice with prawns 251
    rice with red pepper and peas 263
    rice with salami 255
    Roman-style rice with Pecorino cheese 264
    Sicilian oranges – rice balls with a
        savoury filling 260
    soup with rice and peas 52
    spinach and rice mould 255
    stuffed rice balls 254
    three-coloured rice 266
    tiger prawn rice 256
    veal with rice 143
    warm rice with parsley 262
    see also risottos
rich beef in red wine 83
rich veal with pasta shells 236
Ricotta cheese
    artichokes stuffed with cheese 173
    cheese filling for pasta 199
    pasta with Ricotta 205
    Ricotta and spinach lasagne 249
rigatoni
    cauliflower and chicken rigatoni 242
Rimini stew 110

risottos
    bacon risotto 257
    black risotto with squid 259
    chicken and mushroom risotto 258
    chicken and tarragon risotto 261
    chicken risotto with peas 256
    chive and courgette risotto 251
    creamed risotto with lemon 264
    creamy Champagne risotto 264
    creamy ham and mushroom risotto 265
    ham and turkey risotto 250
    ham risotto 254
    Milan-style risotto 258
    milk risotto 258
    mixed mushroom risotto 250
    Naples-style risotto with butter 260
    peasant-style risotto 267
    risotto from Milan 252
    risotto with butter 260
    risotto with Gorgonzola 262
    risotto with melon and prosciutto 261
    risotto with porcini mushrooms 263
    risotto with prawns 257
    risotto with quail 259
    sausage risotto 267
    savoury chicken liver risotto 263
    scampi risotto 254
    Tuscan risotto with raisins 262
    wild mushroom risotto 255
    see also rice
roast garlic and fennel 25
roast monkfish with bacon and marjoram
    sauce 163
roast sea bass 148
roast stuffed turkey roll 109
roast veal and celery sauce 134
roasted fennel 186
roasted peppers 26
Roman chicken 101
Roman kidneys 129
Roman salad 300
Roman-style gnocchi 38
Roman-style rice with Pecorino cheese 264
Roman-style veal escalopes 145
Roman violet liqueur 341
rose vinegar 373
rosemary
    rosemary and ham pizza 279
    rosemary and raspberry sauce 366
    rosemary focaccia bread 287
    rosemary potato chunks 26
royal peach chicken 106
rum cake 327
rump steak, tomatoes and peppers 85
rustic pizza 64
rustic-style tagliatelle 246
saffron
    saffron and olive bread 287
    saffron pancakes with mussels 68
sage

sage polenta discs 67
sage sautéed courgettes 191
salads
    apple and carrot salad 297
    apricot salad 304
    Augusta's vegetable salad 310
    beetroot salad 296
    broad bean and tarragon salad 297
    carrot and chicory salad 297
    carrot salad 298
    celeriac salad 299
    chicory salad 298
    courgette salad 306
    fennel and cucumber salad 308
    fruit and nut salad 299
    Genoese salad 298
    grape salad 299
    haricot bean salad 306
    Italian seafood salad 301
    Jerusalem artichoke salad 297
    lobster salad 310
    Mediterranean salad 301
    Milanese green salad 308
    minted orange salad 301
    mixed bean salad 299
    mixed mushroom salad 310
    Mozzarella salad with ratatouille 302
    orange plum salad 305
    pasta and vegetable salad 304
    pear and Parmesan salad 303
    Piedmont salami salad 304
    plum salad 305
    prawn salad 303
    quick tuna and pepper salad 305
    red radicchio salad 298
    rice and scampi salad 300
    rice salad with olives and tomatoes 296
    Roman salad 300
    red cabbage pickle 300
    salad of capers and anchovies 307
    seafood salad 308
    smoked eel and vegetable salad 309
    spinach with lime dressing 305
    sporty peach salad 302
    springtime pasta salad 302
    strawberry, grape and mint salad 303
    strawberry salad 344
    summer party salad 306
    Tivolian salad 307
    veal and avocado salad 307
    warm courgette salad 306
    warm pasta salad with radishes 300
    white fish salad 309
    yellow pepper salad 304
salami
    Piedmont salami salad 304
    rice with salami 255
    salami and caper tart 124
    salami and Mozzarella pizza 278
    salami pizza 273

    salami slices 27
    salami with beans 26
    thick salami soup 52
Salerno pastry 288
salmon
    pan-fried salmon and pasta 210
    salmon and pepper pie 163
    smoked salmon with green noodles 239
salt cod 152
San Severo pastries 291
sandwiches
    anchovy bread 76
    apricot sandwiches 59
    cheese and tomato bread 62
    crisp herb slices 60
    see also bread
Sanremo-style escalopes 87
sardines
    sardines and coriander sauce 165
    sardines in vine leaves 164
sauces
    Alfred's sauce for fresh pasta 368
    Amaretto sauce 369
    aubergine and mushroom sauce 361
    basic white sauce 357
    basil sauce 357
    butter sauce 357
    caper and tomato sauce 358
    chicken liver sauce 356
    chocolate Mascarpone cream 369
    chunky tomato sauce 357
    classic tomato sauce for pasta 359
    cream of fennel sauce 362
    creamy garlic sauce 361
    creamy walnut and basil sauce 366
    creamy white sauce 366
    dried mushroom sauce 364
    fake meat sauce for pasta 368
    fish sauce 367
    fresh apricot sauce 369
    ham and almond sauce 362
    hazelnut savoury sauce 365
    herb sauce 360
    lemon mint sauce 360
    lemon sauce 360
    lemon topping 372
    Ligurian walnut sauce 369
    lime topping 372
    meat sauce 356
    mushroom and hazelnut sauce 363
    mushroom sauce 363
    Napoli sauce 358
    oil and lemon sauce 368
    Parmesan sauce 361
    peach sauce 370
    pine nut and basil sauce 366
    piquant Chinese sauce 365
    piquant garlic sauce 367
    pistachio butter sauce 362
    quick pasta sauce 364

red pesto sauce 366
rosemary and raspberry sauce 366
sauce of the honey bees 367
savoury Mascarpone cream 359
Sicilian sauce 363
simple lemon sauce 370
sorrel sauce 362
sweet cherry sauce 370
tarragon cream sauce 364
tasty cherry sauce 370
tomato and Ricotta sauce 359
tomato sauce 358
tomato sauce with cream 359
tuna sauce 364
warm mint sauce 360
Sauerkraut
  barley and Sauerkraut soup 56
sausages
  lentils and garlic sausage 126
  mortadella rolls 71
  rice, sausages and tomatoes 253
  sausage and pasta shells 215
  sausage and prosciutto with potato 125
  sausage fritters 119
  sausage pizza 276
  sausage risotto 267
  sausages in wine 125
  sausages with beans 126
savoury chicken liver risotto 263
savoury haricot beans 27
savoury Mascarpone cream 359
savoury meat loaf 87
scallops
  Champagne scallops 150
  grilled scallops 157
  pasta with saffron and scallops 212
  Venetian scallops 167
scampi
  rice and scampi salad 300
  scampi risotto 254
seafood
  crumbly topped seafood 154
  grilled seafood 152
  Italian seafood salad 301
  monkfish with crab and shrimp 153
  pasta with seafood topping 213
  pepper and almond spaghetti with
    seafood 214
  quick seafood pizza 281
  seafood and Mascarpone fettuccine 216
  seafood noodles 239
  seafood pie 166
  seafood salad 308
  seafood spaghetti 238
  seafood with mustard and cheese
    sauce 166
  see also individual types e.g. prawns
seasoned red mullet 165
semolina
  semolina dumplings 39

semolina dumplings in hot soup 54
shallots
  caramelised potatoes, shallots and garlic 12
shortbread
  cheese shortbread 289
  Parmesan shortbread 292
shrimps
  clam and shrimp soup 45
Sicilian bread 289
Sicilian nut and chocolate cake 334
Sicilian oranges – rice balls with a savoury
    filling 260
Sicilian sauce 363
Sicilian spaghetti 217
Sicilian-style aubergine and olive antipasto 40
Sicilian toast 71
Sicilian vegetables 187
simple lemon sauce 370
simple prawns 167
smoked eel and vegetable salad 309
smoked platter with spaghettini 229
smoked salmon with green noodles 239
snacks 59–78
sole
  baked fillet of sole with prawn sauce 148
  baked fillets in wine sauce 146
  sole and Madeira sauce 169
  sole fillets in lime sauce 168
  sole with garlic and tomatoes 169
sorbet, tangerine 354
sorrel
  sorrel and chicken stew 106
  sorrel and courgette fritters 28
  sorrel sauce 362
soufflés
  iced Amaretti soufflé 350
  liver soufflé 127
  mocha soufflé 353
  orange soufflé 312
  walnut soufflé 336
soup with rice and peas 52
soups 41–57
spaghetti
  chicken Bolognese 202
  clams, pesto and spaghetti 152
  crispy fried spaghetti 241
  Mediterranean spaghetti 218
  pepper and almond spaghetti with
    seafood 214
  seafood spaghetti 238
  Sicilian spaghetti 217
  spaghetti Alsacienne 223
  spaghetti and spinach bake 220
  spaghetti Bolognese 216
  spaghetti in Neapolitan sauce 208
  spaghetti meat pie 215
  spaghetti pancakes 219
  spaghetti veal 234
  spaghetti with baby clams 240
  spaghetti with bacon and eggs 217

spaghetti with eggs 247
spaghetti with garlic and oil 221
spaghetti with garlic butter 217
spaghetti with oyster mushrooms 220
spaghetti with peppers, anchovies
    and tomato 241
spaghetti with pork, anchovies and
    tomato 221
spaghettini, smoked platter with 229
spiced carrots 187
spicy broccoli pasta 219
spicy Italian pancakes 27
spicy marinade 375
spicy pappardelle with crab 235
spicy pizza dough 268
spinach
    green gnocchi 38
    mushrooms stuffed with spinach 21
    pasta with spinach and sage 211
    rice and spinach soup 57
    spaghetti and spinach bake 220
    spinach and anchovy pâté 28
    spinach and egg ravioli 222
    spinach and ham fettuccine 223
    spinach and Mozzarella pastry 66
    spinach and rice mould 255
    spinach flan 193
    spinach gnocchi 185
    spinach lamb cutlets 118
    spinach leaf fritters 29
    spinach mushrooms 189
    spinach ring 188
    spinach with lime dressing 305
sporty peach salad 302
springtime pasta salad 302
springtime tagliatelle 247
squid
    black risotto with squid 259
    squid and crayfish 159
    stuffed squid 150
St Joseph's puffs 333
starters see antipasti; salads; soups
steak
    chuck steak in red wine 80
    Florentine steak 88
    Milanese steak 84
    Neapolitan beef 86
    pizzaiola steak 81
    rich beef in red wine 83
    rump steak, tomatoes and peppers 85
    steak filled with aubergine 90
    steak with basil sauce 86
    steak with green peppercorn
        sauce 90
    steak with pasta 229
    see also beef
stews
    fish stew 154
    Rimini stew 110
    sorrel and chicken stew 106

tomato stew 189
strawberries
    frangipane and strawberry pie 339
    fresh strawberry tart 339
    nougat and strawberry mousse 331
    strawberries in balsamic vinegar 330
    strawberries in wine 332
    strawberry, grape and mint salad 303
    strawberry ice cream 354
    strawberry salad 344
stuffed apricots with Mascarpone and
    pistachios 337
stuffed aubergines with ham 30
stuffed breast of veal 137
stuffed chicken thighs 94
stuffed courgettes 23
stuffed fennel with olives 29
stuffed figs 326
stuffed fried olives 15
stuffed olive puffs 31
stuffed onions 30
stuffed peaches 336
stuffed peppers 30
stuffed pizza 278
stuffed rice balls 254
stuffed shoulder of veal 136
stuffed squid 150
stuffed tomatoes 186
stuffed turkey roll 109
stuffed veal slices 135
summer party salad 306
sun-dried dip 34
sun-dried tomato and walnut loaf 293
sun-dried tomato mayonnaise 374
sun-dried tomato pasta 225
sweet almond biscuits 286
sweet-and-sour carrots 31
sweet-and-sour courgettes 185
sweet cherry sauce 370
sweet cream 371
sweet fried pastry balls 337
sweet Genoese bread 288
sweet lime dressing 372
sweet Marsala cream cheese 338
sweet peppers with bagna cauda 31
sweetcorn and chicken pizza 277
tagliarini pasta 198
tagliarini with peas 224
tagliatelle
    almond tagliatelle 312
    chicken and walnut tagliatelle 203
    rustic-style tagliatelle 246
    springtime tagliatelle 247
    tagliatelle crab 240
    tagliatelle with cheese and broccoli 223
    tagliatelle with sun-dried tomatoes and
        cream 224
    tomato and onion tagliatelle 225
tangerine sorbet 354
Taranto peppers 32

tarragon
  tarragon butter 376
  tarragon cream sauce 364
  tarragon lamb 117
  tarragon pesto 367
  tarragon veal 138
  tarragon vinegar 374
  vermicelli with tarragon 244
tarts
  almond tart 332
  baked vegetable tart 177
  courgette and tomato tart 181
  courgette tart 179
  fig tart 318
  frangipane tartlets 319
  fresh strawberry tart 339
  Genoese tart 328
  grape tart 322
  lemon tart 320
  Mediterranean tartlets 63
  Mozzarella tart 76
  orange and frangipane tart 324
  salami and caper tart 124
  vanilla nut tartlets 335
tasty cherry sauce 370
thick fish soup with noodles 55
thick ribbon pasta 198
thick salami soup 52
three-colour fettuccine 202
three-coloured rice 266
thunder and lightning 242
tiger prawn rice 256
tiramisu 329
Tivolian salad 307
toasted goats' cheese 32
tomatoes
  asparagus and tomato pie 173
  buttered tomatoes 174
  caper and tomato sauce 358
  cheese and tomato pie 180
  cheesy tomatoes 194
  chicken in tomato cases 70
  chunky tomato sauce 357
  classic tomato sauce for pasta 359
  courgette and tomato tart 181
  cream of tomato soup 53
  fennel and tomato bake 184
  iced tomato and fennel soup 49
  Italian tomato bread 62
  pasta bows with tomato sauce 204
  pork with tomatoes and onions 125
  quick tomato sauce 374
  red mullet and tomatoes 162
  sole with garlic and tomatoes 169
  stuffed tomatoes 186
  sun-dried dip 34
  tagliatelle with sun-dried tomatoes and
    cream 224
  tomato anchovy soup 53
  tomato and basil soup 48

tomato and mushroom soup 53
tomato and onion tagliatelle 225
tomato and Ricotta sauce 359
tomato-baked macaroni 226
tomato sauce 358
tomato sauce balls 89
tomato sauce with cream 359
tomato stew 189
tomato topped beef 91
tortellini with tomato, caper and onion
  sauce 225
veal with tomatoes 142
Torino ham 126
tortellini
  tortellini and chicken carbonara 232
  tortellini in black butter 245
  tortellini with tomato, caper and onion
    sauce 225
Trebbiano lamb 118
Trentino turnips 179
trifles
  Milanese trifle 330
  trifle 343
trout, almond 147
truffles
  pasta with butter and truffle 221
tuna
  grilled tuna 167
  Ionan tuna 160
  open tuna omelette 76
  penne with tuna and black olives 247
  quick tuna and pepper salad 305
  tuna fish with almonds 169
  tuna lasagne 222
  tuna sauce 364
  veal in tuna sauce 139
turbot
  baked turbot with tomatoes 147
  turbot with fennel 170
turkey
  roast stuffed turkey roll 109
  turkey breast Sanremo 110
  turkey breasts with prosciutto 110
turnips, Trentino 179
Tuscan bean broth 54
Tuscan braised beef 91
Tuscan pappardelle 227
Tuscan risotto with raisins 262
Tuscan veal stew 137
Tuscan-style cheesecake 335
tutti frutti ice cream 350
Umbrian carnival cake 318
vanilla
  fried vanilla bread 61
  vanilla ice cream 345
  vanilla nut tartlets 335
veal
  baked fillet of veal and potatoes 133
  galantine of veal with spinach 145
  Italian veal rolls 135

loin of veal Valdostana-style 144
Milanese-style veal escalope 144
Mozzarella veal 134
Orvietto veal 133
osso buco 134
Parmesan veal cutlets 136
rich veal with pasta shells 236
roast veal and celery sauce 134
Roman-style veal escalopes 145
spaghetti veal 234
stuffed breast of veal 137
stuffed shoulder of veal 136
stuffed veal slices 135
tarragon veal 138
Tuscan veal stew 137
veal and avocado salad 307
veal and juniper pie 141
veal and mushrooms 140
veal Bellagio 138
veal cutlets 142
veal in a cream sauce 141
veal in creamy mushroom sauce 139
veal in soured cream and celery 137
veal in tuna sauce 139
veal patties in wine sauce 140
veal ravioli 236
veal with Gorgonzola 136
veal with lemon and capers 143
veal with macaroni 235
veal with mustard and cheese 142
veal with rice 143
veal with tomatoes 142
wine chops 143
vegetables
    antipasto platter 9
    Augusta's vegetable salad 310
    baked vegetable tart 177
    bean and vegetable loaf 191
    beef roll with vegetables 81
    big vegetable minestrone 42
    cooked mixed vegetables 181
    country vegetable soup 45
    herb vegetables 189
    Italian vegetable parcels 24
    Italian vegetables 188
    Liguria fritters 18
    mixed vegetables and olives 21
    pasta and vegetable salad 304
    pasta bows with roasted vegetables 205
    pasta shells with vegetables 226
    peasant soup 51
    pork and vegetables 122

    Sicilian vegetables 187
    vegetables in green sauce 187
    see also individual types e.g. carrots
Venetian boiled duck 108
Venetian liver 129
Venetian prawns 154
Venetian scallops 167
Venetian-style chicken 99
vermicelli
    vermicelli with peppers 226
    vermicelli with tarragon 244
Verona chickenmeat balls 107
vine leaves
    layered vine leaves 18
    sardines in vine leaves 164
vinegar
    rose vinegar 373
    tarragon vinegar 374
violet liqueur, Roman 341
walnuts
    creamy walnut and basil sauce 366
    Ligurian walnut sauce 369
    walnut and asparagus penne 227
    walnut delights 293
    walnut liqueur 343
    walnut, mushroom and cheese pasta 224
    walnut soufflé 336
warm courgette salad 306
warm mint sauce 360
warm pasta salad with radishes 300
warm rice with parsley 262
whipped Marsala custard 333
white fish
    baked mustard and herb fish 162
    fish and fennel parcels 155
    fish fillets and capers 156
    fish, onion and carrot parcels 156
    fish stew 154
    fishy noodle ring 237
    foiled fish 153
    Italian fried fish 158
    layered fish roast 157
    white fish salad 309
wholemeal pizza dough 269
wild mushroom risotto 255
wine chops 143
wined leg of lamb 112
yeast pastry 283
yellow pepper salad 304
zabaglione
    Lombard zabaglione 344
    whipped Marsala custard 333

Everyday Eating made more exciting

			QUANTITY	AMOUNT
New Classic 1000 Recipes	0-572-02575-0	£5.99		
Classic 1000 Chinese	0-572-01783-9	£5.99		
Classic 1000 Indian	0-572-02807-5	£6.99		
Classic 1000 Italian	0-572-02848-2	£6.99		
Classic 1000 Pasta & Rice	0-572-02300-6	£5.99		
Classic 1000 Vegetarian	0-572-02808-3	£6.99		
Classic 1000 Quick and Easy	0-572-02330-8	£5.99		
Classic 1000 Cake & Bake	0-572-02803-2	£6.99		
Classic 1000 Calorie-counted Recipes	0-572-02405-3	£5.99		
Classic 1000 Microwave Recipes	0-572-01945-9	£5.99		
Classic 1000 Dessert Recipes	0-572-02542-4	£5.99		
Classic 1000 Low-Fat Recipes	0-572-02804-0	£6.99		
Classic 1000 Chicken Recipes	0-572-02646-3	£5.99		
Classic 1000 Seafood Recipes	0-572-02696-X	£5.99		
Classic 1000 Beginners' Recipes	0-572-02734-6	£5.99		

Please allow 75p per book for post & packing in UK   • POST & PACKING

Overseas customers £1 per book.   **TOTAL**

Foulsham books are available from local bookshops. Should you have any difficulty obtaining supplies please send Cheque/Eurocheque/Postal Order (£ sterling only) made out to BSBP or debit my credit card:

☐ ACCESS   ☐ VISA   ☐ MASTER CARD   ☐☐☐☐☐☐☐☐☐☐☐☐☐☐☐☐☐

EXPIRY DATE   SIGNATURE

ALL ORDERS TO:
Foulsham Books, PO Box 29, Douglas, Isle of Man IM99 1BQ
Telephone 01624 836000, Fax 01624 837033, Internet http://www.bookpost.co.uk.

NAME

ADDRESS

Please allow 28 days for delivery.
Please tick box if you do not wish to receive any additional information ☐
Prices and availability subject to change without notice.